3rd Workshop on Multi-lingual Representation Learning (MRL 2023)

Singapore
7 December 2023

ISBN: 978-1-7138-8602-0

Printed from e-media with permission by:

Curran Associates, Inc.
57 Morehouse Lane
Red Hook, NY 12571

CURRAN ASSOCIATES INC.
proceedings
.com

Some format issues inherent in the e-media version may also appear in this print version.

Printed with permission by Curran Associates, Inc. (2024)

For permission requests, please contact the Association for Computational Linguistics at the address below.

Association for Computational Linguistics
209 N. Eighth Street
Stroudsburg, Pennsylvania 18360

Phone: 1-570-476-8006
Fax: 1-570-476-0860

acl@aclweb.org

Additional copies of this publication are available from:

Curran Associates, Inc.
57 Morehouse Lane
Red Hook, NY 12571 USA
Phone: 845-758-0400
Fax: 845-758-2633
Email: curran@proceedings.com
Web: www.proceedings.com

MRL 2023

The 3rd Workshop on Multi-lingual Representation Learning

Proceedings of the Workshop

December 7, 2023

Order copies of this and other ACL proceedings from:

Association for Computational Linguistics (ACL)
209 N. Eighth Street
Stroudsburg, PA 18360
USA
Tel: +1-570-476-8006
Fax: +1-570-476-0860
acl@aclweb.org

Organizing Committee

Organizers

Duygu Ataman, New York University
Hila Gonen, Meta, University of Washington
Sebastian Ruder, Google
David Ifeoluwa Adelani, Google Deepmind and UCL
Gözde Gül Sahin, Koc University
Chris Emezue, TU Munich
Benjamin Muller, Meta
Omer Goldman, Bar-Ilan University
Mammad Hajili, Microsoft
Francesco Tinner, University of Amsterdam
Genta Indra Winata, Bloomberg

Program Committee

Reviewers

Saksham Bassi, New York University
Jannis Vamvas, University of Zurich
Ankur Bapna, Google
Ivan Vulić, University of Cambridge
Biao Zhang, Google
Sneha Kudugunta, Google
Ahmet Ustun, Cohere
Gozde Gul Sahin, Koc University
Duygu Ataman, New York University
Asa Cooper Stickland, New York University
Jonne Saleva, Brandeis University
Richard Yuanzhe Pang, New York University
Genta Winata, Bloomberg
Abhinav Arora, Meta
Constantine Lignos, Brandeis University
Xinyan Yu, University of Southern California
Antonios Anastasopoulos, George Mason University
Abdullatif Koksal, LMU Munich
Holy Lovenia, AISG

Keynote Talk: Orhan Firat

Orhan Firat
Google Deepmind
2023-12-07 09:10 –

Bio: Orhan Firat is a senior research scientist at Google Deepmind where he works on cutting-edge technologies on scalable and multi-lingual language models.

Keynote Talk: Katharina Kann

Katharina Kann
UC Boulder
2023-12-07 09:50 –

Bio: Katharina Kann is an assistant professor at UC Boulder and JGU Mainz and her research focuses on building natural language processing systems that work for all of the world's languages.

Keynote Talk: Sunayana Sitaram

Sunayana Sitaram
Microsoft
2023-12-07 16:00 –

Bio: Sunayana Sitaram is a principal researcher at Microsoft Research India. Her research interests are broadly in democratizing AI and making LLMs more inclusive to more languages and cultures.

Table of Contents

Program

Thursday, December 7, 2023

09:00 - 09:10	*Opening Remarks*
10:30 - 11:00	*Coffee Break*
11:00 - 12:30	*Poster Session*
12:30 - 14:00	*Lunch Break*
14:00 - 14:30	*Shared task session*
14:30 - 15:30	*Best Paper Award Session*
15:30 - 16:00	*Coffee Break*
16:00 - 16:50	*Afternoon Oral Session*
16:50 - 17:00	*Closing Remarks*

Friday, December 8, 2023

09:10 - 10:30 *Morning Oral Session*

UniBriVL: Robust Universal Representation and Generation of Audio Driven Diffusion Models

Sen Fang[1], **Bowen Gao**[2,*], **Yangjian Wu**[3], **Teik Toe Teoh**[4]
[1,2]Victoria University, [3]Hainan University, [4]Nanyang Technological University
{sen.fang, bowen.gao}@live.vu.edu.au, yangjian.wu@hainanu.edu.cn
ttteoh@ntu.edu.sg

Abstract

Multimodal large models have been recognized for their advantages in various performance and downstream tasks. The development of these models is crucial towards achieving general artificial intelligence in the future. In this paper, we propose a novel universal language representation learning method called UniBriVL, which is based on Bridging-Vision-and-Language (BriVL). **Uni**versal **BriVL** embeds audio, image, and text into a shared space, enabling the realization of various multimodal applications. Our approach addresses major challenges in robust language (both text and audio) representation learning and effectively captures the correlation between audio and image. Additionally, we demonstrate the qualitative evaluation of the generated images from UniBriVL, which serves to highlight the potential of our approach in creating images from audio. Overall, our experimental results demonstrate the efficacy of UniBriVL in downstream tasks and its ability to choose appropriate images from audio. The proposed approach has the potential for various applications such as speech recognition, music signal processing, and captioning systems.

1 Introduction

Sound and vision affect people's core cognition in many areas, such as feeling, information processing and communication. Sound and vision are closely related. However, most of the existing methods only have a single cognitive ability, and some only study text-vision, text-voice, etc. Recent studies have shown that leveraging large-scale Internet data for self-supervised pre-training of models offers better results than relying on high-quality or manually labeled data sets (Pan et al., 2022), such as the recently popular chatGPT. Moreover, multiple studies demonstrate the effectiveness of multimodal models over single or bimodal models in several fields and tasks (Chen et al., 2022a), such as Microsoft's latest BEiT3 (Wang et al., 2022), Meta's ImageBind (Girdhar et al., 2023), etc.

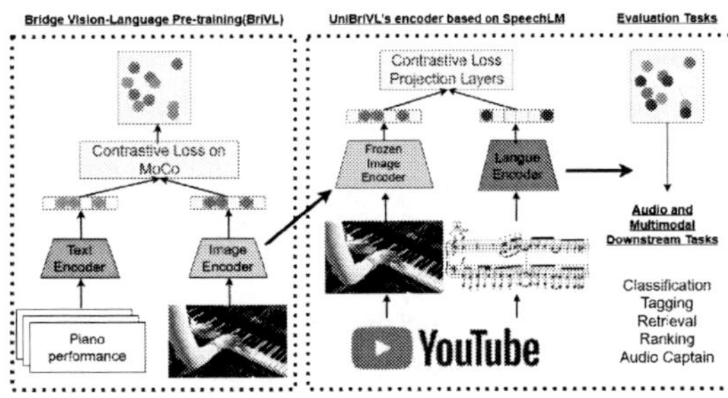

Fig. 1: Our UniBriVL architecture and training flow, we train in conjunction with a SpeechLM encoder, enabling a unified text and audio entry.

Data volume is the basic element for training large-scale language models. Since BERT of Devlin et al. (2018) (perhaps even earlier (Ma and Zhang, 2015)), the pre-training model of NLP has been benefiting from large-scale corpora. According to the theory of Kaplan et al. (2020), the language model gradually reflects a scaling law (the rule that the model capacity increases with the model volume). Manual annotation of large amounts of data in supervised learning is very expensive, so self-supervised learning is valued for large model training. In order to expand the boundary of the research field and break the limitation of the lack of relevant resources (Hsu et al., 2021), we explore a new multimodal self-monitoring model based on the latest excellent work: **Bridging-Vision-and-Language** (Fei et al., 2022). It's a new effort similar to OpenAI CLIP (Radford et al., 2021) and Google ALIGN (Jia et al., 2021). Like CLIP, BriVL can rearrange images based on how well they match text images to find the best match. BriVL[1] model has excellent effect on image and text retrieval tasks, surpassing other common multimodal pre-training models in the same period.

* Collaborator Author.

[1]https://github.com/BAAI-WuDao/BriVL

Proceedings of the The 3rd Workshop on Multi-lingual Representation Learning (MRL), pages 1–11
December 7, 2023 ©2023 Association for Computational Linguistics

In this work, we propose UniBriVL, an audio-visual correspondence model that extracts training from the BriVL model. As shown in Figure 1, the principle of UniBriVL is to freeze the BriVL visual model, run video on the visual stream of the model, and train a new model to predict BriVL embedding independently from the audio stream. The entry point for our selection of the new language modality is Microsoft's latest developed model, SpeechLM (Zhang et al., 2023), which is a fusion model of text and audio. It is capable of outputting text and audio as the same representation. This allows us to input text, audio, or both when using the model. Consequently, this significantly enhances the adaptability of the model to various tasks, such as audio-text retrieval, image retrieval, audio recognition, image captioning, and even theoretically enables better perception of real-life scenarios through simultaneous processing of live speech and text. We conducted a comprehensive evaluation of our model in the aforementioned tasks. The experimental results demonstrate its strong generalizability and excellent performance in the main experiments.

Finally, we use UniBriVL to guide the generation of model Stable Diffusion[2] (Rombach et al., 2022) output images, and intuitively verify that the embedded space is meaningful. Experimental results show that this method can effectively choose appropriate images from audio. This is a significant contribution to the field of multimodal learning, as prior methods mainly focused on generating images from text or image inputs, rather than audio inputs. In addition, compared with other fully supervised models, UniBriVL theoretically requires less data to obtain competitive performance in downstream tasks, that is, it performs pre-training more effectively than competitive methods, because it does not need to completely re learn the visual model, only needs to train the audio model. It is a reproducible and potential application model, and we will provide our model and more code information after publication.

2 Related Works

The impetus for our research is the considerable progress noticed in multimodal learning, specifically during the early part of 2022. The comparison of BriVL's performance with CLIP (Radford et al., 2021) indicates noteworthy improvements across various benchmarks. Likewise, Microsoft's SpeechLM (Zhang et al., 2023) outshines the former Wav2Vec (Baevski et al., 2020) in several dimensions. We posit that fusing the strengths of BriVL and SpeechLM could indeed result in an enhancement over Wav2CLIP[3]. Crucially, the field is presently underexplored in terms of pioneering endeavors concerning the use of audio-guided diffusion models for image generation.

2.1 Audio dependent multimodal models

There have been many multimodal works that have taken audio into account before, and some have replaced text with audio as the main object for matching with images (Ilharco et al., 2019; Chrupała, 2022). In addition to AudioCLIP (Guzhov et al., 2021) and other similar but actually different work, the most similar to us is Wav2CLIP (Wu et al., 2022). For CLIP, the BriVL we use has the following differences and advantages: Firstly,

Fig. 2: Examples of CLIP (top) and BriVL (bottom) to image generation from text, BriVL's labels in x-axis are translated.

BriVL has more weak semantic relevance, so our model is more imaginative (We also use naturally distributed weak semantic data.). For example, here are two groups of graphs in Figure 2 generated by using CLIP and BriVL respectively using GAN for comparison and understanding in the field of text-guided generation. Secondly, for our network architecture, because there is not necessarily a fine-grained area match between the image and audio, we lost the time-consuming target detector and adopted a simple and more efficient dual tower architecture. Thirdly, BriVL designed a cross modal comparative learning algorithm based on the single modal comparative learning method MoCo (He et al., 2020), which has different advantages than CLIP.

[2] https://github.com/CompVis/stable-diffusion

[3] https://github.com/descriptinc/lyrebird-wav2clip

2.2 Audio driven image generation

For many years, people have been trying to give AI people multimodal perception and thinking, and one of the main ideas is to simulate people's impressions of different external inputs, namely image generation. The pursuit of applications and methods for generating different images is the direction of researchers' efforts. With the emergence of different generation models, such as Goodfellow introduced GAN in 2014, there has been a lot of excellent work in the field of GAN-based image generation (Karras et al., 2017; Cudeiro et al., 2019; Yi et al., 2020; Zhang et al., 2021a; Song et al., 2022; Zhang et al., 2021b,c; Wu et al., 2021; Lahiri et al., 2021; Richard et al., 2021; Thies et al., 2020; Wen et al., 2020; Chen et al., 2020b). Then, from single mode to multi-mode, from text guidance about 15 years later to audio guidance (Qiu and Kataoka, 2018) 20 years later (of course, there are more and earlier attempts and exceptions), several impressive works appeared (Xu et al., 2018; Zhu et al., 2021; Hessel et al., 2021; Saharia et al., 2022b,a). At a time when diffusion models have achieved success in many fields, exploring based on this work is meaningful.

2.3 Background information

SpeechLM (Zhang et al., 2023) is a neural network model that combines speech and text information to perform language modeling. It consists of two parts: a Speech Transformer and a Shared Transformer, which are enhanced with a random swapping mechanism. The Speech Transformer uses a standard Transformer with relative position embedding to process the speech waveform into speech features, which are then masked and further processed by the Speech Transformer to obtain higher-level representations. A speech waveform $\boldsymbol{S}$ is first processed into a sequence of speech features $\boldsymbol{X} = (x_1, x_2, \ldots, x_M)$ by a stack of 1-D convolutional layers. They follow HuBERT to mask the speech feature $\boldsymbol{X}$ with the mask probability of 8% and the mask length of 10. Then the masked features, $\hat{\boldsymbol{X}}$, are fed into the Speech Transformer for higher level representations $\boldsymbol{H}^l = \text{Transformer}(\boldsymbol{H}^{l-1})$, where l means the layer and $\boldsymbol{H}^0 = \hat{\boldsymbol{X}}$ indicates the input. The Shared Transformer has the same architecture, but takes in both the encoded speech representations and the embeddings derived from tokenized text units. To better align the speech and text representations in the same latent space, they introduce a random swapping mechanism that randomly replaces some speech features with corresponding text embeddings. They randomly select some positions from the unmasked region of speech and replace the lower representations $h_i^{L/2}$ with the corresponding unit embeddings u_i, where the units are extracted from the input speech sample. In this way, the speech and text modalities can be shuffled into one sequence and treated equally. This is also one of the advantages of our model, we can use it for tasks that require text-image matching as well as voice-image matching, which is very convenient.

3 Methodology And Experiments

BriVL is a model trained on 650 million text image weak semantic datasets. They designed a cross modal comparison learning algorithm based on the monomodal comparison learning method MoCo (He et al., 2020), and maintained the negative sample queue in different training batches through a mechanism called Memory Bank, so as to obtain a large number of negative samples for use in the comparison learning method. In simple terms, it does not incorporate momentum encoders or negative sample queues, instead relying on computing the InfoNCE loss (Oord et al., 2018) within each batch. Specifically, the number of negative samples for each positive image-text pair is determined by the mini-batch size, affording greater flexibility and efficiency in training. It also shows the SOTA results in such scenes as image annotation, image zero sample classification, and input features of other downstream multimodal tasks. Even the guidance generation model has excellent performance.

As mentioned in the introduction, UniBriVL replaces the text encoder with the audio/shared encoder encoder by model of BriVL (In fact, as mentioned in the background information, SpeechLM's feature extraction is shared across text and audio types. The model is retrained after changing the BriVL code, and then fine-tuned together with SpeechLM.), runs the image through it, and trains the new model to predict that only the matching image embedded content is obtained from the audio. We refer to the exclusive multilayer perceptron of BriVL, which can not only enhance performance but also prepare for possible downstream tasks. After the audio encoder is fine-tuned, we freeze it and use it in the UniBriVL image generation task as a qualitative evaluation of our experimental results.

3.1 Dataset for performance test

We select diverse set of data ranging from various number of clips, number of categories, and perform diverse tasks including classification, retrieval, and generation. For evaluation, we use relevant metrics detailed in Table 1 for each task.

3.2 Dataset for training

To train audio-image correspondence, we use the files of the AudioSet (Gemmeke et al., 2017) video datasets as the audio input for our rearrangement of the generated images. AudioSet comprises a growing ontology that encompasses 632 distinct audio event classes and a comprehensive corpus of 2.1 million videos. These clips are annotated by human experts and extracted from YouTube videos, each lasting ten seconds. The ontology is structured as a hierarchical graph of event categories, encompassing a diverse spectrum of human and animal sounds, musical genres and instruments, as well as everyday environmental sounds. We randomly select one image from each sample video, cut them into squares, and sample them down to 64 x 64. The audio sampling rate is 16,000Hz. We use it to train the model, which helps to increase the applicability of the model. In total, we randomly selected 200,000 segments for training and then selected some additional audio for our image generation task.

3.3 Feature extraction processing methods

For image and audio encoders, we use EfficientNet-B7 (Tan and Le, 2019) as the CNN in the image encoder, and the backbone SpeechLM (Zhang et al., 2023) as the basic transformer in the audio encoder. The self concerned block is composed of 4 Transformer encoder layers and MLP block respectively, with two fully connected layers and one ReLU activation layer. For all models, we use grid search to find the best hyperparameter. For other hyperparameters (such as batch size, training steps, learning rate, etc.), we directly use the suggested values in the original papers. Note that for per-instance perturbation, we adopt the appropriate quantity compared to the original epochs.

Picture Encoding. The technique employed by BriVL utilizes random grayscale conversion for the input picture, along with random color jitter for data enrichment. A 720P resolution is utilized for all videos in the dataset, with non-compliant ones being converted to 480P. The pictures are then trimmed to 360 × 360 pixels. Patch features from the picture are captured via a Transformer, followed by employing an average pooling layer for feature integration. To further refine the extraction and depiction of interrelations among the picture patch features, a self-attention (SA) block containing multiple Transformer encoder layers is employed by the BriVL team[4]. Each Transformer encoder layer encompasses a multi-head attention (MHA) layer and a feed-forward network (FFN) layer (Fei et al., 2022):

$$\mathbf{T}' = \text{LayerNorm}(\mathbf{T} + \text{MHA}(\mathbf{T})) \quad (1)$$

$$\mathbf{T} = \text{LayerNorm}(\mathbf{T}' + \text{FFN}(\mathbf{T}')) \quad (2)$$

Post this, they make use of an average pooling layer to amalgamate the extracted patch features:

$$\mathbf{q}^{(i)} = \frac{1}{N_p} \sum_{j=1}^{N_p} \mathbf{T}_j \in \mathbb{R}^c \quad (3)$$

wherein $\mathbf{T}_j$ stands for the j-th column of $\mathbf{T}$. To project $\mathbf{q}^{(i)}$ to the joint cross-modal embedding space, a two-layer MLP block equipped with a ReLU activation layer is used. This results in generating the ultimate d-dimensional picture embedding $\mathbf{y}^{(i)} \in \mathbb{R}^d$.

Audio Encoder. For audio input, we first convert the original audio waveform (1D) into a spectrum (2D) as the input of SpeechLM, and pool the entire 512 dimensional audio sequence to output an embedding. The SpeechLM embedding is computed by the weighted average of outputs from all transformer layers. The SpeechLM[5] model inspired by HuBERT (Hsu et al., 2021) consists of a Speech Transformer and a Shared Transformer, which are enhanced with the random swapping mechanism. The Transformer is optimized to predict the discrete target sequence $\mathbf{z}$, in which each $z_t \in [C]$ is a C-class categorical variable. The distribution over the classes is parameterized with

$$p(c|\mathbf{n}_t) = \frac{\exp(\text{sim}(\mathbf{K}^P \mathbf{n}_t^L, \mathbf{e}_c)/\tau)}{\sum_{c'=1}^{C} \exp(\text{sim}(\mathbf{K}^P \mathbf{n}_t^L, \mathbf{e}_{c'})/\tau)} \quad (4)$$

where $\mathbf{K}^P$ is a projection matrix, $\mathbf{n}_t^L$ is the output hidden state for step t, $\mathbf{e}_c$ is the embedding for class c, $\text{sim}(a, b)$ means the cosine similarity between a and b, and $\tau = 0.1$ scales the logit (Chen

[4]https://github.com/BAAI-WuDao/BriVL

[5]https://aka.ms/SpeechLM

Dataset	Task	Clip (Split)	Class	Metric
ESC-50 (Piczak, 2015)	MC/ZS	2k (5 folds)	50	ACC
UrbanSound8K (Salamon et al., 2014)	MC/ZS	8k (10 folds)	10	ACC
VGGSound (Chen et al., 2020a)	MC/ZS	185k	309	mAP
DESED (Turpault et al., 2019)	AR	2.5k (valid)	10	F1
VGGSound (Chen et al., 2020a)	CMR	15k (test)	309	MRR
Clotho (Drossos et al., 2020)	AC	5k (evaluation)		COCO

Table 1: Downstream tasks, including 1. classification: multi-class (MC), zero-shot (ZS), 2. retrieval: audio (AR) and cross-modal retrieval (CMR), and 3. audio captioning (AC) task, with various of clips, classes, and common metrics.

et al., 2022b). The SpeechLM embedding is calculated by the weighted average of all transformer layer outputs of SpeechLM, where the weights are learned during fine tuning. In the process of fine-tuning, we either update or freeze the parameters of SpeechLM.

3.4 Training process

Adhering to BriVL's method, we employ a similar cross modal comparative loss delineated upon the concept of MoCo (He et al., 2020), a mechanism that facilitates dynamic sample queue formation for contrastive learning. Our approach, with two negative queues, enables a larger negative sample size without equivalent mini-batch size, thereby economizing GPU resources. The cross projection loss function, $CXLoss = L(f(Image), Language) + L(Image, g(Language))$ (f, g: projection functions and L: contrastive loss). For all models, we use grid search to find the best hyperparameter. For other hyperparameters (such as batch size, training steps, learning rate, etc.), we directly use the suggested values in the original papers. Note that for per-instance perturbation, we adopt the appropriate quantity compared to the original epochs. The topk parameter is set to 1, which indicates that we only consider the top-scoring prediction for each input instance. The queue_size parameter is set to 9600, which controls the number of instances that can be processed in parallel. We use a momentum value of 0.99 to stabilize the learning process and prevent oscillations during training. The temperature parameter is set to 0.07, which scales the logits output of the model to control the softness of the predicted probability distribution. Finally, we use a grid_size of 4 to divide the input image into a grid of smaller sub-regions for object detection tasks.

4 Task 1: UniBriVL Performance Test

We begin by discussing the training, development, and evaluation process of the UniBriVL model. We use publicly available datasets of varying sizes and tasks, including classification, retrieval, and audio captioning tasks. We compare UniBriVL with some widely used as strong benchmarks in this field and evaluate its performance in these tasks. Additionally, we investigate the effect of sound volume on the generated images. We hypothesize that the volume of sounds can influence the generated images. Hence, we explore the influence of sound volume on image features extracted from the sound using the sound correlation model. We also perform quantitative image analysis to evaluate the performance of UniBriVL compared to previous work, such as S2I and Pedersoli et al. We test model with five categories from VEGAS (Zhou et al., 2018) and compare its performance with other methods in terms of generating visually plausible images.

4.1 Training, development, and evaluation

We selected publicly available audio classification data of different sizes, which are generally used for evaluation (Cramer et al., 2019), and also included some audio tasks/data, as shown in table 1, including classification, retrieval and audio captioning. ESC-50 (Piczak, 2015) is a simple data set with only 2 thousand samples, while UrbanSound8K (Salamon et al., 2014) is a large environmental data set with 10 categories. VGGSound (Chen et al., 2020a) is a huge set of audio and video materials as we said before, including the widest and most diverse range of audio molds. DESED is used again as an audio extraction (AR) job because DESED can perform sound extraction at the fragment level. Finally, Clotho (Drossos et al., 2020) is a unique set of audio subtitles.

Model	Classification			Retrieval		
	ESC-50	UrbanSound8K	VGGSound	DESED (AR)	VGGSound (CMR)	
	ACC	ACC	mAP	F1	A→I (MRR)	I→A (MRR)
Supervise	0.5200	0.6179	0.4331			
OpenL3	0.733	0.7588	0.3487	0.1170	0.0169	0.0162
Wav2CLIP	0.8595	0.8101	0.4663	0.3955	0.0566	0.0678
UniBriVL	**0.9307**	**0.8722**	**0.4885**	0.4111	**0.0641**	**0.0612**
SOTA	0.959	0.8949	0.544			
UniBriVL (ZS)	0.412	0.4024	0.1001			

Table 2: In the subsequent classification and acquisition work, there will be supervised training, other audio representation modes, OpenL3, and the latest SOTA (Guzhov et al., 2021; Kazakos et al., 2021). ZS is based on UniBriVL as a zero sample size model, some of which are derived from the original literature.

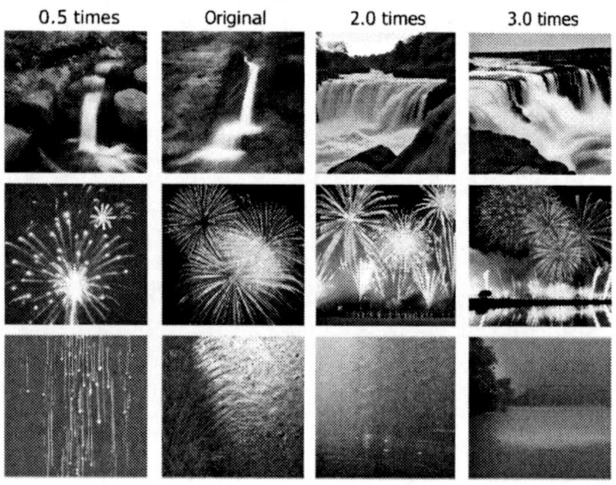

Fig. 3: Generated images by inputting different volumes of sounds. The numbers in the table is the relative loudness to the original sound.

	Method	VEGAS (5 classes)		
		R@1	FID (↓)	IS (↑)
(A)	Pedersoli et al.	23.10	118.68	1.19
(B)	S2I	39.19	114.84	1.45
(C)	S2V	77.58	34.68	4.01
(D)	Ours	**81.31**	**31.48**	**5.42**

Table 3: **Comparison to the baseline:** Pedersoli et al. (2022) and **existing sound-to-image/video method: S2I and S2V** (Fanzeres and Nadeu, 2021; Sung-Bin et al., 2023). Our method outperforms the others both qualitatively and quantitatively in the VEGAS dataset.

For multi-class (MC) classification problems, an MLP-based classifier is employed, with a corresponding number of classes as output. In DESED, we use the way of simulating UniBriVL and sed_eval[6] to realize audio retrieval (AR). At the same time, we also explore the performance of ours when dealing with multimodal tasks, and how to transfer zero samples to other modalities.

4.2 Sound volume

To establish the reliability of our method's capability to learn the connection between sound and vision, we analyzed the influence of sound volume on generated images. Specifically, we explored how changes in sound volume may affect the generated image. To achieve this, we adjusted the sound volume levels during testing and extracted features for the corresponding sound files. These modified sound features were then input into our pre-trained generator, which was trained on a standard volume scale. The final three sets of images can prove our hypothesis that the magnitude of different volume levels is usually positively correlated with the effects and meanings displayed in the images.

4.3 Quantitative image analysis

We conducted a comparative analysis of our proposed model against publicly available prior works S2I[7] (Fanzeres and Nadeu, 2021; Sung-Bin et al., 2023) and Pedersoli et al. (2022). It should be noted that while the latter is not primarily designed for sound-to-image conversion, it employs a VQVAE-based model to generate sound-to-depth or segmentation. We trained our model and Pedersoli et al. using the same training setup as S2I, including five categories in VEGAS, to ensure a fair comparison. As shown in Table 3, our proposed model outperforms all other models while generating visually compelling and recognizable images. We assert that this superior performance can be attributed to the combination of visually enriched audio embeddings and a powerful image generator.

[6] https://github.com/TUT-ARG/sed_eval

[7] https://github.com/leofanzeres/s2i

Model	B1	B4	M	RL	Cr
Baseline	0.389	0.015	0.084	0.262	0.074
Wav2CLIP	0.393	0.054	0.104	0.271	0.100
UniBriVL	**0.434**	**0.107**	**0.115**	**0.268**	**0.126**

Table 4: Results of audio captionin, ASR, compared with baseline (Drossos et al., 2020). We tested some tasks on the test tools we worked on previously[8] and we exclude Bleu2/3, list Bleu1/4 (B1/4), METEOR (M), ROUGEL (RL), CIDEr (Cr).

4.4 Downstream task result analysis

As shown in Tables 2 and 4, in training, we monitor the benchmark by training from scratch on each downlink (with random initialization of the encoder weights). Next, we compare UniBriVL with other publicly available OpenL3 (Cramer et al., 2019) pre-trained on different pretext tasks in OpenL3. OpenL3 multimodal self-monitoring training with AudioSet. It serves as a strong benchmark for different audio tasks, such as audio classification and retrieval. We extract features from OpenL3 (512 dim) and UniBriVL (512 dim) and apply the same training scheme to all downstream classification and retrieval tasks. In the chart, we can see that in the retrieval of classification, we are slightly better than our previous work, with an average increase of about 0.04, and only some deficiencies in AR. But it's only about 0.02. We approach or slightly outperform our previous work in retrieval tasks. On tasks such as BLEU and audio captioning, we have some advantages over the baseline, which to our knowledge are not state-of-the-art, but are sufficient to prove their effectiveness.

In sumary, our model has good effects in both data sets of audio retrieval classification, for the source of our strengths: In the Classification tasks, on the four datasets, three of us achieved good results close to or exceeding SOTA. one of reason may be related to our data, and the other may be the effect of BriVL. As for the lack of excellent performance in AR tasks, it may be due to the excessive divergence of the BriVL dataset. If we retrain the basic model on a large scale, we may achieve better results. In the Retrieva tasks, such mrr tasks from A to I, from I to A we have also achieved excellent results, which mainly comes from the excellent training effect of the previous two towers model and the pre-training model. In addition, we believe that increasing the amount of data has the potential to further improve performance on audio tasks.

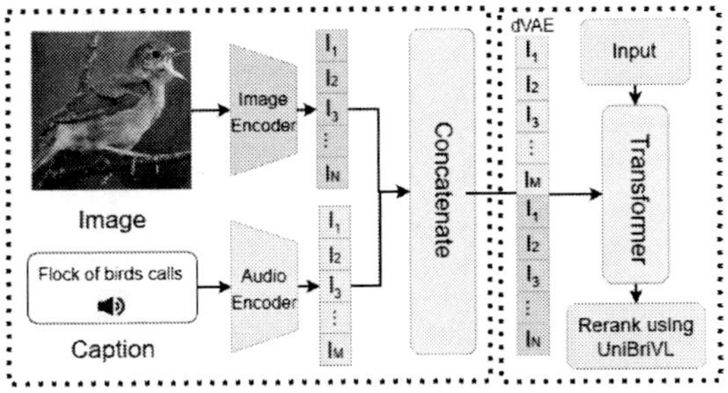

(a) Stage One (b) Stage Two

Fig. 4: UniBriVL controls the concept map of the stable diffusion model after the model matches the image features through the input language.

5 Task2: Speech Generation Picture Based on Diffusion Model

Our method uses the UniBriVL model to guide the generation of Stable Diffusion. This process utilizes meaningful embedding in the embedding space, by calculating the matching score between audio and image to rearrange the image, and this rearrangement idea is like CLIP. Our code is improved from the official model code and similarity calculation tools[9]. In the reasoning stage, as shown in Figure 4, the matching score of the audio and the generated image can be calculated through the pre-trained UniBriVL, ultimately achieving the effect of guiding the generation of the most matched image. The rearranged images are all provided by selecting from the 100th epoch of the same 20 text inputs. We found that this method can generate images that are appropriate for a given audio input, as confirmed by feedback from related experiments.

5.1 Correlation between sounds and images

This section aims to investigate whether the proposed method generates graphs that are also relevant to humans. Because simply proving authenticity is not enough to prove the deep connection between sound and image, to demonstrate the connection between the two, we conducted a test similar to previous work (Ilharco et al., 2019; Wan et al., 2019). Participants were presented with two images, each with different sound categories as input and the image closest to the given sound. We conducted three tests and obtained a series of option values. By collecting participants' options, we aim to evaluate the effectiveness of the model in generating images related to different sound categories.

[9] https://github.com/BAAI-WuDao/BriVL

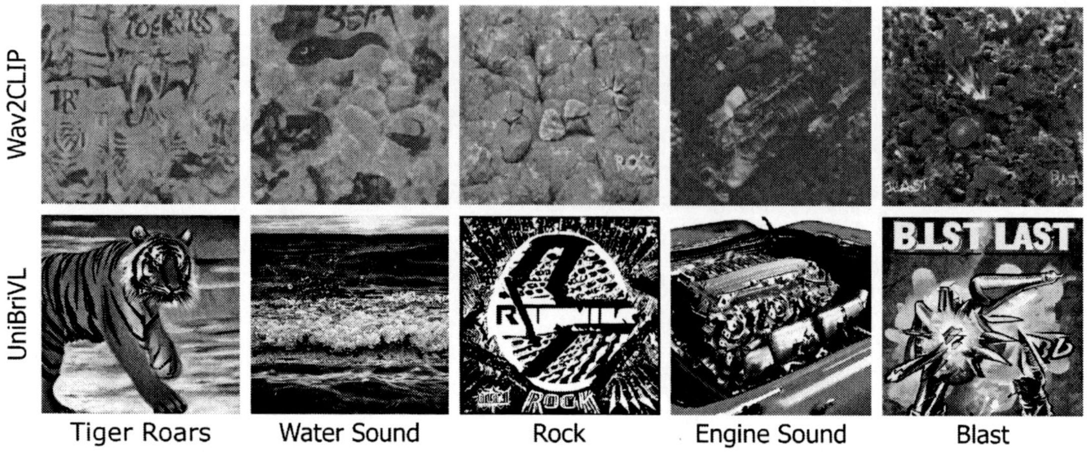

Fig. 5: Images generated from five-piece audio in AudioSet (Gemmeke et al., 2017). Top: Wav2CLIP, Bottom: UniBriVL - corresponding audio input labels in x-axis. Experiments have shown that our tools are effective.

Options	Positive	Negative	Neither
Wav2CLIP	75%	13%	12%
UniBriVL	79%	10%	11%

Table 5: Human scores on correlation between sounds and images, Wav2CLIP works for comparison

The experimental results are shown in Table 5, which collected participants' reactions and classified them as positive, negative, or neutral. A positive option indicates that participants have chosen images generated from input sound, while a negative option indicates their preference for images generated from different categories of sound. Participants who believe that neither of these images represents the sound they hear are considered neutral. Our research results indicate that the majority of participants believe that the generated images are related to the input sound, thus verifying our method's ability to generate images related to a given sound, and it was a good match.

5.2 Comparison with previous work

In previous work, Wav2CLIP also tried to generate text/audio maps. Here are two sets of pictures for comparison with our work. Figure 2 shows the text output image of CLIP and BriVL. Figure 5 shows another group of pictures generated by Wav2CLIP and UniBriVL using audio.

However, in general, they all generated appropriate images, and they have their own characteristics: for example, in their understanding of "Tiger Roads", UniBriVL is more realistic, and WavCLIP is more abstract. When they faced the input of "Water Sound", our work generated a small stream, WavCLIP generated symbolic images similar to fish fossils, and the other images have similar features. Even considering the characteristics of the GAN model, this result can further prove the superiority of our work, which also indicates that our exploration and attempt to generate images using a universal audio guided diffusion model is meaningful; For the generation of audio, they exhibit two characteristics of convergence and divergence between the two models, as we can see, convergence still corresponds to the image. Divergence is reflected in Figure 5 generated by audio, which is more imaginative than Figure 2 generated by text. This is because our BriVL weak semantic text image dataset has strong imagination, and another reason is that audio itself has strong divergence ability, which will enhance the associative ability of audio driven models.

6 Summary & Conclusion

This article introduces a UniBriVL method for generating generic representations. The results show that UniBriVL is able to output general, robust sound representations, and that UniBriVL can be easily transferred to multimodal jobs, such as audio classification, audio retrieval, audio captioning and audio image generation. In future research, we will explore a number of interpretable machine learning methods, consider extending to 6 modalities to our work, just like ImageBind (Girdhar et al., 2023). We will also consider exploring more efficient presentation and using the Consistency Models (Song et al., 2023) and the NeRF (Mildenhall et al., 2020) as the next version of the work and method.

Limitations

We fine-tune the language encoder on SpeechLM-large model, but are limited by the fact that we use part of the AudioSet data, which is a bit less than the original Microsoft training data, perhaps making performance limited. Lastly, it is essential to consider the potential influence of external factors such as background noise, reverberation, or speaker variability on the performance of the speech recognition system. These factors were not extensively addressed in our study, and their impact on the model's performance may be a subject for further investigation.

In summary, our study is subject to limitations concerning the representativeness of the training data, potential language and accent bias, and the focus solely on the language encoder component. These limitations should be taken into account when interpreting our results and considering the application of the model in real-world scenarios. Further research, incorporating diverse datasets and investigating other components of the speech recognition system, would be valuable to overcome these limitations and enhance the overall performance of speech recognition technology.

Ethics Statement

All datasets we train actively exclude harmful, pornographic, and private content, and are only used for research purposes. The participants we recruited, except for some who volunteered, received satisfactory compensation for the rest. The academic tools and human assessment related tests used in this article comply with all regulations or relevant permits.

Biases & Content Acknowledgment Although our ability to generate images through audio is impressive, it should be noted that this model may be influenced by human factors to output content that enhances or exacerbates social biases. In addition, we note a parallel work called WavBriVL, but they are based on simple representation matching, while we use the latest text-audio fusion feature extraction methods and train them with the help of a novel loss. They use Gans to generate images, and we use diffusion models to generate images. Our submission time and their appearance are within three months, so there is no need to compare it to their model or data.

References

Alexei Baevski, Yuhao Zhou, Abdelrahman Mohamed, and Michael Auli. 2020. wav2vec 2.0: A framework for self-supervised learning of speech representations. *Advances in Neural Information Processing Systems*, 33:12449–12460.

Hang Chen, Hengshun Zhou, Jun Du, Chin-Hui Lee, Jingdong Chen, Shinji Watanabe, Sabato Marco Siniscalchi, Odette Scharenborg, Di-Yuan Liu, Bao-Cai Yin, et al. 2022a. The first multimodal information based speech processing (misp) challenge: Data, tasks, baselines and results. In *ICASSP 2022-2022 IEEE International Conference on Acoustics, Speech and Signal Processing (ICASSP)*, pages 9266–9270. IEEE.

Honglie Chen, Weidi Xie, Andrea Vedaldi, and Andrew Zisserman. 2020a. Vggsound: A large-scale audio-visual dataset. In *ICASSP*, pages 721–725. IEEE.

Lele Chen, Guofeng Cui, Celong Liu, Zhong Li, Ziyi Kou, Yi Xu, and Chenliang Xu. 2020b. Talking-head generation with rhythmic head motion. In *European Conference on Computer Vision*, pages 35–51. Springer.

Sanyuan Chen, Chengyi Wang, Zhengyang Chen, Yu Wu, Shujie Liu, Zhuo Chen, Jinyu Li, Naoyuki Kanda, Takuya Yoshioka, Xiong Xiao, et al. 2022b. Wavlm: Large-scale self-supervised pre-training for full stack speech processing. *IEEE Journal of Selected Topics in Signal Processing*.

Grzegorz Chrupała. 2022. Visually grounded models of spoken language: A survey of datasets, architectures and evaluation techniques. *Journal of Artificial Intelligence Research*, 73:673–707.

Jason Cramer, Ho-Hsiang Wu, Justin Salamon, and Juan Pablo Bello. 2019. Look, listen, and learn more: Design choices for deep audio embeddings. In *ICASSP*, pages 3852–3856. IEEE.

Daniel Cudeiro, Timo Bolkart, Cassidy Laidlaw, Anurag Ranjan, and Michael J Black. 2019. Capture, learning, and synthesis of 3d speaking styles. In *Proceedings of the IEEE/CVF Conference on Computer Vision and Pattern Recognition*, pages 10101–10111.

Jacob Devlin, Ming-Wei Chang, Kenton Lee, and Kristina Toutanova. 2018. Bert: Pre-training of deep bidirectional transformers for language understanding. *arXiv preprint arXiv:1810.04805*.

Konstantinos Drossos, Samuel Lipping, and Tuomas Virtanen. 2020. Clotho: An audio captioning dataset. In *ICASSP*.

Leonardo A Fanzeres and Climent Nadeu. 2021. Sound-to-imagination: Unsupervised crossmodal translation using deep dense network architecture. *arXiv preprint arXiv:2106.01266*.

Nanyi Fei, Zhiwu Lu, Yizhao Gao, Guoxing Yang, Yuqi Huo, Jingyuan Wen, Haoyu Lu, Ruihua Song, Xin Gao, Tao Xiang, et al. 2022. Towards artificial general intelligence via a multimodal foundation model. *Nature Communications*, 13(1):1–13.

Jort F. Gemmeke, Daniel P. W. Ellis, Dylan Freedman, Aren Jansen, Wade Lawrence, R. Channing Moore, Manoj Plakal, and Marvin Ritter. 2017. Audio set: An ontology and human-labeled dataset for audio events. In *Proc. IEEE ICASSP 2017*, New Orleans, LA.

Rohit Girdhar, Alaaeldin El-Nouby, Zhuang Liu, Mannat Singh, Kalyan Vasudev Alwala, Armand Joulin, and Ishan Misra. 2023. Imagebind: One embedding space to bind them all.

Andrey Guzhov, Federico Raue, Jörn Hees, and Andreas Dengel. 2021. Audioclip: Extending clip to image, text and audio. *arXiv preprint arXiv:2106.13043*.

Kaiming He, Haoqi Fan, Yuxin Wu, Saining Xie, and Ross Girshick. 2020. Momentum contrast for unsupervised visual representation learning. In *2020 IEEE/CVF Conference on Computer Vision and Pattern Recognition (CVPR)*, pages 9726–9735.

Jack Hessel, Ari Holtzman, Maxwell Forbes, Ronan Le Bras, and Yejin Choi. 2021. Clipscore: A reference-free evaluation metric for image captioning. In *Proceedings of the 2021 Conference on Empirical Methods in Natural Language Processing*, pages 7514–7528.

Wei-Ning Hsu, Benjamin Bolte, Yao-Hung Hubert Tsai, Kushal Lakhotia, Ruslan Salakhutdinov, and Abdelrahman Mohamed. 2021. Hubert: Self-supervised speech representation learning by masked prediction of hidden units. *IEEE/ACM Transactions on Audio, Speech, and Language Processing*, 29:3451–3460.

Gabriel Ilharco, Yuan Zhang, and Jason Baldridge. 2019. Large-scale representation learning from visually grounded untranscribed speech. In *Proceedings of the 23rd Conference on Computational Natural Language Learning (CoNLL)*, pages 55–65, Hong Kong, China. Association for Computational Linguistics.

Chao Jia, Yinfei Yang, Ye Xia, Yi-Ting Chen, Zarana Parekh, Hieu Pham, Quoc Le, Yun-Hsuan Sung, Zhen Li, and Tom Duerig. 2021. Scaling up visual and vision-language representation learning with noisy text supervision. In *International Conference on Machine Learning*, pages 4904–4916. PMLR.

Jared Kaplan, Sam McCandlish, Tom Henighan, Tom B Brown, Benjamin Chess, Rewon Child, Scott Gray, Alec Radford, Jeffrey Wu, and Dario Amodei. 2020. Scaling laws for neural language models. *arXiv preprint arXiv:2001.08361*.

Tero Karras, Timo Aila, Samuli Laine, Antti Herva, and Jaakko Lehtinen. 2017. Audio-driven facial animation by joint end-to-end learning of pose and emotion. *ACM Transactions on Graphics (TOG)*, 36(4):1–12.

Evangelos Kazakos, Arsha Nagrani, Andrew Zisserman, and Dima Damen. 2021. Slow-fast auditory streams for audio recognition. In *ICASSP*, pages 855–859.

Avisek Lahiri, Vivek Kwatra, Christian Frueh, John Lewis, and Chris Bregler. 2021. Lipsync3d: Data-efficient learning of personalized 3d talking faces from video using pose and lighting normalization. In *Proceedings of the IEEE/CVF conference on computer vision and pattern recognition*, pages 2755–2764.

Long Ma and Yanqing Zhang. 2015. Using word2vec to process big text data. In *2015 IEEE International Conference on Big Data (Big Data)*, pages 2895–2897. IEEE.

Ben Mildenhall, Pratul P. Srinivasan, Matthew Tancik, Jonathan T. Barron, Ravi Ramamoorthi, and Ren Ng. 2020. Nerf: Representing scenes as neural radiance fields for view synthesis. In *ECCV*.

Aaron van den Oord, Yazhe Li, and Oriol Vinyals. 2018. Representation learning with contrastive predictive coding. *arXiv preprint arXiv:1807.03748*.

Xichen Pan, Peiyu Chen, Yichen Gong, Helong Zhou, Xinbing Wang, and Zhouhan Lin. 2022. Leveraging unimodal self-supervised learning for multimodal audio-visual speech recognition. In *Proceedings of the 60th Annual Meeting of the Association for Computational Linguistics (Volume 1: Long Papers)*, pages 4491–4503, Dublin, Ireland. Association for Computational Linguistics.

Fabrizio Pedersoli, Dryden Wiebe, Amin Banitalebi, Yong Zhang, and Kwang Moo Yi. 2022. Estimating visual information from audio through manifold learning. *arXiv preprint arXiv:2208.02337*.

Karol J. Piczak. 2015. ESC: Dataset for Environmental Sound Classification. In *ACM Multimedia*, page 1015. ACM Press.

Yue Qiu and Hirokatsu Kataoka. 2018. Image generation associated with music data. In *Proceedings of the IEEE Conference on Computer Vision and Pattern Recognition Workshops*, pages 2510–2513.

Alec Radford, Jong Wook Kim, Chris Hallacy, Aditya Ramesh, Gabriel Goh, Sandhini Agarwal, Girish Sastry, Amanda Askell, Pamela Mishkin, et al. 2021. Learning transferable visual models from natural language supervision. *ICML*.

Alexander Richard, Michael Zollhöfer, Yandong Wen, Fernando De la Torre, and Yaser Sheikh. 2021. Meshtalk: 3d face animation from speech using cross-modality disentanglement. In *Proceedings of the IEEE/CVF International Conference on Computer Vision*, pages 1173–1182.

Robin Rombach, Andreas Blattmann, Dominik Lorenz, Patrick Esser, and Björn Ommer. 2022. High-resolution image synthesis with latent diffusion models. In *Proceedings of the IEEE/CVF Conference on*

Computer Vision and Pattern Recognition (CVPR), pages 10684–10695.

Chitwan Saharia, William Chan, Saurabh Saxena, Lala Li, Jay Whang, Emily L Denton, Kamyar Ghasemipour, Raphael Gontijo Lopes, Burcu Karagol Ayan, Tim Salimans, Jonathan Ho, David J Fleet, and Mohammad Norouzi. 2022a. Photorealistic text-to-image diffusion models with deep language understanding. In *Advances in Neural Information Processing Systems*, volume 35, pages 36479–36494. Curran Associates, Inc.

Chitwan Saharia, William Chan, Saurabh Saxena, Lala Li, Jay Whang, Emily L Denton, Kamyar Ghasemipour, Raphael Gontijo Lopes, Burcu Karagol Ayan, Tim Salimans, et al. 2022b. Photorealistic text-to-image diffusion models with deep language understanding. *Advances in Neural Information Processing Systems*, 35:36479–36494.

J. Salamon, C. Jacoby, and J. P. Bello. 2014. A dataset and taxonomy for urban sound research. In *ACM Multimedia*, pages 1041–1044, Orlando, FL, USA.

Linsen Song, Wayne Wu, Chen Qian, Ran He, and Chen Change Loy. 2022. Everybody's talkin': Let me talk as you want. *IEEE Transactions on Information Forensics and Security*, 17:585–598.

Yang Song, Prafulla Dhariwal, Mark Chen, and Ilya Sutskever. 2023. Consistency models.

Kim Sung-Bin, Arda Senocak, Hyunwoo Ha, Andrew Owens, and Tae-Hyun Oh. 2023. Sound to visual scene generation by audio-to-visual latent alignment.

Mingxing Tan and Quoc Le. 2019. Efficientnet: Rethinking model scaling for convolutional neural networks. In *International conference on machine learning*, pages 6105–6114. PMLR.

Justus Thies, Mohamed Elgharib, Ayush Tewari, Christian Theobalt, and Matthias Nießner. 2020. Neural voice puppetry: Audio-driven facial reenactment. In *European conference on computer vision*, pages 716–731. Springer.

Nicolas Turpault, Romain Serizel, Ankit Parag Shah, and Justin Salamon. 2019. Sound event detection in domestic environments with weakly labeled data and soundscape synthesis. In *DCASE*, New York City, United States.

Chia-Hung Wan, Shun-Po Chuang, and Hung-Yi Lee. 2019. Towards audio to scene image synthesis using generative adversarial network. In *ICASSP 2019 - 2019 IEEE International Conference on Acoustics, Speech and Signal Processing (ICASSP)*, pages 496–500.

Wenhui Wang, Hangbo Bao, Li Dong, Johan Bjorck, Zhiliang Peng, Qiang Liu, Kriti Aggarwal, Owais Khan Mohammed, Saksham Singhal, Subhojit Som, et al. 2022. Image as a foreign language: Beit pretraining for all vision and vision-language tasks. *arXiv preprint arXiv:2208.10442*.

Xin Wen, Miao Wang, Christian Richardt, Ze-Yin Chen, and Shi-Min Hu. 2020. Photorealistic audio-driven video portraits. *IEEE Transactions on Visualization and Computer Graphics*, 26(12):3457–3466.

Haozhe Wu, Jia Jia, Haoyu Wang, Yishun Dou, Chao Duan, and Qingshan Deng. 2021. Imitating arbitrary talking style for realistic audio-driven talking face synthesis. In *Proceedings of the 29th ACM International Conference on Multimedia*, pages 1478–1486.

Ho-Hsiang Wu, Prem Seetharaman, Kundan Kumar, and Juan Pablo Bello. 2022. Wav2clip: Learning robust audio representations from clip. In *ICASSP 2022-2022 IEEE International Conference on Acoustics, Speech and Signal Processing (ICASSP)*, pages 4563–4567. IEEE.

Tao Xu, Pengchuan Zhang, Qiuyuan Huang, Han Zhang, Zhe Gan, Xiaolei Huang, and Xiaodong He. 2018. Attngan: Fine-grained text to image generation with attentional generative adversarial networks. In *Proceedings of the IEEE conference on computer vision and pattern recognition*, pages 1316–1324.

Ran Yi, Zipeng Ye, Juyong Zhang, Hujun Bao, and Yong-Jin Liu. 2020. Audio-driven talking face video generation with learning-based personalized head pose. *arXiv preprint arXiv:2002.10137*.

Chenxu Zhang, Saifeng Ni, Zhipeng Fan, Hongbo Li, Ming Zeng, Madhukar Budagavi, and Xiaohu Guo. 2021a. 3d talking face with personalized pose dynamics. *IEEE Transactions on Visualization and Computer Graphics*.

Chenxu Zhang, Yifan Zhao, Yifei Huang, Ming Zeng, Saifeng Ni, Madhukar Budagavi, and Xiaohu Guo. 2021b. Facial: Synthesizing dynamic talking face with implicit attribute learning. In *Proceedings of the IEEE/CVF international conference on computer vision*, pages 3867–3876.

Zhimeng Zhang, Lincheng Li, Yu Ding, and Changjie Fan. 2021c. Flow-guided one-shot talking face generation with a high-resolution audio-visual dataset. In *Proceedings of the IEEE/CVF Conference on Computer Vision and Pattern Recognition*, pages 3661–3670.

Ziqiang Zhang, Sanyuan Chen, Long Zhou, Yu Wu, Shuo Ren, Shujie Liu, Zhuoyuan Yao, Xun Gong, Lirong Dai, Jinyu Li, and Furu Wei. 2023. Speechlm: Enhanced speech pre-training with unpaired textual data.

Yipin Zhou, Zhaowen Wang, Chen Fang, Trung Bui, and Tamara L Berg. 2018. Visual to sound: Generating natural sound for videos in the wild. In *CVPR*.

Hao Zhu, Man-Di Luo, Rui Wang, Ai-Hua Zheng, and Ran He. 2021. Deep audio-visual learning: A survey. *International Journal of Automation and Computing*, 18(3):351–376.

Meta-learning For Vision-and-language Cross-lingual Transfer

Hanxu Hu
University of Edinburgh
School of Informatics
hanxu.hu@ed.ac.uk

Frank Keller
University of Edinburgh
School of Informatics
keller@inf.ed.ac.uk

Abstract

Current pre-trained vision-language models (PVLMs) achieve excellent performance on a range of multi-modal datasets. Recent work aims at building multilingual versions of such models, and a range of multilingual multi-modal datasets have been introduced for this purpose. However, current PVLMs typically perform poorly on such datasets when used for zero-shot or few-shot cross-lingual transfer, especially for low-resource languages. To alleviate this problem, we propose a novel meta-learning fine-tuning framework. Our framework makes it possible to rapidly adapt PVLMs to new languages by using Model-agnostic Meta-learning (MAML) in a novel cross-lingual multi-modal manner. Experiments show that this new method boosts the performance of current PVLMs in both zero-shot and few-shot settings on four different vision-language tasks across 14 languages.

1 Introduction

Multi-modal models focus on jointly learning representations from multiple modalities, such as vision and language. Many tasks require the integration of information of vision and language, including image captioning (Vinyals et al., 2015), natural language visual reasoning (Zhou et al., 2017; Suhr et al., 2019), and cross-modal retrieval (Zhen et al., 2019). Multi-modal learning captures the interaction between different modalities, allowing the resulting representations to be used in multimedia applications that enhance human-computer interaction.

Recently, pre-trained vision-language models (PVLMs; Chen et al. 2020; Lu et al. 2019; Tan and Bansal 2019) have achieved significant advances in multi-modal tasks. However, the data which PVLMs learn from is mostly for high-resource languages such as English. The resulting models rely on large amounts of training data for good performance, and often the models acquire biases

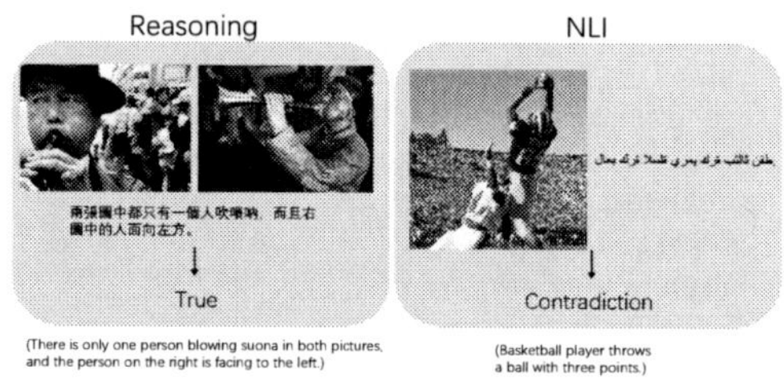

Figure 1: Examples in IGLUE (Bugliarello et al., 2022) benchmark. The left example comes from MaRVL (Liu et al., 2021) dataset, and the right example comes from XVNLI dataset proposed in IGLUE.

that mean they perform poorly in low-resource languages such as Indonesian or Swahili. To address this, several multilingual PVLMs have been proposed (Zhou et al., 2021; Ni et al., 2021). A number of studies have used multilingual multi-modal datasets (Bugliarello et al., 2022; Liu et al., 2021) and Figure 1 shows two examples from such datasets. The authors of these datasets used them to evaluate current famous PVLMs and demonstrated they do not perform well in low-resource cross-lingual transfer settings.

In this paper, we conjecture that meta-learning can mitigate this issue. This is a learning approach that enables machine learning models to adapt quickly to new tasks by learning the learning algorithm itself. Model-agnostic Meta-learning (MAML; Finn et al. 2017) is one of the most widely used meta-learning frameworks. It is based on gradient-descent optimization, does not require multiple models or complex settings, and can be used for a range of models. In previous work (Verma et al., 2020; Finn et al., 2017; Nooralahzadeh et al., 2020), MAML-based methods have been shown to be useful in low-resource and cross-lingual transfer scenarios, including both few-shot and zero-shot cross-lingual tasks. However, prior work has only attempted to use MAML for cross-lingual transfer in **text-only tasks**

Proceedings of the The 3rd Workshop on Multi-lingual Representation Learning (MRL), pages 12–23
December 7, 2023

(Nooralahzadeh et al., 2020).

Inspired by previous works about using MAML for natural language tasks, this paper proposes XVL-MAML, a novel variant of MAML that addresses the limitations of previous PVLMs in **vision-language tasks** for low-resource cross-lingual transfer. Our framework combines a traditional supervised loss for learning down-stream tasks with a contrastive loss to encourage the alignment between modalities, resulting in a cross-lingual, multi-modal MAML optimization procedure.

The intuition underlying our method is that a contrastive loss can align representations of different modalities, and MAML allows the model to generalize quickly to unseen tasks (languages, in our case). We show that XVL-MAML can lead to significant improvements in PVLM performance for cross-lingual transfer. We also find that using contrastive learning in a MAML framework on its own can bring improvements in PVLM performance in unsupervised settings.

In sum, our contributions are as follows: (1) We propose a novel framework called XVL-MAML which is the first meta-learning method specialized for vision-language cross-lingual transfer, and doesn't require the translation or pre-training data. (2) We show that using only contrastive learning in the MAML framework in an unsupervised setting can also be useful. (3) We demonstrate that our proposed framework can boost the performance of current PVLMs across 14 languages and four tasks in both **zero-shot learning** and **few-shot learning**. (4) We conduct an ablation study to verify the effect of contrastive learning in both supervised and unsupervised settings and present an analysis across languages and tasks.

2 Related Work

2.1 Multilingual Vision-and-Language Methods and Tasks

Recent work has investigated vision-and-language cross-lingual transfer tasks. Elliott et al. (2016) proposed Multi30K, an image description dataset which contains descriptions in multiple languages. Previous methods (Gella et al., 2017; Rotman et al., 2018) propose ways of bridging languages through images, but they mainly focus on image-text retrieval and only consider high-resource languages such as English and German. Pfeiffer et al. (2022) built a multilingual visual question answering dataset xGQA. Liu et al. (2021) proposed a multilingual version of the grounded visual reasoning dataset MaRVL, which follow the same setting as the natural language visual reasoning dataset NLVR2 (Su et al., 2019), but considers both cross-lingual transfer and domain shift between languages.

Several pre-trained models are recently proposed for vision-and-language cross-lingual transfer. Ni et al. (2021) proposed M3P, a transformer-based pre-trained model that maps the same concepts in different modalities and languages into a common semantic space. Similar to M3P, Liu et al. (2021) extended UNITER (Chen et al., 2020), proposing mUNITER based on M-BERT (Devlin et al., 2019), and xUNITER based on XLM-R (Conneau et al., 2020). Zhou et al. (2021) proposed UC2, a model using a data augmentation method based on machine translation for cross-lingual cross-modal pre-training. Although pre-training methods have proven powerful across multiple tasks, they require large amounts of training data and show a clear performance gap between English and low-resource languages on the IGLUE benchmark (Bugliarello et al., 2022).

Recently, some adapter-based efficient tuning methods (Pfeiffer et al., 2022; Wang et al., 2023) and translation augmented methods (Qiu et al., 2022) were proposed for multilingual multimodal tasks. But they still require a large amount of data or machine translated data for training. Our method, in contrast, only requires a small amount of auxiliary data.

2.2 Meta-Learning

Meta-learning has been increasingly popular in machine learning. Whereas conventional machine learning methods learn by data points, meta-learning learns by tasks. Previous meta-learning work (Vinyals et al., 2016; Finn et al., 2017) focused on adapting to new tasks quickly. But meta-learning can be applied to other scenarios as well, including semi-supervised learning (Ren et al., 2018), multi-task learning (Yu et al., 2020), and domain generalization (Li et al., 2018).

Prior work has also explored the effectiveness of meta-learning in NLP: Wang et al. (2021) applied meta-learning in semantic parsing for domain generalization based on MAML (Finn et al., 2017; Li et al., 2018). Obamuyide and Vlachos (2019) leveraged meta-learning under limited supervision in a relation classification task. Recently, there have been some applications using MAML in cross-lingual transfer: Gu et al. (2018) and Nooralahzadeh et al. (2020) regard languages as tasks in their meta-learning framework. In contrast to these existing approaches, which explore text-only scenarios, we are the first to utilize meta-learning for cross-lingual transfer in multi-modal tasks.

3 Meta-learning for Vision-and-language Cross-lingual Transfer

We first formally define the problem of vision-and-Language cross-lingual transfer in the context of zero-shot and few-shot scenarios in Section 3.1. Then, we introduce our overall fine-tuning framework in Section 3.2. And we introduce the contrastive learning used for vision-and-language tasks in Section 3.3. Finally, we introduce our XVL-MAML algorithm in Section 3.4.

3.1 Problem Definition

Following the multilingual vision-language IGLUE benchmark (Bugliarello et al., 2022), we formulate the problem of cross-lingual transfer learning in vision-and-language scenarios. For understanding tasks, the input is a pair of an image V and text U, and the output Y is the result inferred by the multi-modal model. We can thus formulate this problem as computing $P_\theta(Y|V,U)$, where θ are the parameters of the PVLMs. During training, the image-text pairs come from datasets D_s in a set of source languages, and our aim is to perform well on datasets D_t for the same task in the target languages. For the zero-shot setup, the pre-trained model fine-tuned on D_s is directly used in inference on D_t for unseen target languages. For the few-shot setup, after training on D_s, the model is continually fine-tuned on several shots of the training set of D_t and then evaluated on the development set of D_t.

3.2 Overall Fine-tuning Framework For Cross-lingual Transfer

The pipeline of our proposed meta-learning fine-tuning framework can be divided into three parts:

1. Fine-tune the pre-trained vision-language model on data of the down-stream task **in English**
2. Fine-tune the model on data in the **auxiliary language** (one language other than English) using our proposed XVL-MAML algorithm.
3. Evaluate the fine-tuned model on data in the **target languages** (languages other than English and the auxiliary language).

The traditional cross-lingual transfer learning procedure described in Bugliarello et al. (2022) only includes part 1 and 3. In part 3, if the setting is zero-shot, the model is evaluated on data in the target language directly, but if the setting is few-shot, the model continues to be fine-tuned on few-shot data in the target languages and is then evaluated. The difference between our framework and the traditional procedure is the additional fine-tuning step of part 2. We will describe it specifically in Section 3.4, but before that, we will introduce contrastive learning for vision-and-language tasks.

3.3 Contrastive Learning for Vision-and-language Tasks

The vision-and-language contrastive learning loss proposed by Zhang et al. (2020) has proven effective in medical image scenarios and is used as the pre-training objective function of CLIP (Radford et al., 2021). It can be regarded as an auxiliary task for representation learning, aiming to enable models to gain better aligned multi-modal representation for downstream tasks. In the contrastive learning scheme, a batch of embeddings of images encoded by the model can be written as $I = \{I_1, ..., I_N\}$, and a batch of embeddings of texts encoded by the model can be written as $T = \{T_1, ..., T_N\}$, where N is the size of batch, (I_i, T_i) is an image-text pair. If the paired image-text data describe the same or similar concepts, then we can assume they are **positive** examples, and non-paired data are **negative** examples. Then, the embeddings of images and texts are fed into two different linear transformation layers separately, W_1 and W_2:

$$U = I \cdot W_1^\top \tag{1}$$

$$V = T \cdot W_2^\top \tag{2}$$

Where U and V represent the batch of image-text pairs. Then the cosine similarity of each pair can be computed as $\langle U_i, V_j \rangle = \frac{U_i^\top V_j}{\|U_i\| \|V_j\|}$. The objective is to maximize the similarity of matched image-text pairs and minimize the similarity of others. So the image-text contrastive loss can be formulated as follows:

$$\mathcal{L}_i^1 = -\log \frac{\exp(\langle U_i, V_i \rangle)}{\sum_{K=1}^{N} \exp(\langle U_i, V_k \rangle)} \tag{3}$$

Following Zhang et al. (2020), the contrastive loss should be symmetric for each modality, and the text-image contrastive loss is:

$$\mathcal{L}_i^2 = -\log \frac{\exp(\langle V_i, U_i \rangle)}{\sum_{K=1}^{N} \exp(\langle V_i, U_k \rangle)} \quad (4)$$

The final contrastive loss of this batch of paired data is then:

$$\mathcal{L}_{CL} = \sum_{i=1}^{N} (\mathcal{L}_i^1 + \mathcal{L}_i^2) \quad (5)$$

Where $\mathcal{L}_{CL}$ is the overall contrastive loss. When we minimize $\mathcal{L}_{CL}$, we maximize the similarity of image-text pairs which are positive examples.

3.4 XVL-MAML

Inspired by the effectiveness of MAML for quickly adapting to new tasks, we propose a novel variant of the MAML algorithm specialized for cross-lingual transfer in vision and language tasks, called XVL-MAML. Specifically, we first integrate contrastive learning into the MAML algorithm, making it specialized for the visual-language task of cross-lingual transfer learning. Our intuition is that we can use MAML with a contrastive loss as its learning objective for quickly adapting vision-language alignment to new languages. In this framework, the alignment between image and text in a specific language can be regarded as a task. Inspired by Nooralahzadeh et al. (2020), we use the data of one auxiliary language for fine-tuning, but with a contrastive loss as objective function in the MAML algorithm.

Specifically, we sample a batch of support data $\mathcal{B}_s$ and a batch of query data $\mathcal{B}_q$ in the data in auxiliary language A for each virtual task $\mathcal{T}$. Assuming the parameters of the model are θ and the contrastive loss on the support data is $\mathcal{L}_{CL}(\theta)_{\mathcal{B}_s}$, then the parameters of the model can be updated by one step of gradient descent:

$$\theta' = \theta - \alpha \nabla_\theta \mathcal{L}_{CL}(\theta)_{\mathcal{B}_s} \quad (6)$$

Following the MAML algorithm, our final objective for this task is to minimize $\mathcal{L}_{CL}(\theta')_{\mathcal{B}_q}$ on the query data $\mathcal{B}_q$ using gradient descent:

$$\theta \leftarrow \theta - \beta \nabla_\theta \mathcal{L}_{CL}(\theta')_{\mathcal{B}_q} \quad (7)$$

$$\theta \leftarrow \theta - \beta \nabla_\theta \mathcal{L}_{CL}(\theta - \alpha \nabla_\theta \mathcal{L}_{CL}(\theta)_{\mathcal{B}_s})_{\mathcal{B}_q} \quad (8)$$

Optimized using this method, pre-trained vision-language models can quickly adapt to new tasks in other languages without using any annotation in the auxiliary language for downstream tasks, so we will refer to this as an **unsupervised scenario**.

In **supervised scenarios**, where the downstream tasks labels in the auxiliary language are available, we combine the loss of the downstream task $\mathcal{L}$ with the vision-language contrastive loss $\mathcal{L}_{CL}$ by adding them together. So during fine-tuning, Equation (8) is modified to:

$$\theta \leftarrow \theta - \beta(\nabla_\theta \mathcal{L}(\theta'')_{\mathcal{B}_q} + \lambda \nabla_\theta \mathcal{L}_{CL}(\theta')_{\mathcal{B}_q}) \quad (9)$$

Where the temporary parameters optimized for one step by the downstream task loss $\mathcal{L}$ on the support set $\mathcal{B}_s$ is θ'', β is the meta-learning rate, and λ is the scale factor of contrastive learning. By simply adding the gradients of the downstream task and contrastive learning in the meta-update, the model learns downstream tasks and vision-language alignment simultaneously for cross-lingual transfer.

4 Experiments

In this section, we introduce both the base PVLMs we use for vision-language cross-lingual transfer, as well as the datasets and metrics we use to evaluate our proposed method. Then we describe how the experiments were conducted and discuss the results.

4.1 Base models

In this paper, we choose xUNITER (Liu et al., 2021) and UC2 (Zhou et al., 2021) as our base models, as they use different pre-training methods. Then we applied XVL-MAML to both models to show that this method works across different models.

xUNITER is a multilingual version of the UNITER model (Chen et al., 2020). It has a similar architecture to UNITER and uses Faster-RCNN (Ren et al., 2015) as a feature extractor for images. The image features are pooled and reshaped as vectors with the same dimensions as text embeddings. UNITER has four pre-training methods: Masked Language Modelling (MLM), Masked Region Modelling (MRM), Image-Text Matching (ITM), and Word Region Alignment (WRA). xUNITER, in addition to these pre-training methods, also uses Masked Language Modelling for multilingual data and uses the same text embedder as XLM-R (Conneau et al., 2020).

Method	Model	XNVLI	xGQA	MaRVL	xFlickr&Co	
					IR	TR
Baseline	mUNITER	53.7	10.0	53.7	8.1	8.9
	xUNITER	59.0	20.8	56.0	13.8	12.5
	UC2	62.5	29.0	56.4	19.7	17.0
	M3P	58.2	28.2	56.0	12.9	11.9
Ours	xUNITER	63.0 (**+4.0**)	22.5 (**+1.7**)	**59.4 (+4.4)**	16.3 (**+2.5**)	14.2 (**+1.7**)
	UC2	**64.4** (+1.9)	**29.9** (+0.9)	57.0 (+0.6)	**21.3** (+1.6)	**18.7 (+1.7)**

Table 1: Zero-shot performance (accuracy) of four baseline models only fine-tuned on English data (Baseline) and two models fine-tuned by our meta-learning method (Ours) on four IGLUE datasets (Bugliarello et al., 2022).

UC2 uses a similar model architecture as UNITER, but different pre-training methods. Specifically, UC2 augments pre-training on English data by constructing a multilingual corpus via machine translation and then uses this augmented data for pre-training. It also proposes the Visual Translation Language Modeling (VTLM) pre-training method, which uses the image as a pivot to learn the relationship between parallel texts in two languages and their corresponding images.

4.2 Datasets and Metrics

We use datasets for four tasks from the IGLUE benchmark (Bugliarello et al., 2022), which includes xGQA (Pfeiffer et al., 2022), MaRVL (Liu et al., 2021), XVNLI, and xFlickr&Co (Plummer et al., 2015; Lin et al., 2014). We show examples from MaRVL and XVNLI in Figure 1. Following the convention in IGLUE, the evaluation metric is accuracy for all tasks except cross-modal retrieval, which uses Recall@1. The task format of these four datasets are described below:

- **MaRVL** is a multicutural vision-language reasoning dataset, following the format of English NLVR2 (Suhr et al., 2019) which namely to judge whether a sentence is correct or not for a pair of images.
- **XVNLI** is a multilingual version of visual natural language inference task, which requires models to predict the relationships between premise and hypothesis based on a given image.
- **xGQA** is a multilingual grounded question answering task based on GQA (Hudson and Manning, 2019) and machine translated question-answer pairs.
- **xFlickr&CO** is a multilingual image-text retrieval dataset collected from Flickr30k (Plummer et al., 2015) and COCO (Lin et al., 2015)

4.3 Implementation and Hyperparameters

We conduct all experiments based on the Visiolinguistic Transformer Architectures framework VOLTA on four 2080Ti GPUs. We implement the MAML algorithm using the Higher library. We use the AdamW (Loshchilov and Hutter, 2018) optimizer to fine-tune all models in PyTorch.

Fine-tuning on English Data Before evaluating models on data in low-resource languages, we firstly fine-tune the pre-trained models on the corresponding English datasets: GQA (Hudson and Manning, 2019), NLVR2 (Suhr et al., 2019), SNLI-VE (Xie et al., 2019), and Flickr30k (Plummer et al., 2015) for xGQA, MaRVL, XVNLI, and xFlickr&Co, respectively, using the procedure of Bugliarello et al. (2022) and Liu et al. (2021). We follow the setting in IGLUE (Bugliarello et al., 2022) and also use the IGLUE hyper-parameters for each task when fine-tuning. We save the parameters of models in each epoch, then pick the best performing model for each task as the initialized parameters θ for the meta-learning fine-tuning stage.

Fine-tuning with Meta-learning For the XVL-MAML algorithm, the size of the support set and the query set is 64. We explore learning rates 5×10^{-5}, 1×10^{-5}, 5×10^{-6} , 1×10^{-6} for both UC2 and xUNITER, and find the best learning rate is 5×10^{-6} for both the normal fine-tuning stage and the meta-update of MAML. For the inner learning rate of XVL-MAML, we explore learning rates 5×10^{-6}, 5×10^{-5}, 5×10^{-4} and 5×10^{-3}, and find that 5×10^{-4} is the best inner learning rate.

For the proposed meta-learning framework, we find that models overfit after 300 iterations in most situations (for each iterations, we sample a batch of data as support set and a batch as query set),

METHOD	ZH	TA	SW	TR	ID	avg
xUNITER						
Base	54.34/4.74	55.40/6.55	56.41/7.61	57.53/10.99	56.44/7.79	56.02/7.54
Ours ($zh \rightarrow X$)	-	59.82/14.10	58.85/9.78	60.93/13.22	61.17/13.48	-
Ours (avg)	58.34/9.88	58.49/10.25	59.59/10.33	60.06/12.03	60.35/12.41	59.37/10.98
Ours (max)	**59.75/10.28**	**59.82/14.10**	**60.83/10.14**	**62.20/15.25**	**61.17/13.48**	**60.75/12.65**
UC2						
Base	57.81/12.25	**60.06/11.15**	51.81/1.09	55.76/7.46	56.56/8.51	56.40/8.09
Ours ($zh \rightarrow X$)	-	58.94/12.13	53.61/7.57	55.34/7.99	56.74/8.03	-
Ours (avg	58.35/13.44	58.35/12.71	53.99/7.93	56.80/9.61	56.54/9.41	56.81/10.62
Ours (max)	**59.59/13.04**	58.94/12.13	**54.60/9.11**	**58.13/13.48**	**56.74/12.60**	**57.60/12.07**

Table 2: Zero-shot performance (accuracy/consistency) of two baseline models fine-tuned only on English data (Base) and then fine-tuned by our meta-learning method (Ours) on the MaRVL dataset (Liu et al., 2021), where the definition of consistency following Liu et al. (2021). Columns indicate target languages. The avg column gives the average performance across all target languages in this row. $zh \rightarrow X$ means the auxiliary language is Chinese, and the target languages is other low-resource languages X. We also show the average and maximum performance across all auxiliary languages for each target language.

so we set the number of iterations to 400 for all our experiments, and evaluate the performance of models for each 25 iterations to guarantee that we can pick the model with best performance of each setting for evaluation.

5 Results and Discussion

5.1 Zero-shot

We report the results of the baseline models and the results for fine-tuning them using our meta-learning framework in Table 1. In our setting, baseline model means that the PVLM is only fine-tuned on the English datasets. For simplicity, we report the averaged results of all combinations of target languages and auxiliary languages for each model and task. We set the value of λ in Equation (8) to 2×10^{-2} for xUNITER and 5×10^{-2} for UC2 to gain the best performance.

The results in the Table 1 indicate the effectiveness of our meta-learning framework and show that our method can boost the zero-shot performance of UC2 and XUNITER on all four datasets in IGLUE. Note that Table 1 shows average performance across all languages. The performance for individual languages can vary, and is shown in detail in Appendix A, Table 4. We also show the differences in improvements when using different auxiliary languages for different target languages in Figure 5.

5.2 Few-shot

We also conduct few-shot experiments following the setting in IGLUE (Bugliarello et al., 2022) for both xUNITER and UC2 on XVNLI and MaRVL. The results are shown in Figure 2, where the horizontal axis represents the number of shots, and the vertical axis represents the accuracy score. The leftmost point of the horizontal axis is zero, which represents the performance in the zero-shot setup. The blue points and lines show the performance of our method. The yellow points and lines represent the performance of the baseline. We have performed five runs and the interval represents the standard error. It is clear that in all four figures, our method achieves better performance across all shots. And it is worth noting that although there is a slight increase from the performance of zero-shot to one-shot, our proposed method, without seeing any data in the target languages, outperforms the baselines in the few-shot setting, except for UC2 on MaRVL. In other words, only a few instances of training data in target languages are not enough to eliminate the advantage of our method. This

Method/Models	UC2	xUNITER
Unsupervised Setting		
Baseline	62.5$\pm$0.1	59.1$\pm$0.1
XVL-MAML(w/o down-stream)	**63.1$\pm$0.1**	**60.8$\pm$0.1**
Supervised Setting		
XVL-MAML(w/o contrastive)	63.8$\pm$0.1	61.6$\pm$0.1
XVL-MAML	**64.4$\pm$0.1**	**62.9$\pm$0.1**

Table 3: Ablation study in the unsupervised setting and supervised setting. The labels of the down-stream task data in the auxiliary language are not given in unsupervised setting and provided in supervised setting.

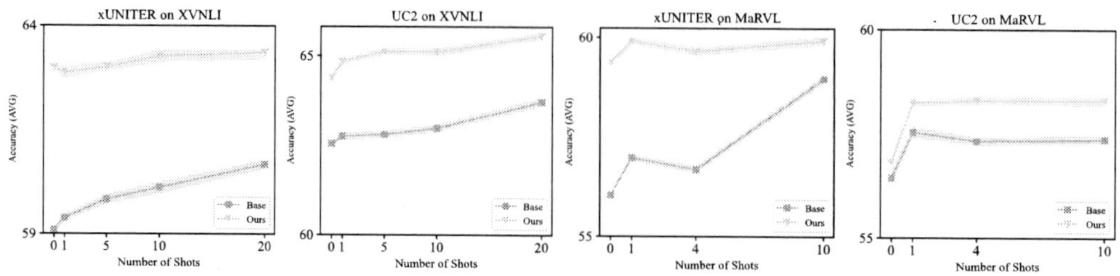

Figure 2: Average few-shot performance (accuracy) across all languages of two baseline models on the XVNLI and MaRVL datasets. The horizontal axis represents the number of shots in the training data.

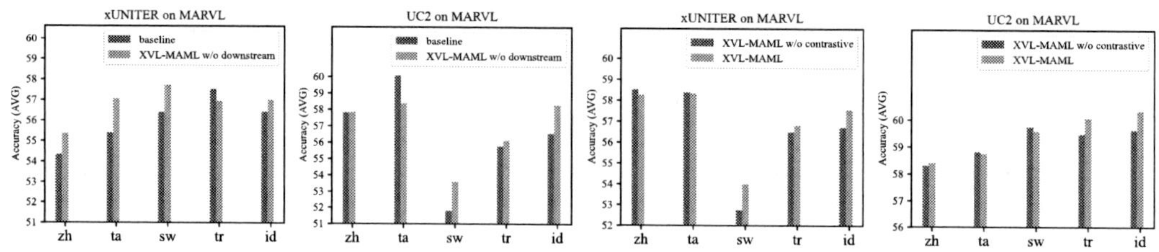

Figure 3: Performance in each target languages averaged across auxiliary languages on the MaRVL dataset.

demonstrates that while our method requires training data in one auxiliary language, there is no need for few-shot data in the target languages.

5.3 Ablation Study and Further Analysis

In this section, we conduct a series of ablation studies which investigate the effect of each part of our proposed meta-learning framework. We have performed five runs for each setting and reported the average and standard error to estimate significant differences.

The Effect of Contrastive Learning We investigate the effect of contrastive learning in our meta-learning fine-tuning framework. Specifically, we fine-tune the model only using a contrastive learning loss in the MAML algorithm (called as "XVL-MAML (w/o down-stream)" in Table 3), where the labels of down-stream task data are not given. We evaluate the performance of UC2 and xUNITER on the XVNLI dataset in this setting and reported them in unsupervised setting part of Table 3. The results indicate that using contrastive learning solely in the MAML algorithm can improve performance. It provides evidence for the hypothesis that contrastive learning can enable models to learn alignments of modalities in cross-lingual transfer, resulting in better representations.

We also compare the performance of the model in the supervised setting where labels of data in auxiliary language are available; hence in the XVL-MAML algorithm, both contrastive loss and down-stream task loss are used. Then we remove the contrastive learning loss in XVL-MAML, only keeping the down-stream task loss. We compare the performance of these two settings in Table 3 to show the effectiveness of the contrastive learning loss in XVL-MAML in the supervised setting. In the "Supervised Setting" part of Table 3, the first row is XVL-MAML without contrastive learning loss, which means only using down-stream task loss when fine-tuning, and the second row is normal XVL-MAML using both contrastive loss and down-stream task loss.

Moreover, we show the difference in performance in each target language separately in Figure 3. Contrastive learning can bring improvements for most of the target languages, especially those whose performance is relatively low when not using contrastive learning. For example, in the left-most plot, performance in *zh*, *ta*, and *sw* is relatively lower than *tr* in the baseline, but gains significant improvements when using our method. The similar effect can be seen in other three plots and Table 2.

Diverse down-stream tasks We report the results of experiments using four diverse multilingual vision-and-language understanding tasks in Table 1. Our method can bring clear improvements across all tasks for both UC2 and xUNITER, indicating that the approach generalises across tasks. Furthermore, these four IGLUE tasks also differ in the distribution of language families and domains, which indicates our method can be useful across

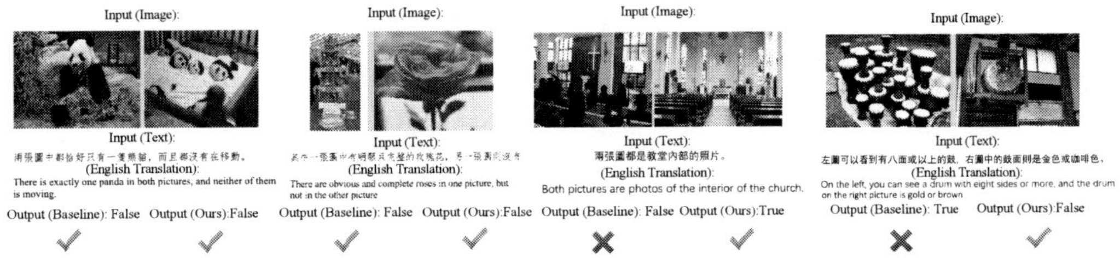

Figure 4: Examples from the Chinese part of the MaRVL dataset and predictions of the baseline and ours method.

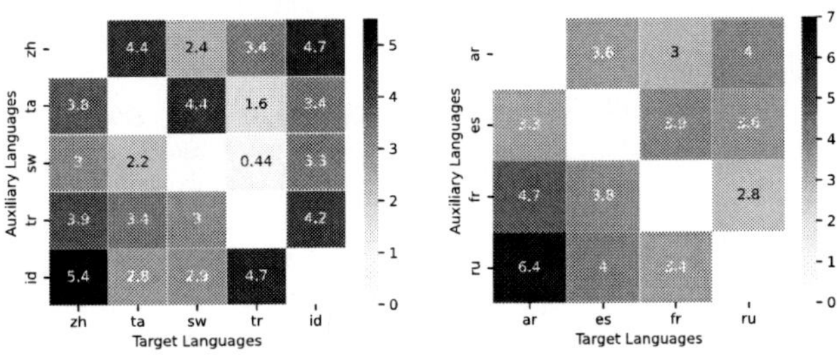

Figure 5: Improvements of zero-shot performance by fine-tuning xUNITER on different auxiliary languages then evaluating on different target languages using our proposed framework compared with baseline. The left heatmap is for MaRVL, and the right is for XVNLI. Rows correspond to auxiliary and columns correspond to target languages.

language families and domains. Moreover, our method can significantly boost the performance of xUNITER even in the challenging MaRVL dataset which encompasses five diverse language families and cultures, improving accuracy by 4.4 points.

Diverse languages We also investigate the difference of performance between languages. Specifically, we take the MaRVL dataset as an example and report results in Table 2, which lists the performance when using Chinese (zh) as the auxiliary language for meta-learning, and the average and maximum performance across all auxiliary languages for each target language respectively. In most situations, our method results in clear improvements. We then visualize the improvements of xUNITER when using different auxiliary languages for different target languages on MaRVL and XVNLI in Figure 5. The improvements we see for MaRVL (which range from 0.44 to 5.4) are smaller than for XVNLI (which range from 2.8 to 6.4), and one possible reason is that the language families of MaRVL are more diverse than those of XVNLI. But in general, our method improves performance for all combinations of auxiliary and target languages, even when they come from different language families. This further indicates that our method is language-agnostic.

5.4 Example Predictions

We show some examples of inputs and predictions for baseline and our method in Figure 4. We use xUNITER to predict the Chinese part of the MaRVL dataset. We have selected two examples where the baseline prediction is incorrect, but our method predicts correctly (the rightmost two examples), and two examples where both our method and baseline method predict correctly (the leftmost two examples). In the two rightmost examples, the label is "True", but the baseline predicts "False". We find that in these two examples, the same concepts ("church" and "drum") described in related texts have different visual features, which makes it more difficult for models to identify them. In the left two examples, however, the concepts (panda and roses) described in the text do not have diverse or obscure visual features when they appear in the images. Therefore, based on these cases, we can surmise that the meta-learning framework makes the model more adaptive to diverse information and resulting in better generalization capabilities when mapping between texts and images.

6 Conclusions

In this paper, we focused on mitigating the problem of poor performance of current PVLMs in vision-language cross-lingual transfer. We proposed a novel MAML framework to adapt pre-trained models for new languages in vision-and-language tasks. Our framework combines contrastive learning and downstream task supervised learning. We verify the effectiveness of our approach in both supervised and unsupervised settings. The key strength of our method is that we leverage contrastive learning in the MAML procedure so that models can quickly learn to align representations from different modalities and adapt them to unseen languages.

Experimental results demonstrate that our proposed meta-learning framework significantly improves the performance of models in vision-and-language cross-lingual transfer both in zero-shot and few-shot setups. We applied our method to two representative PVLMs, UC2 and xUNITER, and verified its effectiveness on four datasets in the IGLUE benchmark in 14 languages. We also conducted an ablation study to explore the effect of contrastive learning, and analysed the effect of different languages and tasks.

Limitations

Our proposed method applies contrastive learning to samples of image-text pairs. The alignments induced in this fashion work best if there is a concept or an object that is both depicted in the image and referred to in the sentence. If this is not the case, then the method may end up learning incorrect alignments; this includes cases where the image or the sentence contain multiple objects or concepts, not all of which can be aligned. To address this limitation, future work should explore how to construct better positive and negative samples and how to enable learning at a more fine-grained level. Besides, current famous PVLMs are encoder-only models, which is different with recent decoder-only LLMs, so meta-learning methods for multi-modal multilingual LLMs is worth to explore as a future work.

Ethics Statement

The use of the IGLUE benchmark in our paper is consistent with its intended use. We have checked the datasets for offensive content by sampling and visualizing examples. There are 14 languages in the datasets we use, we list them in Table 4. More detailed information about the IGLUE dataset can be found in (Bugliarello et al., 2022).

References

Emanuele Bugliarello, Fangyu Liu, Jonas Pfeiffer, Siva Reddy, Desmond Elliott, Edoardo Maria Ponti, and Ivan Vulić. 2022. Iglue: A benchmark for transfer learning across modalities, tasks, and languages. *arXiv preprint arXiv:2201.11732*.

Yen-Chun Chen, Linjie Li, Licheng Yu, Ahmed El Kholy, Faisal Ahmed, Zhe Gan, Yu Cheng, and Jingjing Liu. 2020. Uniter: Universal image-text representation learning. In *European conference on computer vision*, pages 104–120. Springer.

Alexis Conneau, Kartikay Khandelwal, Naman Goyal, Vishrav Chaudhary, Guillaume Wenzek, Francisco Guzmán, Édouard Grave, Myle Ott, Luke Zettlemoyer, and Veselin Stoyanov. 2020. Unsupervised cross-lingual representation learning at scale. In *Proceedings of the 58th Annual Meeting of the Association for Computational Linguistics*, pages 8440–8451.

Jacob Devlin, Ming-Wei Chang, Kenton Lee, and Kristina Toutanova. 2019. Bert: Pre-training of deep bidirectional transformers for language understanding. In *Proceedings of the 2019 Conference of the North American Chapter of the Association for Computational Linguistics: Human Language Technologies, Volume 1 (Long and Short Papers)*, pages 4171–4186.

Desmond Elliott, Stella Frank, Khalil Sima'an, and Lucia Specia. 2016. Multi30k: Multilingual english-german image descriptions. *arXiv preprint arXiv:1605.00459*.

Chelsea Finn, Pieter Abbeel, and Sergey Levine. 2017. Model-agnostic meta-learning for fast adaptation of deep networks. In *International conference on machine learning*, pages 1126–1135. PMLR.

Spandana Gella, Rico Sennrich, Frank Keller, and Mirella Lapata. 2017. Image pivoting for learning multilingual multimodal representations. In *Proceedings of the 2017 Conference on Empirical Methods in Natural Language Processing*, pages 2839–2845, Copenhagen, Denmark. Association for Computational Linguistics.

Jiatao Gu, Yong Wang, Yun Chen, Victor O. K. Li, and Kyunghyun Cho. 2018. Meta-learning for low-resource neural machine translation. In *Proceedings of the 2018 Conference on Empirical Methods in Natural Language Processing*, pages 3622–3631, Brussels, Belgium. Association for Computational Linguistics.

Drew A Hudson and Christopher D Manning. 2019. Gqa: A new dataset for real-world visual reasoning and compositional question answering. In *Proceedings of the IEEE/CVF conference on computer vision and pattern recognition*, pages 6700–6709.

Da Li, Yongxin Yang, Yi-Zhe Song, and Timothy Hospedales. 2018. Learning to generalize: Meta-learning for domain generalization. In *Proceedings of the AAAI conference on artificial intelligence*, volume 32.

Tsung-Yi Lin, Michael Maire, Serge Belongie, Lubomir Bourdev, Ross Girshick, James Hays, Pietro Perona, Deva Ramanan, C. Lawrence Zitnick, and Piotr Dollár. 2015. Microsoft coco: Common objects in context.

Tsung-Yi Lin, Michael Maire, Serge Belongie, James Hays, Pietro Perona, Deva Ramanan, Piotr Dollár, and C Lawrence Zitnick. 2014. Microsoft coco: Common objects in context. In *European conference on computer vision*, pages 740–755. Springer.

Fangyu Liu, Emanuele Bugliarello, Edoardo Maria Ponti, Siva Reddy, Nigel Collier, and Desmond Elliott. 2021. Visually grounded reasoning across languages and cultures. In *Proceedings of the 2021 Conference on Empirical Methods in Natural Language Processing*, pages 10467–10485.

Ilya Loshchilov and Frank Hutter. 2018. Decoupled weight decay regularization. In *International Conference on Learning Representations*.

Jiasen Lu, Dhruv Batra, Devi Parikh, and Stefan Lee. 2019. Vilbert: Pretraining task-agnostic visiolinguistic representations for vision-and-language tasks. *Advances in neural information processing systems*, 32.

Minheng Ni, Haoyang Huang, Lin Su, Edward Cui, Taroon Bharti, Lijuan Wang, Dongdong Zhang, and Nan Duan. 2021. M3p: Learning universal representations via multitask multilingual multimodal pretraining. In *Proceedings of the IEEE/CVF conference on computer vision and pattern recognition*, pages 3977–3986.

Farhad Nooralahzadeh, Giannis Bekoulis, Johannes Bjerva, and Isabelle Augenstein. 2020. Zero-shot cross-lingual transfer with meta learning. In *Proceedings of the 2020 Conference on Empirical Methods in Natural Language Processing (EMNLP)*, pages 4547–4562.

Abiola Obamuyide and Andreas Vlachos. 2019. Model-agnostic meta-learning for relation classification with limited supervision. In *Proceedings of the 57th Annual Meeting of the Association for Computational Linguistics*, pages 5873–5879.

Jonas Pfeiffer, Gregor Geigle, Aishwarya Kamath, Jan-Martin Steitz, Stefan Roth, Ivan Vulić, and Iryna Gurevych. 2022. xgqa: Cross-lingual visual question answering. In *Findings of the Association for Computational Linguistics: ACL 2022*, pages 2497–2511.

Bryan A Plummer, Liwei Wang, Chris M Cervantes, Juan C Caicedo, Julia Hockenmaier, and Svetlana Lazebnik. 2015. Flickr30k entities: Collecting region-to-phrase correspondences for richer image-to-sentence models. In *Proceedings of the IEEE international conference on computer vision*, pages 2641–2649.

Chen Qiu, Dan Oneata, Emanuele Bugliarello, Stella Frank, and Desmond Elliott. 2022. Multilingual multimodal learning with machine translated text. *arXiv preprint arXiv:2210.13134*.

Alec Radford, Jong Wook Kim, Chris Hallacy, Aditya Ramesh, Gabriel Goh, Sandhini Agarwal, Girish Sastry, Amanda Askell, Pamela Mishkin, Jack Clark, et al. 2021. Learning transferable visual models from natural language supervision. In *International Conference on Machine Learning*, pages 8748–8763. PMLR.

Mengye Ren, Eleni Triantafillou, Sachin Ravi, Jake Snell, Kevin Swersky, Joshua B Tenenbaum, Hugo Larochelle, and Richard S Zemel. 2018. Meta-learning for semi-supervised few-shot classification. *arXiv preprint arXiv:1803.00676*.

Shaoqing Ren, Kaiming He, Ross Girshick, and Jian Sun. 2015. Faster r-cnn: Towards real-time object detection with region proposal networks. *Advances in neural information processing systems*, 28.

Guy Rotman, Ivan Vulić, and Roi Reichart. 2018. Bridging languages through images with deep partial canonical correlation analysis. In *Proceedings of the 56th Annual Meeting of the Association for Computational Linguistics (Volume 1: Long Papers)*, pages 910–921, Melbourne, Australia. Association for Computational Linguistics.

Weijie Su, Xizhou Zhu, Yue Cao, Bin Li, Lewei Lu, Furu Wei, and Jifeng Dai. 2019. Vl-bert: Pre-training of generic visual-linguistic representations. In *International Conference on Learning Representations*.

Alane Suhr, Stephanie Zhou, Ally Zhang, Iris Zhang, Huajun Bai, and Yoav Artzi. 2019. A corpus for reasoning about natural language grounded in photographs. In *Proceedings of the 57th Annual Meeting of the Association for Computational Linguistics*, pages 6418–6428.

Hao Tan and Mohit Bansal. 2019. Lxmert: Learning cross-modality encoder representations from transformers. *arXiv preprint arXiv:1908.07490*.

Vinay Kumar Verma, Dhanajit Brahma, and Piyush Rai. 2020. Meta-learning for generalized zero-shot learning. In *Proceedings of the AAAI conference on artificial intelligence*, volume 34, pages 6062–6069.

Oriol Vinyals, Charles Blundell, Timothy Lillicrap, Daan Wierstra, et al. 2016. Matching networks for one shot learning. *Advances in neural information processing systems*, 29.

Oriol Vinyals, Alexander Toshev, Samy Bengio, and Dumitru Erhan. 2015. Show and tell: A neural image caption generator. In *Proceedings of the IEEE conference on computer vision and pattern recognition*, pages 3156–3164.

Bailin Wang, Mirella Lapata, and Ivan Titov. 2021. Meta-learning for domain generalization in semantic parsing. In *Proceedings of the 2021 Conference of the North American Chapter of the Association for Computational Linguistics: Human Language Technologies*, pages 366–379.

Ying Wang, Jonas Pfeiffer, Nicolas Carion, Yann LeCun, and Aishwarya Kamath. 2023. Adapting grounded visual question answering models to low resource languages. In *Proceedings of the IEEE/CVF Conference on Computer Vision and Pattern Recognition*, pages 2595–2604.

Ning Xie, Farley Lai, Derek Doran, and Asim Kadav. 2019. Visual entailment: A novel task for fine-grained image understanding. *arXiv preprint arXiv:1901.06706*.

Tianhe Yu, Saurabh Kumar, Abhishek Gupta, Sergey Levine, Karol Hausman, and Chelsea Finn. 2020. Gradient surgery for multi-task learning. *Advances in Neural Information Processing Systems*, 33:5824–5836.

Yuhao Zhang, Hang Jiang, Yasuhide Miura, Christopher D Manning, and Curtis P Langlotz. 2020. Contrastive learning of medical visual representations from paired images and text. *arXiv preprint arXiv:2010.00747*.

Liangli Zhen, Peng Hu, Xu Wang, and Dezhong Peng. 2019. Deep supervised cross-modal retrieval. In *Proceedings of the IEEE/CVF Conference on Computer Vision and Pattern Recognition*, pages 10394–10403.

Mingyang Zhou, Luowei Zhou, Shuohang Wang, Yu Cheng, Linjie Li, Zhou Yu, and Jingjing Liu. 2021. Uc2: Universal cross-lingual cross-modal vision-and-language pre-training. In *Proceedings of the IEEE/CVF Conference on Computer Vision and Pattern Recognition*, pages 4155–4165.

Stephanie Zhou, Alane Suhr, and Yoav Artzi. 2017. Visual reasoning with natural language. *arXiv preprint arXiv:1710.00453*.

A Appendix

This is a section in the appendix.

	Ar	Bn	De	Es	Id	Fr	Ja	Ko	Pt	Ru	Sw	Ta	Tr	Zh
							MaRVL							
xUNITER (Baseline)	-	-	-	-	56.44	-	-	-	-	-	56.41	55.40	57.53	54.34
UC2 (Baseline)	-	-	-	-	56.56	-	-	-	-	-	51.81	**60.06**	55.76	57.81
xUNITER (Ours)	-	-	-	-	**60.35**	-	-	-	-	-	**59.59**	58.49	**60.06**	**59.75**
UC2 (Ours)	-	-	-	-	56.74	-	-	-	-	-	54.60	58.94	58.13	59.59
							XVNLI							
xUNITER (Baseline)	53.52	-	-	60.05	-	61.60	-	-	-	61.25	-	-	-	-
UC2 (Baseline)	58.36	-	-	**63.86**	-	65.01	-	-	-	64.72	-	-	-	-
xUNITER (Ours)	56.70	-	-	60.91	-	68.64	-	-	-	63.91	-	-	-	-
UC2 (Ours)	**59.94**	-	-	62.97	-	**69.41**	-	-	-	**65,18**	-	-	-	-
							xGQA							
xUNITER (Baseline)	-	11.41	33.21	-	32.38	-	-	13.28	20.51	17.84	-	-	-	17.20
UC2 (Baseline)	-	19.49	33.52	-	29.83	-	-	23.29	31.23	32.61	-	-	-	33.25
xUNITER (Ours)	-	12.46	34.10	-	**33.63**	-	-	15.05	22.71	20.27	-	-	-	19.27
UC2 (Ours)	-	**19.63**	**34.50**	-	29.58	-	-	**24.93**	**32.47**	**33.24**	-	-	-	**35.00**
							Xflickr&Co (IR)							
xUNITER (Baseline)	-	-	14.70	16.40	15.15	-	9.55	-	-	14.75	-	-	8.85	17.20
UC2 (Baseline)	-	-	28.10	14.65	13.55	-	23.70	-	-	18.20	-	-	8.15	31.70
xUNITER (Ours)	-	-	16.20	**18.85**	**18.50**	-	12.10	-	-	17.75	-	-	**11.10**	19.40
UC2 (Ours)	-	-	**29.35**	16.90	14.25	-	**25.15**	-	-	**20.50**	-	-	10.50	**32.10**
							Xflickr&Co (TR)							
xUNITER (Baseline)	-	-	14.2	15.45	13.95	-	8.30	-	-	13.15	-	-	7.75	14.4
UC2 (Baseline)	-	-	23.55	11.90	10.35	-	22.75	-	-	17.50	-	-	6.15	26.85
xUNITER (Ours)	-	-	15.50	**16.15**	**16.70**	-	9.90	-	-	15.70	-	-	**9.50**	15.75
UC2 (Ours)	-	-	**25.30**	13.95	12.45	-	**23.50**	-	-	**19.80**	-	-	8.30	**27.45**

Table 4: Accuracy scores for each target language individually averaged over auxiliary languages.

Counterfactually Probing Language Identity in Multilingual Models

Anirudh Srinivasan[◇*] **Venkata S Govindarajan**[♡*] **Kyle Mahowald**[♡]
[◇]Department of Computer Science [♡]Department of Linguistics
The University of Texas at Austin
{anirudhs,venkatasg,kyle}@utexas.edu

Abstract

Techniques in causal analysis of language models illuminate how linguistic information is organized in LLMs. We use one such technique, AlterRep, a method of counterfactual probing, to explore the internal structure of multilingual models (mBERT and XLM-R). We train a linear classifier on a binary language identity task, to classify tokens between Language X and Language Y. Applying a counterfactual probing procedure, we use the classifier weights to project the embeddings into the null space and push the resulting embeddings either in the direction of Language X or Language Y. Then we evaluate on a masked language modeling task. We find that, given a template in Language X, pushing towards Language Y systematically increases the probability of Language Y words, above and beyond a third-party control language. But it does not specifically push the model towards translation-equivalent words in Language Y. Pushing towards Language X (the same direction as the template) has a minimal effect, but somewhat degrades these models. Overall, we take these results as further evidence of the rich structure of massive multilingual language models, which include both a language-specific and language-general component. And we show that counterfactual probing can be fruitfully applied to multilingual models.

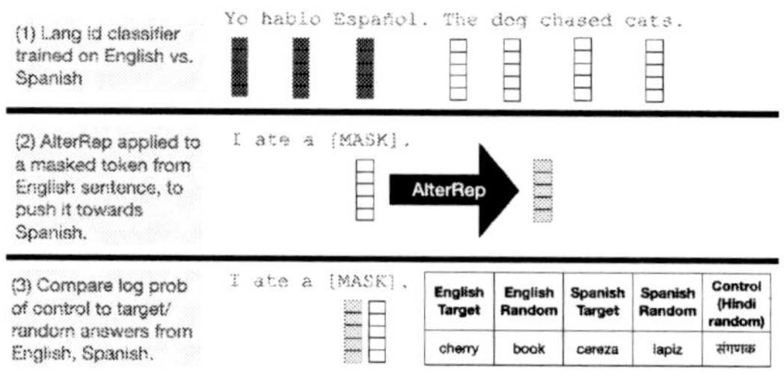

Figure 1: We train a classifier on the language ID task, and then apply AlterRep to the embeddings and examine the change in probabilities. Above, an English template sentence is pushed towards Spanish. We compare the probabilities of the target English answer to its Spanish translation-equivalent, random English and Spanish answers, and a random third-language control.

1 Introduction

Large pretrained multilingual transformer models succeed at a variety of multilingual and monolingual tasks and can be used in transfer learning paradigms, where a model is trained to do a task in one language and then transferred to another language (Lauscher et al., 2020; Conneau et al., 2020b; Wu and Dredze, 2019, 2020; Pires et al., 2019; Vulić et al., 2020; Rust et al., 2021). These abilities have spurred a spate of papers probing the internal workings and capabilities of multilingual models, suggesting that such models may contain language-independent, along with langauge-specific knowledge of interesting linguistic structure (e.g., Chi et al., 2020; Papadimitriou et al., 2021; Ravishankar et al., 2021; Blevins et al., 2022; Gonen et al., 2020).

While the results of this literature are suggestive, probing methods are susceptible to memorizing the original input and may not reflect what information models actually use downstream (Hewitt and Liang, 2019; Elazar et al., 2021; Pimentel et al., 2020; Voita et al., 2021). It is thus desirable to test not only what information can be extracted but what information is actually used (Geiger et al., 2021; Finlayson et al., 2021; Lasri et al., 2022).

To do that we apply AlterRep (Ravfogel et al., 2021), an offshoot of Iterative Nullspace Projection (INLP; Ravfogel et al., 2020; Elazar et al., 2021), in a multilingual setting.[1] The AlterRep method is to train a classifier on the model representations

[*]These authors contributed equally to this work.

[1]Since running these experiments, there is now work showing that linearly removing information as in INLP is suboptimal (Ravfogel et al., 2022). A natural extension would be to explore our paradigm using these newer techniques.

Proceedings of the The 3rd Workshop on Multi-lingual Representation Learning (MRL), pages 24–36
December 7, 2023

to pick out a particular feature and then use the parameters learned by the classifier to *intervene* on the embeddings, pushing them in a particular direction. Ravfogel et al. (2021) use it to intervene on whether a noun phrase is in a relative clause (e.g., training a classifier on whether the noun phrase is in a relative clause and then using projections from the classifier to push the embeddings towards or away from the relative clause direction). Crucially, they then measure how this manipulation affects downstream subject-verb number agreement.

Whereas Ravfogel et al. (2021) use AlterRep to explore syntactic representations in models, our hypothesis is that the same kind of causal manipulation could be informative as to how multilingual models process multilingual text. Doing so necessarily involves separating multilingual embedding space into language-neutral and language-specific components. Libovický et al. (2020) explore the idea of obtaining a language-neutral representation from a multilingual model by computing an "average" representation for each language and subtracting it from the token embedding.

There is some precedent for using INLP to generate language-specific and language-neutral components. Gonen et al. (2020) showed that multilingual models like mBERT have both a language-specific and language-general component and that, by separating them using INLP on a language identification task, one can obtain language-agnostic representations (and, inversely, highly language-specific representations). They show that, by training on an English vs. non-English task and then projecting onto the nullspace using INLP, the generated text on a masked language modeling task (in English) is less likely to be English after INLP. Gonen et al. (2020) also show that, by subtracting an "average" representation of language X from a particular token embedding and then adding the average language Y embedding, one can obtain a translation of the token in language Y by *analogy*. But they do not specifically use INLP to do these translations in a language-to-language way, as we do here.

Using a similar logic but the AlterRep technique instead of the analogical method, we test whether we can do a kind of "translation via AlterRep", effectively "pushing" the embeddings towards a particular language. First, we use the original multilingual model embeddings for a particular token h_t to train a language identity classifier C to classify the language of tokens from Languages X and Y. We then use INLP to null out language ID information, creating null embeddings h_t^N. We can then generate altered embeddings h_t^X and h_t^Y, which go beyond merely nulling out language ID and instead represent embeddings that have been pushed into the direction of Language X or Y, respectively. We use these counterfactual embeddings to generate predictions for masked text and compare the result to the original embeddings.

To make this concrete, imagine training a language identification classifier on English vs. Spanish, as shown in Figure 1. Whereas a multilingual model would typically fill in the [MASK] position in the English sentence "I ate a [MASK]" with an English token, if we use the classifier to push the embeddings in the direction of Spanish, then we might expect a completion like "I ate a *cereza*" to become more likely where *cereza* is the English word for cherry. We would expect the probability of the English word "cherry" to decrease.

Through this work, our hope is not only to illuminate the innerworkings of multilingual models, but also to validate and explore the use of counterfactual probing in a novel domain.

To spoil the result: we show that language identity is encoded in contextual token embeddings and, crucially, that this information is *used* by multilingual models in masked language modeling. In effect, pushing embeddings in the direction of a particular language (and away from another) systematically increases probabilities of words in the PUSHEDTO language and decreases the probabilities in the PUSHEDAWAY language, while leaving words from other languages unchanged. By comparing the changes in probabilities of target words in the PUSHEDTO language (i.e., translation equivalents of the original correct word) to random words in that language, we see that our alterations seem to push the model towards the *prior* of the intended language, without specifically boosting the semantic equivalent.[2]

2 Methods

We run two experiments, with slightly different procedures. In Experiment 1, we train a token-level language ID classifier on a corpus of monolingual sentences from 2 languages, without mixing the languages within-sentence. In Experiment 2, we create artificial code-mixed text (mixing within sentences) and use this for training the classifier. In

[2]We make our code available online here.

both experiments, we evaluate two representative massive multilingual transformer models, Multilingual BERT (mBERT; Devlin et al., 2019) and XLM-RoBERTa Base (XLM-R; Conneau et al., 2020a), and we focus on the last layer for intervention. We describe each step in more detail below.

Models Multilingual BERT (Devlin et al., 2019) and XLM-Roberta Base (Conneau et al., 2020a) span 104 and 100 languages respectively. Both are transformer encoders that have a hidden dimension size of 768.

Classifier For each iteration of INLP, a linear classifier is learned on the representations produced by the encoder to predict language ID (L_1 vs L_2) for each token in the input. We use SVMs as our linear classifiers (as in Ravfogel et al., 2021). While training the classifier, 15% of the tokens are randomly masked. This is done to be more representative of the final evaluation setting where masked inputs are used. The classifier is trained on balanced samples.

INLP and AlterRep INLP is a technique for removing information from embeddings. Specifically, INLP uses the weights learned by each classifier to project the embedding h_t onto the intersection of nullspaces of the classifiers h_t^N (this contains no information for doing the classification). The component orthogonal to this h_t^R, contains all of the information for doing classification. In practice, not all information is removed by the first projection onto the nullspace, so the process is repeated iteratively. The second classifier is learned on top of the embeddings whose information has been nulled out based on the first classifier's weights, and so on. This is repeated m times, yielding m classifiers.

AlterRep (Ravfogel et al., 2021) considers both the nullspace component and the orthogonal component to generate a new embedding h'_t that has been modified to lie on a particular side of the classifier. Suppose that for weight w_i learned by classifier i, $h_t^{w_i}$ is the orthogonal component. The counterfactual vector h'_t is created as follows:

$$h'_t = h_t^N + \alpha \sum_{w_i} S * h_t^{w_i} \quad (1)$$

S is 1 when the given classifier's prediction $w_i^T h_t > 0$ (predicts L_1) and -1 when $w_i^T h_t < 0$ (predicts L_2).

The parameter α controls the direction and magnitude of the alteration. When $\alpha = 0$, it's equivalent to amnesic probing. While training classifiers for INLP, α is always set to 0. α is non zero when we're evaluating on MLM in the subsequent sections. When $\alpha > 0$, the representations will be pushed to the L_1 side of the classifier, irrespective of where they were originally. When $\alpha < 0$, the representations will be pushed to the L_2 side of the classifier, irrespective of where they were originally.

Choosing the number of INLP iterations Determining the number of iterations to run INLP for is tricky as there is tension between removing information and destroying the language model (Elazar et al., 2021). We sought to find a number of iterations that would (a) significantly degrade performance on the language identification task (thus proving removal of language ID information) but (b) not torpedo the performance of the model on the MLM task.

One option for choosing the number of iterations to run INLP is to run it until the classifier performance is at chance on the target task. We found that, if we do this for XLM-R (and to a lesser extent for mBERT), a large number of iterations is required (around 32). This large number of iterations effectively destroys the language model, causing the most likely completions to be jibberish (with a MLM-100 accuracy close to zero).

So, instead, we choose to optimize for removing as much information as possible while still maintaining acceptable (>90%) MLM-100 accuracy. Figure 2 shows the number of iterations plotted against both the MLM-100 measure and against the language ID accuracy. For Experiment 1, we chose 4 iterations for XLM-R and mBERT. For Experiment 2, we run for more iterations (16 for both models) since the code-mixed data is less susceptible to model degradation.

Note that this means that, for our post-INLP models, there is still some language identity information remaining and so these embeddings should not be treated as entirely free of language identity information. But the number of iterations was still sufficiently high to allow us to meaningfully push towards or away from the original language.

Running the INLP classifier for the same number of iterations more catastrophically affects the overall MLM performance for XLM-R than it does mBERT. We leave it to future work to ascertain

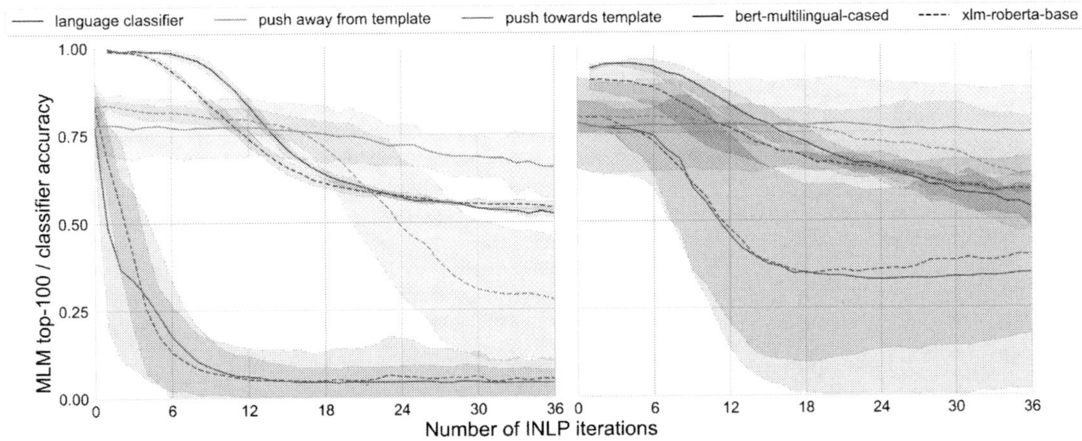

Figure 2: MLM-100 accuracies after intervention, and language ID classifier accuracy plotted over number of INLP iterations for m-BERT and XLM-R. Results are shown with INLP trained on non-code mixed data on the left, and code-mixed data on the right. All MLM results are accuracies averaged over all languages and language pairs

why XLM-R might have its MLM performance more closely tied to language identity information than mBERT.

2.1 Experiment 1: Non-Code-Mixed Sentences

Languages We pair English with each of Korean, Hindi, Spanish, and Finnish, giving us 4 pairwise comparisons. These languages were chosen to form pairs with the same script/family (English-Spanish), same script but different family (English-Finnish) and different script/family (English with Hindi and Korean). We always use English as one of the pairs, which ensures adequate translations using the MUSE dictionaries. But see Experiment 2 for results between non-English pairs.

Table 1 shows the sources and statistics for the data used to train these classifiers. The monolingual sentences for English and Hindi are taken from their corresponding parts of an English-Hindi parallel corpus (Kunchukuttan et al., 2018). The data for Korean is taken from ParaCrawl (Esplà et al., 2019), Spanish and Finnish from EuroParl (Koehn, 2005).

Training/Testing methodology The Language ID classifiers are trained using 1500 sentences from each language. We alternately embed sentences from English and sentences from the other language and then extract the token embeddings. The classifier learns to predict whether a given token is extracted from the English or non-English language.

	Lang	Source	Train	Val	Test
En-Es	En	IITB En-Hi	1500	250	250
	Es	EuroParl	1500	250	250
En-Fi	En	IITB En-Hi	1500	250	250
	Fi	EuroParl	1500	250	250
En-Hi	En	IITB En-Hi	1500	250	250
	Hi	IITB En-Hi	1500	250	250
En-Ko	En	IITB En-Hi	1500	250	250
	Ko	ParaCrawl	1500	250	250

Table 1: Monolingual Data Sources/Sizes

Evaluation of AlterRep is done on a target of 250 sentences from each language, from the test sets of the same corpora used for training the language ID classifiers. But, because we cannot always find a dictionary match for each target word, the number of test sentences ranges in practice from 205 to 243. We take sentences from the language ID classifier test sets and randomly pick a word to mask in each sentence. We treat that word as the *target word* in the original language, and we use MUSE dictionaries (Lample et al., 2018) to find the equivalent of that word in the alternate language. Then, we compare the probability of (a) the target word in the original language, (b) the target word in the other language, (c) a random word in the original language, (d) a random word in the other language, and (e) a random word form a *third* language (which serves as a control). For instance, Figure 1 shows an English sentence "I ate a cherry."

Original sentence	I ate a *cherry*
Masked input to model	I ate a [MASK]
Mask replaced with target language (es) word	I ate a *cereza*
Mask replaced with random target language (es) word	I ate a *lapiz*
Maks replaced with third language (fi) word	I ate a *kirsikka*

Table 2: Example of how we replace a masked word with different words from the target language/third language dictionary

where we mask the token "cherry.". Table 2 shows an example of how we modify the masked word in the sentence in different manners.

When we push that masked token in the direction of Spanish using AlterRep, we then compare the log probability (before and after the intervention) of: the target English word ("cherry"), the Spanish translation-equivalent ("cereza"), a randomly chosen English word, a randomly chosen Spanish word, and a randomly chosen control word from a third language. The random words are all chosen to have the same number of tokens as the target word in that language. As is standard, we obtain log probabilities for multi-token words by averaging (Kassner et al., 2021; Dou and Neubig, 2021).

If the AlterRep procedure works, then if we start with an English template and push the masked token towards Spanish, the probability of Spanish words will rise and the probability of English words will decrease, while the probability of Hindi words will be unaffected. When we start with English and push towards English, we expect little change. If there are shared semantic representations across languages, then we might expect to see the target words in the pushed-towards language (e.g., "cereza", Spanish "cherry") increase more than random ones (e.g., "lapiz", Spanish for "pencil").

2.2 Experiment 2: Mixed-Language Sentences

Languages To assess the robustness of our results, we focus on a scenario where the model is exposed to mixed-language text, as opposed to monolingual text. Existing work (Santy et al., 2021) has probed the abilities of multilingual transformer encoders on code-mixed text and has shown that these models are able to learn language ID in code-mixed scenarios and this experiment serves as a further probe into the cross-lingual abilities of these models. We consider 3 languages: English, Hindi and Korean and consider all 3 pairs using these languages (En-Hi, En-Ko and Hi-Ko).

	Lang	Source	Train	Val	Test
En-Hi	En Hi	IIT En-Hi Word Subn w/ MUSE	3000	500	500
En-Ko	En Ko	IIT En-Hi Word Subn w/ MUSE	3000	500	500
Hi-Ko	Hi Ko	IIT En-Hi Word Subn w/ MUSE	3000	500	500

Table 3: Code Mixed Data Sources/Sizes. To generate code-mixed data, text from the first language is taken and words from the second language using the MUSE dictionary

Training/Testing methodology The language ID classifiers are trained using synthetic code-mixed text generated for these 3 language pairs. Generating training data this way gives us the flexibility in evaluating on any language pair that we want (unlike using real code-mixed which would limit the language pairs we could choose). We created the synthetic code-mixed data by lexical substitution of words in a monolingual sentence using MUSE dictionaries (Lample et al., 2018), substituting so that 30% of the words are in the second language. Table 3 shows the sources and the statistics for the data used to train this.

Evaluation is done using the multilingual mLAMA dataset (Kassner et al., 2021). Based on Wikipedia entity relations, it consists of templates, translated across languages, with slots in which masked language modeling has to be used to fill in the correct mLAMA answer. Thus, in this experiment, the masked token is always the mLAMA answer in a particular language instead of a random word. We thus have the same template in both languages, along with correct answers in both languages that we can use to evaluate AlterRep on. The number of templates used for evaluation are n=7,256 for English-Hindi, 14,204 for English-Korean, 6,496 for Hindi-Korean. Because we are not limited to pairs involving English in this experiment, we focus on all pairwise comparisons between Hindi, English, and Korean for this study

3 Results

Push in dir. of temp.	Answer pushed towards	Third Lang	Target Word	Random Word
		mBERT		
Opposite	Opposite	0.66	0.98	0.93
Opposite	Same	-	0.98	0.98
Same	Opposite	0.10	1.00	0.99
Same	Same	-	0.54	0.77
		XLMR		
Opposite	Opposite	0.37	0.99	0.96
Opposite	Same	-	0.92	0.92
Same	Opposite	0.25	1.00	0.98
Same	Same	-	0.36	0.62

Table 4: Exp 1. Proportion of data points that move in the expected direction, as a function of template matching push direction and answer matching push direction. When "push in dir. of temp" says "opposite", that means we are pushing away from the direction of the template (e.g., pushing an English sentence to Hindi). When "push in dir. of temp says "same", that means we are pushing in the same direction of the template (e.g., pushing an English sentence even further toward English). We break down how often an answer word moves in the expected direction when that answer word is being pushed towards (e.g., an English word in a template that is being pushed towards English) or when that answer word is being pushed away from (e.g., an English word in a template that is being pushed toward Hindi). The Target word is the actual template word or its translation-equivalent. The random word is a random word in the same language. The third-party word is a random word in a third-party language.

Overall, across both Experiments, we find that the AlterRep operation works as expected in the majority of cases. Figure 3 shows data for our Experiment 1, on mBERT and XLM- R. In each subfigure, the top row indicates the language of the template, the 2nd row indicates the direction in which the token embedding is pushed. The plot has dark arrows indicating the change in probability distributions of tokens from the 2 languages (as indicated), with shaded arrows indicating changes for random tokens in those languages. Blue arrows indicate change in probability distributions for random tokens.

We consider separately the case where we push in the opposite direction as the template (e.g., pushing a Korean template in the English direction) (the left 2 subfigures indicate this) vs. the case where we push in the same direction (the right 2 subfigures indicate this). In the analysis below, we focus on the proportion of time that the probabilities shift

Most likely tokens pre-intervention	friend, house, dream, novel, room, bed, book
Most likely tokens after pushing to Spanish	coma, car, man, la, son, del, más
Most likely tokens after pushing to English	house, dream, room, friend, book, tree, memory

Table 5: Example of the most likely tokens predicted for the masked token pre and post-intervention for the English language text "One day while Cat was wandering about, he came to a [MASK]."

in the expected direction after the intervention. The mean change in log probability, before and after intervention, tells a similar story and is shown in Figure 3.

From hereon, we focus on $\alpha = 3$, but see Appendix B for results on sensitivity to this parameter.

3.1 Experiment 1

When we push in the *opposite direction* of the template (e.g., push an English template towards Spanish), **the template language probabilities plummet**, both for the target (99% of the time, across pairs) and random words (93% of the time, across pairs). The fact that the target word decreases more than the random one may not be very meaningful: the target word starts out with very high probability and so it has farther to drop. Crucially, **the PUSHEDTO language probabilities all increase significantly** (98% of the time for target answers, 98% of the time for random answers). **The THIRDLANG control words show little change**, as predicted (decreasing 66% of the time). Thus, this manipulation works as expected: taking a mask from an English language template and pushing it towards Spanish causes the probability of all Spanish words to increase while decreasing the probability of English-language words and leaving other language words (e.g., Korean or Hindi) largely untouched.

When we push in the *same direction* as the template (e.g., we push an English template even further in the English direction), we find that the **ORIGINALLANGUAGE is largely unchanged** (increasing in 54% of pairs for target words and 77% of the time for random words). Here the difference between random and target is likely because the target word is already at ceiling. **The PUSHEDAWAY language drops significantly** for both target and random words (decreases for 100% and 99% of pairs, for both random and target words).

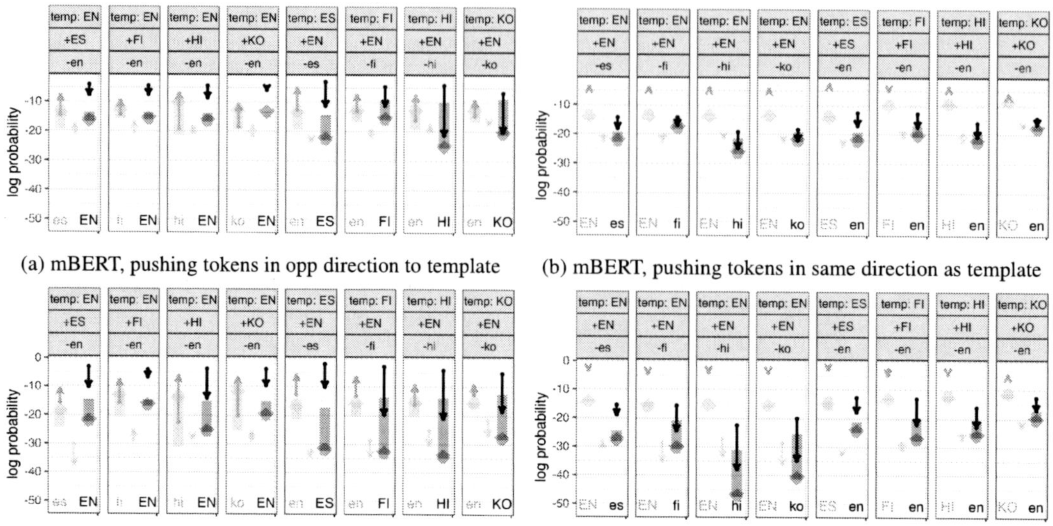

(a) mBERT, pushing tokens in opp direction to template

(b) mBERT, pushing tokens in same direction as template

(c) XLMR, pushing tokens in opp direction to template

(d) XLMR, pushing tokens in same direction as template

Figure 3: Change in language-specific probability distributions for Exp. 1. When we push the token in the opposite language of the template (left two figures), we can see significant changes in the probability distributions for the target (dark arrows) and random words (shaded arrows) from that language, with some cases showing such a large change that tokens from the new language have more probability and will be sampled. Third language controls (blue arrows) and pushing tokens in the same language as the template (right 2 figures) don't show much change.

The THIRDLANG control decreases 90% of the time, suggesting that the probability of a third party language becomes even less likely when we push in the same direction as the template. Taken together, these results suggest that pushing in the same direction as the template does not make the language model better (the target word does not increase substantially), but it does make it more likely to generate words from that language. That is, if we push towards English and the target answer is "dog", pushing towards English will not make "dog" more likely but it will increase the overall Englishness in the model, essentially pushing it towards the English prior while decreasing the probability of generations in other languages.

Table 4 summarizes these results, showing the fraction of templates for which the probabilities move in the expected direction. We see movement in the expected direction in all cases except on words in the pushed-towards language, when we push in the direction of the template. That is, English words don't become *even more likely* when we push towards English in an English template. These results are consistent, regardless of whether we have a language pair with the same script (e.g., English and Finnish) or pairs with different scripts (e.g., English and Hindi). Given the large overlap in shared tokens between any two Latin script languages (and low overlap across scripts), this consistency is notable.

3.2 Experiment 2

Experiment 2 is notable for the fact that we're evaluating the model in a code-mixed setting and testing the model on queries that involve real world factual knowledge (the relations in mLAMA). Results are similar for Experiment 2 (see Figure 4), suggesting robustness to training on code-mixed data and on using non-English pairs. These results are broadly similar to Experiment 1, except that, as we see in Figure 2, the performance of the code-mixed data decays at a very different rate for the code-mixed data. Therefore, we used 16 iterations for both models. Why the code-mixed data is more robust to intervention is potentially interesting, but exploring it is beyond the scope of this work.

Table 6 depicts the proportions of cases in which the probabilities move in the expected direction, and the results are similar. We see that there is not much change when pushing in the same direction as the template and larger changes when pushing in the opposite direction. As with Experiment 1, this likely represents a ceiling effect.

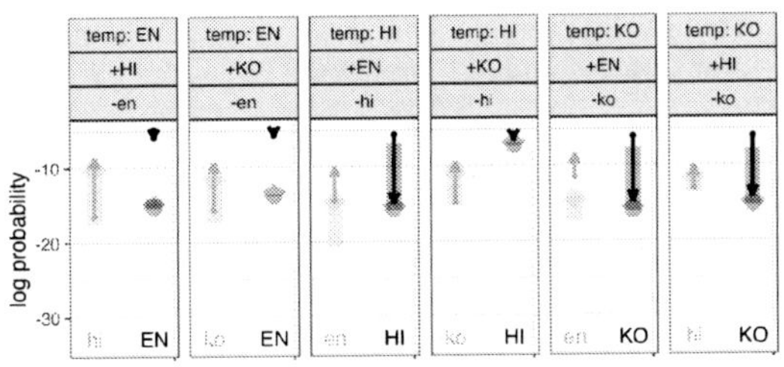

(a) mBERT, pushing tokens in opp direction to template

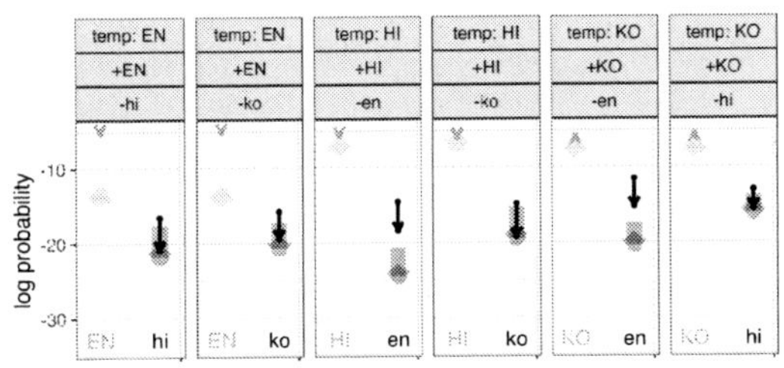

(b) mBERT, pushing tokens in same direction as template

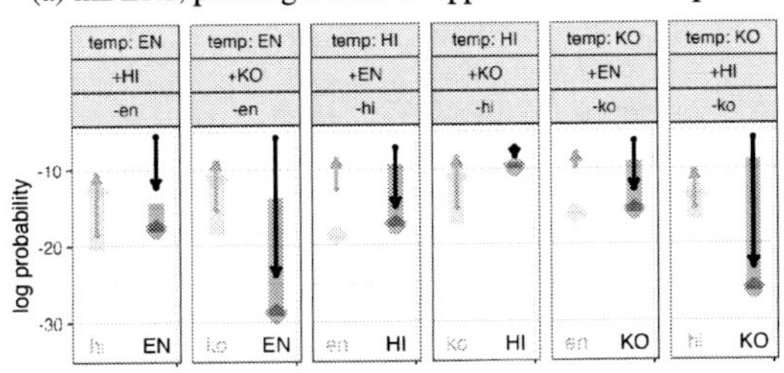

(c) XLMR, pushing tokens in opp direction to template

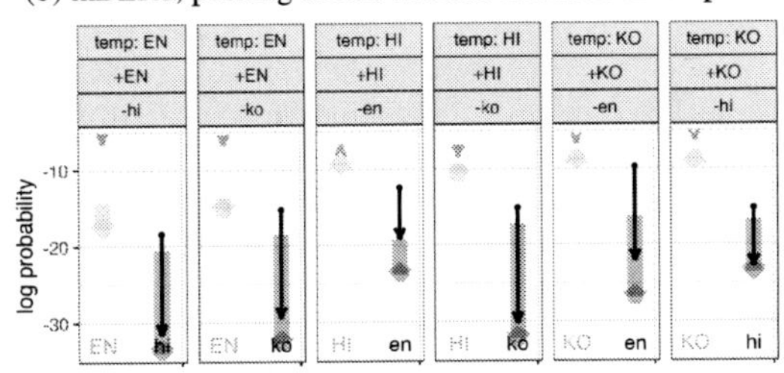

(d) XLMR, pushing tokens in same direction as template

Figure 4: Change in language-specific probability distributions for Exp. 2. As with Exp. 1, when we push the tokens in the opposite direction to the template (left two plots), there are bigger changes in the probability distribution, with the new language sometimes having higher probabilities than the original one. Pushing in the same direction as the template (right two plots) doesn't show any change in the ordering of the two languages.

4 Conclusions

Overall, our results show that, if we take a sentence in Language A, embed it in a multilingual model, and use AlterRep to systematically push a particular word in that sentence towards Language B, the probability of words in Language B will go up. If we push a word in Language A towards Language A, there is little change except that, as shown in Table 5, highly probable words increase in probability overall. Importantly, the probability of words in random control languages do not increase under either intervention.

What can we conclude from this? First, since learning a language ID classifier can be used to causally affect the language of probable masked tokens, we take it as additional evidence (Libovický et al., 2020; Gonen et al., 2020) that mBERT and XLM-R (and likely other models of similar structure) have both a language-specific and language-general component. Second, this language-specific component is linearly extractable and can be used causally to affect the language generated. That said, we did not find evidence that it can be used for translation specifically since translation-equivalent words do not show a boost relative to controls.

In addition to shedding light on multilingual models, we think the method here shows that the AlterRep method (Ravfogel et al., 2021) can be fruitfully applied in settings beyond the syntactic application for which it was originally used. In future work, we could use this method to explore linguistic typology in multilingual model space.

Limitations

Techniques like INLP extract information that is linearly extractable. While we've shown that it is possible to extract and manipulate language information using such simple linear techniques, more complex methods like those proposed by Ravfogel et al. (2022) might be able to manipulate more non-linearly encoded properties.

We have shown that language ID information is extractable and can be used to manipulate embeddings, but we urge caution in concluding that this means it could be used to practical effect (e.g., in machine translation). We leave the translation of these results into practical applications for future work.

The AlterRep procedure, as can be seen in our results and in Ravfogel et al. (2021), is sensitive to parameters like α and the number of INLP iterations. Picking these parameters is tricky and we have done it in a manner that preserves information in the language model. It is possible that a different set of settings not explored here could lead to different results.

The risks associated with this work are the risks

Push in dir. of temp.	Answer pushed towards	Target Word	Random Word
	mBERT		
Opposite	Opposite	.90	.87
Opposite	Same	0.98	0.98
Same	Opposite	1.00	1.00
Same	Same	0.46	0.64
	XLMR		
Opposite	Opposite	.99	.96
Opposite	Same	0.95	0.86
Same	Opposite	1.00	1.00
Same	Same	0.41	0.37

Table 6: Proportion of data points that move in the expected direction, as a function of the template matching push direction and answer matching push direction. When "push in dir. of temp" says "opposite", that means we are pushing away from the direction of the template (e.g., pushing an English sentence to Hindi). When "push in dir. of temp says "same", that means we are pushing in the same direction of the template (e.g., pushing an English sentence towards English). We break down how often an answer word moves in the expected direction when that answer word is being pushed towards (e.g., an English word in a template pushed towards English) or when that answer word is being pushed away from (e.g., an English word in a template that is being pushed toward Hindi). The Target word is the actual template word or its translation-equivalent. The random word is a random word in the same language.

associated with any work dealing with large language models, including potential environmental impacts.

Acknowledgements

We thank Hila Gonen for helpful comments. We thank Tal Linzen for presenting AlterRep to K.M.'s LIN 393 grad seminar and the students of that seminar for helpful comments. K.M. acknowledges funding from NSF Grant 2104995.

References

Terra Blevins, Hila Gonen, and Luke Zettlemoyer. 2022. Analyzing the mono- and cross-lingual pretraining dynamics of multilingual language models. In *Proceedings of the 2022 Conference on Empirical Methods in Natural Language Processing*, pages 3575–3590, Abu Dhabi, United Arab Emirates. Association for Computational Linguistics.

Ethan A. Chi, John Hewitt, and Christopher D. Manning. 2020. Finding universal grammatical relations in multilingual BERT. In *Proceedings of the 58th Annual Meeting of the Association for Computational Linguistics*, pages 5564–5577, Online. Association for Computational Linguistics.

Alexis Conneau, Kartikay Khandelwal, Naman Goyal, Vishrav Chaudhary, Guillaume Wenzek, Francisco Guzmán, Edouard Grave, Myle Ott, Luke Zettlemoyer, and Veselin Stoyanov. 2020a. Unsupervised cross-lingual representation learning at scale. In *Proceedings of the 58th Annual Meeting of the Association for Computational Linguistics*, pages 8440–8451, Online. Association for Computational Linguistics.

Alexis Conneau, Shijie Wu, Haoran Li, Luke Zettlemoyer, and Veselin Stoyanov. 2020b. Emerging cross-lingual structure in pretrained language models. In *Proceedings of the 58th Annual Meeting of the Association for Computational Linguistics*, pages 6022–6034, Online. Association for Computational Linguistics.

Jacob Devlin, Ming-Wei Chang, Kenton Lee, and Kristina Toutanova. 2019. BERT: Pre-training of deep bidirectional transformers for language understanding. In *Proceedings of the 2019 Conference of the North American Chapter of the Association for Computational Linguistics: Human Language Technologies, Volume 1 (Long and Short Papers)*, pages 4171–4186, Minneapolis, Minnesota. Association for Computational Linguistics.

Zi-Yi Dou and Graham Neubig. 2021. Word alignment by fine-tuning embeddings on parallel corpora. In *Proceedings of the 16th Conference of the European Chapter of the Association for Computational Linguistics: Main Volume*, pages 2112–2128, Online. Association for Computational Linguistics.

Yanai Elazar, Shauli Ravfogel, Alon Jacovi, and Yoav Goldberg. 2021. Amnesic probing: Behavioral explanation with amnesic counterfactuals. *Transactions of the Association for Computational Linguistics*, 9:160–175.

Miquel Esplà, Mikel Forcada, Gema Ramírez-Sánchez, and Hieu Hoang. 2019. ParaCrawl: Web-scale parallel corpora for the languages of the EU. In *Proceedings of Machine Translation Summit XVII: Translator, Project and User Tracks*, pages 118–119, Dublin, Ireland. European Association for Machine Translation.

Matthew Finlayson, Aaron Mueller, Sebastian Gehrmann, Stuart Shieber, Tal Linzen, and Yonatan Belinkov. 2021. Causal analysis of syntactic agreement mechanisms in neural language models. In *Proceedings of the 59th Annual Meeting of the Association for Computational Linguistics and the 11th International Joint Conference on Natural Language Processing (Volume 1: Long Papers)*, pages 1828–1843, Online. Association for Computational Linguistics.

Atticus Geiger, Hanson Lu, Thomas Icard, and Christopher Potts. 2021. Causal Abstractions of Neural Networks. In *Advances in Neural Information Process-*

ing Systems, volume 34, pages 9574–9586. Curran Associates, Inc.

Hila Gonen, Shauli Ravfogel, Yanai Elazar, and Yoav Goldberg. 2020. It's not Greek to mBERT: Inducing word-level translations from multilingual BERT. In *Proceedings of the Third BlackboxNLP Workshop on Analyzing and Interpreting Neural Networks for NLP*, pages 45–56, Online. Association for Computational Linguistics.

John Hewitt and Percy Liang. 2019. Designing and interpreting probes with control tasks. In *Proceedings of the 2019 Conference on Empirical Methods in Natural Language Processing and the 9th International Joint Conference on Natural Language Processing (EMNLP-IJCNLP)*, pages 2733–2743, Hong Kong, China. Association for Computational Linguistics.

Nora Kassner, Philipp Dufter, and Hinrich Schütze. 2021. Multilingual LAMA: Investigating knowledge in multilingual pretrained language models. In *Proceedings of the 16th Conference of the European Chapter of the Association for Computational Linguistics: Main Volume*, pages 3250–3258, Online. Association for Computational Linguistics.

Philipp Koehn. 2005. Europarl: A parallel corpus for statistical machine translation. In *Proceedings of Machine Translation Summit X: Papers*, pages 79–86, Phuket, Thailand.

Anoop Kunchukuttan, Pratik Mehta, and Pushpak Bhattacharyya. 2018. The IIT Bombay English-Hindi parallel corpus. In *Proceedings of the Eleventh International Conference on Language Resources and Evaluation (LREC 2018)*, Miyazaki, Japan. European Language Resources Association (ELRA).

Guillaume Lample, Alexis Conneau, Marc'Aurelio Ranzato, Ludovic Denoyer, and Hervé Jégou. 2018. Word translation without parallel data. In *6th International Conference on Learning Representations, ICLR 2018, Vancouver, BC, Canada, April 30 - May 3, 2018, Conference Track Proceedings*. OpenReview.net.

Karim Lasri, Tiago Pimentel, Alessandro Lenci, Thierry Poibeau, and Ryan Cotterell. 2022. Probing for the usage of grammatical number. In *Proceedings of the 60th Annual Meeting of the Association for Computational Linguistics (Volume 1: Long Papers)*, pages 8818–8831, Dublin, Ireland. Association for Computational Linguistics.

Anne Lauscher, Vinit Ravishankar, Ivan Vulić, and Goran Glavaš. 2020. From zero to hero: On the limitations of zero-shot language transfer with multilingual Transformers. In *Proceedings of the 2020 Conference on Empirical Methods in Natural Language Processing (EMNLP)*, pages 4483–4499, Online. Association for Computational Linguistics.

Jindřich Libovický, Rudolf Rosa, and Alexander Fraser. 2020. On the language neutrality of pre-trained multilingual representations. In *Findings of the Association for Computational Linguistics: EMNLP 2020*, pages 1663–1674, Online. Association for Computational Linguistics.

Isabel Papadimitriou, Ethan A. Chi, Richard Futrell, and Kyle Mahowald. 2021. Deep subjecthood: Higher-order grammatical features in multilingual BERT. In *Proceedings of the 16th Conference of the European Chapter of the Association for Computational Linguistics: Main Volume*, pages 2522–2532, Online. Association for Computational Linguistics.

Tiago Pimentel, Josef Valvoda, Rowan Hall Maudslay, Ran Zmigrod, Adina Williams, and Ryan Cotterell. 2020. Information-theoretic probing for linguistic structure. In *Proceedings of the 58th Annual Meeting of the Association for Computational Linguistics*, pages 4609–4622, Online. Association for Computational Linguistics.

Telmo Pires, Eva Schlinger, and Dan Garrette. 2019. How multilingual is multilingual BERT? In *Proceedings of the 57th Annual Meeting of the Association for Computational Linguistics*, pages 4996–5001, Florence, Italy. Association for Computational Linguistics.

Shauli Ravfogel, Yanai Elazar, Hila Gonen, Michael Twiton, and Yoav Goldberg. 2020. Null it out: Guarding protected attributes by iterative nullspace projection. In *Proceedings of the 58th Annual Meeting of the Association for Computational Linguistics*, pages 7237–7256, Online. Association for Computational Linguistics.

Shauli Ravfogel, Grusha Prasad, Tal Linzen, and Yoav Goldberg. 2021. Counterfactual interventions reveal the causal effect of relative clause representations on agreement prediction. In *Proceedings of the 25th Conference on Computational Natural Language Learning*, pages 194–209, Online. Association for Computational Linguistics.

Shauli Ravfogel, Francisco Vargas, Yoav Goldberg, and Ryan Cotterell. 2022. Adversarial concept erasure in kernel space. In *Proceedings of the 2022 Conference on Empirical Methods in Natural Language Processing*, pages 6034–6055, Abu Dhabi, United Arab Emirates. Association for Computational Linguistics.

Vinit Ravishankar, Artur Kulmizev, Mostafa Abdou, Anders Søgaard, and Joakim Nivre. 2021. Attention can reflect syntactic structure (if you let it). In *Proceedings of the 16th Conference of the European Chapter of the Association for Computational Linguistics: Main Volume*, pages 3031–3045, Online. Association for Computational Linguistics.

Phillip Rust, Jonas Pfeiffer, Ivan Vulić, Sebastian Ruder, and Iryna Gurevych. 2021. How good is your tokenizer? on the monolingual performance of multilingual language models. In *Proceedings of the 59th Annual Meeting of the Association for Computational Linguistics and the 11th International Joint Conference on Natural Language Processing (Volume 1:*

Long Papers), pages 3118–3135, Online. Association for Computational Linguistics.

Sebastin Santy, Anirudh Srinivasan, and Monojit Choudhury. 2021. BERTologiCoMix: How does code-mixing interact with multilingual BERT? In *Proceedings of the Second Workshop on Domain Adaptation for NLP*, pages 111–121, Kyiv, Ukraine. Association for Computational Linguistics.

Elena Voita, Rico Sennrich, and Ivan Titov. 2021. Analyzing the source and target contributions to predictions in neural machine translation. In *Proceedings of the 59th Annual Meeting of the Association for Computational Linguistics and the 11th International Joint Conference on Natural Language Processing (Volume 1: Long Papers)*, pages 1126–1140, Online. Association for Computational Linguistics.

Ivan Vulić, Edoardo Maria Ponti, Robert Litschko, Goran Glavaš, and Anna Korhonen. 2020. Probing pretrained language models for lexical semantics. In *Proceedings of the 2020 Conference on Empirical Methods in Natural Language Processing (EMNLP)*, pages 7222–7240, Online. Association for Computational Linguistics.

Shijie Wu and Mark Dredze. 2019. Beto, bentz, becas: The surprising cross-lingual effectiveness of BERT. In *Proceedings of the 2019 Conference on Empirical Methods in Natural Language Processing and the 9th International Joint Conference on Natural Language Processing (EMNLP-IJCNLP)*, pages 833–844, Hong Kong, China. Association for Computational Linguistics.

Shijie Wu and Mark Dredze. 2020. Are all languages created equal in multilingual BERT? In *Proceedings of the 5th Workshop on Representation Learning for NLP*, pages 120–130, Online. Association for Computational Linguistics.

A Implementation

We use `bert-base-multilingual-cased` and `xlm-roberta-base` models from the Huggingface models repository, and the `transformers` package for all of our probing experiments. Language ID classifiers were trained using `LinearSVC` classifier from `sklearn`. For training these classifiers, equal number of tokens from both labels were sampled. We used a batch size of 32, and a maximum sequence length of 256 when performing the intervention experiments.

B Effect of α

For our Experiment 1 results, we plot key measures in Figure 5 as a function of α. Specifically, we plot the proportion of the time we see movement in the expected direction and the mean change in log probability.

When α gets large, the words that we are pushing *away from* continue to move in the expected direction. This is likely because the increased shift can decrease the probability of those words arbitrarily, even while affecting the language model.

For words from the language that we are pushing *towards*, there are diminishing returns to increasing α and in some cases we see decreases (as with the XLM-R purple line, which shows the probability of the target answer when we push towards its language). This is likely because the target answer starts off with high probability, and larger α increasingly degrades the language model, causing the true answer to decrease in probability.

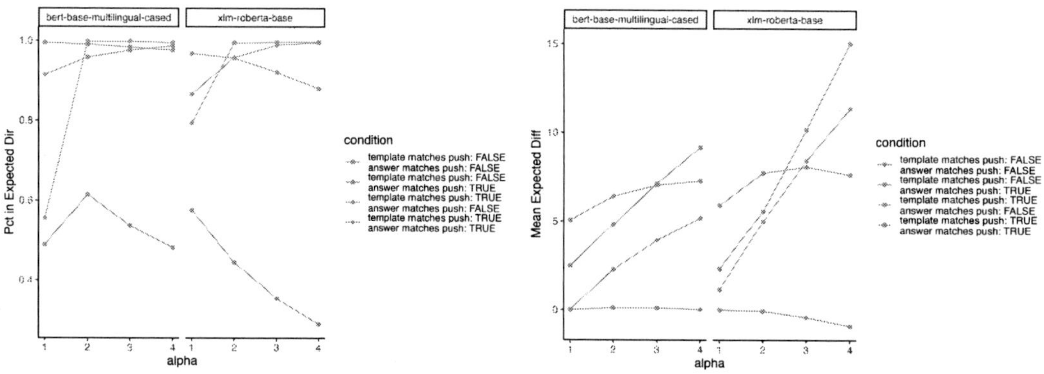

Figure 5: Left: Mean difference in log probability, across languages, in the *expected* direction (positive if pushed to, negative if pushed away from) between before-intervention and after-intervention probabilities of either the pushed-to language or the pushed-away-from language, as a function of α. Right: Proportion of the time, across languages, the intervention causes the probabilities to move in the *expected* direction (positive if pushed *to*, negative if pushed *away from*), as a function of α.

A General-Purpose Multilingual Document Encoder

Onur Galoğlu[1] **Robert Litschko**[2*] **Goran Glavaš**[3]

[1]Independent Researcher
[2]MaiNLP, Center for Information and Language Processing (CIS), LMU Munich, Germany
[3]CAIDAS, University of Würzburg

Abstract

Massively multilingual pretrained transformers (MMTs) have tremendously pushed the state of the art on multilingual NLP and cross-lingual transfer of NLP models in particular. While a large body of work leveraged MMTs to mine parallel data and induce bilingual document embeddings, much less effort has been devoted to training general-purpose (massively) multilingual document encoder that can be used for both supervised and unsupervised document-level tasks. In this work, we pretrain a massively multilingual document encoder as a hierarchical transformer model (HMDE) in which a shallow document transformer contextualizes sentence representations produced by a state-of-the-art pretrained multilingual sentence encoder. We leverage Wikipedia as a readily available source of comparable documents for creating training data, and train HMDE by means of a cross-lingual contrastive objective, further exploiting the category hierarchy of Wikipedia for creation of difficult negatives. We evaluate the effectiveness of HMDE in two arguably most common and prominent cross-lingual document-level tasks: (1) cross-lingual transfer for topical document classification and (2) cross-lingual document retrieval. HMDE is significantly more effective than (i) aggregations of segment-based representations and (ii) multilingual Longformer. Crucially, owing to its massively multilingual lower transformer, HMDE successfully generalizes to languages unseen in document-level pretraining. We publicly release our code and models.[1].

1 Introduction

Massively multilingual Transformers (MMTs) such as XLM-R (Conneau et al., 2020), and mT5 (Xue et al., 2021) have drastically pushed the state-of-the-art in multilingual NLP, especially for medium-resourced languages included in their pretraining, enabling effective cross-lingual transfer of task-specific NLP models from languages with plenty of training data to languages with little or no annotated task data. Being standard transformer-based language models, MMTs process text linearly – as a flat sequence of tokens, which has – in monolingual contexts – been shown suboptimal for document-level tasks (e.g., document classification or retrieval) for two main reasons: (1) it does not correspond to the hierarchical nature of document organization – documents are sequences of (presumably meaningfully ordered) paragraphs, which are in turn sequences of sentences (Zhang et al., 2019; Glavaš and Somasundaran, 2020), and (2) representing documents longer than the MMTs maximal input length requires either document trimming, which leads to loss of potentially task-relevant information, or segmentation, which leading to context fragmentation (Ding et al., 2021).

A number of models that produce document-level representations have been proposed, albeit predominantly in the monolingual (English) realm, with two prominent lines of work. **(1)** Hierarchical encoders (Pappas and Popescu-Belis, 2017; Pappagari et al., 2019; Zhang et al., 2019; Yang et al., 2020; Glavaš and Somasundaran, 2020; Chalkidis et al., 2022) typically contextualize sentence-level representations with additional document-level parameters (e.g., an additional, document-level transformer). These document-level parameters of the encoder, added on top of a pretrained language model like BERT (Devlin et al., 2019), are typically trained on large task-specific datasets, ranging from document classification (Pappagari et al., 2019) to summarization (Zhang et al., 2019) and segmentation (Glavaš and Somasundaran, 2020). Task-specific training of document-level parameters impedes the transfer of such encoders to other tasks. **(2)** Sparse attention models (Child et al., 2019; Zaheer et al., 2020; Beltagy et al., 2020; Tay et al., 2020) modify the attention mechanism in

* Work done while at University of Mannheim

[1]`https://github.com/ogaloglu/pre-training-multilingual-document-encoders`

Proceedings of the The 3rd Workshop on Multi-lingual Representation Learning (MRL), pages 37–49
December 7, 2023 ©2023 Association for Computational Linguistics

order to reduce its computational complexity and consequently be able to encode longer texts. Although flat long-text encoders do not model the hierarchical nature of documents, they allow for flat encoding of substantially longer documents.

In this work, we demonstrate the benefits of hierarchical document representations in multilingual context. We propose to train a hierarchical transformer model (HMDE), coupling (i) a pretrained multilingual sentence encoder as a lower encoder with (ii) an upper transformer that contextualizes sentence representations against each other and from which we derive document representations. Unlike in monolingual setup, where task-specific data is commonly used to train the parameters of the upper transformer (Zhang et al., 2019; Glavaš and Somasundaran, 2020), we exploit the fact that in the multilingual context one can leverage cross-lingual document alignments to guide the *pretraining* of the document encoder, i.e., its upper transformer. To this end, we leverage Wikipedia as a readily available source of quasi-parallel documents, and additionally exploit its hierarchy of categories to create hard negative examples for our contrastive pretraining objective.

We evaluate HMDE in two arguably most prominent (cross-lingual) document-level tasks: (1) cross-lingual transfer for document classification (XLDC) and (2) cross-lingual document retrieval (CLIR). For XLDC, as a supervised task, we fine-tune HMDE on English task-specific data; in CLIR, in contrast, we leverage HDME in an unsupervised fashion, using it to produce static document embeddings (and its lower transformer to produce query embeddings). HDME exhibits performance superior to that of competitive models – MMTs with sliding window and multilingual Longformer (Yu et al., 2021; Sagen, 2021). Crucially, HMDE generalizes well to languages unseen in its document-level pretraining. Our further analyses offer additional insights: (i) that it is important to allow updates from document-level training to propagate to the sentence-level encoder (i.e., not to freeze the parameters of the pretrained sentence encoder) and (ii) that the size of the document-level pretraining corpora matters more than its linguistic diversity (i.e., number of languages it encompasses).

2 Hierarchical Multilingual Encoder

The HMDE architecture, illustrated in Figure 1, is similar to that of hierarchical document encoders trained monolingually in task-specific training (e.g., (Glavaš and Somasundaran, 2020)): a sentence-level (lower) encoder produces sentence embeddings from tokens, whereas the document-level (upper) transformer yields document representation from a sequence of sentence embeddings. We initialize the lower transformer with the pretrained weights of a multilingual sentence encoder (Feng et al., 2022), and train the whole model via a bi-encoder configuration (also known as Siamese architecture) – where we compute a similarity score between representations of two documents produced independently with HDME – using a cross-lingual contrastive objective with both in-batch and hard negatives (Oord et al., 2018).

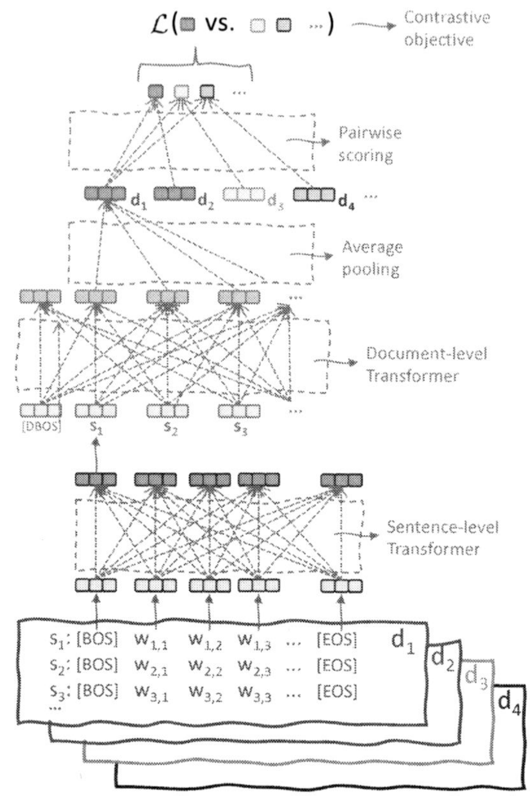

Figure 1: Illustration of HDME: hierarchical transformer architecture coupled with a cross-lingual contrastive objective. Document colors indicate the Wikipedia concepts: d_1 and d_2 are the pages of the same concept (e.g., New York) in two different languages, L_1 and L_2; documents d_3 and d_4 are pages of other concepts in L_1. The pair (d_1, d_2) is a positive pair (i.e., same concept) for the contrastive training objective and pairs (d_1, d_3) and (d_1, d_4) are corresponding negative pairs (i.e., different concepts).

2.1 Hierarchical Encoding

The role of the sentence-level (lower) transformer is to produce sentence representations from sequences of tokens. Because of this, we initialize it with the pretrained weights (including subword embeddings) of LaBSE (Feng et al., 2022), a state-of-the-art multilingual sentence encoder.[2] The sentence embedding is the transformed representation of the special beginning-of-sequence (BOS) token. The sequence of sentence embeddings obtained with the sentence-level transformer is then forwarded to the document-level (upper) transformer, which mutually contextualizes them, prepended with a special document-level beginning-of-sequence token (DBOS, with a randomly initialized embedding). We derive the document representation by average-pooling contextualized sentence embeddings (i.e., output of the last layer of the document-level transformer).[3]

2.2 Multi- and Cross-Lingual Objective

Our training dataset consists of Wikipedia pages written in one of n languages (see §3.1 for details on the creation of different training datasets): let $L = L_1, L_2, \ldots, L_n$ denote our set of training languages. In each training step, we select a batch of N documents pairs, $\{(d_1^{(1)}, d_2^{(1)}), \ldots, (d_1^{(N)}, d_2^{(N)})\}$, where $d_1^{(i)}$ and $d_2^{(i)}$ are Wikipedia pages of the same concept but in two different languages, L_k and $L_m \in L$. Each of the documents $d_1^{(i)}$ (i.e., first document of each pair) is additionally paired with a document $d_{neg}^{(i)}$ – a document in the same language L_k as $d_1^{(i)}$ and from the same Wikipedia category – representing a *hard negative* for $d_1^{(i)}$ (see §3.1 for details). We then compute and minimize a variant of the popular InfoNCE loss (Oord et al., 2018) that incorporates hard negatives, treating all other batch documents $d_2^{(j)}$ as in-batch (easy) negatives for $d_1^{(i)}$:

$$\mathcal{L} = -\sum_{i=1}^{N} \left[\frac{1}{\tau} s(\mathbf{d}_1^{(i)}, \mathbf{d}_2^{(i)}) - \log\left(e^{s(\mathbf{d}_1^{(i)}, \mathbf{d}_{neg}^{(i)})/\tau} + \sum_{j=1}^{N} e^{s(\mathbf{d}_1^{(i)}, \mathbf{d}_2^{(j)})/\tau} \right) \right] \quad (1)$$

with $\mathbf{d} \in \mathbb{R}^h$ as the embedding of d, i.e., the output of the document-level transformer (and h as the hidden size of upper transformer), $s(\mathbf{d}_i, \mathbf{d}_j)$ as the scoring function capturing similarity between the two document embeddings, and τ as the hyperparameter (the so-called temperature) of the InfoNCE loss. Following common practice, we use cosine similarity as the scoring function s.

Note that the loss we compute is both multilingual and cross-lingual: documents $d_1^{(i)}$ come from any of the $|L|$ languages, and positive pairs $(d_1^{(i)}, d_2^{(i)})$ are cross-lingual. Among the in-batch negatives, there will be cross-lingual as well as monolingual pairs (when $d_1^{(i)}$ and $d_2^{(j)}$ happen to be documents written in the same language). Our hard negatives are, by design, always monolingual pairs. While one could create cross-lingual hard negatives in the same manner (e.g., by pairing the English article *"France"* with an Italian article *"Svizzera"* (Switzerland) that covers another concept from the same category *"Country"*), monolingual hard negatives should be *harder* because the two document representations will originate from the same language-specific subspace of the embedding space of the lower (multilingual) transformer (Cao et al., 2020; Wu and Dredze, 2020).

3 Experimental Setup

We first describe how we created the multilingual dataset for HMDE pretraining from Wikipedia (§3.1). We then briefly describe the two evaluation tasks – cross-lingual transfer for document classification and cross-lingual information retrieval – and their respective datasets (§3.2), following with the description of the baselines – a multilingual sentence encoder with a sliding window and a multilingual Longformer (Yu et al., 2021; Sagen, 2021) (§3.3). We provide training and optimization details for all models in the Appendix A.1.

3.1 Data Creation

Wikipedia has been leveraged as a suitable source for mining comparable and parallel corpora for decades (Ni et al., 2009; Plamadă and Volk, 2013; Schwenk et al., 2021, *inter alia*). We add to the body of work that exploits Wikipedia as a massively multilingual text resource by using it to build pretraining data for HMDE. Concretely, for a set of languages $L = \{L_1, L_2, \ldots, L_n\}$, we first fetch

[2]We load LaBSE weights from HuggingFace: `https://huggingface.co/sentence-transformers/LaBSE`

[3]We preliminarily also experimented with the contextualized vector of the DBOS token as the document representation, but that consistently led to lower performance.

monolingual portions from the Wiki-40B corpus.[4] We then identify articles in different languages that are about the same concept (via the wikidata_id field) and keep only those concepts for which pages are found in at least two languages from L. For each such concept with pages $p_1, p_2, \ldots, p_m$ in m different languages, we create all possible cross-lingual pairs of articles (p_i, p_j) covering the same concept. For each pair (p_i, p_j), we then leverage Wikipedia metadata – namely mapping of Wikipedia pages into its hierarchy of categories – to select an article n_i from the same monolingual Wikipedia as p_i (i.e., written in the same language as p_i) that belongs to (at least one) same Wikipedia category as p_i. This yields triples (p_i, p_j, n_i) from which we create cross-lingual positives (p_i, p_j) and their corresponding monolingual hard negatives (p_i, n_i) for our contrastive objective (see §2.2).

On the one hand, the quality of MMTs' representations of a particular language depends on the size of the pretraining corpora of that language (Hu et al., 2020; Lauscher et al., 2020). On the other hand, multilingual model training with instances from linguistically diverse languages may generalize better to unseen languages (Chen et al., 2019; Ansell et al., 2021). Most resourced languages, however, tend to be Indo-European (Joshi et al., 2020), putting corpus size and linguistic diversity at odds. We thus create two different datasets, each emphasis one of these two aspects: (1) XLW-4L is built starting from four high-resource Indo-European languages: English, German, French, and Italian; (12) XLW-12L is built starting from a set of 12 linguistically diverse languages: English, French, Russian, Japanese, Chinese, Hungarian, Finnish, Arabic, Persian, Turkish, Greek, and Malay. With 1.1M triples (p_i, p_j, n_i), XLW-4L is almost twice as large as XLW-12L (which encompasses 592K triples), despite encompassing three times fewer languages: this is primarily because there are many more shared concepts between large Wikipedias of XLW-4L (e.g., German and Italian) than between smaller Wikipedias of XLW-12L (e.g., Turkish and Malay).[5]

3.2 Evaluation Tasks and Datasets

HMDE is meant to be a general-purpose multilingual document encoder. It thus needs to be useful both (1) when fine-tuned for a supervised document-level task, and (2) as a standalone document encoder. We thus evaluate HMDE in (1) zero-shot cross-lingual transfer for supervised document classification (XLDC) and (2) unsupervised cross-lingual document retrieval (CLIR).

XLDOC. Regular MMTs (e.g., mBERT or XLM-R) are primarily used in zero-shot cross-lingual transfer for supervised NLP tasks: an MMT fine-tuned on task-specific training data in a resource-rich language is used to make predictions for language(s) without task data. We evaluate HMDE in exactly the same zero-shot cross-lingual transfer setup, only for a document-level task – topical document classification. We fine-tune HMDE in the standard manner, by stacking a softmax classifier on top the output of the document-level encoder. With $\mathbf{d}$ as HDME's encoding of the input document d, classifier's prediction is computed as:

$$\mathbf{y} = \mathit{softmax}\left(\mathbf{W} \cdot \mathbf{d} + \mathbf{b}\right) \qquad (2)$$

with $\mathbf{W} \in \mathbb{R}^{C \times h}$ and $\mathbf{b} \in \mathbb{R}^{C}$ as classifier's trainable parameters (and C as the number of classes).

We fine-tune HMDE on the English training portion of the MLDOC dataset (Schwenk and Li, 2018) and evaluate its performance on the test portions of all other (target) languages. MLDOC is a subset of the Reuters Corpus Volume 2 (RCV2), with training, development, and test portions in 8 languages (English, Spanish, German, French, Italian, Russian, Japanese and Chinese), consisting of 1000, 1000, and 4000 documents, respectively. News stories are categorized into $C = 4$ semantically closely related classes (*Corporate/Industrial*, *Economics*, *Government/Social*, and *Markets*).

CLIR. We evaluate the effectiveness of HMDE as a standalone document encoder in an unsupervised cross-lingual document retrieval task: queries (short text) in one language are fired against a collection of documents written in another language. We adopt a simple retrieval model: we rank documents in decreasing order of cosine similarity of their embeddings $\mathbf{d}$, produced by the HMDE, with the embedding $\mathbf{q}$ of the query, $\cos(\mathbf{d}, \mathbf{q})$. We obtain the query embedding $\mathbf{q}$ by encoding the query only with HMDE's lower (sentence-level) transformer: $\mathbf{q}$ is the transformed representation of the beginning-of-sequence ([BOS]) token.

We carry out the evaluation on CLEF-2003,[6] a popular CLIR benchmark, including the following

[4] Available in Tensorflow datasets: https://www.tensorflow.org/datasets/catalog/wikipedia

[5] Per-language statistics of the datasets are in the Appendix.

[6] http://catalog.elra.info/en-us/repository/browse/ELRA-E0008/

languages: English (EN), German (DE), Italian (IT), Finnish (FI) and Russian (RU). Following prior work (Glavaš et al., 2019; Litschko et al., 2022), we evaluate HMDE on 9 language pairs (with first language being the query language): EN-FI, DE, IT, RU, DE-FI, IT, RU, FI-IT, RU. For each language pair we work with 60 queries and document collections of following sizes: RU – 17K, FI – 55K, IT – 158K, and DE – 295K.

3.3 Baseline Models

There are two main alternatives to hierarhical (long) document encoding. The first is to (i) fragment the document into smaller segments, (ii) encode each segment with a regular pretrained MMT (e.g., vanilla MMT like XLM-R or a multilingual sentence encoder like LaBSE), and (iii) aggregate the document representation from the embeddings of segments. The second is to train a multilingual sparse-attention encoder, akin to (Sagen, 2021).

MMT with a Sliding Window (LaBSE-Seg). For fair comparison, we use LaBSE (Feng et al., 2022) – the same pretrained MMT that we use for the initialization of the lower transformer in HMDE – to independently encode overlapping segments of the input document. We break down the document into segments of length N_S tokens. Following Dai et al. (2022), who find that overlapping segments alleviate the context fragmentation problem, we make adjacent segments overlap in $N_S/3$ tokens. After encoding each segment with LaBSE, we average-pool the document representation **d** from the set of segment embeddings. In XLDX (topical document classification) this average of segment embeddings is fed into the classification head. In CLIR, it is compared with the LaBSE encoding of the query.

Multilingual Longformer (mLongformer). Longformer architecture (Beltagy et al., 2020) combines local-window attention with global attention, resulting in a hybrid attention mechanism, the memory requirements of which scale linearly with the input length. Beltagy et al. (2020) additionally propose multi-step procedure for initializing Longformer's parameters based on the parameters of a pretrained regular transformer (e.g., in the case of monolingual English Longformer from RoBERTa (Liu et al., 2019)) and then further train the Longformer via masked language modeling (MLM). We train the multilingual Longformer following the same procedure: for fair comparison with HMDE, we initialize its parameters from the parameters of LaBSE and carry out the additional MLM training on XLW-4L, the same corpus on which we train HMDE.

4 Results and Discussion

We first report and discuss the main results we obtain with HMDE on XLDC and CLIR (in §4.1). In a series of follow-up experiments, we further analyze key design choices for HMDE (§4.2).

4.1 Main Results

Cross-lingual Document Classification. Table 1 compares HMDE trained on XLW-4L against several standard and long document multilingual encoders: besides the baselines introduced in §3.3, for completeness we add the results for vanilla LaBSE (i.e., without sliding over the long document) and models based on XLM-R and mBERT reported by Dong et al. (2020) and Zhao et al. (2021), respectively. Expectedly, all long-document encoders outperform all of the standard MMTs. mLongformer and HMDE generally exhibit similar performance, surpassing the performance of segmentation-based LaBSE-Seg for virtually all languages. Comparable performance of mLongformer and HMDE suggests that in the presence of task-specific fine-tuning data it does not really matter whether we aggregate document representations in a flat or hieratrchical fashion. What is particularly encouraging is that both HDME and mLongformer exhibit strong performance for languages that they did not observe in document-level pretraining: Spanish, Russian, Japanese, and Chinese.[7,8]

Cross-lingual Retrieval. The results for unsupervised CLIR are shown in Table 2. Like in XLDC, we additionally report the results for LaBSE that encodes only the beginning of the document (without sliding) as well as for mBERT, reported by Litschko et al. (2022). CLIR, in which multilingual transformers are used as standalone document encoders without any task-specific fine-tuning, tell a very different story from supervised XLDC results. HMDE drastically outperforms mLongformer, indicating that, much like the vanilla MMTs, mLongformer requires fine-tuning and cannot encode reli-

[7]LaBSE, with whose parameters both HMDE and mLongofrmer were initialized before document-level pretraining, however, was exposed to all of these languages in its own sentence-level pretraining.

[8]Performance across languages *not* directly comparable as MLDOC test sets are not parallel across languages.

Model	En	Es	De	Fr	It	Ru	Ja	Zh	AVG
Standard Multilingual Transformers									
LaBSE	95.5	79.0	89.6	87.2	76.8	63.9	**80.8**	86.1	82.4
XLM-R (Dong et al., 2020)	93.0	84.6	**92.5**	87.1	73.2	68.9	78.2	85.8	83.0
mBERT (Zhao et al., 2021)	**96.9**	81.9	88.3	83.1	74.1	72.3	74.6	84.4	82.0
Multilingual Long Document Encoders									
LaBSE-Seg	94.0	82.9	90.2	89.9	78.1	71.9	75.5	88.4	84.0
mLongformer (XLW-4L)	95.8	**87.0**	93.4	91.9	**80.6**	71.7	79.5	88.5	86.1
HMDE (XLW-4L)	95.4	85.6	91.2	**92.0**	78.5	**83.9**	76.3	**89.5**	**86.8**

Table 1: Performance of HDME compared against standard MMTs and baseline multilingual long-document encoders on supervised topical document classification (MLDOC). Performance (except En) for zero-shot cross-lingual transfer: all models are fine-tuned only on English training data. **Bold**: best performance in each column.

Model	En–Fi	En–It	En–Ru	En–De	De–Fi	De–It	De–Ru	Fi–It	Fi–Ru	AVG
Standard Multilingual Transformers										
LaBSE	.247	.224	.131	.138	.247	.214	.135	.211	.125	.186
mBERT (Litschko et al., 2022)	.145	.146	**.167**	.107	.151	.116	**.149**	.117	.128	.136
Multilingual Long Document Encoders										
LaBSE-Seg	.243	.169	.107	.194	.268	.178	.104	.153	.014	.159
mLongformer (XLW-4L)	.150	.088	.094	.082	.190	.072	.120	.097	.091	.109
HMDE (XLW-4L)	**.380**	**.282**	.141	**.326**	**.352**	**.259**	.130	**.238**	**.129**	**.249**

Table 2: Performance of HDME compared against standard MMTs and baseline multilingual long-document encoders on unsupervised cross-lingual document retrieval (CLEF-2003). **Bold**: best performance in each column.

ably encode documents "out of the box". HMDE also substantially outperforms LaBSE-Seg, the long-document encoder based on sliding LaBSE over the document. Interestingly, vanilla LaBSE, which encodes only the beginning of the document, also outperforms its sliding counterpart LaBSE-Seg, which is exposed to the entire document. We believe that this is because (1) in CLEF, retrieval-relevant information often occurs at the beginnings of documents and in such cases (2) LaBSE-Seg's average-pooling over all document segments then dilutes the encoding of query-relevant content. Importantly, HMDE in CLIR also seems to generalize very well to languages unseen in its document-level pretraining (in particular for Finnish documents).

4.2 Further Analysis

We next empirically examine how different choices in HDME's design and pretraining affect its performance, focusing on: (i) linguistic diversity and size of the pretraining corpus (XLW-4L vs. XLW-12L), (ii) freezing of the lower transformer (i.e., LaBSE weights) after initialization, and (iii) initializing it with the weights of XLM-R as the standard MMT (vs. initialization with LaBSE as the sentence encoder). We provide a further ablations on document segmentation (sentences vs. token sequences ignorant of sentence boundaries) in the Appendix A.2.

Pretraining Data: Linguistic Diversity vs. Size. As discussed in §3.1, we prepare two different corpora for HMDE pretraining: XLW-4L, which is larger (1.1M instances) but encompasses only four major Indo-European languages and XLW-12L, which is smaller (590K instances) but has documents from a set of 12 linguistically diverse languages. To control for the size, and assess the effect of linguistic diversity alone, we randomly downsample XLW-4L, creating a 4-language dataset XLW-4L-S that matches in size XLW-12L. Figure 2 shows the downstream performance of HMDE when pretrained on each of these three datasets.

Comparison between XLW-4L and XLW-4L-S (same languages, different dataset size) shows that

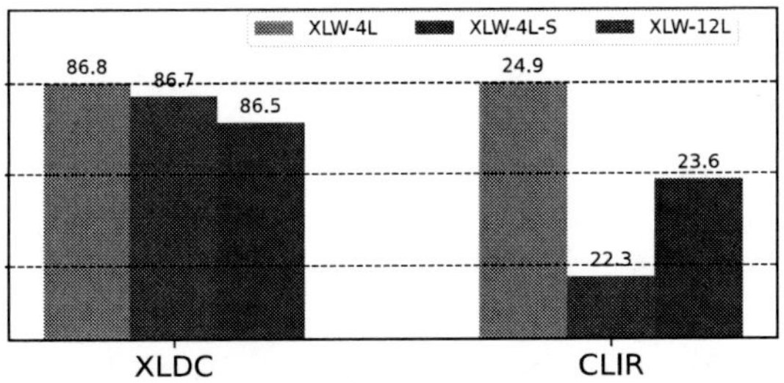

Figure 2: Performance of HMDE when pretrained on different datasets. Results are averages across all test languages (XLDC) and language pairs (CLIR).

our flavor of cross-lingual contrastive pretraining (§2.2) leads to a fairly sample-efficient pre-training: cutting the training data almost in half leads to small performance drops (mere 0.3 accuracy points in XLDC; 1.3 MAP points in CLIR). Comparison between XLW-4L-S and XLW-12L (same size, different language sets) quantifies the role of linguistic diversity in pretraining. Somewhat surprisingly, the more linguistically diverse pretraining on XLW-12L does not bring better performance compared to "Indo-European-only" pretraining on XLW-4L-S: while they perform comparably on XLDC, more diverse pretraining (XLW-12L) leads to worse CLIR performance (-1.3 MAP points on average). We hypothesize that this is due to higher-quality of representation of the four Indo-European languages (EN, DE, FR, IT) in LaBSE (owing to their over-representation in LaBSE's pretraining), with which we initialize the lower transformer of HMDE. We find this result to be particularly encouraging, as – together with the observation that HMDE generalizes well to languages unseen in its document-level pretraining – it suggests that document-level pretraining itself does not necessarily need to be massively multilingual in order to yield successful massively multilingual document encoders.

Lower Transformer. We next investigate two aspects of the lower-transformer: (1) with which weights to initialize it and (2) whether it pays off to update its parameters during the document-level pretraining. For the former, we compare our default LaBSE-based initialization (with LaBSE as a sentence-specialized multilingual encoder) against the initialization with weights of XLM-R, as the vanilla multilingual MMT. To answer the latter, we additionally train HMDE by freezing its lower transformer in document-level pretraining. Table 3 summarizes the results of these ablations.

Model	Updates	XLDC	CLIR
HMDE-LaBSE	*Updated*	**86.8**	**0.249**
HMDE-LaBSE	*Frozen*	85.9	0.167
HMDE-XLM-R	*Updated*	83.9	0.135

Table 3: HMDE results for different choices w.r.t. to initialization and training of the lower transformer. Training for all three variants carried out on XLW-4L. Results are averages across all test languages (XLDC) and language pairs (CLIR).

While freezing the lower transformer after initialization leads to much faster training, it results in poorer document encoder, especially if used for standalone document encoding, without task-specific fine-tuning[9] (HMDE-LaBSE *Updated* vs. *Frozen*; 1 accuracy point drop in XLDC vs. 8 MAP points drop in CLIR). Initializing HDME's lower transformer with LaBSE weights leads to much better downstream performance compared to initialization with XLM-R which is not specialized for sentence-level semantics.

5 Related Work

We position our contributions w.r.t. three related lines of work: (1) pretraining long-document encoders, (2) self-supervised pretraining for retrieval, and (3) mining parallel documents.

Long-Document Encoders. Hierarchical (Zhang et al., 2019; Yang et al., 2020; Glavaš and Somasundaran, 2020) and sparse-attention-based encoders (Beltagy et al., 2020; Zaheer et al., 2020; Tay et al., 2020) already discussed in §1 account for the vast majority of long-document encoding approaches. Dai et al. (2022) extensively compare Longformer (Beltagy et al., 2020) against hierarchical transformers on various long-document classification tasks, showing that the latter exhibit slightly better performance, especially if the lower encoder encodes overlapping segments. Ding et al. (2021) propose a different, segmentation-based model based on recurrence transformers (Dai et al., 2019), designed to remedy for context fragmentation with a retrospective feed mechanism: each segment is encoded twice – after initial left-to-right segment with a recurrent transformer, segment representations are further mutually contextualized

[9]The parameters of the lower-transformer are always updated in XLDC fine-tuning, even if we froze them in document-level pretraining.

bidirectionally. Their training couples MLM-ing with a segment reordering objective.

The vast majority of work on pretraining encoders for long documents focuses on monolingual (mainly English) models. The few multilingual exceptions (Yu et al., 2021; Sagen, 2021) derive a multilingual Longformer from standard MMTs (XLM-R and mBERT) in exactly the same fashion in which the original work (Beltagy et al., 2020) pretrains English Longformer after initialization from RoBERTa weights. In this work, we replicated this effort, evaluating mLongformer as the main baseline for HMDE.

Pretraining for Retrieval. Self-supervised and distantly-supervised approaches have recently been proposed for pretraining documents encoders specifically for the task of document retrieval (Izacard et al., 2022; Yu et al., 2021; Gao et al., 2022). Izacard et al. (2022) pretrain Contriever – a BERT-based document encoder with an objective based on the inverse cloze task (Lee et al., 2019): a positive query-document pair is created by extracting a span of text from the document and using it as a "query"; they train with a contrastive objective that scores the document from which the query was extracted higher than other documents. Gao et al. (2022) feed queries as prompts to a generative language model, which then generates document; they then use Contriever to embed this synthetic document and find most similar real documents in the collection, finally fine-tuning Contriever on query-document pairs obtained this way. In a manner similar to ours, Yu et al. (2021) leverage Wikipedia as a source of quasi-parallel data: while we exploit document-level alignments, they leverage section-level aligments to create positive cross-lingual training instances for paragraph retrieval: a section title ("query") in one language is coupled with the section body ("document") in another language; they then train a multilingual Longformer initialized from mBERT with a combination of query MLM-ing and contrastive relevance ranking. In contrast to these efforts, we create a general-purpose (i.e., task-agnostic) multilingual document encoder that can both be fine-tuned for supervised tasks and used as a standalone document embedder.

Mining Parallel Documents. Mining parallel documents – a task which aims to identify mutual translations in a large document collection and is often used as a first step in extracting parallel sentences (Resnik and Smith, 2003; Uszkoreit et al., 2010; Schwenk, 2018, *inter alia*) – is the task that bears most resemblance to our pretraining. Transformer-based approaches to the task (Guo et al., 2019; El-Kishky and Guzmán, 2020; Gong et al., 2021) typically aggregate document-level representations from multilingual sentence embeddings. The work of Guo et al. (2019) is arguably most related to ours: they train a hierarchical encoder with a simple feed-forward net as the upper encoder that independently transforms precomputed sentence embeddings: document embedding is then the average of feed-forward-transformed sentence embeddings. The model is trained bilingually (English-Spanish and English-French) with a contrastive objective on a huge silver-standard corpus of parallel documents (13M and 6M document pairs, respectively) and evaluated on the very same task of parallel document mining. Our work differs in two crucial aspects: (1) while (Guo et al., 2019) train *bilingual* models for recognizing parallel documents, we train a single general-purpose massively multilingual document encoder; (2) we train on a much smaller corpus of comparable (not parallel) documents, readily available from Wikipedia. Both aspects make HMDE much more widely applicable, for both supervised and unsupervised document-level tasks and any of the languages from LaBSE's pretraining (as HMDE's lower encoder is initialized with LaBSE's weights).

6 Conclusion

In this work, we pretrain a multilingual document encoder based on a hierarchical transformer architecture (HMDE), and initialize its lower-level encoder with the weights of a state-of-the-art multilingual sentence encoder. We leverage Wikipedia as a rich source of quasi-parallel long documents and train HDME with a contrastive cross-lingual document matching objective. We show that the obtained model is a general-purpose multilingual document encoder that can successfully be both (1) fine-tuned for document-level cross-lingual transfer and (2) used as a document embedding model out of the box. Our results render HMDE substantially more effective than both multilingual Longformer and segmentation-based document encoding. Crucially, HMDE generalizes well to languages unseen in its document-level pretraining. Our follow-up experiments reveal that the size of the pretraining corpus affects the performance more than the number and diversity of languages involved, suggesting that reliable massively multilingual document encoders do not necessarily require equally massively multilingual pretraining.

Limitations

Because we initialize the lower transformer of HMDE with LaBSE (Feng et al., 2022), the set of languages that HMDE "supports" out of the box is bound to the set of 109 languages included in LaBSE's pretraining.[10] This means that HMDE will, in principle, be less effective as a document encoder for other languages.[11] HDME, like LaBSE, should in principle be useless for languages written in a script that LaBSE (or in fact, mBERT, from which LaBSE borrows the vocabulary and pretrained subword embeddings) has not seen in its pretraining, as the corresponding tokenizer will produce a sequence of unknown tokens ([UNK]). This means that HMDE, much like the rest of existing multilingual encoders, supports only a small fraction of world's 7000+ languages (Joshi et al., 2020). Moreover, all languages included in our evaluation datasets – MLDOC and CLEF – are covered by this set of 109 languages, which means that the average performance we report is likely a gross overestimate for languages unseen in LaBSE's pretraining. Further, HMDE leverages Wikipedia for training (with sets of either 4 or 12 languages, see 3.1) – the number of Wikipedia pages (and more generally, digital footprint of a language on the web) varies tremendously across languages, effectively limiting the selection of languages for HMDE's document-level pretraining. Our results (see 4.1), however, show that HMDE generalizes well to languages not seen in its document-level pretraining.

Further, HMDE is implemented as a Bi-Encoder (aka Siamese network), which means that for a given pair of documents in a training example (positive or negative pair), it separately encodes each of the documents. Cross-Encoder architecture, in which the documents would be concatenated before encoding, would have the advantage of allowing the encoder to contextualize the token/sentence representations of one document with those of the other before the computation of their similarity score. Cross-encoding architectures have been shown effective, albeit not efficient (i.e., slow) in training for document retrieval, in which the (short) query is concatenated with the (long) document (MacAvaney et al., 2020; Shi et al., 2020; Rosa et al., 2022). We do not explore cross-encoding in our work; in our case, it implies joint encoding of the concatenation of two long documents (in different languages), arguably exploding in GPU memory occupancy and possibly preventing us from fitting even single-instance batches on our GPU cards.

[10]The full list is provided in Table 10 of the Appendix in (Feng et al., 2022).

[11]Not necessarily the case only for unseen that are close relatives to some of the high-resource languages seen in LaBSE's pretraining.

Ethical Considerations

We do not test HMDE explicitly to check whether the representations it produces reflect negative societal biases and stereotypes (e.g., sexism or racism), but given that its lower encoder is initialized from LaBSE's weights, it would not be surprising if this was the case. If so, many of the existing techniques from the literature designed to debias pretrained language models (Qian et al., 2019; Barikeri et al., 2021; Guo et al., 2022) could be applied to HMDE too, and in principle "as-is" (i.e., without special modifications).

References

Alan Ansell, Edoardo Maria Ponti, Jonas Pfeiffer, Sebastian Ruder, Goran Glavaš, Ivan Vulić, and Anna Korhonen. 2021. Mad-g: Multilingual adapter generation for efficient cross-lingual transfer. In *Findings of the Association for Computational Linguistics: EMNLP 2021*, pages 4762–4781.

Soumya Barikeri, Anne Lauscher, Ivan Vulić, and Goran Glavaš. 2021. Redditbias: A real-world resource for bias evaluation and debiasing of conversational language models. In *Proceedings of the 59th Annual Meeting of the Association for Computational Linguistics and the 11th International Joint Conference on Natural Language Processing (Volume 1: Long Papers)*, pages 1941–1955.

Iz Beltagy, Matthew E Peters, and Arman Cohan. 2020. Longformer: The long-document transformer. *arXiv preprint arXiv:2004.05150*.

Steven Cao, Nikita Kitaev, and Dan Klein. 2020. Multilingual alignment of contextual word representations. In *International Conference on Learning Representations*.

Ilias Chalkidis, Xiang Dai, Manos Fergadiotis, Prodromos Malakasiotis, and Desmond Elliott. 2022. An exploration of hierarchical attention transformers for efficient long document classification. *arXiv preprint arXiv:2210.05529*.

Xilun Chen, Ahmed Hassan Awadallah, Hany Hassan, Wei Wang, and Claire Cardie. 2019. Multi-source cross-lingual model transfer: Learning what to share. In *Proceedings of the 57th Conference of the Association for Computational Linguistics (ACL)*.

Rewon Child, Scott Gray, Alec Radford, and Ilya Sutskever. 2019. Generating long sequences with sparse transformers. *arXiv preprint arXiv:1904.10509*.

Alexis Conneau, Kartikay Khandelwal, Naman Goyal, Vishrav Chaudhary, Guillaume Wenzek, Francisco Guzmán, Édouard Grave, Myle Ott, Luke Zettlemoyer, and Veselin Stoyanov. 2020. Unsupervised cross-lingual representation learning at scale. In *Proceedings of the 58th Annual Meeting of the Association for Computational Linguistics*, pages 8440–8451.

Xiang Dai, Ilias Chalkidis, Sune Darkner, and Desmond Elliott. 2022. Revisiting transformer-based models for long document classification. In *Findings of the 2022 Conference on Empirical Methods in Natural Language Processing (EMNLP)*.

Zihang Dai, Zhilin Yang, Yiming Yang, Jaime G Carbonell, Quoc Le, and Ruslan Salakhutdinov. 2019. Transformer-xl: Attentive language models beyond a fixed-length context. In *Proceedings of the 57th Annual Meeting of the Association for Computational Linguistics*, pages 2978–2988.

Jacob Devlin, Ming-Wei Chang, Kenton Lee, and Kristina Toutanova. 2019. Bert: Pre-training of deep bidirectional transformers for language understanding. In *Proceedings of the 2019 Conference of the North American Chapter of the Association for Computational Linguistics: Human Language Technologies, Volume 1 (Long and Short Papers)*, pages 4171–4186.

SiYu Ding, Junyuan Shang, Shuohuan Wang, Yu Sun, Hao Tian, Hua Wu, and Haifeng Wang. 2021. ERNIE-Doc: A retrospective long-document modeling transformer. In *Proceedings of the 59th Annual Meeting of the Association for Computational Linguistics and the 11th International Joint Conference on Natural Language Processing (Volume 1: Long Papers)*, pages 2914–2927, Online. Association for Computational Linguistics.

Xin Dong, Yaxin Zhu, Yupeng Zhang, Zuohui Fu, Dongkuan Xu, Sen Yang, and Gerard de Melo. 2020. Leveraging adversarial training in self-learning for cross-lingual text classification. In *Proceedings of the 43rd International ACM SIGIR Conference on Research and Development in Information Retrieval*, SIGIR '20, page 1541–1544, New York, NY, USA. Association for Computing Machinery.

Ahmed El-Kishky and Francisco Guzmán. 2020. Massively multilingual document alignment with cross-lingual sentence-mover's distance. In *Proceedings of the 1st Conference of the Asia-Pacific Chapter of the Association for Computational Linguistics and the 10th International Joint Conference on Natural Language Processing*, pages 616–625.

Fangxiaoyu Feng, Yinfei Yang, Daniel Cer, Naveen Arivazhagan, and Wei Wang. 2022. Language-agnostic bert sentence embedding. In *Proceedings of the 60th Annual Meeting of the Association for Computational Linguistics (Volume 1: Long Papers)*, pages 878–891.

Luyu Gao, Xueguang Ma, Jimmy Lin, and Jamie Callan. 2022. Precise zero-shot dense retrieval without relevance labels. *arXiv preprint arXiv:2212.10496*.

Goran Glavaš, Robert Litschko, Sebastian Ruder, and Ivan Vulić. 2019. How to (properly) evaluate cross-lingual word embeddings: On strong baselines, comparative analyses, and some misconceptions. In *Proceedings of the 57th Annual Meeting of the Association for Computational Linguistics*, pages 710–721.

Goran Glavaš and Swapna Somasundaran. 2020. Two-level transformer and auxiliary coherence modeling for improved text segmentation. In *Proceedings of the AAAI Conference on Artificial Intelligence*, volume 34, pages 7797–7804.

Hongyu Gong, Vishrav Chaudhary, Yuqing Tang, and Francisco Guzmán. 2021. Lawdr: Language-agnostic weighted document representations from pre-trained models. *arXiv preprint arXiv:2106.03379*.

Mandy Guo, Yinfei Yang, Keith Stevens, Daniel Cer, Heming Ge, Yun-Hsuan Sung, Brian Strope, and Ray Kurzweil. 2019. Hierarchical document encoder for parallel corpus mining. In *Proceedings of the Fourth Conference on Machine Translation (Volume 1: Research Papers)*, pages 64–72.

Yue Guo, Yi Yang, and Ahmed Abbasi. 2022. Autodebias: Debiasing masked language models with automated biased prompts. In *Proceedings of the 60th Annual Meeting of the Association for Computational Linguistics (Volume 1: Long Papers)*, pages 1012–1023.

Dan Hendrycks and Kevin Gimpel. 2016. Gaussian error linear units (gelus). *arXiv preprint arXiv:1606.08415*.

Junjie Hu, Sebastian Ruder, Aditya Siddhant, Graham Neubig, Orhan Firat, and Melvin Johnson. 2020. Xtreme: A massively multilingual multi-task benchmark for evaluating cross-lingual generalisation. In *International Conference on Machine Learning*, pages 4411–4421. PMLR.

Gautier Izacard, Mathilde Caron, Lucas Hosseini, Sebastian Riedel, Piotr Bojanowski, Armand Joulin, and Edouard Grave. 2022. Unsupervised dense information retrieval with contrastive learning. *Transactions on Machine Learning Research*, 8:1–22.

Pratik Joshi, Sebastin Santy, Amar Budhiraja, Kalika Bali, and Monojit Choudhury. 2020. The state and fate of linguistic diversity and inclusion in the nlp world. In *Proceedings of the 58th Annual Meeting of the Association for Computational Linguistics*, pages 6282–6293.

Anne Lauscher, Vinit Ravishankar, Ivan Vulić, and Goran Glavaš. 2020. From zero to hero: On the limitations of zero-shot language transfer with multilingual transformers. In *Proceedings of the 2020 Conference on Empirical Methods in Natural Language Processing (EMNLP)*, pages 4483–4499.

Kenton Lee, Ming-Wei Chang, and Kristina Toutanova. 2019. Latent retrieval for weakly supervised open domain question answering. In *Proceedings of the 57th Annual Meeting of the Association for Computational Linguistics*, pages 6086–6096.

Robert Litschko, Ivan Vulić, Simone Paolo Ponzetto, and Goran Glavaš. 2022. On cross-lingual retrieval with multilingual text encoders. *Information Retrieval Journal*, 25(2):149–183.

Yinhan Liu, Myle Ott, Naman Goyal, Jingfei Du, Mandar Joshi, Danqi Chen, Omer Levy, Mike Lewis, Luke Zettlemoyer, and Veselin Stoyanov. 2019. Roberta: A robustly optimized bert pretraining approach. *arXiv preprint arXiv:1907.11692*.

Ilya Loshchilov and Frank Hutter. 2019. Decoupled weight decay regularization. In *International Conference on Learning Representations*.

Sean MacAvaney, Luca Soldaini, and Nazli Goharian. 2020. Teaching a new dog old tricks: Resurrecting multilingual retrieval using zero-shot learning. In *European Conference on Information Retrieval*, pages 246–254. Springer.

Xiaochuan Ni, Jian-Tao Sun, Jian Hu, and Zheng Chen. 2009. Mining multilingual topics from wikipedia. In *Proceedings of the 18th international conference on World wide web*, pages 1155–1156.

Aaron van den Oord, Yazhe Li, and Oriol Vinyals. 2018. Representation learning with contrastive predictive coding. *arXiv preprint arXiv:1807.03748*.

Raghavendra Pappagari, Piotr Zelasko, Jesús Villalba, Yishay Carmiel, and Najim Dehak. 2019. Hierarchical transformers for long document classification. In *2019 IEEE Automatic Speech Recognition and Understanding Workshop (ASRU)*, pages 838–844. IEEE.

Nikolaos Pappas and Andrei Popescu-Belis. 2017. Multilingual hierarchical attention networks for document classification. In *Proceedings of the Eighth International Joint Conference on Natural Language Processing (Volume 1: Long Papers)*, pages 1015–1025.

Magdalena Plamadă and Martin Volk. 2013. Mining for domain-specific parallel text from wikipedia. In *Proceedings of the Sixth Workshop on Building and Using Comparable Corpora*, pages 112–120.

Yusu Qian, Urwa Muaz, Ben Zhang, and Jae Won Hyun. 2019. Reducing gender bias in word-level language models with a gender-equalizing loss function. In *Proceedings of the 57th Annual Meeting of the Association for Computational Linguistics: Student Research Workshop*, pages 223–228.

Philip Resnik and Noah A Smith. 2003. The web as a parallel corpus. *Computational Linguistics*, 29(3):349–380.

Guilherme Rosa, Luiz Bonifacio, Vitor Jeronymo, Hugo Abonizio, Marzieh Fadaee, Roberto Lotufo, and Rodrigo Nogueira. 2022. In defense of cross-encoders for zero-shot retrieval. *arXiv preprint arXiv:2212.06121*.

Markus Sagen. 2021. Large-context question answering with cross-lingual transfer. Master's thesis, Uppsala University, Department of Information Technology.

Holger Schwenk. 2018. Filtering and mining parallel data in a joint multilingual space. In *Proceedings of the 56th Annual Meeting of the Association for Computational Linguistics (Volume 2: Short Papers)*, pages 228–234, Melbourne, Australia. Association for Computational Linguistics.

Holger Schwenk, Vishrav Chaudhary, Shuo Sun, Hongyu Gong, and Francisco Guzmán. 2021. Wikimatrix: Mining 135m parallel sentences in 1620 language pairs from wikipedia. In *Proceedings of the 16th Conference of the European Chapter of the Association for Computational Linguistics: Main Volume*, pages 1351–1361.

Holger Schwenk and Xian Li. 2018. A corpus for multilingual document classification in eight languages. In *Proceedings of the Eleventh International Conference on Language Resources and Evaluation (LREC 2018)*, Miyazaki, Japan. European Language Resources Association (ELRA).

Peng Shi, He Bai, and Jimmy Lin. 2020. Cross-lingual training of neural models for document ranking. In *Findings of the Association for Computational Linguistics: EMNLP 2020*, pages 2768–2773, Online. Association for Computational Linguistics.

Yi Tay, Dara Bahri, Liu Yang, Donald Metzler, and Da-Cheng Juan. 2020. Sparse sinkhorn attention. In *International Conference on Machine Learning*, pages 9438–9447. PMLR.

Jakob Uszkoreit, Jay M Ponte, Ashok C Popat, and Moshe Dubiner. 2010. Large scale parallel document mining for machine translation. In *Proceedings of the 23rd International Conference on Computational Linguistics*, pages 1101–1109.

Shijie Wu and Mark Dredze. 2020. Do explicit alignments robustly improve multilingual encoders? In *Proceedings of the 2020 Conference on Empirical Methods in Natural Language Processing (EMNLP)*, pages 4471–4482.

Linting Xue, Noah Constant, Adam Roberts, Mihir Kale, Rami Al-Rfou, Aditya Siddhant, Aditya Barua, and Colin Raffel. 2021. mt5: A massively multilingual pre-trained text-to-text transformer. In *Proceedings of the 2021 Conference of the North American Chapter of the Association for Computational Linguistics: Human Language Technologies*, pages 483–498.

Liu Yang, Mingyang Zhang, Cheng Li, Michael Bendersky, and Marc Najork. 2020. Beyond 512 tokens: Siamese multi-depth transformer-based hierarchical encoder for long-form document matching. In *Proceedings of the 29th ACM International Conference on Information & Knowledge Management*, pages 1725–1734.

Puxuan Yu, Hongliang Fei, and Ping Li. 2021. Cross-lingual language model pretraining for retrieval. In *Proceedings of the Web Conference 2021*, pages 1029–1039.

Manzil Zaheer, Guru Guruganesh, Kumar Avinava Dubey, Joshua Ainslie, Chris Alberti, Santiago Ontanon, Philip Pham, Anirudh Ravula, Qifan Wang, Li Yang, et al. 2020. Big bird: Transformers for longer sequences. *Advances in Neural Information Processing Systems*, 33:17283–17297.

Xingxing Zhang, Furu Wei, and Ming Zhou. 2019. HIBERT: Document level pre-training of hierarchical bidirectional transformers for document summarization. In *Proceedings of the 57th Annual Meeting of the Association for Computational Linguistics*, pages 5059–5069, Florence, Italy. Association for Computational Linguistics.

Mengjie Zhao, Yi Zhu, Ehsan Shareghi, Ivan Vulić, Roi Reichart, Anna Korhonen, and Hinrich Schütze. 2021. A closer look at few-shot crosslingual transfer: The choice of shots matters. In *Proceedings of the 59th Annual Meeting of the Association for Computational Linguistics and the 11th International Joint Conference on Natural Language Processing (Volume 1: Long Papers)*, pages 5751–5767, Online. Association for Computational Linguistics.

A Appendix

A.1 Training and Optimization Details

In all training procedures, we use AdamW (Loshchilov and Hutter, 2019) as the optimization algorithm.

HMDE Pretraining. We set the maximal sentence length for HMDE, input to its lower-level transformer (initialized with LaBSE weights) to 128 tokens. For fair comparison, we set the segment size of the LasBSE-Seg baseline also to $N_S = 128$ tokens. For fair comparison against mLongformer, we limit the maximal document length for HMDE to 32 sentences, not to exceed the mLongformer's maximal input length of $4,096$ tokens. In our main set of experiments, the document-level (upper) transformer consists of 2 transformer layers, with GELU activation (Hendrycks and Gimpel, 2016), layer normalization ($\epsilon = 1e^{-12}$), and feed-forward sublayer with hidden size of 2048. The dropout rate for the upper transformer is set to 0.1. We train in batches of size $N = 2$ with the gradient accumulation over 64 batches for 1 full epoch,[12] with the initial learning rate of $1e^{-5}$, linear scheduling and 1000 warm-up steps.

mLongformer Pretraining. We train the mLongformer model (also initialized from LaBSE), also for 1 full epoch via MLM-ing, masking out 15% of tokens. We train with the initial learning rate of $1e^{-5}$ with weight decay of 0.01 and 500 warm-up steps. We train in batches of size 2, accumulating gradients over 32 batches.

XLDC Fine-Tuning. We fine-tune both HMDE and mLongformer for topical document classification with the learning rate of $2e^{-5}$ and without weight decay (with a 200 warm-up steps). We train in batches of size 4 for 50 epochs, accumulating gradients over 8 batches. Model selection was carried out based on the performance on the English validation portion of the MLDOC dataset, with early stopping if validation loss did not improve over 7 epochs.

A.2 Additional Ablation

We additionally test our design decision to segment the document into sentences, and encode sentences with the lower-level transformer (the weights of which are initialized from LaBSE). To this end, we compare our default strategy of segmenting input documents into sentences against a less-informed segmentation into consecutive chunks of 128 tokens. Table 4 shows the results of this comparison. Unsurprisingly – given that the lower encoder is initialized with the weights of a pretrained *sentence* encoder – sentence-based segmentation is more effective, although chunking does not trail by much.

Model	Segmentation	XLDC	CLIR
HMDE-LaBSE	*Sentence*	86.8	0.249
HMDE-LaBSE	*Chunk*	85.4	0.224

Table 4: HMDE results for different choices w.r.t. to document segmentation. Training for both variants carried out on XLW-4L. Results are averages across all test languages (XLDC) and language pairs (CLIR).

[12] Note that batch size $N = 2$ in our contrastive objective (see §2.2) implies only one in-batch negative pair (besides the hard negative) for each positive pair.

Zero-Shot Cross-Lingual Sentiment Classification under Distribution Shift: an Exploratory Study

Maarten De Raedt[◇♣] **Semere Kiros Bitew**[♣] **Fréderic Godin**[◇] **Thomas Demeester**[♣] **Chris Develder**[♣]

[◇] Sinch Chatlayer [♣] Ghent University - imec

{maarten.deraedt, semerekiros.bitew, thomas.demeester, chris.develder}@ugent.be

frederic.godin@sinch.com

Abstract

The brittleness of finetuned language model performance on out-of-distribution (OOD) test samples in unseen domains has been well-studied for English, yet is unexplored for multilingual models. Therefore, we study generalization to OOD test data specifically in zero-shot cross-lingual transfer settings, analyzing performance impacts of both *language* and *domain* shifts between train and test data. We further assess the effectiveness of counterfactually augmented data (CAD) in improving OOD generalization for the cross-lingual setting, since CAD has been shown to benefit in a monolingual English setting. Finally, we propose two new approaches for OOD generalization that avoid the costly annotation process associated with CAD, by exploiting the power of recent large language models (LLMs). We experiment with 3 multilingual models, LaBSE, mBERT, and XLM-R trained on English IMDb movie reviews, and evaluate on OOD test sets in 13 languages: Amazon product reviews, Tweets, and Restaurant reviews. Results echo the OOD performance decline observed in the monolingual English setting. Further, (i) counterfactuals from the original high-resource language do improve OOD generalization in the low-resource language, and (ii) our newly proposed cost-effective approaches reach similar or up to to +3.1% better accuracy than CAD for Amazon and Restaurant reviews.

1 Introduction

To solve Natural Language Processing (NLP) tasks in low-resource languages, using multilingual models is a much adopted strategy (Devlin et al., 2019; Artetxe and Schwenk, 2019; Conneau and Lample, 2019; Feng et al., 2022). A particularly popular paradigm is zero-shot cross-lingual transfer (Ruder et al., 2019; Artetxe et al., 2020b; Hu et al., 2020; Lauscher et al., 2020): pre-trained multilingual models are finetuned on downstream tasks with training data solely from a high-resource language

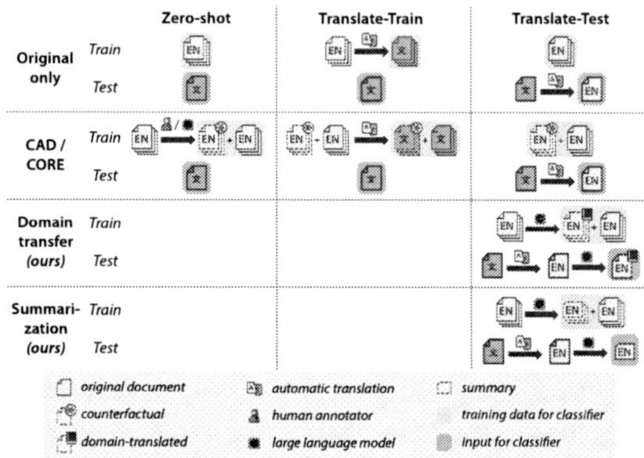

Fig. 1: **Zero-shot cross-lingual transfer setup.** Multiple transfer strategies, including our newly proposed *summarization* and *domain transfer* methods for boosting OOD generalization.

(e.g., English). The resulting finetuned model can then be applied on a low-resource language samples, i.e., without requiring costly training data in the low-resource language.

In such zero-shot cross-lingual transfer, linguistic discrepancy between training and test languages causes a challenge: typically, performance is subpar compared to monolingual models.[1] Several works have looked into narrowing the performance gap stemming from such language-based distribution shift (Liu et al., 2021; Yu and Joty, 2021; Zheng et al., 2021; Artetxe et al., 2023).

Yet, besides the language-based shift, in real-world settings there may also be a domain-shift between training and test samples, i.e., test samples may comprise out-of-distribution (OOD) data (Quiñonero-Candela et al., 2008). For example, a sentiment classifier to predict positive/negative appreciation by a consumer may be trained on movie reviews but applied on product reviews or tweets, where underlying sentiment features are assumed to be invariant (Arora et al., 2021).

[1]Admittedly, such monolingual models do need low-resource training data.

Proceedings of the The 3rd Workshop on Multi-lingual Representation Learning (MRL), pages 50–66
December 7, 2023 ©2023 Association for Computational Linguistics

In a monolingual (English) setting, several studies unsurprisingly found a performance degradation when evaluating on OOD test data rather than on in-distribution (ID) data (Kaushik et al., 2019, 2020; Gardner et al., 2020; Katakkar et al., 2022). One of the underlying causes for that performance drop was found to be the classifier's reliance on spurious features, i.e., patterns that from a human perspective should not be indicative for the classifier's label (Poliak et al., 2018; Gururangan et al., 2018; McCoy et al., 2019; Wang and Culotta, 2020; Joshi et al., 2022): e.g., Wang and Culotta (2020) found the occurrence of "*Spielberg*" to be important for a positive sentiment classification.

A strategy that has been shown to improve OOD generalization in the monolingual English setting is the use of counterfactually augmented data (CAD), where annotators minimally revise training data to flip their labels (Kaushik et al., 2019). Yet, constructing such annotations is costly: Kaushik et al. (2019) report 5 min/sample.

In this paper, we present an exploratory study of OOD generalization specifically in a *cross-lingual* context, since we found this not to be covered in related work (§2). Specifically, we (i) identify the impact of OOD data on zero-shot *cross-lingual* transfer performance, aiming to disentangle performance drops stemming from *language* vs. *domain* shifts between training and test data, and (ii) propose and analyze two new data augmentation strategies to improve OOD generalization that *avoid the costly annotations* associated with using counterfactuals. For both, we present an empirical study (§3) within the domain of binary sentiment analysis. We consider English IMDb reviews (Maas et al., 2011) as in-distribution training data, with out-of-distribution test data spanning 13 languages across the Amazon (Keung et al., 2020), Tweets (Barbieri et al., 2022), and Restaurants (Pontiki et al., 2016) datasets. We further experiment with pre-trained multilingual models mBERT (Devlin et al., 2019), XLM-R (Conneau and Lample, 2019), and LaBSE (Feng et al., 2022).

For (i), we answer a first research question, **(RQ1)** *How well do zero-shot cross-lingual methods trained with English sentiment data generalize to out-of-distribution samples in non-English languages?* To this end, we finetune the multilingual models on the English IMDb sentiment data, and evaluate their performance on OOD test samples in non-English languages.

For (ii), we answer **(RQ2)** *How can zero-shot cross-lingual transfer methods better generalize to out-of-distribution samples, including for non-English languages?* We will consider a CAD baseline as proposed by Kaushik et al. (2019), where annotators minimally revise training data to flip their labels, since training on both original and counterfactual data improves OOD generalization to unseen domains in the monolingual English setting. Specifically, we finetune the multilingual models on both the original English and counterfactually revised English IMDb reviews, and evaluate whether the OOD generalization gains observed in the monolingual setting translate also to OOD test samples in non-English languages.

We then propose (§3.3) two cost-effective alternatives for CAD, using Large Language Models (LLMs): (1) *domain transfer*, and (2) *summarization*, as illustrated in the 2 bottom rows of Fig. 1. For (1), we prompt an LLM to minimally edit both ID training and OOD test samples to map them onto the same, *hypothetical* domain, e.g., books. For (2), we prompt an LLM to abstractly summarize both ID training and OOD test data, since we hypothesize that summaries can capture the core essence of samples while removing non-essential, potentially spurious, information.

Our results (§4) show that in the OOD test setting for non-English languages, model performance of zero-shot cross-lingual transfer substantially declines, aligned with OOD generalization studies in a monolingual English setting. We further find that CAD improves OOD generalization for non-English samples, with gains up to +14.8%, +4.7%, and +7.9% for respectively LaBSE, mBERT, and XLM-R. Finally, our cost-effective *domain transfer* and *summarization* data augmentation methods similarly improve OOD generalization, on par with or even surpassing CAD for *Amazon* and *Restaurants* by up to +3.1% in accuracy.

2 Related Work

Zero-shot cross-lingual transfer: A large part of multilingual NLP research focuses on improving the transfer of multilingual models trained on high-resource language data to low-resource languages. This can be achieved either by (i) cross-lingual pre-training schemes that yield stronger multilingual models (Artetxe and Schwenk, 2019; Conneau and Lample, 2019; Conneau et al., 2020; Xue et al., 2021; Feng et al., 2022; Chi et al., 2022), or (ii) fine-tuning strategies that facilitate better cross-lingual transfer (Liu et al., 2021; Yu and Joty, 2021; Zheng et al., 2021). Recently, Artetxe et al. (2023) revisited the *translate-test* and *translate-train* baselines (Shi et al., 2010; Duh et al., 2011; Artetxe et al., 2020a), where *test* samples are translated into English prior to evaluating them, or, respectively, the *training* samples are translated into the test languages for fine-tuning a multilingual model. Artetxe et al. found that using more recent machine translation systems, e.g., NLLB (Costa-jussà et al., 2022), further boosts performance and often surpasses strong zero-shot cross-lingual methods. Hence, we also experiment with *translate-test* and *translate-train* approaches.

Cross-lingual transfer under distribution shift: The limited research on the robustness of multilingual models has primarily focused on being robust against specific types of *noise*, e.g., adversarial perturbations for Japanese Natural Language Inference (Yanaka and Mineshima, 2021), a combination of general and task-specific text transformations based on manipulating synonyms, antonyms, syntax, etc. (Wang et al., 2021), and introducing errors and noise through Wikipedia edits (Cooper Stickland et al., 2023). Unlike these works, we will evaluate how well zero-shot cross-lingual transfer from English to non-English test samples can generalize in scenarios where there is a shift in *domain* from train to test data: the domain-specific features of test samples may change, whereas the semantic sentiment features remain invariant.

Counterfactually-augmented data (CAD): For English sentiment analysis, CAD is widely adopted to mitigate the effect of spurious patterns. For example, Kaushik et al. (2019, 2020) recruited Mechanical Turk workers to construct counterfactually revised samples by flipping labels with minimal editing, helping classifiers to learn real associations between samples and labels, thereby improving OOD generalization to unseen test domains. Building upon the success of CAD, several works have also studied how to automatically generate counterfactuals for English sentiment analysis (Wang and Culotta, 2021; Yang et al., 2021; Dixit et al., 2022; Howard et al., 2022; De Raedt et al., 2022). We adopt this CAD idea for OOD generalization in a zero-shot cross-lingual setting, which to the best of our knowledge has not been studied yet.

We start by exploring whether augmenting the English training data with the manually constructed counterfactuals from Kaushik et al. (2019) also benefits OOD generalization for non-English test samples. Additionally, we propose two new LLM-based methods as alternatives to constructing counterfactuals, aiming to specifically improve zero-shot transfer to non-English OOD test samples. We benchmark our new LLM-based methods against a CAD setup following Kaushik et al. (2019), thus assessing whether we can achieve similar OOD performance but avoid CAD's costly human annotations. We further contrast classifiers trained on data augmented by our two new LLM-based methods to those trained on counterfactuals generated by CORE (Dixit et al., 2022), the state-of-the-art method in automatic counterfactual generation. CORE first retrieves naturally occurring counterfactual edits from an unlabeled text corpus and then, based on these retrieved edits, instructs an LLM (GPT-3) to counterfactually revise training samples.

3 Experimental Setup

We describe the English ID training data and non-English OOD test data in §3.1. Next, we outline the pre-trained multilingual models and the transfer strategies we experiment with in §3.2. In §3.3, we present our LLM-based *domain transfer* and *summarization* data augmentation methods. We cover finetuning and evaluation in §3.4.

3.1 Datasets

In-distribution (ID) training data: We use the subset of 1,707 English reviews selected by Kaushik et al. (2019) from the IMDb sentiment dataset (Maas et al., 2011) as training data, as well as 245 English validation samples. To better assess the OOD generalization of cross-lingual transfer, we also report in-distribution results of all 13 considered languages on the IMDb test set with 488 samples. However, the test set of Kaushik et al. (2019) is English-only. Hence, we translate the 488 English test samples into each of the 12 other non-English languages, using OpenAI's `ChatGPT-turbo (v0301)` (Ouyang et al., 2022), as it achieves translation quality that is competitive to commercial machine translation tools (e.g., Google Translate or Microsoft Translation Suite) (Jiao et al., 2023; Hendy et al., 2023; Peng et al., 2023), while being more cost-effective. Since we aim to explore the benefits of English CAD for

		Original samples
	IMDB	If you haven't seen this, it's terrible. It is pure trash. I saw this about 17 years ago, and I'm still screwed up from it.
	TWEETS	She just didn't get them in areas were she needed them. Lots of voter supression going on. Hacking & tampering
	AMAZON	The straps are super small, for a very small wrist, and the closure is bad, easy to lose the watch.
	RESTAURANTS	The food is standard, but the person waiting at the door in the style of a manager is cold and unfriendly.
		Domain transferred samples
	IMDB	If you haven't read this book, it's terrible. It is pure trash. I read this about 17 years ago, and I'm still screwed up from it.
	TWEETS	She just didn't get the books in areas where she needed them. Lots of book censorship going on. Piracy & Plagiarism
	AMAZON	The binding of the book is super light, suited for a compact size, and the cover is not secure, easy to lose the pages.
	RESTAURANTS	The books are average, but the person at the front desk in a manager-like role is distant and unapproachable.
		Summarized samples
	IMDB	Terrible and traumatizing movie, avoid it.
	TWEETS	Allegations of voter suppression and tampering.
	AMAZON	Small straps, bad closure, easy to lose.
	RESTAURANTS	Standard food, unfriendly manager.

Table 1: **LLM-based data-augmentation.** *Top:* original ID training and OOD test samples (including English translations). *Middle:* mapping of the diverse domain samples onto the *hypothetical* books domain. *Bottom:* demonstrates how *summarization* retains essential information while removing potentially spurious elements.

OOD generalization also to non-English test samples, we augment the respectively 1,707 and 488 original training and validation samples with their English counterfactually revised counterparts provided by Kaushik et al. (2019). All training, validation, and test sets are equally balanced between positive and negative samples.

Out-of-distribution (OOD) test data: Our OOD test data comprises three non-movie domains: *product reviews*, *tweets* and *restaurant feedback*. We use the MARC dataset (Keung et al., 2020) for Amazon *product reviews* in six languages: English, German, French, Spanish, Japanese, and Chinese. For *tweets*, we use the recent multilingual test sets provided by Barbieri et al. (2022), in eight languages: English, German, French, Spanish, Arabic, Hindi, Portuguese, and Italian. For *restaurant* reviews, we use the multilingual aspect-based sentiment classification dataset for the 2016 SemEval Task 5 (Pontiki et al., 2016), i.e., its restaurant domain data covering six languages: English, Dutch, French, Spanish, Russian, and Turkish. Since SemEval Task 5 concerns aspect-based sentiment, we apply a rule-based mapping to cast it as a binary classification task: included reviews are labeled either as *positive* (if all aspects are positive or a mix of neutral and positive) or *negative* (if all aspects are negative or a mix of neutral and negative). We undersample test examples from the majority sentiment to ensure that all test sets are balanced. Further dataset statistics are provided in Appendix A.

3.2 Zero-shot cross-lingual transfer

Pre-trained multilingual models: We consider the base-cased versions of two multilingual language models pre-trained on masked language model (MLM) objectives: mBERT, i.e., a multilingual variant of BERT (Devlin et al., 2019), and XLM-R, a RoBERTa-based multilingual model (Conneau and Lample, 2019). Additionally, we use the pre-trained multilingual sentence encoder LaBSE (Feng et al., 2022) that maps sentences to 768-dimensional single vector representations.

Transfer strategies: To transfer from the English ID training data to non-English test samples, we use 3 widely adopted strategies (Fig. 1, top row):

(1) *zero-shot*: finetunes the multilingual model on the English ID training and validation set, followed by directly evaluating the OOD test samples in the non-English languages.
(2) *translate-test*: finetunes the multilingual model on the English ID training and validation datasets. However, prior to making predictions for OOD test samples, the samples are translated into English.
(3) *translate-train*: first translates the English ID training and validation datasets to the target OOD test language. Subsequently, the multilingual model is trained on this translated data to then make predictions for the original, untranslated, OOD test samples in that non-English language.

Note that in case where both *translate-train* and CAD are used, the English CAD training and validation data are translated to the target OOD test language. For both *translate-test* and *translate-train*, we use OpenAI's `ChatGPT-turbo (v0301)` (Ouyang et al., 2022) as the LLM to translate from English to non-English languages and vice versa. We adopt OpenAI's default parameter values. See Appendix A for translation prompts.

3.3 LLM-based data-augmentation

We explore whether data augmentation using an LLM, as a cost-effective alternative to CAD, can also boost OOD generalization. We propose two such alternatives: (1) *domain transfer*, and (2) *summarization*. Our focus is on augmenting data for *translate-test*, as recent work has shown it to be more effective than *zero-shot* and *translate-train* (Artetxe et al., 2023). The multilingual models are finetuned on the original English ID, as well as the augmented ID training samples[2], with predictions made solely on augmented test samples. Table 1 provides illustrations for both strategies.

Domain transfer: We align the domains of both the original ID training and OOD test samples *translated* into English to a common *hypothetical* domain. To achieve this, we instruct `ChatGPT-turbo (v0301)` (Ouyang et al., 2022) to minimally change the samples so that they relate to the new *hypothetical* domain, for which we experiment with the domain of *books*. Note that rather than solely mapping OOD test samples to the ID training domain of movies, we use a *hypothetical* domain to transform both training and test samples with an LLM to avoid introducing a new distribution shift caused by the mismatch between the original human-based training and the LLM-generated test samples. See Appendix A for our domain transfer prompt.

Summarization: For our second augmentation strategy, we abstractly summarize both the original English training and the *translated* English OOD test samples. We hypothesize that such concise summaries can retain essential information while omitting non-essential and potentially spurious features, such as, e.g., specific syntax structures and lexical choices, thereby a priori preventing classifiers from relying on such features for prediction. Furthermore, transforming text with language models, i.e., through summarization, may have the added benefit of normalizing the background, non-sentiment related, features. Hence, summarizing the data can lead to more uniform syntax and word choice among test and training samples, potentially further narrowing the distribution mismatch between ID training and OOD test samples. Appendix A lists the exact prompt that we supply to `ChatGPT-turbo (v0301)` (Ouyang et al., 2022), using OpenAI's default parameter values.

[2]To ensure all strategies have the same number of training samples, we train the *original-only* models (without manual counterfactuals or LLM-augmented samples) on twice the number (3.4k) of original IMDb reviews (§3.4).

3.4 Finetuning and evaluation

We finetune the MLM-based models, i.e., mBERT and XLM-R, by adding a classification head to the [`CLS`]-token. We use the Hugging Face Transformers library (Wolf et al., 2020) and train on a single Tesla V100 GPU for 20 epochs, with a batch size of 38, and a learning rate of $5e{-}6$. To select an optimal model, we employ early validation stopping with a loss threshold of 0.01 and a patience of 10. Since we are also interested in measuring the performance of a more compute-efficient model, we freeze LaBSE's parameters and train on CPU a logistic regression model on LaBSE's sentence vectors through five-fold cross-validation. We use the `scikit-learn` library (Pedregosa et al., 2011), with `lbfgs` (Liu and Nocedal, 1989) as the solver, and set the maximum number of iterations to 5,000.

To assess the performance of each transfer strategy, we report the mean accuracy over 5 randomly initialized training runs, i.e., with randomly selected weights and cross-validation folds for respectively mBERT/XLM-R and LaBSE.

Note that classifiers trained on CAD, as well as on data augmented by our two strategies, use respectively 1.7k extra manually constructed counterfactuals and 1.7k extra LLM-generated samples, in addition to the 1.7k original IMDb training samples. To ensure that the OOD generalization gains from CAD and our two augmentation strategies are not solely attributed to the increased number of training samples, we randomly sample an extra 1.7k original English IMDb reviews from the IMDb dataset of Maas et al. (2011) for the *original-only* strategy (i.e., models trained without counterfactuals or augmented data). As such, all considered strategies are trained on 3.4k samples

4 Experimental Results and Discussion

4.1 Zero-shot cross-lingual out-of-distribution generalization

We first address **(RQ1)**, on assessing OOD generalization to non-English samples. In Table 2, we present both ID and OOD accuracies of the *original only* method, which trains solely on (translated) English IMDb movie reviews without data augmentation.

We see that both for English and non-English, all models and transfer strategies decline in perfor-

Method	IMDB EN	IMDB NON-EN	AMAZON EN	AMAZON NON-EN	RESTAURANTS EN	RESTAURANTS NON-EN	TWEETS EN	TWEETS NON-EN
LaBSE								
- ZSHOT	85.0	84.9	66.3	71.9	72.7	74.1	76.3	67.8
- TTRAIN	85.0	85.2	66.3	74.0	72.7	76.4	76.3	66.0
- TTEST	85.0	-	66.3	67.6	72.7	73.1	76.3	68.8
mBERT								
- ZSHOT	89.5	80.8	79.3	72.2	80.2	69.6	75.9	62.8
- TTRAIN	89.5	87.5	79.3	73.5	80.2	74.5	75.9	62.9
- TTEST	89.5	-	79.3	77.8	80.2	78.9	75.9	71.1
XLM-R								
- ZSHOT	92.4	88.4	86.3	85.0	86.0	79.2	84.3	69.2
- TTRAIN	92.4	90.7	86.3	86.0	86.0	83.0	84.3	72.5
- TTEST	92.4	-	86.3	85.6	86.0	81.5	84.3	71.7

Table 2: **In-distribution vs. out-of-distribution** test accuracies for the *original only* strategy trained solely on IMDb reviews (without CAD or data augmentation). Results are presented for English (EN) and non-English (NON-EN) test data, with the latter's accuracies averaged across all non-English languages per test set. Detailed results per language are provided in Appendix A. Note, for English, TTRAIN and TTEST do not involve any translation, hence their EN scores are equivalent to ZSHOT. Further, ID scores for TTEST are omitted as these would involve backtranslating the non-English ID samples (originally translated from English ID test data per §3.1) to English, which would largely assess back-translation quality.

mance when evaluated on OOD rather than ID test samples. For example, the *zero-shot* strategy's drop from English ID to English OOD ($ID_{EN} \rightarrow OOD_{EN}$) ranges from 8.7%–18.7% for LaBSE, 9.3%–13.6% for mBERT, and 6.1%–8.1% for XLM-R. Similarly, for non-English ($ID_{NON\text{-}EN} \rightarrow OOD_{NON\text{-}EN}$), the performance drops for LaBSE, mBERT, and XLM-R vary within the ranges of 10.8%–17.1%, 8.6%–18%, and 3.4%–19.2%, respectively. These findings suggest that model performance decline to OOD test samples in non-English is substantial, as was already known (and here confirmed again) for English. We do not, however, see a consistently stronger decline for non-English than for English, as may be intuitively expected. This is discussed in more detail in the next paragraph.

English vs. non-English OOD generalization: We assess whether multilingual models generalize better to English than non-English OOD test data. Overall, the EN versus NON-EN scores in Table 2 reveal that the MLM-based models mBERT and XLM-R generalize less well to non-English compared to English OOD test samples: the accuracies for non-English languages are lower in most cases. Surprisingly, the converse holds for LaBSE: it has consistently better non-English OOD accuracies compared to English on *Amazon* and *Restaurants*. Note, however, the absolute performance of the three models: LaBSE appears to be the least accurate model in English in most cases. This is consistent with the fact that its encoder remains frozen during training in English, unlike the other encoders, whereas LaBSE's non-English performance is more on par with the other models. While our results suggest that performance decline to OOD test samples in non-English and English is substantial, the disparity among OOD model performance between non-English and English depends on the (i) pre-trained multilingual model or finetuning strategy, and (ii) the type of OOD data.

Impact of the pre-trained multilingual models: We compare the OOD generalization of LaBSE, mBERT, and XLM-R. The results in Table 2 show XLM-R as the top performer, consistently surpassing both LaBSE and mBERT. Despite having only 768 trainable parameters (frozen encoder with trainable logistic regression layer) against mBERT's 110M (fully tuned), it is surprising that LaBSE is at least on par with mBERT on non-English OOD data, except for *translate-test*. This suggests a stronger bias towards English in mBERT compared to LaBSE, also evidenced by an 8.7% drop in mBERT's ID *zero-shot* performance between English and non-English, whereas this difference is just 0.1% for LaBSE.

Impact of the transfer strategies: We assess the *translate-train* and *translate-test* strategies for

	LaBSE						mBERT						XLM-R					
	AMAZON		RESTAURANTS		TWEETS		AMAZON		RESTAURANTS		TWEETS		AMAZON		RESTAURANTS		TWEETS	
Method	EN	NON-EN	EN	NON-EN	EN	NON-EN	EN	NON-EN	EN	NON-EN	EN	NON-EN	EN	NON-EN	EN	NON-EN	EN	NON-EN
Original only																		
- ZSHOT	66.3	71.9	72.7	74.1	76.3	67.8	79.3	72.2	80.2	69.6	75.9	62.8	86.3	85.0	86.0	79.2	84.3	69.2
- TTRAIN	66.3	74.0	72.7	76.4	76.3	66.0	79.3	73.5	80.2	74.5	75.9	62.9	86.3	86.0	86.0	83.0	84.3	72.5
- TTEST	66.3	67.6	72.7	73.1	76.3	68.8	79.3	77.8	80.2	78.9	75.9	71.1	86.3	85.6	86.0	81.5	84.3	71.7
Original + CAD (Kaushik et al., 2019)																		
- ZSHOT	81.2	82.9	84.7	85.7	81.7	74.5	81.7	74.9	81.8	70.9	79.0	67.2	87.0	85.7	87.5	81.9	86.7	75.9
- TTRAIN	81.2	82.3	84.7	83.4	81.7	73.7	81.7	78.2	81.8	75.7	79.0	66.9	87.0	86.4	87.5	84.6	86.7	77.3
- TTEST	81.2	82.4	84.7	85.9	**81.7**	**76.2**	**81.7**	**81.2**	81.8	81.2	**79.0**	**75.0**	87.0	86.8	87.5	87.1	**86.7**	79.6
Original + CORE (Dixit et al., 2022)																		
- ZSHOT	81.0	82.0	85.0	84.9	77.4	71.1	80.2	74.1	80.4	69.6	73.6	64.8	86.8	87.0	89.7	87.5	83.9	77.9
- TTEST	81.0	81.7	85.0	86.3	77.4	74.3	80.2	79.9	80.4	79.9	73.6	72.8	86.8	87.0	89.7	89.1	83.9	**80.5**
Original + Domain transfer (ours)																		
TTEST+TRAN.	81.7	81.9	84.1	84.1	72.3	69.6	81.3	80.3	83.3	81.0	72.4	69.7	87.1	**87.1**	87.2	84.5	72.7	69.7
Original + Summarization (ours)																		
TTEST+SUM.	**86.2**	**84.7**	**91.6**	**88.8**	76.6	74.0	81.1	**81.2**	**87.3**	**84.3**	74.3	73.8	**87.8**	86.8	**92.8**	**90.2**	83.0	75.9

Table 3: **Out-of-distribution generalization with data augmentation.** *Original only*: baseline model trained solely on IMDb reviews, without CAD or data augmentation. +*CAD*: augments IMDb training samples with manually constructed counterfactuals. +*CORE*: augments training samples with automatically generated counterfactuals. +*Domain transfer* and +*Summarization* augment the training data with our newly proposed strategies. **Best** model in bold with the runner-up underlined.

OOD generalization against the *zero-shot* approach. The results in Table 2 reveal large OOD generalization gains for non-English languages using *translate-test* and mBERT, with accuracy gains between +5.6% and +9.3%. This supports our previous discussion of mBERT being more biased towards English. For LaBSE, *translate-train* is most effective on *Amazon* and *Restaurants*, with average accuracy boosts of +2.1% and +2.3% respectively, but not for *Tweets* (−1.8%). For XLM-R, *Restaurants* and *Tweets* benefit most from translation: *translate-train* (*translate-test*) surpass *zero-shot* with respective gains of +3.8% (+2.3%) and +3.3% (+2.5%). In conclusion, while translation-based strategies can further boost the OOD generalization zero-shot cross-lingual transfer, the benefits are dependent on the multilingual model and OOD test data.

4.2 Out-of-distribution generalization with data augmentation

To address **(RQ2)** on achieving better OOD generalization, we first analyze the effect of augmenting training data with the manually constructed counterfactuals of Kaushik et al. (2019). These counterfactuals will serve as an upper baseline against which we will subsequently compare the performance of models trained on (i) counterfactuals generated by the state-of-the-art in automatic counterfactual construction, i.e., CORE (Dixit et al., 2022), and (ii) our LLM *domain transferred* and *summarized* augmented data.

Manually constructed counterfactuals: Comparing the *original + CAD* results in Table 3 to the corresponding *original only* results, reveals that augmenting training data with CAD consistently boosts OOD generalization, across all datasets and both for English and non-English test samples. Accuracy gains averaged over the non-English languages for OOD vary between 7%–14.8%, 1.2%–4.7%, and 0.4%–7.9% for respectively LaBSE, mBERT, and XLM-R. This confirms that the English OOD generalization gains of CAD based training (Kaushik et al., 2019) translate well to non-English OOD test data in a cross-lingual setting.

Impact of LLM-based data augmentation on cross-lingual OOD generalization: As an alternative to costly manually constructed counterfactuals, we investigate the viability of *automatic* data augmentation: CORE from Dixit et al. (2022) (replacing humans with the LLM for counterfactual creation), as well as our newly proposed *domain transfer* and *summarization* strategies described in §3.3. First, we compare the non-English OOD generalization of models trained with augmented data to models trained solely on original data. Table 3 shows clear non-English OOD improvements for all of LaBSE, mBERT, and XLM-R, with respective gains over *original only* ranging from: (i) 3.3%–14.1%, 0%–2.1%, and 1.4%–8.8% for CORE, (ii) 0.8%–14.3%, −1.4%–2.5%, and −2.0%–3% for *domain transfer*, and (iii) 5.2%–17.1%, 2.7%–5.4%, and 1.3%–8.7% for *summarization*. The drops −1.4% and −2.0% for mBERT and XLM-R on *Tweets* suggest that *domain transfer* is less effective when the discrepancy between test and training domains is excessively large: the IMDb training data, similar to the *Amazon* and *Restaurant* domains, comprises reviews, whereas *Tweets* do not.

The bold and underlined scores in Table 3 denote the top two results. Our *summarization* strategy achieves the best non-English OOD generalization on *Amazon* and *Restaurants*, on par with (or surpassing) models trained on CAD. On *Tweets*, while *summarization* still improves models trained solely on the original data, training on CAD or CORE (XLM-R) yields the best results.

These findings support the efficacy of cost-effective data augmentation as a viable alternative to manually constructed counterfactuals for non-English test data. It is worth noting that our *summarization* and *domain transfer* methods scale linearly, only requiring a single transformation of training samples for each class. However, it is doubtful that CAD and CORE can be similarly expanded beyond binary sentiment classification due to their quadratic data complexity: counterfactuals have to be constructed among every pair of classes.

Impact of LLM-based data augmentation on mono-lingual OOD generalization: Thus far, our analysis has primarily focused on the generalization from English ID training data to non-English OOD test data. Here, we investigate whether our *summarization* and *domain transfer* strategies can also help classifiers generalize in the well-studied monolingual setup, i.e., from English training data to English OOD test data. In this setup, the *translate-test* step is omitted: both the English ID training reviews from IMDb and the English OOD test samples are summarized or domain transferred, without any prior translation.

Comparing the EN scores across the different transfer strategies in Table 3 for each of LaBSE, mBERT, and XLM-R, reveals findings similar to the OOD generalization to non-English languages. (i) For *Amazon* and *Restaurants*, all data augmentation approaches deliver classifiers that better generalize OOD compared to the *original only* classifiers trained without augmented data. Our *summarization* strategy achieves the best overall results,

	AMAZON		RESTAURANTS		TWEETS	
Method	EN	NON-EN	EN	NON-EN	EN	NON-EN
LaBSE						
ZSHOT	77.1	79.7	83.6	83.7	81.9	71.8
+TTEST	77.1	78.9	83.6	84.0	**81.9**	73.1
+SUM.	**86.2**	**84.7**	**91.6**	**88.8**	76.6	**74.0**
mBERT						
ZSHOT	80.7	73.6	82.4	72.5	77.8	63.5
+TTEST	80.7	79.6	82.4	80.0	**77.8**	72.0
+SUM.	**81.0**	**81.2**	**87.3**	**84.3**	74.3	**73.8**
XLM-R						
ZSHOT	87.8	87.7	89.4	84.9	86.3	75.1
+TTEST	87.8	**88.0**	89.4	87.1	**86.3**	**77.8**
+SUM.	87.8	86.8	**92.8**	**90.2**	83.0	75.9

Table 4: **Ablations** of our best data augmentation strategy: *summarization*. ZSHOT: trains on the original English and summarized English IMDb reviews. +TTEST: additionally translates test samples to English. +SUM.: further summarizes the English translated test samples prior inference.

surpassing both classifiers trained on CORE and manually constructed counterfactuals (CAD), except for mBERT and *Amazon*, where CAD results in a minor accuracy gain of 0.6% over *summarization*. (ii) Surprisingly, for *Tweets*, only classifiers trained on manually constructed CAD show consistent OOD generalization improvements over *original-only* classifiers. This is in contrast to the results observed for non-English, where CORE and our *summarization* augmentation approach were able to improve upon the *original-only* classifiers.

Overall, these results highlight that our *summarization* strategy can also benefit monolingual OOD generalization, surpassing classifiers augmented either with CAD or CORE generated counterfactuals for *Amazon* and *Restaurants*.

Ablations: We provide ablations in Table 4 for our most effective strategy, i.e., *summarization*, and find that:
(i) The benefits of translating test samples into English (*translate-test*) versus solely augmenting the training data with summaries (*zero-shot*) vary based on the multilingual and/or OOD test data: there are clear OOD improvements to non-English samples for mBERT and XLM-R, but results for LaBSE are mixed and comparable to the *zero-shot* strategy;
(ii) More importantly, further summarizing the English translated test samples improves OOD generalization more than solely translating them to

English, consistently boosting accuracies by up to +5% for LaBSE and +4.3% mBERT, across all datasets. For XLM-R, summarization slightly reduces accuracy, e.g., −1.2% for non-English languages on *Amazon* and −1.9% for *Tweets* compared to translation alone, yet still boosts OOD generalization to *Restaurants* by 3.1% over *translate-test*.

Cost-effectiveness of LLM-based augmentation: To assess the cost-effectiveness of our LLM-based augmentation, we discuss the costs of our best approach, i.e., *summarization*, and compare it to that cost of employing human workers to manually construct counterfactuals. Kaushik et al. (2019) report that human workers spent an average of 5 minutes revising a single IMDb review, with each worker earning $0.65 per revised review. Therefore, manually revising 1.7K training reviews incurs a total cost of ≈$1,105 and ≈141 hours of labor.

In contrast, our summarization strategy costs $0.0003 on average for summarizing a single training IMDb review, totaling $0.51 for all 1.7K training reviews. However, our best OOD generalization is achieved not only by summarizing training reviews, but also by using an LLM during inference to: (1) translate non-English test samples to English (*translate-test*), and (2) further summarize the English translated test samples. For (1), the cost is $0.00015 per OOD sample. For (2), an additional cost of $0.00007 is required per OOD sample.[3] The reported costs per test sample are taken as the average among all OOD test sets and non-English languages.

In conclusion, our *summarization* strategy costs $0.51 to summarize all 1.7K training samples, and $0.00022 (=(1)+(2)) per inference. Thus, for the same cost of employing human workers for CAD creation (≈ $1,105), our *summarization* strategy enables inference for 5M test samples. Note, however, that the best overall performance of classifiers augmented with CAD are achieved for *translate-test*. Therefore, if we also account for translation costs of the CAD-augmented classifiers, our *summarization* method can perform inference for 15M test samples for the same cost as employing human workers for CAD creation. This demonstrates the cost-effectiveness of our *summarization* approach when scaled up to 5M test samples as compared to *zero-shot* +CAD, and up to 15M when compared to *translate-test* +CAD. For future work, exploring open-source LLMs -or translation and summarization models could prove valuable for reducing inference costs.

[3] Summarizing OOD test samples is less costly than summarizing IMDb training samples due to the test samples comprising fewer tokens.

5 Conclusions

We explored the generalization of zero-shot cross-lingual transfer to out-of-distribution (OOD) test data, considering both *language* and *domain* shifts. Our experiments on binary sentiment classification with pre-trained multilingual models LaBSE, mBERT, and XLM-R finetuned on English IMDb movie reviews and evaluated on non-English test samples comprising *Amazon* product reviews, *Restaurant* feedback, and *Tweets*, demonstrate that model performance substantially degrades, aligning with previous OOD generalization studies in a monolingual English setting. We also found that mBERT and XLM-R suffer more from performance reduction on OOD in non-English languages compared to English OOD degradation, while LaBSE's generalization strongly depends on the OOD dataset. Our experiments with models finetuned on original data augmented with manually constructed English counterfactual (CAD) IMDb reviews show that CAD's OOD generalization gains observed in a monolingual English setting also translate well to a zero-shot cross-lingual setup. Finally, to avoid costly manually constructed counterfactuals, we propose two new data augmentation approaches for OOD generalization based on large language models: (i) *domain transfer*, and (ii) *summarization*. Models trained with data augmented by our *summarization* strategy, show substantial gains across all datasets and models, and on *Amazon* and *Restaurants* surpassing models either augmented with (i) manually constructed CAD (Kaushik et al., 2019), or (ii) state-of-the-art generated CORE counterfactuals (Dixit et al., 2022).

Limitations

Task domain: In this exploratory study, we only presented results for zero-shot cross-lingual binary sentiment classification. To investigate whether our findings generalize beyond binary classification, and to other non-classification tasks, further analysis is required. Nevertheless, as mentioned in §4.2, our data augmentation approaches scale better for classification tasks with more than two classes, since it only requires summarizing/transferring the training samples of each class once, whereas it is unclear how to scale counterfactuals to a larger number of classes.

Automatically translated in-distribution test data: Since we followed a similar setup as Kaushik et al. (2019), our experiments used the IMDb movie reviews as in-distribution sentiment data. While the main focus in our study is on out-of-distribution generalization, the in-distribution test set was only provided in English. Hence, we used translation tools to automatically translate the English IMDb test set to the considered non-English languages. This may have caused annotation artifacts in the translated in-distribution tests, making it unclear how well the reported in-distribution results for non-English languages match real-world test data for non-English languages.

Translate-test based on a multilingual model: As our aim was to analyze the out-of-distribution generalization of multilingual models and compare their performance, we did not include results for the *translate-test* based on a monolingual English model. We believe that using such a monolingual model could further boost the accuracy of *translate-test*, as well as for our *summarization* and *domain transfer* strategies. However, we leave exploration thereof for future work.

Applicability to low-resource languages: The effectiveness of the *translate-test* and *translate-train* approaches are highly dependent on the accuracy of the adopted machine translation system. In this study, we used `ChatGPT-turbo (v0301)` as our translation tool, and found it to produce high-quality translations for all languages considered in our experiments, i.e., boosting OOD generalization compared to the *zero-shot* strategy. However, such machine translations systems may not work well for low-resource languages that lack high-quality translation data.

Ethics Statement

Since our data augmentation methods use LLMs to generate summaries or create domain-transferred training (and test) samples, any biases present in the data used to train these LLMs could be transferred to the augmented data. We should therefore be careful to ensure that these biases do not carry over when training models on the augmented data, to avoid models that could discriminate against and/or potentially be harmful to certain demographics.

Acknowledgements

This work was funded in part by Flanders Innovation & Enterpreneurship (VLAIO), through Baekeland project-HBC.2019.2221 in collaboration with Sinch Chatlayer; and in part by the Flemish government under the "Onderzoeksprogramma Artificiële Intelligentie (AI) Vlaanderen" (AI Research Program).

References

Udit Arora, William Huang, and He He. 2021. Types of out-of-distribution texts and how to detect them. In *Proceedings of the 2021 Conference on Empirical Methods in Natural Language Processing*, pages 10687–10701, Online and Punta Cana, Dominican Republic. Association for Computational Linguistics.

Mikel Artetxe, Vedanuj Goswami, Shruti Bhosale, Angela Fan, and Luke Zettlemoyer. 2023. Revisiting machine translation for cross-lingual classification. *arXiv preprint arXiv:2305.14240*.

Mikel Artetxe, Gorka Labaka, and Eneko Agirre. 2020a. Translation artifacts in cross-lingual transfer learning. In *Proceedings of the 2020 Conference on Empirical Methods in Natural Language Processing (EMNLP)*, pages 7674–7684, Online. Association for Computational Linguistics.

Mikel Artetxe, Sebastian Ruder, and Dani Yogatama. 2020b. On the cross-lingual transferability of monolingual representations. In *Proceedings of the 58th Annual Meeting of the Association for Computational Linguistics*, pages 4623–4637, Online. Association for Computational Linguistics.

Mikel Artetxe and Holger Schwenk. 2019. Massively multilingual sentence embeddings for zero-shot cross-lingual transfer and beyond. *Transactions of the Association for Computational Linguistics*, 7:597–610.

Francesco Barbieri, Luis Espinosa Anke, and Jose Camacho-Collados. 2022. XLM-T: Multilingual language models in Twitter for sentiment analysis and beyond. In *Proceedings of the Thirteenth Language Resources and Evaluation Conference*, pages 258–266, Marseille, France. European Language Resources Association.

Zewen Chi, Shaohan Huang, Li Dong, Shuming Ma, Bo Zheng, Saksham Singhal, Payal Bajaj, Xia Song, Xian-Ling Mao, Heyan Huang, and Furu Wei. 2022. XLM-E: Cross-lingual language model pre-training via ELECTRA. In *Proceedings of the 60th Annual Meeting of the Association for Computational Linguistics (Volume 1: Long Papers)*, pages 6170–6182, Dublin, Ireland. Association for Computational Linguistics.

Alexis Conneau, Kartikay Khandelwal, Naman Goyal, Vishrav Chaudhary, Guillaume Wenzek, Francisco Guzmán, Edouard Grave, Myle Ott, Luke Zettlemoyer, and Veselin Stoyanov. 2020. Unsupervised cross-lingual representation learning at scale. In *Proceedings of the 58th Annual Meeting of the Association for Computational Linguistics*, pages 8440–8451, Online. Association for Computational Linguistics.

Alexis Conneau and Guillaume Lample. 2019. Cross-lingual language model pretraining. *Advances in neural information processing systems*, 32.

Asa Cooper Stickland, Sailik Sengupta, Jason Krone, Saab Mansour, and He He. 2023. Robustification of multilingual language models to real-world noise in crosslingual zero-shot settings with robust contrastive pretraining. In *Proceedings of the 17th Conference of the European Chapter of the Association for Computational Linguistics*, pages 1375–1391, Dubrovnik, Croatia. Association for Computational Linguistics.

Marta R Costa-jussà, James Cross, Onur Çelebi, Maha Elbayad, Kenneth Heafield, Kevin Heffernan, Elahe Kalbassi, Janice Lam, Daniel Licht, Jean Maillard, et al. 2022. No language left behind: Scaling human-centered machine translation. *arXiv preprint arXiv:2207.04672*.

Maarten De Raedt, Fréderic Godin, Chris Develder, and Thomas Demeester. 2022. Robustifying sentiment classification by maximally exploiting few counterfactuals. In *Proceedings of the 2022 Conference on Empirical Methods in Natural Language Processing*, pages 11386–11400, Abu Dhabi, United Arab Emirates. Association for Computational Linguistics.

Jacob Devlin, Ming-Wei Chang, Kenton Lee, and Kristina Toutanova. 2019. BERT: Pre-training of deep bidirectional transformers for language understanding. In *Proceedings of the 2019 Conference of the North American Chapter of the Association for Computational Linguistics: Human Language Technologies, Volume 1 (Long and Short Papers)*, pages 4171–4186, Minneapolis, Minnesota. Association for Computational Linguistics.

Tanay Dixit, Bhargavi Paranjape, Hannaneh Hajishirzi, and Luke Zettlemoyer. 2022. CORE: A retrieve-then-edit framework for counterfactual data generation. In *Findings of the Association for Computational Linguistics: EMNLP 2022*, pages 2964–2984, Abu Dhabi, United Arab Emirates. Association for Computational Linguistics.

Kevin Duh, Akinori Fujino, and Masaaki Nagata. 2011. Is machine translation ripe for cross-lingual sentiment classification? In *Proceedings of the 49th Annual Meeting of the Association for Computational Linguistics: Human Language Technologies*, pages 429–433, Portland, Oregon, USA. Association for Computational Linguistics.

Fangxiaoyu Feng, Yinfei Yang, Daniel Cer, Naveen Arivazhagan, and Wei Wang. 2022. Language-agnostic BERT sentence embedding. In *Proceedings of the 60th Annual Meeting of the Association for Computational Linguistics (Volume 1: Long Papers)*, pages 878–891, Dublin, Ireland. Association for Computational Linguistics.

Matt Gardner, Yoav Artzi, Victoria Basmov, Jonathan Berant, Ben Bogin, Sihao Chen, Pradeep Dasigi, Dheeru Dua, Yanai Elazar, Ananth Gottumukkala, Nitish Gupta, Hannaneh Hajishirzi, Gabriel Ilharco, Daniel Khashabi, Kevin Lin, Jiangming Liu, Nelson F. Liu, Phoebe Mulcaire, Qiang Ning, Sameer Singh, Noah A. Smith, Sanjay Subramanian, Reut Tsarfaty, Eric Wallace, Ally Zhang, and Ben Zhou. 2020. Evaluating models' local decision boundaries via contrast sets. In *Findings of the Association for Computational Linguistics: EMNLP 2020*, pages 1307–1323, Online. Association for Computational Linguistics.

Suchin Gururangan, Swabha Swayamdipta, Omer Levy, Roy Schwartz, Samuel Bowman, and Noah A. Smith. 2018. Annotation artifacts in natural language inference data. In *Proceedings of the 2018 Conference of the North American Chapter of the Association for Computational Linguistics: Human Language Technologies, Volume 2 (Short Papers)*, pages 107–112, New Orleans, Louisiana. Association for Computational Linguistics.

Amr Hendy, Mohamed Abdelrehim, Amr Sharaf, Vikas Raunak, Mohamed Gabr, Hitokazu Matsushita, Young Jin Kim, Mohamed Afify, and Hany Hassan Awadalla. 2023. How good are GPT models at machine translation? a comprehensive evaluation. *arXiv preprint arXiv:2302.09210*.

Phillip Howard, Gadi Singer, Vasudev Lal, Yejin Choi, and Swabha Swayamdipta. 2022. NeuroCounterfactuals: Beyond minimal-edit counterfactuals for richer data augmentation. In *Findings of the Association for Computational Linguistics: EMNLP 2022*, pages 5056–5072, Abu Dhabi, United Arab Emirates. Association for Computational Linguistics.

Junjie Hu, Sebastian Ruder, Aditya Siddhant, Graham Neubig, Orhan Firat, and Melvin Johnson. 2020. Xtreme: A massively multilingual multi-task benchmark for evaluating cross-lingual generalisation. In *International Conference on Machine Learning*, pages 4411–4421. PMLR.

Wenxiang Jiao, Wenxuan Wang, Jen-tse Huang, Xing Wang, and Zhaopeng Tu. 2023. Is ChatGPT a good translator? a preliminary study. *arXiv preprint arXiv:2301.08745*.

Nitish Joshi, Xiang Pan, and He He. 2022. Are all spurious features in natural language alike? an analysis through a causal lens. In *Proceedings of the 2022 Conference on Empirical Methods in Natural Language Processing*, pages 9804–9817, Abu Dhabi, United Arab Emirates. Association for Computational Linguistics.

Anurag Katakkar, Clay H. Yoo, Weiqin Wang, Zachary Lipton, and Divyansh Kaushik. 2022. Practical benefits of feature feedback under distribution shift. In *Proceedings of the Fifth BlackboxNLP Workshop on Analyzing and Interpreting Neural Networks for NLP*, pages 346–355, Abu Dhabi, United Arab Emirates (Hybrid). Association for Computational Linguistics.

Divyansh Kaushik, Eduard Hovy, and Zachary Lipton. 2019. Learning the difference that makes a difference with counterfactually-augmented data. In *International Conference on Learning Representations*.

Divyansh Kaushik, Amrith Setlur, Eduard H Hovy, and Zachary Chase Lipton. 2020. Explaining the efficacy of counterfactually augmented data. In *International Conference on Learning Representations*.

Phillip Keung, Yichao Lu, György Szarvas, and Noah A. Smith. 2020. The multilingual Amazon reviews corpus. In *Proceedings of the 2020 Conference on Empirical Methods in Natural Language Processing (EMNLP)*, pages 4563–4568, Online. Association for Computational Linguistics.

Anne Lauscher, Vinit Ravishankar, Ivan Vulić, and Goran Glavaš. 2020. From zero to hero: On the limitations of zero-shot language transfer with multilingual Transformers. In *Proceedings of the 2020 Conference on Empirical Methods in Natural Language Processing (EMNLP)*, pages 4483–4499, Online. Association for Computational Linguistics.

Dong C Liu and Jorge Nocedal. 1989. On the limited memory bfgs method for large scale optimization. *Mathematical programming*, 45(1-3):503–528.

Zihan Liu, Genta Indra Winata, Andrea Madotto, and Pascale Fung. 2021. Preserving cross-linguality of pre-trained models via continual learning. In *Proceedings of the 6th Workshop on Representation Learning for NLP (RepL4NLP-2021)*, pages 64–71, Online. Association for Computational Linguistics.

Andrew L. Maas, Raymond E. Daly, Peter T. Pham, Dan Huang, Andrew Y. Ng, and Christopher Potts. 2011. Learning word vectors for sentiment analysis. In *Proceedings of the 49th Annual Meeting of the Association for Computational Linguistics: Human Language Technologies*, pages 142–150, Portland, Oregon, USA. Association for Computational Linguistics.

Tom McCoy, Ellie Pavlick, and Tal Linzen. 2019. Right for the wrong reasons: Diagnosing syntactic heuristics in natural language inference. In *Proceedings of the 57th Annual Meeting of the Association for Computational Linguistics*, pages 3428–3448, Florence, Italy. Association for Computational Linguistics.

Long Ouyang, Jeffrey Wu, Xu Jiang, Diogo Almeida, Carroll Wainwright, Pamela Mishkin, Chong Zhang, Sandhini Agarwal, Katarina Slama, Alex Gray, et al. 2022. Training language models to follow instructions with human feedback. In *Advances in Neural Information Processing Systems*.

Fabian Pedregosa, Gaël Varoquaux, Alexandre Gramfort, Vincent Michel, Bertrand Thirion, Olivier Grisel, Mathieu Blondel, Peter Prettenhofer, Ron Weiss, Vincent Dubourg, et al. 2011. Scikit-learn: Machine learning in Python. *The Journal Of Machine Learning Research*, 12:2825–2830.

Keqin Peng, Liang Ding, Qihuang Zhong, Li Shen, Xuebo Liu, Min Zhang, Yuanxin Ouyang, and Dacheng Tao. 2023. Towards making the most of ChatGPT for machine translation. *arxiv preprint*.

Adam Poliak, Jason Naradowsky, Aparajita Haldar, Rachel Rudinger, and Benjamin Van Durme. 2018. Hypothesis only baselines in natural language inference. In *Proceedings of the Seventh Joint Conference on Lexical and Computational Semantics*, pages 180–191, New Orleans, Louisiana. Association for Computational Linguistics.

Maria Pontiki, Dimitris Galanis, Haris Papageorgiou, Ion Androutsopoulos, Suresh Manandhar, Mohammad AL-Smadi, Mahmoud Al-Ayyoub, Yanyan Zhao, Bing Qin, Orphée De Clercq, Véronique Hoste, Marianna Apidianaki, Xavier Tannier, Natalia Loukachevitch, Evgeniy Kotelnikov, Nuria Bel, Salud María Jiménez-Zafra, and Gülşen Eryiğit. 2016. SemEval-2016 task 5: Aspect based sentiment analysis. In *Proceedings of the 10th International Workshop on Semantic Evaluation (SemEval-2016)*, pages 19–30, San Diego, California. Association for Computational Linguistics.

Joaquin Quiñonero-Candela, Masashi Sugiyama, Anton Schwaighofer, and Neil D Lawrence. 2008. *Dataset shift in machine learning*. Mit Press.

Sebastian Ruder, Ivan Vulić, and Anders Søgaard. 2019. A survey of cross-lingual word embedding models. *Journal of Artificial Intelligence Research*, 65:569–631.

Lei Shi, Rada Mihalcea, and Mingjun Tian. 2010. Cross language text classification by model translation and semi-supervised learning. In *Proceedings of the 2010 Conference on Empirical Methods in Natural Language Processing*, pages 1057–1067, Cambridge, MA. Association for Computational Linguistics.

Xiao Wang, Qin Liu, Tao Gui, Qi Zhang, Yicheng Zou, Xin Zhou, Jiacheng Ye, Yongxin Zhang, Rui Zheng, Zexiong Pang, Qinzhuo Wu, Zhengyan Li, Chong Zhang, Ruotian Ma, Zichu Fei, Ruijian Cai, Jun Zhao, Xingwu Hu, Zhiheng Yan, Yiding Tan, Yuan Hu, Qiyuan Bian, Zhihua Liu, Shan Qin, Bolin Zhu, Xiaoyu Xing, Jinlan Fu, Yue Zhang, Minlong Peng, Xiaoqing Zheng, Yaqian Zhou, Zhongyu Wei, Xipeng Qiu, and Xuanjing Huang. 2021. TextFlint: Unified multilingual robustness evaluation toolkit for natural language processing. In *Proceedings of the 59th Annual Meeting of the Association for Computational Linguistics and the 11th International Joint Conference on Natural Language Processing: System Demonstrations*, pages 347–355, Online. Association for Computational Linguistics.

Zhao Wang and Aron Culotta. 2020. Identifying spurious correlations for robust text classification. In *Findings of the Association for Computational Linguistics: EMNLP 2020*, pages 3431–3440, Online. Association for Computational Linguistics.

Zhao Wang and Aron Culotta. 2021. Robustness to spurious correlations in text classification via automatically generated counterfactuals. In *Proceedings of the AAAI Conference on Artificial Intelligence*, volume 35, pages 14024–14031.

Thomas Wolf, Lysandre Debut, Victor Sanh, Julien Chaumond, Clement Delangue, Anthony Moi, Pierric Cistac, Tim Rault, Remi Louf, Morgan Funtowicz, Joe Davison, Sam Shleifer, Patrick von Platen, Clara Ma, Yacine Jernite, Julien Plu, Canwen Xu, Teven Le Scao, Sylvain Gugger, Mariama Drame, Quentin Lhoest, and Alexander Rush. 2020. Transformers: State-of-the-art natural language processing. In *Proceedings of the 2020 Conference on Empirical Methods in Natural Language Processing: System Demonstrations*, pages 38–45, Online. Association for Computational Linguistics.

Linting Xue, Noah Constant, Adam Roberts, Mihir Kale, Rami Al-Rfou, Aditya Siddhant, Aditya Barua, and Colin Raffel. 2021. mT5: A massively multilingual pre-trained text-to-text transformer. In *Proceedings of the 2021 Conference of the North American Chapter of the Association for Computational Linguistics: Human Language Technologies*, pages 483–498, Online. Association for Computational Linguistics.

Hitomi Yanaka and Koji Mineshima. 2021. Assessing the generalization capacity of pre-trained language models through Japanese adversarial natural language inference. In *Proceedings of the Fourth BlackboxNLP Workshop on Analyzing and Interpreting Neural Networks for NLP*, pages 337–349, Punta Cana, Dominican Republic. Association for Computational Linguistics.

Linyi Yang, Jiazheng Li, Padraig Cunningham, Yue Zhang, Barry Smyth, and Ruihai Dong. 2021. Exploring the efficacy of automatically generated counterfactuals for sentiment analysis. In *Proceedings of the 59th Annual Meeting of the Association for Computational Linguistics and the 11th International Joint Conference on Natural Language Processing (Volume 1: Long Papers)*, pages 306–316, Online. Association for Computational Linguistics.

Tao Yu and Shafiq Joty. 2021. Effective fine-tuning methods for cross-lingual adaptation. In *Proceedings of the 2021 Conference on Empirical Methods in Natural Language Processing*, pages 8492–8501, Online and Punta Cana, Dominican Republic. Association for Computational Linguistics.

Bo Zheng, Li Dong, Shaohan Huang, Wenhui Wang, Zewen Chi, Saksham Singhal, Wanxiang Che, Ting Liu, Xia Song, and Furu Wei. 2021. Consistency regularization for cross-lingual fine-tuning. In *Proceedings of the 59th Annual Meeting of the Association for Computational Linguistics and the 11th International Joint Conference on Natural Language Processing (Volume 1: Long Papers)*, pages 3403–3417, Online. Association for Computational Linguistics.

	#Test												
Dataset	EN	DE	NL	FR	ES	IT	PT	TU	RU	JA	ZH	AR	HI
AMAZON	4,000	4,000	-	4,000	4,000	-	-	-	-	4,000	4,000	-	-
TWEETS	580	580	-	580	580	580	580	-	-	-	-	580	580
RESTAURANTS	980	-	960	1,268	760	-	-	780	1,012	-	-	-	-

Table 5: **Out-of-distribution** dataset statistics.

IMDB (EN)	#Train	#Val	#Test
Original	1,707	245	488
CAD	1,707	245	-

Table 6: **In-distribution** dataset statistics.

A Appendix

Datasets: Tables 5 and 6 summarize respectively the number of *out-of-distribution* test samples and the number of train, validation and test *in-distribution* test samples. Note that the number of samples for *translate-train* and *translate-test* exactly match those shown in the tables.

Prompts: Figs. 2 and 3 show our adopted prompts for instructing `ChatGPT-turbo` to translate (i) non-English out-of-distribution test samples into English for *translate-test*, and (ii) English in--distribution English training and validation samples into non-English for *translate-train*.

Detailed ID and OOD results per language: The in-distribution and out-of-distribution results per language are presented in Tables 7 and 8. As mentioned in §4.1, the *translate-test* in-distribution scores are not included for non-English languages. This is because these test sets are automatically translated versions of the original English test set. Including *translate-test* scores would require translating the already translated test samples back to English, which would evaluate the quality of back-translation rather than the *translate-test* performance itself. In our pilot experiments, we observed that the backtranslation quality was quite high. As such, small differences in accuracy between the performance of *translate-test* and the model performance on the original English test set appeared overly optimistic. Hence, we opted to exclude them.

Translate-test

Translate from {Language} to English.
{**Language**}: {test sample}
English:

Translate-train

Translate from English to {Language}.
English: {train sample}
{**Language**}:

Fig. 2: **Translation prompts** for `ChatGPT-turbo (v0301)`.

Summarization

Summarize the review in a maximum of 10 words.
Review: {train -or English translated test sample}

Domain transfer

Make minimal changes to adapt the review such that it becomes about books.
Review: {train or English-translated test sample}

Fig. 3: **Data augmentation prompts** for `ChatGPT-turbo (v0301)`. **Left:** *Summarization* prompt. **Right:** *Domain transfer* prompt.

IMDB													
	LaBSE												
Method	EN	DE	NL	FR	ES	IT	PT	TU	RU	AR	HI	JA	ZH
Original only													
- ZSHOT	85.0	85.3	86.0	85.9	86.1	85.4	85.5	83.5	85.1	85.2	81.2	83.5	86.0
- TTRAIN	85.0	86.0	87.0	84.5	87.1	85.4	86.9	83.0	86.5	85.0	81.8	83.9	85.6
Original & CAD (Kaushik et al., 2019)													
- ZSHOT	81.4	82.0	80.1	82.0	82.6	81.6	81.6	80.5	80.1	79.3	80.1	80.3	79.5
- TTRAIN	81.4	83.0	80.7	82.4	83.0	81.8	83.8	82.0	80.7	78.7	78.7	80.7	79.1
Original & CORE (Dixit et al., 2022)													
- ZSHOT	80.1	77.9	80.3	79.3	81.4	79.3	78.7	79.1	78.3	79.9	75.4	79.5	79.1
Domain transfer (ours)													
- ZSHOT♠	83.3	84.5	84.5	84.4	86.0	85.4	85.5	82.3	83.8	84.6	79.0	82.7	83.3
+TRANS.	85.5	-	-	-	-	-	-	-	-	-	-	-	-
Summarization (ours)													
- ZSHOT♠	83.6	84.0	85.9	84.8	85.0	84.0	86.1	82.4	84.2	84.8	80.9	85.7	83.6
+SUM.	86.7	-	-	-	-	-	-	-	-	-	-	-	-
	mBERT												
Method	EN	DE	NL	FR	ES	IT	PT	TU	RU	AR	HI	JA	ZH
Original only													
- ZSHOT	89.5	84.0	77.8	84.2	86.9	83.4	83.2	76.1	80.0	75.2	72.2	81.9	84.8
- TTRAIN	-	87.2	89.1	89.1	90.2	88.7	88.8	87.4	87.8	84.1	81.9	87.1	88.5
Original & CAD (Kaushik et al., 2019)													
- ZSHOT	86.3	82.8	75.8	82.2	83.6	79.4	79.7	72.3	78.5	70.1	69.1	78.9	84.5
- TTRAIN	-	86.0	86.6	86.8	87.6	87.0	86.7	84.5	86.1	83.2	78.8	86.9	87.0
Original & CORE (Dixit et al., 2022)													
- ZSHOT	84.5	79.7	73.0	80.6	78.2	77.4	77.7	70.1	74.7	66.5	65.0	75.6	80.3
Domain transfer (ours)													
- ZSHOT♠	86.7	82.9	76.7	84.1	84.3	82.0	82.0	75.8	77.7	74.3	71.1	79.3	84.4
+TRANS.	87.8	-	-	-	-	-	-	-	-	-	-	-	-
Summarization (ours)													
- ZSHOT♠	87.2	83.1	74.4	82.3	84.4	81.1	82.3	74.4	77.3	73.6	71.0	80.9	82.9
+SUM.	88.2	-	-	-	-	-	-	-	-	-	-	-	-
	XLM-R												
Method	EN	DE	NL	FR	ES	IT	PT	TU	RU	AR	HI	JA	ZH
Original only													
- ZSHOT	92.4	90.4	90.9	89.9	89.8	89.5	90.7	88.5	89.4	84.7	82.3	85.4	89.6
- TTRAIN	-	91.4	92.2	91.7	91.6	91.3	91.8	91.0	90.9	89.2	86.4	89.2	91.1
Original & CAD (Kaushik et al., 2019)													
- ZSHOT	90.4	88.1	88.0	88.1	87.8	87.0	87.4	86.8	86.8	81.6	82.2	85.9	88.3
- TTRAIN	-	88.9	88.5	89.8	89.7	89.3	89.8	89.2	88.9	88.2	85.7	87.9	88.8
Original & CORE (Dixit et al., 2022)													
- ZSHOT	88.1	86.9	87.5	87.2	87.5	87.2	86.7	86.1	87.0	83.6	82.4	85.4	85.9
Domain transfer (ours)													
- ZSHOT♠	90.5	89.6	89.9	89.2	89.3	88.4	89.8	87.5	88.7	83.6	82.8	86.7	89.2
+TRANS.	91.1	-	-	-	-	-	-	-	-	-	-	-	-
Summarization (ours)													
- ZSHOT♠	91.4	89.5	90.3	89.9	89.5	89.1	88.8	88.3	88.8	83.6	81.7	85.1	89.7
+SUM.	89.9	-	-	-	-	-	-	-	-	-	-	-	-

Table 7: **In-distribution** accuracies for LaBSE, mBERT, and XLM-R. ♠: ablations. Scores for *translate-test* are omitted due to the English ID test sets being translated into the respective non-English languages. Note, for English, TTRAIN does not involve any translation, hence its EN scores are equivalent to ZSHOT.

LaBSE																							
	IMDB → AMAZON							IMDB → RESTAURANTS							IMDB → TWEETS								
Method	EN	DE	FR	ES	JA	ZH	AVG.	EN	NL	FR	ES	RU	TU	AVG.	EN	DE	FR	ES	AR	HI	IT	PT	AVG.
Original only																							
- ZSHOT	66.3	75.3	70.6	70.0	69.5	73.9	71.9	72.7	75.0	73.6	74.9	74.6	72.6	74.1	76.3	70.5	67.6	72.3	60.3	61.6	72.1	70.2	67.8
- TTRAIN	66.3	71.6	74.2	72.5	77.0	74.8	74.0	72.7	76.2	77.5	76.7	76.1	75.4	76.4	76.3	66.3	67.1	70.1	56.1	62.3	69.3	71.1	66.0
- TTEST	66.3	70.0	67.6	66.4	66.4	67.5	67.6	72.7	75.6	72.5	73.8	70.4	73.3	73.1	76.3	70.6	64.8	72.4	60.6	67.7	73.3	72.4	68.8
Original & CAD (Kaushik et al., 2019)																							
- ZSHOT	81.2	85.4	85.3	85.0	80.4	78.5	<u>82.9</u>	84.7	86.8	86.4	88.6	83.5	83.3	85.7	81.7	76.6	72.2	80.3	71.6	67.8	75.2	77.8	<u>74.5</u>
- TTRAIN	81.2	85.0	83.5	84.5	80.0	78.7	82.3	84.7	84.4	81.6	88.6	80.8	81.5	83.4	81.7	77.6	72.6	81.0	67.4	64.7	74.8	77.8	73.7
- TTEST	81.2	84.4	84.9	83.7	79.8	79.3	82.4	84.7	88.0	86.4	87.9	82.2	85.0	85.9	**81.7**	79.8	71.7	81.6	71.0	74.8	75.0	79.3	**76.2**
Original & CORE (Dixit et al., 2022)																							
- ZSHOT	81.0	84.8	84.2	84.6	80.2	76.3	82.0	85.0	84.6	85.4	88.7	84.7	81.2	84.9	77.4	71.2	67.6	76.0	66.9	64.0	75.7	76.0	71.1
- TTEST	81.0	84.4	83.9	83.2	79.8	77.1	81.7	<u>85.0</u>	86.5	85.3	89.5	84.1	86.2	<u>86.3</u>	<u>77.4</u>	77.9	69.8	80.5	65.3	72.8	76.0	77.8	74.3
Original & Domain transfer (ours)																							
- ZSHOT♠	76.0	82.5	79.5	79.1	77.7	75.8	78.9	81.4	83.1	81.2	82.6	82.0	78.4	81.5	80.9	72.3	68.1	76.2	65.2	64.7	74.8	74.3	70.8
+TTEST♠	76.0	80.6	79.8	79.2	76.6	75.6	78.4	81.4	84.4	82.8	81.6	80.7	81.6	82.2	80.9	72.7	69.1	75.4	66.3	74.1	74.3	74.3	72.3
+TRAN.	<u>81.7</u>	83.6	83.7	83.0	81.1	78.0	81.9	84.1	85.9	84.2	85.2	83.1	82.1	84.1	72.3	69.1	62.0	74.9	62.6	71.0	71.1	76.5	69.6
Original & Summarization (ours)																							
- ZSHOT♠	77.1	82.5	80.7	81.2	77.8	76.2	79.7	83.6	85.2	83.7	84.7	84.2	80.5	83.7	81.9	73.4	70.9	77.9	65.0	66.2	75.5	74.0	71.8
+TTEST♠	77.1	81.1	80.4	80.2	76.6	76.1	78.9	83.6	86.7	83.5	83.0	84.1	82.6	84.0	81.9	74.7	69.3	77.6	68.1	75.3	73.1	73.4	73.1
+SUM.	**86.2**↑	86.3↑	87.6↑	87.5↑	82.6↑	79.7↑	**84.7**	**91.6**↑	89.5↑	89.1↑	89.5	89.2↑	86.5↑	**88.8**	76.6↓	74.7↓	73.3↑	81.0↑	70.2↑	74.3↑	71.7↓	73.1↓	74.0

mBERT																							
	IMDB → AMAZON							IMDB → RESTAURANTS							IMDB → TWEETS								
Method	EN	DE	FR	ES	JA	ZH	AVG.	EN	NL	FR	ES	RU	TU	AVG.	EN	DE	FR	ES	AR	HI	IT	PT	AVG.
Original only																							
- ZSHOT	79.3	72.2	73.1	74.5	71.6	69.8	72.2	80.2	69.8	68.8	72.2	73.3	64.1	69.6	75.9	60.5	66.2	64.0	61.4	58.3	65.8	63.4	62.8
- TTRAIN	79.3	72.6	77.6	76.8	71.0	69.4	73.5	80.2	75.4	75.3	78.4	76.8	66.7	74.5	75.9	57.7	69.5	66.7	64.3	52.6	66.9	62.4	62.9
- TTEST	79.3	78.9	79.8	80.3	75.2	74.6	77.8	80.2	79.4	78.2	82.2	79.2	75.4	78.9	75.9	67.4	67.1	73.8	68.3	72.0	73.5	75.7	71.1
Original & CAD (Kaushik et al., 2019)																							
- ZSHOT	81.7	76.0	76.0	77.7	73.1	71.9	74.9	81.8	68.6	71.2	77.1	72.7	64.9	70.9	79.0	64.3	74.9	68.9	69.0	61.0	68.3	64.2	67.2
- TTRAIN	81.7	79.0	80.5	80.4	76.5	74.5	78.2	81.8	75.9	76.6	81.5	74.5	69.9	75.7	79.0	64.9	75.6	71.2	65.0	54.8	70.4	66.7	66.9
- TTEST	**81.7**	82.7	83.3	83.2	79.4	77.4	**81.2**	81.8	81.4	81.5	83.9	79.1	79.9	<u>81.2</u>	**79.0**	73.9	74.1	78.3	75.5	73.3	72.6	77.5	**75.0**
Original & CORE (Dixit et al., 2022)																							
- ZSHOT	80.2	74.3	75.3	77.2	73.6	70.2	74.1	80.4	65.3	72.1	75.3	71.2	63.9	69.6	73.6	59.4	72.0	70.3	62.7	59.3	68.3	61.5	64.8
- TTEST	80.7	81.3	80.4	82.5	79.2	76.3	79.9	80.4	79.2	79.7	82.9	78.5	79.4	79.9	73.6	70.6	70.0	77.9	73.0	70.1	73.0	75.1	72.8
Original & Domain transfer (ours)																							
- ZSHOT♠	79.6	73.2	74.8	76.4	72.3	71.0	73.5	80.2	70.8	70.4	73.6	73.1	63.9	70.4	78.1	60.5	69.0	63.8	62.6	58.8	66.0	64.9	63.7
+TTEST♠	79.6	80.3	81.0	80.8	76.8	75.8	78.9	80.2	78.2	77.8	80.9	78.3	76.4	78.3	<u>78.1</u>	68.8	68.2	73.9	72.3	72.7	72.9	75.6	72.1
+TRAN.	81.3	81.4	81.6	81.9	79.5	77.0	<u>80.3</u>	<u>83.3</u>	81.0	80.4	83.6	80.4	79.6	81.0	72.4	67.5	66.2	72.2	65.1	70.6	70.3	75.9	69.7
Original & Summarization (ours)																							
- ZSHOT♠	80.7	74.1	75.4	77.1	72.3	69.2	73.6	82.4	71.1	72.4	76.8	75.5	66.6	72.5	77.8	60.6	67.1	66.8	61.5	59.5	65.3	63.8	63.5
+TTEST♠	80.7	81.5	82.3	82.4	76.7	75.3	79.6	82.4	80.0	80.2	83.0	79.7	77.3	80.0	77.8	70.1	67.5	75.6	70.8	72.4	71.4	76.2	72.0
+SUM.	<u>81.0</u>↑	82.3↑	83.6↑	84.0↑	78.1↓	77.8↑	**81.2**	**87.3**↑	84.6↑	85.5↑	87.3↑	83.6↑	80.4↑	**84.3**	74.3↑	73.0↑	72.1↑	76.9↓	76.1↑	71.6↑	69.9↓	77.0↑	<u>73.8</u>

XLM-R																							
	IMDB → AMAZON							IMDB → RESTAURANTS							IMDB → TWEETS								
Method	EN	DE	FR	ES	JA	ZH	AVG.	EN	NL	FR	ES	RU	TU	AVG.	EN	DE	FR	ES	AR	HI	IT	PT	AVG.
Original only																							
- ZSHOT	86.3	86.7	85.0	83.9	86.9	82.4	85.0	86.0	81.2	78.6	80.7	81.9	73.4	79.2	84.3	75.5	66.0	72.9	68.4	63.6	70.0	68.0	69.2
- TTRAIN	86.3	86.9	86.5	88.2	87.1	81.4	86.0	86.0	85.9	79.2	86.7	85.5	77.9	83.0	84.3	75.4	66.9	82.1	71.3	66.6	71.6	73.6	72.5
- TTEST	86.3	86.7	87.8	86.6	85.5	81.4	85.6	86.0	81.6	82.2	86.0	79.8	79.8	81.5	84.3	76.6	67.5	77.3	70.2	70.0	69.4	71.2	71.7
Original & CAD (Kaushik et al., 2019)																							
- ZSHOT	87.0	86.9	86.3	86.3	86.2	82.7	85.7	87.5	82.5	81.8	83.3	82.1	79.6	81.9	86.7	77.6	76.1	82.7	78.2	67.9	74.2	74.6	75.9
- TTRAIN	87.0	87.6	87.8	88.4	87.0	81.0	86.4	87.5	85.3	83.5	87.6	85.0	81.7	84.6	86.7	80.4	75.1	85.0	79.6	68.4	75.6	77.0	77.3
- TTEST	87.0	87.8	88.8	88.4	86.9	82.1	86.8	87.5	87.3	86.5	89.2	85.8	86.9	87.1	**86.7**	81.4	77.6	84.3	79.6	76.0	77.8	80.6	<u>79.6</u>
Original & CORE (Dixit et al., 2022)																							
- ZSHOT	86.8	88.1	87.7	88.7	88.9	81.6	87.0	89.7	88.8	87.2	90.4	89.1	81.9	87.5	83.9	75.7	79.4	82.9	80.9	67.8	79.9	78.8	77.9
- TTEST	86.8	88.4	89.0	89.0	87.6	81.1	87.0	<u>89.7</u>	89.2	89.0	91.2	88.0	88.1	<u>89.1</u>	83.9	81.1	77.6	86.2	82.2	75.4	79.6	81.2	**80.5**
Original & Domain transfer (ours)																							
- ZSHOT♠	86.4	86.9	85.5	84.6	87.1	82.0	85.2	85.4	80.1	79.2	81.7	82.3	74.4	79.5	85.2	75.7	69.2	75.6	70.6	65.6	71.1	69.7	71.1
+TTEST♠	86.4	88.1	89.0	88.0	87.5	81.7	86.9	85.4	84.0	83.4	85.7	83.0	83.7	84.0	85.2	78.4	71.8	80.4	74.9	73.8	73.5	74.7	75.4
+TRAN.	<u>87.1</u>	88.3	89.2	88.4	87.1	82.5	<u>87.1</u>	87.2	84.3	85.0	87.0	82.8	83.4	84.5	72.7	72.4	66.0	73.7	65.8	70.0	66.4	73.9	69.7
Original & Summarization (ours)																							
- ZSHOT♠	87.8	89.1	89.3	88.7	88.1	83.3	87.7	89.4	86.1	83.8	86.5	86.5	81.7	84.9	86.3	76.6	71.7	81.6	75.8	69.0	75.7	75.2	75.1
+TTEST♠	87.8	89.5	90.5	89.5	88.0	82.4	**88.0**	89.4	87.5	87.7	88.6	85.8	85.7	87.1	<u>86.3</u>	79.8	73.7	83.0	77.1	75.7	75.1	80.4	77.8
+SUM.	**87.8**↑	87.6↓	89.7↑	89.2↑	86.1↓	81.2↑	86.8↓	**92.8**↑	91.0↑	90.1↑	91.8↑	89.5↑	88.8↑	**90.2**	83.0↓	78.0↓	74.6↓	80.0↓	76.0↓	74.1↓	71.4↓	77.0↓	75.9

Table 8: **Out-of-distribution** accuracies for LaBSE, mBERT, and XLM-R. **Best** model in bold with the <u>runner-up</u> underlined. ♠: ablations. For English, TTRAIN and TTEST do not involve any translation, hence their EN scores are equivalent to ZSHOT. Highlighted rows show a 1-on-1 comparison between classifiers augmented with (i) our (*summarization*) strategy, and (ii) the state-of-the-art generated CORE counterfactuals.

To token or not to token: A Comparative Study of Text Representations for Cross-Lingual Transfer

Md Mushfiqur Rahman, Fardin Ahsan Sakib, Fahim Faisal, Antonios Anastasopoulos
Department of Computer Science, George Mason University
{mrahma45,fsakib,ffaisal,antonis}@gmu.edu

Abstract

Choosing an appropriate tokenization scheme is often a bottleneck in low-resource cross-lingual transfer. To understand the downstream implications of text representation choices, we perform a comparative analysis on language models having diverse text representation modalities including 2 segmentation-based models (BERT, mBERT), 1 image-based model (PIXEL), and 1 character-level model (CANINE). First, we propose a scoring Language Quotient (LQ) metric capable of providing a weighted representation of both zero-shot and few-shot evaluation combined. Utilizing this metric, we perform experiments comprising 19 source languages and 133 target languages on three tasks (POS tagging, Dependency parsing, and NER). Our analysis reveals that image-based models excel in cross-lingual transfer when languages are closely related and share visually similar scripts. However, for tasks biased toward word meaning (POS, NER), segmentation-based models prove to be superior. Furthermore, in dependency parsing tasks where word relationships play a crucial role, models with their character-level focus, outperform others. Finally, we propose a recommendation scheme based on our findings to guide model selection according to task and language requirements. [1]

1 Introduction

The performance of multilingual language models varies substantially across languages, with low-resource languages demonstrating particularly sub-optimal results compared to their high-resource counterparts. This disparity poses a global challenge for deploying effective NLP applications, given the diverse linguistic landscape worldwide (Blasi et al., 2022).

To address this challenge, cross-lingual transfer has emerged as a promising solution. By leveraging knowledge from high-resource languages, cross-lingual transfer aims to enhance the performance of low-resource ones. However, the effectiveness of cross-lingual knowledge transfer is not uniformly observed across all language pairs. It is influenced by various factors, including language style, structure, origin, dataset quality (Yu et al., 2022; Kreutzer et al., 2022), and the specific relationship between the source and target languages (Ahmad et al., 2019; He et al., 2019). On top of that, the selection of an appropriate language model becomes crucial to achieve successful cross-lingual knowledge transfer. While most state-of-the-art models rely on tokenization (Schuster and Nakajima, 2012; Gage, 1994), yielding high scores for various linguistic downstream tasks, their performance in terms of cross-lingual transfer has room for further investigation. Considering that word formation can significantly vary across different languages, differences in tokenization techniques can hinder the transfer of linguistic capabilities between languages (Hofmann et al., 2022). Hence, the exploration of tokenization-free models is also imperative.

This study thoroughly investigates the role and effectiveness of both tokenization-based (Devlin et al., 2019a) and tokenization-free models (Rust et al., 2022) in cross-lingual knowledge transfer. Our selection of models encompasses BERT and mBERT (Devlin et al., 2019a), which uses traditional subword-based segmentation. In addition, we delve into tokenization-free models such as CANINE (Clark et al., 2022) and PIXEL (Rust et al., 2022). CANINE leverages character-level information to accommodate the diverse word formations and structures found in different languages. On the other hand, PIXEL represents texts using visual elements, introducing new possibilities for script-based transfer in visually similar languages.

In this study, we perform standard syntactic task evaluation in both zero-shot and few-shot manner

[1] The code for reproducing our results is available here https://github.com/mushfiqur11/tokenfreetransfer.

Proceedings of the The 3rd Workshop on Multi-lingual Representation Learning (MRL), pages 67–84
December 7, 2023 ©2023 Association for Computational Linguistics

to evaluate the cross-lingual transfer capabilities of these models. While accuracy, F1 score, Labeled Attachment Score (LAS), etc. are all effective evaluation indicators of the goodness of a model, they are not particularly representative of how much a model has learned in a short span of training. We utilize these common metrics over zero-shot and few-shot steps and propose the Learning Quotient (LQ) metric, a novel scoring metric that depends on the relation between the zero-shot and few-shot scores. The metric evaluates the linguistic characteristics of the languages with the model's performance on the tasks. This metric enables a comprehensive evaluation of cross-lingual transfer capabilities, offering valuable insights into the strengths and weaknesses of the models. Our findings suggest contrastive downstream performance that relates to the model architecture. Furthermore, we present a decision tree framework, based on this extensive analysis providing practical guidance for selecting appropriate models based on specific task requirements and language relationships. This framework serves as a tool for researchers and practitioners seeking to harness the potential of NLP applications across diverse languages.

2 Methodology

Problem formulation In this work, we use pre-trained language models and fine-tune them on source languages followed by few-shot training on the target languages. Consider the sets of target $T = \{t_1, t_2, \ldots, t_m\}$ and source languages $S = \{s_1, s_2, \ldots, s_n\}$. We assume source languages $s \in S$ have adequate resources for effective language model training. Conversely, target languages $t \in T$ are low-resource languages with limited data. For any language pair (s, t), we aim to quantify how efficiently a language model can learn the target language t using knowledge transferred from the source language s. Given the scarcity of data for t, our focus lies on the model's performance in the early stages of fine-tuning it, denoted by the evaluation score E.

Let $(M)_s^\infty$ represents a language model M fully finetuned on the language s and $(M)_t^c$ represents the model finetuned up to c steps. We investigate how fast can a model learn the language t in the early steps if it was previously finetuned on s. Essentially, we measure the performance of the model $((M)_s^\infty)_t^c$ where c is a small positive integer. It's important, however, to acknowledge that the efficiency of this method can be influenced by factors such as the similarities between the source and target languages, as well as the quality and quantity of data available for both.

Our methodology can be broadly divided into two steps:

Fine-tuning on Sources Following the pre-trained model selection, each system is fine-tuned using the selected source languages. This fine-tuning stage allows each system to adjust and optimize its parameters based on specific requirements. Once fine-tuned, the systems are prepared for the evaluation phase in a cross-lingual transfer scenario.

Evaluation and Scoring The last step involves evaluating each system's performance on target language tasks after undergoing a certain amount of fine-tuning. Two scores are measured at this point: zero-shot and few-shot scores. To measure the final score, we calculate the LQ-score (§2). This score allows us to determine the speed and efficiency at which each system learns a new language based on the knowledge transferred from the source language.

Learning Quotient(LQ) metric Let us denote $E_s^{(t_c)}$ as the score achieved by the model $(M)s^\infty$ on the language t after c steps of training on t. For different tasks, E can be different. We use accuracy for POS tagging and NER, and Labeled Attachment Score (LAS) for dependency parsing. $E_s^{(t_0)}$ stands for the zero-shot score of the model on t. Using the same logic, $\frac{1}{n}\sum_{i=0}^{n} E_i^{(t_0)}$ is the average zero-shot score across all source languages, denoted as Z_A.

Now, let's introduce our proposed scoring metric, applicable for any pair of languages $t \in T$ and $s \in S$:

$$LQ(t, s) = \frac{\left(E_s^{(t_c)} - Z_A\right)\left(E_s^{(t_c)} + E_s^{(t_0)}\right)}{Z_A + \epsilon} \quad (1)$$

$LQ(t, s)$ is comprised of two primary terms, along with a normalization factor. The first term measures the performance of the model after few-shot training on language t, relative to the average zero-shot scores for that target language. The second term simply sums the zero-shot and the few-shot scores. To normalize the metric value, we employ the average zero-shot score, Z_A. A minute value ϵ is added to the denominator to avoid division by zero cases.

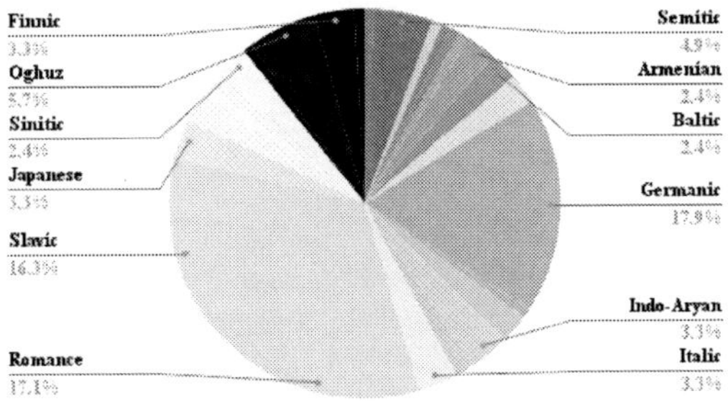

Figure 1: Distribution of the languages according to their sub-families. The majority of these are of Indo-European origin. The languages belong to 28 sub-families spanning 13 different families

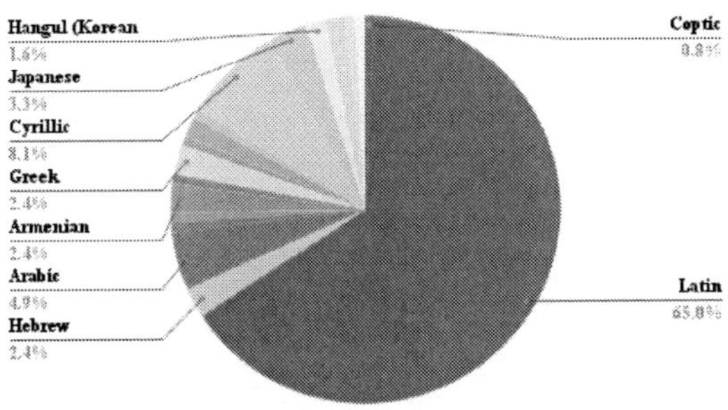

Figure 2: Distribution of the languages according to their scripts. The majority of these use Latin script. The languages use 19 different scripts

The LQ score provides positive reinforcement for both zero-shot and few-shot scores. Any few-shot score that falls below the zero-shot average incurs a substantial penalty. This metric proves effective in quantifying the *pace* at which a model adapts to a new language.[2]

3 Experimentation

Task Selection We perform the evaluation on three downstream tasks that heavily depend on fundamental linguistic capabilities and syntactic structure: Dependency Parsing, Part-of-Speech (POS) tagging and Named Entity Recognition (NER). These tasks can work as indicators of a model's understanding of language dynamics and its ability to comprehend and interpret linguistic information (Chen and Manning, 2014; Manning, 2011; Lample et al., 2016)

Language and Dataset Selection For the execution of POS tagging and Dependency Parsing, we utilized the Universal Dependencies (UD) Dataset (Nivre et al., 2017, 2020). To maintain focus and ensure a meaningful study, we selected 9 languages (as listed in Figure 3(a)) as our source languages and 123 languages as our target languages for the experiments[3]. All the models were comprehensively fine-tuned on the selected source languages, thereby establishing a baseline for performance comparison[4]. For NER, we utilized the MashakhaNER dataset (Adelani et al., 2021) and all its associated languages as sources and targets (as described in Figure 3(b)). MasakhaNER mainly focuses on a few African languages. These languages are quite low-resource. Hence, these were perfect for this research.

Model Selection To ensure a fair comparison, we use `BERT`, `mBERT`, `CANINE`, and `PIXEL` as our choice of pre-trained models. `BERT` and `mBERT` use subword segmentation whereas `CANINE` is a character-based model. Unlike these, `PIXEL` represents text using visual elements rather than traditional tokens. We selected `BERT`, as it is the most well-established tokenization-based model that aligns with `PIXEL`'s pre-training dataset. On the other hand, character-level models provide another perspective for understanding and processing languages, capturing the distinct attributes of word formations. `CANINE`, with its pre-training on 104 languages, emerged as a strong candidate. As a counterpart, we chose `mBERT`, which shares a similar scope of pre-training languages.

Experimental Setup Our experiments involved two major training phases followed by a result extraction step. In the first training phase, each language model was fully fine-tuned on each of the source languages for each task. The experimental setup maintained a high computational standard to ensure robust training and evaluation. All experiments were conducted on a remote server equipped with an A100 GPU. The analysis was conducted over 4 (models) x 9 (source languages) x 123 (target languages) data points for Dependency Parsing and POS tagging. For NER, the analysis was conducted over all 4 (models) x 12 (source languages) x 12 (target languages) data points. We used 10 fine-tuning steps (for §1, set $c = 10$) for the target languages for all tasks.

For reproducing the results, the language models can be fully fine-tuned on the source languages (our

[2]The proof can be found in Appendix A.2

[3]A detailed list is provided in appendix A.5

[4]All fine-tuned models are available on HuggingFace for further research and investigation

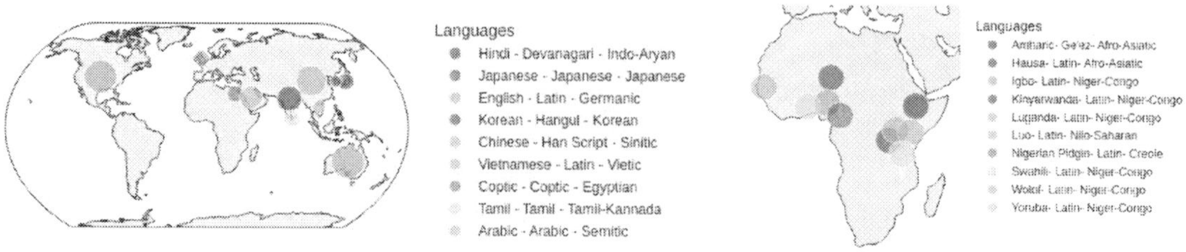

(a) POS tagging and Dependency Parsing tasks

(b) Named Entity Recognition

Figure 3: Geographic distribution of source languages (with script and family) used in the analysis across tasks.

finetuned versions can be used directly from HuggingFace) to get the zero-shot results. These models can then be finetuned on the target languages for 10 steps to get the few-shot score.

4 Results and Discussion

First, we break down the results by several key variables including the visual similarity of languages, their lexical correspondence, and the type of language task. Then, we discuss the performance of these models in light of these variables, revealing patterns regarding model characteristics.

4.1 Visual similarity is all you need

Case1 (English → European) Both of PIXEL and BERT are pre-trained in English. Therefore, for a fair comparison with other models, we perform a comparison where English is the only source language. For evaluation, we consider various European languages, taking into account both lexical similarity and the LQ score on the POS tagging task. Figure 4 represent the LQ scores of PIXEL and CANINE when English is used as the source language and various other languages as the targets. Here, in Figure 4(a) we observe the proficiency of PIXEL in handling tasks between languages sharing a similar script. For example, English shares similar degrees of lexical similarity with French (0.27) and Russian (0.24) (§A.5 and §A.6). However, when considering the LQ scores, French significantly outperforms Russian for PIXEL. Moreover, despite Spanish and Portuguese exhibiting low lexical similarity coefficients with English, they both have achieved high LQ scores. A key factor contributing to these scores is the usage of the Latin script. French, Spanish, and Portuguese, which have all garnered high scores, also use the Latin script. Russian employs a different (Cyrillic) script, which likely explains its relatively lower score. Finnish, despite its use of the Latin script, belongs to a different language family compared to English, which may account for the less impressive performances. Moreover, when the script is non-Latin as presented in Figure 4(b), CANINE has an edge over PIXEL. The lexical similarities between different European languages are outlined in Table 8 in the appendix.

POS Tagging				
	Hindi→Urdu		Hindi→Marathi	
Model	Score	Rank	Score	Rank
PIXEL	-0.4	94	17.9	5
CANINE	96.1	3	14.6	15
mBERT	102.2	2	7.3	112

Table 1: Comparison between different language models on Hindi as the source and Urdu and Marathi as target shows CANINE and mBERT massively favor linguistically similar languages. PIXEL favors visual similarity

Case2 (Hindi → Urdu | Marathi) Despite the high mutual intelligibility and substantial grammatical and linguistic similarities between Hindi and Urdu, as acknowledged in the literature (Bhatt, 2005), the LQ score on the POS tagging task attained by PIXEL for this language pairing is not as high as one would anticipate (ranked 94th). The relatively low performance can be attributed to their disparate scripts, underscoring the importance of visual similarity when using image-based language models such as PIXEL. However, for the other three models, with Hindi as the source, Urdu ranked in the top 3 target languages. Table 1 represents this phenomenon.

On the flip side, Hindi and Marathi are not mutually intelligible. But both of these languages use the Devanagari script. Sorting the LQ scores for Hindi as the source language, Marathi comes out as one of the top-performing target languages (4th).

Case3 (Arabic → X) In the case of Arabic as the source language, PIXEL received the highest scores for Persian (ranked 2nd) and Urdu (ranked 3rd) as

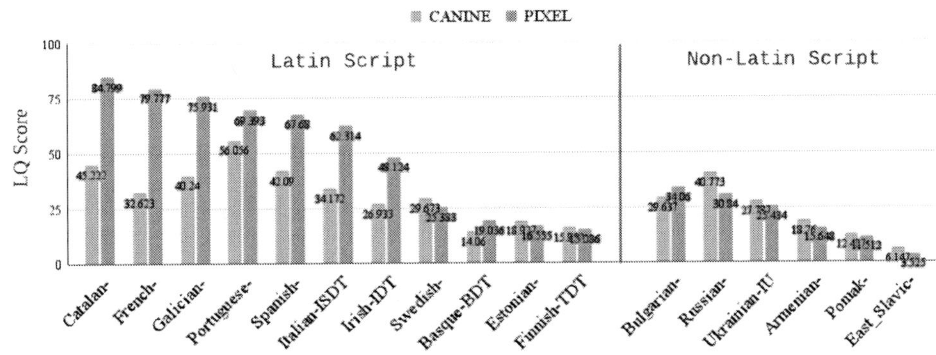

Figure 4: LQ score obtained by PIXEL and CANINE on Latin and non-Latin scripts on POS tagging. PIXEL outperforms CANINE on the POS tagging task when both source and target use the same script (on the left portion of the graph). Conversely, PIXEL does not outperform CANINE when the scripts are dissimilar (on the right portion of the graph)

Arabic→X (POS Tagging)				
Lang. (X)	CANINE LQ Score, (Rank)	PIXEL LQ Score, (Rank)	Script Similarity	Linguistics Similarity
Maltese	5.9 (24)	1.5 (80)	Dissimilar	Very Close
Persian	15.7 (6)	42.8 (2)	Same	Dissimilar
Hebrew	43.1 (3)	36.9 (3)	Close	Related
Urdu	0.3 (74)	24.1 (6)	Same	Dissimilar

Table 2: LQ score and rank of PIXEL with Arabic as the source language shows PIXEL receives a high score when scripts are visually similar rather than when languages are only linguistically similar.

respective source languages. Persian and Urdu are both Indo-European languages and are not at all lexically similar to Arabic. However, these are both written using Arabic script. On the contrary, like Arabic, Maltese is an Afro-Asiatic language with Semitic origin. But PIXEL performed extremely poorly in the case of Maltese (ranked 81st). This, we suspect, is due to the use of Latin script in Maltese, which further emphasizes the effect of visual similarity for PIXEL.

In the case of mBERT and CANINE, these patterns of favoring similar-looking scripts were absent. Rather, we saw an average score for the languages irrespective of the script.

Case4 (African → African) We've compared all four models using 10 African languages from the MasakhaNER dataset for the Named Entity Recognition (NER) task. Aside from Amharic, which uses the Ge'ez script, all other languages use the Latin script. Figure 5 shows the average LQ score obtained by PIXEL and CANINE models for each language as sources. The Table shows Amharic as an unfit choice for the source language when the target languages are in Latin script. Comparing PIXEL and CANINE, we notice CANINE outperforms PIXEL. Since PIXEL was only pre-trained on English, it is comparatively difficult for PIXEL to perform well on African languages. Conversely, CANINE was pre-trained on Yoruba (an African language) which has strong linguistic similarities with other African languages.

Observation Clearly, the above findings highlight the positive correlation between the performance of PIXEL, an image-based language model, and the visual similarity between languages. It is logical to expect that visually similar language would demonstrate better performance in cross-lingual transfer when utilizing PIXEL. The findings in the CANINE and mBERT comparison further reinforce the notion that language models that do not rely on visual representations do not exhibit a strong correlation between their scores and the visual similarity of the source and target languages.

4.2 Task Specific Performance

POS tagging In general, mBERT learns quickly compared to other models. This can be attributed to several reasons. First of all, mBERT operates on token-level representations and manifests heavy reliance on word-level semantics. So it is easier to associate the word or subword tokens with their respective POS tags, compared to character-level models like CANINE. Moreover, mBERT's predefined vocabulary, which includes commonly used subwords can potentially expedite the learning process

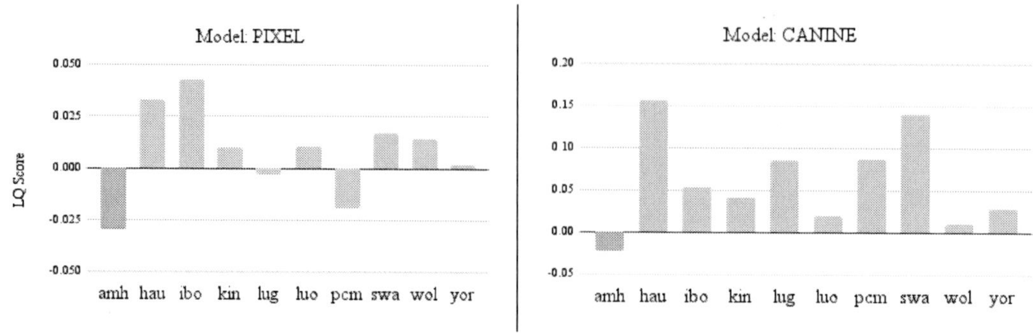

Figure 5: Average LQ scores with each language as sources for NER task (for PIXEL and CANINE) shows Amharic (only non-Latin script) pairs significantly worse with other languages that use Latin script

as the model can leverage semantic associations between these known tokens and their POS tags. On the contrary, character-level models have larger input sequence lengths and may require more examples to adequately learn the pattern in data which can lead to slower learning as compared to the tokenization-based models.

In addition, mBERT is trained on multilingual data. So it is more efficient than BERT at transferring knowledge from a high-resource language to a low-resource language, enhancing its few-shot learning capabilities for POS tagging tasks across different languages.

Coptic→X (POS tagging)			
Lang. (X)	**mBERT**	**CANINE**	**BERT**
Telegu	38.84	37.45	55.76
French	20.73	26.93	50.59
Italian	22.63	26.07	47.12
Russian	33.48	27.15	43.55
Persian Seraji	23.21	21.26	43.53

Table 3: Few-shot accuracy for POS tagging task with Coptic as the source language highlighting the performance of BERT (monolingually pre-trained) over mBERT and CANINE. Coptic is the only source language (in our analysis) that is not part of the pre-training languages of mBERT and CANINE and the only language where BERT significantly outperforms mBERT and CANINE

Dependency Parsing Interestingly, CANINE performs better than mBERT or BERT. This may be partly attributed to the nature of the task. Parsing is centered more on understanding the syntactic relationships between words in a sentence rather than on the meanings of individual words. As CANINE works on character level, it is more equipped to capture finer-grained patterns in these relationships, outperforming mBERT, exactly because the necessary information is marked with affixal morphemes in many languages. Moreover, CANINE operates without a predefined vocabulary, and its language independence might be advantageous when parsing sentences in a low-resource language or multilingual context. As a result, it can transfer knowledge across languages more fluidly. On top of that, the occurrence of out-of-vocabulary words or rare words can impact the parsing accuracy. As a character-level model, CANINE is better equipped in handling out-of-vocabulary words, which might be the reason for its improved performance in parsing in few-shot scenarios.

Named Entity Recognition NER, like POS tagging, leans heavily on understanding the meanings of individual words in order to accurately identify and classify named entities. This semantic nature of the task presents an advantage for segmentation-based models such as mBERT over character-level models like CANINE. Despite the multilingual strength of CANINE, its focus on character-level patterns may not sufficiently capture the semantic nuances needed for effective NER. Conversely, mBERT, with its token-based approach, can better handle the word meanings central to NER tasks. Therefore, in our analysis, mBERT demonstrates slightly superior performance in NER compared to CANINE. This suggests that while character-level models may excel in tasks centered on syntactic relationships, segmentation-based models may still hold the edge in tasks with a strong semantic dependency.

4.3 Unseen Languages

BERT performs better than mBERT and CANINE on some languages that these multilingual models

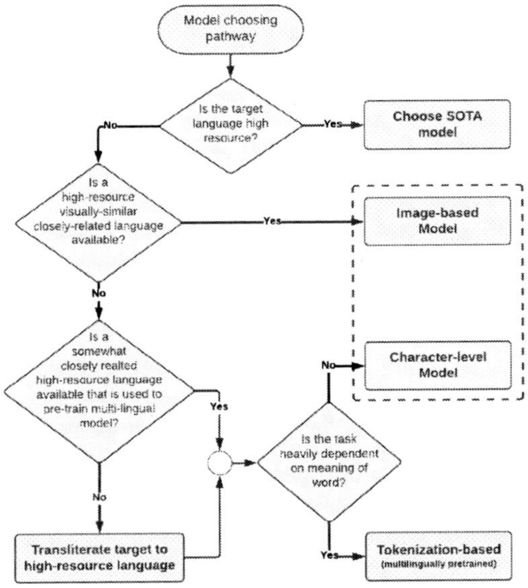

Figure 6: Model Recommendation Tree

were not pre-trained on. For example, consider the case study of Coptic. In comparison to CANINE and mBERT, BERT has better scores for POS tagging when Coptic is used as the source language (Table 3). Multilingual models like CANINE and mBERT underperform in this case. Among all the source languages used in our analysis, Coptic is the only source that is not part of the pre-training languages of CANINE and mBERT. It is also the only language where BERT has consistently outperformed the multi-lingually pre-trained models.

This inability to effectively adapt to a new unseen language could be attributed to the influence of the scripts of those languages. In these cases, transliterating the target to a high-resource language has been shown to improve performance on downstream tasks (Muller et al., 2021).

5 Model Recommendation Tree

Based on our findings, we propose a model selection pathway predicated on three primary considerations: resource availability for the target language, the presence of a visually similar high-resource language, and the task's semantic dependency.

High Resource Languages In the context of high-resource languages, we recommend employing the most advanced models. Our research indicates that both character-based models like CANINE and tokenization-based models like mBERT exhibit superior performances in this setting. Generally, multilingual pre-training grants these models a notable edge over their monolingually trained counterparts, making them well-suited for tasks involving high-resource languages and ensuring efficient performance.

Visual Similarity In cases where the target language is resource-poor but visually resembles a high-resource language, our suggestion is to undertake a cross-lingual transfer from the high-resource language using a tokenization-free model like the PIXEL. PIXEL is explicitly designed to discern and capitalize on visual correspondences between languages, which makes it an optimal choice in instances where such resemblances can be exploited.

Semantic Dependency If a high-resource language somewhat closely related to the target language has been used in pre-training a multilingual model, the choice between different models should be guided by the task's semantic content requirements. If the task depends heavily on semantic understanding, models like mBERT or similar tokenization-based models are advisable. These models excel in scenarios where deep semantic comprehension is key. Conversely, if the task doesn't require a strong understanding of semantics, character-based models like CANINE may be a more efficient choice. These models typically perform well in scenarios where semantic dependence is lower.

Special Cases For scenarios that do not fall within the purview of the above-mentioned conditions, a multitude of factors come into play. For instance, when the source language was not part of the pre-training set for the multilingual model, we suggest transliterating the target language to a high-resource language. Transliterating those languages substantially enhances the performance of these multilingual models on downstream tasks.

6 Related Work

Cross-lingual transfer Cross-lingual transfer has emerged as a valuable approach to enhance model performance in low-resource languages without requiring extensive amounts of target language data (Conneau et al., 2020). XLM-R, proposed by Conneau et al., demonstrates the effectiveness of pre-training on a large-scale masked language model trained on 100 languages from CommonCrawl data. It outperforms multilingual

BERT (mBERT) on various cross-lingual benchmarks. Similarly, Devlin et al. and Xue et al. propose finetuning approaches for existing pre-trained language models (PLMs). Recently, another approach by Lee et al. employs adapters for cross-lingual transfer in low-resource languages. Fusing Multiple Adapters for Cross-Lingual Transfer (FAD-X) utilizes language adapters and task adapters to address the imbalance in lower-resource languages. MAD-X (Pfeiffer et al., 2020) is another adapter-based method that employs language, task, and invertible adapters. Moreover, this similar setting coupled with language phylogeny information proved to be useful for low-resource cross-lingual transfer (Faisal and Anastasopoulos, 2022).

Tokenization-free models Tokenization-based models such as **BERT** (Devlin et al., 2019b), RoBERTa (Liu et al., 2019), GPT-3 (Brown et al., 2020), ALBERT (Lan et al., 2020), T5 (Raffel et al., 2020) and ELECTRA (Clark et al., 2020b) are leading the field when it comes to performance across a broad range of natural language processing tasks. However, tokenization-based models like BERT demonstrate poor performance in unexplored domains (Boukkouri et al., 2020) and lack resilience to noisy data such as typos and missed clicks (Sun et al., 2020).

Studies have shown that models using visual text representations are more robust (Salesky et al., 2021). PIXEL (Rust et al., 2022) proposes the use of visual embeddings for language modeling, eliminating the need for a fixed vocabulary. Research suggests that models utilizing visual text representations exhibit greater resilience to noisy texts and enable rapid adaptation to new languages while maintaining performance.

CANINE (Clark et al., 2022), a character-based model, provides an alternative approach that eliminates the reliance on predefined vocabularies. CANINE surpasses vanilla BERT on the TyDiQA benchmark (Clark et al., 2020a) by downsampling input sequences to achieve similar speeds.

ByT5 (Xue et al., 2021a) introduces a modified version of the standard transformer that processes byte sequences, addressing the limitations of a finite vocabulary. Similarly, CHARFORMER (Tay et al., 2021) proposes a gradient-based sub-word tokenization method that operates directly on a byte level. It performs on par with tokenizer-based approaches and outperforms most byte-level methods.

Language Similarity Metrics Several researchers have proposed different methodologies to quantify similarity among languages. For instance, (Petroni and Serva, 2010) introduced a measure of lexical distance, which quantifies the difference between languages based on their vocabulary. On the other hand, (Chiswick and Miller, 2005) suggests a metric of linguistic distance that represents how challenging it is for English speakers to learn other languages. However, this method relies on English speakers' learning difficulty, making it language-biased and not generalizable for speakers of other languages.

A different approach is presented by Ciobanu and Dinu, who propose an automated method for identifying pairs of cognates (words with a common etymology) across languages. But this cognate identification method requires a known list of cognates, limiting its usefulness for less-studied languages, and it may overlook non-lexical aspects of language similarity.

Another common tool is the Automated Similarity Judgment Program (Automated Similarity Judgment Program, 2023) which uses a comprehensive database of vocabulary to analyze linguistic relationships but has been criticized for its simplified standard orthography and its reliance on a limited vocabulary list.

7 Conclusion

This study provides pivotal insights into the practical application of tokenization-based as well as tokenization-free models in cross-lingual transfer tasks, accentuating the importance of context and task-based model selection. However, there's an abundance of uncharted territory awaiting exploration. The gaps in our understanding of tokenization-free models such as PIXEL and CANINE present a significant opportunity for further research. These models, though promising, are still in their early stages of development. This paves the way for studies aiming to enhance their performance, potentially through the integration of advanced learning algorithms or novel feature extraction techniques.

Additionally, investigating the role of tokenization in handling different language families could provide profound insights. For instance, how do these models perform with agglutinative languages like Turkish or Finnish, or with logographic languages like Chinese? Exploring such linguistic diversity could further clarify the strengths and weaknesses of different model types. An iterative inclusion of extinct or less commonly spoken languages is also essential at this point.

In summary, this study marks a significant step in understanding the capabilities and limitations of different models in cross-lingual transfer tasks. It opens several doors for future research, promising an exciting trajectory for the evolution of language modeling and translation tasks. The journey ahead, albeit challenging, presents a wealth of opportunities for innovation and discovery.

Limitations

This research, while extensive, presents certain limitations. Our study focuses primarily on syntactic tasks, leaving semantic tasks unexplored. While our work delves into the performance of specific models like BERT, mBERT, PIXEL, and CANINE, other models, especially emerging ones like decoder-based language models, remain unexamined in this context. The research also predominantly concerns low-resource languages, potentially limiting the applicability of our findings to high-resource contexts. Moreover, the consideration of different language families, such as agglutinative or logographic languages, is lacking in this analysis. Looking ahead, we plan to address these limitations by incorporating a broader range of language tasks, investigating a wider array of language models, and expanding our research to include high-resource languages and different language families. This will allow us to present a more holistic understanding of cross-lingual transfer in future studies.

Acknowledgements

We are thankful to the anonymous reviewers for their constructive feedback. Fahim Faisal and Antonios Anastasopoulos are generously supported by the National Science Foundation through grant IIS-2125466.

References

David Ifeoluwa Adelani, Jade Abbott, Graham Neubig, Daniel D'souza, Julia Kreutzer, Constantine Lignos, Chester Palen-Michel, Happy Buzaaba, Shruti Rijhwani, Sebastian Ruder, Stephen Mayhew, Israel Abebe Azime, Shamsuddeen H. Muhammad, Chris Chinenye Emezue, Joyce Nakatumba-Nabende, Perez Ogayo, Aremu Anuoluwapo, Catherine Gitau, Derguene Mbaye, Jesujoba Alabi, Seid Muhie Yimam, Tajuddeen Rabiu Gwadabe, Ignatius Ezeani, Rubungo Andre Niyongabo, Jonathan Mukiibi, Verrah Otiende, Iroro Orife, Davis David, Samba Ngom, Tosin Adewumi, Paul Rayson, Mofetoluwa Adeyemi, Gerald Muriuki, Emmanuel Anebi, Chiamaka Chukwuneke, Nkiruka Odu, Eric Peter Wairagala, Samuel Oyerinde, Clemencia Siro, Tobius Saul Bateesa, Temilola Oloyede, Yvonne Wambui, Victor Akinode, Deborah Nabagereka, Maurice Katusiime, Ayodele Awokoya, Mouhamadane MBOUP, Dibora Gebreyohannes, Henok Tilaye, Kelechi Nwaike, Degaga Wolde, Abdoulaye Faye, Blessing Sibanda, Orevaoghene Ahia, Bonaventure F. P. Dossou, Kelechi Ogueji, Thierno Ibrahima DIOP, Abdoulaye Diallo, Adewale Akinfaderin, Tendai Marengereke, and Salomey Osei. 2021. MasakhaNER: Named entity recognition for African languages. *Transactions of the Association for Computational Linguistics*, 9:1116–1131.

Wasi Uddin Ahmad, Zhisong Zhang, Xuezhe Ma, Eduard Hovy, Kai-Wei Chang, and Nanyun Peng. 2019. On difficulties of cross-lingual transfer with order differences: A case study on dependency parsing. In *Proceedings of NAACL-HLT*, pages 2440–2452.

Automated Similarity Judgment Program. 2023. Automated similarity judgment program — Wikipedia, the free encyclopedia. [Online; accessed 18-June-2023].

Rajesh Bhatt. 2005. Long distance agreement in hindi-urdu. *Natural Language & Linguistic Theory*, 23(4):757–807.

Damian Blasi, Antonios Anastasopoulos, and Graham Neubig. 2022. Systematic inequalities in language technology performance across the world's languages. In *Proceedings of the 60th Annual Meeting of the Association for Computational Linguistics (Volume 1: Long Papers)*, pages 5486–5505, Dublin, Ireland. Association for Computational Linguistics.

Hicham El Boukkouri, Olivier Ferret, Thomas Lavergne, Hiroshi Noji, Pierre Zweigenbaum, and Junichi Tsujii. 2020. Characterbert: Reconciling elmo and bert for word-level open-vocabulary representations from characters.

Tom B. Brown, Benjamin Mann, Nick Ryder, Melanie Subbiah, Jared Kaplan, Prafulla Dhariwal, Arvind Neelakantan, Pranav Shyam, Girish Sastry, Amanda Askell, Sandhini Agarwal, Ariel Herbert-Voss, Gretchen Krueger, Tom Henighan, Rewon Child, Aditya Ramesh, Daniel M. Ziegler, Jeffrey Wu, Clemens Winter, Christopher Hesse, Mark Chen, Eric Sigler, Mateusz Litwin, Scott Gray, Benjamin Chess, Jack Clark, Christopher Berner, Sam McCandlish, Alec Radford, Ilya Sutskever, and Dario Amodei. 2020. Language models are few-shot learners.

Danqi Chen and Christopher D Manning. 2014. A fast and accurate dependency parser using neural networks. In *Proceedings of the 2014 conference on empirical methods in natural language processing (EMNLP)*, pages 740–750.

Barry R. Chiswick and Paul W. Miller. 2005. Linguistic distance: A quantitative measure of the distance between english and other languages. *Journal of Multilingual and Multicultural Development*, 26(1):1–11.

Alina Maria Ciobanu and Liviu P. Dinu. 2014. Automatic detection of cognates using orthographic alignment. In *Proceedings of the 52nd Annual Meeting of the Association for Computational Linguistics (Volume 2: Short Papers)*, pages 99–105, Baltimore, Maryland. Association for Computational Linguistics.

Jonathan H. Clark, Eunsol Choi, Michael Collins, Dan Garrette, Tom Kwiatkowski, Vitaly Nikolaev, and Jennimaria Palomaki. 2020a. Tydi qa: A benchmark for information-seeking question answering in typologically diverse languages.

Jonathan H. Clark, Dan Garrette, Iulia Turc, and John Wieting. 2022. Canine: Pre-training an efficient tokenization-free encoder for language representation. *Transactions of the Association for Computational Linguistics*, 10:73–91.

Kevin Clark, Minh-Thang Luong, Quoc V. Le, and Christopher D. Manning. 2020b. Electra: Pre-training text encoders as discriminators rather than generators.

Alexis Conneau, Kartikay Khandelwal, Naman Goyal, Vishrav Chaudhary, Guillaume Wenzek, Francisco Guzmán, Edouard Grave, Myle Ott, Luke Zettlemoyer, and Veselin Stoyanov. 2020. Unsupervised cross-lingual representation learning at scale. In *Proceedings of the 58th Annual Meeting of the Association for Computational Linguistics*, pages 8440–8451, Online. Association for Computational Linguistics.

Jacob Devlin, Ming-Wei Chang, Kenton Lee, and Kristina Toutanova. 2019a. BERT: Pre-training of deep bidirectional transformers for language understanding. In *Proceedings of the 2019 Conference of the North American Chapter of the Association for Computational Linguistics: Human Language Technologies, Volume 1 (Long and Short Papers)*, pages 4171–4186, Minneapolis, Minnesota. Association for Computational Linguistics.

Jacob Devlin, Ming-Wei Chang, Kenton Lee, and Kristina Toutanova. 2019b. Bert: Pre-training of deep bidirectional transformers for language understanding.

Ethnologue. 2023. Ethnologue. [Online; accessed 18-June-2023].

Fahim Faisal and Antonios Anastasopoulos. 2022. Phylogeny-inspired adaptation of multilingual models to new languages. In *Proceedings of the 2nd Conference of the Asia-Pacific Chapter of the Association for Computational Linguistics and the 12th International Joint Conference on Natural Language Processing (Volume 1: Long Papers)*, pages 434–452, Online only. Association for Computational Linguistics.

Yimin Fan, Yaobo Liang, Alexandre Muzio, Hany Hassan, Houqiang Li, Ming Zhou, and Nan Duan. 2021. Discovering representation sprachbund for multilingual pre-training.

Philip Gage. 1994. A new algorithm for data compression. *C Users J.*, 12(2):23–38.

Junxian He, Zhisong Zhang, Taylor Berg-Kirkpatrick, and Graham Neubig. 2019. Cross-lingual syntactic transfer through unsupervised adaptation of invertible projections. *arXiv preprint arXiv:1906.02656*.

Valentin Hofmann, Hinrich Schuetze, and Janet Pierrehumbert. 2022. An embarrassingly simple method to mitigate undesirable properties of pretrained language model tokenizers. In *Proceedings of the 60th Annual Meeting of the Association for Computational Linguistics (Volume 2: Short Papers)*, pages 385–393, Dublin, Ireland. Association for Computational Linguistics.

Julia Kreutzer, Isaac Caswell, Lisa Wang, Ahsan Wahab, Daan van Esch, Nasanbayar Ulzii-Orshikh, Allahsera Tapo, Nishant Subramani, Artem Sokolov, Claytone Sikasote, Monang Setyawan, Supheakmungkol Sarin, Sokhar Samb, Benoî t Sagot, Clara Rivera, Annette Rios, Isabel Papadimitriou, Salomey Osei, Pedro Ortiz Suarez, Iroro Orife, Kelechi Ogueji, Andre Niyongabo Rubungo, Toan Q. Nguyen, Mathias Müller, André Müller, Shamsuddeen Hassan Muhammad, Nanda Muhammad, Ayanda Mnyakeni, Jamshidbek Mirzakhalov, Tapiwanashe Matangira, Colin Leong, Nze Lawson, Sneha Kudugunta, Yacine Jernite, Mathias Jenny, Orhan Firat, Bonaventure F. P. Dossou, Sakhile Dlamini, Nisansa de Silva, Sakine Çabuk Ballı, Stella Biderman, Alessia Battisti, Ahmed Baruwa, Ankur Bapna, Pallavi Baljekar, Israel Abebe Azime, Ayodele Awokoya, Duygu Ataman, Orevaoghene Ahia, Oghenefego Ahia, Sweta Agrawal, and Mofetoluwa Adeyemi. 2022. Quality at a glance: An audit of web-crawled multilingual datasets. *Transactions of the Association for Computational Linguistics*, 10:50–72.

Guillaume Lample, Miguel Ballesteros, Sandeep Subramanian, Kazuya Kawakami, and Chris Dyer. 2016. Neural architectures for named entity recognition. *arXiv preprint arXiv:1603.01360*.

Zhenzhong Lan, Mingda Chen, Sebastian Goodman, Kevin Gimpel, Piyush Sharma, and Radu Soricut. 2020. Albert: A lite bert for self-supervised learning of language representations.

Jaeseong Lee, Seung-won Hwang, and Taesup Kim. 2022. FAD-X: Fusing adapters for cross-lingual transfer to low-resource languages. In *Proceedings of the 2nd Conference of the Asia-Pacific Chapter of the Association for Computational Linguistics and the*

12th International Joint Conference on Natural Language Processing (Volume 2: Short Papers), pages 57–64, Online only. Association for Computational Linguistics.

Yinhan Liu, Myle Ott, Naman Goyal, Jingfei Du, Mandar Joshi, Danqi Chen, Omer Levy, Mike Lewis, Luke Zettlemoyer, and Veselin Stoyanov. 2019. Roberta: A robustly optimized bert pretraining approach.

Christopher D Manning. 2011. Part-of-speech tagging from 97% to 100%: is it time for some linguistics? In *International conference on intelligent text processing and computational linguistics*, pages 171–189. Springer.

Benjamin Muller, Antonios Anastasopoulos, Benoît Sagot, and Djamé Seddah. 2021. When being unseen from mBERT is just the beginning: Handling new languages with multilingual language models. In *Proceedings of the 2021 Conference of the North American Chapter of the Association for Computational Linguistics: Human Language Technologies*, pages 448–462, Online. Association for Computational Linguistics.

Joakim Nivre, Marie-Catherine de Marneffe, Filip Ginter, Jan Hajič, Christopher D. Manning, Sampo Pyysalo, Sebastian Schuster, Francis Tyers, and Daniel Zeman. 2020. Universal Dependencies v2: An evergrowing multilingual treebank collection. In *Proceedings of the Twelfth Language Resources and Evaluation Conference*, pages 4034–4043, Marseille, France. European Language Resources Association.

Joakim Nivre, Daniel Zeman, Filip Ginter, and Francis Tyers. 2017. Universal Dependencies. In *Proceedings of the 15th Conference of the European Chapter of the Association for Computational Linguistics: Tutorial Abstracts*, Valencia, Spain. Association for Computational Linguistics.

Filippo Petroni and Maurizio Serva. 2010. Measures of lexical distance between languages. *Physica A: Statistical Mechanics and its Applications*, 389(11):2280–2283.

Jonas Pfeiffer, Ivan Vulic, Iryna Gurevych, and Sebastian Ruder. 2020. MAD-X: an adapter-based framework for multi-task cross-lingual transfer. *CoRR*, abs/2005.00052.

Colin Raffel, Noam Shazeer, Adam Roberts, Katherine Lee, Sharan Narang, Michael Matena, Yanqi Zhou, Wei Li, and Peter J. Liu. 2020. Exploring the limits of transfer learning with a unified text-to-text transformer.

Phillip Rust, Jonas F. Lotz, Emanuele Bugliarello, Elizabeth Salesky, Miryam de Lhoneux, and Desmond Elliott. 2022. Language modelling with pixels.

Elizabeth Salesky, David Etter, and Matt Post. 2021. Robust open-vocabulary translation from visual text representations.

Mike Schuster and Kaisuke Nakajima. 2012. Japanese and korean voice search. In *2012 IEEE International Conference on Acoustics, Speech and Signal Processing (ICASSP)*, pages 5149–5152.

Lichao Sun, Kazuma Hashimoto, Wenpeng Yin, Akari Asai, Jia Li, Philip Yu, and Caiming Xiong. 2020. Adv-bert: Bert is not robust on misspellings! generating nature adversarial samples on bert.

Yi Tay, Vinh Q. Tran, Sebastian Ruder, Jai Gupta, Hyung Won Chung, Dara Bahri, Zhen Qin, Simon Baumgartner, Cong Yu, and Donald Metzler. 2021. Charformer: Fast character transformers via gradient-based subword tokenization.

Linting Xue, Aditya Barua, Noah Constant, Rami Al-Rfou, Sharan Narang, Mihir Kale, Adam Roberts, and Colin Raffel. 2021a. Byt5: Towards a token-free future with pre-trained byte-to-byte models.

Linting Xue, Noah Constant, Adam Roberts, Mihir Kale, Rami Al-Rfou, Aditya Siddhant, Aditya Barua, and Colin Raffel. 2021b. mT5: A massively multilingual pre-trained text-to-text transformer. In *Proceedings of the 2021 Conference of the North American Chapter of the Association for Computational Linguistics: Human Language Technologies*, pages 483–498, Online. Association for Computational Linguistics.

Xinyan Velocity Yu, Akari Asai, Trina Chatterjee, Junjie Hu, and Eunsol Choi. 2022. Beyond counting datasets: A survey of multilingual dataset construction and necessary resources.

+

A Appendix

A.1 Frequently Asked Questions

1. Q: What did the authors mean by 'few-shot' and 'zero-shot'?
   A: The term 'few-shot' is quite loosely used in this paper. Each model is at first fully trained on a source language and then evaluated on some target language. In the evaluation phase, the model is either (i) directly evaluated on the target language (termed as zero-shot), or (ii) fine-tuned for a few steps on the target language (termed as few-shot).

2. Q: How can LQ score be negative and what does it imply?
   A: The LQ score does not have strong bounds. So it can have negative scores. Since it is a relative metric rather than an absolute one, having a negative score does not create any issue. It implies that the model is performing worse for the source-target pair compared to other sources in the system.

3. Q: Can LQ metric be used to compare different models?
   A: Yes, LQ metric can be used to compare different models if the same pair of source and target languages are considered.

A.2 LQ Score

Proof of Effectiveness of LQ Score Let $E_s^{(t_c)} = F$, $E_s^{(t_0)} = Z_0$, and $Z_A = \frac{1}{n}\sum_{i=1}^{n} E_i^{(t_0)}$. We can rewrite the LQ score as:

$$LQ(x, k) = \frac{(F - Z_A)(F + Z_0))}{Z_A + \epsilon} \quad (2)$$

We assume that a score would effectively measure the cross-lingual transfer capabilities if it gets positively rewarded for a higher score after a few shots of training in comparison to other language pairs and in comparison to the state before few-shot training. That means the growth of F from Z_0 and the difference of F with Z_A should play a high impact on the score.

Simplifying the right-hand-side of Eqn 1, we get,

$$\frac{F^2 - FZ_A + FZ_0 - Z_A Z_0}{Z_A + \epsilon} \quad (3)$$

$$= F\frac{F}{Z_A} - F + F\frac{Z_0}{Z_A} - Z_0 \quad (4)$$

$$= F\left(\frac{F + Z_0}{Z_A}\right) - F\left(1 + \frac{Z_0}{F}\right) \quad (5)$$

In equation 5, the term $(F + Z_0)/Z_A$ will be greater than 1 when either F is very large or Z_0 is significantly larger than Z_A. That means a strong positive score can be obtained when the few-shot score is very high or the leap from zero-shot to few-shot is high. The remaining term $F\left(1 + \frac{Z_0}{F}\right)$ ensures the stability of the score. So, if a model learns quickly and gains good accuracy/las in the early steps of training, the LQ score will give out a strong score. If a model achieves a good score in zero-shot learning, it also receives a good LQ score.

Limitations of LQ Score The score utilizes a normalizing term that averages the zero-shot scores across all source languages. So, for any pair of languages, x and k, the LQ score will not always be the same. It will vastly depend on the list of source languages used in the experimentation. So, the numeric value of the LQ score does not have a direct meaning. However, for a given source, the relation between the target languages is indicative of how compatible the source and target are. On the flip side, for a target language, the relation between the source languages is also meaningful.

A.3 Hyper-parameters

A.3.1 Dependency Parsing

Full Fine-tuning (on source)
- Train batch size: 32
- Max Training Steps: 15000
- Early Stopping: Yes
- Learning Rate: 5e-5
- Maximum Sequence Length: 256
- Eval metric: LAS

Few-shot Fine-tuning (on targets)
- Train batch size: 32
- Max Training Steps: 10
- Learning Rate: 5e-5
- Maximum Sequence Length: 256
- Eval metric: LAS

A.3.2 POS Tagging

Full Fine-tuning (on source)
- Train batch size: 32
- Max Training Steps: 15000
- Early Stopping: Yes
- Learning Rate: 5e-5
- Maximum Sequence Length: 256
- Eval metric: Accuracy

Few-shot Fine-tuning (on targets)
- Train batch size: 32
- Max Training Steps: 10
- Learning Rate: 5e-5
- Maximum Sequence Length: 256
- Eval metric: Accuracy

A.3.3 Named Entity Recognition

Full Fine-tuning (on source)
- Train batch size: 32
- Max Training Steps: 15000
- Early Stopping: Yes
- Learning Rate: 5e-5
- Maximum Sequence Length: 256
- Eval metric: Accuracy

Few-shot Fine-tuning (on targets)
- Train batch size: 32
- Max Training Steps: 10
- Learning Rate: 5e-5
- Maximum Sequence Length: 256

- Eval metric: Accuracy

A.4 Source languages as target languages

Table 4 provides a comprehensive analysis of the PIXEL model's performance in terms of accuracy in the POS-tagging task, evaluated in both zero-shot and few-shot scenarios. Here, the set of source languages also serves as the target languages, creating a self-referential evaluation method. This unique approach further allows for a deeper understanding of the model's strengths and weaknesses when dealing with identical sources and target languages.

A.5 List of target languages

Tables 5, 6, and 7 give an elaborate list of languages and their scripts along with their respective families. The languages are spread across multiple scripts and multiple families.

A.6 Lexical Similarity

Lexical similarity is the percentage obtained by comparing standardized wordlists from two linguistic varieties and tallying words similar in form and meaning (Ethnologue, 2023). It ranges from 0 to 100, representing the vocabulary overlap between two languages. Values over 85% often suggest the speech variant may be a dialect of the compared language. The proportion of lexical similarity between two kinds of language is calculated by comparing standardized lists of words and tallying the forms that demonstrate similarity in both structure and meaning.

Table 8 gives the similarity scores between different European Language pairs (Ethnologue, 2023; Fan et al., 2021).

B Additional Materials

Target Language	English	Arabic	Korean	Vietnamese	Tamil	Chinese	Japanese	Coptic	Hindi	Average (Z_A)
English	**0.967**	0.238	0.297	0.284	0.255	0.149	0.297	0.289	0.219	0.33
Arabic	0.238	**0.958**	0.412	0.379	0.289	0.152	0.403	0.177	0.07	0.34
Korean	0.28	0.382	**0.944**	0.476	0.284	0.23	0.413	0.329	0.172	0.39
Vietnamese	0.286	0.341	0.47	**0.86**	0.3	0.234	0.458	0.321	0.233	0.39
Tamil	0.135	0.3	0.388	0.331	**0.817**	0.224	0.37	0.25	0.223	0.34
Chinese	0.336	0.32	0.428	0.412	0.3	**0.93**	0.525	0.3	0.274	0.43
Japanese	0.276	0.294	0.376	0.349	0.229	0.303	**0.973**	0.226	0.179	0.36
Coptic	0.103	0.144	0.189	0.188	0.154	0.056	0.162	**0.962**	0.093	0.23
Hindi	0.229	0.215	0.292	0.302	0.24	0.202	0.274	0.209	**0.964**	0.33

(a) Accuracy for POS task at zero-shot

	Arabic	Chinese	Coptic	English	Hindi	Japanese	Korean	Tamil	Vietnamese
Arabic	**0.958**	0.328	0.337	0.396	0.277	0.34	0.388	0.337	0.355
Chinese	0.371	**0.93**	0.339	0.366	0.395	0.531	0.414	0.328	0.391
Coptic	0.191	0.11	**0.962**	0.183	0.163	0.188	0.193	0.166	0.229
English	0.25	0.219	0.324	**0.968**	0.283	0.304	0.292	0.265	0.29
Hindi	0.311	0.288	0.331	0.319	**0.964**	0.264	0.261	0.257	0.349
Japanese	0.417	0.403	0.295	0.374	0.334	**0.973**	0.385	0.295	0.364
Korean	0.42	0.373	0.416	0.404	0.403	0.409	**0.943**	0.384	0.47
Tamil	0.328	0.303	0.298	0.33	0.298	0.302	0.39	**0.817**	0.337
Vietnamese	0.385	0.312	0.328	0.379	0.395	0.439	0.454	0.336	**0.859**

(b) Accuracy for POS task at few-shot

Table 4: Accuracy of PIXEL model (on POS-tagging task) of zero-shot evaluation and few-shot evaluation of 9 source languages on the same languages as targets

Language Name	Script	Language Family	Sub-family
Armenian-ArmTDP	Armenian	Indo-European	Armenian
Armenian-BSUT	Armenian	Indo-European	Armenian
Western_Armenian-ArmTDP	Armenian	Indo-European	Armenian
Latvian-LVTB	Latin	Indo-European	Baltic
Lithuanian-ALKSNIS	Latin	Indo-European	Baltic
Lithuanian-HSE	Latin	Indo-European	Baltic
Irish-IDT	Latin	Indo-European	Celtic
Scottish_Gaelic-ARCOSG	Latin	Indo-European	Celtic
Welsh-CCG	Latin	Indo-European	Celtic
Afrikaans-AfriBooms	Latin	Indo-European	Germanic
Danish-DDT	Latin	Indo-European	Germanic
Dutch-Alpino	Latin	Indo-European	Germanic
Dutch-LassySmall	Latin	Indo-European	Germanic
English-Atis	Latin	Indo-European	Germanic
English-ESL	Latin	Indo-European	Germanic
English-EWT	Latin	Indo-European	Germanic
English-GUM	Latin	Indo-European	Germanic
English-GUMReddit	Latin	Indo-European	Germanic
English-LinES	Latin	Indo-European	Germanic
English-ParTUT	Latin	Indo-European	Germanic
Faroese-FarPaHC	Latin	Indo-European	Germanic
German-GSD	Latin	Indo-European	Germanic
German-HDT	Latin	Indo-European	Germanic
Icelandic-IcePaHC	Latin	Indo-European	Germanic
Icelandic-Modern	Latin	Indo-European	Germanic
Norwegian-Bokmaal	Latin	Indo-European	Germanic
Norwegian-Nynorsk	Latin	Indo-European	Germanic
Norwegian-NynorskLIA	Latin	Indo-European	Germanic
Swedish-LinES	Latin	Indo-European	Germanic
Swedish-Talbanken	Latin	Indo-European	Germanic
Gothic-PROIEL	Gothic	Indo-European	Germanic
Turkish_German-SAGT	Latin	Indo-European	Germanic (German)
Ancient_Greek-Perseus	Greek	Indo-European	Hellenic
Ancient_Greek-PROIEL	Greek	Indo-European	Hellenic
Greek-GDT	Greek	Indo-European	Hellenic
Hindi_English-HIENCS	Devanagari and Latin	Indo-European	Indo-Aryan
Hindi-HDTB	Devanagari	Indo-European	Indo-Aryan
Marathi-UFAL	Devanagari	Indo-European	Indo-Aryan
Urdu-UDTB	Arabic	Indo-European	Indo-Aryan
Persian-PerDT	Arabic	Indo-European	Iranian
Persian-Seraji	Arabic	Indo-European	Iranian
Latin-ITTB	Latin	Indo-European	Italic
Latin-LLCT	Latin	Indo-European	Italic

Table 5: List of Target Languages (Part 1)

Language Name	Script	Language Family	Sub-family
Latin-PROIEL	Latin	Indo-European	Italic
Latin-UDante	Latin	Indo-European	Italic
Catalan-AnCora	Latin	Indo-European	Romance
French-FTB	Latin	Indo-European	Romance
French-GSD	Latin	Indo-European	Romance
French-ParTUT	Latin	Indo-European	Romance
French-Rhapsodie	Latin	Indo-European	Romance
French-Sequoia	Latin	Indo-European	Romance
Galician-CTG	Latin	Indo-European	Romance
Italian-ISDT	Latin	Indo-European	Romance
Italian-MarkIT	Latin	Indo-European	Romance
Italian-ParTUT	Latin	Indo-European	Romance
Italian-PoSTWITA	Latin	Indo-European	Romance
Italian-TWITTIRO	Latin	Indo-European	Romance
Italian-VIT	Latin	Indo-European	Romance
Old_French-SRCMF	Latin	Indo-European	Romance
Portuguese-Bosque	Latin	Indo-European	Romance
Portuguese-GSD	Latin	Indo-European	Romance
Romanian-Nonstandard	Latin	Indo-European	Romance
Romanian-RRT	Latin	Indo-European	Romance
Romanian-SiMoNERo	Latin	Indo-European	Romance
Spanish-AnCora	Latin	Indo-European	Romance
Spanish-GSD	Latin	Indo-European	Romance
Croatian-SET	Latin	Indo-European	Slavic
Czech-CAC	Latin	Indo-European	Slavic
Czech-CLTT	Latin	Indo-European	Slavic
Czech-FicTree	Latin	Indo-European	Slavic
Czech-PDT	Latin	Indo-European	Slavic
Polish-LFG	Latin	Indo-European	Slavic
Polish-PDB	Latin	Indo-European	Slavic
Slovak-SNK	Latin	Indo-European	Slavic
Slovenian-SSJ	Latin	Indo-European	Slavic
Old_Church_Slavonic-PROIEL	Glagolitic and Cyrillic	Indo-European	Slavic
Belarusian-HSE	Cyrillic	Indo-European	Slavic
Bulgarian-BTB	Cyrillic	Indo-European	Slavic
Old_East_Slavic-Birchbark	Cyrillic	Indo-European	Slavic
Old_East_Slavic-TOROT	Cyrillic	Indo-European	Slavic
Pomak-Philotis	Cyrillic	Indo-European	Slavic
Russian-GSD	Cyrillic	Indo-European	Slavic
Russian-SynTagRus	Cyrillic	Indo-European	Slavic
Russian-Taiga	Cyrillic	Indo-European	Slavic
Serbian-SET	Cyrillic	Indo-European	Slavic
Ukrainian-IU	Cyrillic	Indo-European	Slavic

Table 6: List of Target Languages (Part 2)

Language Name	**Script**	**Language Family**	**Sub-family**
Coptic-Scriptorium	Coptic	Afro-Asiatic	Egyptian
Maltese-MUDT	Latin	Afro-Asiatic	Semitic
Ancient_Hebrew-PTNK	Hebrew	Afro-Asiatic	Semitic
Hebrew-HTB	Hebrew	Afro-Asiatic	Semitic
Hebrew-IAHLTwiki	Hebrew	Afro-Asiatic	Semitic
Arabic-NYUAD	Arabic	Afro-Asiatic	Semitic
Arabic-PADT	Arabic	Afro-Asiatic	Semitic
Vietnamese-VTB	Latin	Austroasiatic	Vietic
Indonesian-GSD	Latin	Austronesian	Malayo-Polynesian
Tamil-TTB	Tamil	Dravidian	Tamil-Kannada
Telugu-MTG	Telugu	Dravidian	Telugu-Kui
Japanese-BCCWJ	Japanese (Kanji, Hiragana, Katakana)	Japonic	Japanese
Japanese-BCCWJLUW	Japanese (Kanji, Hiragana, Katakana)	Japonic	Japanese
Japanese-GSD	Japanese (Kanji, Hiragana, Katakana)	Japonic	Japanese
Japanese-GSDLUW	Japanese (Kanji, Hiragana, Katakana)	Japonic	Japanese
Korean-GSD	Hangul and Hanja	Koreanic	Korean
Korean-Kaist	Hangul and Hanja	Koreanic	Korean
Basque-BDT	Latin	Language Isolate	Language Isolate
Naija-NSC	Latin	Niger-Congo	Benue-Congo
Wolof-WTB	Latin	Niger-Congo	Senegambian
Swedish_Sign_Language	Swedish Sign Language (SignWriting)	Sign Language	Sign Language
Chinese-GSDSimp	Simplified Chinese (Han script)	Sino-Tibetan	Sinitic
Classical_Chinese-Kyoto	Classical Chinese (Han script)	Sino-Tibetan	Sinitic
Chinese-GSD	Chinese (Han script)	Sino-Tibetan	Sinitic
Uyghur-UDT	Arabic	Turkic	Karluk
Turkish-Atis	Latin	Turkic	Oghuz
Turkish-BOUN	Latin	Turkic	Oghuz
Turkish-FrameNet	Latin	Turkic	Oghuz
Turkish-IMST	Latin	Turkic	Oghuz
Turkish-Kenet	Latin	Turkic	Oghuz
Turkish-Penn	Latin	Turkic	Oghuz
Turkish-Tourism	Latin	Turkic	Oghuz
Estonian-EDT	Latin	Uralic	Finnic
Estonian-EWT	Latin	Uralic	Finnic
Finnish-FTB	Latin	Uralic	Finnic
Finnish-TDT	Latin	Uralic	Finnic
Hungarian-Szeged	Latin	Uralic	Ugric

Table 7: List of Target Languages (Part 3)

	Catalan	English	French	German	Italian	Portuguese	Romanian	Russian	Spanish
Catalan	1	-	0.85	-	0.87	0.85	0.73	-	0.85
English	-	1	0.27	0.6	-	-	-	0.24	-
French	0.85	0.27	1	0.29	0.89	0.75	0.75	-	0.75
German	-	0.6	0.29	1	-	-	-	-	-
Italian	0.87	-	0.89	-	1	0.8	0.77	-	0.82
Portuguese	0.85	-	0.75	-	0.8	1	0.72	-	0.89
Romanian	0.73	-	0.75	-	0.77	0.72	1	-	0.71
Russian	-	0.24	-	-	-	-	-	1	-
Spanish	0.85	-	0.75	-	0.82	0.89	0.71	-	1

Table 8: Lexical similarity among European languages (Ethnologue, 2023; Fan et al., 2021)

	mBERT	CANINE	BERT
UD_Telugu-MTG	38.83	37.45	55.76
UD_French-ParTUT	20.37	26.93	50.52
UD_Italian-ParTUT	22.63	26.07	47.12
UD_French-Sequoia	22.57	27.72	46.64
UD_Spanish-AnCora	24.10	24.17	46.09
UD_French-GSD	22.94	28.09	46.03
UD_Galician-CTG	27.80	22.67	45.95
UD_Italian-ISDT	23.07	26.80	45.62
UD_Italian-VIT	24.43	27.54	44.61
UD_Spanish-GSD	22.55	23.2	43.80
UD_Russian-GSD	33.48	27.15	43.54
UD_Persian-Seraji	23.21	21.26	43.54
UD_Catalan-AnCora	22.42	23.93	43.41
UD_Turkish-Kenet	32.31	32.29	43.21
UD_Portuguese-Bosque	26.99	22.92	42.51
UD_Portuguese-GSD	26.36	22.36	41.95
UD_Italian-MarkIT	21.57	26.19	41.78
UD_Turkish-FrameNet	33.33	32.45	41.38
UD_Turkish-Penn	29.87	30.68	41.25
UD_French-Rhapsodie	27.63	32.16	40.88
UD_Hebrew-IAHLTwiki	26.53	19.43	40.13
UD_Russian-SynTagRus	33.16	27.29	40.09
UD_Polish-PDB	30.01	25.15	39.90
UD_Lithuanian-ALKSNIS	34.08	25.40	39.78
UD_Arabic-PADT	30.52	19.67	39.62
UD_Belarusian-HSE	30.87	23.30	38.41
UD_Polish-LFG	30.18	29.38	38.24
UD_Ukrainian-IU	30.56		37.60
UD_Hebrew-HTB	23.88	17.32	37.58
UD_Vietnamese-VTB	21.60	25.97	37.52
UD_Turkish-BOUN	30.42	25.66	37.35
UD_Greek-GDT	25.18	15.39	37.26
UD_Latvian-LVTB	32.35	24.42	37.24
UD_Romanian-SiMoNERo	34.12	21.87	37.23

Table 9: LQ scores of different models (using Coptic as source language)

Adapt and Prune Strategy for Multilingual Speech Foundational Model on Low-resourced Languages

Hyeon Soo Kim*, **Chunghyeon Cho***, **Hyejin Won*** and **Kyung Ho Park**†
SOCAR AI Research, Seoul, Republic of Korea
{lucci, yoplait, cheese, kp}@socar.kr

Abstract

While foundational speech models such as Whisper demonstrate state-of-the-art performance across various benchmarks, it necessitates an adaptation process for specific downstream tasks, particularly in low-resourced languages. Classical full fine-tuning (FFT) successfully adapts the model to downstream tasks, but requires computational resources proportional to the extensive model size. Parameter-efficient fine-tuning (PEFT) methods introduced to address this issue effectively adapt a given model with less trainable parameters, but demand higher inference complexities for the increased number of overall parameters. In response to these issues, we propose **PEPSI**—a **P**arameter-**E**fficient ada**P**tation for the Speech foundat**I**onal model. Our PEPSI integrates a compact adapter module into the decoder layers of the foundational model and removes neurons irrelevant to the downstream task. Through experiments, we showcase that PEPSI achieves performance surpassing PEFT methods and comparable to FFT, while significantly reducing trainable and inference parameters to utilize Whisper on low-resourced languages that require additional adaptation.

1 Introduction

Recent advancements in speech foundational models pre-trained on large-scale, multilingual data have facilitated the resolution of speech recognition tasks to human standards in a wide array of languages. However, such models, including the recently introduced Whisper (Radford et al., 2023) and Universal Speech Model(USM) (Zhang et al., 2023), tend to exhibit suboptimal performance in languages like *Swahili* or *Malayalam* that cover only a small portion of their pre-training data. A prevalent strategy to address this limitation involves adapting these models to the target language of interest (Singh et al., 2023). Full fine-tuning (FFT) involves updating all the parameters within the model, demanding substantial computational resources. Parameter Efficient Fine-Tuning (PEFT) methods, proposed to reduce the training costs required for FFT, introduce additional small-scale, trainable parameters referred to as adapters into the model's architecture (Houlsby et al., 2019; Liu et al., 2021). These techniques, such as Low-Rank Adaption (Hu et al., 2021), update only the adapter parameters while freezing the backbone model. While significantly reducing the computational resources for training, such methods hold drawbacks of increasing the parameter number during inference.

Another avenue to mitigate computational costs involves model compression and pruning. These approaches propose methods to reduce the model size by eliminating specific neurons from model weight matrices (LeCun et al., 1989). These subnetworks are identified by assessing magnitude changes before and after training the model, removing neurons with low weight magnitudes as they are considered less crucial (Han et al., 2015; Frankle and Carbin, 2018). Although these pruning methods succeeded in reducing the weight of foundational models, the resulting task performances were not adequate for practical utilization.

1.1 Main Idea and Its Novelty

Building upon previous research by (Wang et al., 2020; Houston and Kirchhoff, 2023), which uncovered the existence of language-specific parameters and multilingual interference within Large Language Models (LLMs), we propose that a similar phenomenon may also be present in the foundational speech recognition model, Whisper. We hypothesize that not all neurons are essential for addressing ASR tasks in a specific target language. Hence, eliminating these non-essential neurons could alleviate computational load while maintain-

*Equal Contribution
†Corresponding author

Proceedings of the The 3rd Workshop on Multi-lingual Representation Learning (MRL), pages 85–94
December 7, 2023 ©2023 Association for Computational Linguistics

ing task performance. Furthermore, we postulate that not all layers are language-dependent and question whether incorporating adapters into the text-related layers (decoders) could enhance predicting text token outputs.

In this context, we introduce **PEPSI**, a Parameter-Efficient adaPtation for the Speech foundatIonal model, designed to address ASR tasks for a specific language. We adopt the established PEFT method introduced in Hu et al. (2021) to align the foundational model's knowledge with the target language. Subsequently, we maintain the LoRA adapter attached to the Whisper and remove language-irrelevant neurons.

We emphasize the novelty of our work. While prior studies have focused on pruning models followed by fine-tuning or simultaneous pruning and fine-tuning, we take a step further by identifying language-relevant parameters and retaining adapter-friendly neurons to enable efficient adaptation. Unlike previous research that concentrated on showcasing Whisper's capabilities or enhancing its performance during adaptation, our study addresses the practical concern of reducing computation overhead during adaptation, an aspect that has received limited attention.

Secondly, we identify that the language-relevant components of Whisper are associated with text-related decoders, rather than speech-related encoders. Building on this insight, we pioneer the application of the LoRA adapter to Whisper, exclusively integrating adapters at decoder layers. This is in contrast to prior adapter studies that focused on incorporating adapters throughout all layers of the parent model. Lastly, we introduce PEPSI as an innovative approach that combines LoRA and model pruning to achieve a streamlined utilization of Whisper. Notably, our experimental focus centers on Whisper, the only available open-sourced model that achieves state-of-the-art performance. Through experiments, we confirm the effectiveness of our approach in adapting the Whisper model to a target language or a specific domain that are low-resourced. PEPSI outperforms LoRA and matches FFT, but with significantly less active parameters.

1.2 Key Contributions

- We discover language-specific networks within Whisper, which can be solely utilized to perform comparably to FFT with significant parameter reduction.
- From analyzing the effect of LoRA on different layers, we demonstrate that ASR task relies heavily on text decoder layers, especially on the attention heads.
- Upon the above findings, we propose PEPSI, a novel paradigm to adapt multilingual speech foundational models to a target language.
- We conduct experiments on 5 low-resourced languages to demonstrate that our approach outperforms the commonly used LoRA and matches FFT while reducing the number of parameters up to 50% on specific languages.

2 Related Works

2.1 Automatic Speech Recognition

Automatic Speech Recognition (ASR), or Speech to Text (STT), transcribes a given audio into text. Previous ASR systems utilize RNNs and CNNs as backbone networks to improve performance (Hannun et al., 2014; Schneider et al., 2019). Further research demonstrated that Transformer architecture achieves a competitive recognition rate compared to prior models (Baevski et al., 2019). Recent works following the Scaling Laws (Kaplan et al., 2020) of the NLP domain demonstrated that the same applies to the speech domain; large speech models pre-trained on web-scale data can solve ASR tasks at human standards. An example is Whisper, which effectively addresses the challenge of weakly supervised pre-training by utilizing a large amount of labeled audio data collected from the web. Nevertheless, such models demand high computational complexity and latency due to the scale of their parameters. To address this concern, researchers explore methods to lightly fine-tune the large model to mitigate the cost associated with full fine-tuning large parameter models (Shao et al., 2023; Gong et al., 2023). We share the same goal with the full fine-tuning scheme, but our approach employs distinct methods.

2.2 Parameter-Efficient Fine-Tuning

Several studies have been proposed to rectify the limitations of full fine-tuning when applied to downstream tasks in Pre-trained Language Models(PLMs). Liu et al. (2021) and Li and Liang (2021) optimize the input word embedding by transforming it into a trainable continuous prompt embedding vector. In work by Houlsby et al. (2019), the bottleneck adapter with a transformer-based

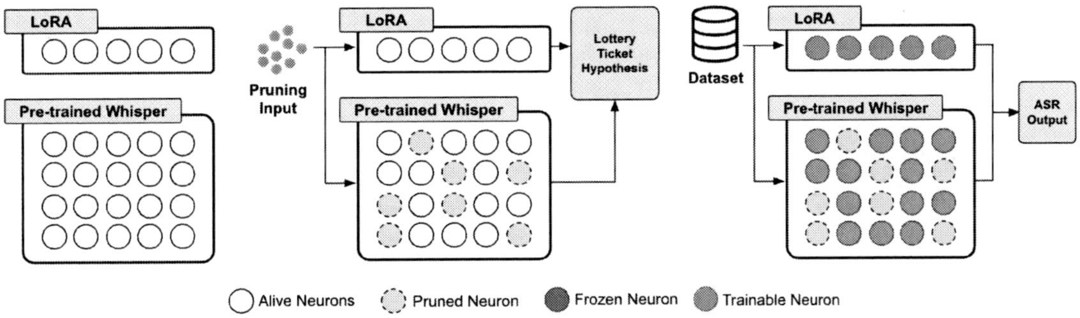

Figure 1: The three steps of PEPSI: (**Left**): Attaching LoRA onto the Whisper model. (**Middle**): Pruning the Whisper neurons irrelevant to the target language; LTH is applied with the pruning input dataset in the target language. (**Right**): Adapting the new language-specific model onto the target dataset.

model was proposed to improve diverse text classification tasks. To concurrently accommodate multiple linguistic target tasks, Bapna and Firat (2019) adds small task-specific adapter layers into the frozen language model. Hu et al. (2021) proposed LoRA, which is trainable low-rank decomposition matrics within PLMs to diminish the trainable parameters for downstream tasks. Our approach adopts a similar strategy to LoRA, utilizing an injected adapter layer. However, while LoRA integrates attention layers into the language model, we enhance the STT performance by integrating a compact adapter module into the decoder.

2.3 Pruning

The pruning technique implicates removing unnecessary weights from neural networks, reducing the number of parameters while minimizing the decrease in performance. LeCun et al. (1989) first introduced the pruning technique using second derivatives. Recently, Han et al. (2015) and Frankle and Carbin (2018) showed that by repeatedly removing weights with low magnitudes, the size of image networks can be significantly reduced. In addition, there are various pruning heuristics, such as activations (Hu et al., 2016), redundancy (Mariet and Sra, 2015), per-layer second derivatives (Dong et al., 2017), and energy/computation efficiency (Yang et al., 2017).

The Lottery Ticket Hypothesis (LTH) (Frankle and Carbin, 2018) goes against the shared wisdom of pruning after training (Han et al., 2015). LTH demonstrates the existence of subnetworks that reach similar performance comparable to the original network and are independently trainable from scratch.LTH has been studied in many fields. Early follow-up efforts have been researched in vision tasks (Frankle et al., 2020; Renda et al., 2020). Then, with the emergence of studies proving LTH is applicable in NLP and RL tasks (Renda et al., 2020; Yu et al., 2019), its scope extends. In particular, it is shown that LTH can be applied in Transformer architecture, commonly used as large models in NLP downstream (Chen et al., 2020). Furthermore, the first research, *Audio Lottery*, proposed applying LTH in speech tasks appeared (Ding et al., 2021). Although we share a common topic and scope, the difference lies in that while *Audio Lottery* pruned a model for a single language, we applied the LTH to a multilingual model, Whisper (Radford et al., 2023). Additionally, in contrast to conventional research that conducts pruning on the entire model, our approach involves using a pruning technique that improves the performance of models with adapters attached.

3 Discovering Language-specific Neurons

As preliminary analyses, we investigate the existence of language-specific neurons within Whisper and whether using only these neurons damages the ASR performance on the target language. We conducted two experiments on the widely utilized ASR dataset *Commonvoice 13* (Ardila et al., 2020). We selected 5 languages (i.e., *Korean, Malayalam, Japanese, Swahili, Chinese*) that cover only a small portion in the pre-training data of Whisper, and compared with *English*, a language that covers the most portion.

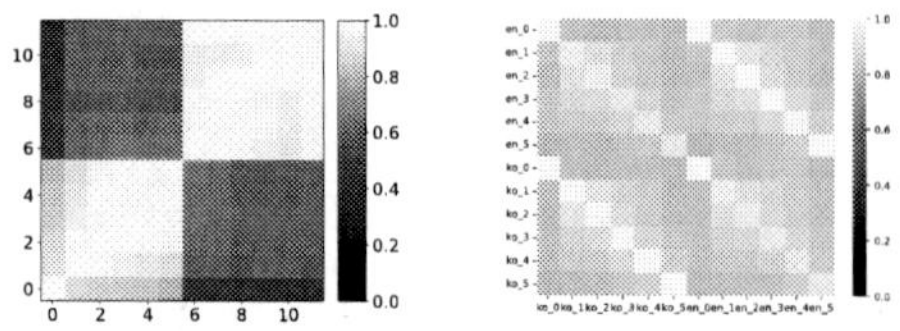

(a) CKA(ko vs. en)   (b) NeuronSim

Figure 2: Visualized representation similarity between different language tokens. Note that (b) is conducted on Whisper's decoder module. Both experiments were conducted using $\text{Whisper}_{\text{Tiny}}$ as the base model.

3.1 Does language token influence the network?

Setup In this study, we investigate the impact of language tokens on both representation and activation patterns within the Whisper model. The prompt utilized in Whisper is as follows: $< |sot| >< |language| >< |task| >< |notimestamps| >$, where $< |language| >$ corresponds to the language token of interest. We alter the language tokens as $< |ko| >$ for *Korean* and $< |en| >$ for *English*, then quantitatively assess the influence of its variations. We employ Centered Kernel Alignment (CKA) (Kornblith et al., 2019) and NeuronSim (Wu et al., 2020) to analyze activation patterns. CKA evaluates representation similarity between layers, producing a score from 0 to 1, while NeuronSim quantifies neuron activation similarity on a scale from 0 to 1, where 0 indicates dissimilarity. It is noteworthy that CKA focuses on representation similarity, whereas NeuronSim concentrates on neuron activation similarity, distinguishing between these two concepts.

Results Figure 2 shows that different patterns are discovered by changing the decoder input of the model under the same audio signal conditions. Comparing the heatmaps of similarity layers, (a) CKA exhibits high level of similarity, whereas (b) NeuronSim reveals a discernible block-diagonal heatmap. We attribute this phenomenon to the Whisper's representation varies depending on the decoder input language. Building upon prior research, we can deduce that two models may have similar representations but different individual neurons (Wu et al., 2020).

	pruned on	**Alive params %**		
		100.0%	81.0%	65.7%
$\text{Whisper}_{\text{Small}}$	Korean	10.5	10.2	12.9
	Malayalam	10.5	10.8	15.2

Table 1: Zero-shot CER (%) results on *Korean* when pruned with each language. The 100.0% is the unpruned Whisper model.

3.2 Impact of Pruning Language-irrelevant Neurons

Setup The previous experiment confirmed that each language's parameters are activated differently in Whisper. Therefore, we identify crucial parameters for the specific language and determine if achieving reasonable performance compared with the original model is possible using only these significant parameters. We use $\text{Whisper}_{\text{Small}}$ as our backbone model. We employ iterative weight magnitude pruning (IMP), a widely used algorithm in previous LTH literature (Frankle and Carbin, 2018; Renda et al., 2020; Ding et al., 2021), to detect subnetworks. To identify subnetworks, IMP carries out the following three steps: (1) Train an unpruned model to completion on a dataset $\mathcal{D}$; (2) Remove a portion of unimportant weights with the globally smallest magnitudes; (3) Rewind model weights to θ ($\theta = \theta_{pre}$, the weights from a pre-trained model; or $\theta = \theta_t$, the weights from t training step) and fine-tune the subnetworks to converge. Steps (2) and (3) typically require iterative repetition to discover highly competitive winning tickets. In all experiments, we set $s_i\% = (1 - 0.9^i) \times 100\%$, where i is the number of iterations and s_i is the remaining weights after pruning. We conducted three experiments to identify parameters that operate differently for each language in Whisper.

3.2.1 Results

Language-specific Subnetworks We use LTH to determine if we can identify significant parameters for specific languages in the Whisper model. We pruned the model separately for *Korean* and *Malayalam*, low-resource languages in *Commonvoice*. After identifying subnetworks for each language, we conducted zero-shot evaluation on *Korean*. In Table 1, we report our results on CER with $\text{Whisper}_{\text{Small}}$ model. We observe that the model pruned in *Korean* is better than that pruned by *Malayalam* in all subnetworks. Furthermore, the subnetworks exhibit reasonable performance

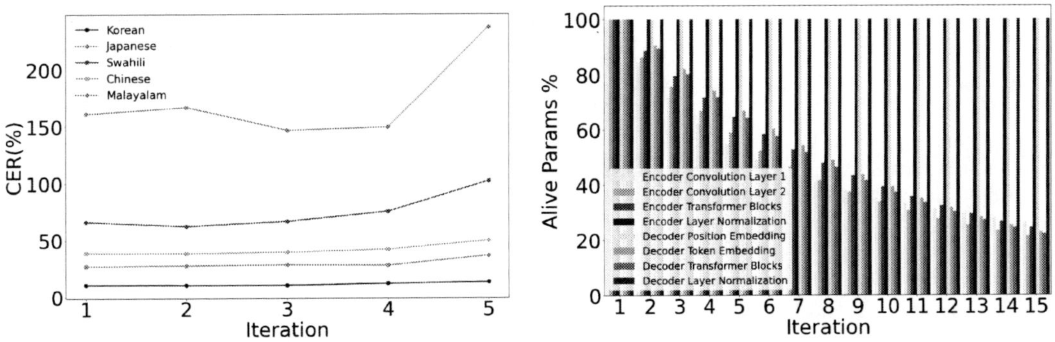

(a) CER curves for each language

(b) Alive parameters percentage bar chart

Figure 3: **(a) CER curves** for each language. We conduct Whisper$_{\text{Small}}$ pruned on *Korean* on the *Commonvoice* dataset. Also, we use IMP to prune the model. **(b) Alive parameters percentage bar chart** per iteration for each model layer. We prune Whisper$_{\text{Small}}$ based on *Korean*.

compared to the unpruned Whisper model. This fact demonstrates that the model pruned in *Korean* has more appropriate parameters for *Korean* data, and we can detect subnetworks for Whisper. In other words, it is evident that there are significant parameters for specific languages in Whisper, and we can identify subnetworks composed of these parameters.

Zero-Shot CER for each Languages Also, in Figure 3(a), we evaluated the zero-shot CER of the model pruned in *Korean* across 5 languages except English, which covers majority of Whisper's pre-training data. We prune the model iteratively at the same ratio to create subnetworks. Then, we calculate each language's zero-shot CER from the subnetworks found at each iteration. As a result, the best CER score is observed in Korean and shows minimal performance drop in all iterations, while other languages exhibit notable performance degradation. These results also mean that essential parameters for specific languages exist within Whisper and can be identified.

Layer-Wise Analysis of Pruning Ratios To gain a more detailed understanding of Whisper pruning, we investigated the pruning ratios for each layer. As shown in Figure 3(b), we divide the model's layers into eight distinct segments, and analyze the pruning ratios of each layer at each iteration. In Figure 3(b), we observe that no pruning occurs in *Encoder Layer Normalization, Decoder Position Embedding,* and *Decoder Layer Normalization*. Furthermore, the trend in the pruned ratio of each layer changes as the iteration progresses. Initially, the encoder convolution layers (i.e., *Encoder Convolution Layer 1* and *Encoder Convolution Layer 2*) are the dominantly pruned layers, while the decoder layers (i.e., *Decoder Token Embedding* and *Decoder Transformer Blocks*) are pruned more significantly as the iteration increases. As a result, we can deduce that subnetworks exist for specific languages, even within the encoder convolution layers responsible for processing audio. Also, we find that the transformer blocks in the decoder layers, which handle text processing, are mainly pruned.

4 Our Method: PEPSI

Upon our findings from above sections, we design and propose PEPSI, a Parameter-Efficient adaptation scheme for the Speech foundational model. We illustrate the overall architecture of our method in Figure 1. As can be seen, our method is composed of three parts. The first phase injects lightweight adapters into the Whisper model for efficient adaptation in the following steps. Next, LTH is conducted to determine the Whisper neurons relevant to a particular language and remove those irrelevant. In the last step, we align the model representation with the distribution of the target language dataset of interest by tuning the adapters injected in the model.

4.1 Injecting Adapters to Whisper

The first part of PEPSI injects a lightweight adapter in the Whisper model for efficient adaptation in the following steps. We adopt LoRA as the adapter architecture as it was shown in Hu et al. (2021) to be the most effective in their works. Whisper follows an encoder-decoder transformer architecture with an audio encoder attached with cross attention to a text decoder. The adapter is injected into the

	KO	ML	JA	SW	ZH-CN	EN
Train	192	509	7,071	34,980	29,383	1,013,968
Test	131	215	4,961	11,271	10,624	16,372

Table 2: Statistics of each language in Commonvoice 13; the abbreviations represent *Korean*, *Malayalam*, *Japanese*, *Swahili*, *Chinese* and *English*, in the respective order.

decoder attention layers following our hypothesis that the text decoder requires further adaptation than the audio encoders for an ASR task. We conduct experiments to verify this hypothesis in the sections to follow.

4.2 Model Pruning

We carry out pruning on the Whisper model parameters to ease the increase in the number of parameters brought by the addition of LoRA. Specifically, LTH is conducted on the Whisper parameters only, without pruning any of the adapter neurons and the Whisper neurons attached to the adapters. This way, the parameters and neurons of Whisper required for connecting with LoRA remains unpruned. The process of pruning follows the previous settings, where we constantly remove unimportant weights every iteration while fine-tuning the model. We prune 50% of Whisper parameters as we figure it is the maximum possible prune percentage to maintain ASR performance on a specific language.

4.3 Tuning LoRA

Through the first and second steps of Adapter Injection and Model Pruning, we obtain a language-specific Whisper model which is able to perform close to the original Whisper without training. Still, the adaptation process on the target language is required to enhance its performance. Hence, we train the pruned model but only the added LoRA adapters for computational efficiency. Low-Rank Adaptation (LoRA) enables training injected intermediate layers within a neural network by optimizing rank decomposition matrices while maintaining the pre-trained Whisper weights in a frozen state—the formulation of adapter in equation 1.

$$output = W(x) + BA(x) \tag{1}$$

where $W(\cdot)$ represents the frozen pre-trained weight, with the weight matrix denoted as $W \in \mathbb{R}^{d\times k}$, matrices $B \in \mathbb{R}^{d\times r}, A \in \mathbb{R}^{r\times k}$, and the rank $r \ll min(d, k)$.

5 Experiments

Setup We conduct experiments to test the effectiveness of our proposed method on 5 low-resourced languages and compare with the high-resourced *English*. We aim to verify 2 objectives in our experiments: 1) To prove our proposed method does indeed bring competitive ASR performances on a specific target language despite the significant reduction in the number of active parameters. 2) To confirm the proposed method eliminates unnecessary neurons for a target language, and the knowledge left in the model is transferable to other datasets of the same language.

Implementation Details Following the prior works of Choi and Park (2022), we evaluate our method on *Commonvoice*, a standard evaluation suite for multilingual ASR models. The detailed statistics of each train/test set is summarized in Table 2. As for the second objective of our experiment, we test the transferability of our pruned model by measuring the ASR performance on a separate dataset with the same language. The model is first pruned with the *Korean* dataset in *Commonvoice*, then adapted to *Clovacall* (Ha et al., 2020) dataset, a Korean speech dataset mainly containing words and phrases from contact centers.

For PEPSI, we use $\text{Whisper}_{\text{Large}}$ as our base model, and prune 50% of its parameters. LoRA is used as the adapter architecture and is added to the attention heads in the text decoder. For the LTH stage, we observe the magnitude change in the Whisper parameters by training the model for 2 epochs with a learning rate of 1e-5. During LoRA adaptation phase, we train the LoRA parameters using the target language set using a learning rate of 1e-3 using the AdamW optimizer.

Baselines We compare the results of PEPSI with the following baselines:

- **Whisper zero-shot**: We compare the ASR performance with zero-shot Whisper, and show the model is not competent to be used as-is for low-resource languages.
- **Whisper Full Fine-tuning**: To test the efficiency of our approach, we compare the number of parameters in comparison to the ASR performance with the standard Whisper FFT.
- **Whisper LoRA**: We compare the number of train/test parameters with the typical LoRA, a widely used PEFT method.

Model	# train param	# test param	KO		ML		JA		SW		ZH-CN		EN	
			CER	WER	CER	WER	CER	WER	CER	WER	CER	WER	CER	WER
whisper zero-shot	-	1.5B	6.71	22.76	102.4	117.8	17.30	96.13	36.02	83.38	25.56	98.70	5.88	11.78
whisper FFT	1.5B	1.5B	**6.12**	**20.54**	**21.67**	**67.78**	**16.88**	**80.52**	**6.72**	**27.53**	**13.56**	**69.33**	**5.78**	**11.45**
whisper LoRA	2.6M	1.5B	6.32	21.33	31.46	76.79	22.36	91.70	11.38	35.46	16.67	73.42	5.81	11.52
whisper LTH	-	0.77B	8.10	30.47	46.89	96.62	30.41	93.44	15.98	38.70	16.12	75.59	6.12	13.22
whisper LTH FT	0.77B	0.77B	7.83	28.67	33.84	84.47	28.38	92.37	14.67	34.51	15.96	83.36	5.99	12.01
OURS	2.6M	0.77B	6.28	21.39	30.96	76.54	18.91	90.31	11.95	35.02	14.03	71.71	5.84	11.52

Table 3: ASR performance comparison of our method (PEPSI) with baselines on each language dataset. We use $\text{Whisper}_{\text{Large}}$ as the base model and prune 50% of its parameters for LTH and PEPSI. The scores are written in %.

- **Whisper LTH**: We apply sole LTH on Whisper using the target language dataset to compare its efficiency with ours. The metric is measured under zero-shot settings after pruning is complete.
- **Whisper LTH FT**: To test the effect of tuning a pruned model, we adapt the Whisper LTH model with the target language dataset.

We observe the effectiveness of each method using the standard CER / WER plus the number of active parameters during training and inference, and the results are summarized in Tables 3 and 4. Note that we set the above methods as baselines as our work is mainly focused on effectively utilizing a multilingual speech foundational model on a specific target language; comparison with monolingual models (Baevski et al., 2020) are beyond the scope of our study.

5.1 Enhanced Parameter Efficiency

Observing the results in Table 3, it is foremost visible that the Whisper model itself exhibits low performance and cannot be utilized as-is for low-resourced languages such as *Malayalam* or *Swahili* while showing supreme performance on the high-resourced *English*. While the FFT scheme on Whisper yields promising results across most datasets, it requires a considerable amount of both training and inference parameters. On the contrary, LoRA achieves error rates almost as low as the FFT paradigm while only requiring the number of parameters corresponding to the adapter itself. Still, it can be observed that LoRA requires more test time parameters than the FFT during inference time. The LTH methods introduced to reduce the test time parameters generally exhibit higher error rates than the abovementioned methods. Our method, PEPSI, mitigates the drawbacks of each work by reducing both train and test time parameters while matching the performance of FFT. As

Model	# train param	# test param	pruned (Y/N)	trained on	CER
whisper zero-shot	-	1.5B	N	-	10.19
whisper FFT	1.5B	1.5B	N	Clovacall	**5.07**
whisper LoRA	2.6M	1.5B	N	Clovacall	6.71
whisper LTH	-	0.77B	Y	-	11.25
whisper LTH FT	0.77B	0.77B	Y	Clovacall	10.75
OURS	2.6M	0.77B	Y	Clovacall	6.29

Table 4: ASR Results on *Clovacall*. For pruned models, the models are pruned on *Commonvoice* Korean then trained on *Clovacall*. The scores are written in %.

can be seen in Table 3, our method achieves error rates lower than the commonly used LoRA for lower-resourced languages, and shows results comparable to FFT for low-resourced languages.

5.2 Transferability on Other Datasets

Aside from the performances on *Commonvoice*, we measure the transferability of models pruned on a general speech dataset to a more specific domain with the same language of interest, such as *Clovacall*. Table 4 shows that the Whisper zero-shot shows high error rates on the *Clovacall* dataset, hinting that the domain knowledge for contact centers is not well-formed within the Whisper model itself. The FFT scheme is able to inject the domain knowledge into the model but at high computational costs. LoRA shows comparable results with low training and high inference costs, sharing the identical takeaways from the above experiment. Unlike the original Whisper model, the model pruned on *Commonvoice Korean* causes higher error rates than the original Whisper model under the same zero-shot settings. Fine-tuning the pruned model does lower the error rates, but only to a slight degree. Our method, PEPSI, while sharing the same two phases of pruning and adapting, lowers the error rates further to match that of FFT but with fewer parameters. The result suggests that the mismatching scale of the large-scale Whisper model and a low-resourced language may cause overfitting. It necessitates a more parameter-efficient training scheme such as LoRA to prevent

		# train param	CER	WER
Encoder	fc1	246K	26.77	59.01
	fc2	246K	25.21	57.40
	attn	98K	27.48	60.62
	fc1+attn	344K	27.01	58.71
	fc2+attn	344K	27.58	61.13
Decoder	fc1	246K	24.53	54.28
	fc2	246K	24.35	53.27
	attn	98K	24.11	53.98
	fc1+attn	344K	24.79	53.37
	fc2+attn	344K	24.27	54.68

Table 5: ASR performance of LoRA injected in each layer. *attn* refers to the attention layers while *fc1* and *fc2* refer to the fully connected layers. The scores are written in %.

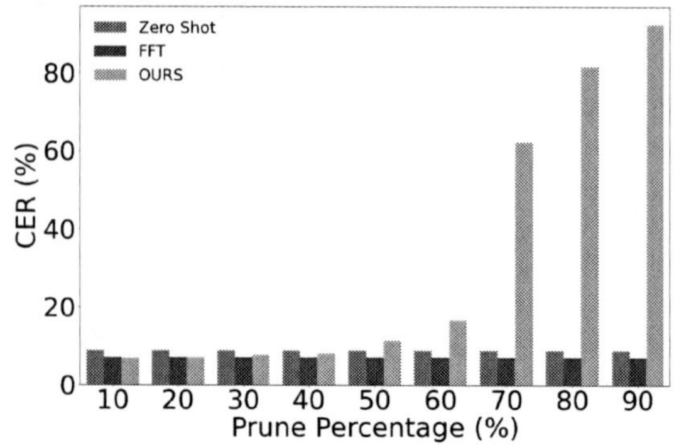

Figure 4: Change in the ASR performance of PEPSI according to the prune percentage.

such phenomena and compression techniques to reduce the model size to match the dataset size.

6 Ablations

6.1 Optimal Injection Point for LoRA

We excavate the optimal positioning approach for integrating the LoRA adapter throughout the Whisper. We assume the adequate adaptation location will differ from the language model to which the original LoRA is applied. In default settings, LoRA is applied to each attention layer in the model. However, we apply the adapters to each attention and MLP layer to discover the optimal injection location. We trained the model on *Commonvoice Korean*. For LoRA parameter settings, we establish the alpha at 64 and the dropout at 0.05. We summarize our results in Table 5.

We find that the components excelling in the encoder differ from those in the decoder. Injecting LoRA in the decoder significantly enhances the STT performance more than the encoder. We presume the underlying reason behind these phenomena is the architectural difference in the Whisper. In this framework, the encoder transforms input audio into a representation vector while the decoder predicts the corresponding text caption.

6.2 Trade-off between Pruned Neurons and Performance

We aim to observe the correlation between the ratio of neurons and performance in the $\text{Whisper}_{\text{Large}}$ model. By measuring the change in zero-shot CER with respect to the increase in prune percentage, we can estimate the ratio of the neurons essential to solving ASR tasks in a particular language. During inference, we apply our proposed PEPSI, which involves applying LTH to the Whisper model alongside LoRA adapters, and we assess its performance using the *Commonvoice Korean*. The prune percentage is gradually incremented from 10 to 90, with a step size of 10. For each prune percentage, we conduct IMP with two epochs to obtain the pruning masks. The masks are applied to the updated weights of the Whisper+LoRA model, and the zero-shot performance is measured on the test set of each language; the results are illustrated in Figure 4.

By analyzing the overall trend between prune percentage and CER, we observe that the Whisper model can maintain its performance until approximately 50% of its neurons/parameters are pruned. We assume that 50% of the parameters are composed of the parameters heavily relevant to the target language, plus those containing the general reasoning ability the model gains from large-scale pretraining, as similarly suggested in Lu et al. (2022).

7 Conclusion

In this paper, we proposed PEPSI, a parameter-efficient adaptation strategy for the speech foundation model in low-resource language, demonstrating competitiveness with high-parameter multilingual models. The method incorporates compact adapter modules into the decoder layers of the pretrained model and then eliminates neurons irrelevant to the target language by LTH-based pruning. For adaptation, only the parameters of the added LoRA are updated for efficient tuning. We exhibit the efficiency of our approach by comparing the ASR error rates with existing Whisper baselines in 5 low-resourced languages. We expect our study to serve as a practical guideline for lightweight tuning with speech foundation models and be applied to various low-resource language research.

Limitations

Our method achieves performance surpassing the commonly used LoRA approach with fewer inference parameters. The results are comparable to the standard FFT but with significantly less computational burden. Although our proposed PEPSI exhibits promising results, several improvement avenues exist. While PEPSI applies LoRA with LTH, future works might utilize other adapter architectures or pruning methodologies. Moreover, enhancements to our PEPSI method might involve integration with other speech foundational models, such as USM (Zhang et al., 2023).

Ethics Statement

We hereby clarify that our work complies with ACL Ethics policy. As potential social harms, our method utilizes a well-pretrained Whisper model; thus, any bias or fairness issues in the original pretrained Whisper model can be carried out during our experiments on ASR. We encourage candidate researchers or any users to thoroughly examine the base model to prevent bias and fairness issues.

References

R. Ardila, M. Branson, K. Davis, M. Henretty, M. Kohler, J. Meyer, R. Morais, L. Saunders, F. M. Tyers, and G. Weber. 2020. Common voice: A massively-multilingual speech corpus. In *Proceedings of the 12th Conference on Language Resources and Evaluation (LREC 2020)*, pages 4211–4215.

Alexei Baevski, Steffen Schneider, and Michael Auli. 2019. vq-wav2vec: Self-supervised learning of discrete speech representations. *arXiv preprint arXiv:1910.05453*.

Alexei Baevski, Yuhao Zhou, Abdelrahman Mohamed, and Michael Auli. 2020. wav2vec 2.0: A framework for self-supervised learning of speech representations. *Advances in neural information processing systems*, 33:12449–12460.

Ankur Bapna and Orhan Firat. 2019. Simple, scalable adaptation for neural machine translation. In *Proceedings of the 2019 Conference on Empirical Methods in Natural Language Processing and the 9th International Joint Conference on Natural Language Processing (EMNLP-IJCNLP)*, pages 1538–1548.

Tianlong Chen, Jonathan Frankle, Shiyu Chang, Sijia Liu, Yang Zhang, Zhangyang Wang, and Michael Carbin. 2020. The lottery ticket hypothesis for pretrained bert networks. *Advances in neural information processing systems*, 33:15834–15846.

Kwanghee Choi and Hyung-Min Park. 2022. Distilling a pretrained language model to a multilingual asr model. *arXiv preprint arXiv:2206.12638*.

Shaojin Ding, Tianlong Chen, and Zhangyang Wang. 2021. Audio lottery: Speech recognition made ultra-lightweight, noise-robust, and transferable. In *International Conference on Learning Representations*.

Xin Dong, Shangyu Chen, and Sinno Pan. 2017. Learning to prune deep neural networks via layer-wise optimal brain surgeon. *Advances in neural information processing systems*, 30.

Jonathan Frankle and Michael Carbin. 2018. The lottery ticket hypothesis: Finding sparse, trainable neural networks. *arXiv preprint arXiv:1803.03635*.

Jonathan Frankle, Gintare Karolina Dziugaite, Daniel Roy, and Michael Carbin. 2020. Linear mode connectivity and the lottery ticket hypothesis. In *International Conference on Machine Learning*, pages 3259–3269. PMLR.

Yuan Gong, Sameer Khurana, Leonid Karlinsky, and James Glass. 2023. Whisper-at: Noise-robust automatic speech recognizers are also strong general audio event taggers. *arXiv preprint arXiv:2307.03183*.

Jung-Woo Ha, Kihyun Nam, Jingu Kang, Sang-Woo Lee, Sohee Yang, Hyunhoon Jung, Hyeji Kim, Eunmi Kim, Soojin Kim, Hyun Ah Kim, et al. 2020. Clovacall: Korean goal-oriented dialog speech corpus for automatic speech recognition of contact centers. *arXiv preprint arXiv:2004.09367*.

Song Han, Jeff Pool, John Tran, and William Dally. 2015. Learning both weights and connections for efficient neural network. *Advances in neural information processing systems*, 28.

Awni Hannun, Carl Case, Jared Casper, Bryan Catanzaro, Greg Diamos, Erich Elsen, Ryan Prenger, Sanjeev Satheesh, Shubho Sengupta, Adam Coates, et al. 2014. Deep speech: Scaling up end-to-end speech recognition. *arXiv preprint arXiv:1412.5567*.

Neil Houlsby, Andrei Giurgiu, Stanislaw Jastrzebski, Bruna Morrone, Quentin De Laroussilhe, Andrea Gesmundo, Mona Attariyan, and Sylvain Gelly. 2019. Parameter-efficient transfer learning for nlp. In *International Conference on Machine Learning*, pages 2790–2799. PMLR.

Brady Houston and Katrin Kirchhoff. 2023. Exploration of language-specific self-attention parameters for multilingual end-to-end speech recognition. In *2022 IEEE Spoken Language Technology Workshop (SLT)*, pages 755–762. IEEE.

Edward J Hu, Phillip Wallis, Zeyuan Allen-Zhu, Yuanzhi Li, Shean Wang, Lu Wang, Weizhu Chen, et al. 2021. Lora: Low-rank adaptation of large language models. In *International Conference on Learning Representations*.

Hengyuan Hu, Rui Peng, Yu-Wing Tai, and Chi-Keung Tang. 2016. Network trimming: A data-driven neuron pruning approach towards efficient deep architectures. *arXiv preprint arXiv:1607.03250*.

Jared Kaplan, Sam McCandlish, Tom Henighan, Tom B Brown, Benjamin Chess, Rewon Child, Scott Gray, Alec Radford, Jeffrey Wu, and Dario Amodei. 2020. Scaling laws for neural language models. *arXiv preprint arXiv:2001.08361*.

Simon Kornblith, Mohammad Norouzi, Honglak Lee, and Geoffrey Hinton. 2019. Similarity of neural network representations revisited. In *International conference on machine learning*, pages 3519–3529. PMLR.

Yann LeCun, John Denker, and Sara Solla. 1989. Optimal brain damage. *Advances in neural information processing systems*, 2.

Xiang Lisa Li and Percy Liang. 2021. Prefix-tuning: Optimizing continuous prompts for generation. In *Proceedings of the 59th Annual Meeting of the Association for Computational Linguistics and the 11th International Joint Conference on Natural Language Processing (Volume 1: Long Papers)*, pages 4582–4597.

Xiao Liu, Yanan Zheng, Zhengxiao Du, Ming Ding, Yujie Qian, Zhilin Yang, and Jie Tang. 2021. Gpt understands, too. *arXiv preprint arXiv:2103.10385*.

Yizhou Lu, Mingkun Huang, Xinghua Qu, Pengfei Wei, and Zejun Ma. 2022. Language adaptive cross-lingual speech representation learning with sparse sharing sub-networks. In *ICASSP 2022-2022 IEEE International Conference on Acoustics, Speech and Signal Processing (ICASSP)*, pages 6882–6886. IEEE.

Zelda Mariet and Suvrit Sra. 2015. Diversity networks: Neural network compression using determinantal point processes. *arXiv preprint arXiv:1511.05077*.

Alec Radford, Jong Wook Kim, Tao Xu, Greg Brockman, Christine McLeavey, and Ilya Sutskever. 2023. Robust speech recognition via large-scale weak supervision. In *International Conference on Machine Learning*, pages 28492–28518. PMLR.

Alex Renda, Jonathan Frankle, and Michael Carbin. 2020. Comparing rewinding and fine-tuning in neural network pruning. *arXiv preprint arXiv:2003.02389*.

Steffen Schneider, Alexei Baevski, Ronan Collobert, and Michael Auli. 2019. wav2vec: Unsupervised pre-training for speech recognition. *arXiv preprint arXiv:1904.05862*.

Hang Shao, Wei Wang, Bei Liu, Xun Gong, Haoyu Wang, and Yanmin Qian. 2023. Whisper-kdq: A lightweight whisper via guided knowledge distillation and quantization for efficient asr. *arXiv preprint arXiv:2305.10788*.

Abhayjeet Singh, Arjun Singh Mehta, Jai Nanavati, Jesuraja Bandekar, Karnalius Basumatary, Sandhya Badiger, Sathvik Udupa, Saurabh Kumar, Prasanta Kumar Ghosh, Priyanka Pai, et al. 2023. Model adaptation for asr in low-resource indian languages. *arXiv preprint arXiv:2307.07948*.

Zirui Wang, Zachary C Lipton, and Yulia Tsvetkov. 2020. On negative interference in multilingual models: Findings and a meta-learning treatment. *arXiv preprint arXiv:2010.03017*.

John Wu, Yonatan Belinkov, Hassan Sajjad, Nadir Durrani, Fahim Dalvi, and James Glass. 2020. Similarity analysis of contextual word representation models. In *Proceedings of the 58th Annual Meeting of the Association for Computational Linguistics*, pages 4638–4655.

Tien-Ju Yang, Yu-Hsin Chen, and Vivienne Sze. 2017. Designing energy-efficient convolutional neural networks using energy-aware pruning. In *Proceedings of the IEEE conference on computer vision and pattern recognition*, pages 5687–5695.

Haonan Yu, Sergey Edunov, Yuandong Tian, and Ari S Morcos. 2019. Playing the lottery with rewards and multiple languages: lottery tickets in rl and nlp. *arXiv preprint arXiv:1906.02768*.

Yu Zhang, Wei Han, James Qin, Yongqiang Wang, Ankur Bapna, Zhehuai Chen, Nanxin Chen, Bo Li, Vera Axelrod, Gary Wang, et al. 2023. Google usm: Scaling automatic speech recognition beyond 100 languages. *arXiv preprint arXiv:2303.01037*.

Multilingual Word Embeddings for Low-Resource Languages using Anchors and a Chain of Related Languages

Viktor Hangya[1,2], **Silvia Severini**[1], **Radoslav Ralev**[3],
Alexander Fraser[1,2] and **Hinrich Schütze**[1,2]
[1]Center for Information and Language Processing, LMU Munich, Germany
[2]Munich Center for Machine Learning,
[3]Technical University of Munich
{hangyav, silvia, fraser}@cis.lmu.de,
radoslav.ralev@tum.de

Abstract

Very low-resource languages, having only a few million tokens worth of data, are not well-supported by multilingual NLP approaches due to poor quality cross-lingual word representations. Recent work showed that good cross-lingual performance can be achieved if a source language is related to the low-resource target language. However, not all language pairs are related. In this paper, we propose to build multilingual word embeddings (MWEs) via a novel language chain-based approach, that incorporates intermediate related languages to bridge the gap between the distant source and target. We build MWEs one language at a time by starting from the resource rich source and sequentially adding each language in the chain till we reach the target. We extend a semi-joint bilingual approach to multiple languages in order to eliminate the main weakness of previous works, i.e., independently trained monolingual embeddings, by anchoring the target language around the multilingual space. We evaluate our method on bilingual lexicon induction for 4 language families, involving 4 very low-resource ($\leq$ 5M tokens) and 4 moderately low-resource ($\leq$ 50M) target languages, showing improved performance in both categories. Additionally, our analysis reveals the importance of good quality embeddings for intermediate languages as well as the importance of leveraging anchor points from all languages in the multilingual space.

1 Introduction

Cross-lingual word representations are shared embedding spaces for two – *Bilingual (BWEs)* – or more languages – *Multilingual Word Embeddings (MWEs)*. They have been shown to be effective for multiple tasks including machine translation (Lample et al., 2018c) and cross-lingual transfer learning (Schuster et al., 2019). They can be created by jointly learning shared embedding spaces (Lample et al., 2018a; Conneau et al., 2020) or via mapping approaches (Artetxe et al., 2018; Schuster et al., 2019). However, their quality degrades when low-resource languages are involved, since they require an adequate amount of monolingual data (Adams et al., 2017), which is especially problematic for languages with just a few millions of tokens (Eder et al., 2021).

Recent work showed that building embeddings jointly by representing common vocabulary items of the source and target languages with a single embedding can improve representations (Wang et al., 2019; Woller et al., 2021). On the other hand, these approaches require the source and target to be related, which in practice means high vocabulary overlap. Since for many distant language pairs this requirement is not satisfied, in this paper, we propose to leverage a chain of intermediate languages to overcome the large language gap. We build MWEs step-by-step, starting from the source language and moving towards the target, incorporating a language that is related to the languages already in the multilingual space in each step. Intermediate languages are selected based on their linguistic proximity to the source and target languages, as well as the availability of large enough datasets.

Since our main targets are languages having just a few million tokens worth of monolingual data, we take static word embeddings (Mikolov et al., 2013a) instead of contextualized representations (Devlin et al., 2019) as the basis of our method, due to the generally larger data requirements of the latter. Additionally, the widely used mapping-based approaches (Mikolov et al., 2013b), including multilingual methods (Kementchedjhieva et al., 2018; Jawanpuria et al., 2019; Chen and Cardie, 2018), require good quality monolingual word embeddings. Thus, to incorporate a single language to the multilingual space in each step we rely on the anchor-based approach of Eder et al. (2021). We refer to this method as ANCHORBWES. It builds the

Proceedings of the The 3rd Workshop on Multi-lingual Representation Learning (MRL), pages 95–105
December 7, 2023

target embeddings and aligns them to the source space in one step using anchor points, thus not only building cross-lingual representations but a better quality target language space as well. We extend this bilingual approach to multiple languages. Instead of aligning the target language to the source in one step, we maintain a multilingual space (initialized by the source language), and adding each intermediate and finally the target language to it sequentially. This way we make sure that the language gap between the two spaces in each step stays minimal.

We evaluate our approach (CHAINMWES) on the Bilingual Lexicon Induction (BLI) task for 4 language families, including 4 very ($\leq$ 5 million tokens) and 4 moderately low-resource ($\leq$ 50 million) languages and show improved performance compared to both bilingual and multilingual mapping based baselines, as well as to the bilingual ANCHORBWES. Additionally, we analyze the importance of intermediate language quality, as well as the role of the number of anchor points during training. In summary, our contributions are the following:

- we propose to strengthen word embeddings of low-resource languages by employing a chain of intermediate related languages in order to reduce the language gap at each alignment step,
- we extend ANCHORBWES of Eder et al. (2021) to multilingual word representations which does not take the distance between the source and target languages into consideration,
- we test our approach on multiple low-resource languages and show improved performance,
- we make our code available for public use.[1]

2 Related Work

Bilingual lexicon induction is the task of inducing word translations from monolingual corpora in two languages (Irvine and Callison-Burch, 2017), which became the de facto task to evaluate the quality of cross-lingual word embeddings. There are two main approaches to obtain MWEs: mapping and joint learning. Mapping approaches aim at computing a transformation matrix to map the embedding space of one language onto the embedding space of the others (Ravi and Knight, 2011; Artetxe et al., 2017; Lample et al., 2018b; Artetxe et al., 2018; Lample et al., 2018a; Artetxe et al., 2019, inter alia). Alternatively, joint learning approaches aim at learning a shared embedding space for two or more languages simultaneously. Luong et al. (2015) learn sentence and word-level alignments jointly and create BWEs by modifying the Skip-gram model. The Skip-gram model is also used by Vulic and Moens (2015) who train it on a pseudo-bilingual corpus obtained by merging two aligned documents. Artetxe and Schwenk (2019) use a large parallel corpus to train a bidirectional LSTM and jointly learn representations for many languages. Most recently, transformer based large LMs are trained jointly on multiple languages using a shared subword vocabulary to obtain contextualized cross-lingual representations (Devlin et al., 2019; Conneau et al., 2020). However, large LMs require more training data than static word embeddings, thus we focus on the latter in our work.

Ruder et al. (2019) provided a survey paper on cross-lingual word embedding models and identified three sub-categories within static word-level alignment models: mapping-based approaches, pseudo-multilingual corpus-based approaches and joint methods, highlighting their advantages and disadvantages. To combine the advantages of mapping and joint approaches Wang et al. (2019) proposed to first apply joint training followed by a mapping step on overshared words, such as false friends. Similarly, a hybrid approach was introduced in (Woller et al., 2021) for 3 languages, which first applies joint training on two related languages which is then mapped to the distant third language. A semi-joint approach was introduced in (Ormazabal et al., 2021) and (Eder et al., 2021), which using a fixed pre-trained monolingual space of the source language trains the target space from scratch by aligning embeddings close to given source anchor points. We utilize (Eder et al., 2021) in our work, since it is evaluated on very low-resource languages which is the main interest of our work.

Most work on cross-lingual word embeddings is English-centric. Anastasopoulos and Neubig (2019) found that the choice of hub language to which others are aligned to can significantly affect the final performance. Other methods leveraged multiple languages to build MWEs (Kementched-

[1]https://cistern.cis.lmu.de/anchor-embeddings

jhieva et al., 2018; Chen and Cardie, 2018; Jawanpuria et al., 2019), showing that some languages can help each other to achieve improved performance compared to bilingual systems. However, these approaches rely on pre-trained monolingual embeddings, which could be difficult to train in limited resource scenarios. In our work we also leverage multiple languages, but mitigate the issue of poor quality monolingual embeddings.

Søgaard et al. (2018) showed that embedding spaces do not tend to be isomorphic in case of distant or low-resource language pairs, making the task of aligning monolingual word embeddings harder than previously assumed. Similarly, Patra et al. (2019) empirically show that etymologically distant language pairs are hard to align using mapping approaches. A non-linear transformation is proposed in (Mohiuddin et al., 2020), which does not assume isomorphism between language pairs, and improved performance on moderately low-resource languages. However, Michel et al. (2020) show that for a very low-resource language such as Hiligaynon, which has around 300K tokens worth of available data, good quality monolingual word embeddings cannot be trained, meaning that they can neither be aligned with other languages. Eder et al. (2021) found that mapping approaches on languages under 10M tokens achieve under 10% P@1 score when BLI is performed. In our work, we focus on such low-resource languages and propose to combine the advantages of related languages in multilingual spaces and hybrid alignment approaches.

3 Method

The goal of our approach is to reduce the distance between two languages which are being aligned at a time. Thus instead of directly aligning the source and target languages we incorporate a chain of intermediate related languages in order for a reduced distance. Our approach starts from the source language as the initial multilingual space and iteratively adds the languages in the chain till it reaches the target language. We build upon the bilingual ANCHORBWES algorithm presented in (Eder et al., 2021) by extending it to multilingual setting. First, we discuss the ANCHORBWES approach, followed by our proposed intermediate language-based CHAINMWES method.

3.1 ANCHORBWES

The anchor-based method assumes that the source language is high-resource, thus starts by training source monolingual word embeddings with a traditional static word embedding approach, more precisely *word2vec* (Mikolov et al., 2013a). Using this vector space it trains an embedding space for the low-resource target language by aligning them at the same time, this way the properties of the good quality source space, such as similar embeddings for words with similar meaning, is transferred to the target space. Given a seed dictionary defining word translation pairs, the source side of the pairs are defined as the anchor points. Instead of randomly initializing all target language words at the beginning of the training process, the method initializes target words in the seed dictionary using their related anchor points. The rest of the training process follows the unchanged algorithm of either CBOW or Skip-gram on the target language corpus. This approach significantly outperforms previous methods in low-resource bilingual settings, as demonstrated by strong results on both simulated low-resource language pairs (English-German) and true low-resource language pairs (English-Hiligaynon). Additionally, Eder et al. (2021) shows that not only the cross-lingual performance is improved, but the monolingual space is of better quality compared when the target space is trained independently of the source language.

3.2 CHAINMWES

We extend ANCHORBWES by first defining a chain of languages $C = [c_1, c_2, ..., c_n]$, starting from the high-resource source language (c_1) and ending at the low-resource target language (c_n), including intermediate languages that are related to the preceding and following nodes. As described in Section 4, we define chains in which the lower-resource languages are of the same language family. The intuition is to interleave the source and target with languages that are similar in terms of linguistic properties. After selecting the intermediate languages, our method comprises five steps as depicted in Figure 1:

1. As the first step ($i = 1$), we construct the initial monolingual embedding space (E_1) for the source language (c_1) using its monolingual corpus (D_1), by training a Word2Vec (Mikolov et al., 2013a) model. We consider this space as the initial multilingual space

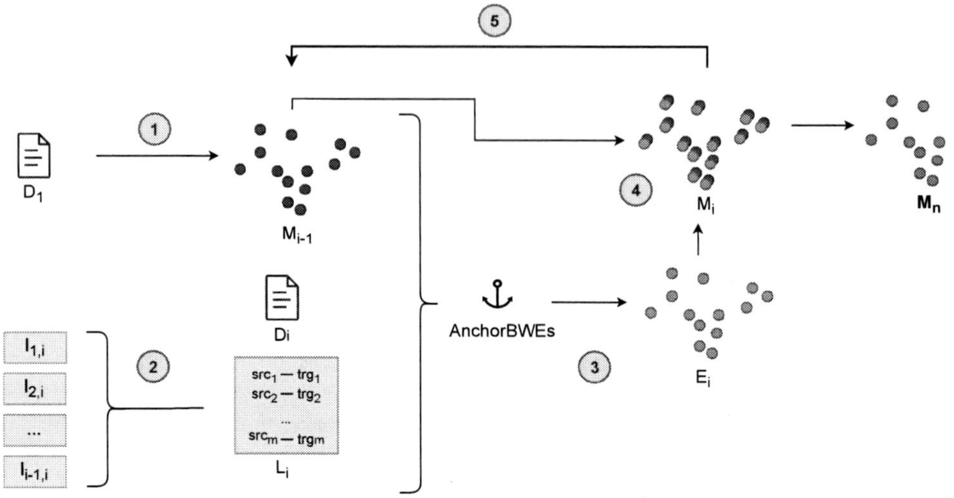

Figure 1: Visual depiction of our CHAINMWEs method. The resulting embedding (M_n in green) is multilingual involving all languages in the chain.

($M_1 := E_1$) which we extend in the following steps.

2. In the next step ($i = i + 1$), we collect the seed lexicon (L_i) for training embeddings for the next language in the chain (c_i) by concatenating the seed lexicons of all the languages before c_i in the chain paired with c_i. More precisely:

$$L_i = \bigcup_{k=1}^{i-1} l_{k,i}$$

where $l_{k,i}$ is the seed lexicon between languages k and i. Since Eder et al. (2021) showed that ANCHORBWEs performs better as the number of available anchor points increase, our goal is to take all available anchor points already in M_{i-1}.

3. Apply ANCHORBWEs using M_{i-1} as the source embedding space, D_i as the training corpus and L_i as the anchors to build embeddings (E_i) for c_i.

4. Since ANCHORBWEs builds embeddings for c_i which are aligned with the maintained multilingual space, we simply concatenate them $M_i = M_{i-1} \cup E_i$.

5. Goto step 2 until the target language is reached.

By strategically integrating intermediate languages, we enrich the quality of the multilingual space by making sure that the distance between two languages at any alignment step is minimal. Our experiments show that without the intermediate languages the quality of the embeddings built by ANCHORBWEs is negatively affected by the large gap between the source and target.

4 Experimental Setup

In this section, we describe the experimental setup, including the selection of languages, datasets, and model parameters used in our study.

4.1 Data

We select four language families of different geographic locations for evaluation. Figure 2 depicts the language similarities in 2D using *lang2vec* language embeddings based on their syntactic features (Malaviya et al., 2017). We discuss their relevance on the final results in Section 5. Although, we selected low-resource target and intermediate languages based on language families, we stepped over their boundaries in order to have intermediate languages related to the source language as well by considering the influence some languages had on others, e.g., during the colonial era. Our source language is English in each setup, and sort the intermediate languages based on their monolingual corpora sizes. We present the exact chains of these languages in section 5.

Austronesian We select two languages spoken in the Philippines: Tagalog as moderately and Hiligaynon as very low-resource target languages, with Indonesian and Spanish as the intermediates. Spanish being an Indo-European language is related to English. Additionally, due to colonization, it influenced the selected Austronesian languages to a varying degree. Furthermore, Indonesian, Tagalog and Hiligaynon show similarities, especially the two languages of the Philippines, due to their close proximity.

Turkic languages using the Cyrillic script. We take Kazakh as moderately, and Chuvash and Yakut as very low-resource languages. Since they use the Cyrillic alphabet and mostly spoken in Russia, we use Russian as the intermediate language. Due to Russian being high-resource, it can be well aligned with English.

Scandinavian We select Icelandic and Faroese as two very low-resource languages, with Norwegian and Swedish as the intermediates that are related to both of them and to English.

Atlantic-Congo Finally, we select Swahili as a moderately low-resource language, which has a high number of loanwords from Portuguese and German which we take as the intermediate languages. We note that we experimented with the very low-resource Zulu and Xhosa languages as well, however due to difficulties acquiring good quality lexicons for training and evaluation, we achieved near zero performance, thus we do not present them in this paper.

The embeddings were trained on Wikipedia dumps for all languages except Hiligaynon, which was trained on the corpus used in (Michel et al., 2020) due to comparison reasons. Hiligaynon is extremely low-resource, having 345K tokens in its monolingual corpus. Corpus sizes for each language are presented in Table 1. Bilingual dictionaries for training and testing are taken from the Wiktionary based resource released in (Izbicki, 2022). As mentioned in the previous section, at each iteration of our approach we take training dictionaries between the current language and all languages which are already in the multilingual vector space. Since, Izbicki (2022) only release resources for English paired with various target languages, we build dictionaries for the other language pairs through

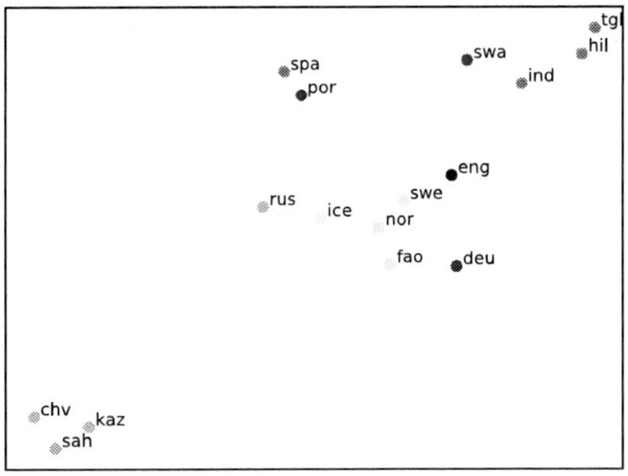

Figure 2: Visualization of language embeddings using *lang2vec* syntax features. Colors indicate different language families: Austronesian in turquoise, Turkic in green, Scandinavian in yellow and Atlantic-Congo in blue.

pivoting, more precisely:

$$l_{k,i} = \{(trg_{e,k}, trg_{e,i}) \mid (src_{e,k}, trg_{e,k}, src_{e,i}, trg_{e,i}) \in l_{e,k} \times l_{e,i}, src_{e,i} = src_{e,k}\}$$

where $l_{e,x}$ is a dictionary between English (e) and an arbitrary language (x), while $src_{x,y}$ and $trg_{x,y}$ is a source (x) and target (y) language translation pair. Number of dictionary entries for each language pair is presented in Table 2.

4.2 Baselines and Model Parameters

We compare our approach to the mapping-based bilingual *VecMap* (Artetxe et al., 2018) and multilingual *UMWE* (Chen and Cardie, 2018) approaches. Additionally, we run ANCHORBWES (Eder et al., 2021) as our joint alignment baseline.

We trained word2vec embeddings (Mikolov et al., 2013a) with a maximum vocabulary size of 200 000 in every setup, i.e., for the mapping-based baselines as well as in ANCHORBWES and CHAINMWES. The training was performed using standard hyperparameters included in the Gensim Word2Vec package (Řehůřek and Sojka, 2010): context window of 5, dimensionality of 300 and for 5 epochs, with the exception that we used minimum word frequency of 3 due to the small corpora for the target languages. Additionally, since Eder et al. (2021) showed that CBOW outperforms SG in ANCHORBWES, we used the former in our experiments.

	Language	ISO	# tokens (M)
intermediate	English	eng	3 044
	German	deu	1 124
	Spanish	spa	836
	Russian	rus	717
	Portuguese	por	377
	Swedish	swe	252
	Indonesian	ind	128
	Norwegian	nor	127
moderate	Kazakh	kaz	32
	Tagalog	tgl	11
	Icelandic	ice	10
	Swahili	swa	9
very-low	Chuvash	chv	4
	Yakut	sah	3
	Faroese	fao	2
	Hiligaynon	hil	0.35

Table 1: Selected intermediate as well as moderately and very low-resource languages. Monolingual corpora sizes are shown in millions.

lang.	train	test	lang.	train
en-de	65 120	-	es-id	19 952
en-es	88 114	-	es-tl	26 088
en-ru	67 397	-	es-hil	4 661
en-pt	53 336	-	ru-kk	21 147
en-sv	25 214	-	ru-cv	1 212
en-id	9 868	-	ru-sah	6 913
en-no	18 916	-	pt-sw	13 197
en-kk	8 990	2 358	sv-no	15 843
en-tl	15 242	2 597	sv-is	13 749
en-is	17 004	2 568	sv-fo	6 425
en-sw	5 203	2 132	id-tl	6 089
en-cv	170	823	id-hil	1 575
en-sah	1 202	2 065	no-is	10 759
en-fo	4 505	1 786	no-fo	4 917
en-hil	1 132	200	kk-cv	160
de-pt	44 791	-	kk-sah	1 000
de-sv	34 659	-	tl-hil	1 683
de-sw	14 818	-	is-fo	5 587

Table 2: Number of unique words in the train and test dictionaries of the used language pairs.

We use the MUSE evaluation tool (Lample et al., 2018b) to report precision at 1, 5, and 10, using the nearest neighbor search. For the mapping based approaches we leverage the CSLS similarity score as it was shown to perform better by handling the hubness problem (Lample et al., 2018b). However, similarly to (Woller et al., 2021) we found that jointly trained embeddings do not benefit from the CSLS method, thus we use simple cosine similarity (NN) based search for both ANCHORBWEs and CHAINMWEs.

5 Results

We present our results in Table 3 split into the moderately and very low-resource language groups and sorted based on the size of available monolingual data for each target language (Table 1). Overall, the results show the difficulties of building cross-lingual word embeddings for the selected target languages, since the performance is much lower compared to high resource languages in general, which for example is around 50% P@1 for English-German on the Wiktionary evaluation set (Izbicki, 2022). Comparing the multilingual UMWE approach to the bilingual VecMap the results support the use of related languages, since they improve the performance on most source-target language pairs. However, this is most apparent on the moderately low-resource languages. The results on the very low-resource languages are very poor for the mapping-based approaches, which as discussed depend on the quality of pre-trained monolingual embeddings. In contrast, the semi-joint anchor-based approaches can significantly improve the embedding quality showing their superiority in the very low-resource setups.

Our proposed CHAINMWEs method outperforms mapping-based approaches on 7 out of 8 target languages, and ANCHORBWEs on 6 target languages, which is most apparent when retrieving more than one translation candidate (P@5 and P@10). Interestingly when looking at P@1, the systems are close to each other, indicating that our method improves the general neighborhood relations of the embedding space instead of just improving the embeddings of a few individual words. This is further supported in the case of Kazakh and Icelandic where UMWE outperforms CHAINMWEs in terms of P@1, however it performs lower when a larger neighborhood is leveraged for the translation. This property is caused by the combination of the semi-joint anchor-based training, instead of relying on independently trained monolingual spaces, and the smaller distances between aligned languages.

When comparing moderately and very low-resource languages, we found similar trends in the two groups. In both cases CHAINMWEs outperforms ANCHORBWEs on 3 out of 4 languages, however in case of Hiligaynon, which has less than 1 million tokens, the results are mixed, i.e., ANCHORBWEs tends to perform better when the smaller neighborhood of P@5 is considered, but it is the opposite when P@10 is measured.

	Method	Intermediate	P@1	P@5	P@10
		Moderately low-resource			
Kazakh	VecMap	-	12.37	23.06	29.42
	UMWE	rus	**14.58**	25.18	29.95
	ANCHORBWEs	-	12.79	24.51	31.22
	CHAINMWEs	rus	14.37	**26.90**	**33.16**
Tagalog	VecMap	-	7.63	14.94	17.76
	UMWE	esp - ind	15.59	24.69	29.08
	ANCHORBWEs	-	15.38	26.57	32.01
	CHAINMWEs	esp - ind	**15.90**	**28.66**	**33.79**
Icelandic	VecMap	-	4.48	9.26	12.68
	UMWE	swe - nor	**12.35**	18.23	21.02
	ANCHORBWEs	-	8.77	17.94	21.67
	CHAINMWEs	swe - nor	8.17	**18.75**	**23.19**
Swahili	VecMap	-	2.29	7.08	10.68
	UMWE	deu - por	**13.38**	**24.05**	**28.07**
	ANCHORBWEs	-	10.23	21.44	26.22
	CHAINMWEs	deu - por	10.99	20.78	25.90
		Very low-resource			
Chuvash	VecMap	-	0.00	0.00	0.00
	UMWE	rus	0.00	0.30	0.30
	ANCHORBWEs	-	**0.31**	0.61	1.53
	CHAINMWEs	rus	**0.31**	**0.92**	**2.75**
Yakut	VecMap	-	0.00	0.25	0.38
	UMWE	rus	0.76	1.78	2.42
	ANCHORBWEs	-	**2.92**	**7.49**	**9.90**
	CHAINMWEs	rus	2.03	6.98	9.14
Faroese	VecMap	-	0.00	0.51	0.63
	UMWE	swe - nor	1.01	3.42	3.93
	ANCHORBWEs	-	4.09	9.20	12.26
	CHAINMWEs	swe - nor	**4.21**	**9.96**	**13.67**
Hiligaynon	VecMap	-	0.00	0.00	0.00
	UMWE	esp - ind	0.00	0.00	0.00
	ANCHORBWEs	-	**5.08**	**7.63**	8.47
	CHAINMWEs	esp - ind	**5.08**	6.78	**10.17**

Table 3: Precision at $k \in \{1, 5, 10\}$ values for the target languages paired with English as the source in each case. The *Intermediate* column shows the languages in between the source and target (e.g., line 2 shows the chain *English→Russian→Kazakh*

Furthermore, UMWE tends to be more competitive with ANCHORBWEs on the moderately low-resource languages, e.g., it performs better in case of Kazakh, while it does not improve over CHAINMWEs. Overall however, we found no strong correlation between the available monolingual resources for a given language and on which target language CHAINMWEs achieved the best results, since the two cases where it did not improve over the baselines are the 3rd (Yakut) and 5th (Swahili) lowest resource languages. Looking at the visualization of language embeddings in Figure 2, the negative results on Swahili can be explained by the relatively large distance between its two intermediate pairs. Although Swahili has a large number of German and Portuguese loan words, the syntactic properties of the languages seem to be too different. Similarly, Yakut (sah) is the furthest away from Russian which could explain our negative results.

	Method	Inter.	P@1	P@5	P@10
sah	CHAINMWEs	rus	2.03	6.98	9.14
	CHAINMWEs	rus - kaz	1.78	5.58	8.12
fao	CHAINMWEs	swe - nor	4.21	9.96	13.67
	CHAINMWEs	swe - nor - ice	3.83	7.15	8.81
hil	CHAINMWEs	esp - ind	5.08	6.78	10.17
	CHAINMWEs	esp - ind - tgl	5.08	6.78	7.63

Table 4: Experiments on adding related moderately low-resource languages to the language chains of very low-resource languages.

5.1 Adding Moderate Resource Languages

Since some moderately low-resource languages are related to the very low-resource ones (Kazakh to Yakut[2], Icelandic to Faroese and Tagalog to Hiligaynon), we add them to the language chain in the experiments presented in Table 4. The results show, that although these languages are closely related, they do not contribute positively to the quality of the resulting MWEs. These results indicate, that the languages involved in the language-chains as intermediate steps should have good quality embeddings (the BLI performance P@5 for the Russian, Swedish, Norwegian and Spanish range between 45% and 65%), thus embedding quality is more important than language closeness. Additionally, Figure 2 shows that Tagalog is less similar to Indonesian and Spanish than to Hiligaynon, and Icelandic is less similar to Faroese than to Norwegian or Swedish.

5.2 Ablation Study

An advantage of the sequential nature of our approach is that as we add more languages to the multilingual space step-by-step, the number of potential anchor points for aligning the language next in line increases. We exploit this by accumulating all word translation pairs from the dictionaries between all languages already in the multilingual space and the currently trained language (Step 2). Although this requires dictionaries between all language pairs, we mitigated this requirement by pivoting through English. In Table 5 we present an ablation study, where we turn dictionary accumulation off, by using dictionaries only between the trained language and its preceding neighbor. The results show that this has a sizable impact on the performance. Although there are a few cases where P@1 is marginally improved (Icelandic, Swahili, Chuvash and Yakut), both P@5 and P@10 are decreased in most cases even where P@1 is improved except Chuvash. The least impacted by the accumulated dictionaries are Turkic languages which indicates their strong relation to Russian and distance from English which could stem from their different scripts. Overall, these findings align with the results of (Eder et al., 2021), who showed that the embedding quality improves as more dictionary entries are available.

[2] Kazakh is also related to Chuvash which we omitted in these experiments due to low results on Chuvash in general.

	Method	Inter.	P@1	P@5	P@10
	Moderately low-resource				
kaz	CHAINMWEs	rus	14.37	26.90	33.16
	CHAINMWEs*	rus	13.67	26.19	31.22
tgl	CHAINMWEs	esp - ind	15.90	28.66	33.79
	CHAINMWEs*	esp - ind	13.28	23.43	28.66
ice	CHAINMWEs	swe - nor	8.17	18.75	23.19
	CHAINMWEs*	swe - nor	8.27	15.42	19.96
swa	CHAINMWEs	deu - por	10.99	20.78	25.90
	CHAINMWEs*	deu - por	11.21	20.67	24.92
	Very low-resource				
chv	CHAINMWEs	rus	0.31	0.92	2.75
	CHAINMWEs*	rus	0.61	1.53	3.67
sah	CHAINMWEs	rus	2.03	6.98	9.14
	CHAINMWEs*	rus	2.28	6.85	9.01
fao	CHAINMWEs	swe - nor	4.21	9.96	13.67
	CHAINMWEs*	swe - nor	3.96	8.56	12.52
hil	CHAINMWEs	esp - ind	5.08	6.78	10.17
	CHAINMWEs*	esp - ind	4.24	5.93	8.47

Table 5: Results of the ablation experiments, where we turn training dictionary accumulation off in CHAINMWEs*, by using only the dictionary between a given language and its preceding neighbor.

6 Conclusion

In this paper we proposed CHAINMWEs, a novel method for enhancing multilingual embeddings of low-resource languages by incorporating intermediate languages to bridge the gap between distant source and target languages. Our approach extends ANCHORBWEs, the bilingual approach of Eder et al. (2021) to MWEs by employing chains of related languages. We evaluate CHAINMWEs on 4 language families involving 4 moderately and 4 very low-resource languages using bilingual lexicon induction. Our results demonstrate the effectiveness of our method showing improvements on 6 out of 8 target languages compared to both bilingual and multilingual mapping-based, and the ANCHORBWEs baselines. Additionally, we show the importance of involving only those intermediate languages for which building good quality embeddings is possible.

Limitations

One limitation of our work is the manual selection of intermediate languages. Although, the selection and ordering of languages in the chains was straightforward based on language family information, such as Glottolog (Nordhoff and Hammarström, 2011), and available data size, it could be possible that other languages which we did not consider in our experiments are also helpful in improving the quality of MWEs. Additionally, we did not consider all possible ordering of intermediate languages, such as the order of English→Norwegian→Swedish→Faroese instead of English→Swedish→Norwegian→Faroese, in order to save resources. Thus, a wider range of chains could uncover further improvements.

Acknowledgements

We thank the anonymous reviewers for their helpful feedback and the Cambridge LMU Strategic Partnership for funding for this project.[3] The work was also funded by the European Research Council (ERC; grant agreements No. 740516 and No. 640550) and by the German Research Foundation (DFG; grant FR 2829/4-1).

References

Oliver Adams, Adam Makarucha, Graham Neubig, Steven Bird, and Trevor Cohn. 2017. Cross-lingual word embeddings for low-resource language modeling. In *Proceedings of the 15th Conference of the European Chapter of the Association for Computational Linguistics: Volume 1, Long Papers*, pages 937–947, Valencia, Spain. Association for Computational Linguistics.

Antonios Anastasopoulos and Graham Neubig. 2019. Should All Cross-Lingual Embeddings Speak English? In *Proceedings of the 58th Annual Meeting of the Association for Computational Linguistics*, pages 8658–8679.

Mikel Artetxe, Gorka Labaka, and Eneko Agirre. 2017. Learning bilingual word embeddings with (almost) no bilingual data. In *Proceedings of the 55th Annual Meeting of the Association for Computational Linguistics (Volume 1: Long Papers)*, pages 451–462, Vancouver, Canada. Association for Computational Linguistics.

[3]https://www.cambridge.uni-muenchen.de

Mikel Artetxe, Gorka Labaka, and Eneko Agirre. 2018. A robust self-learning method for fully unsupervised cross-lingual mappings of word embeddings. In *Proceedings of the 56th Annual Meeting of the Association for Computational Linguistics (Volume 1: Long Papers)*, pages 789–798, Melbourne, Australia. Association for Computational Linguistics.

Mikel Artetxe, Gorka Labaka, and Eneko Agirre. 2019. Bilingual lexicon induction through unsupervised machine translation. In *Proceedings of the 57th Annual Meeting of the Association for Computational Linguistics*, pages 5002–5007, Florence, Italy. Association for Computational Linguistics.

Mikel Artetxe and Holger Schwenk. 2019. Massively multilingual sentence embeddings for zero-shot cross-lingual transfer and beyond. *Transactions of the Association for Computational Linguistics*, 7:597–610.

Xilun Chen and Claire Cardie. 2018. Unsupervised multilingual word embeddings. In *Proceedings of the 2018 Conference on Empirical Methods in Natural Language Processing*, pages 261–270, Brussels, Belgium. Association for Computational Linguistics.

Alexis Conneau, Kartikay Khandelwal, Naman Goyal, Vishrav Chaudhary, Guillaume Wenzek, Francisco Guzmán, Edouard Grave, Myle Ott, Luke Zettlemoyer, and Veselin Stoyanov. 2020. Unsupervised cross-lingual representation learning at scale. In *Proceedings of the 58th Annual Meeting of the Association for Computational Linguistics*, pages 8440–8451.

Jacob Devlin, Ming-Wei Chang, Kenton Lee, and Kristina Toutanova. 2019. BERT: Pre-training of deep bidirectional transformers for language understanding. In *Proceedings of the 2019 Conference of the North American Chapter of the Association for Computational Linguistics: Human Language Technologies, Volume 1 (Long and Short Papers)*, pages 4171–4186.

Tobias Eder, Viktor Hangya, and Alexander Fraser. 2021. Anchor-based bilingual word embeddings for low-resource languages. In *Proceedings of the 59th Annual Meeting of the Association for Computational Linguistics and the 11th International Joint Conference on Natural Language Processing (Volume 2: Short Papers)*, pages 227–232.

Ann Irvine and Chris Callison-Burch. 2017. A comprehensive analysis of bilingual lexicon induction. *Computational Linguistics*, 43(2):273–310.

Mike Izbicki. 2022. Aligning word vectors on low-resource languages with wiktionary. In *Proceedings of the Fifth Workshop on Technologies for Machine Translation of Low-Resource Languages (LoResMT 2022)*, pages 107–117.

Pratik Jawanpuria, Arjun Balgovind, Anoop Kunchukuttan, and Bamdev Mishra. 2019. Learning multilingual word embeddings in latent metric space: a geometric approach. *Transaction of the Association for Computational Linguistics (TACL)*, 7:107–120.

Yova Kementchedjhieva, Sebastian Ruder, Ryan Cotterell, and Anders Søgaard. 2018. Generalizing Procrustes analysis for better bilingual dictionary induction. In *Proceedings of the 22nd Conference on Computational Natural Language Learning*, pages 211–220, Brussels, Belgium. Association for Computational Linguistics.

Guillaume Lample, Alexis Conneau, Ludovic Denoyer, and Marc'Aurelio Ranzato. 2018a. Unsupervised machine translation using monolingual corpora only. In *International Conference on Learning Representations*.

Guillaume Lample, Alexis Conneau, Marc'Aurelio Ranzato, Ludovic Denoyer, and Hervé Jégou. 2018b. Word translation without parallel data. In *International Conference on Learning Representations*.

Guillaume Lample, Myle Ott, Alexis Conneau, Ludovic Denoyer, and Marc'Aurelio Ranzato. 2018c. Phrase-based & neural unsupervised machine translation. In *Proceedings of the 2018 Conference on Empirical Methods in Natural Language Processing*, pages 5039–5049, Brussels, Belgium. Association for Computational Linguistics.

Minh-Thang Luong, Hieu Pham, and Christopher D Manning. 2015. Bilingual word representations with monolingual quality in mind. In *Proceedings of the 1st workshop on vector space modeling for natural language processing*, pages 151–159.

Chaitanya Malaviya, Graham Neubig, and Patrick Littell. 2017. Learning language representations for typology prediction. In *Proceedings of the 2017 Conference on Empirical Methods in Natural Language Processing*, pages 2529–2535.

Leah Michel, Viktor Hangya, and Alexander Fraser. 2020. Exploring bilingual word embeddings for Hiligaynon, a low-resource language. In *Proceedings of the Twelfth Language Resources and Evaluation Conference*, pages 2573–2580, Marseille, France. European Language Resources Association.

Tomas Mikolov, Kai Chen, Greg Corrado, and Jeffrey Dean. 2013a. Efficient estimation of word representations in vector space.

Tomas Mikolov, Quoc V. Le, and Ilya Sutskever. 2013b. Exploiting similarities among languages for machine translation.

Tasnim Mohiuddin, M Saiful Bari, and Shafiq Joty. 2020. Lnmap: Departures from isomorphic assumption in bilingual lexicon induction through non-linear mapping in latent space. In *Proceedings of the 2020 Conference on Empirical Methods in Natural Language Processing (EMNLP)*, pages 2712–2723.

Sebastian Nordhoff and Harald Hammarström. 2011. Glottolog/langdoc: Defining dialects, languages, and language families as collections of resources. In *First International Workshop on Linked Science 2011-In conjunction with the International Semantic Web Conference (ISWC 2011)*.

Aitor Ormazabal, Mikel Artetxe, Aitor Soroa, Gorka Labaka, and Eneko Agirre. 2021. Beyond offline mapping: Learning cross-lingual word embeddings through context anchoring. In *Proceedings of the 59th Annual Meeting of the Association for Computational Linguistics and the 11th International Joint Conference on Natural Language Processing (Volume 1: Long Papers)*, pages 6479–6489, Online. Association for Computational Linguistics.

Barun Patra, Joel Ruben Antony Moniz, Sarthak Garg, Matthew R. Gormley, and Graham Neubig. 2019. Bilingual lexicon induction with semi-supervision in non-isometric embedding spaces. In *Proceedings of the 57th Annual Meeting of the Association for Computational Linguistics*, pages 184–193.

Sujith Ravi and Kevin Knight. 2011. Deciphering foreign language. In *Proceedings of the 49th Annual Meeting of the Association for Computational Linguistics: Human Language Technologies*, pages 12–21, Portland, Oregon, USA. Association for Computational Linguistics.

Radim Řehůřek and Petr Sojka. 2010. Software Framework for Topic Modelling with Large Corpora. In *Proceedings of the LREC 2010 Workshop on New Challenges for NLP Frameworks*, pages 45–50, Valletta, Malta. ELRA. `http://is.muni.cz/publication/884893/en`.

Sebastian Ruder, Ivan Vulić, and Anders Søgaard. 2019. A survey of cross-lingual word embedding models. *Journal of Artificial Intelligence Research*, 65:569–631.

Tal Schuster, Ori Ram, Regina Barzilay, and Amir Globerson. 2019. Cross-lingual alignment of contextual word embeddings, with applications to zero-shot dependency parsing. In *Proceedings of the 2019 Conference of the North American Chapter of the Association for Computational Linguistics: Human Language Technologies, Volume 1 (Long and Short Papers)*, pages 1599–1613, Minneapolis, Minnesota. Association for Computational Linguistics.

Anders Søgaard, Sebastian Ruder, and Ivan Vulić. 2018. On the limitations of unsupervised bilingual dictionary induction. In *Proceedings of the 56th Annual Meeting of the Association for Computational Linguistics (Volume 1: Long Papers)*, pages 778–788, Melbourne, Australia. Association for Computational Linguistics.

Ivan Vulic and Marie-Francine Moens. 2015. Bilingual word embeddings from non-parallel document-aligned data applied to bilingual lexicon induction.

In *Proceedings of the 53rd Annual Meeting of the Association for Computational Linguistics (ACL 2015)*, volume 2, pages 719–725. ACL; East Stroudsburg, PA.

Zirui Wang, Jiateng Xie, Ruochen Xu, Yiming Yang, Graham Neubig, and Jaime G Carbonell. 2019. Cross-lingual alignment vs joint training: A comparative study and a simple unified framework. In *International Conference on Learning Representations*.

Lisa Woller, Viktor Hangya, and Alexander Fraser. 2021. Do not neglect related languages: The case of low-resource Occitan cross-lingual word embeddings. In *Proceedings of the 1st Workshop on Multilingual Representation Learning*, pages 41–50, Punta Cana, Dominican Republic. Association for Computational Linguistics.

TalaMT: Multilingual Machine Translation for Cabécar-Bribri-Spanish

Alex Jones
Dartmouth College
alexander.g.jones.23@dartmouth.edu

Rolando Coto-Solano
Dartmouth College
Department of Linguistics
rolando.a.coto.solano@dartmouth.edu

Guillermo González Campos
University of Costa Rica, Atlantic Branch, Turrialba
guillermo.gonzalezcampos@ucr.ac.cr

Abstract

In this paper, we experiment with building multilingual neural machine translation models to translate the extremely under-resourced Indigenous Costa Rican languages Cabécar and Bribri — members of the Viceitic branch of the Chibchan family — to and from Spanish. We explore a variety of techniques, including: (1) training trilingual models that can translate Bribri or Cabécar to and from Spanish; (2) performing self-supervised training, such as denoising autoencoding and masked sequence-to-sequence reconstruction; (3) adding data from a bilingual lexicon as additional parallel data; and (4) prepending indicator tokens to source sentences that tell the model which language it is translating to (`<2tgt>`) or from (`<4src>`). We observe some modest gains from self-supervised training and adding lexical data in this extremely under-resourced setting, and also find that trilingual models can outperform bilingual models, including models trained to translate in just one direction. We also see that prepending `<2tgt>` *and* `<4src>` tokens to source sentences yields modest gains. Our best model achieves around 26 CHRF averaged across the four directions (Spanish ↔ Cabécar, Bribri ↔ Spanish), despite being trained on only 8K parallel sentences for Bribri-Spanish and 4K for Cabécar-Spanish.

1 Introduction

This paper focuses on building neural machine translation (NMT) systems that translate two Indigenous Costa Rican languages to and from Spanish: Cabécar and Bribri. Cabécar and Bribri both fall under the Viceitic branch of the Chibchan language family. The Chibchan family is native to the Isthmo-Colombian Area, stretching from eastern Honduras to northern Colombia, including Costa Rica, Panama, and Nicaragua. There are hundreds of thousands of Chibchan speakers spread throughout this region. Along with Teribe, Cabécar and Bribri are the only living languages in the Viceitic branch. Cabécar and Bribri, like the other Chibchan languages, tend to have rich and complex morphology, compounding the challenge of building machine translation systems for them.

The Cabécar people live in the Chirripó and Talamanca regions in Eastern and Southern Costa Rica. As of 2011, the population numbered around $14,000$ (INEC, 2011), and there are an estimated $11,100$ native speakers of Cabécar presently. The Bribri people live in southern Costa Rica and northern Panama. Their population is around $17,000$ (INEC, 2011), with approximately $7,000$ speakers of the language. Both languages are classified as vulnerable (Moseley, 2010; Sánchez Avendaño, 2013).

There are a number of objectives we have in mind with this work, some of them purely technical and some of them related to language documentation and revitalization. On the technical side, we aim to see whether multilingual MT training and/or self-supervised training can improve translation performance for extremely under-resourced languages. Unlike other works that attempt these techniques at massive scale, involving hundreds of languages and billions of sentences, we wish to put multilingual training and self-supervision to the test using realistic under-resourced conditions: only three languages, four translation directions, and tens of thousands of parallel sentences. We hope that in training models with both Bribri *and* Cabécar the model will leverage linguistic similarity to improve performance in one or both languages.

On the documentation and revitalization side, we ultimately want to build systems that Indigenous people can use to engage with content in their community's language, e.g. by translating Spanish web text to Cabécar or Bribri. This capability becomes increasingly important as indigenous cultures adopt digital technologies and come into contact with content in other languages. If people cannot continue

Proceedings of the The 3rd Workshop on Multi-lingual Representation Learning (MRL), pages 106–117
December 7, 2023

using their culture's language in the digital age, the language may lose even more domains of usage and ultimately become dormant (Jany, 2018; Stern, 2018; Cruz and Waring, 2019; Zhang et al., 2022; Orynycz, 2022). On the flip side, translating in the other direction (e.g. {Bribri, Cabécar} → Spanish) can facilitate communication or help outsiders learn indigenous languages.

The contributions of this work are as follows:

1. We train and evaluate a multilingual NMT system that translates Cabécar and Bribri to and from Spanish. To our knowledge, we are the first to train and evaluate an MT system with Cabécar, and among the first to train multilingual NMT systems tailored to Indigenous languages of the Americas.

2. We compare a number of methods for enhancing multilingual NMT performance on extremely under-resourced languages, including self-supervised methods like denoising autoencoding and masked reconstruction, as well as other techniques like `<4src>` tagging or using bilingual lexicon entries as additional parallel data.

3. We provide comparisons between unidirectional bilingual models and bidirectional bilingual models, as well as between bilingual and trilingual models. Notably, we show that multilingual NMT models can beat bilingual models, even in an extremely resource-poor setting.

2 Related Work

2.1 MT and NLP for indigenous languages of the Americas

There are a number of previous efforts that have looked at machine translation and other NLP tasks for Indigenous languages of the Americas. For an extensive list of works in this area, we recommend the `Naki` GitHub page[1]. We will provide a brief overview of some recent work, with a focus on MT.

The closest work to ours, who our project is in part a follow-up to, is Feldman and Coto-Solano (2020), which experimented with training NMT models with back-translation for Bribri → Spanish and Spanish → Bribri. We use an extended version of Bribri-Spanish parallel dataset from their paper, but there are a number of differences: (1) we train on Cabécar-Spanish data as well; (2) we train multilingual, multidirectional models, rather than only unidirectional bilingual models; and (3) we experiment with self-supervised training on monolingual data.

There have been various other efforts at MT for other Amerindian languages. Some recent works include: Zhang et al. (2020), who work with Cherokee-English translation; Le and Sadat (2020), who work with Inuktitut-English translation; Montoya (2019), who work with Shipibo Konibo-Spanish translation; and Hois (2017), who work with Wixarika-Spanish translation. These works deploy a number of techniques for training low-resource MT models, such as incorporating language models and back-translation (Zhang et al., 2020), morphologically segmenting polysynthetic words before training (Le and Sadat, 2020), and leveraging related-language data from higher-resource languages to effect transfer learning (Montoya, 2019). Due to the extremely low level of resources for these languages, some of these works experiment with statistical machine translation, either in addition to NMT (e.g. Zhang et al. (2020)) or in place of it (e.g. Hois (2017)). In the AmericasNLP (Mager et al., 2021) shared task on MT for Indigenous languages of the Americas, various authors built and evaluated systems for a diverse set of languages, namely: Asháninka, Aymara, Bribri, Guarani, Nahuatl, Otomí, Quechua, Rarámuri, Shipibo-Konibo, and Wixarika.

Also of note is a recent collaborative effort between many NLP researchers who work on Indigenous languages of the Americas, called AmericasNLI (Ebrahimi et al., 2022). This paper examined the natural language understanding capabilities of pretrained multilingual models on Indigenous language data, investigating both zero-shot transfer and continued pretraining on these languages. They found that the pretrained multilingual models' performance was poor on the 10 Indigenous languages they examined, although continued pretraining offered substantial improvements. This is one of the few large-scale collaborative efforts for Indigenous NLP in the Americas, but there will hopefully be more projects of this sort that focus on other tasks such as MT.

2.2 Multilingual NMT

Multilingual NMT refers to training machine translation models on many languages, in many direc-

[1] `https://github.com/pywirrarika/naki`

tions, with a single set of parameters and a shared vocabulary. Currently, the largest industry labs with the most data and compute resources (e.g. Google, Meta, Microsoft) can train models capable of translating hundreds of directions, a procedure known as "massively multilingual machine translation" (Johnson et al., 2017; Aharoni et al., 2019; Fan et al., 2020; NLLB Team et al., 2022; Bapna et al., 2022). This is how state-of-the-art production MT systems are now trained.

Multilingual NMT has a number of appeals compared to training bilingual models. For one, the parameter efficiency is much greater. The number of possible language pairs scales quadratically with the number of languages, and if one wants the option of translating between all possible language pairs then the number of bilingual models required would scale quadratically as well. For instance, accommodating all possible language pairs for 30 languages would require 435 bilingual models. By contrast, a single model could be trained on all 30 languages, with parallel data for some language pairs, and then there is also the possibility of performing zero-shot translation for some of the language pairs not seen in training (Johnson et al., 2017). Multilingual models of course must be larger than bilingual models, but not so much larger that their use of parameters is less efficient.

Another appeal of multilingual MT systems is the potential for transfer learning. Specifically, it is possible for the model to improve on translating under-resourced languages by being trained on the rich data for higher-resource languages. Notably, however, this type of positive transfer is most likely to happen when the languages are closely related to each other genealogically (Ko et al., 2021; Khatri et al., 2021). In our case, we do not have a high-resource Chibchan language that we can use to bootstrap training for Cabécar and Bribri (and this is probably the case for most language families in the world). However, it is still theoretically possible to see gains on one or both languages due to their relatedness, even if they are both very under-resourced.

Although multilingual NMT has been spearheaded by large industry labs, there have been a number of recent efforts at training multilingual models specifically for low-resource languages. Among these are Yigezu et al. (2021), Emezue and Dossou (2022), and Vegi et al. (2022). All three of these papers build systems for African languages. Multilingual NMT hasn't been attempted for many Indigenous languages in other parts of the world, and certainly not for the Chibchan languages. It is promising, however, that industry labs are beginning to introduce Indigenous languages (of the Americas and elsewhere) into both research and production MT systems, e.g. Aymara and Guarani for Google Translate, and Yucatec Maya and Inuktitut for Microsoft Translator.

2.3 Self-supervised training

The other class of techniques we experiment with in this paper is self-supervised training. Self-supervised training refers to feeding the model some manipulated (e.g. noised or masked) form of monolingual sentences to the model and then tasking the model with reconstructing the original sentences. There are two types of self-supervised training methods we experiment with in this paper: denoising autoencoding and masked reconstruction[2].

The denoising autoencoding training we do is inspired by BART (Lewis et al., 2019) and mBART (Liu et al., 2020). In these works, sequence-to-sequence models are fed noisy (e.g. randomly shuffled) sentences and made to reconstruct the original sentences. By pretraining on this task in multiple languages, Liu et al. (2020) showed that the resulting model could be finetuned to perform well on MT.

The second self-supervised task we experiment with is MASS, or MAsked Sequence-to-Sequence pretraining (Song et al., 2019). In this method, the masked language modeling objective is generalized such that spans of arbitrary length are masked and the model has to predict either the masked tokens or reconstruct the entire original sentence. We opt for the latter approach (reconstructing the whole sentence), and try two different masking variants (see Section 4.2.2).

Self-supervised training has been shown to be successful in training massively multilingual NMT models, improving performance on low-resource and unsupervised languages in particular (Bapna et al., 2022; Siddhant et al., 2022; NLLB Team et al., 2022). A limited number of works have also looked at self-supervised training for MT in low-resource settings, and found it to be beneficial (Kuwanto et al., 2021; Dhar et al., 2022).

[2]Our masked sequence-to-sequence reconstruction task could be viewed as denoising autoencoding as well, but we keep it separate from our other denoising task for clarity.

3 Data

We have two parallel datasets at our disposal for this work: one for Bribri-Spanish, one for Cabécar-Spanish. The Bribri-Spanish dataset contains $\approx$ 8600 sentence pairs. These come from textbooks for Spanish speakers to learn Bribri (Constenla et al., 2004; Jara Murillo and García Segura, 2013), bilingual dictionaries (Margery, 2005), grammar books (Jara Murillo, 2018a), compilations of transcribed oral literature (Constenla, 2006, 1996; García Segura, 2016; Jara Murillo, 2018b), pedagogical textbooks (Sánchez Avendaño, 2020), and a digitized and transcribed oral corpus with traditional stories and songs (Flores Solórzano, 2017). Most of these sentences belong to general domains (e.g. *Ye' dör bua'ë* 'I am doing well'), but they also include technical passages from narrations about mythology and traditional practices. This corpus is available at the AmericasNLP 2021 repository[3].

The Cabécar-Spanish dataset contains $\approx$ 4200 sentence pairs. These come from the bilingual dictionary by González Campos and Obando Martínez (2020). This corpus is also composed of general sentences (e.g. *Yís sḛ́r dä él da* 'I live with my brother'). These were gathered from the authors' fieldwork and pedagogical books (González Campos et al., 2020; González Campos and Obando Martínez, 2018).

For both language pairs, we use a 90/5/5 train/validation/test split. Due to the lack of monolingual data for Bribri or Cabécar (besides Biblical data, which we deliberately do not use due to its linguistic and topical skew), we use the sentences from the parallel datasets as our monolingual data for the self-supervised (denoising/MASS) tasks as well. We also have a small bilingual lexicon available for Cabécar-Spanish, containing 1350 entries. We use this as additional parallel data in training a bidirectional Cabécar $\leftrightarrow$ Spanish model (see Section 5.2).

4 Methods

4.1 Model

We use the OpenNMT (Klein et al., 2017) implementation of the Transformer (Vaswani et al., 2017) model for all our experiments. Each model has $\approx$ 50M parameters and we tokenize our data using the OpenNMT implementation of BPE (Sennrich et al., 2016) with `n_symbols` = 10000. Unless indicated otherwise, we train our models with Adam optimization (Kingma and Ba, 2015) for 4000 steps with a batch size of 4096, a learning rate of 2.0, 6 hidden layers, 8 attention heads, a hidden layer dimension of 512, a feedforward layer dimension of 2048, and a dropout probability of 0.1. We train on one NVIDIA A100 GPU provided by Google Colab, which took around 20-30 minutes per model. Full hyperparameters are given in Section B of the Appendix.

4.2 Training Techniques

We experiment with a variety of training techniques to arrive at the best method, or combination of methods. First, we train two types of *bilingual* models: unidirectional models, which only translate one language to another, and bidirectional models that translate two languages in both directions. Because we have Cabécar-Spanish bilingual lexicon data, we also experiment with adding that as additional parallel signal. Second, we experiment with training *trilingual* models, which translate Bribri $\leftrightarrow$ Spanish and Cabécar $\leftrightarrow$ Spanish.

Next, we experiment with several different self-supervised training schemes to improve the trilingual models. These methods are described below.

4.2.1 Multilingual Training

One of our main interests in this paper is training multilingual models that translate Bribri $\leftrightarrow$ Spanish and Cabécar $\leftrightarrow$ Spanish. The only modification we make to the training data for training the baseline trilingual model is prepending a `<2tgt>` token that tells the model which language to translate to, as in Bapna et al. (2022). For example, when translating Spanish to Cabécar we use the tag `<2cjp>`. The models are then trained in all four directions with a cross-entropy loss.

4.2.2 Self-supervised Training

We also experiment with self-supervised training using monolingual data (taken from the parallel datasets).

Denoising autoencoding One of the self-supervised tasks we try is denoising autoencoding, where the model is fed a noisy version of a sentence and has to reconstruct the original sentence. As our noising function, we randomly shuffle the order of words in a sentence, similar to Lewis et al. (2019); Liu et al. (2020). Once again following Bapna et al. (2022), we add a `<2task>` tag to all

[3] https://github.com/AmericasNLP/americasnlp2021

sentences in the dataset to help the model distinguish the denoising task from the MT task. In this case, that token is `<2denoise>` for the denoising task and `<2translate>` for the MT task.

MASS The second self-supervised training technique we experiment with is MASS (Song et al., 2019). This method involves masking tokens in the source sentence and having the model try to reconstruct the original sentence. Bapna et al. (2022); Siddhant et al. (2022) show this can be used to improve performance for many low-resource and unsupervised languages in massively multilingual MT systems. We employ two variants of MASS. In the first, text spans of arbitrary length in the source are replaced with a single `[MASK]` token (following Lewis et al. (2019)). In the second, each masked token is replaced with its own `[MASK]` token. In either case, we mask 50% of the words in each sentence and train on the task for all three languages. The `<2task>` token we use here is `<2mass>`.

4.2.3 Using bilingual lexicons

We also experiment with adding bilingual lexicon entries as extra parallel data. For this, we use a Cabécar-Spanish bilingual lexicon to help train a bidirectional Cabécar $\leftrightarrow$ Spanish model. Once again, `<2lang>` tags are used so the model knows which language to translate to.

5 Experiments

All models use the hyperparameters described in Section 4.1 and Section B of the Appendix unless stated otherwise. We arrive at these hyperparameters through manual tuning of `train_steps`, `learning_rate`, `warmup_steps`, `enc/dec_layers`, `heads`, `hidden_size`, and `transformer_ff`. The remaining hyperparameters are left as the defaults selected by OpenNMT.

5.1 Unidirectional bilingual models

The simplest models we train are unidirectional bilingual models: models which just translate one language to one other language, e.g. Spanish $\rightarrow$ Bribri. These models act as baselines against which to compare our bidirectional bilingual models, described below. No modification to the training data is necessary for these models. The models here are referred to as **Cabécar $\rightarrow$ Spanish**, **Spanish $\rightarrow$ Cabécar**, **Bribri $\rightarrow$ Spanish**, and **Spanish $\rightarrow$ Bribri**.

5.2 Bidirectional bilingual models

The second type of models we train are bidirectional bilingual models, which translate two languages in both directions, e.g. Cabécar $\leftrightarrow$ Spanish. For these models, we add a `<2tgt>` tag to the training data so the model knows which language to translate to. The models here are referred to as **Bribri+Spanish** and **Cabécar+Spanish**.

We also train a Cabécar $\leftrightarrow$ Spanish model using bilingual lexicon entries as additional parallel data, which we will refer to as the **Cabécar+Spanish+bilingual lexicon data** model.

5.3 Trilingual models

We train multilingual models that translate Bribri $\leftrightarrow$ Spanish and Cabécar $\leftrightarrow$ Spanish as well.

Baseline In the baseline setup, we simply use the hyperparameters from 4.1 to train a three-language, four-directional model. This model is called **Trilingual baseline**. We also train two additional models, which are trained for 8000 steps and 12000 steps but otherwise use the same hyperparameters as the baseline. We do these as basic checks for approximately how long it takes the model to converge.

`<4src>` tagging Although all our trilingual models have `<2tgt>` tags to indicate which language to translate to, we also experiment with adding `<4src>` tags to tell the model which language it's translating *from* (e.g. `<4cjp>` when translating from Cabécar). The motivation here is that the model could potentially get confused between Cabécar and Bribri due to their similarity, and an explicit tag may mitigate some of this confusion. The source sentences for this model took the form `<4src> <2tgt> word1 word2...wordN`. This model is referred to as the **Baseline+`<4src>` tagging** model.

Joint denoising training We also experiment with jointly training the model on the denoising autoencoding task and the MT task. We try two variants of this: in the first, we simply train the model on both tasks simultaneously for 4000 steps. This model is called **Baseline+joint denoising training**. In the second variant, we do the same but then continue finetuning the model on the MT task, with the same data, for an extra 4000 steps. This variant is called **Baseline+joint denoising training, MT finetuning**.

Joint MASS training Additionally, we try jointly training the model on the MASS task and the MT task. We use two different variants of MASS: in the first, we replace spans of arbitrary length in the source with a single [MASK] token. This model is called **Baseline+joint MASS training (replace span)**. In the second, we replace *each* ablated token with a [MASK] token. This model is called **Baseline+joint MASS training (replace token)**.

6 Results

The results are summarized in Tables 1 and 2. Table 1 shows a comparison between the unidirectional and bidirectional bilingual models. Table 2 gives a comparison between the bilingual and trilingual models.

The first thing to note is that the bidirectional models outperform unidirectional models in all directions. Across all four directions, the average improvement (Δ CHRF) of the best-performing bidirectional model was $+4.9$. The model with bilingual lexicon data performs best on Spanish $\rightarrow$ Cabécar ($+5.2$ over unidirectional baseline), although it slightly underperforms the vanilla bilingual model on Cabécar $\rightarrow$ Spanish ($+0.1$ vs $+1.2$).

Next, there are a number of takeaways from the comparison between the bilingual and trilingual models. First, note that *at least one* trilingual model outperformed each bilingual baseline except in the Bribri $\rightarrow$ Spanish direction, where the next-best model got -5.7 CHRF relative to the bilingual Bribri+Spanish model. The reason for this deviation from the general trend is not clear to us. There were five trilingual models that improved over the bilingual baselines in at least one direction: **Trilingual baseline**, **Trilingual baseline+8000 steps**, **Trilingual baseline+12000 steps**, **Baseline+<4src> tagging**, and **Baseline+joint denoising training, MT finetuning**. The remaining models failed to improve over the bilingual baselines in any direction.

Looking at average CHRF across all four directions—denoted μ_4 in Table 2—we see a near three-way tie between **Baseline+joint denoising training, MT finetuning** (26.1 CHRF), **Baseline+8000 steps** (26.0 CHRF), and **Baseline+<4src> tagging** (25.9 CHRF). Just looking at the averages, it appears that these three techniques work pretty well in our training setting: (1) simply training the model a bit longer; (2) performing joint denoising training, followed by MT finetuning; and (3) adding <4src> tags to the beginning of source sentences.

Next, we examine each translation direction separately. For Cabécar-Spanish, the model with <4src> tagging wins in both directions, with gains of $+3.9$ CHRF in the Cabécar $\rightarrow$ Spanish direction and $+1.9$ in the Spanish $\rightarrow$ Cabécar direction. For Bribri-Spanish, the results are somewhat less clear-cut. For Bribri $\rightarrow$ Spanish, the bilingual baseline performs best, netting 30.8 CHRF. For Spanish $\rightarrow$ Bribri, the 8000 steps model does best, improving $+1.2$ CHRF over the bilingual baseline.

The models co-trained on the MASS task performed poorly, seeing huge losses across the board. There are a number of reasons why this might have happened. One is that we simply did not have enough data for the model to learn from the task effectively. The MASS task has been shown to work well for very high-resource settings on models with hundreds of millions or billions of parameters, and this result might simply not scale to the extremely low-resource, small model scenario. Another possibility is that there are different ways to implement MASS that would be more amenable to datasets of the size studied here. In personal correspondence with various authors on Bapna et al. (2022), we learned that the MASS task can be difficult to implement properly given the description in Song et al. (2019). Further experimentation with the MASS task in resource-poor settings is left for future work.

In regard to the denoising autoencoding task, it is interesting to note that while model performance decreased relative to the trilingual baseline using the **Baseline+joint denoising training** setup, we were able to see gains by adding in 4000 steps of MT finetuning following the joint dual-task training. It could be that this is a quirk of very low-resource training, as the extra finetuning step isn't necessary to see substantial improvements on large, high-resource, massively multilingual models (Bapna et al., 2022; Siddhant et al., 2022). In our setting, it seems that the model does indeed learn from the denoising task but that it needs more training passes on the MT data for it to really make use of those gains on unseen MT queries at inference time.

7 Discussion

There are a number of contributions that our experiments make from both a technical and a social angle. On the technical side, our experiments

	Cabécar → Spanish	Spanish → Cabécar	Bribri → Spanish	Spanish → Bribri
		Unidirectional		
Cabécar → Spanish	21.3	–	–	–
Spanish → Cabécar	–	23.8	–	–
Bribri → Spanish	–	–	24.9	–
Spanish → Bribri	–	–	–	21.2
		Bidirectional		
Cabécar+Spanish	**22.5**	26.4	–	–
+bilingual lexicon data	21.4	**29.0**	–	–
Bribri+Spanish	–	–	**30.8**	**28.6**

Table 1: A comparison between unidirectional and bidirectional bilingual models (CHRF). All models are trained for 4000 steps with identical hyperparameters. The "+bilingual lexicon data" model was trained with 1352 Cabécar-Spanish bilingual lexicon entries as additional parallel data.

	μ_4	cab → spa	spa → cab	bri → spa	spa → bri
		Bilingual			
Cabécar+Spanish (4000 steps)	–	22.5	26.4	–	–
+bilingual lexicon data	–	21.4	29.0	–	–
Bribri+Spanish (4000 steps)	–	–	–	**30.8**	28.6
		Trilingual			
Trilingual baseline (4000 steps)	24.2	21.8	28.8	18.9	27.3
Trilingual baseline with additional training (8000 steps)	26.0	24.2	29.3	20.5	**29.8**
Trilingual baseline with additional training (12000 steps)	25.1	24.2	28.3	19.6	28.2
Trilingual baseline+<4src> tagging	25.9	**26.4**	**30.9**	19.1	27.3
Trilingual baseline+joint denoising training	22.0	20.2	25.5	18.8	23.3
Trilingual baseline+joint denoising training, MT finetuning	**26.1**	22.1	29.5	25.1	27.7
Trilingual baseline+joint MASS training (replace span)	11.1	9.0	14.7	11.5	9.3
Trilingual baseline+joint MASS training (replace token)	8.6	6.7	9.5	9.8	8.5

Table 2: A comparison between the bilingual and trilingual models that translate Cabécar and Bribri to/from Spanish (performance is measured in CHRF). Green-colored indicate improvements over the baseline, with bright green cells being the best performers. Red-colored cells indicate losses relative to the bilingual baselines. μ_4 indicates the average performance across all 4 directions.

are noteworthy because they put to the test techniques that have been shown to work for giant-scale machine translation models trained with copious amounts of data, but haven't been rigorously examined in very under-resourced settings. Namely, the two classes of techniques we investigate here are (1) multilingual machine translation, and (2) self-supervised training, namely denoising autoencoding and masked reconstruction (MASS).

Our results show that we can get benefits from multilingual training even in this resource-scarce scenario, as well as from denoising autoencoding training. The first of these results suggests that there is some transfer learning happening between Bribri and Cabécar even with $<$ 10K sentences for each. Of course, these are closely related languages, and we would not expect such transfer to happen between distantly related languages with such little data. But this is a promising result for extremely low-resource MT nonetheless.

The fact that denoising autoencoding training did reasonably well, especially when followed by MT finetuning, is also interesting. The upshot here is that even a small amount of monolingual data for a low-resource language can potentially yield benefits on the MT task. By contrast, it is puzzling that our implementation of MASS yielded poor results. This could be an indication that the MASS task requires a certain amount of data to benefit MT training, and that we were well below that threshold, but this hypothesis needs further investigation in future work. It is also possible that a different implementation of the MASS task could work better for extremely low-resource settings, e.g. one where only tokens at the beginning or end of source sentences are masked.

Lastly, although MT performance on under-resourced languages is far from where it needs to be to suit the demands of actual speakers, we see our work on these indigenous languages as a step in the right direction. Whenever an NLP method is shown to help high-resource, politically and economically dominant languages like English, Spanish, or Chinese, that same method should be tested on under-resourced languages, which constitute the vast majority of the world's languages (Joshi et al., 2020). If the method works, then that is a step toward making language technology better and more inclusive. If it doesn't, then that shows a fundamental limitation in state-of-the-art techniques, because it suggests they don't scale to down to the languages that much of the world speaks. What we have seen in this paper is a mixture of both these results. We hope that these findings are helpful for the research community and, ultimately, the indigenous speaker communities for whom this technology is made.

8 Conclusions

In this paper, we have experimented with training multilingual neural machine translation models that translate the indigenous Costa Rican languages Cabécar and Bribri to and from Spanish. First, we provide a comparison between unidirectional bilingual models and bidirectional bilingual models, showing that the latter can outdo the former in all directions. Next, we show that the trilingual models we train beat the bilingual baselines in all but one of the four translation directions (namely Bribri $\rightarrow$ Spanish). In training the trilingual models, we experiment with a number of variables: (1) training for more steps; (2) prepending a `<4src>` tag to source sentences to tell the model what language it's translating from, in addition to the `<2tgt>` tag we use for all multidirectional models; (3) adding in self-supervised training on monolingual data, either denoising autoencoding or masked reconstruction (MASS); and (4) finetuning models on the MT task following joint training on denoising autoencoding and MT. Out of these, the most promising findings are that `<4src>` tags appear useful (especially for Cabécar $\leftrightarrow$ Spanish) and that joint denoising training followed by MT finetuning is an efficacious approach. We also show that adding bilingual lexicon entries as additional parallel data improves performance somewhat on Spanish $\rightarrow$ Cabécar.

Future work should look at combining these strategies with other techniques, such as back-translation. Additionally, with the increasing capabilities of Large Language Models as general NLP systems, much work must be done to see how their translation abilities on under-resourced languages can be evaluated and improved.

Limitations

One limitation of this work is the small number of languages explored. While it is important to examine the members of the Chibchan language family individually due to the extreme scarcity of attention they've been given in the NLP literature, it is true that the results in our paper are only directly applicable to Cabécar, Bribri, and Spanish. To mitigate this narrowness, future work should incorporate Chibchan languages into broader multilingual NLP efforts.

Another limitation of this work is the small amount of training data available. Of course, this is simply the state of affairs for extremely under resourced languages like Cabécar and Bribri, and it is part of the experimental design itself. However, future efforts should focus on data resource creation in addition to modeling in order to improve the state of technology for these languages.

Finally, a limitation of this work at present is the fact that some of the data we used is not yet open-source, due to intellectual property restrictions. However, it is our hope that all the data associated with this project will soon be released for public use.

Ethics Statement

Perhaps the greatest ethical concern in working on language technology for Indigenous languages is the European colonialist history that looms over these languages and their associated cultures. This history is one of violence, genocide, cultural theft and destruction, exploitation, and bigotry. Countless Indigenous languages across the world have been suppressed, stigmatized, diminished, or altogether wiped out in the wake of colonialism. These, of course, are only the linguistic consequences of a history that has been violent in many distinct ways.

First and foremost, the purpose of building technology for Indigenous languages should be to benefit the speakers themselves. The features and potential applications of the technology should be guided by the speakers' needs and desires. It is our hope that our research will lead to technologies that the Cabécar, Bribri, and other peoples can use and benefit from, and that they can develop these tools themselves in the near future.

Building Indigenous language technologies ethically entails more than just constructing useful systems. It also entails respect for concerns such as data sovereignty and the ways in which the speakers want their language to be used (for instance, whether they would like outsiders to interact with their language). While some of these matters are not particular to Indigenous languages, they are especially pertinent to these languages because of the colonialist history described above.

Acknowledgments

We would like to thank Isaac Caswell, Ankur Bapna, and Xavier García on the Google Translate team for their correspondence regarding this project. We would also like to thank Franklin Morales, Freddy Obando, and Samantha Wray for their help.

References

Roee Aharoni, Melvin Johnson, and Orhan Firat. 2019. Massively multilingual neural machine translation. In *Proceedings of the 2019 Conference of the North American Chapter of the Association for Computational Linguistics: Human Language Technologies, Volume 1 (Long and Short Papers)*, pages 3874–3884, Minneapolis, Minnesota. Association for Computational Linguistics.

Ankur Bapna, Isaac Caswell, Julia Kreutzer, Orhan Firat, Daan van Esch, Aditya Siddhant, Mengmeng Niu, Pallavi Baljekar, Xavier Garcia, Wolfgang Macherey, Theresa Breiner, Vera Axelrod, Jason Riesa, Yuan Cao, Mia Xu Chen, Klaus Macherey, Maxim Krikun, Pidong Wang, Alexander Gutkin, Apurva Shah, Yanping Huang, Zhifeng Chen, Yonghui Wu, and Macduff Hughes. 2022. Building machine translation systems for the next thousand languages.

Adolfo Constenla. 1996. *Poesía tradicional indígena costarricense*. Editorial Universidad de Costa Rica.

Adolfo Constenla. 2006. *Poesía bribri de lo cotidiano: 37 cantos de afecto, devoción, trabajo y entretenimiento*. Editorial Universidad de Costa Rica.

Adolfo Constenla, Feliciano Elizondo, and Francisco Pereira. 2004. *Curso Básico de Bribri*. Editorial de la Universidad de Costa Rica.

Hilaria Cruz and Joseph Waring. 2019. Deploying technology to save endangered languages.

Prajit Dhar, Arianna Bisazza, and Gertjan van Noord. 2022. Evaluating pre-training objectives for low-resource translation into morphologically rich languages. In *Proceedings of the Thirteenth Language Resources and Evaluation Conference*, pages 4933–4943, Marseille, France. European Language Resources Association.

Abteen Ebrahimi, Manuel Mager, Arturo Oncevay, Vishrav Chaudhary, Luis Chiruzzo, Angela Fan, John Ortega, Ricardo Ramos, Annette Rios, Ivan Vladimir Meza Ruiz, Gustavo Giménez-Lugo, Elisabeth Mager, Graham Neubig, Alexis Palmer, Rolando Coto-Solano, Thang Vu, and Katharina Kann. 2022. AmericasNLI: Evaluating zero-shot natural language understanding of pretrained multilingual models in truly low-resource languages. In *Proceedings of the 60th Annual Meeting of the Association for Computational Linguistics (Volume 1: Long Papers)*, pages 6279–6299, Dublin, Ireland. Association for Computational Linguistics.

Chris C. Emezue and Bonaventure F. P. Dossou. 2022. Mmtafrica: Multilingual machine translation for african languages. *CoRR*.

Angela Fan, Shruti Bhosale, Holger Schwenk, Zhiyi Ma, Ahmed El-Kishky, Siddharth Goyal, Mandeep Baines, Onur Celebi, Guillaume Wenzek, Vishrav Chaudhary, Naman Goyal, Tom Birch, Vitaliy Liptchinsky, Sergey Edunov, Edouard Grave, Michael Auli, and Armand Joulin. 2020. Beyond english-centric multilingual machine translation. *CoRR*, abs/2010.11125.

Isaac Feldman and Rolando Coto-Solano. 2020. Neural machine translation models with back-translation for the extremely low-resource indigenous language Bribri. In *Proceedings of the 28th International Conference on Computational Linguistics*, pages 3965–3976, Barcelona, Spain (Online). International Committee on Computational Linguistics.

Sofía Flores Solórzano. 2017. Corpus oral pandialectal de la lengua bribri.

Alí García Segura. 2016. *Ditsö Rukuö Identity of the Seeds: Learning from Nature*. IUCN.

Guillermo González Campos and Freddy Obando Martínez. 2018. *Fonología y ortografía del Cabécar*. Editorial de la Universidad Estatal a Distancia.

Guillermo González Campos and Freddy Obando Martínez. 2020. *Diccionario Escolar del Cabécar de Chirripó - Ditsá duchíwák kté chulíí i yuäklä*. Universidad de Costa Rica, Vicerrectoría de Acción Social, Sede del Atlántico.

Guillermo González Campos, Freddy Obando Martínez, and Arturo Peña Hurtado. 2020. *Itsó Pákë - Historia de Itsó*. Universidad de Costa Rica, Vicerrectoría de Acción Social, Sede del Atlántico.

Jesús Manuel Mager Hois. 2017. *Traductor híbrido Wixarika - Español con escasos recursos bilingües*. Ph.D. thesis, Universidad Autónoma Metropolitana Azcapotzalco, Mexico City, Mexico.

INEC. 2011. Población total en territorios indígenas por autoidentificación a la etnia indígena y habla de alguna lengua indígena, según pueblo y territorio indígena. In Instituto Nacional de Estadística y Censos, editor, *Censo 2011*. INEC Costa Rica.

Carmen Jany. 2018. The role of new technology and social media in reversing language loss. *Speech, Language and Hearing*, 21(2):73–76.

Carla Victoria Jara Murillo. 2018a. *Gramática de la Lengua Bribri*. EDigital.

Carla Victoria Jara Murillo. 2018b. *I Ttè Historias Bribris*, second edition. Editorial de la Universidad de Costa Rica.

Carla Victoria Jara Murillo and Alí García Segura. 2013. *Se' ttö' bribri ie Hablemos en bribri*. EDigital.

Melvin Johnson, Mike Schuster, Quoc V. Le, Maxim Krikun, Yonghui Wu, Zhifeng Chen, Nikhil Thorat, Fernanda Viégas, Martin Wattenberg, Greg Corrado, Macduff Hughes, and Jeffrey Dean. 2017. Google's multilingual neural machine translation system: Enabling zero-shot translation. *Transactions of the Association for Computational Linguistics*, 5:339–351.

Pratik Joshi, Sebastin Santy, Amar Budhiraja, Kalika Bali, and Monojit Choudhury. 2020. The state and fate of linguistic diversity and inclusion in the NLP world. In *Proceedings of the 58th Annual Meeting of the Association for Computational Linguistics*, pages 6282–6293, Online. Association for Computational Linguistics.

Jyotsana Khatri, Nikhil Saini, and Pushpak Bhattacharyya. 2021. Language relatedness and lexical closeness can help improve multilingual NMT: IITBombay@MultiIndicNMT WAT2021. In *Proceedings of the 8th Workshop on Asian Translation (WAT2021)*, pages 217–223, Online. Association for Computational Linguistics.

Diederik P. Kingma and Jimmy Ba. 2015. Adam: A method for stochastic optimization. In *3rd International Conference on Learning Representations, ICLR 2015, San Diego, CA, USA, May 7-9, 2015, Conference Track Proceedings*.

Guillaume Klein, Yoon Kim, Yuntian Deng, Jean Senellart, and Alexander Rush. 2017. OpenNMT: Open-source toolkit for neural machine translation. In *Proceedings of ACL 2017, System Demonstrations*, pages 67–72, Vancouver, Canada. Association for Computational Linguistics.

Wei-Jen Ko, Ahmed El-Kishky, Adithya Renduchintala, Vishrav Chaudhary, Naman Goyal, Francisco Guzmán, Pascale Fung, Philipp Koehn, and Mona Diab. 2021. Adapting high-resource NMT models to translate low-resource related languages without parallel data. In *Proceedings of the 59th Annual Meeting of the Association for Computational Linguistics and the 11th International Joint Conference on Natural Language Processing (Volume 1: Long Papers)*, pages 802–812, Online. Association for Computational Linguistics.

Garry Kuwanto, Afra Feyza Akyürek, Isidora Chara Tourni, Siyang Li, Alexander Jones, and Derry Wijaya. 2021. Low-resource machine translation for low-resource languages: Leveraging comparable data, code-switching and compute resources. *CoRR*, abs/2103.13272.

Tan Ngoc Le and Fatiha Sadat. 2020. Low-resource NMT: an empirical study on the effect of rich morphological word segmentation on Inuktitut. In *Proceedings of the 14th Conference of the Association for Machine Translation in the Americas (Volume 1: Research Track)*, pages 165–172, Virtual. Association for Machine Translation in the Americas.

Mike Lewis, Yinhan Liu, Naman Goyal, Marjan Ghazvininejad, Abdelrahman Mohamed, Omer Levy, Veselin Stoyanov, and Luke Zettlemoyer. 2019. BART: denoising sequence-to-sequence pre-training for natural language generation, translation, and comprehension. *CoRR*, abs/1910.13461.

Yinhan Liu, Jiatao Gu, Naman Goyal, Xian Li, Sergey Edunov, Marjan Ghazvininejad, Mike Lewis, and Luke Zettlemoyer. 2020. Multilingual denoising pre-training for neural machine translation. *CoRR*, abs/2001.08210.

Manuel Mager, Arturo Oncevay, Abteen Ebrahimi, John Ortega, Annette Rios, Angela Fan, Ximena Gutierrez-Vasques, Luis Chiruzzo, Gustavo Giménez-Lugo, Ricardo Ramos, Ivan Vladimir Meza Ruiz, Rolando Coto-Solano, Alexis Palmer, Elisabeth Mager-Hois, Vishrav Chaudhary, Graham Neubig, Ngoc Thang Vu, and Katharina Kann. 2021. Findings of the AmericasNLP 2021 shared task on open machine translation for indigenous languages of the Americas. In *Proceedings of the First Workshop on Natural Language Processing for Indigenous Languages of the Americas*, pages 202–217, Online. Association for Computational Linguistics.

Enrique Margery. 2005. *Diccionario Fraseológico Bribri-Español Español-Bribri*, second edition. Editorial de la Universidad de Costa Rica.

Héctor Erasmo Gómez Montoya. 2019. *A crowd-powered conversational assistant for the improvement of a Neural Machine Translation system in native Peruvian language*. Ph.D. thesis, Pontifica Universidad Católica Del Perú, Lima, Peru.

Christopher Moseley. 2010. *Atlas of the World's Languages in Danger*. Unesco.

NLLB Team, Marta R. Costa-jussà, James Cross, Onur Çelebi, Maha Elbayad, Kenneth Heafield, Kevin Heffernan, Elahe Kalbassi, Janice Lam, Daniel Licht, Jean Maillard, Anna Sun, Skyler Wang, Guillaume Wenzek, Al Youngblood, Bapi Akula, Loic Barrault, Gabriel Mejia Gonzalez, Prangthip Hansanti, John Hoffman, Semarley Jarrett, Kaushik Ram Sadagopan, Dirk Rowe, Shannon Spruit, Chau Tran, Pierre Andrews, Necip Fazil Ayan, Shruti Bhosale, Sergey Edunov, Angela Fan, Cynthia Gao, Vedanuj Goswami, Francisco Guzmán, Philipp Koehn, Alexandre Mourachko, Christophe Ropers, Safiyyah Saleem, Holger Schwenk, and Jeff Wang. 2022. No language left behind: Scaling human-centered machine translation.

Petro Orynycz. 2022. Say it right: AI neural machine translation empowers new speakers to revitalize Lemko. In *Artificial Intelligence in HCI: 3rd International Conference, AI-HCI 2022, Held as Part of the 24th HCI International Conference, HCII 2022, Virtual Event, June 26 – July 1, 2022, Proceedings*, page 567–580, Berlin, Heidelberg. Springer-Verlag.

Carlos Sánchez Avendaño. 2013. Lenguas en peligro en Costa Rica: vitalidad, documentación y descripción. *Revista Káñina*, 37(1):219–250.

Rico Sennrich, Barry Haddow, and Alexandra Birch. 2016. Neural machine translation of rare words with subword units. In *Proceedings of the 54th Annual Meeting of the Association for Computational Linguistics (Volume 1: Long Papers)*, pages 1715–1725, Berlin, Germany. Association for Computational Linguistics.

Aditya Siddhant, Ankur Bapna, Orhan Firat, Yuan Cao, Mia Xu Chen, Isaac Caswell, and Xavier Garcia. 2022. Towards the next 1000 languages in multilingual machine translation: Exploring the synergy between supervised and self-supervised learning. *CoRR*, abs/2201.03110.

Kaitao Song, Xu Tan, Tao Qin, Jianfeng Lu, and Tie-Yan Liu. 2019. MASS: masked sequence to sequence pre-training for language generation. *CoRR*, abs/1905.02450.

Alissa J. Stern. 2018. Can the internet revitalize local languages? *Stanford Social Innovation Review*.

Carlos Sánchez Avendaño. 2020. *Se' Dalì Diccionario y Enciclopedia de la Agricultura Tradicional Bribri*. DIPALICORI.

Ashish Vaswani, Noam Shazeer, Niki Parmar, Jakob Uszkoreit, Llion Jones, Aidan N. Gomez, Lukasz Kaiser, and Illia Polosukhin. 2017. Attention is all you need. *CoRR*, abs/1706.03762.

Pavanpankaj Vegi, Sivabhavani J, Biswajit Paul, Prasanna K R, and Chitra Viswanathan. 2022. ANVITA-African: A multilingual neural machine translation system for African languages. In *Proceedings of the Seventh Conference on Machine Translation (WMT)*, pages 1090–1097, Abu Dhabi, United Arab Emirates (Hybrid). Association for Computational Linguistics.

Mesay Gemeda Yigezu, Michael Melese Woldeyohannis, and Atnafu Lambebo Tonja. 2021. Multilingual neural machine translation for low resourced languages: Ometo-english. In *2021 International Conference on Information and Communication Technology for Development for Africa (ICT4DA)*, pages 89–94.

Shiyue Zhang, Ben Frey, and Mohit Bansal. 2022. How can NLP help revitalize endangered languages? a case study and roadmap for the Cherokee language. In *Proceedings of the 60th Annual Meeting of the Association for Computational Linguistics (Volume 1: Long Papers)*, pages 1529–1541, Dublin, Ireland. Association for Computational Linguistics.

Shiyue Zhang, Benjamin Frey, and Mohit Bansal. 2020. ChrEn: Cherokee-English machine translation for endangered language revitalization. In *Proceedings of the 2020 Conference on Empirical Methods in Natural Language Processing (EMNLP)*, pages 577–595, Online. Association for Computational Linguistics.

A Appendix: Sample outputs

Table 3 shows some examples of outputs from each of our models in each direction.

B Hyperparameters

The full list of hyperparameters for all our models, except where stated otherwise, is as follows:

1. `train_steps = 4000`
2. `batch_size = 4096`
3. `valid_batch_size = 600`
4. `optimizer = adam`
5. `learning_rate = 2.0`
6. `warmup_steps = 8000`
7. `decay_method = noam`
8. `adam_beta2 = 0.998`
9. `label_smoothing = 0.1`
10. `position_encoding = true`
11. `enc_layers = 6`
12. `dec_layers = 6`
13. `heads = 8`
14. `hidden_size = 512`
15. `word_vec_size = 512`
16. `transformer_ff = 2048`
17. `dropout_steps = [0]`
18. `dropout = 0.1`
19. `attention_dropout = 0.1`
20. `share_vocab = true`
21. `share_embeddings = true`
22. `share_decoder_embembeddings = true`
23. `seed = 1234`

	Cabécar → Spanish
Source	¿Bikö matsílí ta Túrí rä?
Reference	¿A qué distancia queda Turrialba?
Unidirectional baseline	Vendí la carga para Turrialba.
Bidirectional bilingual baseline	¿Qué hora es?
Trilingual	¿Usted conoce la casa de Turrialba?
Trilingual + <4src> tagging	¿Cuánto es para Turrialba?
Trilingual + joint denoising training	¿La caña agria tiene hueba?
Previous model + MT finetuning	¿Juta tiene usted?
Trilingual + joint MASS training	rä?
Trilingual, 8K training steps	¿Cele con Turrialba.
Trilingual, 12K training steps	¿Qué tiene mucha saliva .
	Spanish → Cabécar
Source	Llegó un hombre con mucho tamaño.
Reference	Ékla jäyí dëju wákëi ta tái.
Unidirectional baseline	I jäyí bätsä káte.
Bidirectional bilingual baseline	Ékla jäyí dëju ju ska.
Trilingual	Jäyí dëkájuná tái.
Trilingual + <4src> tagging	Ékla jäyí dëju ju ska dí yäklä.
Trilingual + joint denoising training	jäyí júna kono wa.
Previous model + MT finetuning	Mulítä jénáká tái.
Trilingual + joint MASS training	I kjuátká ámijia.
Trilingual, 8K training steps	Jäyí butsaná tái.
Trilingual, 12K training steps	Jäyí butsaná tái.
	Bribri → Spanish
Source	E’ ku̱é̱ki̱ e’ mè̱kèa̱ttke se’ ia̱, tö na̱i̱’ rö se’ kutà, kë̀ rö katàno̱k.
Reference	Por eso él nos dejó eso, que la danta es nuestra hermana, no es para comer.
Unidirectional baseline	eso ya iba a dejar eso establecido para nosotros, que la danta es nuestra hermana. no es para comer.
Bidirectional bilingual baseline	Por eso ya iba a dejar eso establecido para nosotros, que la danta es nuestra hermana, no es para comer.
Trilingual	Cuando el búho suena a los bejucos , para que se transformó en lengua ;
Trilingual + <4src> tagging	Al principio , por eso se debe decir que en la nariz , vea.
Trilingual + joint denoising training	A la hermana se les duelen las ví, las plantas.
Previous model + MT finetuning	por eso ahora , a partir de una persona , no eran para comer ,
Trilingual + joint MASS training	Por que majarse usa el cuerpo para bañar , y eso se usa la hermana ,
Trilingual, 8K training steps	¿Cuándo se apagan los bribris de monte?
Trilingual, 12K training steps	por eso las deidades siguen haciendo a la señora con un pedazo de piedra , porque era aprovechado
	Spanish → Bribri
Source	En la actualidad los jóvenes no conocen los taparrabos
Reference	Î̱ñe̱ ta̱ se’ duládulapa kë̀ wa̱ kipàdawo sù̱ne̱ i̱a̱.
Unidirectional baseline	iñ e alàrala i chèke. ema e’ kuéki.
Bidirectional bilingual baseline	Skámoköl kë yö r ia dinamu súrule.
Trilingual	Nañéwe ta îñe kë ye’ wa káse se se se lo que ".
Trilingual + <4src> tagging	Ká batá kë wa ya kë wa kapá taî táwa.
Trilingual + joint denoising training	Sä diëi yäklä ra, ká sá káwäta köchi chálí bu
Previous model + MT finetuning	Ká i’ ki kë a’ wa jóvenes ök..
Trilingual + joint MASS training	Chakì ye’ chka’ awá ta̱ .
Trilingual, 8K training steps	Káwö wéle ta akëkëpa bák alambre yëuk.
Trilingual, 12K training steps	Skámoköl kë yör ktöm se’ tabèla wa.

Table 3: Example model outputs. Green words are those that appear in the reference.

24. valid_steps = 1000
25. accum_count = 3
26. accum_steps = 0

These hyperparameters were passed to the `translate.py` function in OpenNMT-py[4].

[4] https://opennmt.net/OpenNMT-py/options/translate.html

Mergen: The First Manchu-Korean Machine Translation Model Trained on Augmented Data

Jean Seo, Sungjoo Byun, Minha Kang, Sangah Lee
Seoul National University
{seemdog, byunsj, alsgk1123, sanalee}@snu.ac.kr

Abstract

The Manchu language, with its roots in the historical Manchurian region of Northeast China, is now facing a critical threat of extinction, as there are very few speakers left. In our efforts to safeguard the Manchu language, we introduce *Mergen*, the first-ever attempt at a Manchu-Korean Machine Translation (MT) model. To develop this model, we utilize valuable resources such as the Mǎnwén Lǎodàng(a historical book) and a Manchu-Korean dictionary. Due to the scarcity of a Manchu-Korean parallel dataset, we expand our data by employing word replacement guided by GloVe embeddings, trained on both monolingual and parallel texts. Our approach is built around an encoder-decoder neural machine translation model, incorporating a bi-directional Gated Recurrent Unit (GRU) layer. The experiments have yielded promising results, showcasing a significant enhancement in Manchu-Korean translation, with a remarkable 20-30 point increase in the BLEU score.

1 Introduction

Efforts to conserve and revive endangered languages have surged, with modern advancements in Natural Language Processing (NLP) playing a pivotal role. Zhang et al. (2020) introduce ChrEn, a Cherokee-English parallel dataset, and examine methodologies like Statistical Machine Translation (SMT) and Neural Machine Translation (NMT). Zhang et al. (2020) aid the conservation of Cherokee, a critically endangered Native American dialect. On a similar note, Luo et al. (2020) present a decipherment model for lost languages that addresses challenges posed by non-segmented scripts and undetermined proximate languages, leveraging linguistic constraints and the International Phonetic Alphabet (IPA) for phonological patterns.

Manchu language, originated from the historical Manchurian region in Northeast China, stands as a highly endangered Tungusic language of East Asia (Tsunoda, 2006). There are merely few Manchu speakers left nowadays, leading Manchu to be labeled 'nearly extinct' by UNESCO (Kim et al., 2008). The Manchu spell checker (You, 2014) and the Manchu corpus with morphological annotations (Choi et al., 2023a,b) are the only prior approaches to embrace Manchu in the field of NLP. We introduce *Mergen*, the first Manchu-Korean machine translation model, which marks the pioneering effort to apply MT to the Manchu language.

We employ two sets of parallel corpora for machine translation from Manchu to Korean, as detailed in Kim et al. (2019). Initially, we train an adapted version of the NMT model (Bahdanau et al., 2016). Assuming the unexpectedly low performance is due to the scarcity of Manchu-Korean data, we augment the size of parallel data several fold utilizing GloVe (Pennington et al., 2014). Our findings suggest that this data augmentation methodology substantially enhances translation quality.

Despite the constrained availability of resources, our goal is to enhance Manchu-Korean machine translation performance. To symbolize our commitment to the field of Manchu NLP, we christen our model *Mergen*, denoting a sage or a wise individual in the Manchu lexicon. Our translation approach, which employs a data augmentation technique, not only seeks to improve Manchu-Korean translation performance but also aims to eventually serve as a potential model for addressing NLP challenges in other extremely low-resource scenarios as addressed in King (2015).

2 Related Work

2.1 Low-Resource Machine Translation

MT necessitates parallel data of source and target languages to be trained effectively. However, the majority of language pairs face a scarcity of resources. As a result, there has been various research

Proceedings of the The 3rd Workshop on Multi-lingual Representation Learning (MRL), pages 118–124
December 7, 2023

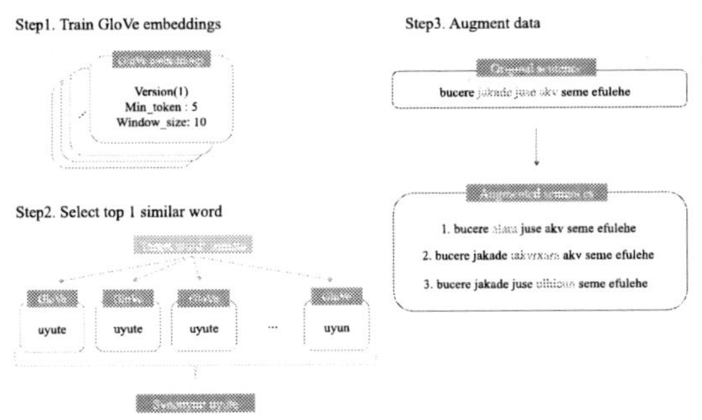

Figure 1: Our data augmentation methodology. First, we train ten versions of GloVe embedding models, varying in the minimum token length of source data and window size. Then, the presumable synonym for the target word is selected via comparing the frequency of outputs from each model. Finally, we augment data through replacing original words with synonyms if possible. The pair of original and substituted words are in the same color.

endeavors aimed at developing translation models in low-resource scenarios. Extended language models such as XLM-RoBERTa (Conneau et al., 2019), mBART (Tang et al., 2021), multilingual BERT (mBERT) (Pires et al., 2019), and mT5 (Xue et al., 2021) are trained on diverse languages. Yet, most of these multilingual language models tend not to incorporate endangered languages. This leads to an increasing disparity in NLP resources, where less-resourced languages are further marginalized. Numerous strategies have been attempted in low-resource machine translation. Gibadullin et al. (2019) and Siddhant et al. (2020) employ monolingual data in low-resource NMT. Additionally, utilization of pre-trained word embeddings (Qi et al., 2018) and application of transfer learning with pre-trained language models like XLM (Lample and Conneau, 2019) and mBART (Liu et al., 2020) have been employed. Furthermore, Lakew et al. (2018) enhance the zero-shot translation capability of low-resource languages.

2.2 Typological Similarities between Manchu and Korean

There are several typological motivations for translating Manchu to Korean using a Machine Translation model. The genetic affinity between Manchu and Korean is not proven, but it is well-known that Manchu has a similar structure to that of Korean. The word order of Manchu and Korean mostly coincide, including the order of 'noun-particle,' 'modifier-modified,' and 'object-verb,' etc. (Park, 2018). Substitutes in Korean, *kes*, and Manchu, *-ngge*, have analogous grammatical functions and positions (Choi, 2009). The two languages both show factivity alternation by using the attitude verb 'to know' (Lee, 2019) and have parallel subordinated clause structures (Malchukov and Czerwinski, 2020). These typological similarities between Manchu and Korean arouse interest in understanding and linguistically translating each other. In fact, studies of the Manchu language are active in Korea (Ko, 2023).

3 Data

3.1 Materials

The Manchu corpora used in this study comprise all of the digitized textual data available and can be categorized as either parallel or monolingual. The parallel corpora are *Mănwén Lăodàng* (1774-1778) and the Manchu-Korean dictionary. These corpora consist of Manchu texts and their corresponding translations in Korean. We only utilize a section of the *Mănwén Lăodàng* and its translations from Kim et al. (2019), which details the history of Nurhaci, the Emperor Taizu of Qing dynasty. Additionally, we refer to the dictionary from Lee (2017) and select sentences with a minimum of three words.

The monolingual texts of Manchu include the remaining part of *Mănwén Lăodàng*, Manchu-Manchu dictionaries, and several pieces of literature. The part of *Mănwén Lăodàng* left over is the chronicle of Hong Taiji, the Emperor Taizong of Qing. The Manchu-Manchu dictionaries we use are *Yùzhì Qīngwénjiàn* (1708) and *Yùzhì Zēngdìng Qīngwénjiàn* (c.1771).

The other data is composed of novels, *Ilan gurun i bithe* (c.1723-1735) and *Gin ping mei bithe* (1708). *Ilan gurun i bithe* is the translated version of *The Romance of the Three Kingdoms*. *Gin ping mei bithe* is translated from the Chinese naturalistic novel, *The Plum in the Golden Vase*. The size

Monolingual data	Number of sentences
Mănwén Lăodàng–Taizong	2,220
Ilan gurun i bithe	41,904
Gin ping mei bithe	21,376
Yùzhì Qīngwénjiàn	11,954
Yùzhì Zēngdìng Qīngwénjiàn	18,420
Parallel data (Man-Kor)	
Mănwén Lăodàng–Taizu	22,578
Manchu-Korean Dictionary	40,583

Table 1: The size of each material

description of each data can be found in Table 1.

3.2 Romanization of Manchu script and Hangul

To create a more sufficient translation model, the script of each language should be unified in one writing system. That is, both the source and target language should undergo transliteration to the Latin alphabet, so-called 'romanization'. For the romanization of Manchu, we apply Abkai Latin transliteration. The Abkai romanization suggested by An (1993) is a Pinyin-based writing system. We also use the system of Seong (1977) for the special characters in the Manchu script. Transliteration of Manchu to the Latin alphabet is reversible except for a couple of letters. For the Latin transliteration of Korean, we employ Yale romanization system (Martin, 1992) and develop the corresponding Python library[1]. See Appendix A for examples.

3.3 Data Augmentation

The lack of available Manchu linguistic data poses challenges not only for the pre-training of transformer-based models but also for the training of simpler and more lightweight models, such as encoder-decoder models. Inspired by TinyBERT (Jiao et al., 2020), we adopt a novel data augmentation approach. While the data augmentation method in TinyBERT (Jiao et al., 2020) combines both BERT (Devlin et al., 2019) and GloVe (Pennington et al., 2014), we exclusively employ GloVe embeddings. This decision stems from the absence of a pre-trained BERT model tailored to Manchu and the significant difficulty of pre-training a BERT model from scratch due to the limited amount of available textual data.

Our methodology involves training GloVe embedding models with two different versions of the dataset: (1) a dataset comprising sentences with at least 3 words, and (2) a dataset comprising sentences with at least 5 words. The dataset includes both monolingual and parallel text data. Various window sizes, specifically 1, 3, 5, 7, and 10, are used during the training process, resulting in a total of 10 distinct variations of GloVe embeddings.

For each word in the training dataset, we gather the most similar word predicted by each individual GloVe embedding. Amongst the list of 10 words generated from these separate models, the word with the highest frequency is considered the most suitable synonym for the target word. Following this, we substitute a single word in each sentence from parallel text data with the identified synonym. The augmentation steps are described in Figure 1. This procedure leads to the creation of two augmented versions of the original dataset: full augmentation and half augmentation. The first version involves replacing every word possible in each sentence with its corresponding synonym, significantly expanding the dataset size relative to the average sentence length. The second version is generated by replacing half of the words in each sentence with their respective synonyms, resulting in a dataset expansion about half the size of the first method. Additional details regarding the original and augmented dataset are available in Table 2.

[1] anonymous author github

augmentation	Mǎnwén Lǎodàng –Taizu (train)	Man-Kor Dict
Before augmentation	20,320	40,583
Full augmentation	179,843	154,404
Half augmentation	99,506	100,694

Table 2: The number of sentences of parallel text data before and after augmentation

4 Experiments

4.1 Task Details

In the experiment, we merge *Mǎnwén Lǎodàng* with Manchu-Korean dictionary and shuffle them together. The combined dataset is then divided into training, validation, and testing subsets. These subsets are split in an 8:1:1 ratio. In the augmentation process, we first shuffle and then augment the data to even out the word distributions, finally splitting into subsets.

4.2 Model

We adopt the sequence-to-sequence (seq2seq) framework, a deep learning approach designed to transform one sequence into another. Our model is based on the encoder-decoder structure of the NMT (Bahdanau et al., 2016), implemented with bidirectional Gated Recurrent Unit (GRU) layer (Cho et al., 2014). We incorporate two techniques to enhance the performance: packed padded sequences and masking. Packed padded sequences ensure that the RNN processes only the genuine elements of the input sentence, excluding the padded ones. Masking directs the model to deliberately overlook specific components, like attention weights assigned to padded sections.

Train	Test	BLEU	PPL
Before augmentation (No augmentation)			
Mănwén Lăodàng	Mănwén Lăodàng	0.0	72.50
Man-Kor Dict	Man-Kor Dict	0.0	59.34
Combined	Mănwén Lăodàng	0.0	61.83
	Man-Kor Dict	0.0	61.16
	Combined	0.0	69.62
Half augmentation			
Mănwén Lăodàng	Mănwén Lăodàng	38.38	147.07
Man-Kor Dict	Man-Kor Dict	0.0	174.94
Combined	Mănwén Lăodàng	36.05	192.95
	Man-Kor Dict	**2.37**	36.14
	Combined	27.59	29.22
Full augmentation			
Mănwén Lăodàng	Mănwén Lăodàng	**38.95**	1549.40
Man-Kor Dict	Man-Kor Dict	0.0	158.25
Combined	Mănwén Lăodàng	**37.17**	447.59
	Man-Kor Dict	2.26	46.54
	Combined	**28.00**	41.97

Table 3: Manchu-Korean Translation Performance

4.3 Results and Discussions

We perform machine translation and evaluate the performance on all the available combinations of parallel corpora: *Mănwén Lăodàng*, Manchu-Korean dictionary, and the combined dataset. In particular, we augment the training sets of each corpus to alleviate the data scarcity problem. Table 3 shows the performance of our Manchu-Korean translation models, with BLEU score (Papineni et al., 2002) and Perplexity (PPL) as the metrices. We train each model for 5 epochs and report the one with the best performance.

The first block of Table 3 shows the translation performance based on the original Manchu-Korean parallel corpora. All the experiments here show BLEU scores of 0.0, which represent that none of the test sentences are accurately translated. Most of the predicted translations include the special symbol '<UNK>' instead of proper Korean tokens, possibly due to the small dataset and vocabulary size.

The second block shows the experiment results from the augmented version of the parallel corpora, where up to 50% of the tokens in each sentence are replaced for data augmentation. The third block displays experiments on another augmented version where all tokens with substitutes are replaced. The augmentation procedure increases the size of the training set, resulting in a significant rise in the translation performance. BLEU scores exceed 38 on the *Mănwén Lăodàng* test set, and around 28 on the combined test set. The two versions of the augmented dataset show comparable performance, but replacing all the possible words in the corpus resulted in slightly higher BLEU scores.

Due to data augmentation, the vocabulary for each model is expanded; for example, the original *Mănwén Lăodàng* vocabulary includes 4,335 words, while the full-augmented dataset constructs an expanded vocabulary with 11,089 words. A larger vocabulary and training set may have helped the language model's representation and result in better translation performance. Additionally, most newly induced words are from the augmentation sources which include monolingual Manchu texts, different from our parallel corpora. This expansion of word diversity may have also affected the models' perplexity to increase when they predicted the next words in each sentence.

On the other hand, results on the Manchu-Korean dictionary are consistently very low, and this may have influenced the lower performance of the combined test set. We suppose that it is because the corpus is a dictionary, where each line is a unique word or phrase. The training set and the test set would have much fewer overlaps in their vocabularies, and this could cause a number of '<UNK>' generations in the model prediction.

5 Conclusion

In our exploration of the critically endangered Manchu language, we have made significant strides towards development of low-resource NLP through the development of the Manchu-Korean MT system, "Mergen." Our endeavor to train this model, despite the challenges posed by the scarcity of a Manchu-Korean parallel dataset, demonstrates the potential of an innovative data augmentation strategy. This attempt is also significant in that we have collected all the digitized Manchu text data. By leveraging resources such as "Mănwén Làodăng" and a Manchu-Korean dictionary, and by adopting a word substitution techniqus guided by GloVe embeddings, we have not only built a functional MT system but have also considerably enhanced its accuracy, as evidenced by the increase in the BLEU score. Our encoder-decoder NMT model, equipped with a bi-directional GRU layer, has shown promising results, offering hope for the preservation and accessibility of the Manchu language to future generations. We anticipate that this research will serve as a foundation for further innovations in the realm of endangered language preservation.

Limitations

The main limitation of this study is the scarcity of resources. Numerous Manchu literatures exist in East Asia (Vovin, 2023), including China (Elliott, 2001), Korea (Ko and You, 2012), and Mongolia (Choi, 2014). However, most of them lack an electronic version. The only publicly available Manchu language database is the Manchu Dictionary and Literature DB, created by Seoul National University and supported by the National Research Foundation of Korea.[2] Furthermore, the majority of these resources have not been translated into Korean. To address this gap, we intend to provide supplementary parallel texts translated into Korean for further study. In addition, we plan to implement a cutting-edge method of Transformer-based language model including Manchu language. Knowledge Distillation could be a way for modeling endangered languages, training a small student model based on those languages and improving it with a teacher model based on high-resource languages (Heffernan et al., 2022).

Ethics Statement

The Manchu language, classified as critically endangered, remains underrepresented due to its scarce resources. As such, it has yet to be incorporated into any multilingual language models. This study pioneers Manchu translation efforts, an endeavor previously uncharted. Our primary research objective as NLP practitioners is to prevent the extinction of Manchu language and ensure its preservation. We have no intention of commercializing the translation model. Instead, by making the model publicly available, we aim to facilitate and encourage as many individuals as possible to learn Manchu using our translator. We are committed to continuous collaboration with Manchu language researchers. We endeavor to enhance the performance of our translator and regularly update it with new Manchu data to ensure its accuracy.

References

Shuangcheng An. 1993. *Man Han Da Ci Dian*. Liaoning Minzhu Chubanshe, Shenyang.

Dzmitry Bahdanau, Kyunghyun Cho, and Yoshua Bengio. 2016. Neural machine translation by jointly learning to align and translate.

Kyunghyun Cho, Bart van Merrienboer, Çaglar Gülçehre, Fethi Bougares, Holger Schwenk, and Yoshua Bengio. 2014. Learning phrase representations using RNN encoder-decoder for statistical machine translation. *CoRR*, abs/1406.1078.

Donggeun Choi. 2014. A study of Manchu language literatures in Mongolia. *The journal of humanities*, 25:275–303.

Dongguen Choi. 2009. A comparative study of substitute - Korean *keos*, Mongolian *yum*, Manchu *-ngge* -. *Mongolian Studies*, 27:205–228.

Woonho Choi, Sunghoon Jung, and Jeongup Do. 2023a. Construction of the Manchu corpus: focusing on *Manwen laodang Taidzu*. *Altai Hakpo*, 33:67–87.

Woonho Choi, Sunghoon Jung, and Jeongup Do. 2023b. Word embeddings for *Manwen laodang* corpus with focus on names of countries and articles. In *Proceedings of the 16th Seoul International Altaistic Conference*, pages 189–204. The Altaic Society of Korea.

Alexis Conneau, Kartikay Khandelwal, Naman Goyal, Vishrav Chaudhary, Guillaume Wenzek, Francisco Guzmán, Edouard Grave, Myle Ott, Luke Zettlemoyer, and Veselin Stoyanov. 2019. Unsupervised cross-lingual representation learning at scale. *CoRR*, abs/1911.02116.

Jacob Devlin, Ming-Wei Chang, Kenton Lee, and Kristina Toutanova. 2019. Bert: Pre-training of deep bidirectional transformers for language understanding.

Mark C Elliott. 2001. The manchu-language archives of the qing dynasty and the origins of the palace memorial system. *Late Imperial China*, 22(1):1–70.

Ilshat Gibadullin, Aidar Valeev, Albina Khusainova, and Adil Khan. 2019. A survey of methods to leverage monolingual data in low-resource neural machine translation. *CoRR*, abs/1910.00373.

Kevin Heffernan, Onur Çelebi, and Holger Schwenk. 2022. Bitext mining using distilled sentence representations for low-resource languages.

Xiaoqi Jiao, Yichun Yin, Lifeng Shang, Xin Jiang, Xiao Chen, Linlin Li, Fang Wang, and Qun Liu. 2020. Tinybert: Distilling bert for natural language understanding.

Juwon Kim, Dongho Ko, Gyeyeong Choe, Sangchul Park, Jeongup Do, Hyungmi Lee, Hui Jin, and Jaehong Shim. 2019. *Tongki Fuka Sindaha Hergen i Dangse - The Chronicles of Early Qing Dynasty: Taizu Vol. 1 2*. Seoul National University Press, Seoul.

Juwon Kim, Dongho Ko, Youfeng Han, Lianyu Piao, and B. V. Boldyrev. 2008. *Materials of spoken Manchu*. unesco.

[2]NFR-2012S1A5B4A01035397, available at `http://ffr.krm.or.kr/base/td037/intro_db.html`

Benjamin Philip King. 2015. *Practical Natural Language Processing for Low-Resource Languages*. Ph.D. thesis.

Dongho Ko. 2023. Manchu-tungus studies in korea: Focusing on the studies of third-generation scholars. *Reosiahag*, 26:1–27.

Dongho Ko and Hyunjo You. 2012. For building a database of written Manchu. *Kenci Inmwunhak*, 8:5–30.

Surafel Melaku Lakew, Quintino F. Lotito, Matteo Negri, Marco Turchi, and Marcello Federico. 2018. Improving zero-shot translation of low-resource languages. *CoRR*, abs/1811.01389.

Guillaume Lample and Alexis Conneau. 2019. Cross-lingual language model pretraining. *CoRR*, abs/1901.07291.

Chungmin Lee. 2019. Factivity alternation of attitude 'know' in Korean, Mongolian, Uyghur, Manchu, Azeri, etc. and content clausal nominals. *Journal of Cognitive Science*, 20(4):449–503.

Hoon Lee. 2017. *Manju Solho Gisun Kamcibuha Buleku Bithe - Manhan-sacen*. Korea University Press, Seoul.

Yinhan Liu, Jiatao Gu, Naman Goyal, Xian Li, Sergey Edunov, Marjan Ghazvininejad, Mike Lewis, and Luke Zettlemoyer. 2020. Multilingual denoising pre-training for neural machine translation. *Transactions of the Association for Computational Linguistics*, 8:726–742.

Jiaming Luo, Frederik Hartmann, Enrico Santus, Yuan Cao, and Regina Barzilay. 2020. Deciphering undersegmented ancient scripts using phonetic prior. *CoRR*, abs/2010.11054.

Andrej Malchukov and Patryk Czerwinski. 2020. Complex constructions in the Transeurasian languages. In Martine Robbeets and Alexander Savelyev, editors, *The Oxford Guide to the Transeurasian Languages*, pages 625–644. Oxford University Press, Oxford.

Samuel E. Martin. 1992. *A Reference Grammar of Korean*. Charles E. Tuttle, Rutland, VT and Tokyo.

Kishore Papineni, Salim Roukos, Todd Ward, and Wei-Jing Zhu. 2002. Bleu: a method for automatic evaluation of machine translation. In *Proceedings of the 40th Annual Meeting of the Association for Computational Linguistics*, pages 311–318, Philadelphia, Pennsylvania, USA. Association for Computational Linguistics.

Sangchul Park. 2018. The function of Modern Korean as in discourse. *Eoneohag*, 81:243–264.

Jeffrey Pennington, Richard Socher, and Christopher Manning. 2014. GloVe: Global vectors for word representation. In *Proceedings of the 2014 Conference on Empirical Methods in Natural Language Processing (EMNLP)*, pages 1532–1543, Doha, Qatar. Association for Computational Linguistics.

Telmo Pires, Eva Schlinger, and Dan Garrette. 2019. How multilingual is multilingual bert? *CoRR*, abs/1906.01502.

Ye Qi, Devendra Sachan, Matthieu Felix, Sarguna Padmanabhan, and Graham Neubig. 2018. When and why are pre-trained word embeddings useful for neural machine translation? In *Proceedings of the 2018 Conference of the North American Chapter of the Association for Computational Linguistics: Human Language Technologies, Volume 2 (Short Papers)*, pages 529–535, New Orleans, Louisiana. Association for Computational Linguistics.

Baegin Seong. 1977. Romanization of the special letters of manchu. *Eoneohag*, 2:185–197.

Aditya Siddhant, Ankur Bapna, Yuan Cao, Orhan Firat, Mia Xu Chen, Sneha Reddy Kudugunta, Naveen Arivazhagan, and Yonghui Wu. 2020. Leveraging monolingual data with self-supervision for multilingual neural machine translation. *CoRR*, abs/2005.04816.

Yuqing Tang, Chau Tran, Xian Li, Peng-Jen Chen, Naman Goyal, Vishrav Chaudhary, Jiatao Gu, and Angela Fan. 2021. Multilingual translation from denoising pre-training. In *Findings of the Association for Computational Linguistics: ACL-IJCNLP 2021*, pages 3450–3466.

Tasaku Tsunoda. 2006. *Language endangerment and language revitalization: An introduction*. De Gruyter Mouton.

Alexander Vovin. 2023. Written Manchu. In Alexander Vovin, José Andrés Alonso de la Fuente, and Juha Janhunen, editors, *The Tungusic Languages*, pages 103–138. Routledge, New York.

Linting Xue, Noah Constant, Adam Roberts, Mihir Kale, Rami Al-Rfou, Aditya Siddhant, Aditya Barua, and Colin Raffel. 2021. mt5: A massively multilingual pre-trained text-to-text transformer.

Hyun-Jo You. 2014. A manchu speller: With a practical introduction to the natural language processing of minority languages. *Altai Hakpo*, 24:39–67.

Shiyue Zhang, Benjamin Frey, and Mohit Bansal. 2020. Chren: Cherokee-english machine translation for endangered language revitalization.

A Example Appendix

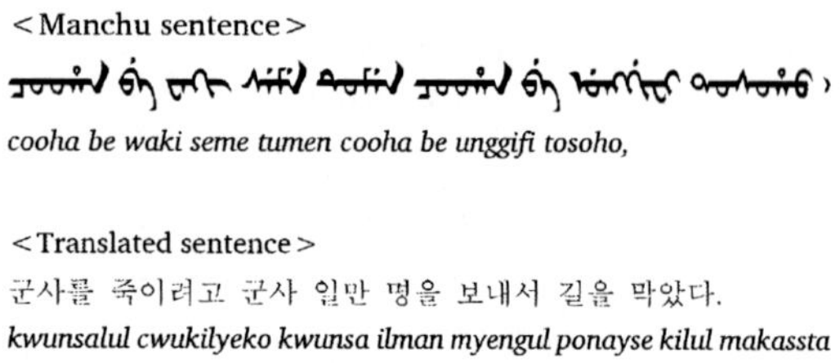

Figure 2: Example of Romanizations of Manchu text and Korean text

Improving Cross-Lingual Transfer for Open Information Extraction with Linguistic Feature Projection

Youmi Ma[1], Bhushan Kotnis[2], Carolin Lawrence[3], Goran Glavaš[4], Naoaki Okazaki[1]
[1]Tokyo Institute of Technology, Japan [2]Coresystems AG, Switzerland
[3]NEC Laboratories Europe, Germany [4]CAIDAS, University of Würzburg, Germany
{youmi.ma@nlp., okazaki@}c.titech.ac.jp
bhushan.kotnis@coresystems.ch, carolin.lawrence@neclab.eu
goran.glavas@uni-wuerzburg.de

Abstract

Open Information Extraction (OpenIE) structures information from natural language text in the form of (*subject*, *predicate*, *object*) triples. Supervised OpenIE is, in principle, only possible for English, for which plenty of labeled data exists. Recent research efforts tackled multilingual OpenIE by means of zero-shot transfer from English, with massively multilingual language models as vehicles of transfer. Given that OpenIE is a highly syntactic task, such transfer tends to fail for languages that are syntactically more complex and distant from English. In this work, we propose two Linguistic Feature Projection strategies to alleviate the situation, having observed the failure of transferring from English to German, Arabic, and Japanese. The strategies, namely (i) reordering of words in source-language utterances to match the target language word order and (ii) code-switching, lead to training data that contains features of both the source (English) and target language. Experiments render both strategies effective and mutually complementary on German, Arabic, and Japanese. Additionally, we propose a third strategy tailored for English-Japanese transfer by (iii) inserting Japanese case markers into English utterances, which leads to further performance gains[1].

1 Introduction

Open Information Extraction (OpenIE) is the task of structuring relational information from natural language text into (*subject*, *predicate*, *object*) triples (Banko et al., 2007). The task distinguishes itself from other Information Extraction tasks by being schema-free, i.e., requiring no pre-defined ontologies for entities and relations (Mausam, 2016).

Recently, neural OpenIE models – effectively supervised OpenIE models based on pretrained language models (LMs) – have attracted much attention from the community (Stanovsky et al., 2018; Cui et al., 2018; Kolluru et al., 2020). These models yield reasonable OpenIE performance for English, the only language for which labeled OpenIE data is plentiful. The lack of labeled data prevents training similarly performant OpenIE models for most other languages. The issue of limited resources for non-English languages has also been observed in other structured prediction tasks due to their complexity to annotate (Yu et al., 2022). As a result, approaches that aim to support multilingual OpenIE, e.g., Multi2OIE (Ro et al., 2020) and MILIE (Kotnis et al., 2022), resort to (zero-shot) cross-lingual transfer of the model trained on English OpenIE data, exploiting massively multilingual LMs such as mBERT (Devlin et al., 2019) or XLM-R (Conneau et al., 2020) as the vehicle of transfer. Cross-lingual transfer with multilingual LMs, especially for lower-level syntactic tasks, has been shown ineffective for target languages that are linguistically distant from English as the source language (Pires et al., 2019; Lauscher et al., 2020). Kotnis et al. (2022) also show that cross-lingual transfer for OpenIE based on mBERT is also far from robust: massive performance drops have been witnessed for target languages that exhibit syntactical dissimilarities with respect to English, i.e., German and Arabic.

Language	Family	Word Order	Script
German	IE: Germanic	SOV	Latin
Arabic	Afro-Asiatic	VSO	Arabic
Japanese	Japonic	SOV	Kanji/Kana
English	IE: English	SVO	Latin

Table 1: Target languages and their properties. **IE** is short for Indo-European.

In this work, we set out to improve the cross-lingual transferability of neural OpenIE from English (EN) to syntactically dissimilar languages, using German (DE), Arabic (AR), and Japanese (JA) as representatives. Table 1 summarizes the property of each language of interest. In addition to German

[1]The source code and benchmark are publicly available at https://github.com/nec-research/OpenIE_LFP

Proceedings of the The 3rd Workshop on Multi-lingual Representation Learning (MRL), pages 125–138
December 7, 2023 ©2023 Association for Computational Linguistics

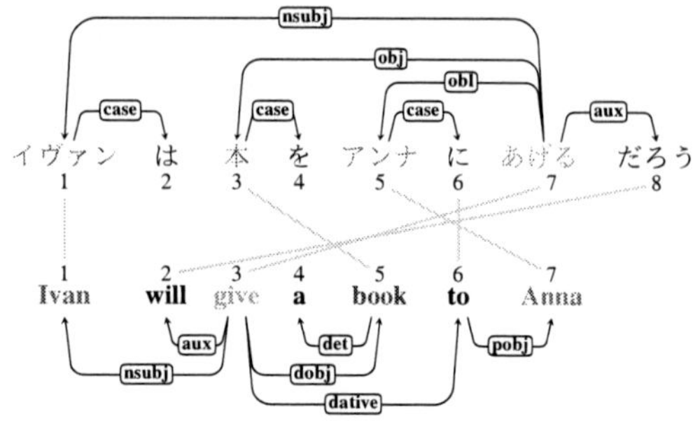

Figure 1: Dependency parsing trees (SpaCy, Honnibal and Montani (2017)) of an EN-JA parallel sentence pair. Gray lines in between represent alignment results from a token-level aligner (Dou and Neubig, 2021). As a visual aid, we highlight content words with the same semantic meaning using the same color.

and Arabic where low cross-lingual transferability from English has been witnessed, Japanese, as one of the most distant languages from English in linguistics (Chiswick and Miller, 2004), is also one of our focuses. As showcased in Figure 1, differences in word order and syntactic structure are evident for an English and Japanese parallel sentence pair.

We thus propose to bridge the gap between the source (English) and target language (L^{tgt}) to promote the cross-lingual transfer, by employing several linguistic feature projection (LFP) strategies. The LFP strategies we employ facilitate the transfer by constructing an intermediate language (to which we refer as *pseudo-English*), which effectively interpolates between the English and L^{tgt}. Concretely, we investigate two LFP strategies:

(1) *reordering* (RO): reorder words in the English sentences to match the word order of the translation in L^{tgt} (see Figure 2); (2) *code-switching* (CS): replace some of the English tokens with their aligned counterparts in L^{tgt} (see Figure 3). While code-switching has no effect on syntactical alignment, we expect it to push pseudo-English closer to L^{tgt} lexically. In addition to the language-agnostic strategies RO and CS, we propose a language-specific LFP strategy tailored for Japanese: (3) *case marker insertion* (CM). CM pushes pseudo-English closer to Japanese by inserting case markers, i.e., special Japanese linguistic units that give important hints about the grammatical roles of noun phrases, into the English sentence (see Figure 4).

To verify the effectiveness of proposed LFP strategies, we train the state-of-the-art neural OpenIE system on the generated pseudo-English training data. Evaluation on BenchIE (Gashteovski et al., 2022) renders all strategies effective and mutually complementary, significantly improving the F_1 scores of German, Arabic, and Japanese over existing methods.

2 Preliminaries

2.1 OpenIE: Task Definition

OpenIE is the task of collecting structured facts in the form of (s, p, o) from natural language texts, where s, p, and o stand for subject, predicate, and object, respectively. Here, we define all components of structured facts as text spans extracted from the original text. Given a natural language sentence $S = w_1, w_2, \ldots, w_n$, the goal is to extract all structured facts in S as a set of triples $T = \{(s_1, p_1, o_1), (s_2, p_2, o_2), \ldots, (s_k, p_k, o_k)\}$.

In this work, we choose BenchIE (Gashteovski et al., 2022) as the benchmark. BenchIE is a multilingual benchmark that estimates OpenIE performance more reliably than measures based on token overlaps leveraged by prior benchmarks like OIE2016 (Stanovsky and Dagan, 2016) and CaRB (Bhardwaj et al., 2019). BenchIE defines fact synsets that group all (s, p, o) valid extractions that describe the same fact (Table 2). If the extraction perfectly matches any one of the gold extractions of a synset, then the corresponding fact is regarded as correctly extracted. Being complete, BenchIE rewards only exact matches against some gold extractions and avoids excessive rewarding of systems that produce highly overlapping extractions that describe the same fact.

2.2 Preprocessing

Throughout this paper, we adopt English as the source language for cross-lingual transfer and denote the target language as L^{tgt}. Similar to existing techniques (Fei et al., 2020; Kolluru et al., 2022), we adopt two off-the-shelf systems to assist the transfer: a machine translator (MT) and a token aligner. Here we introduce the overall process of machine translation and token alignment, leaving details of selected systems to §4.

Machine Translation. We first generate texts in L^{tgt} parallel to English texts to serve as points of reference for linguistic features of L^{tgt}. Specifically, for each sentence $S^{\text{en}} = t_1^{\text{en}}, t_2^{\text{en}}, \ldots, t_n^{\text{en}}$ with n tokens, we obtain its translation in L^{tgt}: $S^{\text{tgt}} = t_1^{\text{tgt}}, t_2^{\text{tgt}}, \ldots, t_m^{\text{tgt}}$ with m tokens.

id	subject	predicate	object
Sentence: A large gravestone was erected in 1866, over 100 years after his death.			
1	[A] [large] gravestone	was erected in	1866
	[A] [large] gravestone	was	erected in 1866
	[A] [large] gravestone	was erected	in 1866
2	[A] [large] gravestone	was erected [over 100 years] after	his death
	[A] [large] gravestone	was erected [over 100 years]	after his death

Table 2: An example sentence in English BenchIE (Gashteovski et al., 2022) with 2 fact synsets. A fact synset contains one or more gold extractions. Tokens in brackets ([]) are optional and can be omitted in extractions.

Token Alignment. Next, we perform token alignment between S^{en} and S^{tgt} with the help of a pretrained aligner. This way, we effectively split English tokens into two disjoint groups: (1) $T^{\text{en}\to\text{tgt}}$: English tokens with one (or more) L^{tgt} tokens aligned to them, and (2) $T^{\text{en}\not\to\text{tgt}}$: English tokens not aligned to any L^{tgt} tokens.

2.3 Baseline OpenIE Transfer Methods

We first evaluate the performance of MILIE (Kotnis et al., 2022) – a state-of-the-art OpenIE system – on BenchIE, after subjecting it to two standard transfer techniques for token level tasks: (i) zero-shot cross-lingual transfer and (ii) annotation projection. We show the performance for these standard transfer approaches in the first part of Table 3 (see §4).

Zero-Shot Transfer. We evaluate MILIE trained on English OpenIE data directly on L^{tgt} portion of BenchIE. Our setting differs from that of Kotnis et al. (2022) in that we adopt XLM-R instead of mBERT as the vehicle of transfer, hence higher cross-lingual transferability could be expected. Unfortunately, the model still scores low on German (5.9% F_1), Arabic (2.8% F_1), and Japanese (1.5% F_1). Given that the model scores 28.6% F_1 on English BenchIE (see Appendix C.1), we confirm our suspicion that zero-shot OpenIE transfer between syntactically dissimilar languages fails. Further, we observe that the difficulty of cross-lingual transfer varies among languages, with Japanese being the most challenging, followed by Arabic and German.

Annotation Projection. We carry out a second pilot experiment, facilitating the transfer by means of annotation projection (AP, Yarowsky et al. (2001); Akbik et al. (2015); Aminian et al. (2019)). Here, we utilize the token alignments to transfer the token-level labels (which belong to the standard BIO scheme for sequence labeling) to the automatically translated sentence in L^{tgt}. For example, consider the subject span (labeled in the original English sentence) $s^{\text{en}} = (t_i^{\text{en}}, t_{i+1}^{\text{en}}, t_{i+2}^{\text{en}})$ with the induced EN-TGT token alignment $(t_i^{\text{en}}, t_j^{\text{tgt}})$, $(t_{i+2}^{\text{en}}, t_{j-1}^{\text{tgt}})$; note that t_{i+1}^{en} is not aligned with any token in L^{tgt} in this case. The corresponding subject span in L^{tgt} is then $s^{\text{tgt}} = (t_{j-1}^{\text{tgt}}, t_j^{\text{tgt}})$. The obtained L^{tgt} triple is then considered to be a "gold" extraction from the automatically-translated sentence in L^{tgt}. We then use this label-projected noisy OpenIE corpus in L^{tgt} to train MILIE. While better than zero-shot transfer, AP still yields moderate performance on German (9.6% F_1) and Arabic (8.7% F_1). On Japanese, AP yields even lower than zero-shot transfer (0.7% F_1). Looking closely at the projected Japanese corpus, we identified many triples with discontinuous spans, resulting in bad labels that violate the assumption of the BIO tagging scheme. The discontinuity comes from the syntactic dissimilarity between English and Japanese, where spans in English are likely to be projected into multiple discontinuous segments in Japanese.

3 Linguistic Feature Projection

Based on insights of previous works (K et al., 2020; Gashteovski et al., 2022; Kotnis et al., 2022), as well as our own observation in §2.3, it is reasonable to conclude that transfer failure is due to systematic syntactic discrepancies between English and L^{tgt}. We propose to remedy this with Linguistic Feature Projection (LFP), that is, by converting labeled English sentences into pseudo-English that reflects the syntactic properties of L^{tgt}. This way, we aim to (i) emulate syntax of L^{tgt} in our training data while, unlike with annotation projection, and (ii) retaining clean token-level OpenIE labels. Concretely, we propose two LFP strategies: reordering (RO) and code-switching (CS). RO is meant to bridge the difference in word order between the languages, while CS brings additional lexico-semantic alignment. Additionally, having witnessed the challenges in EN-JA cross-lingual transfer (§ 2.3), we introduce another strategy specifically designed for Japanese, case marker insertion (CM), which caters for both

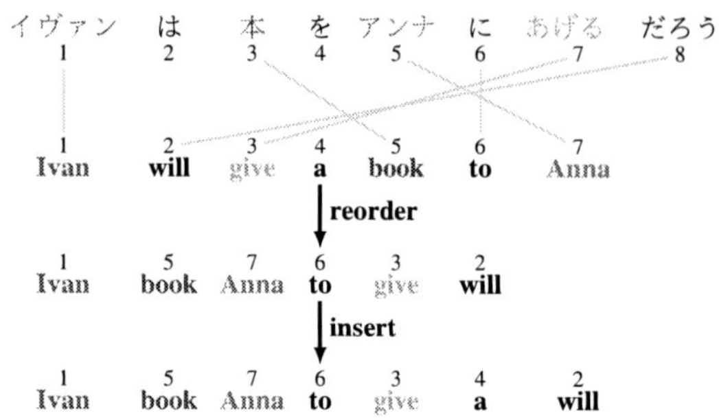

Figure 2: The reordering strategy.

syntactic and lexical differences.

Throughout this section, we use the following English sentence as a running example: *"Ivan will give a book to Anna"*, with its Japanese translation shown in Figure 1. The example contains a knowledge fact that can be structured as a triple (Ivan, give a book to, Anna). Note that although we introduce the strategies with EN-JA examples, RO and CS are language-agnostic and can be applied to any language pair.

3.1 Reordering

Sentences. For each English sentence S^{en}, our goal is to reorder the words to form a new sentence $S^{\text{en}}_{\text{RO}}$ that reflects the word order of the translation S^{tgt}. We first reorder English tokens based on the order of their aligned L^{tgt} counterparts. We reposition each aligned English token $t^{\text{en}}_i \in T^{\text{en}\rightarrow\text{tgt}}$ according to the index of its alignment t^{tgt}_j in S^{tgt}. If t^{en}_i is aligned with multiple tokens in S^{tgt}, we choose the token for which the alignment model yielded the highest confidence. This treatment holds for all proposed LFP strategies. As shown in the example in Figure 2, 'give' is placed after 'book' because 'give' is aligned to 'あげる' and 'book' is aligned to '本', and '本' comes after 'あげる' in the Japanese translation. In the second step, we insert English tokens without alignment $t^{\text{en}}_j \in T^{\text{en}\not\rightarrow\text{tgt}}$ into the reordered sentence: for each such token, we place it directly after the closest preceding aligned token $t^{\text{en}}_i \in T^{\text{en}\rightarrow\text{tgt}}$. In the example from Figure 2, we place 'a' after 'give' as its closest preceding token.

Triples. Tokens within each triple element (i.e., subject, predicate, and object) are then reordered to match the token ordering of the new, reordered pseudo-English sentence. In the example, the triple (Ivan, give a book to, Anna) becomes (Ivan, book to give a, Anna).

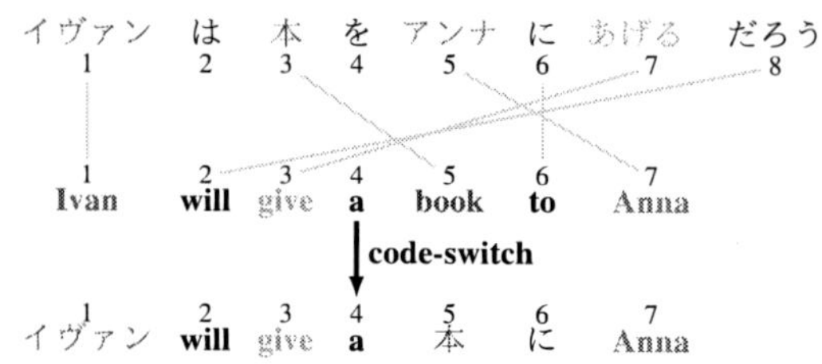

Figure 3: The code-switching strategy.

3.2 Code-Switching

Code-switching, or code-mixing, is a common phenomenon in multilingual communities, with speakers seamlessly switching between two or more languages, even within sentences. Inspired by Krishnan et al. (2021), we adopt code-switching to produce sentences comprising tokens in both English and L^{tgt}. Training on the code-switched sentences, we expect the MILIE (and its underlying LM) to establish better and task-specific lexico-semantic alignments between the two languages. Training on code-switched data is thus expected to improve target language performance, compared to training on English (or pseudo-English) sentences alone.

Sentences. For each English sentence S^{en}, we replace words with their alignments in S^{tgt} to form a code-switched sentence $S^{\text{en}}_{\text{CS}}$. For each English token $t^{\text{en}} \in T^{\text{en}\rightarrow\text{tgt}}$ aligned to a token t^{tgt}_j, we replace it by t^{tgt}_j with probability p, a hyperparameter controlling the percentage of aligned English tokens to be replaced with their alignments in S^{tgt}. As shown in Figure 3, if we set $p = 0.5$, half of the aligned English tokens will be replaced by their alignments in S^{tgt}. In this specific example, we have 'Ivan' replaced by 'イヴァン', 'to' replaced by 'に', and 'book' replaced by '本', while 'will', 'give', and 'Anna' stay unchanged.

Triples. We switch tokens according to their replacements (or lack thereof) in $S^{\text{en}}_{\text{CS}}$. In this example, the triple (Ivan, give a book to, Anna) becomes (イヴァン, give a 本 に, Anna).

3.3 Inserting Case Markers

Our last LFP strategy is specifically tailored for Japanese, and focuses on *case markers*, a special class of functional tokens in Japanese.

Case Markers in Japanese. Case markers (*kakujoshi*) are special functional tokens that immediately follow noun phrases (NP) they refer to. Case

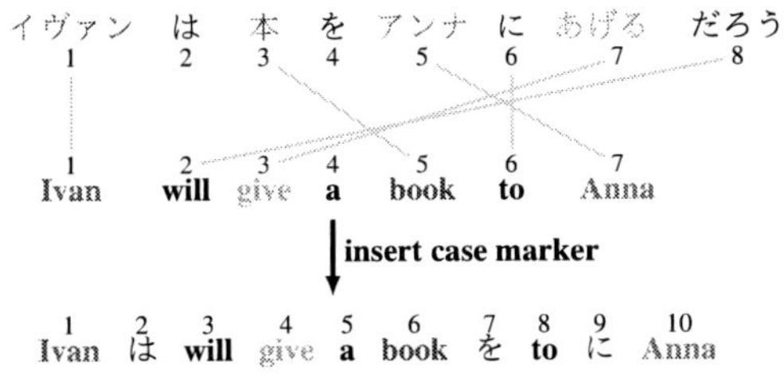

Figure 4: The case marker insertion strategy.

markers indicate the grammatical role of their respective NPs, and thus provide important signals for syntactic tasks like OpenIE. In the example from Figure 1, the 4th Japanese token, 'を(*wo*)' is a case marker that commonly accompanies the object of an action. In this example, 'を(*wo*)' indicates that '本(*book*)' is the object of 'あげる(*give*)'. Case markers thus reveal a lot about the syntactic structure of Japanese sentences: e.g., the Universal Dependency (UD) annotations for Japanese have rules that determine dependency labels based on case markers (Tanaka et al., 2016; Asahara et al., 2018; Omura and Asahara, 2018). Under UD, the case marker and the NP it modifies are connected by a dependency arc labeled `case`, as in Figure 1.

Sentences. For each English sentence S^{en}, our goal is to insert Japanese case markers at the adequate position, resulting in a new sentence $S^{\text{en}}_{\text{CM}}$. For each English token $t^{\text{en}} \in T^{\text{en}\rightarrow\text{ja}}$ that is aligned to a Japanese token t^{ja}_j, we check whether t^{ja}_{j+1}, following t^{ja}_j, is a case marker or not. If so, we insert t^{ja}_{j+1} directly after t^{en}. In the example from Figure 4, given the word alignment pairs (Ivan, イヴァン), (book, 本) and (Anna, アンナ), we insert case markers 'は', 'を' and 'に' after 'Ivan', 'book' and 'Anna', respectively, into the English sentence.

Triples. To preserve the contiguity of each span, we also insert case markers in the triples. In this example, the triple corresponding to sentence $S^{\text{en}}_{\text{CM}}$ is (Ivan は, give a book を, Anna に).

4 Experiments

We have introduced the LFP strategies to bridge the gap between English and syntactically-dissimilar languages, both structurally and lexically. In this section, we describe the experiments conducted to verify the effectiveness of the proposed strategies.

4.1 Settings

Dependent Systems. As mentioned in §2.3, we need two off-the-shelf systems to perform cross-lingual transfer: a machine translator and a token aligner. For the machine translator, we adopt NLLB (No-Language-Left-Behind, Costa-jussà et al. (2022))[2], a neural machine translation system eligible for translating between any pair of 200 languages. For the token aligner, we adopt AWESOME (Dou and Neubig, 2021)[3], the state-of-the-art multilingual token aligner.

Multilingual LMs (mLMs). We by default base our experiments on mBERT (Devlin et al., 2019), arguably the most widely used massively multilingual LM. XLM-Roberta (XLM-R, Conneau et al. (2020)), another multilingual LM believed to transfer better than mBERT, is also included for comparison. We employ XLM-R *base* whose model architecture is the same as mBERT.

Training. We obtain training data by applying the proposed LFP strategies on English OpenIE4 training set (Zhan and Zhao, 2020), commonly used in prior work (Ro et al., 2020; Kotnis et al., 2022). For each target language, we create a proxy dataset for every possible combination of the proposed LFP strategies. This results in 3 proxy datasets for German and Arabic and 7 proxy datasets for Japanese. We train a MILIE model on each of the proxy datasets, with the batch size, learning rate, and number of epochs set to 128, 3e-5, and 2.0, respectively, following Kotnis et al. (2022). For code-switching, we decide the replacement rate for each target language by searching over the grid $\{0.2, 0.5, 1.0\}$. More details, including dataset statistics, model parameters, and computational budgets, are described in Appendix B.

Evaluation. We evaluate MILIE trained on each proxy dataset on German, Arabic, and Japanese BenchIE. All reported scores are averages over three runs corresponding to initializations with different random seeds. Notably, while previous works have collected German and Arabic BenchIE (Gashteovski et al., 2022; Kotnis et al., 2022), a Japanese version was absent. We thus create Japanese BenchIE, which will be made publicly available, following the same data-collecting

[2] `https://github.com/facebookresearch/fairseq/tree/nllb/examples/nllb`

[3] `https://github.com/neulab/awesome-align`

	mLM	German (DE) P	R	F_1	Arabic (AR) P	R	F_1	Japanese (JA) P	R	F_1
Baselines										
zero-shot	mBERT	12.70	3.84	5.89	10.71	1.51	2.64	0.00	0.00	0.00
	XLM-R	12.26	3.90	5.91	12.35	1.57	2.79	9.66	0.83	1.53
AP	mBERT	**22.47**	6.69	10.31	24.89	5.27	8.70	18.61	0.33	0.65
	XLM-R	18.52	4.36	7.06	**27.95**	6.84	11.00	**29.25**	0.36	0.71
LFP Strategies										
RO + CS (+ CM)	mBERT	17.05	**8.63**	**11.45**	22.21	**9.65**	**13.45**	19.71	**7.26**	**10.61**
	XLM-R	17.75	7.74	10.78	22.56	9.58	**13.45**	16.95	5.69	8.51
RO	mBERT	15.77	3.96	6.32	21.83	5.27	8.46	12.52	2.02	3.47
CS	mBERT	13.43	5.65	7.95	9.92	3.29	4.93	0.06	0.03	0.04

Table 3: Precision (P), Recall (R), and F_1 scores (%) of MILIE on BenchIE. **mLM** is short for multilingual Language Model and **AP** is short for annotation projection. **RO**, **CS**, **CM** refer to reordering, code-switching, and case marker insertion (only for JA), respectively.

process as other non-English versions, with details described in Appendix A.

4.2 Main Results

We summarize the experiment results of all target languages in Table 3. In addition to the results of MILIE trained on the proxy dataset combining all LFP strategies, two ablations are also provided: reordering (RO) only and code-switching (CS) only.

LFP strategies improve cross-lingual transfer for OpenIE. We observe the same tendency for all target languages: training MILIE on data created by combining all LFP strategies yields the best performance. Specifically, when using mBERT as the mLM, a combination of RO and CS improves MILIE over zero-shot performance by 5.6% F_1 for DE, 10.8% F_1 for AR, and 10.6 % F_1 for JA. These are improvements over the current state-of-the-art, as MILIE is a state-of-the-art system on BenchIE. The superiority is still evident even compared to the zero-shot performance of MILIE on top of XLM-R, especially for languages distant from English, i.e., AR and JA. Interestingly, with MILIE as the OpenIE model, AP exhibits high precision and low recall, yielding few but decent predictions. Systems trained under AP are thus unavailing for practical OpenIE applications, e.g., knowledge base population (Gashteovski et al., 2020).

LFP strategies benefit cross-lingual transfer the most on distant language pairs. Under zero-shot setting, XLM-R exhibits higher cross-lingual transferability than mBERT. Notably, for EN-JA, while transferring with mBERT totally fails (0.0% F_1), XLM-R brings the performance up to 1.5% F_1. However, the performance still lags far behind that of other language pairs. The low transferability from EN to JA of both mLMs is backed by existing works (Pires et al., 2019; Lauscher et al., 2020), where mLMs are found less effective on distant language pairs. Proxy datasets, consisting of pseudo-English sentences with features of both EN and the target language, can thus act as an intermediary between the language pair. By fine-tuning on the proxy dataset, mLMs no longer need to transfer from English to an extremely distant language but can "land" halfway on the pseudo-English, reducing the burden of cross-lingual transfer. As shown in Table 3, when adopting the LFP strategies, we observe more performance gains on languages distant from English, i.e., AR and JA, than languages closer to English, i.e., DE.

Bridging syntactic differences matters the most. We observe that RO is the key to promoting cross-lingual transfer, especially for distant target languages like AR and JA. RO alone improves the performance by 5.7% F_1 for AR and 1.9% F_1 for JA over the zero-shot baselines. While CS helps less independently, it brings substantial further gains when combined with RO. The above observation confirms that neural OpenIE models heavily rely on word order signals. This explains why transferring to DE, AR, and JA, whose word order differs from English, is harder than transferring to, e.g., Chinese.[4] We thus conclude that bridging syntactical differences plays a more essential role in cross-lingual transfer for OpenIE than lexical alignment.

4.3 Effect of Dependent Systems

Similar to existing translation-based cross-lingual transfer techniques (Faruqui and Kumar, 2015; Fei

[4]Chinese obtains 16.3% F_1, whereas our best scores for German, Arabic, and Japanese are 11.5%, 13.5%, and 10.6%, respectively.

MT	IWSLT17 (BLEU)	Transfer Technique	BenchIE (F_1)
German (DE)			
NLLB	**32.34**	AP	10.16
		RO + CS	11.45
WMT19	30.95	AP	9.59
		RO + CS	**11.54**
Japanese (JA)			
NLLB	**12.60**	AP	0.65
		RO + CS + CM	**10.61**
JParaCrawl	11.18	AP	1.08
		RO + CS + CM	8.48

Table 4: F_1 scores (%) on BenchIE when applying cross-lingual transfer based on different MT systems.

et al., 2020; Kolluru et al., 2022), our proposed method depends on a machine translator (MT). Here, we investigate how using different MTs will influence the performance of the OpenIE model, namely MILIE, on BenchIE.

Settings. We focus on EN-DE and EN-JA as few EN-AR MTs are publicly available. For EN-DE, we employ the MT trained on WMT19 (Barrault et al., 2019) provided by fairseq (Ng et al., 2019)[5]; for EN-JA, we employ the MT trained on JParaCrawl released by Morishita et al. (2020)[6]. The performance of each MT system is evaluated on IWSLT17 test set (Cettolo et al., 2017)[7].

Effectiveness of LFP relates to the quality of translations. As shown in Table 4, using better MT systems for cross-lingual transfer results in better OpenIE systems for Japanese. However, the situation is not the same for German: NLLB scores higher than WMT19, while LFP based on WMT19 yields slightly better performance on BenchIE. The discrepancy possibly results from the divergent difficulty of EN-DE and EN-JA translations. While EN-DE MTs are good enough to yield fair translations with BLEU scores over 30, the translations of EN-JA MTs score below 15. Given that EN-JA MTs struggle to generate good translations, the 1.4-point improvement on BLEU (from 11.2 to 12.6) becomes more crucial as some critical errors may be eliminated. This is especially important for succeeding token-level alignment and projections. In contrast, the difference in BLEU scores of EN-DE MTs can be less important, as the translations are already good enough and unlikely to contain many critical errors.

[5]https://github.com/facebookresearch/fairseq/blob/main/examples/translation/

[6]http://www.kecl.ntt.co.jp/icl/lirg/jparacrawl/

[7]https://huggingface.co/datasets/iwslt2017, we use SacreBLEU (Post, 2018) to compute the scores.

4.4 Language-Specific Investigations

Here we focus on EN-JA transfer, with the following purposes: (i) To analyze the effectiveness of case-marker insertion (CM), the LFP strategy tailored for Japanese; (ii) To compare our method with even stronger baselines, namely the state-of-the-art cross-lingual transfer technique for OpenIE dubbed Alignment-Augmented Constrained Translation (AACTrans, Kolluru et al. (2022)). AACTrans is a sequence-to-sequence model for transferring OpenIE training data from source to target language, improving consistency between the transferred sentence and triples by ensuring that triples consist of only tokens present in the sentence.

Settings. In addition to an MT system and a token aligner, a parallel corpus between the source and target language is necessary to train AACTrans, for which we employ The Kyoto Free Translation Task dataset (KFTT, Neubig (2011)). We adopt the MT system trained on JParaCrawl for translation and AWESOME for token alignment. We train three different neural OpenIE models – GenOIE, Gen2OIE, both proposed together with AACTrans, and MILIE – on data generated by AACTrans via Cross-Lingual Projection (CLP, Faruqui and Kumar (2015)), a variant of annotation projection. It is worth noting that transferring OpenIE training data with AACTrans (via CLP) is time-consuming as it requires multiple rounds of MT training.[8] The evaluation results are shown in Table 5.

AACTrans+CLP fails on EN-JA transfer. Much like zero-shot transfer and annotation projection, AACTrans (with CLP) exhibits near-zero performance on Japanese BenchIE, irrespective of the underlying OpenIE model (GenOIE/Gen2OIE, or MILIE). We believe this is because CLP, as a variant of AP, also fails between English and Japanese: as noted in §2.3 and also Kolluru et al. (2022), CLP implicitly and strongly assumes that contiguous spans in the source language correspond to contiguous spans in the target language, which is rarely the case between English and Japanese. As depicted in Figure 1, "give a book" at indices (3,4,5) in the English sentence is aligned to a discontiguous span "本 あげる" (indices 3,7) in the Japanese sentence.

[8]It took us ca. 10 GPU-days to carry out EN-JA data transfer. We refer the reader to Kolluru et al. (2022) for more details on AACTrans (with CLP).

			Model	P	R	F_1
Baselines						
zero-shot			MILIE	0.00	0.00	0.00
AP			MILIE	**21.57**	0.55	1.08
AACTrans			GenOIE	0.00	0.00	0.00
AACTrans			Gen2OIE	0.25	0.11	0.16
AACTrans			MILIE	20.44	0.58	1.13
LFP Strategies						
RO	**CS**	**CM**				
✓	✓	✓	MILIE	15.75	**5.80**	**8.48**
✓		✓	MILIE	19.27	4.81	7.69
✓	✓		MILIE	13.06	4.34	6.51
✓			MILIE	15.03	2.44	4.17
	✓	✓	MILIE	1.50	0.44	0.68
		✓	MILIE	2.74	0.11	0.21
	✓		MILIE	0.07	0.03	0.04

Table 5: Precision (P), Recall (R) and F_1 scores (%) on Japanese BenchIE. AACTrans is with CLP as described in Kolluru et al. (2022).

This leads to incomplete extractions in the Japanese dataset created by AACTrans.

CM promotes cross-lingual transfer when combined with RO. Similar to CS, we observe that CM improves the performance of MILIE when combined with RO, while it does not help on its own. However, CM is more effective than CS, as RO + CM outperforms RO + CS for 1.2% F_1. We believe CM is more powerful than CS because CM bridges EN and JA both structurally and lexically, while CS merely brings lexical alignments.

5 Related Work

OpenIE. Although OpenIE has been a heated topic since proposed by Banko et al. (2007), most of the discussions are focused on English (Mausam et al., 2012; Del Corro and Gemulla, 2013; Angeli et al., 2015; Mausam, 2016; Stanovsky et al., 2018; Kolluru et al., 2020). While some efforts have been made on non-English languages, these methods are rule-based, relying heavily on pre-defined syntactic rules (Zhila and Gelbukh, 2014; Guarasci et al., 2020; Wang et al., 2021). The rules, however, are highly language-dependent and hard to transfer between different languages. More recently, neural OpenIE systems trained with supervised data exhibit reasonable performance (Stanovsky et al., 2018; Kolluru et al., 2020). Similar to most neural systems, these systems are free from hand-crafted rules, while a large scale of training data guarantees their performance. Developing multi- and cross-lingual OpenIE systems has hence become increasingly important, reducing the cost of collecting human annotation in non-English languages.

Multilingual OpenIE. Faruqui and Kumar (2015) proposed translating non-English sentences into English, extracting relations with existing English systems, and projecting the extracted labels back to the non-English language. However, Claro et al. (2019) pointed out that cross-lingual transfer depending solely on machine translation is unreliable. Ro et al. (2020) and Kotnis et al. (2022) designed and trained OpenIE systems on top of multilingual BERT (mBERT, Devlin et al. (2019)) with English data, relying on mBERT to capture language-agnostic representations. Although these systems exhibited reasonable zero-shot performance on some languages, the performance gap between different languages is severe. Specifically, the performance on German and Arabic is worse than that on Chinese and Galician (Kotnis et al., 2022). We postulated that the performance gap is due to drastic syntactical differences, such as the word order, between these languages and English. This assumption has been confirmed in our experiments, where the reordering of English sentences proved to be especially effective in bridging the gap between such languages and English. More recently, Kolluru et al. (2022) proposed AACTrans to automatically generate training data in the target language by translating English sentences and their extractions. However, we observed the approach suffers from low recalls. In contrast, our proposed LFP strategies promote cross-lingual transfer vastly, outperforming this baseline by over 7 F_1 points on EN-JA cross-lingual transfer. It is also notable that AACTrans is more time-consuming than our proposed methods.

6 Conclusion

This work tackles the issue of transferring knowledge about OpenIE from English to a syntactically-different language, using German, Arabic, and Japanese as representatives. We propose to promote cross-lingual transfer between each language pair by combating their differences. Specifically, we introduced three Linguistic Feature Projection (LFP) strategies for generating a proxy dataset that contains the linguistic features of both English and the target language. Experiment results confirmed that OpenIE systems trained on the generated proxy dataset outperform all baselines and existing systems on German, Arabic, and Japanese. Ablation studies showed that reordering English words to resemble the typical word order of the target language was the most important ingredient for encouraging cross-lingual transfer on OpenIE.

Future directions include building OpenIE systems that are less sensitive to word order and extending the strategies to syntax levels.

Limitations

Although this work improves cross-lingual transfer between English and another distant language, several limitations exist.

Firstly, the proposed linguistic feature projection (LFP) strategies presume the accessibility of pre-trained machine translation systems and token aligners. The cross-lingual transfer could be difficult for low-resource language pairs where these pre-trained systems are unavailable.

Secondly, the issue of projected triples with discontinuous spans has not been completely resolved. Although proposed LFP strategies can resolve discontinuity to some degree, they do not directly tackle the issue. Some projected extractions in the proxy dataset still contain discontinuous spans and are thus excluded during training. To make full use of the projected data, an explicit approach that tackles discontinuous spans needs to be developed.

Thirdly, how recent large language models (LLMs) perform on OpenIE has not been measured in this work. As LLMs are attracting increasing attention from the community, a comparison between the proposed method against LLMs is potentially helpful.

Ethics Statement

Although we do not foresee a substantial ethical concern in our proposed strategies, there may be a side effect passed down from the pre-trained systems. It is thus important to choose nontoxic and reliable machine translation and word alignment systems during pre-processing.

Note that during data collection, we obey the General Data Protection Regulation (GDPR) law[9] that protects both the annotators and the data.

[9] `https://gdpr.eu/`

References

Alan Akbik, Laura Chiticariu, Marina Danilevsky, Yunyao Li, Shivakumar Vaithyanathan, and Huaiyu Zhu. 2015. Generating high quality proposition Banks for multilingual semantic role labeling. In *Proceedings of the 53rd Annual Meeting of the Association for Computational Linguistics and the 7th International Joint Conference on Natural Language Processing (Volume 1: Long Papers)*, pages 397–407, Beijing, China. Association for Computational Linguistics.

Maryam Aminian, Mohammad Sadegh Rasooli, and Mona Diab. 2019. Cross-lingual transfer of semantic roles: From raw text to semantic roles. In *Proceedings of the 13th International Conference on Computational Semantics - Long Papers*, pages 200–210, Gothenburg, Sweden. Association for Computational Linguistics.

Gabor Angeli, Melvin Jose Johnson Premkumar, and Christopher D. Manning. 2015. Leveraging linguistic structure for open domain information extraction. In *Proceedings of the 53rd Annual Meeting of the Association for Computational Linguistics and the 7th International Joint Conference on Natural Language Processing (Volume 1: Long Papers)*, pages 344–354, Beijing, China. Association for Computational Linguistics.

Masayuki Asahara, Hiroshi Kanayama, Takaaki Tanaka, Yusuke Miyao, Sumire Uematsu, Shinsuke Mori, Yuji Matsumoto, Mai Omura, and Yugo Murawaki. 2018. Universal Dependencies version 2 for Japanese. In *Proceedings of the Eleventh International Conference on Language Resources and Evaluation (LREC 2018)*, Miyazaki, Japan. European Language Resources Association (ELRA).

Michele Banko, Michael J. Cafarella, Stephen Soderland, Matt Broadhead, and Oren Etzioni. 2007. Open information extraction from the web. In *Proceedings of the 20th International Joint Conference on Artifical Intelligence*, IJCAI'07, page 2670–2676, San Francisco, CA, USA. Morgan Kaufmann Publishers Inc.

Loïc Barrault, Ondřej Bojar, Marta R. Costa-jussà, Christian Federmann, Mark Fishel, Yvette Graham, Barry Haddow, Matthias Huck, Philipp Koehn, Shervin Malmasi, Christof Monz, Mathias Müller, Santanu Pal, Matt Post, and Marcos Zampieri. 2019. Findings of the 2019 conference on machine translation (WMT19). In *Proceedings of the Fourth Conference on Machine Translation (Volume 2: Shared Task Papers, Day 1)*, pages 1–61, Florence, Italy. Association for Computational Linguistics.

Sangnie Bhardwaj, Samarth Aggarwal, and Mausam Mausam. 2019. CaRB: A crowdsourced benchmark for open IE. In *Proceedings of the 2019 Conference on Empirical Methods in Natural Language Processing and the 9th International Joint Conference on Natural Language Processing (EMNLP-IJCNLP)*, pages 6262–6267, Hong Kong, China. Association for Computational Linguistics.

Mauro Cettolo, Marcello Federico, Luisa Bentivogli, Jan Niehues, Sebastian Stüker, Katsuhito Sudoh, Koichiro Yoshino, and Christian Federmann. 2017. Overview of the IWSLT 2017 evaluation campaign. In *Proceedings of the 14th International Conference on Spoken Language Translation*, pages 2–14, Tokyo, Japan. International Workshop on Spoken Language Translation.

Barry Chiswick and Paul Miller. 2004. Linguistic distance: A quantitative measure of the distance between english and other languages. IZA Discussion Papers 1246, Institute of Labor Economics (IZA).

Daniela Barreiro Claro, Marlo Souza, Clarissa Castellã Xavier, and Leandro Oliveira. 2019. Multilingual open information extraction: Challenges and opportunities. *Information*, 10(7).

Alexis Conneau, Kartikay Khandelwal, Naman Goyal, Vishrav Chaudhary, Guillaume Wenzek, Francisco Guzmán, Edouard Grave, Myle Ott, Luke Zettlemoyer, and Veselin Stoyanov. 2020. Unsupervised cross-lingual representation learning at scale. In *Proceedings of the 58th Annual Meeting of the Association for Computational Linguistics*, pages 8440–8451, Online. Association for Computational Linguistics.

Marta R. Costa-jussà, James Cross, Onur Çelebi, Maha Elbayad, Kenneth Heafield, Kevin Heffernan, Elahe Kalbassi, Janice Lam, Daniel Licht, Jean Maillard, Anna Sun, Skyler Wang, Guillaume Wenzek, Al Youngblood, Bapi Akula, Loic Barrault, Gabriel Mejia Gonzalez, Prangthip Hansanti, John Hoffman, Semarley Jarrett, Kaushik Ram Sadagopan, Dirk Rowe, Shannon Spruit, Chau Tran, Pierre Andrews, Necip Fazil Ayan, Shruti Bhosale, Sergey Edunov, Angela Fan, Cynthia Gao, Vedanuj Goswami, Francisco Guzmán, Philipp Koehn, Alexandre Mourachko, Christophe Ropers, Safiyyah Saleem, Holger Schwenk, and Jeff Wang. 2022. No language left behind: Scaling human-centered machine translation.

Lei Cui, Furu Wei, and Ming Zhou. 2018. Neural open information extraction. In *Proceedings of the 56th Annual Meeting of the Association for Computational Linguistics (Volume 2: Short Papers)*, pages 407–413, Melbourne, Australia. Association for Computational Linguistics.

Luciano Del Corro and Rainer Gemulla. 2013. Clausie: Clause-based open information extraction. In *Proceedings of the 22nd International Conference on World Wide Web*, WWW '13, page 355–366, New York, NY, USA. Association for Computing Machinery.

Jacob Devlin, Ming-Wei Chang, Kenton Lee, and Kristina Toutanova. 2019. BERT: Pre-training of deep bidirectional transformers for language understanding. In *Proceedings of the 2019 Conference of the North American Chapter of the Association for Computational Linguistics: Human Language Technologies, Volume 1 (Long and Short Papers)*, pages 4171–4186, Minneapolis, Minnesota. Association for Computational Linguistics.

Zi-Yi Dou and Graham Neubig. 2021. Word alignment by fine-tuning embeddings on parallel corpora. In *Proceedings of the 16th Conference of the European Chapter of the Association for Computational Linguistics: Main Volume*, pages 2112–2128, Online. Association for Computational Linguistics.

Manaal Faruqui and Shankar Kumar. 2015. Multilingual open relation extraction using cross-lingual projection. In *Proceedings of the 2015 Conference of the North American Chapter of the Association for Computational Linguistics: Human Language Technologies*, pages 1351–1356, Denver, Colorado. Association for Computational Linguistics.

Hao Fei, Meishan Zhang, and Donghong Ji. 2020. Cross-lingual semantic role labeling with high-quality translated training corpus. In *Proceedings of the 58th Annual Meeting of the Association for Computational Linguistics*, pages 7014–7026, Online. Association for Computational Linguistics.

Niklas Friedrich, Kiril Gashteovski, Mingying Yu, Bhushan Kotnis, Carolin Lawrence, Mathias Niepert, and Goran Glavaš. 2022. AnnIE: An annotation platform for constructing complete open information extraction benchmark. In *Proceedings of the 60th Annual Meeting of the Association for Computational Linguistics: System Demonstrations*, pages 44–60, Dublin, Ireland. Association for Computational Linguistics.

Kiril Gashteovski, Rainer Gemulla, Bhushan Kotnis, Sven Hertling, and Christian Meilicke. 2020. On aligning openie extractions with knowledge bases: A case study. In *Proceedings of the First Workshop on Evaluation and Comparison of NLP Systems*, pages 143–154.

Kiril Gashteovski, Mingying Yu, Bhushan Kotnis, Carolin Lawrence, Mathias Niepert, and Goran Glavaš. 2022. BenchIE: A framework for multi-faceted fact-based open information extraction evaluation. In *Proceedings of the 60th Annual Meeting of the Association for Computational Linguistics (Volume 1: Long Papers)*, pages 4472–4490, Dublin, Ireland. Association for Computational Linguistics.

Raffaele Guarasci, Emanuele Damiano, Aniello Minutolo, Massimo Esposito, and Giuseppe De Pietro. 2020. Lexicon-grammar based open information extraction from natural language sentences in italian. *Expert Systems with Applications*, 143:112954.

Matthew Honnibal and Ines Montani. 2017. spaCy 2: Natural language understanding with Bloom embeddings, convolutional neural networks and incremental parsing. To appear.

Karthikeyan K, Zihan Wang, Stephen Mayhew, and Dan Roth. 2020. Cross-lingual ability of multilingual bert: An empirical study. In *International Conference on Learning Representations*.

Keshav Kolluru, Samarth Aggarwal, Vipul Rathore, Mausam, and Soumen Chakrabarti. 2020. IMoJIE: Iterative memory-based joint open information extraction. In *Proceedings of the 58th Annual Meeting of the Association for Computational Linguistics*, pages 5871–5886, Online. Association for Computational Linguistics.

Keshav Kolluru, Muqeeth Mohammed, Shubham Mittal, Soumen Chakrabarti, and Mausam . 2022. Alignment-augmented consistent translation for multilingual open information extraction. In *Proceedings of the 60th Annual Meeting of the Association for Computational Linguistics (Volume 1: Long Papers)*, pages 2502–2517, Dublin, Ireland. Association for Computational Linguistics.

Bhushan Kotnis, Kiril Gashteovski, Daniel Rubio, Ammar Shaker, Vanesa Rodriguez-Tembras, Makoto Takamoto, Mathias Niepert, and Carolin Lawrence. 2022. MILIE: Modular & iterative multilingual open information extraction. In *Proceedings of the 60th Annual Meeting of the Association for Computational Linguistics (Volume 1: Long Papers)*, pages 6939–6950, Dublin, Ireland. Association for Computational Linguistics.

Jitin Krishnan, Antonios Anastasopoulos, Hemant Purohit, and Huzefa Rangwala. 2021. Multilingual code-switching for zero-shot cross-lingual intent prediction and slot filling. In *Proceedings of the 1st Workshop on Multilingual Representation Learning*, pages 211–223, Punta Cana, Dominican Republic. Association for Computational Linguistics.

Anne Lauscher, Vinit Ravishankar, Ivan Vulić, and Goran Glavaš. 2020. From zero to hero: On the limitations of zero-shot language transfer with multilingual Transformers. In *Proceedings of the 2020 Conference on Empirical Methods in Natural Language Processing (EMNLP)*, pages 4483–4499, Online. Association for Computational Linguistics.

Mausam, Michael Schmitz, Stephen Soderland, Robert Bart, and Oren Etzioni. 2012. Open language learning for information extraction. In *Proceedings of the 2012 Joint Conference on Empirical Methods in Natural Language Processing and Computational Natural Language Learning*, pages 523–534, Jeju Island, Korea. Association for Computational Linguistics.

Mausam Mausam. 2016. Open information extraction systems and downstream applications. In *Proceedings of the Twenty-Fifth International Joint Conference on Artificial Intelligence*, IJCAI'16, page 4074–4077. AAAI Press.

Makoto Morishita, Jun Suzuki, and Masaaki Nagata. 2020. JParaCrawl: A large scale web-based English-Japanese parallel corpus. In *Proceedings of the Twelfth Language Resources and Evaluation Conference*, pages 3603–3609, Marseille, France. European Language Resources Association.

Graham Neubig. 2011. The Kyoto free translation task. http://www.phontron.com/kftt.

Nathan Ng, Kyra Yee, Alexei Baevski, Myle Ott, Michael Auli, and Sergey Edunov. 2019. Facebook FAIR's WMT19 news translation task submission. In *Proceedings of the Fourth Conference on Machine Translation (Volume 2: Shared Task Papers, Day 1)*, pages 314–319, Florence, Italy. Association for Computational Linguistics.

Mai Omura and Masayuki Asahara. 2018. UD-Japanese BCCWJ: Universal Dependencies annotation for the Balanced Corpus of Contemporary Written Japanese. In *Proceedings of the Second Workshop on Universal Dependencies (UDW 2018)*, pages 117–125, Brussels, Belgium. Association for Computational Linguistics.

Telmo Pires, Eva Schlinger, and Dan Garrette. 2019. How multilingual is multilingual BERT? In *Proceedings of the 57th Annual Meeting of the Association for Computational Linguistics*, pages 4996–5001, Florence, Italy. Association for Computational Linguistics.

Matt Post. 2018. A call for clarity in reporting BLEU scores. In *Proceedings of the Third Conference on Machine Translation: Research Papers*, pages 186–191, Brussels, Belgium. Association for Computational Linguistics.

Youngbin Ro, Yukyung Lee, and Pilsung Kang. 2020. Multi^2OIE: Multilingual open information extraction based on multi-head attention with BERT. In *Findings of the Association for Computational Linguistics: EMNLP 2020*, pages 1107–1117, Online. Association for Computational Linguistics.

Gabriel Stanovsky and Ido Dagan. 2016. Creating a large benchmark for open information extraction. In *Proceedings of the 2016 Conference on Empirical Methods in Natural Language Processing*, pages 2300–2305, Austin, Texas. Association for Computational Linguistics.

Gabriel Stanovsky, Julian Michael, Luke Zettlemoyer, and Ido Dagan. 2018. Supervised open information extraction. In *Proceedings of the 2018 Conference of the North American Chapter of the Association for Computational Linguistics: Human Language Technologies, Volume 1 (Long Papers)*, pages 885–895, New Orleans, Louisiana. Association for Computational Linguistics.

Takaaki Tanaka, Yusuke Miyao, Masayuki Asahara, Sumire Uematsu, Hiroshi Kanayama, Shinsuke Mori, and Yuji Matsumoto. 2016. Universal Dependencies for Japanese. In *Proceedings of the Tenth International Conference on Language Resources and Evaluation (LREC'16)*, pages 1651–1658, Portorož, Slovenia. European Language Resources Association (ELRA).

Chengyu Wang, Xiaofeng He, and Aoying Zhou. 2021. Open relation extraction for chinese noun phrases. *IEEE Transactions on Knowledge and Data Engineering*, 33(6):2693–2708.

David Yarowsky, Grace Ngai, and Richard Wicentowski. 2001. Inducing multilingual text analysis tools via robust projection across aligned corpora. In *Proceedings of the First International Conference on Human Language Technology Research*.

Xinyan Yu, Trina Chatterjee, Akari Asai, Junjie Hu, and Eunsol Choi. 2022. Beyond counting datasets: A survey of multilingual dataset construction and necessary resources. In *Findings of the Association for Computational Linguistics: EMNLP 2022*, pages 3725–3743, Abu Dhabi, United Arab Emirates. Association for Computational Linguistics.

Junlang Zhan and Hai Zhao. 2020. Span model for open information extraction on accurate corpus. *Proceedings of the AAAI Conference on Artificial Intelligence*, 34(05):9523–9530.

Alisa Zhila and Alexander Gelbukh. 2014. Open information extraction for Spanish language based on syntactic constraints. In *Proceedings of the ACL 2014 Student Research Workshop*, pages 78–85, Baltimore, Maryland, USA. Association for Computational Linguistics.

A Japanese BenchIE

We create a Japanese portion of BenchIE following the annotation process described in Gashteovski et al. (2022). We ask a bilingual annotator native in Japanese and fluent in English to (i) first translate sentences from English BenchIE to Japanese and then (ii) label the fact synsets using an annotation tool, AnnIE (Friedrich et al., 2022). Finally, following the annotation guidelines of BenchIE, we detect and optionalize some tokens that do not affect the meaning of clauses.[10] To aid the annotation process, we detect optional Japanese tokens automatically based on their positions in dependency trees: these are the dependent tokens linked to their governors with the dependency relation aux from the Japanese UD label set (Tanaka et al., 2016; Asahara et al., 2018). We also make optional *case markers*, a special type of functional token present in Japanese (we provide more details in §3.3).

B Detailed Experiment Settings

B.1 Dataset Statistics

The basis of our training data is the OpenIE corpus provided by Zhan and Zhao (2020).[11] The dataset contains 1,109,411 English sentences with 2,175,294 corresponding triples. For the zero-shot baseline, we adopt the dataset as-it-is, while for other approaches, we apply cross-lingual transfer techniques on the dataset to create proxy data. Final training data is collected after several steps of pre-processing as described in Kotnis et al. (2022).

[10]This is important in order not to unnecessarily penalize OpenIE systems. For more details, we refer the reader to Gashteovski et al. (2022).

[11]https://github.com/zhanjunlang/Span_OIE

	#Sentences	#Fact Synsets	#Ext./#Syn.
EN	300	1,350	101.00
DE	300	1,086	75.27
AR	100	487	5,064.86
JA	298	1,207	45,693.83

Table 6: Statistics of multilingual BenchIE. **Ext.** is short for gold extractions and **Syn.** is short for fact synsets. We only include languages discussed in this paper.

For evaluation, we test our systems on BenchIE (Gashteovski et al., 2022). The statistics of BenchIE are shown in Table 6. Notably, Japanese BenchIE has more instances due to the massive number of case markers being automatically optionalized in the gold annotations. As a future direction, it is meaningful to improve Japanese BenchIE by revising the annotation guideline and recruiting more human annotators.

B.2 Model Parameters

In this work, we adopt pre-trained machine translation systems (600M model for NLLB) and neural token aligners without finetuning, training only OpenIE systems. Notably, we hide the dependency label information from MILIE, further reducing the number of trainable parameters. Hiding such information also makes our experiment result slightly different from those reported in the original paper. As a result, the system has 177.9M trainable parameters in total. We introduce one extra hyperparameter, i.e., the replacement rate p for code-switching. The parameter is independently determined through a grid search over $\{0.2, 0.5, 1.0\}$. As a result, we have $p = 0.2$ for German and Japanese and $p = 0.5$ for Arabic.

B.3 Computational Budgets

Throughout this paper, we conduct experiments on NVIDIA TITAN RTX GPUs (24GB RAM). As preprocessing, we automatically translate sentences in the English training data into the target language using a machine translation system. The translation takes approximately 48 GPU hours. After that, we perform token alignments between the original sentence and the automatically translated sentence, taking approximately 10 GPU hours. Note that both the machine translation and the token align-

	Precision	Recall	F_1
EN	$38.93_{\pm 0.65}$	$21.95_{\pm 0.34}$	$28.61_{\pm 0.47}$
ZH	$22.82_{\pm 0.27}$	$12.64_{\pm 0.62}$	$16.26_{\pm 0.52}$
DE	$17.08_{\pm 0.22}$	$8.72_{\pm 0.23}$	$11.54_{\pm 0.26}$
AR	$22.21_{\pm 0.46}$	$9.65_{\pm 0.54}$	$13.45_{\pm 0.53}$
JA	$19.71_{\pm 1.21}$	$7.26_{\pm 0.05}$	$10.61_{\pm 0.20}$

Table 7: Precision, Recall, and F_1 scores (%) of BenchIE on multiple languages. For EN and ZH, we report the performance of MILIE trained on English data. For DE, AR, and JA, we report the best performance of systems trained on the proxy dataset generated from LFP. Values after $\pm$ show the standard derivation over 3 runs.

ment need to be performed only once for each language pair. The automatically translated sentence and the token alignments are reused for all experiments regarding the language pair. The training on each proxy dataset created using the proposed strategies takes up to 20 hours on a single GPU.

C Additional Experiment Results

C.1 Difficulty of BenchIE

Here, we show the performance of MILIE on BenchIE to show the difficulty of BenchIE quantitively. As in Table 7, MILIE, the current state-of-the-art neural OpenIE system, scores no more than 30 F_1 points on English BenchIE. Given that the system is trained on the same language, i.e., English, as it is evaluated, we witness the difficulty of BenchIE. Therefore, we emphasize the success of our proposed LFP strategies in bringing up the system's performance on German, Arabic, and Japanese BenchIE without using any human-annotated data.

C.2 Descriptive Statistics

In this section, we visualize the experiment results reported in Table 3 with the standard deviation, as shown in Figure 5. The results are arranged in descending order of F_1 scores.

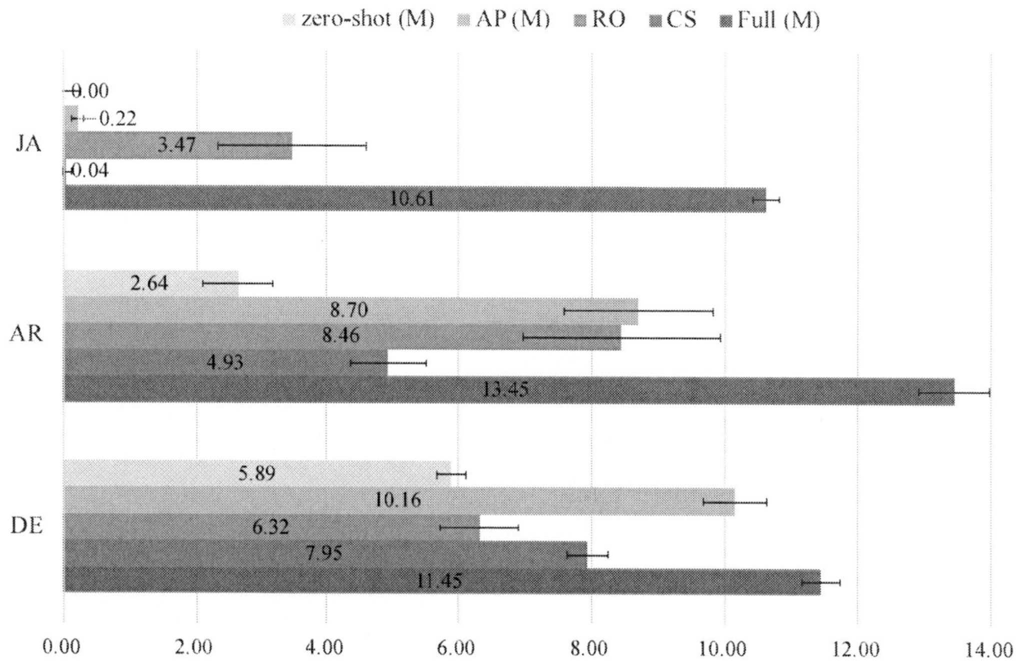

Figure 5: Evaluation results of MILIE on German, Arabic, and Japanese BenchIE. Error bars demonstrate the standard derivations. **M** stands for using mBERT as the encoder.

Geographic and Geopolitical Biases of Language Models

Fahim Faisal, Antonios Anastasopoulos
Department of Computer Science, George Mason University
{ffaisal,antonis}@gmu.edu

Abstract

Pretrained language models (PLMs) often fail to fairly represent target users from certain world regions because of the under-representation of those regions in training datasets. With recent PLMs trained on enormous data sources, quantifying their potential biases is difficult, due to their black-box nature and the sheer scale of the data sources. In this work, we devise an approach to study the geographic bias (and knowledge) present in PLMs, proposing a Geographic-Representation Probing Framework adopting a self-conditioning method coupled with entity-country mappings. Our findings suggest PLMs' representations map surprisingly well to the physical world in terms of country-to-country associations, but this knowledge is unequally shared across languages. Last, we explain how large PLMs despite exhibiting notions of geographical proximity, over-amplify geopolitical favouritism at inference time.[1]

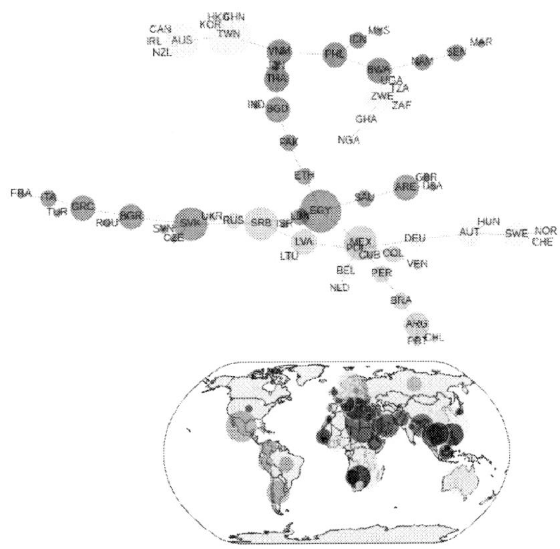

Figure 1: Example of a Geographic Representation network and it's corresponding location clusters (colored) recovered from the top-50 country-"expert" neurons of BLOOM. Notice that connected countries are either geographically or culturally close (e.g. south American cluster in light blue, African countries in yellow, South-East Asian countries in dark blue). *Note: node size is proportional to its degree in the graph.*

1 Introduction

Large pretrained language models (PLMs) are capable of generating meaningful texts beyond English and very likely, models like GPT-4, Llama 2 (Brown et al., 2020; Shliazhko et al., 2022; Zhang et al., 2022; Workshop et al., 2023; OpenAI, 2023; Touvron et al., 2023) will form the go-to base model for automating tasks like summarizing texts, generating datasets given certain instructions (Schick and Schütze, 2021) or perhaps even evaluating the generated texts (Yuan et al., 2021). While these PLMs continue to expand their utility, it is crucial that one also examines the potential biases that these PLMs exhibit. Moreover, the utility of these PLMs should be equitable to their target users so that they perform evenly for all speakers of the languages it is primarily trained on. Otherwise, the disparity that lies in the model (if any) will propagate further. To better illustrate these dynamics, consider a L_1 Spanish speaker from Peru, who is using a prompt-based PLM (like that of Wang et al. (2022, 2021)) to generate a localized synthetic dataset for some downstream task. They may use Spanish *as used in the local context* to form their seed data/prefix/prompts. Now, if this language model has already skewed preferences towards geopolitically dominant countries, it is likely the generated texts will reflect the skewness, thus not appropriately reflecting the local, Peruvian context that the practitioner is interested in. However, the quantification of this presumed geographic disparity in PLMs is not yet explored. Though given the well-documented western-country bias (or Global North bias) exhibited in most NLP benchmarks and

[1]Code and data are publicly available: https://github.com/ffaisal93/geoloc_lm

Proceedings of the The 3rd Workshop on Multi-lingual Representation Learning (MRL), pages 139–163
December 7, 2023

datasets (Faisal et al., 2022, *inter alia*), we hypothesize that text generation models might also suffer from the similar pitfall. On top of that, given a multilingual model, how language variety impact the encoded geographic knowledge is also underexplored.

Herein, we perform an evidence-based study to unfold the underlying geographic distribution of multilingual PLMs. We propose a pipeline to probe the Text-Generative PLMs using prompt-based inference for Geographic-Knowledge as well as existing domain-variant disparity (geography in our case). Our research questions and key findings are:

- **RQ1:** *To what extent is geographic proximity encoded in the PLMs?* **F:** PLMs can infer geographic proximity surprisingly well in terms of country-country association (see Figure 1). However, we observe an over-representation of certain countries during text generation.
- **RQ2:** *What is the influence of multilinguality in PLM's knowledge distribution of geographic proximity?* **F:** The shared multilingual representation space of PLMs has an uneven distribution of knowledge across languages.
- **RQ3:** *What is the effect of prompting using a geographic identifier (eg. "In Colombia" <generate text>) on multilingual text generation?* **F:** Prompting with certain geographic identifiers can even alter the language of free-form generated text.

2 Background and Related Work

A substantial amount of work has investigated existing social bias (eg. gender, racial, ethnic, occupational) identification and mitigation approaches in PLMs including, reducing token sensitivity during text generation (Liang et al., 2021), investigating model sensitivity (Immer et al., 2022), prompting using natural sentences (Alnegheimish et al., 2022) and probing via embedding lookup (Ahn and Oh, 2021). On the other hand, representing space and time utilizing maps and language is a long-standing domain of research (Louwerse and Benesh, 2012; Gatti et al., 2022; Anceresi et al., 2023). More recently, numerous studies are experimenting with geoadaptation of PLMs (Hofmann et al., 2023), what behavior these PLMs exhibit while probing with geographic-context, cultural-commonsense as well as temporal reasoning (Yin et al., 2022; Ghosh et al., 2021; Thapliyal et al., 2022; Hlavnova and Ruder, 2023; Shwartz, 2022; Tan et al., 2023) or how large PLMs learn the representation of space and time (Gurnee and Tegmark, 2023). However, for our goal task, first, we need to identify specific model units sensitive to certain geographic concepts. Then we would like to prioritize those units to generate output text for evaluation. A self-conditioning pre-trained model (Suau et al., 2022) is one such approach enabling us to perform the required experiments.

Self-conditioning Method Suau et al. (2022) propose an approach that extracts PLM weights having certain polarity and then prioritize those weights during text generation. Based on the generated text, they can quantify gender and occupation bias encoded by the PLM. As an example, consider a binary sentence classification task where positive class examples contain the mention of a concept word (eg. doctor) and vice-versa. A PLM is able to provide scores to these positive and negative examples. Looking at the average precision scores and the scores given by different model weights from each layer, we can identify the ones providing higher scores towards the positive examples. Suau et al. (2022) refer to these model weights as *expert units*.

Now, we can prioritize these identified expert units during text generation by artificially simulating the presence of the concept word "doctor" in the input. Basically, at every step of text generation, we replace the actual response of expert units with the typical one where the concept word is present in the input. As a result, the PLM now generates texts relevant to the concept word. In the work of Suau et al. (2022), by comparing the generated texts, they easily quantify the presence of gender-specific words thus evaluating the presence of gender bias in the PLM (for example, consider the number of sentences where the context relates to the word "doctor" and mentions male-gender words compared to female-gender words). This approach serves two main purposes: (1) Identifying expert units: model parameters responsible for generating text related to the target concept (i.e. doctor). (2) Triggering specific behaviour in text generation without explicit mentioning of the target context, which inadvertently influences the behaviour of the model.

3 Geographic Representation Probing

In our study, we use this Self Conditioning Method to first extract expert units (i.e. model weights)

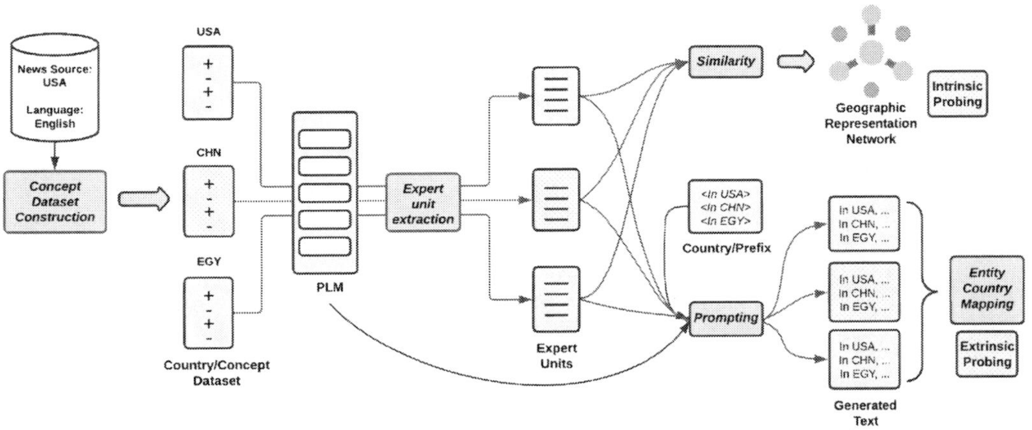

Figure 2: Geographic Representation Probing Framework. First we construct the *Country/Concept* dataset. Then we extract *Expert Units* from the base PLM and use similarity measurement to prepare our Geographic Representation Network to perform Intrinsic Probing. In Parallel, we prompt the self-conditioned PLM with Geographic Identifiers (i.e. *Country/Prefix*). Finally, we map the generated-text entities to countries to perform Extrinsic Probing.

which encode geographic knowledge. Then we use those units to generate relevant texts given different geographic identifier-based prompts. An example: Using some sentences with the mention as well as absence of the word *"China"* to extract expert units and then, prioritize these units during text generation with the prompt *"In USA ..."*. The aim here is to simulate an environment where we evaluate the model knowledge (*Concept-Country*-specific *Expert Units*) by asking what it knows about other countries (i.e *Prefix-Country*). This allows us to quantify existing geographic bias towards certain attributes present in a PLM. Our probing framework contains five steps (see Figure 2): (1) Concept Dataset Construction (2) Expert Unit Extraction (3) Geographic-Representation Network Construction (4) Prompt-based Text Generation (5) Entity Country Mapping.

Concept Dataset Construction First of all, we prepare our concept dataset in a binary classification fashion using which, we later perform self-conditioning a PLM on geographic concepts. To make it quantifiable, we define *country* to be our main unit of reference and construct concept datasets where each "concept" is loosely centered around a country. An additional requirement for these datasets is that the data have not been used as part of the pretraining data of the PLMs. Hence, we turn to recent news articles (scrapped using Google news api[2]): as we can control the date on which these data became public, we can be sure that they were not used in any pre-training process (so far). Such a dataset should also allow us to get a reasonable representation of current geopolitical affairs. Depending on the news-source country and language, we build several such *Concept-Country* datasets. A *Concept-Country* dataset `{C}-{l}` contains news about several $(c_1, c_2, ..c_i..c_n)$ countries in `{l}` language where the news-source is `{C}` country. Each *Concept-Country* c_i has 100 positive examples (mention of c_i) sentences and 300 negative examples (no mention) sentences. For example, `USA-eng` *Concept-Country* dataset (Figure 7) contains data from US sources, in English, which either mention other countries (there are 100 positive examples for each country c_i) or are random sentences not mentioning any countries (negative examples). See App. C for the constructed dataset details with examples.

Expert Unit Extraction Using the self-conditioning method, we identify high performing *Expert Units* for each *Concept-Country*. These are the model weights that provide higher scores for the presence of a specific concept (i.e. country in our case). For example, Consider the *Concept-Country* `India` from the dataset `USA-eng`. Essentially, we have positive examples (text mentioning India or relevant entities) and negative examples (random other sentences not mentioning India) which we can use to identify the model's *Expert Units*. These units are the neurons that can be used as predictors to identify the presence of a concept (i.e. positive examples mentioning "India"). The self-conditioning

[2] https://github.com/ranahaani/GNews

lang	*Template -> Prefix*	English Meaning
ara	في <country> -> في إسبانيا	In Spain
ben	গতকাল <country> এ -> গতকাল স্পেন এ	Yesterday, in Spain
eng	*However, in <country> -> However in Spain*	However in Spain
fra	*<country> est connu pour -> Espagne est connu pour*	Spain is known for
hin	<country> में, -> स्पेन में,	In Spain
kor	<country>에서 -> 스페인에서	In Spain
rus	*Вчера <country> -> Вчера Испания*	Yesterday Spain
zho	昨天 <country> -> 昨天西班牙	Yesterday Spain

Figure 3: Prefix construction using Multilingual Prefix-Templates. Here we replace the **<country>** position with "Spain" in the given language. Complete list of multilingual prefix templates in Appendix D.

framework computes these neurons and uses the average-precision score to rank their predictive expertise thus allowing us to select the top-k (eg. 10, 50) *Expert Units* from each layer. Observing the average precision scores, we select the top-k (eg. 10, 50) *Expert Units* from each PLM layer. A comprehensive theoretical explanation of the self-conditioning method and the *Expert Unit* extraction process is presented in App. B.

Geographic-Representation Network Now utilizing all these model *Expert Units*, we construct our Geographic-Representation Networks. We use jaccard similarity to measure the similarity between any given *Concept-Country* pairs c_i and c_j and their corresponding *Expert Units*. Then, utilizing these similarity measurement scores as edges in a graph (the countries being the nodes), we prepare a PLM-specific Geographic Representation network for each of our *Expert Units* set. This network is a Minimum-Spanning Tree graph highlighting the internal country-country associations. We further make it easier to digest by identifying the community clusters of countries using the Louvain Community Detection method (Blondel et al., 2008). In Figure 1 we show the network obtained with the USA-eng dataset from the BLOOM (Workshop et al., 2023) *Expert Units*. Effectively, we can recover a very good geographical representation of the countries straight from the network weights.

Prompt-based Text Generation With the *Concept-Country*-specific *Expert Units* at hand, we can now investigate what happens when we use the PLM for text generation. The self-conditioning method (Suau et al., 2022) uses sequential decoding and prioritize the *Expert Units* by approximating their scores from the average precision values predicted for a certain *Concept-Country*. This allows us to artificially simulate the presence of a country name and it's related context during text generation. Now we perform text generation with one more twist: we provide one country-mention as part of the prefix/prompt (i.e. *Prefix-Country*). The idea here is to simulate an environment where we evaluate the model knowledge (*Concept-Country*-specific *Expert Units*) by asking what it knows about other countries (i.e *Prefix-Country*). We generate several template-based multilingual prompts (the prefix construction process is depicted in Table 3) where we replace the <country> tag with different country names.

Entity Country Mapping Finally, to investigate the existence of geopolitical favouritism, we quantify the geographic biases of the generated texts by mapping any entities appearing in the text to corresponding countries. We use the Dataset Geography framework of Faisal et al. (2022), which uses multilingual entity linking to map entities to Wikidata entries and then to countries.

4 Experimental Settings

Terminologies Based on our Framework description, let us list some terminologies that we use for the remainder of the paper, to describe the experimental settings and results.

1. ***Concept-Country***: These are the countries for which we collect news.
2. **Source Country**: These are the country of origin *from* where the news data is produced.
3. **Prefix**: This is the text that we use to prompt the model, which may include a country mention. This country is the *Prefix-Country*.
4. ***Expert Units***: The model units that are specific to a country concept c_i and are extracted from the language models.

Models and Languages We use GPT2-medium (Radford et al., 2019), mGPT (Shliazhko et al., 2022) and BLOOM-560m (Workshop et al., 2023), all models available through huggingface. For the English dataset sourced from the US-News Platform (USA-eng) we extract *Expert Units* from all three models. For non-English datasets, we perform *Expert Units* extraction on BLOOM and mGPT. For the generation-level analysis step, we use BLOOM and GPT2 (focusing on English) expert units and report results for conditioning *Concept-Country* datasets in 8 languages: (ara, ben, eng, fra, hin, kor, rus, zho).

Datasets As mentioned before, each concept in our dataset contains 100 positive and 300 negative examples. In some cases, we use up-sampling by repeating the example sentences multiple times when we do not have 100 distinct examples mentioning the *Concept-Country* name. In total, we prepare 31 *Concept-Country* Datasets (22 Country News-Sources, 13 Languages) and extract expert units conditioning over these datasets. Detailed dataset statistics are in Appendix Table C.3.

Generative Scheme: On average we generate `112,225` sentences for a given model and *Concept-Country* Dataset. For 67 *Concept-Country Expert Units*, we randomly choose 5 prefix templates; replace those with all 67 country name and generate 5 sentences with the lowest perplexity per *Prefix-Country*; thus `67x5x67x5=112,225` sentences.

Probing Metrics We analyze both the Geographic Representation Networks (intrinsic/parameter probing) and the generated texts (extrinsic/generation probing) to answer our Research Questions where we utilize the aid of visualization and three additional quantitative metrics as follows:

1. Neighbourhood Score: We propose a proximity-based metric to quantify the inherent encoding of Geographic Proximity present inside an LM by looking at the country-country associations and compare them with the physical world. For example, in Figure 1, South-American neighbouring countries are clustered together thus preserving a factually consistent representation. To capture this, we compute the number of neighbours one country node is connected within a 2-hop distance given a Geographic-Representation Network. To better illustrate, consider in a Geographic-Representation Network G, country node $c_5 \in G$ is connected with 4 other country nodes $\{c_1, c_2, c_3, c_4\} \in G$. Among these 4 connected nodes, c_5 shares sea or land borders with only 2 countries $N_5 = \{c_2, c_3\}$ in real world thus making $|N_5| = 2$. Similarly, we can compute $|N_2|$ and $|N_3|$ for countries c_2 and c_3 respectively. So, the Neighbourhood Score $n_s(c_5) = |N_5| + |N_2| + |N_3|$ which we can generalize and aggregate at the network level as follows:

$$\begin{aligned} N_s(G) &= \sum_{c_i \in G} n_s(c_i) \\ &= \sum_{c_i \in G} (|N_i| + \sum_{j \in N_i} |N_j|) \end{aligned}$$

2. Representation Score: We quantify the overall command of prefix, concept or top-represented countries at the *language* level (i.e. for all generated text in a language). Consider we have *Expert Units* already computed for *Concept-Country* c_i. We use these units to generate text while providing a *Prefix-Country* p_j. Later, we map the entities of generated text to countries. So if we have a total of $L = \{l_1, l_2, ..l_k..l_n\}$ countries with respective entity counts, we can get the top represented countries $T(c_i, p_j)$ for each concept-prefix pair (c_i, p_j):

$$T(c_i, p_j) = \arg\max_{l_k \in L} (P(l_k | c_i, p_j))$$

Having this set of highly represented countries for each concept-prefix pair at hand, we can now compute in how many cases a *Concept-Country*, *Prefix-Country* or the top-10 most represented countries are present in the set $T(c_i, p_j)$ for all $c_i \in \mathcal{N}$, $p_j \in \mathcal{M}$ where $\mathcal{N} = \{\text{Concept Countries}\}$, $\mathcal{M} = \{\text{Prefix Countries}\}$. So given one output-country-distribution B:

$$\text{RS}(B, x) = \sum_{c_i \in \mathcal{N}} \sum_{p_j \in \mathcal{M}} |T(c_i, p_j) \in A_x| \quad \text{where}$$

$$A_x = \{\text{prefix } p_j, \text{ concept } c_i \text{ or top-10 country}\}$$

The intuition here is to quantify how much the influence of *Concept-Country*, *Prefix-Country* or overly represented countries varies across languages. For example, if we observe that the score for *Prefix-Country* is higher than the scores for *Concept-Country* across all settings, it means *Prefix-Country* is a more influencing factor than *Concept-Country* in the geographical relatedness of the text generation. For comparative analysis, we consider top-3 represented countries instead of just one while computing $T(c_i, p_j) \in A_x$.

3. Skewness[3]: We compare the symmetry of the generated country-entity distribution for both generated and the concept dataset texts. The ones that are more skewed one the ones containing amplified bias towards certain country-origin entities.

5 Findings

RQ1: *To what extent the geographic proximity is encoded in the PLMs?*

Intrinsic Findings: Based on our analysis of the Geographic-Representation Networks, it is evident that model parameters respond similarly for

[3] `https://docs.scipy.org/doc/scipy/reference/generated/scipy.stats.skew.html`

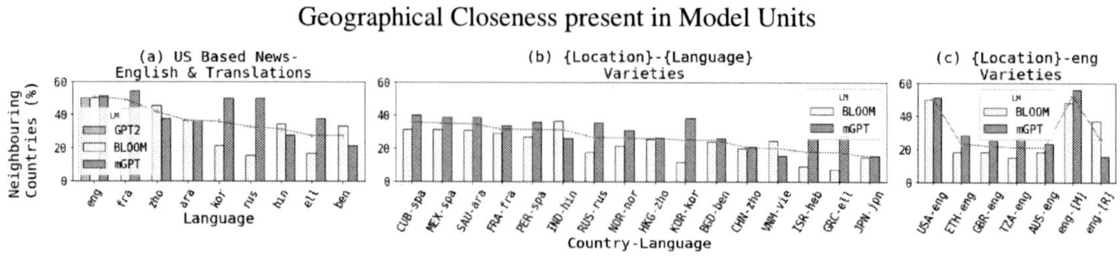

Figure 4: (a) The variation of neighbourhood score for different set of expert units. Notice at (a.1) we get the best score for USA-eng and it decreases when we translate the concept dataset. This also varies across languages, models (a.2) and the precise identification of expert units using high-quality concept-dataset also matters (a.3).

closely related (culturally or geographically) countries. For example, consider the Network in Figure 1 from BLOOM *Expert Units* conditioned using the USA-eng *Concept-Country* dataset. The Latin-American, African and European blocks are fairly clear. The Indian Subcontinent countries (BGD, PAK, IND), or countries of the British Commonwealth (AUS, NZL, CAN) are also clustered together. In addition, from the communities identified with the Louvain Community Detection algorithm, as visualized in the world map plot, we observe that community clusters are mainly formed around countries with proximity. We prepare similar kinds of Geographic-Representation Networks for all sets of *Expert Units* conditioned on different *Concept-Country* datasets (see Appendix E).

Concept	Genareted		Expert Units		
	gpt2	bloom	gpt2	mgpt	bloom
USA	USA	USA	*SRB*	*SWE*	*SWE*
GBR	GBR	FRA	*POL*	*HUN*	*HUN*
FRA	CHN	IND	BGR	AUT	*SVN*
CHN	IND	GBR	*SVK*	*SVK*	*GRC*
UKR	FRA	CHN	*SWE*	CHN	*SVK*
RUS	CAN	RUS	PER	*GRC*	*POL*
DEU	RUS	JPN	LVA	*POL*	*ARG*
ESP	AUS	KOR	*HUN*	*SVN*	COL
AUS	JPN	DEU	*ARG*	CHL	BRA
JPN	ISR	ESP	TZA	*TUR*	*TUR*

Table 1: Top represented countries across concepts and generated text. For BLOOM we aggregate across all eight languages; GPT-2 is English only. For expert units, we report the countries with the highest degree of similarity associations. (The common countries in at-least two model settings are in italic font.)

Extrinsic Findings: Next we investigate *whether the encoded geographic proximity gets modified due to geopolitical favouritism* by performing entity-country mapping on a large pool of generated texts in eight languages (112,255 avg. sentences per language). Evidently, we observe a strong presence of *geopolitical favouritism* which we define as the over-amplification of certain country representation (eg. countries with higher GDP, geopolitical stability, military strength etc). For comparison, we use the distribution of the *Concept-Country* dataset as it contains the actual news text reflecting real-world affairs.

In Table 1 (two left sections), we contrast the top represented countries aggregating the counts from all *Concept-Country* datasets to the ones in the generated text. All top-10 most represented countries in generated texts are present within the top-16 ranks of geopolitically significant countries.[4] This resemblance of higher geopolitically powerful country distribution is visible across all forms (Generated text Country Maps in Appendix F). However, when we compare these top-10 country representations (%) in generated text with the one from the concept dataset, we observe *geopolitical favouritism*. The result is presented in Figure 6 where in all language country-entity distributions, the top-10 country percentage is always higher compared to real-world news (Figure 6(a)). A similar pattern is apparent for the other 7 languages (except Korean) in terms of data skewness (Figure 6(b)). Last, we performed Kolmogorov–Smirnov and Shapiro statistical significance tests to ensure that the generated text country distribution follows a log-normal distribution. The striking fact here is, though this distribution contains entity mention from 246 countries in total, around **11.5%** of all generated entities are from the USA alone. This phenomenon can be further quantified using the neighbourhood score reported in Figure 4. For example, as shown in Figure 4(a), we find that all 3 models (GPT2, BLOOM, mGPT) Geographic-Representation Networks built from the English dataset conditioned *Expert Units* have around 50% of the countries connected with their real-world 2-hop neighbours.

RQ2: *What is the influence of multilinguality in PLM's knowledge distribution of geographic proximity?*

[4]worldpopulationreview-powerful-countries

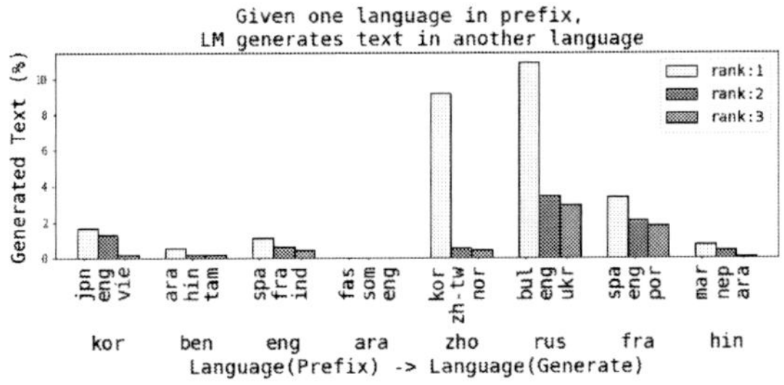

Figure 5: Percentage of generated text (top-3) in different language given the Prefix being in another language.

Intrinsic Findings: By now, we have evidence that Geographic proximity is directly encoded in PLMs in the form of shared expert units. So how this knowledge differs across languages? Ideally, multilingual PLMs should provide equitable utility for their intended users being consistent cross-lingually. To evaluate this, we automatically translate[5] our USA-eng dataset, to avoid any confounders from news content discrepancies from across the world. This way, the content used for identifying the expert units is thematically and semantically the same across languages. The result, in Figure 4(a), shows noticeable disparities in Neighbourhood Score percentages across languages in terms of Neighbourhood Scores. When we find *Expert Units* using Latin-script based *Concept-Country* datasets (English, French), the *Expert Units* make the most of associations among closely related neighbours, while the scores are less than half for Russian, Greek, or Korean in models like mGPT or BLOOM.

RQ3: *What is the effect of prompting with geographic identifier (eg. "In Colombie" <generate text>) on multilingual text generation?*

Extrinsic Findings: To answer this question, we look into the language of the generated texts using spaCy language identifier[6]. On average, BLOOM generates around 5.85% sentences (52k out of our 898k generated sentences) in a language different than the one of the prefix. This anomaly happens mostly in a larger percentage in Russian, Chinese, and French (Figure 5). We observe that every language has a specific second language preference (i.e. rank:1 in Figure 5) which can ignore the given prefix and generate a sentence in that language (eg. kor → jap, ben→ara, eng→spa, ara→far, zho→kor, rus→bgr, etc). This language preference is not reflexive (eg. kor→jap whereas zho→kor).

Observing the amount of text generated in different languages, it might seem insignificant at first sight. However, we need to keep in mind that there is one geographic identifier in the prefix (*Prefix-Country*) as well as given *Concept-Country* units. So when we look into which concept-prefix pair usually changes the direction of language, we observe interesting cultural correlations. In Table 2, given a *Prefix-Country*, we show how certain country mentions instigate text generation in a different direction (up to 50% of total generated text, given a prefix-concept pair). This happens frequently when a prefix token is shared among those languages ("in" exists both in English and Spanish; detailed examples in Appendix G) and when the country is closely tied with the language. For example, the fra→spa and eng→spa directions (French/English prefixes continued in Spanish) include country mentions of Cuba, Argentina, Colombia, or Chile which are all Spanish-speaking countries. We hypothesize that the shared representation space of multilingual decoder often ties language with geographic entity thus changing the favoured generation language.

5.1 Further Analysis

Data Origin Because we are experimenting with real-world multilingual news data without going through any extensive data cleaning process, we also need to quantify the dataset-level significance: *how does Concept-Country data quality impact the identification of Expert Units?*

The scrapping method we use for dataset construction returns localized news depending on the source location. For example, USA news source provides a higher amount of global news with many country mentions. On the other hand, a news source from Bangladesh provides news mostly about its close geopolitical neighbours (eg. India, and China). Thus, the entity frequency distribution of USA-eng and BGD-ben would not be similar.

In addition, we have variations in the amount of upsampling and the negative instance domain. So in Figures 4(b) and 4(c), we report Neighbourhood Scores for geographic-source varied on non-English and English datasets respectively. Like before, the association knowledge for USA-eng sourced Geographic-Representation Network remains the most truthful. For Spanish news sourced from different locations (Cuba, Mexico, Peru),

[5]Using `https://translate.google.com/`

[6]spacy-language-detection

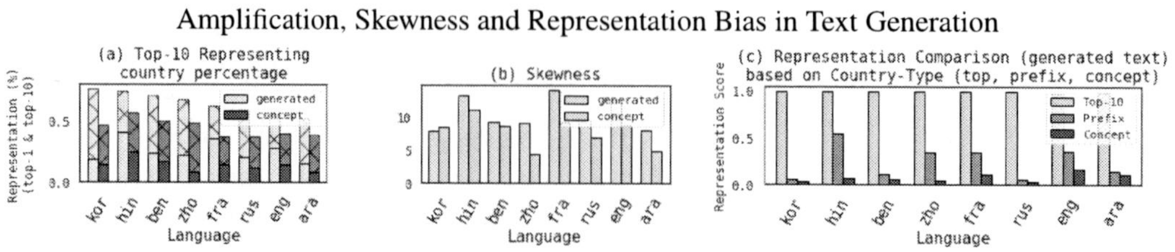

Figure 6: (a) Compared to the concept dataset which is real-world news text, the generated text always overly represents the top-represented countries (eg. USA). (b) This is also true for Skewness (except Korean). In (c) we plot the representation scores depicting the overall influence of prefixes, concepts or top countries. Top countries are over-amplified, irrespective of language. The next dominating factor is prefix but it varies across languages.

Direction	Concept	Prefix	Direction	Concept	Prefix
ben→ara	LVA	PAK	fra→spa	CHL	CUB
eng→spa	ARG	COL	fra→vie	AUT	VNM
eng→ind	IDN	KOR	fra→por	PRT	PRT
zh-cn→ko	UGA	NZL	fra→cat	CHL	SGP
rus→bul	AUS	BGR	fra→eng	CHL	BGD
rus→eng	ETH	JPN	hin→mar	BGR	ARE

Table 2: Given prefix in language A, the LM generates in a different language B (A→B), influenced by the concept and prefix countries. These are the cases where the percentage of language change is more than 50%.

scores are rather similar. Interestingly, the score drops significantly for CHN-zho compared to the translated USA-zho from Figure 4(a).[7]

For the English dataset sourced from different geographic locations (Figure 4(c)), we get poor association scores for any other locale except the USA, confirming the fact that the in-domain distance between positive and negative examples matters given a fixed language. To dig in further, we perform an ablation study by creating one additional augmented English dataset: eng-[M]: By Masking Country, Name and Organization entities in the USA-eng dataset using Spacy NER. Surprisingly, eng-[M] shows the highest percentage of geographic associations even surpassing the original USA-eng one for mGPT. We conclude that small semantic incoherence does not hurt the *Expert Units* extraction and that more contrastive positive-negative class difference (absence of other entity types) helps.

Model Comparison In terms of Neighbourhood Score, mGPT *Expert Units* encode **23.5%** more geographic expertise over BLOOM-560m model on translation datasets (similar text, different language). This improvement is increased **30%** when we consider the multilingual datasets (text and language: both different). GPT-2 units perform similarly on the English dataset.

We conduct another ablation study to quantify how to prune these models towards randomness and semantic incoherence. We prepare another augmented English dataset eng-[R], by putting random semantically incoherent texts while maintaining the positive-negative class difference. The bar showing the Neighbourhood Score is at Figure 4(c). Now BLOOM *Expert Units* are almost as good as before, whereas mGPT *Expert Units* are way worse; only in 3 other cases do BLOOM-560m units represent better associations in total. This reveals that these models contain different distributions even though they were trained with similar objectives, showing different magnitude responses towards data attribute variations, including noise, semantic coherence, data quantity and language.

Influence of *Concept-Country* and *Prefix-Country* We simulate an environment where we provide *Expert Units* about one geographic entity (*Concept-Country*) and ask a PLM about another geographic entity (*Prefix-Country*). By now, we have shown that the PLM encodes geographic proximity but also exhibits geopolitical favouritism during inference. The question we ask at this point is: *Given that PLM is biased, how do the Concept-Country and Prefix-Country influence text generation?*

To answer this question, we compute Representation Score on generated texts varying the language (Figure 6(c)). As always, top-10 country Representation Score is evident in all languages while the second most influencing factor is *Prefix-Country*. In Hindi, *Concept-Country* has the highest influence of geographic mention in a prompt-based generation. However, this scenario does not hold for the cases of Korean, Bengali, and Russian. On the other hand, *Concept-Country* plays the part of a subtle representative but fails to compete with

[7]While investigating this anomaly, we found that the fixed sequence length for both models (BLOOM, mGPT) rejects several positive examples during tokenization process thus hurting the *Expert Units* extraction quality. We corrected this issue by substituting the long examples with shorter ones.

Prefix-Country and geopolitical significant countries. One fact to note here is, our experiment contains a small number of examples while generating a large pool of texts. Nevertheless, we believe that it will require intensive data creation efforts to mitigate the biases that coexist with the geographic knowledge in PLMs.

6 Conclusion and Future Work

In this study, we perform an experimental analysis on identifying the inherent geographic knowledge and inference bias of prompt-based decoder models. Our experiments strongly suggest that current PLMs are able to encode geographic proximity quiet well. However, almost always geopolitical favouritism overshadows the encoded proximity during inference. This finding raises concerns as well as the need to perform bias-mitigation steps if we want to generate geo-specific texts. Our additional findings on the impact of multilinguality on prompting points out how encoded geographic proximity is unevenly distributed across languages and how even just a mention of geographic identifiers may influence the language of free-form text generation. We believe these findings still leave issues to be addressed in current practice and that there should be a a fundamental multilingual-bias mitigation step included in any NLP task workflow. Keeping this in mind, we want to expand the domain of our proposed probing framework and assess its applicability beyond geography. In addition, we aim to perform contrastive training to efficiently extract expert units thus stepping forward with the effort of reducing the inequality inherent in multilingual language models.

Limitations

First of all, selecting country as geographic entities is inherently lossy and ideally, we would be able to perform the experiments with further granularity. We rely on Wikidata for entity linking, which is already somewhat biased towards western countries. In addition, our experiments are limited to 69 countries and 13 languages (8 for generating text) (by necessity and due to computing costs), ignoring other countries as well as languages, especially low-resource ones. In the future, we want to further expand our study to include more languages and cultures, as well as digging deeper in multi-cultural countries.

Acknowledgements

We are thankful to the anonymous reviewers for their constructive feedback. This work is generously supported by the National Science Foundation under grants FAI-2040926, IIS-2125466, and IIS-2127901.

References

2021. Ip2location™ country multilingual database. Online resource.

Jaimeen Ahn and Alice Oh. 2021. Mitigating language-dependent ethnic bias in BERT. In *Proceedings of the 2021 Conference on Empirical Methods in Natural Language Processing*, pages 533–549, Online and Punta Cana, Dominican Republic. Association for Computational Linguistics.

Sarah Alnegheimish, Alicia Guo, and Yi Sun. 2022. Using natural sentence prompts for understanding biases in language models. In *Proceedings of the 2022 Conference of the North American Chapter of the Association for Computational Linguistics: Human Language Technologies*, pages 2824–2830, Seattle, United States. Association for Computational Linguistics.

Giorgia Anceresi, Daniele Gatti, Tomaso Vecchi, Marco Marelli, and Luca Rinaldi. 2023. A map of words: Retrieving the spatial layout of underground stations from natural language.

Vincent D Blondel, Jean-Loup Guillaume, Renaud Lambiotte, and Etienne Lefebvre. 2008. Fast unfolding of communities in large networks. *Journal of Statistical Mechanics: Theory and Experiment*, 2008(10):P10008.

Tom B Brown, Benjamin Mann, Nick Ryder, Melanie Subbiah, Jared Kaplan, Prafulla Dhariwal, Arvind Neelakantan, Pranav Shyam, Girish Sastry, Amanda Askell, et al. 2020. Language models are few-shot learners. arXiv:2005.14165.

Sumanth Dathathri, Andrea Madotto, Janice Lan, Jane Hung, Eric Frank, Piero Molino, Jason Yosinski, and Rosanne Liu. 2020. Plug and play language models: A simple approach to controlled text generation.

Fahim Faisal, Yinkai Wang, and Antonios Anastasopoulos. 2022. Dataset geography: Mapping language data to language users. In *Proceedings of the 60th Annual Meeting of the Association for Computational Linguistics (Volume 1: Long Papers)*, pages 3381–3411, Dublin, Ireland. Association for Computational Linguistics.

Daniele Gatti, Marco Marelli, Tomaso Vecchi, and Luca Rinaldi. 2022. Spatial representations without spatial computations. *Psychological Science*, 33(11):1947–1958. PMID: 36201754.

Sayan Ghosh, Dylan Baker, David Jurgens, and Vinodkumar Prabhakaran. 2021. Detecting cross-geographic biases in toxicity modeling on social media. In *Proceedings of the Seventh Workshop on Noisy User-generated Text (W-NUT 2021)*, pages 313–328, Online. Association for Computational Linguistics.

Wes Gurnee and Max Tegmark. 2023. Language models represent space and time.

Ester Hlavnova and Sebastian Ruder. 2023. Empowering cross-lingual behavioral testing of NLP models with typological features. In *Proceedings of the 61st Annual Meeting of the Association for Computational Linguistics (Volume 1: Long Papers)*, pages 7181–7198, Toronto, Canada. Association for Computational Linguistics.

Valentin Hofmann, Goran Glavaš, Nikola Ljubešić, Janet B. Pierrehumbert, and Hinrich Schütze. 2023. Geographic adaptation of pretrained language models.

Alexander Immer, Lucas Torroba Hennigen, Vincent Fortuin, and Ryan Cotterell. 2022. Probing as quantifying inductive bias. In *Proceedings of the 60th Annual Meeting of the Association for Computational Linguistics (Volume 1: Long Papers)*, pages 1839–1851, Dublin, Ireland. Association for Computational Linguistics.

Paul Pu Liang, Chiyu Wu, Louis-Philippe Morency, and Ruslan Salakhutdinov. 2021. Towards understanding and mitigating social biases in language models.

Max M. Louwerse and Nick Benesh. 2012. Representing spatial structure through maps and language: Lord of the rings encodes the spatial structure of middle earth. *Cognitive Science*, 36(8):1556–1569.

OpenAI. 2023. Gpt-4 technical report. *ArXiv*, abs/2303.08774.

Alec Radford, Jeff Wu, Rewon Child, David Luan, Dario Amodei, and Ilya Sutskever. 2019. Language models are unsupervised multitask learners.

Timo Schick and Hinrich Schütze. 2021. Generating datasets with pretrained language models. In *Proceedings of the 2021 Conference on Empirical Methods in Natural Language Processing*, pages 6943–6951, Online and Punta Cana, Dominican Republic. Association for Computational Linguistics.

Oleh Shliazhko, Alena Fenogenova, Maria Tikhonova, Vladislav Mikhailov, Anastasia Kozlova, and Tatiana Shavrina. 2022. mgpt: Few-shot learners go multilingual.

Vered Shwartz. 2022. Good night at 4 pm?! time expressions in different cultures. In *Findings of the Association for Computational Linguistics: ACL 2022*, pages 2842–2853, Dublin, Ireland. Association for Computational Linguistics.

Xavier Suau, Luca Zappella, and Nicholas Apostoloff. 2022. Self-conditioning pre-trained language models. *International Conference on Machine Learning*.

Qingyu Tan, Hwee Tou Ng, and Lidong Bing. 2023. Towards benchmarking and improving the temporal reasoning capability of large language models. In *Proceedings of the 61st Annual Meeting of the Association for Computational Linguistics (Volume 1: Long Papers)*, pages 14820–14835, Toronto, Canada. Association for Computational Linguistics.

Ashish V. Thapliyal, Jordi Pont Tuset, Xi Chen, and Radu Soricut. 2022. Crossmodal-3600: A massively multilingual multimodal evaluation dataset. In *Proceedings of the 2022 Conference on Empirical Methods in Natural Language Processing*, pages 715–729, Abu Dhabi, United Arab Emirates. Association for Computational Linguistics.

Hugo Touvron, Louis Martin, Kevin Stone, Peter Albert, Amjad Almahairi, Yasmine Babaei, Nikolay Bashlykov, Soumya Batra, Prajjwal Bhargava, Shruti Bhosale, Dan Bikel, Lukas Blecher, Cristian Canton Ferrer, Moya Chen, Guillem Cucurull, David Esiobu, Jude Fernandes, Jeremy Fu, Wenyin Fu, Brian Fuller, Cynthia Gao, Vedanuj Goswami, Naman Goyal, Anthony Hartshorn, Saghar Hosseini, Rui Hou, Hakan Inan, Marcin Kardas, Viktor Kerkez, Madian Khabsa, Isabel Kloumann, Artem Korenev, Punit Singh Koura, Marie-Anne Lachaux, Thibaut Lavril, Jenya Lee, Diana Liskovich, Yinghai Lu, Yuning Mao, Xavier Martinet, Todor Mihaylov, Pushkar Mishra, Igor Molybog, Yixin Nie, Andrew Poulton, Jeremy Reizenstein, Rashi Rungta, Kalyan Saladi, Alan Schelten, Ruan Silva, Eric Michael Smith, Ranjan Subramanian, Xiaoqing Ellen Tan, Binh Tang, Ross Taylor, Adina Williams, Jian Xiang Kuan, Puxin Xu, Zheng Yan, Iliyan Zarov, Yuchen Zhang, Angela Fan, Melanie Kambadur, Sharan Narang, Aurelien Rodriguez, Robert Stojnic, Sergey Edunov, and Thomas Scialom. 2023. Llama 2: Open foundation and fine-tuned chat models.

Yufei Wang, Can Xu, Qingfeng Sun, Huang Hu, Chongyang Tao, Xiubo Geng, and Daxin Jiang. 2022. PromDA: Prompt-based data augmentation for low-resource NLU tasks. In *Proceedings of the 60th Annual Meeting of the Association for Computational Linguistics (Volume 1: Long Papers)*, pages 4242–4255, Dublin, Ireland. Association for Computational Linguistics.

Zirui Wang, Adams Wei Yu, Orhan Firat, and Yuan Cao. 2021. Towards zero-label language learning.

BigScience Workshop, :, Teven Le Scao, Angela Fan, Christopher Akiki, Ellie Pavlick, Suzana Ilić, Daniel Hesslow, Roman Castagné, Alexandra Sasha Luccioni, François Yvon, Matthias Gallé, Jonathan Tow, Alexander M. Rush, Stella Biderman, Albert Webson, Pawan Sasanka Ammanamanchi, Thomas Wang, Benoît Sagot, Niklas Muennighoff, Albert Villanova del Moral, Olatunji Ruwase, Rachel Bawden,

Stas Bekman, Angelina McMillan-Major, Iz Beltagy, Huu Nguyen, Lucile Saulnier, Samson Tan, Pedro Ortiz Suarez, Victor Sanh, Hugo Laurençon, Yacine Jernite, Julien Launay, Margaret Mitchell, Colin Raffel, Aaron Gokaslan, Adi Simhi, Aitor Soroa, Alham Fikri Aji, Amit Alfassy, Anna Rogers, Ariel Kreisberg Nitzav, Canwen Xu, Chenghao Mou, Chris Emezue, Christopher Klamm, Colin Leong, Daniel van Strien, David Ifeoluwa Adelani, Dragomir Radev, Eduardo González Ponferrada, Efrat Levkovizh, Ethan Kim, Eyal Bar Natan, Francesco De Toni, Gérard Dupont, Germán Kruszewski, Giada Pistilli, Hady Elsahar, Hamza Benyamina, Hieu Tran, Ian Yu, Idris Abdulmumin, Isaac Johnson, Itziar Gonzalez-Dios, Javier de la Rosa, Jenny Chim, Jesse Dodge, Jian Zhu, Jonathan Chang, Jörg Frohberg, Joseph Tobing, Joydeep Bhattacharjee, Khalid Almubarak, Kimbo Chen, Kyle Lo, Leandro Von Werra, Leon Weber, Long Phan, Loubna Ben allal, Ludovic Tanguy, Manan Dey, Manuel Romero Muñoz, Maraim Masoud, María Grandury, Mario Šaško, Max Huang, Maximin Coavoux, Mayank Singh, Mike Tian-Jian Jiang, Minh Chien Vu, Mohammad A. Jauhar, Mustafa Ghaleb, Nishant Subramani, Nora Kassner, Nurulaqilla Khamis, Olivier Nguyen, Omar Espejel, Ona de Gibert, Paulo Villegas, Peter Henderson, Pierre Colombo, Priscilla Amuok, Quentin Lhoest, Rheza Harliman, Rishi Bommasani, Roberto Luis López, Rui Ribeiro, Salomey Osei, Sampo Pyysalo, Sebastian Nagel, Shamik Bose, Shamsuddeen Hassan Muhammad, Shanya Sharma, Shayne Longpre, Somaieh Nikpoor, Stanislav Silberberg, Suhas Pai, Sydney Zink, Tiago Timponi Torrent, Timo Schick, Tristan Thrush, Valentin Danchev, Vassilina Nikoulina, Veronika Laippala, Violette Lepercq, Vrinda Prabhu, Zaid Alyafeai, Zeerak Talat, Arun Raja, Benjamin Heinzerling, Chenglei Si, Davut Emre Taşar, Elizabeth Salesky, Sabrina J. Mielke, Wilson Y. Lee, Abheesht Sharma, Andrea Santilli, Antoine Chaffin, Arnaud Stiegler, Debajyoti Datta, Eliza Szczechla, Gunjan Chhablani, Han Wang, Harshit Pandey, Hendrik Strobelt, Jason Alan Fries, Jos Rozen, Leo Gao, Lintang Sutawika, M Saiful Bari, Maged S. Al-shaibani, Matteo Manica, Nihal Nayak, Ryan Teehan, Samuel Albanie, Sheng Shen, Srulik Ben-David, Stephen H. Bach, Taewoon Kim, Tali Bers, Thibault Fevry, Trishala Neeraj, Urmish Thakker, Vikas Raunak, Xiangru Tang, Zheng-Xin Yong, Zhiqing Sun, Shaked Brody, Yallow Uri, Hadar Tojarieh, Adam Roberts, Hyung Won Chung, Jaesung Tae, Jason Phang, Ofir Press, Conglong Li, Deepak Narayanan, Hatim Bourfoune, Jared Casper, Jeff Rasley, Max Ryabinin, Mayank Mishra, Minjia Zhang, Mohammad Shoeybi, Myriam Peyrounette, Nicolas Patry, Nouamane Tazi, Omar Sanseviero, Patrick von Platen, Pierre Cornette, Pierre François Lavallée, Rémi Lacroix, Samyam Rajbhandari, Sanchit Gandhi, Shaden Smith, Stéphane Requena, Suraj Patil, Tim Dettmers, Ahmed Baruwa, Amanpreet Singh, Anastasia Cheveleva, Anne-Laure Ligozat, Arjun Subramonian, Aurélie Névéol, Charles Lovering, Dan Garrette, Deepak Tunuguntla, Ehud Reiter, Ekaterina Taktasheva, Ekaterina Voloshina, Eli Bogdanov, Genta Indra Winata, Hailey Schoelkopf, Jan-Christoph Kalo, Jekaterina Novikova, Jessica Zosa Forde, Jordan Clive, Jungo Kasai, Ken Kawamura, Liam Hazan, Marine Carpuat, Miruna Clinciu, Najoung Kim, Newton Cheng, Oleg Serikov, Omer Antverg, Oskar van der Wal, Rui Zhang, Ruochen Zhang, Sebastian Gehrmann, Shachar Mirkin, Shani Pais, Tatiana Shavrina, Thomas Scialom, Tian Yun, Tomasz Limisiewicz, Verena Rieser, Vitaly Protasov, Vladislav Mikhailov, Yada Pruksachatkun, Yonatan Belinkov, Zachary Bamberger, Zdeněk Kasner, Alice Rueda, Amanda Pestana, Amir Feizpour, Ammar Khan, Amy Faranak, Ana Santos, Anthony Hevia, Antigona Unldreaj, Arash Aghagol, Arezoo Abdollahi, Aycha Tammour, Azadeh HajiHosseini, Bahareh Behroozi, Benjamin Ajibade, Bharat Saxena, Carlos Muñoz Ferrandis, Daniel McDuff, Danish Contractor, David Lansky, Davis David, Douwe Kiela, Duong A. Nguyen, Edward Tan, Emi Baylor, Ezinwanne Ozoani, Fatima Mirza, Frankline Ononiwu, Habib Rezanejad, Hessie Jones, Indrani Bhattacharya, Irene Solaiman, Irina Sedenko, Isar Nejadgholi, Jesse Passmore, Josh Seltzer, Julio Bonis Sanz, Livia Dutra, Mairon Samagaio, Maraim Elbadri, Margot Mieskes, Marissa Gerchick, Martha Akinlolu, Michael McKenna, Mike Qiu, Muhammed Ghauri, Mykola Burynok, Nafis Abrar, Nazneen Rajani, Nour Elkott, Nour Fahmy, Olanrewaju Samuel, Ran An, Rasmus Kromann, Ryan Hao, Samira Alizadeh, Sarmad Shubber, Silas Wang, Sourav Roy, Sylvain Viguier, Thanh Le, Tobi Oyebade, Trieu Le, Yoyo Yang, Zach Nguyen, Abhinav Ramesh Kashyap, Alfredo Palasciano, Alison Callahan, Anima Shukla, Antonio Miranda-Escalada, Ayush Singh, Benjamin Beilharz, Bo Wang, Caio Brito, Chenxi Zhou, Chirag Jain, Chuxin Xu, Clémentine Fourrier, Daniel León Periñán, Daniel Molano, Dian Yu, Enrique Manjavacas, Fabio Barth, Florian Fuhrimann, Gabriel Altay, Giyaseddin Bayrak, Gully Burns, Helena U. Vrabec, Imane Bello, Ishani Dash, Jihyun Kang, John Giorgi, Jonas Golde, Jose David Posada, Karthik Rangasai Sivaraman, Lokesh Bulchandani, Lu Liu, Luisa Shinzato, Madeleine Hahn de Bykhovetz, Maiko Takeuchi, Marc Pàmies, Maria A Castillo, Marianna Nezhurina, Mario Sänger, Matthias Samwald, Michael Cullan, Michael Weinberg, Michiel De Wolf, Mina Mihaljcic, Minna Liu, Moritz Freidank, Myungsun Kang, Natasha Seelam, Nathan Dahlberg, Nicholas Michio Broad, Nikolaus Muellner, Pascale Fung, Patrick Haller, Ramya Chandrasekhar, Renata Eisenberg, Robert Martin, Rodrigo Canalli, Rosaline Su, Ruisi Su, Samuel Cahyawijaya, Samuele Garda, Shlok S Deshmukh, Shubhanshu Mishra, Sid Kiblawi, Simon Ott, Sinee Sang-aroonsiri, Srishti Kumar, Stefan Schweter, Sushil Bharati, Tanmay Laud, Théo Gigant, Tomoya Kainuma, Wojciech Kusa, Yanis Labrak, Yash Shailesh Bajaj, Yash Venkatraman, Yifan Xu, Yingxin Xu, Yu Xu, Zhe Tan, Zhongli Xie, Zifan Ye, Mathilde Bras, Younes Belkada, and Thomas Wolf. 2023. Bloom: A 176b-parameter open-access multilingual language model.

Da Yin, Hritik Bansal, Masoud Monajatipoor, Liunian Harold Li, and Kai-Wei Chang. 2022. Geomlama: Geo-diverse commonsense probing on multilingual pre-trained language models. In *EMNLP*.

Weizhe Yuan, Graham Neubig, and Pengfei Liu. 2021. Bartscore: Evaluating generated text as text generation. In *Advances in Neural Information Processing Systems*, volume 34, pages 27263–27277. Curran Associates, Inc.

Susan Zhang, Stephen Roller, Naman Goyal, Mikel Artetxe, Moya Chen, Shuohui Chen, Christopher Dewan, Mona Diab, Xian Li, Xi Victoria Lin, Todor Mihaylov, Myle Ott, Sam Shleifer, Kurt Shuster, Daniel Simig, Punit Singh Koura, Anjali Sridhar, Tianlu Wang, and Luke Zettlemoyer. 2022. Opt: Open pre-trained transformer language models.

A Frequently asked questions

A.1 What does it mean by the term geographic biases, geographic favouritism and what are their relationships with fairness?

In general, geographic bias means the over-representation of certain geographic attributes. In this study, we use *"geographic bias"* and *"geographic favouritism"* interchangeably as the over-amplification of certain country representation (eg. countries with higher GDP, geopolitical stability, military strength etc) during PLM prediction or text-generation. We believe the overall system utility of a language model should be equitable according to the needs of the intended users with different demographic and geographic origin. Thus ensuring their geographic characteristics are well-represented and not over-shadowed because of geographic favouritism is defined as *"geographic fairness"* in this study.

A.2 What's the reason for using the self-conditioning approach of Suau et al. (2022) for studying biases? There had been many other bias measures in NLP before Suau et al. (2022). Are they not suitable for the study of geographic and geopolitical biases?

A number of previous studies experimented with the behavior different PLMs exhibits while probing with geographic-context as well as cultural-commonsense (Yin et al., 2022; Ghosh et al., 2021). However, we need to extract the specific model weights responsible for these observable polarity. Then using those weights in a controlled setting, we might be able to unfold how PLMs encode geographic knowledge as well as explain the exhibition of geographic-bias during inference. The self-conditioning model proposed by Suau et al. (2022) is one such study that fits to our intended needs perfectly. This approach serves two main purposes: (1) Identifying expert units: model parameters responsible for generating text related to the target concept (i.e. doctor). (2) Triggering specific behaviour in text generation without explicit mentioning or fine-tuning of the target context, which inadvertently influences the behaviour of the model utilizing the encoded-knowledge of PLM.

A.3 What are the practical takeaways from this? Yes, different models encode geographic knowledge, so what? Should we be concerned, should we do something about it?

We recall the example presented earlier: consider a L_1 Spanish speaker from Peru, who is using a prompt-based PLM (like that of Wang et al. (2022, 2021)) to generate a localized synthetic dataset for some downstream task. They may use Spanish *as used in the local context* to form their seed data/prefix/prompts. Now, if this language model has already skewed preferences towards geopolitically important countries, it is likely the generated texts will reflect this skewness, thus not appropriately reflecting the local, Peruvian context that the practitioner is interested in. In this study we address this concern of geographic bias being one of the most-significant yet ignored attributes in practice. Moreover, we show how this is further amplified when we go beyond English and similar languages. Basically we need effective bias-mitigation module as part of the regular NLP workflow which is currently non-existent.

A.4 Why we need to extract the *Expert Units* and how *Concept-Country* helps in this regard?

One of our aims is to unfold the geographic representation using relevant PLM units without external fine-tuning. So, we need to find or extract these relevent units which are basically model parameters. So, we can use our *Concept-Country* datasets as binary classification dataset (positive class contains sentences mentioning certain*Concept-Country*) to find these highly responsive weights (i.e. *Expert Units*) to certain *Concept-Country*. Then we perform self-conditioning on the PLMs using these *Expert Units* to generate texts having the influence of these *Concept-Country*s.

A.5 Explain *Concept-Country* dataset creation process.

We scrape news using a Google news api[8] to capture the current affairs. Importantly, we can select news not just from a given date range, but also news originating in a specific country and a specific language. Such a dataset should allow us to get a reasonable representation of current geopolitical affairs. As such,

[8] https://github.com/ranahaani/GNews

each of the concept datasets we create reflects *"current news about a country reported by the mainstream platforms from another country"*. Hence, a *Concept-Country* dataset `{C}-{l}` contains news about several $(c_1, c_2, ..c_n)$ countries in `{l}` language where the news-source is `{C}` country. For example, `USA-eng` contains data from US sources, in English, which either mention other countries (there are 100 positive examples for each country c_i) or are random sentences not mentioning any countries (negative examples).

A.6 Explain the *Expert Units* extraction process.

Consider the *Concept-Country* `India` from the dataset `USA-eng`. Essentially, we have positive examples (text mentioning India or relevant entities) and negative examples (random other sentences not mentioning India) which we can use to identify the model's *Expert Units*. These units are the neurons which can be used as predictors to identify the presence of a concept (i.e. positive examples mentioning "India"). The self-conditioning framework computes these neurons and uses the average-precision score to rank their predictive expertise thus allowing us to select the top-k (eg. 10, 50) *Expert Units* from each layer.

A.7 What does Geographic Representation Network actually represents?

Note that these networks are produced using the uncovered original PLM expert units, without any external data fine-tuning or prompting. Hence, they provide a view of the *inherent* geographic knowledge present inside the PLM parameter space.

A.8 Why we need to use *Expert Units* during text generation?

We have a setting where we can provide certain *Concept-Country* as part of the generation condition and the specific *Expert Units* from the model itself are supposed to be capable enough to influence the generated text. Our aim is to evaluate the geographic knowledge specific model weights or *Expert Units* by asking those about other *Prefix-Country*. This will unfold whether the geopolitical favouritism happens for geopolitically important countries or the geographical proximity (eg. neighbouring countries) takes the precedence or there exist no such patterns.

A.9 What are the factors considered while constructing the *Concept-Country* dataset?

There are two relevant factors: (1) For the negative examples in USA-eng *Concept-Country* dataset, we use news from a completely different domain (eg. automobile, sport), whereas for different geographic-sourced datasets, negative examples come from randomly sampling news of different locations. (2) The intensity of text-noise and positive example up-sampling amount varies across different news-sourced *Concept-Country* datasets.

A.10 Why 2-hop distance while calculating the neighbourhood-score?

We did experiment with n-hop scoring and they follow similar trends. We choose 2-hop is it is less complex for scoring and at the same-time, sufficient to point out the disparity across multiple languages.

A.11 Comparison to news: although these models are trained on web text, which contain news articles, they are not guaranteed to generate text like a news article. Thus the distribution of entities within the text will be different.

Yes, that is correct but our aim is to capture the learned distribution and evaluate (1) whether that distribution is skewed or not, (2) Whether there is resemblance with the real-world scenario or not. We believe, this assessment is important for a PLM which will be used for solving real-world practical tasks and having news-text for comparison might be the closest viable source we can get in a limited resource setting.

A.12 What does it mean by: *"the model weights which provide higher scores for the presence of a concept"*

In sort, a language model can provide scores to the positive and negative examples of a binary classification dataset (eg. our country-concept dataset). Looking at the average precision scores and the outputs given by different model weights from each layer, we can identify the ones providing higher scores towards the positive examples and these model weights are referred as expert units.

B Self-conditioning Method: Theoretical Definition

Here we provide a theoretical description concerning the working procedure of the self-conditioning method (Suau et al., 2022). First, we provide an overview of the usual generative mechanism followed by the expert unit extraction procedure. Then we talk about creating the simulated environment where the expert units are prioritized to instigate text generation in a specific direction.

Generative Mechanism During autoregressive text generation, a language model maximizes the probability of a sentence $x = \{x_i\}$ as $p(x) = p(x_1, ..x_T) = \prod_{t=1}^{T} p(x_t|x_{<t})$. A conditional generative model can use a joint probability distribution to maximize the probability such that: $p(x, y) = p(y|x)p(x)$. Here, x is the generated sentence while y is a conditional variable (i.e. imposing the presence of a concept word). Dathathri et al. (2020), adopted this setting in a conditional generation where, $p(y|x)$ determines the condition and $p(x)$ ensures constraint on the generated text as it progresses. In this setting, instead of the joint distribution, the condition can even be fixed beforehand as follows:

$$p(x|y = c) \approx p(y = c|x)p(x) \tag{1}$$

Suau et al. (2022), hypothesize that the conditional maximization of $p(x|y = c)$ in Eq. (1) can be done by exploiting the internal mechanism of a PLM (e.g. expert unit extraction and prioritizing them by changing their responses during text generation).

Expert Unit Extraction Suau et al. (2022) defines expert units as the neurons contributing to the conditional model $p(y = c|x)$ in Eq. (1). They extract certain expert units which can further be used as the predictors of the concept presence identification task given an input. Formally, we define z_m^c as the set of outputs of a single neuron m to sentences $\{s_i^c\}$. We can formulate z_m^c as the prediction score of a binary sentence classification task $b^c[0, 1]$ where s_i^c is an input sentence and z_m^c varies depending on the presence/absence of a concept c in s_i^c. Now having the prediction score z_m^c in hand, we can compute the expertise of a unit m for the task $b^c[0, 1]$ by looking at the average precision score so that $AP_m^c = AP(z_m^c, b^c) \in [0, 1]$ (i.e. area under the precision-recall curve). At this point, the top k expert units are identified by ranking all the units from each model layer based on AP_m^c.

Conditional Text Generation The final step is to prioritize the identified expert units to generate texts having specific behaviors. This can be done using a $do(c, k)$ intervention which ensures the influence of concept c while prioritizing the top $k-$expert units. These top $k-$expert units previously performed as the best predictors for c concept identification from sentences. In (Suau et al., 2022), $do(c, k)$ is formulated as follows:

$$do(c, k) : \{z_c^m := E_x^c[z_c^m|b^c = 1]\forall m \in Q_k\} \tag{2}$$

This $do(c, k)$ intervention always replaces the response of an expert unit with the typical value where the concept c was present in an input sentence (i.e. $E_x^c[z_c^m|b^c = 1]$). Here, Q_k is the set of indices of all top-performing k-expert units. Now in Eq. (1), the $p(y = c|x)$ can be maximized by increasing the number of relevant expert units (i.e. k) using the $do(c, k)$ intervention according to the adopted hypothesis of (Suau et al., 2022). As a result, by just exploiting the internal conditioning mechanism of a PLM text generation and without any out-source data training, an artificial environment is created where the presence of concept c is inspired.

C Datasets

In Table 3 we present the concept dataset details. Each dataset here contains 43 to 69 country concept files (The complete list of countries is presented in Table 4).

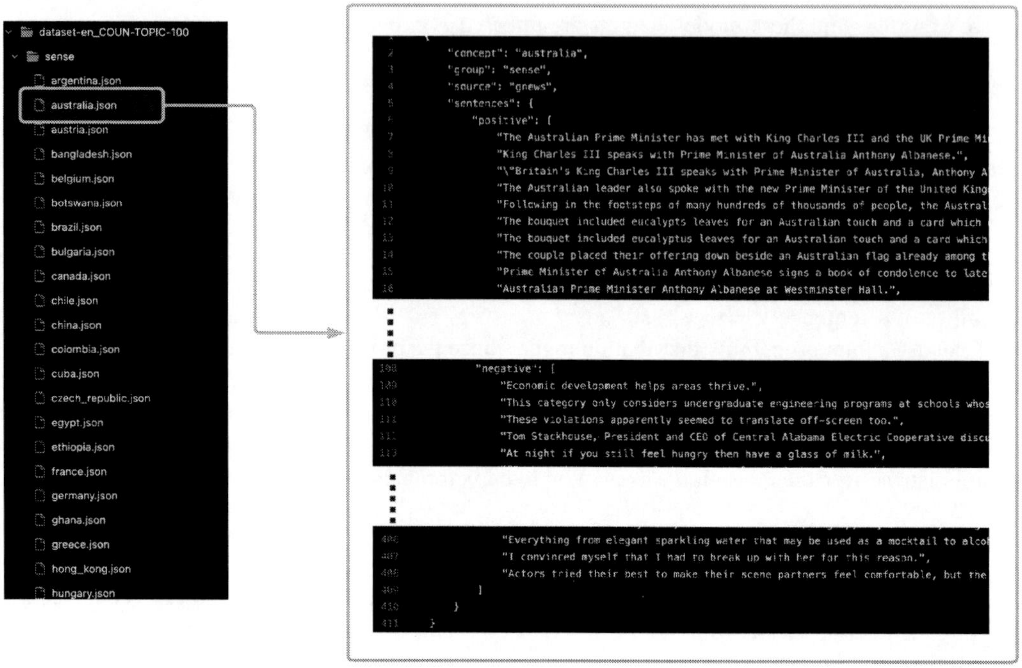

Figure 7: A snap-shot of the *USA-eng* dataset. Each json file contains postive-negative news about one specific country. For example, the `australia.json` contains positive sentences having mention of the country name extracted from the news articles. Whereas, the negative 300 sentences are also collected from news domain having no mention of the word *austrailia*.

A snapshot of the *USA-eng* dataset is presented in Figure 7 to provide a better understanding of how the concept dataset is formatted. This specific dataset contains English news about various countries while the news-originating country is the USA. From the figure, we observe the mention of country-named json files (i.e. the country concept files). Each json file contains positive 100 sentences about that specific country. Whereas, the negative 300 sentences contain no mention of the specific country. Moreover, we can take a further look at the `australia.json` file where the positive instances are sentences selected from Australia-related recent news articles.

In Table 4, The `Type-2` datasets are the translated version of USA-eng dataset. In `Type-3`, we mask USA-eng entities using a NER tagger and `Type-4` is constructed using random english texts.

D Prefix Templates

For each of the eight languages, we generate prefix replacing templates with *Prefix-Country* names. Per language, we have six template prefix. The complete list is presented in Table 5

E Additional Geographic Representation Networks

In Figures (8, 9, 10, 11) we present Geographic-Representation Networks (News Source-language: USA-eng, SAU-ara, FRA-fra, RUS-rus, BGD-ben, KOR-kor, CHN-zho, IND-hin) constructed using the *Expert Units* from GPT2, BLOOM and mGPT.

F Geography Maps on generated text

We present Country Maps on the generated outputs for eight languages. The maps are presented in Figure 12.

Dataset Names	#	Description
Type 1: {News_Source_Location}-{Language}		
USA-eng, GRC-ell, *KOR-kor*, *SAU-ara*, ETH-eng, TZA-eng, JPN-jpn, *BGD-ben*, ISR-heb, MEX-spa, VNM-vie, GBR-eng, *FRA-fra*, *RUS-rus*, *CHN-zho*, *IND-hin*, NOR-nor, AUS-eng, HKG-zho, PER-spa, CUB-spa	21	These 21 datasets are scrapped from news sources originating from 21 different countries in different languages. Each one of these datasets contain country concept sets describing news about specific countries. Each country concept are prepared using 100 positive sentence examples and 300 negative sentence examples. We use upsampling by repetition when we have less examples than the required counts. For only `USA-eng` dataset, we use english news from other topic search (eg. *Automotive, Sport*) to construct the negative examples while, for other 20 datasets we use news about other countries (i.e. in domain) as negative examples.
Type 2: {News_Source_USA}-{Translations}		
USA-ara, USA-hin, USA-zho, USA-ben, USA-kor, USA-fra, USA-ell, USA-rus	8	These 8 datasets are created using translation from the USA-eng dataset. We use Google Translation API[1] to translate the texts from source language to target language.
Type 3: {USA-eng}-{Masked Entities}		
USA-eng-[M]	1	We augment `USA-eng` dataset by masking all additional entities in positive examples for each country concepts using spaCy[2].
Type 4: {USA-eng}-{Random Text}		
eng-[R]	1	We randomly use text instead of original text in `USA-eng` dataset while maintaining the positive negative class distinction but without any semantic coherence.

[1] `https://translate.google.com/`

[2] `https://spacy.io/`

Table 3: Country Concept Datasets sourced from Google News texts. We extracted expert units from language models: gpt-2 (only english), bloom and mgpt for all of these. Among these, we perform text generation using the expert units sourced from *8 datasets* (The underline ones).

ISO	Country	ISO	Country	ISO	Country
AUS	Australia	BWA	Botswana	CAN	Canada
ETH	Ethiopia	GHA	Ghana	IND	India
IDN	Indonesia	IRL	Ireland	ISR	Israel
KEN	Kenya	LVA	Latvia	MYS	Malaysia
NAM	Namibia	NZL	New Zealand	NGA	Nigeria
PAK	Pakistan	PHL	Philippines	SGP	Singapore
ZAF	South Africa	TZA	Tanzania	UGA	Uganda
GBR	United Kingdom	USA	United States	ZWE	Zimbabwe
CZE	Czech Republic	DEU	Germany	AUT	Austria
CHE	Switzerland	ARG	Argentina	CHL	Chile
COL	Colombia	CUB	Cuba	MEX	Mexico
PER	Peru	VEN	Venezuela	BEL	Belgium
FRA	France	MAR	Morocco	SEN	Senegal
ITA	Italy	LTU	Lithuania	HUN	Hungary
NLD	Netherlands	NOR	Norway	POL	Poland
BRA	Brazil	PRT	Portugal	ROU	Romania
SVK	Slovakia	SVN	Slovenia	SWE	Sweden
VNM	Vietnam	TUR	Turkey	GRC	Greece
BGR	Bulgaria	RUS	Russia	UKR	Ukraine
SRB	Serbia	ARE	United Arab Emirates	SAU	Saudi Arabia
LBN	Lebanon	EGY	Egypt	BGD	Bangladesh
THA	Thailand	CHN	China	TWN	Taiwan
HKG	Hong Kong	JPN	Japan	KOR	Republic of Korea
None	None	None	None	None	None

Table 4: List of Countries we conducted experiments on.

G Geographic Identifier and Language Direction

see Table 6 for examples of generated text examples given the prefix "In Cuba" with *Concept-Country*:Argentina. Though the *Concept-Country* dataset here we use is in English, the model generates highly frequent Spanish sentences compared to english.

lang	Templates	lang	Templates
eng	➤ 'In <country>,' ➤ '<country> is known for' ➤ 'Inside <country>' ➤ "In <country>'s" ➤ 'However, in <country>' ➤ 'Yesterday <country>'	ara	➤ 'في <country> ،' ➤ '<country> معروف بـــ' ➤ 'داخل <country>' ➤ 'في <country>' ➤ 'ومع ذلك ، في <country>' ➤ 'أمس <country>'
rus	➤ 'В <country>,', ➤ '<country> известна', ➤ 'Внутри <country>', ➤ 'В <country>', ➤ 'Однако в <country>', ➤ 'Вчера <country>'	kor	➤ '<country>에서는' ➤ '<country>는' ➤ '<country> 내부' ➤ '<country>에서' ➤ '그러나 <country>에서' ➤ '어제 <country>'
ben	➤ '<country>,' ➤ '<country> এর জন্য পরিচিত' ➤ '<country> এর ভিতরে' ➤ '<country> এর' ➤ 'তবে, <country>' ➤ 'গতকাল <country> এ'	hin	➤ '<country> में,' ➤ '<country> के लिए जाना जाता है' ➤ 'अंदर <country>' ➤ "<country>'एस . में" ➤ 'हालांकि, <country> . में' ➤ 'कल <country>'
zho	➤ '在<country>, ' ➤ '<country> 以' ➤ '<country>内部' ➤ '在<country>的' ➤ '但是, 在 <country>' ➤ '昨天 <country>'	fra	➤ 'En <country>,' ➤ '<country> est connu pour' ➤ "À l'intérieur de <country>" ➤ 'En <country>', ➤ 'Cependant, en <country>' ➤ 'Hier <country>'

Table 5: Prefix templates we use for Multilingual Text Generation. We replace the **<country>** with the corresponding country name in generator language. For example, To construct one USA-mention Chinese prefix, we replace **<country>** with 美国. We use a multilingual country-name dataset (cna, 2021) to query country names.

Language Direction	Generated Text
eng→spa	*In Colombia, beginning in 1991,* Ley de Pesca y Tierra Naranja tiene como una estrategia de Economía Indígena presenta como Ley de Conservación y Desarrollo Agrícola
eng→eng	*In Colombia, patients with PO are routinely referred to the Pediatric Critical Care Units (PC from 1996) because they are mostly after peak twice* ***a los to*** *participating in*
eng→spa	In Colombia, donde está en etapa de vacunación las primeras etapas las personas que llegan en el jueves (figuana para el millón y ultimaniano casos y el
eng→spa	In Colombia, la noticia odia a Dios. Es una religión que no santifica. Esta seccionalizada del 4Chanuto para algunos países, a sociedad que
eng→spa	In Colombia, el mercado de la carne, considerado el segundo mayor productor de cortes de carne bovina en la región, es de caña de insumo a nivel
eng→spa	In Colombia, el partido del "9-3" ha sido en la decisión del colombiano, la celebración de Luis Zubeldense Humberto Bloom (peruano, quien abrió
eng→spa	In Colombia, afloró por las fronteras de Argentina. Entre 1985 y 1993, de la República Dominicana, Bolivia, después llegó a Colombia y Ecuador. El entrenador
eng→spa	In Colombia, execuções entre elites, o Partido Comunista y sindicatos de esos países vecinos elites a partiran llevan la denuncia que derrochales. Las
eng→spa	In Colombia, una estrecha relación entre Washington y Venezuela tiene un mensaje claro sobre Bolsonaro. Así mismo, aunque no ve la necesidad de revisar lo que de no hacerlo de
eng→spa	In Colombia, a 0.70 por ciento de la población de niños mueren prematuros de gripe por sobrepeso ha sido diagnosticada. El representante del tamaño real de
eng→spa	In Colombia, PDOT, que hace más de 10 años había significado cerca de 160 actividades laborales para sus miembros, al día e instalaciones de 14 mili 300 personas
eng→spa	In Colombia, made del Derecho penal, es la máxima parte de la violación a través de los notaria Núcleo de medidas contra la descripción de la Justicia y
eng→spa	In Colombia, Cristina Kirchner — la vicepresidenta del fallecido expresidente Néstor Kirchner— ha confesado que "en las últimas horas pasó todo como una enfermedad que no se registró su mujer
eng→spa	In Colombia, el Código Penal declaró cierto grado de subordinación de la salud mental de las víctimas de trabajadores a responsables funcionalistas, no profesionales por el Estado como se
eng→eng	*In Colombia, the majority of women are Catholic. But in the country is still refuses to accept the Catholic counseling school, and, penalizes women after to leave*
eng→eng	*In Colombia, for example, we observed a significantly lower prevalence of chronic bronchoalveolar or peritonitis, bronchobronchial hypertrophy than mon*
eng→spa	In Colombia, un importante sector de las diezañeras vuelve a poner en valor de la importancia el anonimato de las producciones francesas cuando, una mezcla que habían obtenido a
eng→eng	*In Colombia, the EMA has regular royalties on a $27,800 per fee,800 day to $39,000 protein products at the expert. The fair*
eng→eng	*In Colombia, in turn, the mass distributions represent very low prevalence, being around 4. The USA around 35 40-47% and in the usual, and 45%*
eng→spa	In Colombia, el gobierno presentó este miércoles un proyecto de ley en la primera lectura online para eximir controles y renegociación internacional e internacional de suscripto de divisas con

Table 6: Example Generated Sentences with the prefix "In Colombia" and "Country/Concept" Argentina.

Geographic Representation Networks and Corresponding Community Maps

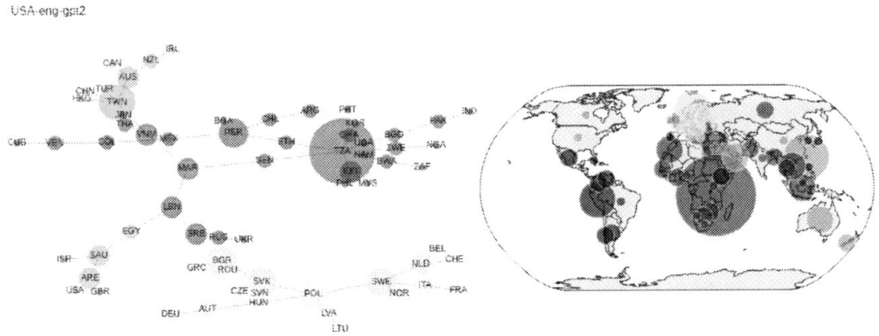

(1)

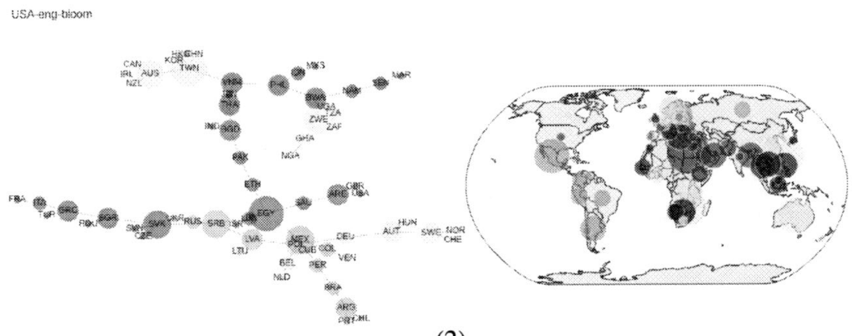

(2)

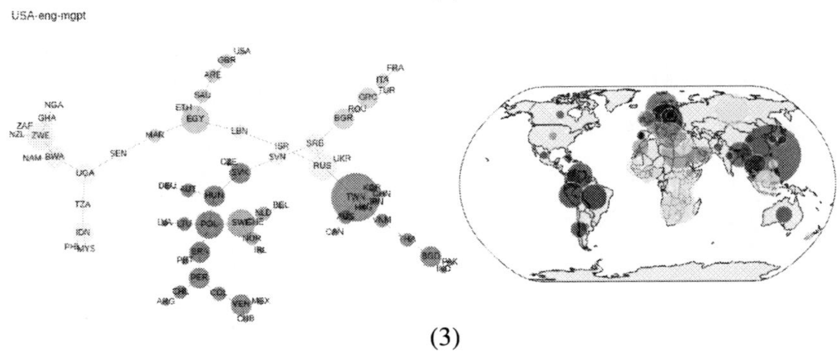

(3)

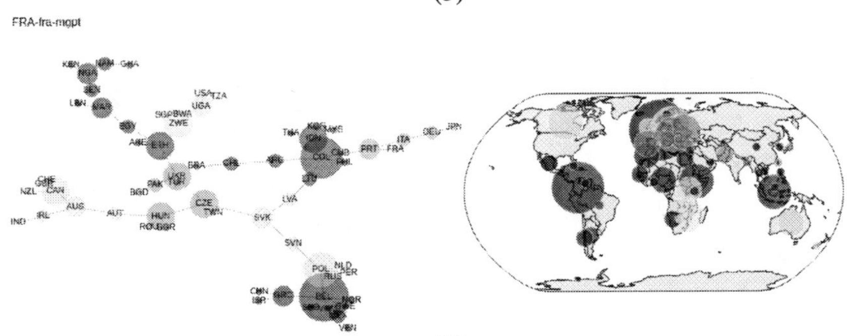

(4)

Figure 8: Geographic Representation Network and Corresponding Community Map for different Expert Unit set Associations. The language models we use are GPT2 (only English), mGPT and BLOOM.

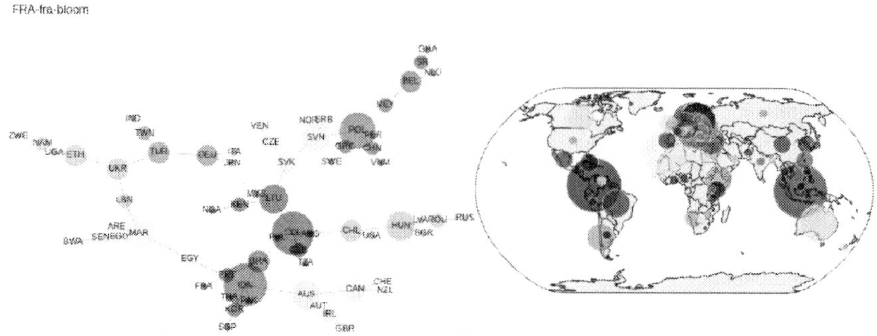

(5)

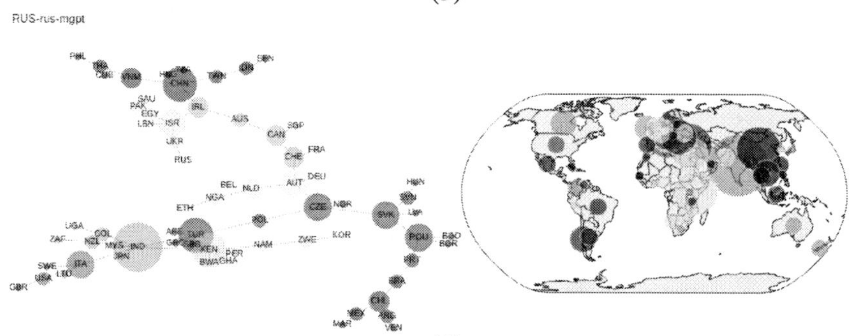

(6)

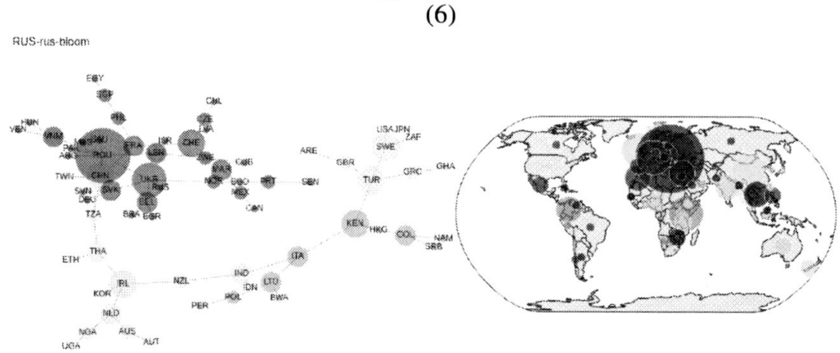

(7)

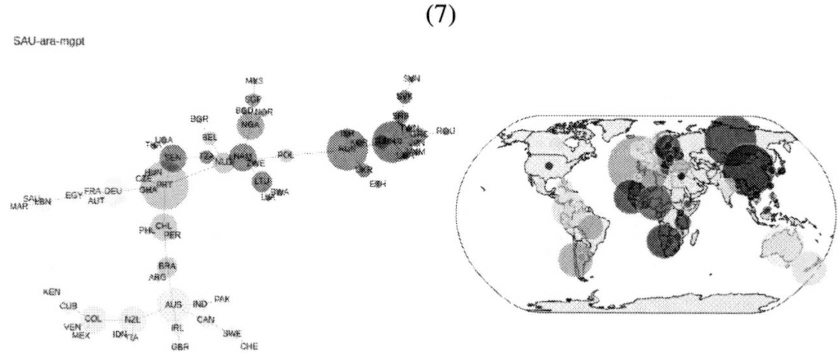

(8)

Figure 9: Geographic Representation Network and Corresponding Community Map for different Expert Unit set Associations. The language models we use are GPT2 (only English), mGPT and BLOOM.

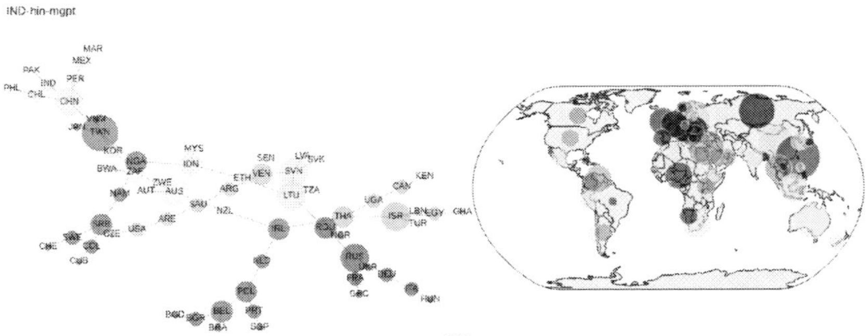

(9)

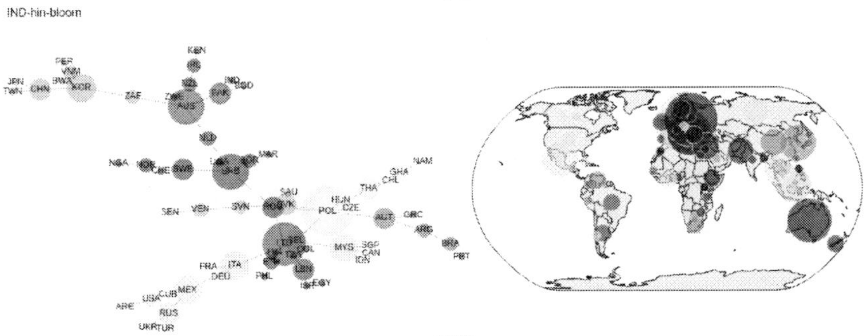

(10)

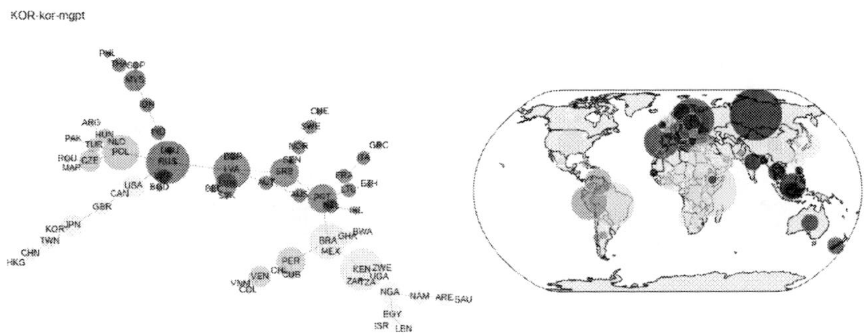

(11)

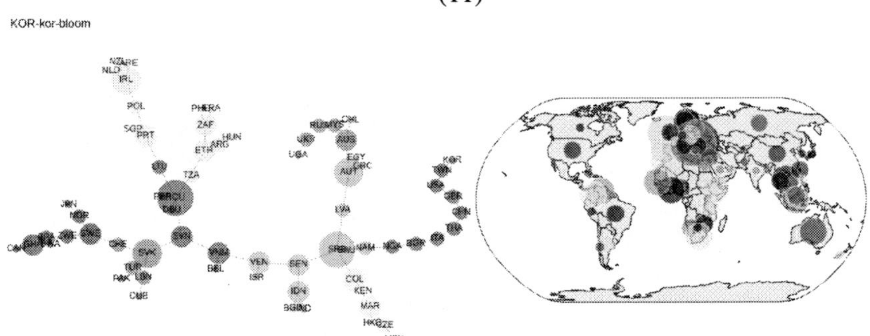

(12)

Figure 10: Geographic Representation Network and Corresponding Community Map for different Expert Unit set Associations. The language models we use are GPT2 (only English), mGPT and BLOOM.

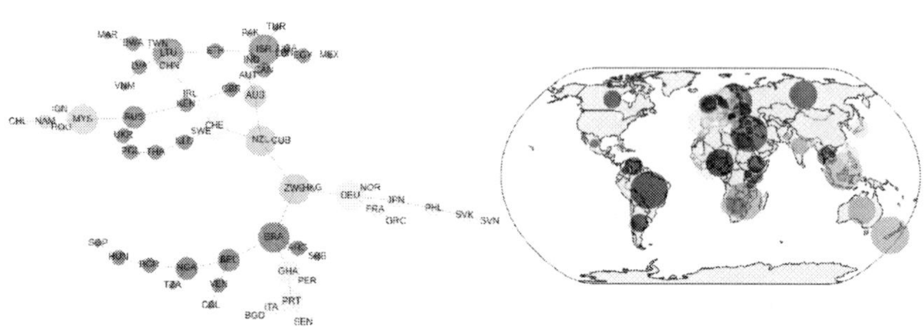

(13)

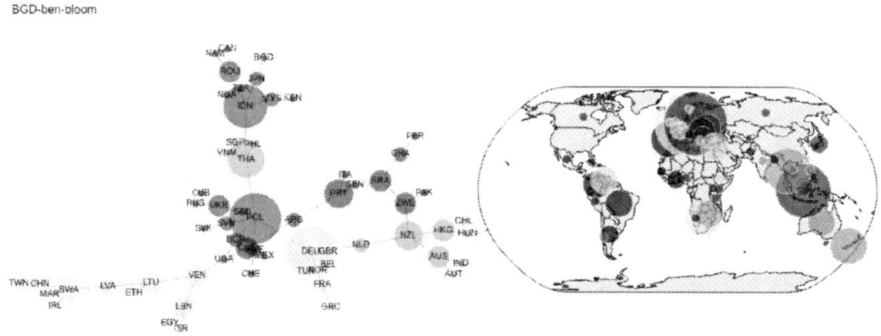

(14)

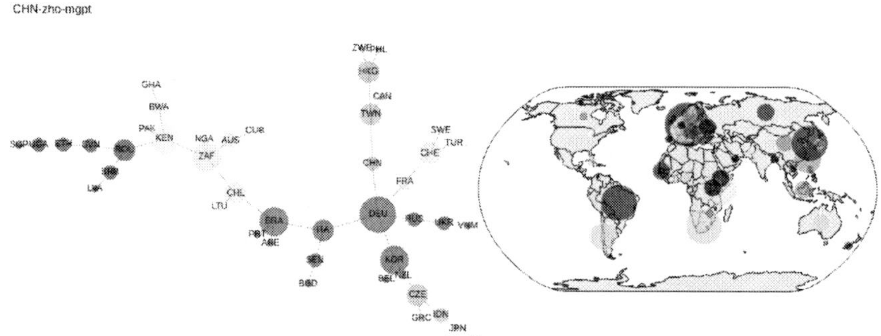

(15)

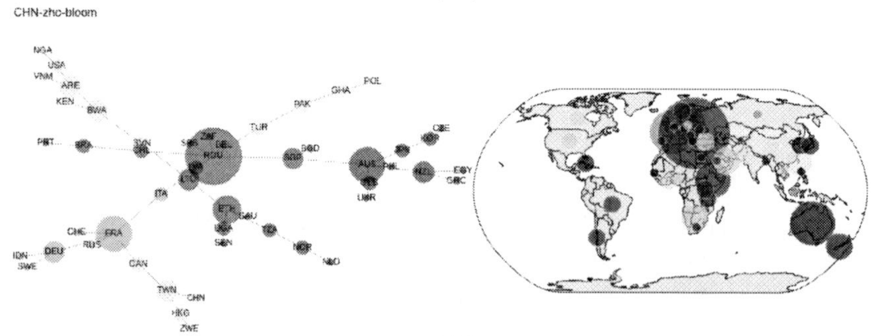

(16)

Figure 11: Geographic Representation Network and Corresponding Community Map for different Expert Unit set Associations. The language models we use are GPT2 (only English), mGPT and BLOOM.

Geographic Representation Networks and Corresponding Community Maps

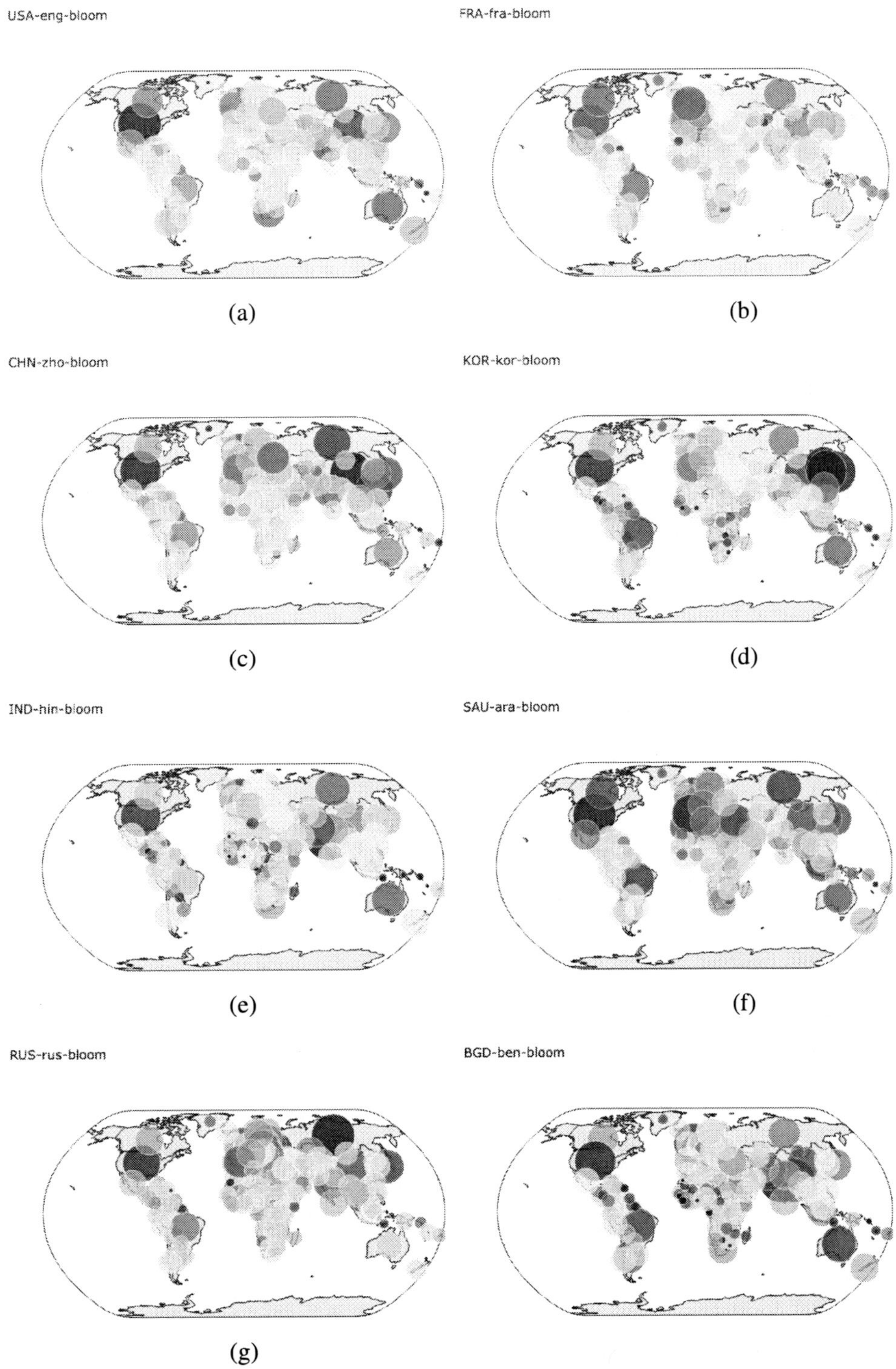

Figure 12: Graphs prepared using entity-country mapping on generated texts using BLOOM. Here We take the log-frequency distribution of entity counts. In all cases, the most frequent country remains the geopolitical favoured ones with the additon of Country/Concept Dataset News Source-country (the darker red ones)

Task-Based MoE for Multitask Multilingual Machine Translation

Hai Pham
Carnegie Mellon University
htpham@cs.cmu.edu

Young Jin Kim
Microsoft
youki@microsoft.com

Subhabrata Mukherjee*
Hippocratic AI

David P. Woodruff
Carnegie Mellon University
dwoodruf@cs.cmu.edu

Barnabás Póczos
Carnegie Mellon University
bapoczos@cs.cmu.edu

Hany Hassan Awadalla
Microsoft
hanyh@microsoft.com

Abstract

Mixture-of-experts (MoE) architecture has been proven a powerful method for diverse tasks in training deep models in many applications. However, current MoE implementations are task agnostic, treating all tokens from different tasks in the same manner. In this work, we instead design a novel method that incorporates task information into MoE models at different granular levels with shared dynamic task-based adapters. Our experiments and analysis show the advantages of our approaches over the dense and canonical MoE models on multitask multilingual machine translations. With task-specific adapters, our models can additionally generalize to new tasks efficiently.

1 Introduction

Mixture-of-Experts (MoE), while not being a novel machine learning algorithm (Yüksel et al., 2012), has revived to combine with deep learning, particularly transformer (Vaswani et al., 2017) and has recently pushed forward various tasks such as natural language processing, computer vision, speech recognition, multimodal and multitask learning due to its advantage in scalability in distributed environments (Fedus et al., 2022). The main advantages of MoE stem from its ensemble design while maintaining the sparsity in computation (Fedus et al., 2021). And with proper design such as using sharded experts (Lepikhin et al., 2020; Fedus et al., 2021), the possibility for enterprise-level scalability is almost boundless. As a result, this method has been more and more widely adopted in many applications that require distributed and intensive workloads.

However, most of the current methods are task-agnostic, only optimizing for performance based on lower levels in the architecture such as at system or communication levels (Rajbhandari et al., 2022). In the case of multitask learning where a single model is required to learn from heterogeneous tasks, however, the task-specific data could be inherently diverse and vary largely from one to another (Wu et al., 2020). As a result, treating data from such different sources the same makes the learning ineffective, as also evidenced recently by the interference between different task data (Pfeiffer et al., 2022).

As a result, in this work, we design a novel MoE approach where task information is used during training and inference for assigning experts based on individual task information. The intuition is to make the training more task-aware so those similar tasks would be routed to the same group of experts and vice versa. From the architectural perspective, we incorporate high-level application-specific information with the system-level information to make the model become task-aware and hence have a better strategy in allocating experts based on the characteristics of distinct tasks, as also illustrated in Figure 1.

Our proposed architecture allows for grouping experts based on the similarity of tasks, i.e. similar tasks should use a similar group of experts and otherwise for different tasks, by using shared-task adapters. Our design of putting those adapters on top of MoE layers allows for flexibility in future extensions: if we want the model to acquire new tasks while still having similar resources, we only finetune new adapters, and if we want to scale the hardware resources, e.g. for more speed, we simply deal with MoE layers with such new resources.

Our experiments and analysis show the advantages of using task information in MoE architectures in multiple settings including multitask multilingual machine translations, as well as its generalization in few-shot learning. In summary, our contributions are as follows.

- First, we design novel MoE architectures that dynamically allocate experts based on task information in the context of multilingual mul-

* Work done while at Microsoft (contact email: subhabrata.mukherjee.ju@gmail.com).

Proceedings of the The 3rd Workshop on Multi-lingual Representation Learning (MRL), pages 164–172
December 7, 2023 ©2023 Association for Computational Linguistics

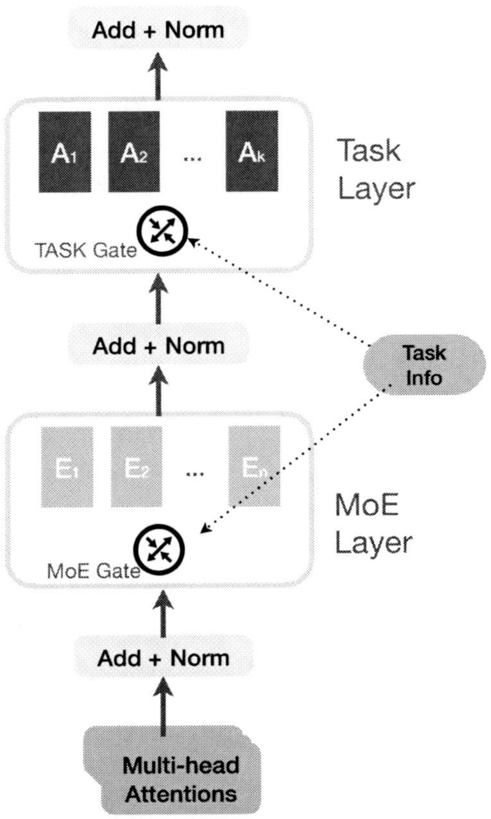

Figure 1: Extended from the typical MoE approaches that do not discriminate tokens from different tasks, we create shared task-related adapters that are trained to route tokens from similar tasks to the same shared adapters, and vice versa.

titask machine translation, with many variations.

- Second, we thoroughly study the pros and cons of our approaches in training from scratch, finetuning as well as transfer learning.
- Third, we implement our models on top of well-proven infrastructres for practicality and scalability including deepspeed (Rasley et al., 2020), `fairseq` (Ott et al., 2019) and `transformer` (Vaswani et al., 2017).

2 Related Work

MoE Basic Transformer-based Mixture-of-Experts (MoE) architecture essentially sparsifies transformer architecture by replacing the heavy feed-forward network (FFN) with a sparse MoE layer with top-1 or top-2 gates (Shazeer et al., 2017). However, increasing the number of experts does not simply increase the performance (Fedus et al., 2021; Clark et al., 2022), many approaches have been proposed together to tackle the large-scale MoE deployment, such as in (Kim et al., 2021). In large-scale deployment, however, additional techniques should also be employed to battle with memory issues such as "sharding" experts (Lepikhin et al., 2020) or stabilizing the training (Zoph et al., 2022), since the models are often deployed on separate nodes that mainly used GPUs with limited memory. The architecture in this work inherits all of those techniques, and in addition incorporates task information into MoE routing, which in turn directs data into separate task adapters. This kind of routing is, however, hardware-agnostic, unlike some other work such as in (Zheng et al., 2022; Chen et al., 2023; Zeng and Xiong, 2023).

MoE Routing Techniques Gating is critical to MoE layer, which works as a weighted sum of the experts and serves for the ultimate purpose of load balancing of all available experts during both training and inference. Unlike the originally proposed top-k experts (Shazeer et al., 2017; Du et al., 2021), it was studied in SwitchTransformer that a single expert can preserve the quality if chosen properly, while significantly reducing the communication and computation cost (Fedus et al., 2021). In more detail, SwitchTransformer first divides evenly amongst all experts with an optional buffer for imbalanced cases and then applies an auxiliary loss to enforce load balancing. Another alternative approach, which is more computationally efficient is to get rid of such extra-heavy complicated loss and instead use a hash function to route every token to its matched expert, which tends to balance the output (Roller et al., 2021). Another interesting approach is to permit each token to appear in the top-k list of multiple experts (Zhou et al., 2022), which has been proven to help, although not applicable for auto-regressive applications. Yet because of the inherent problem of load imbalance, another approach is to replace the gating mechanism with a stochastic selection method, which randomly activates an input during processing (Zuo et al., 2021). The intuition is somewhat similar to the hash approach since it relies on the "fair" randomness to solve the balance problem while keeping the blueprint more lightweight than enforcing an auxiliary loss. Along similar lines, research directions have explored the random dropping of outputs from MoE layers (Liu et al., 2022; Elbayad et al., 2022). Unlike all of those routing techniques which are application agnostic, our proposed model connects the application level (i.e. task information) with the lower-level MoE layers for better dealing with interference of different tasks in the context of multilingual multitask applications.

Task-level Routing Recently task information has been used for improving MoE, e.g. in (Liu et al., 2023). Our model is, however, much simpler and can be trained end-to-end unlike their approach, which requires clustering to be made for off-the-shelf shared representation learning. Probably the most related work to ours is Mod-Squad (Chen et al., 2022) which shares the motivation with us while having several differences. First, their approach has multiple aids to make the task-based MoE work with an additional loss for regularization, while we instead rely mainly on the simple motivation of incorporating task information into MoE. Second, we still stick to a single gate for routing, while they allocate multiple gates, each *per* task. Third, they additionally have MoE attention blocks, which make their architecture more complicated. Finally, our focused application is text-based machine translation, unlike computer vision settings in both works mentioned.

3 Models

Transformer architecture (Vaswani et al., 2017) has been proven to be the core backbone of the pervasive successes in natural language processing, computer vision, and other artificial intelligence fields. The main bottleneck to this architecture is, however, its heavy blueprint leading to intensive resources in training and inference, and is difficult to scale up. MoE is one powerful method to alleviate those problems in transformers.

3.0.1 Sparse Mixture-of-Experts (MoE)

MoE, which was first introduced before the deep learning era (Jacobs et al., 1991), was recently borrowed to address those drawbacks in transformer architecture (Lepikhin et al., 2020). In a nutshell, MoE creates an ensemble of experts in multi-layer transformer blocks in place of a single expert, typically in the form of a feed-forward neural network (FFN) that is dense with many parameters.

In terms of formality, given an original FFN layer called $\tilde{E}$, we clone it into another layer containing a set of N experts with exactly the same architecture $\{E_i\}_{i=1}^{N}$. Likewise, the number of parameters for this particular layer is increased by a factor of N.

The typical granular level of applying those experts in the context of natural language processing is the token level. Given a token x, its learned representation before MoE layer is a vector $\mathbf{x}$, its post-MoE output $\mathbf{y}$ is the weighted average of those experts' output

$$o_i = E_i(\mathbf{x}) \tag{1}$$

$$\mathbf{y} = \sum_{i=1}^{N} W_i o_i, \tag{2}$$

where W_i is the weight (importance) of the corresponding expert E_i.

The key to MoE power and its well-proven successes in tandem with transformer architecture is its sparsity design: only one or few experts are activated (i.e. having non-zero weight) at any point in time in spite of many more parameters just introduced due to the ensemble. Typically the component responsible for this sparsity is a gate that was co-trained with experts to route tokens to their target expert(s), and eventually assigns only a single or few non-zero weights across all experts *per* token to its output $G(\mathbf{x})$ typically using softmax and top-k method

$$g_{out} = \text{softmax}\,(W_g\mathbf{x}) \tag{3}$$

$$G(\mathbf{x}) = \text{Top\_K}\,(g_{out}) \tag{4}$$

With $G(\mathbf{x})$ being a set of K chosen experts, equation 2 becomes

$$\mathbf{y} = \sum_{i \in G(\mathbf{x})} W_i o_i \tag{5}$$

The main architectural problem with this design is its scalability: the memory will be quickly used up as we increase experts, given the limitation of current compute resources allocated to a single compute node in any distributed environment. GShard (Lepikhin et al., 2020) was born to fix this issue by trading the memory for communication: allocating each expert to a single node and only aggregating them when needed, e.g. gradient averaging in training or weight averaging when saving a model. This elegant design has unlocked MoE's unlimited scalability and practicality in enterprise-level deployments, especially with the following-up work in optimizing for better architecture in computation and communication, as mentioned in Section 2.

3.1 Task-based Adapters

Yet another problem on which we are focusing is not at the system level but more at the higher application level. As mentioned, in the multitask setting, the interference amongst tasks that are inherently different from each other could lead to the ineffectiveness of training. As a result, we employ *task-based adapters* to separate those different tasks into different adapters. Likewise, data (or tokens) from similar tasks should be routed to a similar group of adapters. There are three modes for those adapters.

First and the simplest is to allocate each adapter for each individual task. Although this setting is straightforward and requires no additional computation for data routing, it has the drawback of acquiring new unseen tasks. The reason is the model has to allocate a new adapter for each new task and fine-tune it with some amount of new data. Another potential problem is memory limitation if we want to extend to many new tasks in the future. This mode is called `static`, as shown in Figure 2a.

To enforce efficient learning of representation of similar task data, as well as alleviating memory problems, we have `dynamic` (Figure 2b) where the number of adapters is less than the number of tasks. As a result, we intentionally guide the model to learn better cross-task representation in terms of similarity and dissimilarity. In other words, data from similar tasks should be routed to the same adapters and vice versa. In practice, we choose the number of adapters to be $\log_2(n)$ with n being the number of tasks.

3.2 Task-based Adapters with MoE

In this section, we formulate the task-based adapters mentioned in Section 3.1 in combination with MoE, both of which are our core architecture components.

Given M tasks, we allocate them into L shared-task adapters ($L < M$). For every single token x, we have the associated task information t that makes up an input tuple $(\mathbf{x}, \mathbf{t})$ per token. As before, $\mathbf{x}$ is the representation vector from input, and $\mathbf{t}$ is the task representation vector learned by task embedding.

Similar to MoE, we use a learnable task gate G_t that is responsible for this routing with input being the concatenation of the input components

$$G_t(x,t) = \text{Top\_K}(\mathbf{x} \oplus \mathbf{t}) \tag{6}$$

$$\mathbf{y} = \sum_{i \in G_t(\mathbf{x},\mathbf{t})} W_i o_i \tag{7}$$

And since the number of adapters $L < M$, the number of tasks, we call this setting `dynamic`, as demonstrated in Figure 2b, as opposed to `static` (Figure 2a), where each task will go to each individual adapter.

Our main model uses the shared task embedding representation for the task gate as well as MoE gate, which we call `shared-dynamic`, as shown in Figure 2c.

4 Experiment Setup

4.1 Data

We tackle the problem of multitask multilingual machine translation using the data consisting of 10 different languages ranging from high-resource to low-resource ones including English (En), French (Fr), German (De), Czech (Cs), Finnish (Fi), Latvian (Lv), Estonian (Et), Romanian (Ro), Hindi (Hi), Turkish (Tr), and Gujarati (Gu). In more detail, the data for training, validation, and testing are listed in Table 1 where we can see besides the high-resource ones, we have low-resource languages such as Estonian, Hindi, or Gujarati.

Those data are in the form of Bitext in which there is always English. As a result, we denote EX as the translation from English (E) to another language (X), and similarly for the other way around, XE. Those data are populated from the popular WMT corpus [1]. For the given 1 English and 9 other languages, there are consequently 9 EX and 9XE tasks. More information about data can be found in Table 4 in Appendix A.

4.2 Task and Model Training

In this section, we describe the task information, evaluation metrics, and how we deal with data and models for training.

Task Our task is multitask multilingual machine translation (MMMT) which uses the EX and XE pairs. Our single model is trained with two main capacities. First, this single model can translate all the training pairs with high accuracy. Second, the model is able to quickly acquire new translation pairs with only zero or a few shots.

[1] `https://www.statmt.org/wmt20/index.html`

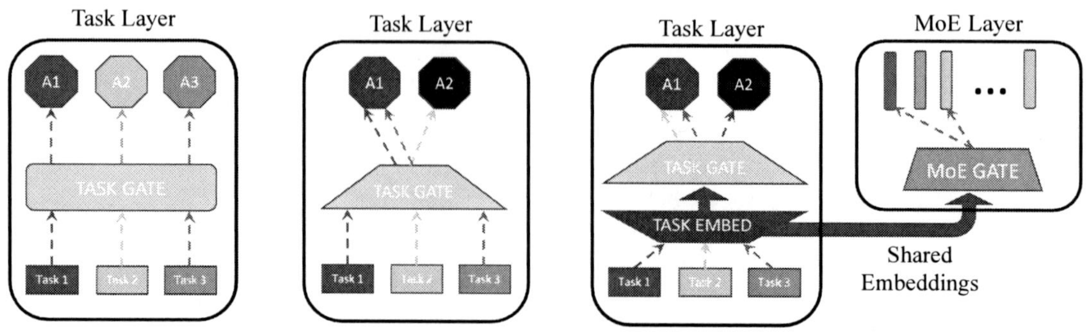

(a) Static (b) Dynamic (c) Shared-Dynamic

Figure 2: Our MoE models with variants. (a) `Static` means for each task, there is a separate adapter associated with it. (b) In the `Dynamic` mode, there is less number of adapters than the number of tasks, in order to learn the shared representation of similar tasks. (c) The last variant is `Shared-Dynamic` where the gates for task adapters and MoE share the same embedding for their routing decisions.

		Task Data								
Split	Unit	de-en	fr-en	cs-en	et-en	fi-en	gu-en	hi-en	lv-en	ro-en
Training	M	4.6	10	10.3	0.7	4.8	0.9	0.3	1.4	0.5
Validation	K	3.0	3.0	3.0	2.0	1.4	2.0	0.5	2.0	2.0
Testing	K	3.0	3.0	3.0	2.0	1.4	2.0	0.5	2.0	2.0

Table 1: Training, Validation, and Testing sizes for all XE tasks (the data for EX are exactly the same). Note that the unit for training is million (M) while that for both validation and testing are thousand (K), and the sizes are the same for validation and testing.

	XE Tasks									
Model	de-en	fr-en	cs-en	et-en	fi-en	gu-en	hi-en	lv-en	ro-en	**Avg**
1. Dense	29.9	31.2	28	22.4	21.4	22.3	21.4	24.5	36.1	26.4
2. MoE Token	27.9	29.5	26.3	19.9	19.6	18.9	17.7	22.3	33.8	24.0
3. MoE Sentence	27.9	29.9	26.2	21.4	19.9	17.9	15.9	23.2	34.4	24.1
4. MoE Task-Static	**32.1**	**33.3**	**30.7**	**24.3**	**23.4**	20.6	**22.5**	**27.2**	**38.8**	**28.1**
5.MoE Task-Dynamic	**31.4**	**32.0**	**29.1**	**23.4**	**22.1**	18.9	20.5	**25.5**	**37.2**	**26.7**
	EX Tasks									
	en-de	en-fr	en-cs	en-et	en-fi	en-gu	en-hi	en-lv	en-ro	
1. Dense	25.4	28.3	22.4	23.3	20.9	28.4	29.0	26.5	31.5	26.2
2. MoE Token	22.9	25.1	19.5	20.1	17.9	26.2	26.3	24.0	29.0	23.4
3. MoE Sentence	23.2	25.7	20.4	22.4	18.7	26.4	27.1	24.2	29.7	24.2
4. MoE Task-Static	**29.5**	**32.5**	**27.9**	**27.4**	**25.8**	**28.8**	**30.8**	**32.2**	**34.6**	**29.9**
5.MoE Task-Dynamic	**27.3**	**29.6**	**25.0**	**24.7**	**22.7**	27.7	**29.3**	**28.4**	**32.7**	**27.5**

Table 2: Comparison of task-based MoE models (models 4 & 5) to task-agnostic MoE models (models 2 & 3) and the non-MOE (Dense) model (model 1) in BLEU scores. With the help of task information, task-based MoE models show their outperforming BLEU scores over all other types across most of the tasks including both high-resource and low-resource ones.

Evaluation While there are many evaluation metrics, we mainly use BLEU score due to its popularity and credibility in evaluating machine translation tasks. This evaluation is implemented by SacreBLEU[2]. We note that, unlike all available public implementations that we found, our implementation evaluates all BLEU scores on the fly along with the training, so there is no disruption for

[2]`https://github.com/mjpost/sacrebleu`

offline evaluation. That also helps in early stopping based on the BLEU scores on the validation sets.

Pre-Processing and Post-Processing In terms of preprocessing, we first encode the data using the Byte-Pair encoding (BPE) method and generate shared dictionaries where all the language pairs use the same vocabulary of size 64K, before feeding to the model. To get accurate scores, for post-processing, we again use BPE decoding for reconstructing the whole translated sentences before comparing them with the original sentences before BPE pre-processing. Likewise, we treat all the processing and model manipulation as a black box for calculating the scores.

Model Configuration and Implementation We use transformer architecture (Vaswani et al., 2017) with 12 layers for both encoder and decoder phases, each of which uses a word embedding layer of dimension 1024 and a non-linear layer of dimension 4096. There are 16 attention heads and a dropout rate of 30%. For MoE, all jobs are trained on Azure cloud machines with 8 GPUs, each of which takes around 2 weeks for a model covering 18 aforementioned tasks to reach decent scores. We apply early stopping based on the validation BLEU scores, in which a non-increasing score after 2 epochs is the condition. For task-based information, we have a task embedding dimension of 64 and a task adapter hidden dimension of 256 for every single task adapter. Our implementation inherits the lower-level infrastructure code from Microsoft Deepspeed and Fairseq. [3]

As for the implementation, an important practical issue with MoE is load balancing among experts for the best utilization of the infrastructure systems. For enforcing the training to have a balanced load, as a result, we employ the auxiliary loss from Lepikhin et al. (2020).

4.2.1 Baselines

In order to show the performance of the task-based MoE models, the following baselines are selected:

Dense This is the traditional transformer model without any MoE layer, i.e., no change to the fully connected (FFN) layer in each layer of encoders or decoders.

MoE - Token This is the MoE model that is usually considered the default option where each FFN layer is replaced by an MoE layer. In our experiments, each MoE layer comprises 8 experts (each has the same size as the original FFN being replaced) and a gate for routing purposes.

[3] https://github.com/facebookresearch/fairseq

MoE - Sentence This is yet another MoE architecture with exactly the same architecture configuration as the MoE - Token baseline. The difference is in the routing layer, which functions at a different granularity: sentences instead of tokens. In more detail, while the gate decides which expert for each token separately in MoE - Token model, it instead routes all tokens belonging to a single sentence to the same chosen expert.

5 Results and Discussions

5.1 Multitask Multilingual Machine Translation

We first present the main results for models capable of translating 18 tasks (see Section 4.2) concurrently. As shown in Table 2, our models that incorporate MoE layers and are enhanced with task information show great advantages over all the baseline models on most tasks, in both directions EX and XE, in accordance with our hypothesis that using task adapters in conjunction with MoE is helpful in multilingual multitask translation.

An outstanding drawback with which the task-based MoE models are facing, however, is for the low-resource translation pairs, e.g. Gu-En, Hi-En, or En-Gu. As we can see from the results in Table 2, training those pairs with Dense models seems to benefit more than with MoE models. We hypothesize the problem is due to the undersampling of the training data for those languages, which have much less data than their high-resource counterparts. In more detail, our training routine concatenates all the tasks' data in a single big dataset before drawing batches. However, without adjusting the sampling process, high-resource language pairs are being trained significantly more given their much larger data in place. In particular, for the case of Gujarati where the Task-Dynamic MoE model underperforms in comparison to the baselines, our hypothesis is that linguistically, this language is the most different from all other languages, which makes the models very hard to learn effective shared representation with any other pairs.

In the future, we plan to explore ideas such as custom sampling or contrastive representation learning to tackle with such issues with the low-resource language pairs, in order to make MoE work as well for those languages as in high-resource pairs.

Model	Design		Routing		Tasks				Average
	MoE	Task	MoE	Task	de-en	fr-en	et-en	fi-en	
MoE	Y	N	Token	-	32.4	33.7	24.2	23.6	28.5
Dense + Task Static	N	Y	Task	Static	32.2	33.7	21.0	22.8	27.4
Dense + Task Dynamic				Dynamic	31.9	33.0	22.0	22.5	27.4
MoE + Task Static	Y	Y		Static	30.7	32.0	19.9	20.8	25.9
MoE + Task Dynamic				Dynamic	**32.6**	**33.9**	24.0	**23.9**	**28.6**
MoE + Task Shared-Dynamic				Shared-Dynamic	32.2	33.3	**24.3**	**24.5**	**28.6**

Table 3: Performance of different models with changes on whether MoE layers exist, whether Task Adapters exist, and how routing for those components is undertaken. The scores better than the baseline are highlighted. Task-based MoE shows advantages, especially with shared-dynamic adapters between MoE and Task Adapters on the low-resource language pair.

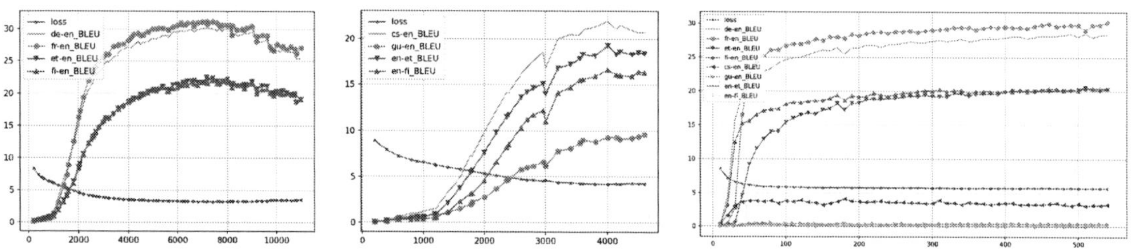

(a) model 1 (b) model 2 (c) merged model

Figure 3: Ablation study about merging 2 checkpointed models of different capabilities. Model 1 is trained with 4 tasks: de-en, fr-en, et-en and fi-en. Model 2 is trained with the other 4 tasks: cs-en, gu-en, en-et, and en-fi. Although those 2 models are under-trained with only a few thousand steps, in the merged model that has the capabilities of those two combined, many pairs have quickly picked up to a similar levels as in the previous single models.

5.2 Ablation Study

5.2.1 Implications of Different Task Layers and MoE Layers

In this study, we limit the number of tasks to four (De-En, Fr-En, Et-En, and Fi-En), which can be divided into 2 groups of similar tasks: (De-En, Fr-En) is the first group and (Et-En, Fi-En) is the second one, to study the performance implications of different model variants when there is a task layer and/or MoE layer.

As illustrated in Table 3, we again see that combining MoE and Task Adapters yields the best models, the same trend as shown in Table 2, particularly when the dynamic adapters are used to enforce similar tasks to share the same representations.

However, when task adapters are not used in conjunction with MoE, the performance is worse than MoE alone. This also means MoE should be the foundational infrastructure, and on top of that, task adapters should be used. It concurs with the motivation that the interference of different tasks or languages makes the training of experts difficult. In other words, there is not so much help when there is only one expert for all the tasks (i.e. Dense models).

5.2.2 Flexibility of Task-based MoE in Merging Two Trained Models

One of the important capabilities in multitask learning and in general learning problems is how to quickly acquire new capabilities given current models with minimal resources and effort. Aligned with this goal, this ablation explores how quickly our task-based MoE models can be merged with each other from 2 different models to newly establish only 1 model that has the combination of their capabilities.

In merging those two models, we restore two respective checkpoints and merge layer-by-layer as follows. First, task-based adapters are kept and combined with each other: each model has 2 adapters (for 4 tasks in the model) and the combined model has 4 adapters (for 8 tasks in combination). Second, the task routers will also be merged and changed so that the routing of each data will now have 4 selections instead of 2 outputs as in the previous models. Finally, the rest of the transformer and MoE layers will have their weights averaged.

The tasks in the original two models are handpicked as in Section 5.2.1 to have 2 different groups, each of which has 2 similar tasks. Model 1 has de-en, fr-en, et-en, and fi-en, while Model 2 has cs-en, gu-en, en-et and en-fi.

As shown in Figure 3, while two original models have been trained with just a few thousand steps (a couple of hours), the combined model shows that it can quickly pick up their original capabilities with just a few hundred steps after merging. Although there are a few uncommon pairs that seem to fail, such as gu-en or en-et, the chart shows the optimistic result of combining trained models with our flexible task-based MoE architectures.

6 Conclusion

In the era of large language models, more efficient and effective modeling techniques are essential to, where MoE in combination with transformer-based models has proven its great advantages. It is, however, complicated to enable that implementation in practice due to the difficulties of training a single model serving diverse tasks. The proposed task-based MoE, which employs both task adapters in tandem with MoE has shown its promising advantages in the application of multitask multilingual machine translations. This novel design enforces shared representation of similar tasks and separates different task data to counter the interference effects. In addition, it also offers the flexibility of changing adapters based on new tasks or changing the MoE infrastructure without affecting the application level. Besides outperforming the traditional approaches using Dense models, however, our MoE models still need to improve on low-resource language pairs. To tackle that issue, in the future, exploring custom sampling for those pairs, and enforcing the shared representation learning explicitly using such additional techniques as contrastive learning or mutual information are worth exploring.

7 Acknowledgements

The authors would like to thank the great feedback and help from Yiren Wang, Muhammad ElNokrashy, Alex Muzio, Akiko Eriguchi and other members of Microsoft's Machine Translation Group.

References

Chang-Qin Chen, Min Li, Zhihua Wu, Dianhai Yu, and Chao Yang. 2023. Ta-moe: Topology-aware large scale mixture-of-expert training. *ArXiv*, abs/2302.09915.

Z. Chen, Yikang Shen, Mingyu Ding, Zhenfang Chen, Hengshuang Zhao, Erik G. Learned-Miller, and Chuang Gan. 2022. Mod-squad: Designing mixture of experts as modular multi-task learners. *ArXiv*, abs/2212.08066.

Aidan Clark, Diego de Las Casas, Aurelia Guy, Arthur Mensch, Michela Paganini, Jordan Hoffmann, Bogdan Damoc, Blake A. Hechtman, Trevor Cai, Sebastian Borgeaud, George van den Driessche, Eliza Rutherford, T. W. Hennigan, Matthew G. Johnson, Katie Millican, Albin Cassirer, Chris Jones, Elena Buchatskaya, David Budden, L. Sifre, Simon Osindero, Oriol Vinyals, Jack W. Rae, Erich Elsen, Koray Kavukcuoglu, and Karen Simonyan. 2022. Unified scaling laws for routed language models. In *International Conference on Machine Learning*.

Nan Du, Yanping Huang, Andrew M. Dai, Simon Tong, Dmitry Lepikhin, Yuanzhong Xu, Maxim Krikun, Yanqi Zhou, Adams Wei Yu, Orhan Firat, Barret Zoph, Liam Fedus, Maarten Bosma, Zongwei Zhou, Tao Wang, Yu Emma Wang, Kellie Webster, Marie Pellat, Kevin Robinson, Kathleen S. Meier-Hellstern, Toju Duke, Lucas Dixon, Kun Zhang, Quoc V. Le, Yonghui Wu, Z. Chen, and Claire Cui. 2021. Glam: Efficient scaling of language models with mixture-of-experts. *ArXiv*, abs/2112.06905.

Maha Elbayad, Anna Sun, and Shruti Bhosale. 2022. Fixing moe over-fitting on low-resource languages in multilingual machine translation. *arXiv preprint arXiv:2212.07571*.

William Fedus, Jeff Dean, and Barret Zoph. 2022. A review of sparse expert models in deep learning. *ArXiv*, abs/2209.01667.

William Fedus, Barret Zoph, and Noam M. Shazeer. 2021. Switch transformers: Scaling to trillion parameter models with simple and efficient sparsity. *J. Mach. Learn. Res.*, 23:120:1–120:39.

Robert A. Jacobs, Michael I. Jordan, Steven J. Nowlan, and Geoffrey E. Hinton. 1991. Adaptive mixtures of local experts. *Neural Computation*, 3:79–87.

Young Jin Kim, Ammar Ahmad Awan, Alexandre Muzio, Andrés Felipe Cruz-Salinas, Liyang Lu, Amr Hendy, Samyam Rajbhandari, Yuxiong He, and Hany Hassan Awadalla. 2021. Scalable and efficient moe training for multitask multilingual models. *ArXiv*, abs/2109.10465.

Dmitry Lepikhin, HyoukJoong Lee, Yuanzhong Xu, Dehao Chen, Orhan Firat, Yanping Huang, Maxim Krikun, Noam M. Shazeer, and Z. Chen. 2020. Gshard: Scaling giant models with conditional computation and automatic sharding. *ArXiv*, abs/2006.16668.

Rui Liu, Young Jin Kim, Alexandre Muzio, and Hany Hassan. 2022. Gating dropout: Communication-efficient regularization for sparsely activated transformers. In *International Conference on Machine Learning*, pages 13782–13792. PMLR.

Zhili Liu, Kai Chen, Jianhua Han, Lanqing Hong, Hang Xu, Zhenguo Li, and James Tin-Yau Kwok. 2023. Task-customized masked autoencoder via mixture of cluster-conditional experts. In *International Conference on Learning Representations*.

Myle Ott, Sergey Edunov, Alexei Baevski, Angela Fan, Sam Gross, Nathan Ng, David Grangier, and Michael Auli. 2019. fairseq: A fast, extensible toolkit for sequence modeling. In *North American Chapter of the Association for Computational Linguistics*.

Jonas Pfeiffer, Naman Goyal, Xi Victoria Lin, Xian Li, James Cross, Sebastian Riedel, and Mikel Artetxe. 2022. Lifting the curse of multilinguality by pre-training modular transformers. In *North American Chapter of the Association for Computational Linguistics*.

Samyam Rajbhandari, Conglong Li, Zhewei Yao, Minjia Zhang, Reza Yazdani Aminabadi, Ammar Ahmad Awan, Jeff Rasley, and Yuxiong He. 2022. Deepspeed-moe: Advancing mixture-of-experts inference and training to power next-generation ai scale. In *International Conference on Machine Learning*.

Jeff Rasley, Samyam Rajbhandari, Olatunji Ruwase, and Yuxiong He. 2020. Deepspeed: System optimizations enable training deep learning models with over 100 billion parameters. *Proceedings of the 26th ACM SIGKDD International Conference on Knowledge Discovery & Data Mining*.

Stephen Roller, Sainbayar Sukhbaatar, Arthur Szlam, and Jason Weston. 2021. Hash layers for large sparse models. In *Neural Information Processing Systems*.

Noam Shazeer, Azalia Mirhoseini, Krzysztof Maziarz, Andy Davis, Quoc Le, Geoffrey Hinton, and Jeff Dean. 2017. Outrageously large neural networks: The sparsely-gated mixture-of-experts layer. *arXiv preprint arXiv:1701.06538*.

Ashish Vaswani, Noam M. Shazeer, Niki Parmar, Jakob Uszkoreit, Llion Jones, Aidan N. Gomez, Lukasz Kaiser, and Illia Polosukhin. 2017. Attention is all you need. In *NIPS*.

Sen Wu, Hongyang Zhang, and Christopher Ré. 2020. Understanding and improving information transfer in multi-task learning. *ArXiv*, abs/2005.00944.

Seniha Esen Yüksel, Joseph N. Wilson, and Paul D. Gader. 2012. Twenty years of mixture of experts. *IEEE Transactions on Neural Networks and Learning Systems*, 23:1177–1193.

Zhiyuan Zeng and Deyi Xiong. 2023. Scomoe: Efficient mixtures of experts with structured communication. In *International Conference on Learning Representations*.

Lianmin Zheng, Zhuohan Li, Hao Zhang, Yonghao Zhuang, Zhifeng Chen, Yanping Huang, Yida Wang, Yuanzhong Xu, Danyang Zhuo, Joseph Gonzalez, and Ion Stoica. 2022. Alpa: Automating inter- and intra-operator parallelism for distributed deep learning. *ArXiv*, abs/2201.12023.

Yan-Quan Zhou, Tao Lei, Han-Chu Liu, Nan Du, Yanping Huang, Vincent Zhao, Andrew M. Dai, Zhifeng Chen, Quoc V. Le, and James Laudon. 2022. Mixture-of-experts with expert choice routing. *ArXiv*, abs/2202.09368.

Barret Zoph, Irwan Bello, Sameer Kumar, Nan Du, Yanping Huang, Jeff Dean, Noam M. Shazeer, and William Fedus. 2022. St-moe: Designing stable and transferable sparse expert models.

Simiao Zuo, Xiaodong Liu, Jian Jiao, Young Jin Kim, Hany Hassan, Ruofei Zhang, Tuo Zhao, and Jianfeng Gao. 2021. Taming sparsely activated transformer with stochastic experts. *arXiv preprint arXiv:2110.04260*.

A WMT Data Information

Code	Language	Test Split
de	German	wmt2013
fr	French	wmt2013
cs	Czech	wmt2013
et	Estonian	wmt2018dev
fi	Finish	wmt2015
gu	Gujarati	wmt2019dev
hi	Hindi	wmt2014dev
lv	Latvian	wmt2017dev
ro	Romanian	wmt2016dev

Table 4: More details about our datasets for comparison and reproducibility.

Does the English Matter? Elicit Cross-lingual Abilities of Large Language Models

Giulia Pucci and Leonardo Ranaldi
Human-Centric ART Group, Department of Enterprise Engineering,
University of Rome Tor Vergata.
[first_name].[last_name]@uniroma2.it,

Abstract

Large Language Models reveal diverse abilities across different languages due to the disproportionate amount of English data they are trained on. Their performances on English tasks are often more robust than in other languages.

In this paper, we propose a method to empower the cross-lingual abilities of instruction-tuned LLMs (It-LLMs) by building semantic alignment between languages. To achieve this, we introduce translation-following demonstrations to elicit better semantic alignment across languages. Our evaluations on multilingual question-answering benchmarks reveal that our models, tested in five distinct languages, outperform the performance of It-LLMs trained on monolingual datasets. The findings highlight the impact of translation-following demonstrations on non-English data, eliciting instruction-tuning and empowering semantic alignment.

1 Introduction

Large Language Models (LLMs) achieve comprehensive language abilities through pre-training on large corpora (Brown et al., 2020). Hence, the acquired language abilities follow the corpora features, primarily available in English (Lin et al., 2021; Zhang et al., 2023; Zhu et al., 2023). This phenomenon produces an imbalance in pre-training (Blevins and Zettlemoyer, 2022) and fine-tuning (Le et al., 2021). Thus, performance is usually lower for non-English languages, especially for low-resource ones (Huang et al., 2023; Bang et al., 2023). The most common approaches to mitigate this problem propose continuing pre-training with large-scale monolingual data (Imani et al., 2023; Cui et al., 2023; Yang et al., 2023), which requires considerable data and computational resources.

In this paper, we propose an approach to empower the It-LLM that elicits semantic alignment between English and other languages. We focus on exploiting the latent multilingual abilities of It-LLMs by empowering the pivotal phase of instruction-tuning using instruction-following demonstrations. To this end, we explore the potential of cross-lingual alignment by integrating translation-following demonstrations to refine the instruction-tuning process.

In our experiments, we use *Llama-7b* (Touvron et al., 2023) as the foundational LLM and target five languages. In instances where data is lacking, we undertake translation tasks. We use the Stanford Alpaca dataset (Taori et al., 2023) and its translated versions in the corresponding languages, while for the translation-following, we use a publicly available translation resource (Tiedemann, 2012), the most accessible and extendable to multiple languages (i.e., *translation-following demonstrations* on Figure 1).

Following the instruction-tuning phase, we assessed the efficacy of our five distinct *Alpaca* tailored for specific languages. Our evaluation leveraged four benchmarks: two inherently multilingual, i.e., XQUAD (Artetxe et al., 2019) and MLQA (Lewis et al., 2020), and two intrinsically monolingual, MMLU (Hendrycks et al., 2021) and BBH (Suzgun et al., 2022). The empirical results indicate that when trained using language-specific instructions combined with translation data, the instruction-tuned models significantly surpass the performance of models trained exclusively with non-English demonstrations. While our models bridge the gap among performances, the translation-following models exhibit optimal alignments. This highlights the pronounced proficiency of Llama when trained on English-centered datasets compared to non-English ones. Furthermore, the semantic alignment effort significantly strengthens the cross-lingual abilities of It-LLMs.

Our findings can be summarized as follows:

- The learning abilities of LLMs on non-English instruction-tuning tasks are limited;
- The multi-lingual abilities of instruction-tuned

Proceedings of the The 3rd Workshop on Multi-lingual Representation Learning (MRL), pages 173–183
December 7, 2023 ©2023 Association for Computational Linguistics

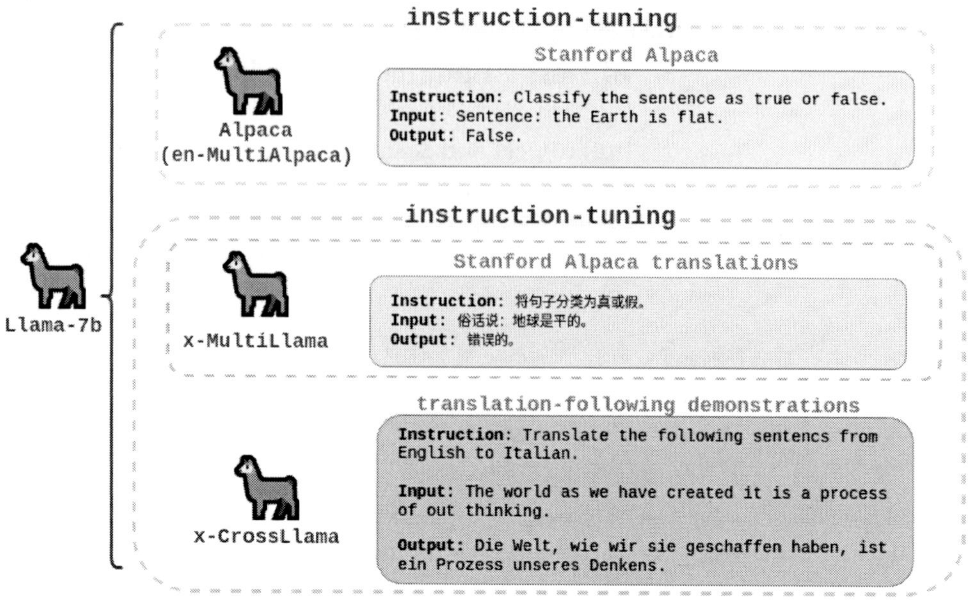

Figure 1: Our *x-CrossLlama* are instruction-tuned on instruction-following and translation-following demonstrations.

LLMs could be empowered through cross-lingual alignment;

- Thus, we propose to elicit the instruction-tuning approach for non-English models based on instruction-following and translation-following demonstrations for the target language. Hence, we show that It-LLMs can semantically align through cross-lingual translation-following demonstrations via an extensive evaluation.

2 Methods

Pre-training from scratch a Large Language Model (LLM) to fill the imbalance language problem is cost-prohibitive for data collection and parameter learning. This is why the trend is to do further fine-tuning to empower the models' abilities in a specific language (Tanti et al., 2021; Moslem et al., 2023). Hence, we aim to elicit the abilities of pre-trained LLMs for non-English languages by further improving the alignment between English and the target language. In the following Sections, we investigate the difficulties of fine-tuning a monolingual scenario (Section 2.1). Based on this, we propose our approach to empower the cross-lingual abilities of It-LLMs (Section 2.2).

2.1 Alpaca Instruction-tuning

The restricted availability and clarity of premium API services for cutting-edge LLMs have driven researchers to focus on creating open-source alternatives. Using the instruction-tuning paradigm, presented in Section 5.2, and resources as Stanford Alpaca (Taori et al., 2023) that is a corpus consisting of 52k of English instruction-output pairs generated by `text-davinci-003`, several instruction-tuned versions of instructed-Llama were released.

Following this approach, multiple monolingual versions of instructed-Llama were proposed by translating the Stanford Alpaca data into the specific language. Table 1 shows a set of versions available as open source. Following an analysis of the translated versions of instructed-Llama in official repositories[1], the languages of the benchmark datasets, and the translation pairs present in news_commentary, which will be introduced later, we selected the speeches that share the most already available data. Table 1 shows the custom versions used in this work, which for simplicity will be renamed *x*-MultiLlama, where *x* indicates the specific language.

2.2 Cross-lingual Instruction-tuning

Although monolingual techniques (presented in Section 2.1) play a key role in enhancing the multilingual strengths of LLMs, simply focusing on translated versions of Alpacas for specific languages does not allow the non-English capabilities

[1]official versions on `https://github.com/tloen/alpaca-lora` and `https://huggingface.co/models`

Model	Language	Name
Alpaca (Taori et al., 2023)	English	en-Llama
Alpaca-Chinese (Chen et al., 2023)	Chinese	zh-Llama
Camoscio (Santilli and Rodolà, 2023)	Italian	it-Llama
German (Thissen, 2023)	German	de-Llama
Arabic (Yasbok)	Arabic	ar-Llama

Table 1: The monolingual Instruction-tuned Large Language Models that use a language-specific version of *MultiLlama* as instruction-tuning data.

of LLMs to be exploited. To overcome this overlaps, we present CrossLlama, shown in Figure 1). This method empowers cross-lingual instruction-tuning by integrating translation-following demonstrations. We aim to elicit LLMs' English and non-English abilities by stimulating a semantic alignment challenge.

Instruction-following Although the version of the Alpaca dataset is in English, there are many derivatives. However, derived versions of the Alpaca dataset, as described in 2.1, have been produced with translation systems. Our work starts with the instruction-tuned Llama on Alpaca (native English) and its versions adapted for distinct languages (which we called *x-MultiLlama*). We also propose the *CrossLlama* variations, built from Alpaca translations specific to each language and augmented with translations (explained further). With this methodology, we intend to elicit the LLM backbone's capability to interpret multilingual instructions and ensure cross-lingual consistency.

Translation-following Challenge Using general instruction information is a logical approach when creating models to tackle multiple tasks guided by instructions(Wang et al., 2023; Zeng et al., 2023). Nevertheless, data from translations might aid in grasping semantic alignment.

We use publicly available sentence-level translation datasets, such as *news_commentary* (Tiedemann, 2012), to construct the translation task instruction demonstrations. We also propose extending this to additional languages, which we release as an open-source dataset. In particular, for each specific language, we constructed specific sets of demonstrations. Hence, following the Alpaca style (Instruction, Input, and Output) (see Table 1), we selected the same number of English to non-English translations non-English to English translations.

3 Experiments

In order to observe the English and non-English abilities of Large Language Models (LLMs) and the impact of the instruction-tuning approach in cross-lingual scenarios, we propose *CrossLlama*. Our approach is based on instruction-tuning on language-specific data augmented with a cross-lingual semantic alignment. Hence, we set several baseline models explained in Section 3.1, which we augmented with our approach introduced in Section 3.2. Finally, we performed a series of systematic evaluations (Section 3.3.1) to observe the impact of the proposed method.

3.1 Baseline LLMs

The common denominator among the It-LLMs shown in Table 1 is the LLM backbone Llama-7b (Touvron et al., 2023). Starting from instruction-following data from the original Alpaca (Taori et al., 2023) and its open-source non-English versions[2], we reproduced *x-MultiLlama* for *x* specific languages: Chinese (zh), Italian (it), Arabic (ar), German (de) and the original English version (en).

3.2 Cross-lingual LLMs

Our method produces *x-CrossLlama* that are instruction-tuned on standard instruction-following empowered with translation-following demonstrations.

Our approach generates a series of instruction-tuned versions of the data shown in Figure 1. We have named the versions *x-CrossLlama*.

3.3 Experimental Setup

To assess the performance of the *x-CrossLlama*, we defined several benchmarks (Section 3.3.1) on which we applied systematic instruction-tuning pipelines in Section 3.3.2.

3.3.1 Benchmarks

To evaluate the performance of the It-LLMs and the impact of the semantic alignment approach, we used two cross-lingual (XQUAD (Artetxe et al., 2019), MLQA (Lewis et al., 2020)) and two multi-task (MMLU (Hendrycks et al., 2021) and BBH (Suzgun et al., 2022)) benchmarks. While XQUAD and MLQA are very focused and require the model to reason about the given context and answer the given question, MMLU, and BBH are much more

[2] open-source code is available on `https://github.com/tloen/alpaca-lora`

Instruction
Translate the following sentences from **English** to **German**.
Input
The world as we have created it is a process of our thinking. It cannot be changed without changing our thinking.
Output
Die Welt, wie wir sie geschaffen haben, ist ein Prozess unseres Denkens. Es kann nicht geändert werden, ohne unser Denken zu ändern.

Instruction
Translate the following sentences from **German** to **English**.
Input
Die Welt, wie wir sie geschaffen haben, ist ein Prozess unseres Denkens. Es kann nicht geändert werden, ohne unser Denken zu ändern.
Output
The world as we have created it is a process of our thinking. It cannot be changed without changing our thinking.

Table 2: Examples of translation-following demonstrations. In particular, in this example, there are two demonstrations with the same directions from English to German (en-x).

open but require the models' ability to solve logical mathematical tasks less related to the language.

However, we decided to introduce them to observe whether our approach degrades performance in these tasks. The first two datasets selected are appropriately constructed for multi-language testing, while the second two are available only in English. Hence, we do a preliminary translation step as outlined below. Thus, descriptions of the benchmarks follow in the next paragraphs:

MultiLingual Question Answering (MLQA) (Lewis et al., 2020) evaluates cross-lingual question answering performance using 5K extractive QA instances in the SQuAD (Rajpurkar et al., 2016) format in several languages. MLQA is highly parallel, with QA instances aligned across four languages on average. Although comprising different languages, some languages, such as Italian, are not represented. To conduct the experiments uniformly, we have translated the examples as also done in the forthcoming MMLU and BBH.

Cross-lingual Question Answering Dataset (XQUAD) (Artetxe et al., 2019) consists of a subset of 240 paragraphs and 1190 question-answer pairs from the development set of SQuAD v1.1 (Rajpurkar et al., 2016) with their manual translations into several languages. Consequently, the dataset is entirely parallel across 11 languages.

Massive Multitask Language Understanding (MMLU) (Hendrycks et al., 2021) measures knowledge of the world and problem-solving problems in multiple subjects with 57 subjects across STEM, humanities, social sciences, and other areas. The benchmark is native in English; however, we translated it into five additional languages[3].

BIG-Bench Hard (BBH) (Suzgun et al., 2022) is a subset of challenging tasks related to navigation, logical deduction, and fallacy detection. Again, the benchmark is native English, and we have translated it into five languages[??].

3.3.2 Models Setup & Evaluation

We used the alpaca_LoRA (Hu et al., 2021a) code[2], adopting the same hyperparameters to align the results with the state-of-the-art models.

We performed the fine-tuning with a single epoch and a batch-size of 128 examples, running our experiments on a workstation equipped with one Nvidia RTX A6000 with 48 GB of VRAM.

As an evaluation metric, we use accuracy. Hence, we estimate accuracy by measuring exact match values in the zero-shot setting. The parts of benchmarks related to the specific language are used for each model.

[3]We performed translations using the Google translator API from English to Chinese (zh), Italian (it), Arabic (ar), and German (de).

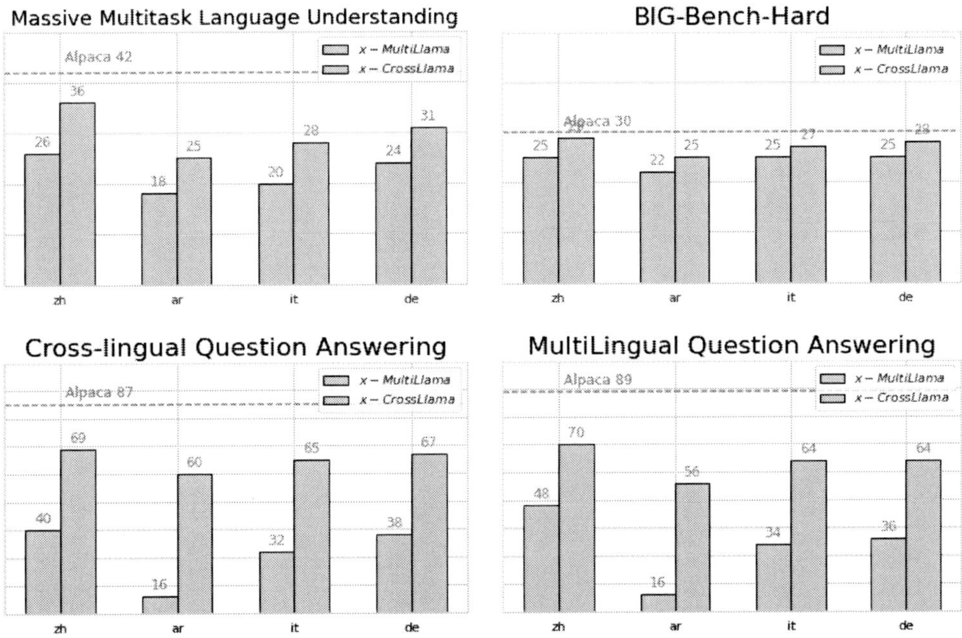

Figure 2: Accuracies (%) on proposed benchmarks. The dotted line represents the performance of the original version of Llama instructed on English data (Taori et al., 2023), which we call Alpaca.

4 Results & Discussion

Eliciting non-English abilities in instruction-tuned Large Language Models (It-LLMs) remains challenging. However, our *x-CrossLlama* revealed improved results in cross-lingual Question Answering (QA) benchmarks. Moreover, at the same time, the instructed models maintained logical-mathematical skills. From the results of Figure 2, it is possible to observe the weaknesses emerging from the fine-tuning of the translated versions of Alpaca (Section 4.1), the improvement obtained from the alignment phase is encouraging (Section 4.2) but it is not enough to outperform the English one.

The fine-grained analysis highlighted the importance of cross-lingual alignment data and the critical issues with non-English data. This opens the way for new hypotheses regarding the imbalance of pre-training languages and learning abilities via instruction-tuning.

4.1 Alpacas problems on Translations

The Instruction-tuning task on LLMs, in our case, Llama-7b, is primarily pre-trained in English, and has implications for the derivated models. As shown in Figure 2, both MLQA and XQUAD benchmarks reveal a notable disparity, with an average point gap of 55 and 53, respectively, between the original tuned Llama-7b (called Alpaca) and the various x-MultiLlama. This discrepancy is attenuated in the case of MMLU and BBH, where the average gaps are 18 and 14 points. Hence, relying exclusively on translations of Alpaca-style demonstrations for instruction in various languages only sometimes yields optimal effects. However, models, for example, zh-MultiLlama and de-MultiLlama, have exhibited better performances. This variation may be attributed to the volume of pre-training data available for the respective languages and, consequently, the inherent abilities of Llama. In future work, we aim to expand our analysis to include LLMs beyond Llama to see if similar, less pronounced, or more accentuated trends emerge.

QA Task	en-Llama	avg-Llama	avg-CrossLlama	δ
MLQA	*0.89*	0.34	0.64	+0.30
XQUAD	*0.97*	0.31	0.65	+0.30
MMLU	*0.42*	0.24	0.32	+0.08
BBH	*0.30*	0.24	0.28	+0.04

Table 3: Averages accuracies on proposed benchmarks.

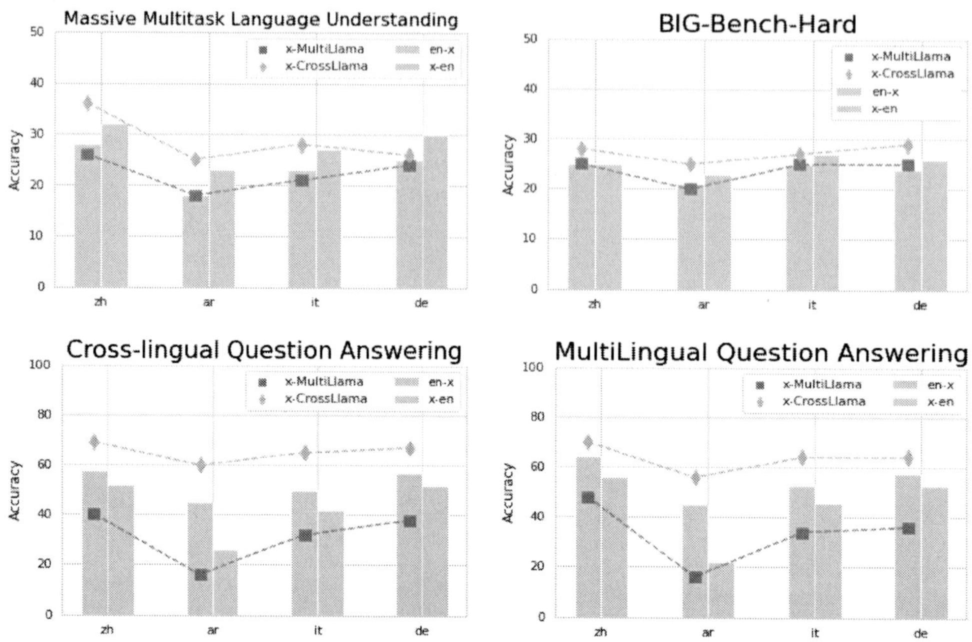

Figure 3: Accuracies (%) of proposed benchmarks using one-direction Translation-following demonstrations. For en-x for English-foreigner and x-en for foreign English.

4.2 A Cross-lingual solution

Using the translation-following demonstrations close to instruction-following ones during instruction-tuning significantly empowers the cross-lingual performances of It-LLMs. In fact, *x-CrossLlama* consistently surpassed the x-MultiLlama, obtaining an improvement of 30 average points on MLQA, 34 on XQUAD, 8 on MMLU, and 4 on BBH, as detailed in Table 3. This approach brought their performance metrics closer to the benchmark set by the original version of Llama (Alpaca), bridging the gap in different situations. For MMLU and BBH, the performance difference was even more marginal, with average gaps of 10 and 2 points, respectively, as indicated in Table 3 and the 'en-Llama vs avg-CrossLlama'.

The inclusion of translation-following demonstrations has undeniably elevated the cross-lingual abilities of It-LLMs. Moreover, specific models, specifically the Chinese and German, surpassed the Arabic version by a significant margin. This disparity might be attributed to the varied representation of corpora within the pre-training datasets, as highlighted in (Yang et al., 2023). Consequently, cross-lingual strategies might not yield as pronounced benefits for underrepresented languages during the initial pre-training stages of the language model.

In conclusion, our strategy shifted to be high-performance and sustainable. As regards the performances, as merely discussed following the systematic analysis, we found empirical evidence to support this statement. While sustainability, our method uses a limited number of demonstrations, around 20k, which, combined with those of Alpaca, around 52k, remain a meager number, allowing the downstream models to obtain performances comparable to those of more robust models.

4.3 Ablation Study

Our *CrossLlama*, distinguished by the construction of the demonstrations pairs presented in Section 3.2, achieves significant performance improvements and contributes to closing the gap between the original version of tuned Llama and a series of x-MultiLlama in different languages. We propose an additional analysis. Working on the translation-following part (defined by half en-x and half x-en demonstrations), we analyze the impact of the demonstrations by splitting the experiments into en-x and x-en (Section 4.3.1).

4.3.1 Demonstration Direction matters

The evaluations in Figure 3 shed light on the impact of varying the directionality of translation-following demonstrations. In particular, demonstrations that transition from English to a non-English language (en-x) appear to have a more pronounced positive effect on subsequent models. On the other hand, demonstrations transitioning from a foreign language to English (x-en) exhibit superior performance compared to baseline models, yet they lag behind when juxtaposed with demonstrations in the reverse direction.

However, as further illustrated in Figure 3, the x-CrossLlama consistently maintains its edge in performance. The observed trend, where translation-following demonstrations in one specific direction seem more influential, is intriguing. Mirroring our prior ablation analysis observations, multi-task benchmarks do not exhibit substantial variances. This observation lends further credence to the hypothesis that cross-lingual capabilities predominantly influence models in tasks heavily imbued with natural language elements.

5 Related Work

In the NLP field, multilingual and cross-linguistic methods have solid foundations and a long-standing tradition, with in-depth studies on feature adaptation (Section 5.1). However, the new Large Language Models (LLMs) no longer require such interventions. After extensive pre-training on massive corpora, cross-linguistic skills are inherently present in LLMs (Section 5.2 and Section 5.3). Nevertheless, although these abilities appear embedded, most LLMs must be elicited to show them exhaustively. Our study introduces a method to empower these cross-linguistic abilities through a cross-linguistic semantic alignment approach (Section 5.4).

5.1 Multilingual Pre-training

The next token prediction based on the prefix sequence, also well-known as language modeling, is the everlasting task of modern NLP (Tenney et al., 2019). The profound linguistic knowledge embedded within today's Large Language Models (LLMs) depends on the billions of neurons trained on large-scale corpora with derivatives of the language modeling task (Zanzotto et al., 2020; Ranaldi et al., 2022). Consequently, the pre-training corpora are predominantly in English, e.g., BooksCorpus (Zhu et al., 2015), MEGATRON-LM (Shoeybi et al., 2019), Gutenberg Dataset (Lahiri, 2014) therefore, LLMs usually have much better knowledge of English than other languages.

Researchers like Aulamo and Tiedemann (2019); Abadji et al. (2022) have proposed forward corpora translated into multiple languages to address this linguistic imbalance. However, these translated datasets, while valuable, are not as voluminous as their English-focused counterparts. The absence of extensive parallel data in these pre-training corpora further hinders the ability of LLMs to align and understand diverse languages effectively (Li et al., 2023).

5.2 Instruction-tuning Paradigm

Ouyang et al. (2022); Wei et al. (2022) fine-tuned LLMs using the instruction-tuning method based on instruction-tuning data, which are instruction-response corpora, to make LLMs more scalable and improve zero-shot performance. In this method, the LLM backbone is fed with data from the instruction (I, X, Y), where I is an instruction describing the task's requirements, X is the input, which can be optional, and Y is the output for the given task. The method aims to minimize the function $f(Y)$ based on the log likelihood with model parameters θ.

Earlier studies show that the instruction-tuning method of LLMs with both human (Wang et al., 2023) and synthetic-generated instructions (Taori et al., 2023; Xu et al., 2023) empowers the ability of LLMs to solve considerable tasks in zero-shot scenarios.

However, we state that the generally used instruction-tuning datasets, alpaca (Taori et al., 2023), Self-Instruct (Wang et al., 2023), Self-Chat (Xu et al., 2023), conceived in English, which limits the prospect of LLMs to follow non-English instructions and therefore solve related tasks.

5.3 Instruction-tuning is at hand

While Large Language Models (LLMs) have achieved remarkable outcomes using prevalent techniques like instruction-tuning, their vastness limits the breadth of the scientific community that can actively experiment with them.

Recent innovations aimed at democratizing access to these models and techniques focus on optimizing parameter tuning. One such method, Parameter-Efficient Tuning (PEFT), strategically adjusts a subset of the model's parameters while keeping the rest static. The overarching objective is to substantially curtail computational and storage overheads without compromising the performance exhibited by the original models (Ranaldi et al., 2023b). Established methodologies under the

PEFT umbrella include LoRA (Hu et al., 2021b), Prefix Tuning (Li and Liang, 2021), and P-Tuning (Liu et al., 2022). The fundamental principle behind these techniques is to retain the weights of the pre-trained model and integrate low-rank matrices at each architectural layer. This strategy considerably diminishes the parameter count that necessitates training for subsequent tasks, thereby enhancing efficiency. Such foundational advancements play a pivotal role in leveling the playing field for the scientific community, eliciting equitable research opportunities, and catalyzing the proliferation of open-source contributions.

5.4 Multilingual Instruction-tuning

Recent studies have highlighted the impressive capabilities of LLMs in assimilating instructions across diverse languages. Researchers such as Santilli and Rodolà (2023); Chen et al. (2023) have ventured into monolingual fine-tuning of Llama, focusing on instructions translated specifically to each language. Adopting optimization techniques elaborated further in Section 5.3, to design bespoke adapters tailored for various tasks has gained momentum. In exploring the cross-lingual potential of It-LLMs, Zhang et al. (2023) emphasized the benefits of enhancing instruction demonstrations.

In this paper, we propose *CrossLlama*, with a series of It-LLMs models with the Llama-7b backbone as the common denominator. The factor of our method is based on the inclusion of translation-following demonstrations that elicit semantic alignment between languages. We present empirical evidence underscoring the expansive cross-lingual learning prowess of It-LLMs. Through evaluations of four benchmarks, we demonstrate that the inherent limitations of It-LLMs can be effectively mitigated using cross-lingual alignment strategies when trained on non-English data. Consequently, our investigation seeks to elucidate the significance of instruction-following and translation-following demonstrations in bridging the linguistic divide, thereby enhancing the adaptability of LLMs to languages beyond English.

6 Future Works

The multilingual abilities of instruction-tuned Large Language Models (It-LLMs) are supported by LLMs, as seen with the Llama backbone in Alpaca's instance. Interestingly, small data-level stimuli improve downstream skills. Our experiments yielded significant insights when introducing strategic demonstrations, specifically translation-following demonstrations. We achieved these outcomes by fine-tuning Llama-7b, following the approach used in Taori et al. (2023).

In subsequent research, we aim to delve deeper by extending the number of parameters in Llama and integrating more backbone models. We are also intrigued by the potential effects on languages with limited resources. Furthermore, we aspire to fully understand the results from specific experiments by applying epistemic approaches (Ranaldi et al., 2023a,c) to It-LLMs.

In parallel, plans include analyzing the translation abilities of general It-LLMs and those empowered with translation tasks, including some specialized translation tasks among our evaluation benchmarks. Finally, we would like to investigate the learning abilities of the original Alpaca as the translation data changes, proposing different probing experiments on (original) English data enhanced with translations. Finally, we would like to investigate explainability techniques to understand better the underlying mechanisms, as done in (Ranaldi and Pucci, 2023), that enable these models to solve multiple tasks in complex scenarios using a small number of instances.

7 Conclusion

In this paper, we proposed *CrossLlama*, a novel methodology designed to empower the instruction-tuning of LLMs for non-English datasets. Our approach uniquely integrates instruction-following demonstrations, reminiscent of the Alpaca style, with translation-following demonstrations. The primary objective of this method is to elicit the LLM towards achieving semantic alignment between English and non-English languages, thereby outperforming models that are instructed using non-English texts. Leveraging the proposed demonstrations led to marked performance enhancements across four Question Answering benchmarks: XQUAD, MLQA, MMLU, and BBH. Furthermore, the depth of semantic alignment amplifies with the direction of the translation data, underscoring the inherent abilities of It-LLMs to assimilate from instruction-following demonstrations. Our innovative approach and the ensuing findings pave the way for advanced research, eliciting the development of more adept LLMs tailored for non-English linguistic contexts.

Limitations

Although the performance achieved by our method is consistently superior to that of several Instruction-tuned on custom corpora, our work has limitations:

- The proposed method was only analyzed on the Large Language Model Llama-7b; consequently, we can only report the results. We intend to extend our work using larger and different models in future developments.
- Although the proposed method performed well, it is only sometimes applicable as it requires an additional data set, the translation-following set.
- Finally, a significant limitation is that it is impossible to conduct correlations between the composition percentages of the training data and the downstream results, as the corpora used for pre-training are not always accessible, and the technical reports do not essay precise estimations.

Ethical Statement

This work used open-source corpora that do not deal with hate speech or inequality topics. The evaluation phase was also done on solid benchmarks commonly used for evaluation in Large Language Models. Finally, the concept of 'disparity' in the multilingual abilities of the Large Language Models in this work is understood as unbalancing the pre-training data used in the training phase.

References

Julien Abadji, Pedro Ortiz Suarez, Laurent Romary, and Benoît Sagot. 2022. Towards a cleaner document-oriented multilingual crawled corpus. In *Proceedings of the Thirteenth Language Resources and Evaluation Conference*, pages 4344–4355, Marseille, France. European Language Resources Association.

Mikel Artetxe, Sebastian Ruder, and Dani Yogatama. 2019. On the cross-lingual transferability of monolingual representations. In *Annual Meeting of the Association for Computational Linguistics*.

Mikko Aulamo and Jörg Tiedemann. 2019. The OPUS resource repository: An open package for creating parallel corpora and machine translation services. In *Proceedings of the 22nd Nordic Conference on Computational Linguistics*, pages 389–394, Turku, Finland. Linköping University Electronic Press.

Yejin Bang, Samuel Cahyawijaya, Nayeon Lee, Wenliang Dai, Dan Su, Bryan Wilie, Holy Lovenia, Ziwei Ji, Tiezheng Yu, Willy Chung, Quyet V. Do, Yan Xu, and Pascale Fung. 2023. A multitask, multilingual, multimodal evaluation of chatgpt on reasoning, hallucination, and interactivity.

Terra Blevins and Luke Zettlemoyer. 2022. Language contamination helps explains the cross-lingual capabilities of english pretrained models. In *Conference on Empirical Methods in Natural Language Processing*.

Tom B. Brown, Benjamin Mann, Nick Ryder, Melanie Subbiah, Jared Kaplan, Prafulla Dhariwal, Arvind Neelakantan, Pranav Shyam, Girish Sastry, Amanda Askell, Sandhini Agarwal, Ariel Herbert-Voss, Gretchen Krueger, Tom Henighan, Rewon Child, Aditya Ramesh, Daniel M. Ziegler, Jeffrey Wu, Clemens Winter, Christopher Hesse, Mark Chen, Eric Sigler, Mateusz Litwin, Scott Gray, Benjamin Chess, Jack Clark, Christopher Berner, Sam McCandlish, Alec Radford, Ilya Sutskever, and Dario Amodei. 2020. Language models are few-shot learners.

Wei-Lin Chen, Cheng-Kuang Wu, and Hsin-Hsi Chen. 2023. Traditional-chinese alpaca: Models and datasets. `https://github.com/ntunlplab/traditional-chinese-alpaca`.

Yiming Cui, Ziqing Yang, and Xin Yao. 2023. Efficient and effective text encoding for chinese llama and alpaca.

Dan Hendrycks, Collin Burns, Steven Basart, Andy Zou, Mantas Mazeika, Dawn Song, and Jacob Steinhardt. 2021. Measuring massive multitask language understanding.

Edward J. Hu, Yelong Shen, Phillip Wallis, Zeyuan Allen-Zhu, Yuanzhi Li, Shean Wang, Lu Wang, and Weizhu Chen. 2021a. Lora: Low-rank adaptation of large language models.

Edward J. Hu, Yelong Shen, Phillip Wallis, Zeyuan Allen-Zhu, Yuanzhi Li, Shean Wang, Lu Wang, and Weizhu Chen. 2021b. Lora: Low-rank adaptation of large language models.

Haoyang Huang, Tianyi Tang, Dongdong Zhang, Wayne Xin Zhao, Ting Song, Yan Xia, and Furu Wei. 2023. Not all languages are created equal in llms: Improving multilingual capability by cross-lingual-thought prompting.

Ayyoob Imani, Peiqin Lin, Amir Hossein Kargaran, Silvia Severini, Masoud Jalili Sabet, Nora Kassner, Chunlan Ma, Helmut Schmid, André F. T. Martins, François Yvon, and Hinrich Schütze. 2023. Glot500: Scaling multilingual corpora and language models to 500 languages.

Shibamouli Lahiri. 2014. Complexity of Word Collocation Networks: A Preliminary Structural Analysis. In *Proceedings of the Student Research Workshop at the*

14th Conference of the European Chapter of the Association for Computational Linguistics, pages 96–105, Gothenburg, Sweden. Association for Computational Linguistics.

Hang Le, Juan Miguel Pino, Changhan Wang, Jiatao Gu, Didier Schwab, and Laurent Besacier. 2021. Lightweight adapter tuning for multilingual speech translation. In *Proceedings of the 59th Annual Meeting of the Association for Computational Linguistics (ACL)*, pages 817–824. Association for Computational Linguistics.

Patrick Lewis, Barlas Oguz, Ruty Rinott, Sebastian Riedel, and Holger Schwenk. 2020. MLQA: Evaluating cross-lingual extractive question answering. In *Proceedings of the 58th Annual Meeting of the Association for Computational Linguistics*, pages 7315–7330, Online. Association for Computational Linguistics.

Jiahuan Li, Hao Zhou, Shujian Huang, Shanbo Cheng, and Jiajun Chen. 2023. Eliciting the translation ability of large language models via multilingual finetuning with translation instructions.

Xiang Lisa Li and Percy Liang. 2021. Prefix-tuning: Optimizing continuous prompts for generation. In *Proceedings of the 59th Annual Meeting of the Association for Computational Linguistics and the 11th International Joint Conference on Natural Language Processing (Volume 1: Long Papers)*, pages 4582–4597, Online. Association for Computational Linguistics.

Zehui Lin, Xiao Pan, Mingxuan Wang, Xipeng Qiu, Jiangtao Feng, Hao Zhou, and Lei Li. 2021. Pre-training multilingual neural machine translation by leveraging alignment information.

Xiao Liu, Kaixuan Ji, Yicheng Fu, Weng Tam, Zhengxiao Du, Zhilin Yang, and Jie Tang. 2022. P-tuning: Prompt tuning can be comparable to fine-tuning across scales and tasks. In *Proceedings of the 60th Annual Meeting of the Association for Computational Linguistics (Volume 2: Short Papers)*, pages 61–68, Dublin, Ireland. Association for Computational Linguistics.

Yasmin Moslem, Rejwanul Haque, John D. Kelleher, and Andy Way. 2023. Adaptive machine translation with large language models.

Long Ouyang, Jeff Wu, Xu Jiang, Diogo Almeida, Carroll L. Wainwright, Pamela Mishkin, Chong Zhang, Sandhini Agarwal, Katarina Slama, Alex Ray, John Schulman, Jacob Hilton, Fraser Kelton, Luke Miller, Maddie Simens, Amanda Askell, Peter Welinder, Paul Christiano, Jan Leike, and Ryan Lowe. 2022. Training language models to follow instructions with human feedback.

Pranav Rajpurkar, Jian Zhang, Konstantin Lopyrev, and Percy Liang. 2016. Squad: 100,000+ questions for machine comprehension of text.

Federico Ranaldi, Elena Sofia Ruzzetti, Felicia Logozzo, Michele Mastromattei, Leonardo Ranaldi, and Fabio Massimo Zanzotto. 2023a. Exploring linguistic properties of monolingual berts with typological classification among languages.

Leonardo Ranaldi, Aria Nourbakhsh, Arianna Patrizi, Elena Sofia Ruzzetti, Dario Onorati, Francesca Fallucchi, and Fabio Massimo Zanzotto. 2022. The dark side of the language: Pre-trained transformers in the darknet.

Leonardo Ranaldi and Giulia Pucci. 2023. Knowing knowledge: Epistemological study of knowledge in transformers. *Applied Sciences*, 13(2).

Leonardo Ranaldi, Elena Sofia Ruzzetti, Davide Venditti, Dario Onorati, and Fabio Massimo Zanzotto. 2023b. A trip towards fairness: Bias and de-biasing in large language models.

Leonardo Ranaldi, Elena Sofia Ruzzetti, and Fabio Massimo Zanzotto. 2023c. Precog: Exploring the relation between memorization and performance in pre-trained language models.

Andrea Santilli and Emanuele Rodolà. 2023. Camoscio: an italian instruction-tuned llama.

Mohammad Shoeybi, Mostofa Ali Patwary, Raul Puri, Patrick LeGresley, Jared Casper, and Bryan Catanzaro. 2019. Megatron-LM: Training multi-billion parameter language models using model parallelism. *ArXiv*, abs/1909.08053.

Mirac Suzgun, Nathan Scales, Nathanael Schärli, Sebastian Gehrmann, Yi Tay, Hyung Won Chung, Aakanksha Chowdhery, Quoc V Le, Ed H Chi, Denny Zhou, , and Jason Wei. 2022. Challenging big-bench tasks and whether chain-of-thought can solve them. *arXiv preprint arXiv:2210.09261*.

Marc Tanti, Lonneke van der Plas, Claudia Borg, and Albert Gatt. 2021. On the language-specificity of multilingual bert and the impact of fine-tuning.

Rohan Taori, Ishaan Gulrajani, Tianyi Zhang, Yann Dubois, Xuechen Li, Carlos Guestrin, Percy Liang, and Tatsunori B. Hashimoto. 2023. Stanford alpaca: An instruction-following llama model. `https://github.com/tatsu-lab/stanford_alpaca`.

Ian Tenney, Dipanjan Das, and Ellie Pavlick. 2019. BERT rediscovers the classical NLP pipeline. In *Proceedings of the 57th Annual Meeting of the Association for Computational Linguistics*, pages 4593–4601, Florence, Italy. Association for Computational Linguistics.

Martin Thissen. 2023. Fine-tune alpaca for any language. `https://github.com/thisserand/alpaca-lora-finetune-language`.

Jörg Tiedemann. 2012. Parallel data, tools and interfaces in OPUS. In *Proceedings of the Eighth International Conference on Language Resources and*

Evaluation (LREC'12), pages 2214–2218, Istanbul, Turkey. European Language Resources Association (ELRA).

Hugo Touvron, Thibaut Lavril, Gautier Izacard, Xavier Martinet, Marie-Anne Lachaux, Timothée Lacroix, Baptiste Rozière, Naman Goyal, Eric Hambro, Faisal Azhar, Aurelien Rodriguez, Armand Joulin, Edouard Grave, and Guillaume Lample. 2023. Llama: Open and efficient foundation language models.

Yizhong Wang, Yeganeh Kordi, Swaroop Mishra, Alisa Liu, Noah A. Smith, Daniel Khashabi, and Hannaneh Hajishirzi. 2023. Self-instruct: Aligning language models with self-generated instructions.

Jason Wei, Maarten Bosma, Vincent Y. Zhao, Kelvin Guu, Adams Wei Yu, Brian Lester, Nan Du, Andrew M. Dai, and Quoc V. Le. 2022. Finetuned language models are zero-shot learners.

Canwen Xu, Daya Guo, Nan Duan, and Julian McAuley. 2023. Baize: An open-source chat model with parameter-efficient tuning on self-chat data. *arXiv preprint arXiv:2304.01196*.

Wen Yang, Chong Li, Jiajun Zhang, and Chengqing Zong. 2023. Bigtranslate: Augmenting large language models with multilingual translation capability over 100 languages.

Yasbok. Alpaca Instruction Fine-Tuning for Arabic. https://huggingface.co/Yasbok .

Fabio Massimo Zanzotto, Andrea Santilli, Leonardo Ranaldi, Dario Onorati, Pierfrancesco Tommasino, and Francesca Fallucchi. 2020. KERMIT: Complementing transformer architectures with encoders of explicit syntactic interpretations. In *Proceedings of the 2020 Conference on Empirical Methods in Natural Language Processing (EMNLP)*, pages 256–267, Online. Association for Computational Linguistics.

Jiali Zeng, Fandong Meng, Yongjing Yin, and Jie Zhou. 2023. Tim: Teaching large language models to translate with comparison.

Shaolei Zhang, Qingkai Fang, Zhuocheng Zhang, Zhengrui Ma, Yan Zhou, Langlin Huang, Mengyu Bu, Shangtong Gui, Yunji Chen, Xilin Chen, and Yang Feng. 2023. Bayling: Bridging cross-lingual alignment and instruction following through interactive translation for large language models.

Wenhao Zhu, Hongyi Liu, Qingxiu Dong, Jingjing Xu, Shujian Huang, Lingpeng Kong, Jiajun Chen, and Lei Li. 2023. Multilingual machine translation with large language models: Empirical results and analysis.

Yukun Zhu, Ryan Kiros, Rich Zemel, Ruslan Salakhutdinov, Raquel Urtasun, Antonio Torralba, and Sanja Fidler. 2015. Aligning books and movies: Towards story-like visual explanations by watching movies and reading books. In *The IEEE International Conference on Computer Vision (ICCV)*.

CAPIVARA: Cost-Efficient Approach for Improving Multilingual CLIP Performance on Low-Resource Languages

Gabriel Oliveira dos Santos[1*], Diego A. B. Moreira[1*], Alef Iury Ferreira[2], Jhessica Silva[1], Luiz Pereira[1], Pedro Bueno[1], Thiago Sousa[2], Helena Maia[1], Nádia da Silva[2], Esther Colombini[1], Helio Pedrini[1], Sandra Avila[1]

[1]Instituto de Computação, Universidade Estadual de Campinas (UNICAMP), Brasil
[2]Instituto de Informática, Universidade Federal de Goiás (UFG), Brasil

Abstract

This work introduces CAPIVARA, a cost-efficient framework designed to enhance the performance of multilingual CLIP models in low-resource languages. While CLIP has excelled in zero-shot vision-language tasks, the resource-intensive nature of model training remains challenging. Many datasets lack linguistic diversity, featuring solely English descriptions for images. CAPIVARA addresses this by augmenting text data using image captioning and machine translation to generate multiple synthetic captions in low-resource languages. We optimize the training pipeline with LiT, LoRA, and gradient checkpointing to alleviate the computational cost. Through extensive experiments, CAPIVARA emerges as state of the art in zero-shot tasks involving images and Portuguese texts. We show the potential for significant improvements in other low-resource languages, achieved by fine-tuning the pre-trained multilingual CLIP using CAPIVARA on a single GPU for 2 hours. Our model and code is available at `https://github.com/hiaac-nlp/CAPIVARA`.

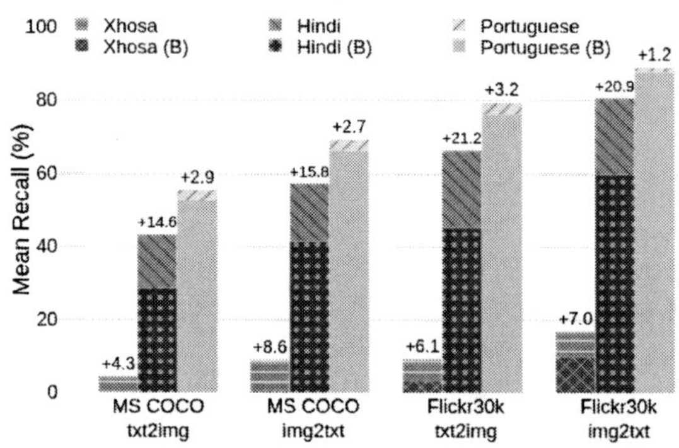

Figure 1: Improving multilingual CLIP Performance in Low-Resource Languages: Xhosa, Hindi, and Portuguese. This figure illustrates CAPIVARA's effectiveness in enhancing the performance of pre-trained multilingual CLIP models, the OPEN-CLIP baseline (B), for low-resource languages. The percentage point increase in mean recall for text-to-image (txt2img) and image-to-text (img2txt) retrieval with low-resource languages on Flickr30k and MS COCO datasets is highlighted above the respective bars. CAPIVARA significantly improves the model's baseline performance with only 2 hours of training and 8.5 GB of GPU memory.

1 Introduction

The challenge of learning a joint multimodal representation for vision and language has developed various pre-trained models in recent years (Wang et al., 2021; Gao et al., 2021; Yang et al., 2022b; Geng et al., 2022; Li et al., 2023). Remarkably, CLIP (Radford et al., 2021) has gained attention for achieving state of the art on zero-shot vision-language tasks through contrastive learning to align images and text within a multimodal embedding.

Training models such as CLIP requires massive data and computational resources despite their good generalization capacity. These models are typically trained with datasets containing hundreds of millions of image-text pairs, often collected from the web. However, many datasets only provide images paired with English descriptions; as a result, the research community focuses excessively on English texts, whereas other languages are neglected, reinforcing cultural, regional, and linguistic biases (Bender et al., 2021). While recent advancements include approaches for languages beyond English (Bianchi et al., 2021; Yang et al., 2022a; Ko and Gu, 2022) and multilingual methods (Carlsson et al., 2022; Chen et al., 2023), they primarily focus on high-resource languages. There is a scarcity of approaches considering low-resource languages, and even models including them show performance disparities in tasks involving these languages compared to tasks with English texts.

*Equal contribution. Corresponding authors: G.O.S. (gabriel.santos@ic.unicamp.br), D.A.B.M. (diego.moreira@ic.unicamp.br) and S.A. (avilas@unicamp.br).

Proceedings of the The 3rd Workshop on Multi-lingual Representation Learning (MRL), pages 184–207
December 7, 2023 ©2023 Association for Computational Linguistics

We propose a cost-efficient approach for improving multilingual CLIP performance in low-resource languages (CAPIVARA), addressing the performance gap with English and reducing computational requirements. Our approach relies on the assumption that datasets may contain images annotated with noisy descriptions. In this way, our framework utilizes BLIP2 (Li et al., 2023) to generate multiple synthetic captions for each image, addressing noisy annotations and limited language diversity challenges. Using the re-annotated dataset, we translate both the original and generated captions into the target language and conduct fine-tuning on the multilingual model. To mitigate the computational cost associated with CLIP model training, we propose to optimize the training pipeline with LiT strategy (Zhai et al., 2022), wherein the image encoder remains frozen during training, gradient checkpointing (Chen et al., 2016) and LoRA (Hu et al., 2021). Figure 1 demonstrates that substantial improvements in low-resource language can be achieved by fine-tuning the pre-trained multilingual CLIP with CAPIVARA.

Our main contributions are as follows:

- We introduce CAPIVARA, a low-cost data-centric framework that leverages image captioning models to enhance the annotation of existing datasets to improve the performance of pre-trained multilingual CLIP in low-resource languages. We report the carbon footprint of our method.
- To the best of our knowledge, we are the first to employ LoRA for language adaptation in CLIP models, considerably reducing the number of trainable parameters.
- We show that augmenting text data, by generating multiple image-conditioned captions with image captioning models, can boost CLIP performance in low-resource language.
- We achieve state of the art in many zero-shot tasks involving images and Portuguese texts. This work aims to push forward the multimodal learning literature in the Portuguese-speaking community[1].
- We make available the re-annotated CC3M with descriptions in Portuguese and English for seamless utilization by other researchers as a data augmentation resource. We also provide the annotations translated to Portuguese for Flickr30k, MS COCO, CC3M, ImageNet-1k, and ELEVATER datasets.

[1]Portuguese, despite being ranked fifth among world languages in the number of native speakers, is a low-resource language from a machine-learning perspective.

2 Related Work

CLIP. The multimodal vision and language model known as CLIP (Contrastive Language-Image Pre-training) (Radford et al., 2021) rapidly gained attention for its simplicity, scalability, and impressive results. It is pre-trained on 400 million image-text pairs to learn a contrastive representation of images and texts in a multimodal space.

OpenCLIP (Ilharco et al., 2021) is an open-source initiative that provides CLIP models trained on large datasets. It offers well-trained and robust models for pre-training purposes. Based on the original CLIP architecture, OpenCLIP maintains similar accuracy when trained on the same dataset. However, it extends its training to datasets like LAION-400M, LAION-2B, and DataComp-1B. Unlike the original CLIP, OpenCLIP introduces various image and text encoder configurations, including the OPENCLIP VIT-B/32 XLM-ROBERTA BASE used in this work.

Non-English CLIPs. Bianchi et al. (2021) introduce the first non-English CLIP-based models. The Italian CLIP model, unlike the original CLIP model, is trained using networks previously pre-trained in text and image tasks. It employs 1.4 million samples from translated datasets.

The Chinese CLIP (Yang et al., 2022a) explores different training approaches. The most effective architecture combines a pre-trained model with the LiT (Locked-image text Tuning) strategy (Zhai et al., 2022), freezing the text encoder until stability and extensive parameter training. Training data comprises 200 million image-text pairs.

The Korean CLIP (KELIP) model (Ko and Gu, 2022) focuses on training from scratch using substantial data and language-specific techniques. It involves self-supervised pre-training of the image encoder and alignment with the English CLIP version. The training dataset comprises 1.1 billion examples, including 708 million Korean samples.

Multilingual CLIPs. M-CLIP (Multilingual CLIP) (Carlsson et al., 2022) builds on the pre-trained CLIP model, using its text encoder while discarding the visual encoder. It employs a teacher-learning technique to transfer knowledge from a pre-trained teacher network to new language models. M-CLIP is applied to 68 languages, translated versions of datasets by the MarianMT model (Junczys-Dowmunt et al., 2018).

AltCLIP (Altering the Language Encoder in CLIP) (Chen et al., 2023) introduces a bilingual model for Chinese and a multilingual one for 11 languages. Like M-CLIP, the teacher-learning technique uses only the textual model across various languages. However, AltCLIP differs by incorporating English text distillation, human-curated translations, and a final fine-tuning phase. It also uses the LiT strategy to freeze the image encoder.

Data-Centric Approaches. Multimodal learning has been mainly explored through algorithmic designs, often treating datasets as monolithic. Santurkar et al. (2023) reveal that CLIP's performance depends on three pre-training datasets properties: dataset size, caption descriptiveness, and caption variability for each image. They employ BLIP (Bootstrapping Language-Image Pre-training) (Li et al., 2022b) to generate new captions to address limited text diversity, improving CLIP performance. Similarly, Fan et al. (2023) propose LaCLIP (Language augmented CLIP) that uses LLM (Large Language Model) to rewrite captions to increase the text diversity within text-image pairs in the pre-training dataset. However, the decoupled text-generation process might limit effectiveness in datasets with non-descriptive captions (Nguyen et al., 2023).

Our work is related to Fan et al. (2023) and Nguyen et al. (2023). However, their studies focus on English captions during training and require extensive computational resources. In contrast, our research addresses a constrained scenario with limited computational power — a single GPU — and a lack of annotated datasets in the target language. We leverage multilingual OpenCLIP and English-annotated open datasets to enhance model performance in Portuguese. Our method, centered on Portuguese-translated captions, can be extended to other languages, making it well-suited for low-resource language challenges.

3 Method

This section details our approach, including generating captions, translating them into Portuguese, and integrating these new captions into the training pipeline. It also describes optimization through LoRA and gradient checkpointing, effectively reducing the computational resources for CLIP model training. Figure 2 illustrates the main components of CAPIVARA.

3.1 Model Architecture

We use the pre-trained multilingual model OPENCLIP VIT-B/32 XLM-ROBERTA BASE[2] (OPENCLIP for short). This model utilizes XLM-RoBERTa Base (Conneau et al., 2020) and ViT Base (Dosovitskiy et al., 2020) with 32×32 resolution as text and image encoder, respectively. The model was pre-trained on LAION-5B (Schuhmann et al., 2022) for 12.8B steps and a batch size of 90k. We employ base versions of the encoders, as larger models would demand significantly greater computational resources for both training and inference. This consideration is crucial when addressing the low-resource language community.

3.2 Datasets

We use CC3M (Sharma et al., 2018) and modifications over it to fine-tune the OPENCLIP model to improve its performance in Portuguese. For zero-shot text-to-image and image-to-text retrieval tasks, we use PraCegoVer (dos Santos et al., 2022), which is composed of images annotated originally with Portuguese texts, and our Portuguese-translated versions of MS COCO (Lin et al., 2014) and Flickr30k (Plummer et al., 2017). We also translate the labels from ImageNet (Deng et al., 2009) and the ELEVATER benchmark datasets (Li et al., 2022a) for image classification.

3.3 Dataset Filtering

Similar to Schuhmann et al. (2022); Gadre et al. (2023), we apply CLIP score filtering. Thus, we discard examples where the cosine similarity, computed by OPENCLIP VIT-B/32 XLM-ROBERTA BASE, between the image and text embeddings is lower than 0.20. We employ this method to CC3M, naming the resulting dataset as CC3M-Filtered. We also apply this method to PraCegoVer[3], used as a test set, to remove unrelated image-text pairs.

3.4 Dataset Re-annotation & Translation

CLIP is a framework based on contrastive learning to train a multimodal model. In its pipeline, a large batch of image-text pairs (x_I, x_T) is sampled at each training step. Then, the image and

[2]https://huggingface.co/laion/CLIP-ViT-B-32-xlm-roberta-base-laion5B-s13B-b90k

[3]PraCegoVer filtered version: https://zenodo.org/records/7548638.

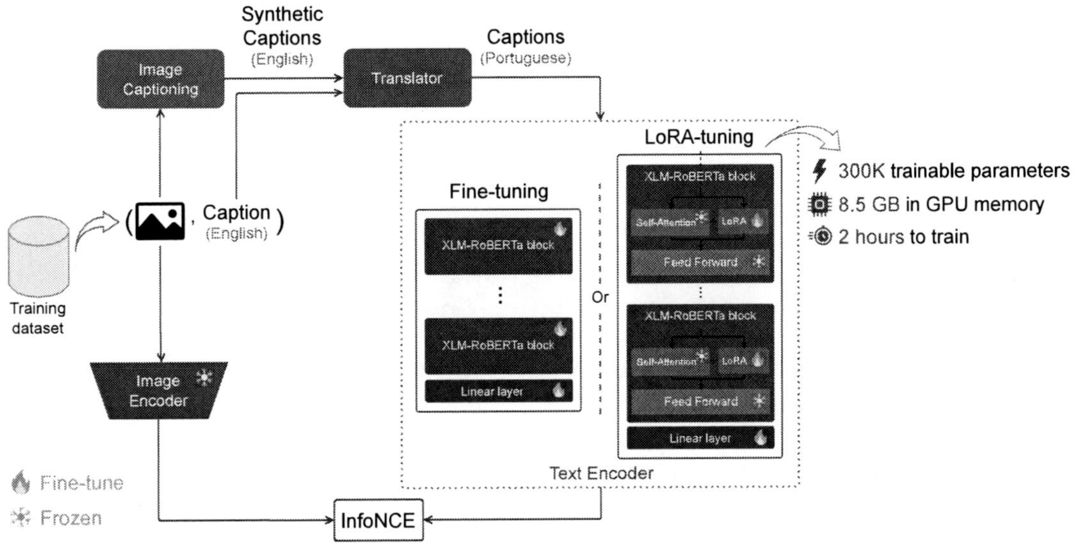

Figure 2: CAPIVARA overview. In our framework, the training dataset comprehends images annotated with English captions. To enhance the annotations, we use an image captioning model to generate synthetic captions for the images. Then, both original and synthetic captions are translated from English to the target language, in our case, Portuguese. We freeze the image encoder and fine-tune the text encoder using the translated captions to align the visual representation by optimizing the InfoNCE loss. While it is possible to fine-tune the entire text encoder, such an approach is resource-intensive. Thus, we propose an optimization method based on LoRA-tuning that can significantly reduce the associated computational cost and speed up the training time.

text features are extracted by the respective encoders f_T and f_I and are used to compute InfoNCE loss (Oord et al., 2018) as follows:

$$L_{\text{InfoNCE}}(x,y) = -\sum_{i=1}^{B} \log \frac{\exp(\text{sim}(x^i, y^i)/\tau}{\sum_{j=1}^{B} \exp(\text{sim}(x^i, y^j))/\tau}, \quad (1)$$

$$L_{\text{CLIP}} = L_{\text{InfoNCE}}(f_I(\text{aug}(x_I)), f_T(x_T)), \quad (2)$$

where B is the batch size, τ is a learnable temperature to scale the logits, $\text{sim}(\cdot)$ and $\text{aug}(\cdot)$ stands for cosine similarity and augmentation operation, respectively.

In the original proposal, only images are augmented as indicated in Equation 2, which might limit the text guidance to the image encoder. Fan et al. (2023) propose to use LLM to augment texts in addition to the image augmentation, as shown in Equation 3. However, this text-generation process does not consider the image content.

$$L_{\text{text aug.}} = L_{\text{InfoNCE}}(f_I(\text{aug}(x_I)), f_T(\text{aug}(x_T))). \quad (3)$$

We propose to use BLIP2[4] to generate new captions conditioned on the images from CC3M. In contrast to Nguyen et al. (2023), and drawing inspiration from LaCLIP (Fan et al., 2023), we propose to generate multiple captions for each image in the dataset by passing different prefixes to BLIP2. Our approach addresses the limitation of LaCLIP and has the advantage of generating multiple captions per image, which is a drawback of Nguyen et al. (2023). Still, as BLIP2 is a monolingual model, we decided to generate the captions in English and then translate them into Portuguese using Google Translate[5]. Therefore, our text augmentation comprehends generating English captions with BLIP2 and translating them into Portuguese. During training, for each image, we randomly sample a caption among the original and the generated ones to fine-tune the text encoder. Hence, at each epoch, a different text can be selected for each image. For evaluation, we translate the annotations from Flickr30k and MS COCO, and the labels from ImageNet and ELEVATER.

3.5 Training

This work takes place within the context of limited computational resources. We apply many techniques to reduce the cost of fine-tuning the OPEN-

[4] https://huggingface.co/Salesforce/blip2-opt-2.7b

[5] https://translate.google.com.br

CLIP. First, we use Gradient Checkpointing (Chen et al., 2016), which reduces the memory usage to $O(\sqrt{n})$ when training n layers. This method removes the layers' activation after the forward pass and recalculates them during the backward pass if necessary. Using this technique, we achieved a considerable reduction in GPU memory usage.

Another method contributing to memory reduction is LiT (Zhai et al., 2022), which only trains the text encoder while keeping the image encoder frozen. The motivation for training only the text encoder is that the image encoder has already undergone extensive pre-training and can produce good representations for images. Hence, we train the text encoder with captions in Portuguese so that this model learns to align the text embeddings to fixed image features, producing a multimodal embedding space. This strategy speeds up training and reduces memory since the image encoder does not compute gradients.

Finally, we also apply LoRA (Hu et al., 2021) to reduce the number of trainable parameters, reducing the memory needed to train the models and the training time. LoRA involves a re-parameterization of the dense layers as follows:

$$h = W_o x + \frac{\alpha}{r} B A x, \tag{4}$$

where $W_o \in \mathbb{R}^{d_1 \times d_2}$ is the frozen pre-trained weight matrix, h is the result of the re-parameterization, $A \in \mathbb{R}^{r \times d_2}$ and $B \in \mathbb{R}^{d_1 \times r}$ are decomposition matrices and $r < \min(d_1, d_2)$ is the low-dimensional rank of the decomposition, an α is a hyperparameter for scale. Similar to Hu et al. (2021), we use LoRA in the query (Q) and value (V) self-attention modules from the text encoder.

The original OPENCLIP consists of 366M parameters. Applying LiT strategies reduces this number to 88M trainable parameters (24% of the total). Further integration of LoRA reduces the trainable parameters to only 0.1% (300k). We report all the training hyperparameters in Appendix A.1.

3.6 Evaluation

To evaluate the proposed framework's generalization capacity, we follow the typical procedure of evaluating pre-trained models (Radford et al., 2021; Yang et al., 2022a; Ko and Gu, 2022) in zero-shot cross-modal retrieval (text-to-image and image-to-text retrieval) and zero-shot image classification.

Zero-shot Cross-modal Retrieval: We evaluate our methods on three cross-modal retrieval datasets: PraCegoVer, MS COCO, and Flickr30k. PraCegoVer is a multimodal dataset with native Portuguese captions based on Instagram posts. We built upon the conventional MS COCO and Flickr30k datasets, using Google Translate to translate all captions to Portuguese. To assess cross-modal retrieval performance, we adopted the recall@K evaluation metric, where $K = \{1, 5, 10\}$, and the mean recall, representing the average recall value across the recall@K instances.

Zero-shot Image Classification: We evaluate our pre-trained models on ImageNet-1k (Deng et al., 2009) and on ELEVATER image classification toolkit (Li et al., 2022a). It contains 20 datasets designed for image classification tasks across various domains and an easy-to-use toolkit to evaluate pre-trained language-augmented visual models. To accommodate evaluation in the Portuguese language, we manually translated the labels for each dataset, as well as the templates, following the methodology outlined in (Radford et al., 2021). In the evaluation process, ImageNet-1k employs the top-1 accuracy metric. Appendix A.2 provides the specific metrics for each dataset in ELEVATER benchmark.

4 Experiments and Results

This section presents a comprehensive set of experiments designed to investigate the effects of dataset filtering and the specific influence of each module within our framework, CAPIVARA. To reduce the effects of randomness, we ran each experiment setup three times. We also focus on zero-shot tasks involving images and Portuguese texts. Since no CLIP model is publicly available for Portuguese, we adopt as baseline the pre-trained multilingual model OPENCLIP due to its state-of-the-art performance in many tasks with Portuguese captions.

Dataset Filtering & CAPIVARA. We investigate two data-centric approaches: filter the training set by selecting promising samples capable of removing noise, and annotation enhancement with our proposed framework. Using CAPIVARA, for each image in CC3M, we add 10 synthetic captions, generated with BLIP2, besides the original caption. We comprehensively analyze the impact of the dataset filtering presented in Sec. 3.3 and the effectiveness of CAPIVARA in cross-modal retrieval tasks on Flickr30k, MS COCO (with Portuguese-translated captions), and PraCegoVer datasets.

Table 1 shows the results of the text-to-image (txt2img) and image-to-text (img2txt) retrieval tasks conducted on OPENCLIP. These results encompass models fine-tuned and trained using the CAPIVARA framework on the original CC3M dataset and its filtered version, CC3M-Filtered. In Table 1, the columns "Synth." and "Trans." indicate which settings include synthetic captions and whether or not the captions are translated.

Employing the CC3M with translated captions, fourth row in Table 1, for fine-tuning increases the mean recall score by roughly 2 percentage points (*pp.*) in text-to-image and image-to-text retrieval tasks on Flickr30k and MS COCO, compared to the baseline, OPENCLIP. However, for the PraCegoVer dataset, a decline of 1.6 *pp.* in text-to-image retrieval and a more significant drop of 9.3 *pp.* in image-to-text retrieval are observed. Comparing the fine-tuning using CC3M and CC3M-Filtered, one can note an average enhancement of 0.9 *pp.* in mean recall score for text-to-image retrieval and a 0.4 *pp.* improvement for image-to-text retrieval across all three datasets.

In addition, as an intermediate step in our architecture, we employ synthetic captions to mitigate noise in the training data. To illustrate the performance gains, we compare the results of only translating the training set and translating and generating synthetic captions (CAPIVARA), fourth and sixth rows in Table 1, respectively. For the Flickr30k dataset, we observe a 1.1 *pp.* improvement in text-to-image retrieval with synthetic captions, with no significant difference in image-to-text retrieval. On the MS COCO dataset, we note a 1.5 *pp.* increase in text-to-image retrieval and a 1.2 *pp.* gain in image-to-text retrieval. Additionally, when evaluating the PraCegoVer dataset under the same conditions, we find a 2.6 *pp.* improvement in text-to-image retrieval and a 4.7 *pp.* gain in image-to-text retrieval. Thus, in most cases, using synthetic data as a means of data augmentation and noise reduction yields a positive impact. Details about the impact of the number of synthetic captions in the performance are shown in Table A6 (Appendix A.3).

The most significant performance gains over the baseline are achieved using CAPIVARA. For instance, the model trained on CC3M with CAPIVARA, sixth row, yields a 3.5 *pp.* improvement in text-to-image retrieval for Flickr30k and MS COCO and 1 *pp.* enhancement on PraCegoVer. Notably, in image-to-text retrieval, CAPIVARA (CC3M) increases 2 *pp.* on Flickr30k and it has a remarkable 4.7 *pp.* gain on MS COCO over the baseline. Also, models trained on CC3M and CC3M-Filtered with CAPIVARA demonstrate similar performance levels. These experiments demonstrate the effectiveness of our proposal, CAPIVARA, in enhancing multilingual CLIP performance in Portuguese.

Caption Translation. We also investigate the impacts of automatic translations of captions in the final model performance for Portuguese texts. We conducted experiments training the model on datasets containing only English annotations (i.e., CC3M + no-translation and CC3M + no-translation + synthetic captions), and their counterparts translated into Portuguese using Google Translate (i.e., CC3M + translation and CC3M + translation + synthetic captions). The evaluation comprehends Flickr30k, MS COCO, and PraCegoVer datasets with only Portuguese captions, particularly images in PraCegoVer that are originally annotated in Portuguese. We present the results in Table 1.

One can note a substantial improvement when translating annotations within the training dataset. Specifically, models trained on datasets containing Portuguese annotations exhibit an average increase of 2.5 *pp.* in text-to-image mean recall scores compared to their English-trained counterparts. Similarly, employing Portuguese-translated captions leads to a mean recall improvement of 1.6 *pp.* for image-to-text retrieval on both the Flickr30k and MS COCO datasets. Fine-tuning with the original CC3M (i.e., CC3M + no-translation) hampers text-to-image performance across all three datasets and drops notable 7 *pp.* the mean recall in image-to-text on PraCegoVer. By training the model on translated synthetic captions, CAPIVARA consistently outperformed all the other settings. Our method increases the average performance in 3.2 *pp.* compared to fine-tuning on the original CC3M dataset. This experiment highlights the importance of including the automatic translation of captions into the target language, Portuguese, in our training pipeline.

Training Pipeline Optimization. This work is inserted in a context of restricted computational resources, in which only a single RTX Quadro 8000 GPU is available. In this way, we propose a method to optimize our training pipeline, detailed in Sec. 3.5. It combines LiT, Gradient Checkpointing (G. Checkpt), and LoRA techniques. In this section, we investigate the impacts of this optimization in terms of model performance and cost

Table 1: Impact analysis of synthetic captions (Synth.) and translation (Trans.) on our framework. This table compares the performance of CLIP fine-tuning on English and Portuguese-translated texts, both with and without the addition of synthetic captions. It shows the experimental results in cross-modal retrieval on Flickr30k and MS COCO with captions translated into Portuguese, and PraCegoVer. We report the average and standard deviation of mean recall for text-to-image (txt2img) and image-to-text (img2txt) retrieval tasks. Our CAPIVARA achieves the best performance across datasets, highlighting its efficacy in enhancing pre-trained multilingual CLIP.

				Flickr30k		MS COCO		PraCegoVer	
Method/Model	Training dataset	Synth.	Trans.	txt2img	img2txt	txt2img	img2txt	txt2img	img2txt
OPENCLIP (Baseline)				76.23	87.93	52.62	66.55	65.36	**69.43**
OPENCLIP + Fine-tuning	CC3M	✗	✗	75.78 ± 0.02	88.78 ± 0.04	52.28 ± 0.01	68.18 ± 0.01	61.41 ± 0.00	62.35 ± 0.01
	CC3M	✓	✗	77.08 ± 0.02	89.01 ± 0.03	53.87 ± 0.01	70.04 ± 0.02	64.01 ± 0.01	66.43 ± 0.01
	CC3M	✗	✓	78.42 ± 0.02	**90.02 ± 0.05**	54.77 ± 0.01	70.06 ± 0.01	63.79 ± 0.01	60.10 ± 0.00
	CC3M-Filtered	✗	✓	79.02 ± 0.01	89.49 ± 0.02	55.46 ± 0.01	69.52 ± 0.02	65.11 ± 0.01	62.29 ± 0.01
CAPIVARA	CC3M	✓	✓	**79.56 ± 0.01**	**89.95 ± 0.04**	**56.27 ± 0.01**	**71.24 ± 0.01**	**66.40 ± 0.01**	64.75 ± 0.01
	CC3M-Filtered	✓	✓	**79.67 ± 0.01**	**89.97 ± 0.04**	**56.32 ± 0.01**	**71.06 ± 0.01**	**66.55 ± 0.01**	65.06 ± 0.01

Table 2: Impact of optimization techniques. We evaluate training models on CC3M with CAPIVARA combined with many optimization techniques. We report the experimental results in terms of mean recall in text-to-image (txt2img), and image-to-text (img2txt) and memory (M) and training time cost (T). Our optimization method leads to the best training time and computational cost while performing similarly to other approaches.

		Flickr30k		MS COCO		PraCegoVer		M	T
	Optimization	txt2img	img2txt	txt2img	img2txt	txt2img	img2txt	(GB)	(h)
	OPENCLIP (Baseline)	76.23	87.93	52.62	66.55	65.36	69.43	-	-
CAPIVARA	LiT + G.Checkpt	79.56 ± 0.01	89.95 ± 0.04	56.27 ± 0.01	71.24 ± 0.01	66.44 ± 0.01	66.57 ± 0.01	38	31
	LiT + G.Checkpt + LoRA	79.51 ± 0.04	89.50 ± 0.03	55.56 ± 0.01	69.63 ± 0.04	67.07 ± 0.02	68.14 ± 0.01	21.5	16
	LiT + G.Checkpt + LoRA + 1500 steps + BS=1000	79.39 ± 0.05	89.13 ± 0.08	55.49 ± 0.06	69.26 ± 0.05	66.89 ± 0.04	67.93 ± 0.01	8.5	2

Table 3: Summary of the models and resources invested in their training, considering the dataset size, the GPU/TPU used, and the required training time.

Model	Language	# Dataset size	GPU/TPU	Training time
Italian CLIP	Italian	1.4M	2 TPUs	14 days
Chinese CLIP	Chinese	200M	128 V100 (2048 GB)	7.5 days
Korean CLIP	Korean	708M	80 A100 (640 GB)	15.7 days
LaCLIP	English	365M	32 V100 (512 GB)	–
AltCLIP	Multilingual	38M/115M	–	–
M-CLIP	Multilingual	3.3M	–	–
CAPIVARA	**Portuguese**	**3.3M**	**1 Quadro RTX 8000 (48 GB)**	**2 hours**

reduction. All experiments include LiT and gradient checkpointing, otherwise, we could not run the training in our infrastructure. In addition, we conducted experiments to assess the impact of including LoRA in our training pipeline. To compare the computational cost among the settings, we fixed the GPU architecture, and we trained the models with batch size (BS) equal to 2816 for 5863 steps, except for LiT + G. Checkpt + LoRA + 1500 steps + BS=1000, trained with a batch size of 1000 samples for only 1500 steps. Still, we demonstrate that it is possible to reduce the batch size and the number of training steps and reach a competitive performance.

Table 2 shows experimental results. Our initial attempt to fine-tune the complete CLIP model encountered infrastructure limitations, hindering its execution. We overcame this constraint by utilizing LiT and gradient checkpointing, which enabled the training process. Comparison between the setups, namely LiT + G. Checkpt and LiT + G. Checkpt + LoRA, reveals that LoRA substantially reduces memory usage by over 40% and cuts training time in half. The model trained with LoRA had a performance similar to the one that fine-tunes the entire text encoder on Flickr30k, but it decreases by 1.2 *pp.* the average performance on MS COCO.

In addition, the model trained with our optimization technique LiT + G. Checkpt + LoRA + 1500 steps + BS=1000 presented a decline of 0.2 *pp.* compared to LiT + G. Checkpt + LoRA. Using our optimization method can remarkably reduce the GPU memory (from 38 GB to 8.5 GB) and training time (from 31h to 2h), yet outperform the baseline by 2.5 *pp.* across the tasks. Our training pipeline requires very modest computational resources compared to the literature, as shown in Table 3. These experiments demonstrate that our optimization method can effectively reduce the cost of fine-tuning CLIP, allowing researchers with restricted computing resources to conduct experiments.

Low-resource Languages. To demonstrate the effectiveness of CAPIVARA in improving pre-trained multilingual CLIP performance on low-resource languages, we expand our investigation to include Xhosa and Hindi. Figure 1 compares the performance between the pre-trained OPENCLIP (baseline) and the models trained by employing the whole CAPIVARA optimized pipeline, which refers to the setting LiT + G. Checkpt + LoRA + 1500 steps + BS=1000, named CAPIVARA + Opt., for text-to-image and image-to-text retrieval tasks on Flickr30k and MS COCO. This experiment employs our optimized training pipeline (Sec. 4), training models for 2 hours on a single GPU Quadro RTX 8000 with a memory usage of 8.5 GB.

The baseline presents the weakest performance in Xhosa across all tasks, with mean recall close to zero in MS COCO and 3 and 10 in text-to-image and image-to-text on Flickr30k, respectively. CAPIVARA increases the average performance in this language by 6.5 *pp.* on Flickr30k and MS COCO. The most significant improvement can be noted in Hindi. A remarkable increase of 15 *pp.* on MS COCO and 21 *pp.* on Flickr30k is obtained with CAPIVARA. This experiment shows that CAPIVARA effectively boosts the pre-trained multilingual CLIP's performance in other low-resource languages with a low computational cost.

Image Classification. In addition to zero-shot cross-modal retrieval tasks, we also evaluate our models in zero-shot image classification across 21 datasets. The results are presented in Table 4. In the context of ELEVATER, training CLIP with CAPIVARA yielded an average improvement of 0.6 *pp.* over our baseline. We plot the bar chart in Figure A1 to thoroughly analyze the performance gap between the baseline and the model trained with CAPIVARA for each dataset within ELEVATER. Our method consistently surpassed the baseline across most datasets, yielding substantial accuracy improvements of 5.53 *pp.*, 5.15 *pp.*, and 3.07 *pp.* for KITTI-Distance, MNIST, and GTSRB, respectively. Regarding ImageNet-1k, CAPIVARA exhibited a performance gain of 0.2 *pp.* compared to the baseline. In addition, the model's performance trained with CAPIVARA + Opt. is close to our baseline. Hence, LoRA-tuning for 1500 steps keeps the average performance on zero-shot image classification, whereas it improves considerably the performance on zero-shot cross-modal retrieval.

Carbon Footprint. Despite the remarkable achievements of large language models, their deployment requires substantial computational power, resulting in significant energy usage. For instance, models such as GPT-3 and BLOOM consumed approximately 1,287 MWh and 433 MWh, respectively, in their training, corresponding to 502 tonnes of CO_2 and 25 tonnes of CO_2 emissions (Maslej et al., 2023). The BLOOM model's carbon footprint alone surpasses an average American's annual carbon emissions by 1.4 times. The energy consumed during BLOOM's training could power a household in the United States for up to 41 years.

Table 4: Zero-shot image classification performance on ELEVATER and ImageNet-1k.

Dataset	OpenCLIP (Baseline)	CAPIVARA	CAPIVARA + Opt.
Caltech-101	84.53 ± 0.00	82.97 ± 0.03	83.68 ± 0.02
CIFAR-10	93.99 ± 0.00	93.85 ± 0.00	93.93 ± 0.03
CIFAR-100	68.44 ± 0.00	69.37 ± 0.01	68.87 ± 0.01
Country-211	17.82 ± 0.00	17.61 ± 0.00	17.32 ± 0.02
DTD	41.17 ± 0.00	42.34 ± 0.04	41.79 ± 0.07
EuroSAT	47.16 ± 0.00	47.77 ± 0.02	48.85 ± 0.12
FER-2013	48.65 ± 0.00	46.68 ± 0.05	46.85 ± 0.13
FGVC-Aircraft	26.30 ± 0.00	25.49 ± 0.01	25.54 ± 0.09
Food-101	65.06 ± 0.00	64.58 ± 0.01	64.46 ± 0.00
GTSRB	43.27 ± 0.00	46.34 ± 0.01	44.66 ± 0.06
Hateful-Memes	56.50 ± 0.00	56.17 ± 0.00	56.81 ± 0.03
KITTI-Distance	28.41 ± 0.00	33.94 ± 0.13	28.27 ± 0.11
MNIST	54.99 ± 0.00	60.14 ± 0.04	55.00 ± 0.10
Oxford Flowers-102	50.88 ± 0.00	49.93 ± 0.02	51.99 ± 0.12
Oxford-IIIT Pets	81.56 ± 0.00	79.37 ± 0.00	80.90 ± 0.09
PatchCamelyon	50.96 ± 0.00	51.71 ± 0.01	52.39 ± 0.07
Rendered-SST2	54.20 ± 0.00	54.82 ± 0.03	52.94 ± 0.04
RESISC-45	58.51 ± 0.00	59.71 ± 0.01	56.93 ± 0.01
Stanford-Cars	84.93 ± 0.00	85.10 ± 0.02	84.90 ± 0.06
PASCAL VOC-2007	82.09 ± 0.00	82.29 ± 0.00	81.99 ± 0.02
Average	56.97 ± 0.00	**57.51** $\pm$ **0.02**	56.90 ± 0.06
ImageNet-1k	45.84 ± 0.00	**46.06** $\pm$ **0.01**	45.65 ± 0.02

Table 5: Average costs per trained model in terms of energy consumption and equivalent CO_2 emissions (CO_2-eq), compared with the number of trainable parameters (# Param.). All the models were trained with a batch size (BS) of 2816 for 5863 steps, except for CAPIVARA + LoRA + 1500 steps / BS=1000.

Model	# Param.	Energy	CO_2-eq
Gopher	280 B	1,066 MWh	352 tonnes
BLOOM	176 B	433 MWh	25 tonnes
GPT-3	175 B	1,287 MWh	502 tonnes
OPT	175 B	324 MWh	70 tonnes
CAPIVARA	278 M	6.49 kW	0.50 kg
CAPIVARA + LoRA	1.9 M	5.67 kW	0.43 kg
CAPIVARA + LoRA +1500 steps / BS=1000	1.9 M	0.22 kW	0.017 kg

To compare energy consumption between our model and larger language models, we employed the codecarbon tool (Courty et al., 2023). The results are shown in Table 5. As other CLIP-like models do not provide energy and carbon expenditure data, we present a comparison with other large language models for which such data is available in the literature (Maslej et al., 2023). For the baseline model, the energy usage amounted to 6.4 kW, resulting in 0.5 kg of CO_2 equivalent emissions. Applying LoRA and reducing the number of training steps decreased energy consumption to 5.6 kW and 1.8 kW, respectively, resulting in 0.4 kg and 0.1 kg of CO_2 equivalent emissions. These calculations are based on Brazil's energy mix, where hydropower is the primary energy source. This calculation does not include the carbon footprint of the initial pre-training performed by OpenCLIP, but only the training with CAPIVARA. We aim to advance sustainable AI systems development by employing these techniques and optimizing training times.

5 Conclusion

This work demonstrates the potential challenges of fine-tuning multilingual CLIP models within low-resource languages due to noisy annotations. To address this issue, we introduce CAPIVARA, a cost-effective framework that leverages image captioning models to enhance the dataset annotations. We conducted extensive experiments involving dataset filtering, re-annotation, and automatic translation. CAPIVARA effectively boosts OPENCLIP performance for Portuguese texts, achieving state-of-the-art results in many zero-shot tasks. Our findings show the importance of dataset re-annotation and automatic translation.

We also propose optimizing our training pipeline using LiT, including LoRA and gradient checkpointing. Our results show a substantial improvement in Portuguese performance by fine-tuning the pre-trained OPENCLIP in a single GPU for 2 hours, and only 8.5 GB of memory — considerably modest compared to literature. Moreover, we demonstrate that our framework is readily extensible to other low-resource languages.

A direction for future research involves investigating the scalability of the proposed approach in terms of dataset and model size, building upon its success with base models. We also plan to explore different image captioning models and text decoding methods. Due to the cost of generating synthetic captions and translating them to Portuguese, there is interest in automating the process, possibly by improving BLIP2's performance in Portuguese. Besides, due to the success of LoRA, other parameter-efficient fine-tuning can be explored. Lastly, an interesting research question remains open: "how many examples annotated in a low-resource language are necessary to achieve a performance comparable to English?".

Limitations

Model. Unlike other studies that compare models with varying architectures and sizes (Radford et al., 2021; Yang et al., 2022a; Li et al., 2022c; Mu et al., 2022), our research focuses on specific choices: the ViT-B/32 as image encoder and the XLM-Roberta Base as text encoder. Future work will explore different model sizes within our budget and consider alternative fine-tuning approaches, such as Parameter-Efficient Fine-Tuning (PEFT) (Liao et al., 2023).

Data. Recent efforts to adapt CLIP for specific languages (Ko and Gu, 2022; Yang et al., 2022a; Bianchi et al., 2021) have typically used datasets much larger than our study. Investigating scalability using training datasets could reveal the optimal trade-off between cost and performance.

Generating captions in languages such as Portuguese involves two steps: caption generation and machine translation; due to the lack of robust non-English image captioning models. Hence, future research could focus on fine-tuning image captioning models for target languages to streamline the process and improve accuracy. Our study used the BLIP2 model for caption generation, but exploring alternative models could enhance results.

An additional limitation is the prevalent use of machine-translated datasets in various multilingual datasets (Carlsson et al., 2022; Jain et al., 2021; Yang et al., 2022a; Bianchi et al., 2021). However, these datasets may not effectively capture unique expressions, cultural nuances, and proper nouns, leading to bias over-amplification, where biases from the source text become exaggerated in the translated output (Hovy and Prabhumoye, 2021; Prabhumoye et al., 2021; Hovy et al., 2020).

Ethics Statement

CAPIVARA is a cost-efficient framework designed to enhance the performance of multilingual CLIP models in low-resource languages. For this purpose, CAPIVARA augments text data using image captioning and machine translation to generate multiple synthetic captions in low-resource languages, and the training pipeline is optimized with LiT, LoRA, and gradient checkpointing to alleviate the computational cost. Intended to be used for general tasks, the model learns to represent in a joint space texts and images. It can be employed in text-to-image, image-to-text retrieval, and image classification tasks. The developed model is particularly intended for scientific researchers.

Based on known problems with image and language models, the model may present lower performance for under-represented and minority groups (Bender et al., 2021). To adapt the model to low-resource languages, we use texts translated from English; thus, the model does not represent the cultural and local aspects of the countries that speak these target languages. This can lead to linguistic biases and a lack of representativeness for the target groups.

The datasets used comprehend texts from the internet and carry biases; thus, the model may perform differently for data collected from other sources. Also, the datasets may contain data with cultural, political, or religious positioning.

Furthermore, CAPIVARA does not generate any type of data that could pose a risk to human life. However, our model can be adapted for other specific tasks, e.g., image or text generation, which could contribute to generating false information and harming people. CAPIVARA is a framework that aims to improve performance for low-resource languages. However, our results show that despite the significant improvements achieved with CAPIVARA, there is still a considerable gap between the model performance with English texts and texts in low-resource languages. Further research is needed to improve performance across languages and incorporate cultural and linguistic elements into the model.

Since language models require large computational, environmental, and financial resources (Bender et al., 2021), CAPIVARA optimizes its training pipeline, resulting in a smaller carbon footprint than traditional fine-tuning. More details about ethical considerations can be found in Model Cards (Appendix A.6).

Acknowledgements

This project was supported by the Ministry of Science, Technology, and Innovation of Brazil, with resources granted by the Federal Law 8.248 of October 23, 1991, under the PPI-Softex. The project was coordinated by Softex and published as Intelligent agents for mobile platforms based on Cognitive Architecture technology [01245.013778/2020-21].

D.A.B.M. is partially funded by FAPESP 2023/05939-5. A.I.F., T.S., N.S. are partially funded by Centro de Excelência em Inteligência Artificial (CEIA), da Universidade Federal de Goiás (UFG). E.L.C. is partially funded by CNPq 315468/2021-1. H.P. is partially funded by CNPq 304836/2022-2. S.A. is partially funded by CNPq 315231/2020-3, FAPESP 2013/08293-7, 2020/09838-0, Google Award for Inclusion Research 2022.

References

Emily M Bender, Timnit Gebru, Angelina McMillan-Major, and Shmargaret Shmitchell. 2021. On the dangers of stochastic parrots: Can language models be too big? In *ACM Conference on Fairness, Accountability, and Transparency*, pages 610–623.

Federico Bianchi, Giuseppe Attanasio, Raphael Pisoni, Silvia Terragni, Gabriele Sarti, and Sri Lakshmi. 2021. Contrastive language-image pre-training for the italian language. *arXiv:2108.08688*. ArXiv:2108.08688 [cs].

Lukas Bossard, Matthieu Guillaumin, and Luc Van Gool. 2014. Food-101–mining discriminative components with random forests. In *European Conference on Computer Vision*, pages 446–461. Springer.

Fredrik Carlsson, Philipp Eisen, Faton Rekathati, and Magnus Sahlgren. 2022. Cross-lingual and multilingual clip. In *Language Resources and Evaluation Conference*, page 6848–6854.

Tianqi Chen, Bing Xu, Chiyuan Zhang, and Carlos Guestrin. 2016. Training deep nets with sublinear memory cost. *arXiv preprint arXiv:1604.06174*.

Zhongzhi Chen, Guang Liu, Bo-Wen Zhang, Qinghong Yang, and Ledell Wu. 2023. AltCLIP: Altering the language encoder in CLIP for extended language capabilities. In *Findings of the Association for Computational Linguistics*, pages 8666–8682. Association for Computational Linguistics.

Gong Cheng, Junwei Han, and Xiaoqiang Lu. 2017. Remote sensing image scene classification: Benchmark and state of the art. *Proceedings of the IEEE*, 105(10):1865–1883.

Mircea Cimpoi, Subhransu Maji, Iasonas Kokkinos, Sammy Mohamed, and Andrea Vedaldi. 2014. Describing textures in the wild. In *IEEE Conference on Computer Vision and Pattern Recognition*, pages 3606–3613.

Alexis Conneau, Kartikay Khandelwal, Naman Goyal, Vishrav Chaudhary, Guillaume Wenzek, Francisco Guzmán, Edouard Grave, Myle Ott, Luke Zettlemoyer, and Veselin Stoyanov. 2020. Unsupervised cross-lingual representation learning at scale. In *Annual Meeting of the Association for Computational Linguistics*, pages 8440–8451. Association for Computational Linguistics.

Benoit Courty, Victor Schmidt, Goyal-Kamal, Marion-Coutarel, Boris Feld, Jérémy Lecourt, SabAmine, Kngoyal, Mathilde Léval, Alexis Cruveiller, Ouminasara, Franklin Zhao, Aditya Joshi, Alexis Bogroff, Inimaz, Amine Saboni, Hugues De Lavoreille, Niko Laskaris, Edoardo Abati, LiamConnell, Douglas Blank, Ziyao Wang, Armin Catovic, Michał Stęchły, Alencon, JPW, MinervaBooks, SangamSwadiK, Christian Bauer, and M. Hervé. 2023. *mlco2/codecarbon: v2.3.0*. Zenodo.

Jia Deng, Wei Dong, Richard Socher, Li-Jia Li, Kai Li, and Li Fei-Fei. 2009. Imagenet: A large-scale hierarchical image database. In *IEEE Conference on Computer Vision and Pattern Recognition*, pages 248–255. IEEE.

Li Deng. 2012. The MNIST database of handwritten digit images for machine learning research [best of the web]. *IEEE Signal Processing Magazine*, 29(6):141–142.

Gabriel Oliveira dos Santos, Esther Luna Colombini, and Sandra Avila. 2022. #PraCegoVer: A Large Dataset for Image Captioning in Portuguese. *Data*, 7(2).

Alexey Dosovitskiy, Lucas Beyer, Alexander Kolesnikov, Dirk Weissenborn, Xiaohua Zhai, Thomas Unterthiner, Mostafa Dehghani, Matthias Minderer, Georg Heigold, and Sylvain Gelly. 2020. An image is worth 16x16 words: Transformers for image recognition at scale. *arXiv preprint arXiv:2010.11929*.

Mark Everingham, Luc Van Gool, Christopher KI Williams, John Winn, and Andrew Zisserman. 2010. The pascal visual object classes (voc) challenge. *International Journal of Computer Vision*, 88:303–338.

Lijie Fan, Dilip Krishnan, Phillip Isola, Dina Katabi, and Yonglong Tian. 2023. Improving clip training with language rewrites. *arXiv preprint arXiv:2305.20088*.

Li Fei-Fei, Rob Fergus, and Pietro Perona. 2004. Learning generative visual models from few training examples: An incremental bayesian approach tested on 101 object categories. In *Conference on Computer Vision and Pattern Recognition Workshop*, pages 178–178. IEEE.

Jannik Fritsch, Tobias Kuehnl, and Andreas Geiger. 2013. A new performance measure and evaluation benchmark for road detection algorithms. In *International Conference on Intelligent Transportation Systems*, pages 1693–1700. IEEE.

Samir Yitzhak Gadre, Gabriel Ilharco, Alex Fang, Jonathan Hayase, Georgios Smyrnis, Thao Nguyen, Ryan Marten, Mitchell Wortsman, Dhruba Ghosh, and Jieyu Zhang. 2023. Datacomp: In search of the next generation of multimodal datasets. *arXiv preprint arXiv:2304.14108*.

Peng Gao, Shijie Geng, Renrui Zhang, Teli Ma, Rongyao Fang, Yongfeng Zhang, Hongsheng Li, and Yu Qiao. 2021. Clip-adapter: Better vision-language models with feature adapters. *arXiv preprint arXiv:2110.04544*.

Shijie Geng, Jianbo Yuan, Yu Tian, Yuxiao Chen, and Yongfeng Zhang. 2022. Hiclip: Contrastive language-image pretraining with hierarchy-aware attention. In *The Eleventh International Conference on Learning Representations*.

Ian J Goodfellow, Dumitru Erhan, Pierre Luc Carrier, Aaron Courville, Mehdi Mirza, Ben Hamner, Will Cukierski, Yichuan Tang, David Thaler, and Dong-Hyun Lee. 2013. Challenges in representation learning: A report on three machine learning contests. In *International Conference on Neural Information Processing*, pages 117–124. Springer.

Patrick Helber, Benjamin Bischke, Andreas Dengel, and Damian Borth. 2019. Eurosat: A novel dataset and deep learning benchmark for land use and land cover classification. *IEEE Journal of Selected Topics in Applied Earth Observations and Remote Sensing*, 12(7):2217–2226.

Dirk Hovy, Federico Bianchi, and Tommaso Fornaciari. 2020. "you sound just like your father" commercial machine translation systems include stylistic biases. In *58th Annual Meeting of the Association for Computational Linguistics*, pages 1686–1690.

Dirk Hovy and Shrimai Prabhumoye. 2021. Five sources of bias in natural language processing. *Language and Linguistics Compass*, 15(8):e12432.

Edward J Hu, Phillip Wallis, Zeyuan Allen-Zhu, Yuanzhi Li, Shean Wang, Lu Wang, and Weizhu Chen. 2021. Lora: Low-rank adaptation of large language models. In *International Conference on Learning Representations*.

Gabriel Ilharco, Mitchell Wortsman, Ross Wightman, Cade Gordon, Nicholas Carlini, Rohan Taori, Achal Dave, Vaishaal Shankar, Hongseok Namkoong, John Miller, Hannaneh Hajishirzi, Ali Farhadi, and Ludwig Schmidt. 2021. Openclip.

Aashi Jain, Mandy Guo, Krishna Srinivasan, Ting Chen, Sneha Kudugunta, Chao Jia, Yinfei Yang, and Jason Baldridge. 2021. MURAL: Multimodal, multitask representations across languages. In *Findings of the Association for Computational Linguistics*, page 3449–3463. Association for Computational Linguistics.

Marcin Junczys-Dowmunt, Roman Grundkiewicz, Tomasz Dwojak, Hieu Hoang, Kenneth Heafield, Tom Neckermann, Frank Seide, Ulrich Germann, Alham Fikri Aji, Nikolay Bogoychev, André F. T. Martins, and Alexandra Birch. 2018. Marian: Fast neural machine translation in C++. In *ACL 2018, System Demonstrations*, pages 116–121. Association for Computational Linguistics.

Douwe Kiela, Hamed Firooz, Aravind Mohan, Vedanuj Goswami, Amanpreet Singh, Pratik Ringshia, and Davide Testuggine. 2020. The hateful memes challenge: Detecting hate speech in multimodal memes. *Advances in Neural Information Processing Systems*, 33:2611–2624.

Byungsoo Ko and Geonmo Gu. 2022. Large-scale bilingual language-image contrastive learning. *arXiv:2203.14463*. ArXiv:2203.14463 [cs].

Jonathan Krause, Michael Stark, Jia Deng, and Li Fei-Fei. 2013. 3d object representations for fine-grained categorization. In *IEEE International Conference on Computer Vision Workshops*, pages 554–561.

Alex Krizhevsky and Geoffrey Hinton. 2009. Learning multiple layers of features from tiny images. Technical report, Toronto, ON, Canada.

Chunyuan Li, Haotian Liu, Liunian Li, Pengchuan Zhang, Jyoti Aneja, Jianwei Yang, Ping Jin, Houdong Hu, Zicheng Liu, and Yong Jae Lee. 2022a. Elevater: A benchmark and toolkit for evaluating language-augmented visual models. *Advances in Neural Information Processing Systems*, 35:9287–9301.

Junnan Li, Dongxu Li, Silvio Savarese, and Steven Hoi. 2023. Blip-2: Bootstrapping language-image pre-training with frozen image encoders and large language models. *arXiv:2301.12597*. ArXiv:2301.12597 [cs].

Junnan Li, Dongxu Li, Caiming Xiong, and Steven Hoi. 2022b. Blip: Bootstrapping language-image pre-training for unified vision-language understanding and generation. In *International Conference on Machine Learning*, pages 12888–12900. PMLR.

Yangguang Li, Feng Liang, Lichen Zhao, Yufeng Cui, Wanli Ouyang, Jing Shao, Fengwei Yu, and Junjie Yan. 2022c. Supervision exists everywhere: A data efficient contrastive language-image pre-training paradigm. In *International Conference on Learning Representations*.

Baohao Liao, Yan Meng, and Christof Monz. 2023. Parameter-efficient fine-tuning without introducing new latency. In *Annual Meeting of the Association for Computational Linguistics*.

Tsung-Yi Lin, Michael Maire, Serge Belongie, James Hays, Pietro Perona, Deva Ramanan, Piotr Dollár, and C Lawrence Zitnick. 2014. Microsoft coco: Common objects in context. In *European Conference on Computer Vision*, pages 740–755. Springer.

Subhransu Maji, Esa Rahtu, Juho Kannala, Matthew Blaschko, and Andrea Vedaldi. 2013. Fine-grained visual classification of aircraft. *arXiv preprint arXiv:1306.5151*.

Nestor Maslej, Loredana Fattorini, Erik Brynjolfsson, John Etchemendy, Katrina Ligett, Terah Lyons, James Manyika, Helen Ngo, Juan Carlos Niebles, Vanessa Parli, Yoav Shoham, Russell Wald, Jack Clark, and Raymond Perrault. 2023. The AI Index 2023 Annual Report. Technical report, AI Index Steering Committee, Institute for Human-Centered AI, Stanford University.

Margaret Mitchell, Simone Wu, Andrew Zaldivar, Parker Barnes, Lucy Vasserman, Ben Hutchinson, Elena Spitzer, Inioluwa Deborah Raji, and Timnit Gebru. 2019. Model cards for model reporting. In *Proceedings of the conference on fairness, accountability, and transparency*, pages 220–229.

Norman Mu, Alexander Kirillov, David Wagner, and Saining Xie. 2022. Slip: Self-supervision meets language-image pre-training. In *European Conference on Computer Vision*, pages 529–544. Springer.

Thao Nguyen, Samir Yitzhak Gadre, Gabriel Ilharco, Sewoong Oh, and Ludwig Schmidt. 2023. Improving multimodal datasets with image captioning. *arXiv preprint arXiv:2307.10350*.

Maria-Elena Nilsback and Andrew Zisserman. 2008. Automated flower classification over a large number of classes. In *Sixth Indian Conference on Computer Vision, Graphics & Image Processing*, pages 722–729. IEEE.

Aaron van den Oord, Yazhe Li, and Oriol Vinyals. 2018. Representation learning with contrastive predictive coding. *arXiv preprint arXiv:1807.03748*.

Omkar M Parkhi, Andrea Vedaldi, Andrew Zisserman, and CV Jawahar. 2012. Cats and dogs. In *IEEE Conference on Computer Vision and Pattern Recognition*, pages 3498–3505. IEEE.

Bryan A. Plummer, Liwei Wang, Chris M. Cervantes, Juan C. Caicedo, Julia Hockenmaier, and Svetlana Lazebnik. 2017. Flickr30k entities: Collecting region-to-phrase correspondences for richer image-to-sentence models. *International Journal of Computer Vision*, 123(1):74–93.

Shrimai Prabhumoye, Brendon Boldt, Ruslan Salakhutdinov, and Alan W Black. 2021. Case study: Deontological ethics in NLP. In *Conference of the North American Chapter of the Association for Computational Linguistics: Human Language Technologies*, pages 3784–3798. Association for Computational Linguistics.

Alec Radford, Jong Wook Kim, Chris Hallacy, Aditya Ramesh, Gabriel Goh, Sandhini Agarwal, Girish Sastry, Amanda Askell, Pamela Mishkin, and Jack Clark. 2021. Learning transferable visual models from natural language supervision. In *International Conference on Machine Learning*, pages 8748–8763. PMLR.

Shibani Santurkar, Yann Dubois, Rohan Taori, Percy Liang, and Tatsunori Hashimoto. 2023. Is a caption worth a thousand images? a study on representation learning. In *The Eleventh International Conference on Learning Representations*.

Christoph Schuhmann, Romain Beaumont, Richard Vencu, Cade Gordon, Ross Wightman, Mehdi Cherti, Theo Coombes, Aarush Katta, Clayton Mullis, and Mitchell Wortsman. 2022. Laion-5b: An open large-scale dataset for training next generation image-text models. *Advances in Neural Information Processing Systems*, 35:25278–25294.

Piyush Sharma, Nan Ding, Sebastian Goodman, and Radu Soricut. 2018. Conceptual captions: A cleaned, hypernymed, image alt-text dataset for automatic image captioning. In *56th Annual Meeting of the Association for Computational Linguistics (Volume 1: Long Papers)*, pages 2556–2565.

Johannes Stallkamp, Marc Schlipsing, Jan Salmen, and Christian Igel. 2011. The german traffic sign recognition benchmark: a multi-class classification competition. In *International Joint Conference on Neural Networks*, pages 1453–1460. IEEE.

Bastiaan S Veeling, Jasper Linmans, Jim Winkens, Taco Cohen, and Max Welling. 2018. Rotation equivariant cnns for digital pathology. In *21st International Conference on Medical Image Computing and Computer Assisted Intervention*, pages 210–218. Springer.

Jue Wang, Haofan Wang, Jincan Deng, Weijia Wu, and Debing Zhang. 2021. Efficientclip: Efficient cross-modal pre-training by ensemble confident learning and language modeling. *arXiv preprint arXiv:2109.04699*.

Peng Xu, Wenqi Shao, Kaipeng Zhang, Peng Gao, Shuo Liu, Meng Lei, Fanqing Meng, Siyuan Huang, Yu Qiao, and Ping Luo. 2023. LVLM-eHub: A comprehensive evaluation benchmark for large vision-language models. *arXiv preprint arXiv:2306.09265*.

An Yang, Junshu Pan, Junyang Lin, Rui Men, Yichang Zhang, Jingren Zhou, and Chang Zhou. 2022a. Chinese clip: Contrastive vision-language pretraining in chinese. *arXiv:2211.01335*. ArXiv:2211.01335 [cs].

Jinyu Yang, Jiali Duan, Son Tran, Yi Xu, Sampath Chanda, Liqun Chen, Belinda Zeng, Trishul Chilimbi, and Junzhou Huang. 2022b. Vision-language pre-training with triple contrastive learning. In *IEEE/CVF Conference on Computer Vision and Pattern Recognition*, pages 15671–15680.

Xiaohua Zhai, Xiao Wang, Basil Mustafa, Andreas Steiner, Daniel Keysers, Alexander Kolesnikov, and Lucas Beyer. 2022. Lit: Zero-shot transfer with locked-image text tuning. In *IEEE/CVF Conference on Computer Vision and Pattern Recognition*, page 18102–18112, New Orleans, LA, USA. IEEE.

A Appendix

Authors' Contributions

G.O.S., D.A.B.M., and A.I.F. collaborated on dataset translation, designing and implementing the proposed pipeline, analyzing the results, and writing the manuscript. G.O.S. also conducted experiments related to dataset filtering, re-annotation, translation, and low-resource languages. D.A.B.M. worked on constructing training datasets, focused on experiments to optimize the pipeline and conducted a carbon footprint analysis. A.I.F. executed inferences for zero-shot image classification. In collaboration with G.O.S., D.A.B.M., and A.I.F., J.S. wrote the Ethics Statement and Model Cards sections. L.P. helped in the result analysis. P.B. contributed to dataset translation. T.S. helped in constructing training datasets. H.M. contributed to the discussion with the team and the result analysis. N.S. advised A.I.F. and T.S. throughout all tasks. E.C. advised G.O.S. throughout all tasks. H.P. advised the team on all tasks and contributed to the writing process. S.A. served as the principal advisor of the team, providing guidance on all tasks and contributing to the writing process. All authors reviewed the manuscript and provided critical feedback to enhance its quality.

A.1 Hyperparameters

To facilitate the reproducibility of the work, we present Tables A1 and A2. These tables contain the hyperparameters used for the best models evaluated in the different experiments. Table A1 contains only the hyperparameters used in the fine-tuning of the OPENCLIP model for Portuguese. Table A2 considers the hyperparameters with the LoRA-tuning for the models with optimizations and 1500 steps, in Portuguese, Hindi and Xhosa.

Table A1: Hyperparameters used in the fine-tuning.

Hyperparameters	Value
Batch size	2816
Maximum token length	77
Optimizer	Adam
Weight decay	0.2
Adam ϵ	1e-8
Adam β	[0.9, 0.98]
Learning rate schedule	CosineWarmupLR
Maximum learning rate	5e-7
Minimum learning rate	1e-7
# Steps	5863

Table A2: Hyperparameters used in LoRA-tuning.

Hyperparameters	Value
LoRA r	8
LoRA Alpha	8
LoRA dropout	0
bias	None
Target modules	(query, value)
Modules to save	projection
Batch size	1000
Maximum token length	77
Optimizer	Adam
Weight decay	0.2
Adam ϵ	1e-8
Adam β	[0.9, 0.98]
Learning rate schedule	CosineWarmupLR
Maximum learning rate	1e-5
Minimum learning rate	1e-6
# Steps	1500

A.2 Results on ELEVATER and ImageNet-1k

In our supplementary experiments on ELEVATER and ImageNet-1k benchmarks, summarized in Table A3, we consistently observe that our approach outperforms the baseline model across various setups, with the exception of CAPIVARA + Opt. This suggests that more training steps might be necessary to fully leverage LoRA's potential in fine-tuning. Furthermore, Table A3 reveals the effect of caption generation and filtering on the efficacy of our method. By analyzing the scenarios with synthetic captions, one can note that training with multiple captions per image outperforms training on only OPENCLIP + Fine-tuning both with or without filtering. Notably, the optimal configuration involves training with CAPIVARA on CC3M-Filtered, resulting in a performance boost of 0.6 *pp.* over the baseline. Still, similar to the cross-modal retrieval in Sec. A.3.1, we do not observe a significant performance gain by augmenting the number of generated captions. Table A4 provides the specific metrics for each dataset in ELEVATER benchmark.

Figure A1 presents the difference in performance between fine-tuning with CAPIVARA and the baseline, OPENCLIP. It can be noted that the majority of datasets exhibit positive differences in performance, indicating a favorable improvement over the baseline with CAPIVARA. Notably, the model trained with CAPIVARA led to substantial improvements of 5.53 and 5.15 *pp.* in two datasets, namely KITTI-Distance and MNIST, respectively. However, it is important to acknowledge instances where the performance of our model under this configuration falls short. Noteworthy cases include the Oxford-IIIT Pets dataset, encompassing 37 distinct

Table A3: Results on ELEVATER benchmark. Ablation without LoRA and with LoRA.

Dataset	OpenCLIP (Baseline)	OpenCLIP + Fine-tuning	OpenCLIP + Fine-tuning (CC3M-Filtered)	CAPIVARA (CC3M-Filtered)	CAPIVARA	CAPIVARA + 5 synth. captions	CAPIVARA + 1 synth. caption	OpenCLIP + Fine-tuning + LoRA	CAPIVARA + LoRA	CAPIVARA + Opt.
Caltech-101	84.53 ±0.00	82.50 ±0.01	82.23 ±0.01	82.90 ±0.00	82.97 ±0.03	82.66 ±0.00	82.87 ±0.01	83.06 ±0.07	83.70 ±0.01	83.68 ±0.02
CIFAR-10	93.99 ±0.00	94.10 ±0.00	93.93 ±0.00	93.94 ±0.00	93.85 ±0.00	93.87 ±0.00	93.96 ±0.00	94.05 ±0.01	93.96 ±0.01	93.93 ±0.03
CIFAR-100	68.44 ±0.00	69.13 ±0.01	68.98 ±0.01	69.33 ±0.01	69.37 ±0.01	69.37 ±0.01	69.27 ±0.01	69.07 ±0.00	68.97 ±0.01	68.87 ±0.01
Country-211	17.82 ±0.00	17.80 ±0.01	17.73 ±0.01	17.63 ±0.01	17.61 ±0.00	17.79 ±0.00	17.78 ±0.00	17.63 ±0.00	17.36 ±0.02	17.32 ±0.02
DTD	41.17 ±0.00	42.36 ±0.03	42.59 ±0.03	42.59 ±0.05	42.34 ±0.04	42.62 ±0.03	42.61 ±0.00	41.52 ±0.05	41.95 ±0.05	41.79 ±0.07
EuroSAT	47.16 ±0.00	50.45 ±0.04	50.51 ±0.02	48.14 ±0.03	47.77 ±0.02	49.19 ±0.05	50.03 ±0.03	48.21 ±0.02	48.53 ±0.08	48.85 ±0.12
FER-2013	48.65 ±0.00	46.08 ±0.03	46.78 ±0.02	46.93 ±0.03	46.68 ±0.05	46.80 ±0.01	46.44 ±0.01	47.93 ±0.01	47.00 ±0.06	46.85 ±0.13
FGVC-Aircraft	26.30 ±0.00	25.56 ±0.02	25.70 ±0.01	25.52 ±0.04	25.49 ±0.01	25.74 ±0.02	25.70 ±0.01	26.45 ±0.01	26.23 ±0.03	25.54 ±0.09
Food-101	65.06 ±0.00	63.83 ±0.00	64.27 ±0.01	64.54 ±0.01	64.58 ±0.01	64.52 ±0.00	64.21 ±0.02	64.52 ±0.01	64.67 ±0.00	64.46 ±0.00
GTSRB	43.27 ±0.00	46.06 ±0.02	46.95 ±0.01	46.81 ±0.03	46.34 ±0.01	46.33 ±0.03	46.62 ±0.02	44.64 ±0.01	44.88 ±0.06	44.66 ±0.06
Hateful-Memes	56.50 ±0.00	56.06 ±0.01	56.25 ±0.01	56.09 ±0.01	56.17 ±0.00	55.98 ±0.01	56.03 ±0.00	57.01 ±0.01	56.64 ±0.02	56.81 ±0.03
KITTI-Distance	28.41 ±0.00	30.80 ±0.00	30.24 ±0.11	33.19 ±0.11	33.94 ±0.13	32.21 ±0.00	29.96 ±0.00	26.30 ±0.00	28.36 ±0.07	28.27 ±0.11
MNIST	54.99 ±0.00	53.64 ±0.04	54.83 ±0.02	61.86 ±0.02	60.14 ±0.04	59.57 ±0.01	56.06 ±0.03	55.68 ±0.04	55.37 ±0.06	55.00 ±0.10
Oxford Flowers-102	50.88 ±0.00	49.98 ±0.00	49.72 ±0.03	49.74 ±0.02	49.93 ±0.02	50.03 ±0.02	50.07 ±0.00	51.26 ±0.01	51.91 ±0.04	51.99 ±0.12
Oxford-IIIT Pets	81.56 ±0.00	79.52 ±0.02	80.69 ±0.01	79.60 ±0.03	79.37 ±0.00	79.24 ±0.02	79.46 ±0.01	81.29 ±0.02	81.24 ±0.03	80.90 ±0.09
PatchCamelyon	50.96 ±0.00	57.15 ±0.01	55.70 ±0.01	51.93 ±0.00	51.71 ±0.01	52.56 ±0.03	55.49 ±0.02	52.86 ±0.02	52.23 ±0.01	52.39 ±0.07
Rendered-SST2	54.20 ±0.00	53.05 ±0.04	53.82 ±0.09	53.67 ±0.03	54.82 ±0.03	54.35 ±0.03	53.03 ±0.03	53.47 ±0.03	53.14 ±0.07	52.94 ±0.04
RESISC-45	58.51 ±0.00	58.78 ±0.01	58.92 ±0.02	59.56 ±0.01	59.71 ±0.01	59.25 ±0.02	58.88 ±0.01	57.06 ±0.00	57.21 ±0.02	56.93 ±0.01
Stanford-Cars	84.93 ±0.00	85.00 ±0.01	85.04 ±0.01	85.10 ±0.00	85.10 ±0.02	85.08 ±0.01	85.08 ±0.01	85.35 ±0.02	84.99 ±0.03	84.90 ±0.06
PASCAL VOC-2007	82.09 ±0.00	82.73 ±0.00	82.31 ±0.00	82.24 ±0.01	82.29 ±0.00	82.39 ±0.00	82.67 ±0.01	82.35 ±0.00	82.00 ±0.01	81.99 ±0.02
Average	56.97 ±0.00	57.23 ±0.02	57.36 ±0.02	57.57 ±0.02	57.51 ±0.02	57.48 ±0.02	57.31 ±0.01	56.99 ±0.02	57.02 ±0.03	56.90 ±0.06
ImageNet-1k	45.84 ±0.00	46.23 ±0.01	46.32 ±0.02	46.09 ±0.00	46.06 ±0.01	46.19 ±0.00	46.33 ±0.01	45.89 ±0.01	45.90 ±0.01	45.65 ±0.02

Table A4: Details of the image classification datasets on the ELEVATER benchmark.

Dataset	#Labels	Test Size	Metric
Caltech-101 (Fei-Fei et al., 2004)	101	6,084	Mean-per-class
CIFAR-10 (Krizhevsky and Hinton, 2009)	10	10,000	Accuracy
CIFAR-100 (Krizhevsky and Hinton, 2009)	100	10,000	Accuracy
Country-211 (Radford et al., 2021)	211	21,100	Accuracy
DTD (Cimpoi et al., 2014)	47	1,880	Accuracy
EuroSAT (Helber et al., 2019)	10	5,000	Accuracy
FER-2013 (Goodfellow et al., 2013)	7	3,589	Accuracy
FGVC-Aircraft (Maji et al., 2013)	100	3,333	Mean-per-class
Food-101 (Bossard et al., 2014)	101	25,250	Accuracy
GTSRB (Stallkamp et al., 2011)	43	12,630	Accuracy
Hateful-Memes (Kiela et al., 2020)	2	500	ROC AUC
KITTI-Distance (Fritsch et al., 2013)	4	711	Accuracy
MNIST (Deng, 2012)	10	10,000	Accuracy
Oxford Flowers-102 (Nilsback and Zisserman, 2008)	102	6,149	Mean-per-class
Oxford-IIIT Pets (Parkhi et al., 2012)	37	3,669	Mean-per-class
PatchCamelyon (Veeling et al., 2018)	2	32,768	Accuracy
Rendered-SST2 (Radford et al., 2021)	2	1,821	Accuracy
RESISC-45 (Cheng et al., 2017)	45	25,200	Accuracy
Stanford-Cars (Krause et al., 2013)	196	8,041	Accuracy
Pascal VOC-2007 (Everingham et al., 2010)	20	4,952	11-point mAP
Total	1,151	192,677	-

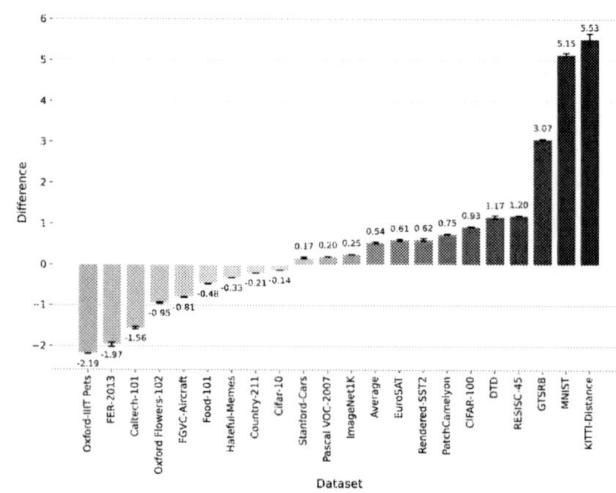

Figure A1: Difference between the OpenCLIP fine-tuned with CAPIVARA on CC3M, and the baseline (OpenCLIP), considering the ELEVATER benchmark and ImageNet-1k.

breeds of cats and dogs, and the FER-2013 dataset, featuring a range of human emotional expressions. Also, our model presented a performance decline on these datasets, with respective decrements of 2.19 and 1.97 *pp.* in comparison to the baseline.

Figures A2 to A5 offer a deeper dive into these observations, presenting normalized confusion matrices that provide granular insights into datasets where CAPIVARA underperformed the baseline. Specifically, Figures A2 and A3 unveil nuances in accurate and erroneous predictions within the Fer-2013 dataset. Notably, the baseline model excels in recognizing neutral expressions, while the fine-tuned model performs well in identifying expressions of sadness. However, the fine-tuned model is also more likely to confound emotions such as sadness and neutral expressions. Figures A4 and A5 present normalized confusion matrices for the Oxford-IIIT Pets Dataset, highlighting the fine-tuned model's tendency to amplify confusion between cat breeds British Shorthair and Russian Blue, as well as dog breeds Leonberger and Newfoundland, leading to reduced overall correctness.

A.3 Ablation Study

A.3.1 Impact of Multiple Captions & Generated Caption Selection

To further validate the contributions of synthetic captions, we analyze the influence of multiple captions per image and how to select proper captions for each image. This latter aspect is related to BLIP2's hallucination, i.e., the model generates a text that does not match the associated image (Xu et al., 2023). The use of these synthetic annotations can introduce noise to the dataset. To address this issue, we implement the Captioning and Filtering

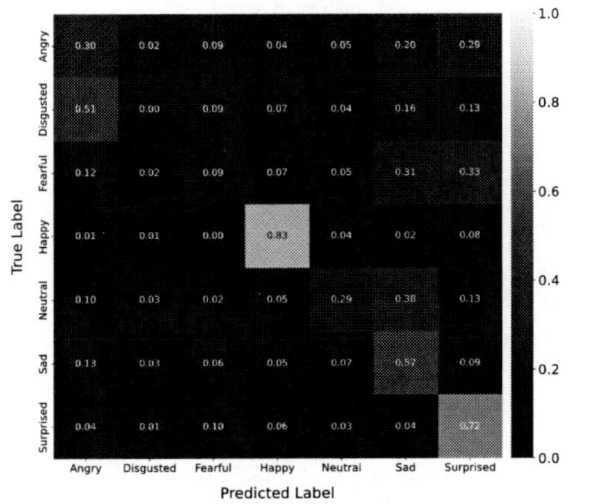

Figure A2: Normalized confusion matrix of the FER-2013 dataset for the OPENCLIP baseline model.

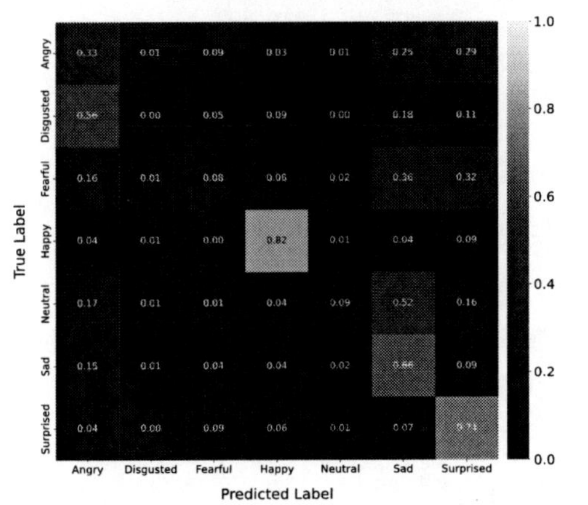

Figure A3: Normalized confusion matrix of the FER-2013 dataset for CAPIVARA.

(CapFilt) (Li et al., 2022b, 2023) method with three different selection strategies: rank-based, threshold-based, and threshold-based + near-duplication removal. All strategies rely on similarity scores produced by OPENCLIP VIT-B/32 XLM-ROBERTA BASE model.

Rank-based: We rank the synthetic captions along with the original descriptions based on the image-text similarity and select the top-k examples; in our tests, we adopted $k = 5$.

Threshold-based: We select the texts among the original and generated captions based on their similarity to the associated image. Then, a caption is selected if the similarity between it and the image is greater than or equal to a given threshold; in this case, the threshold is 0.15.

Threshold-based + near-duplication removal: We first apply the threshold-based filter, and then we remove the near-duplicate captions using the algorithm described in Algorithm 1, keeping a minimum of $k_{min} = 3$ captions per image. Algorithm 1 first computes the text similarity matrix. Then, it computes the cost of removing a text t_i as $c(t_i) = \sum_{j=1}^{B} sim(t_i, t_j), \forall i \neq j$. At each step, it removes the text with the highest cost and updates the cost array. The algorithm stops when all similarity scores are lower than a given threshold or the minimum number of captions is reached. In this way, the algorithm can keep the maximum diversity among the texts.

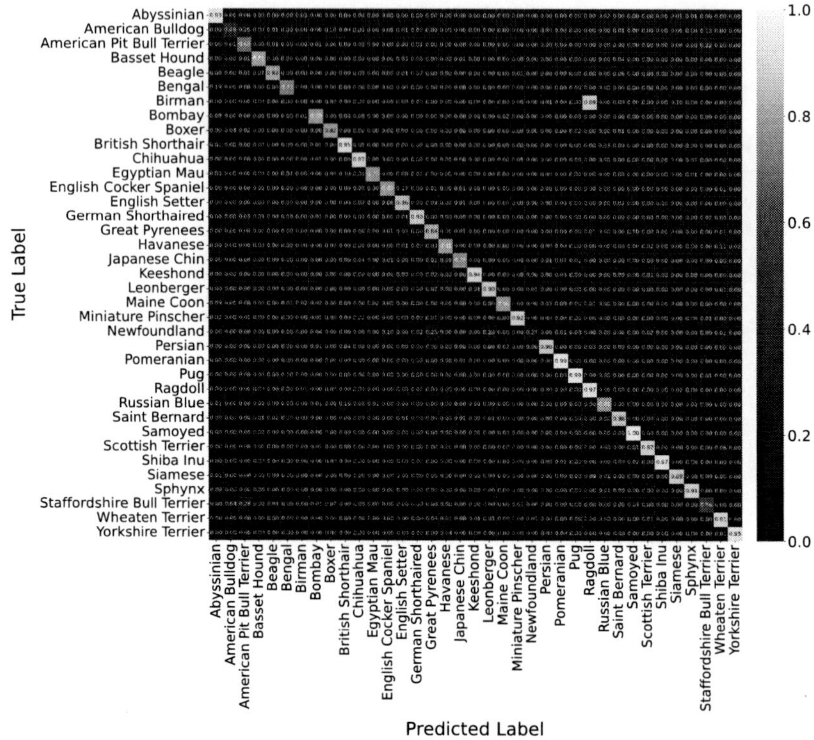

Figure A4: Normalized confusion matrix of the Oxford-IIIT Pets dataset for OPENCLIP baseline model.

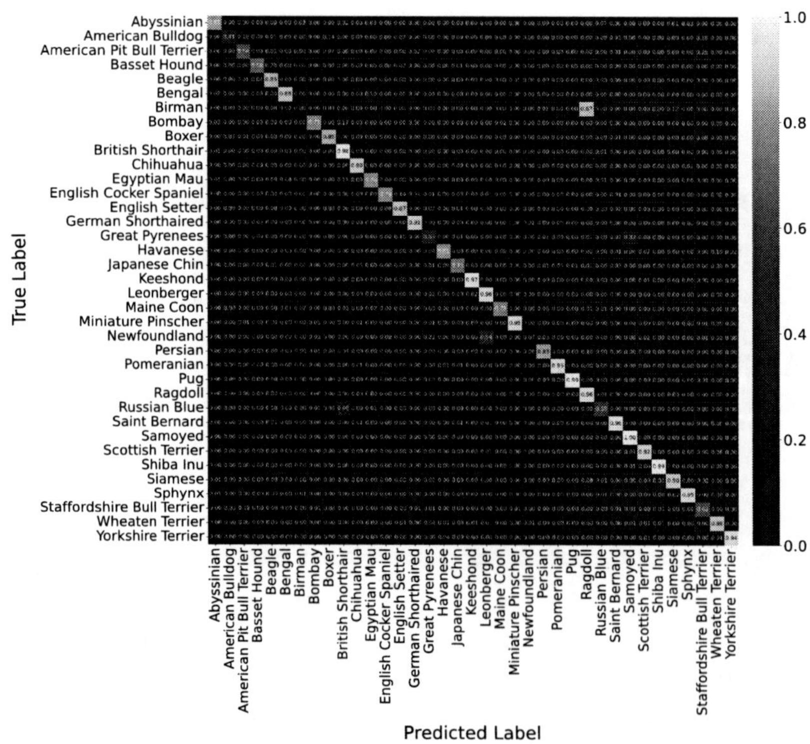

Figure A5: Normalized confusion matrix of the Oxford-IIIT Pets dataset for the OPENCLIP + Fine-tuning model with 10 generated annotations.

```
# captions: image captions
# k_min: minimum number of texts to keep
# thr: maximum similarity between texts
#      allowed

# Remove similar texts keeping the
# maximum diversity among them
def remove_similar(captions, k_min=3,
    thr=0.3):
  if len(captions) < k_min:
    return captions

  sim_matrix = text_similarity(captions)
  n_texts = sim_matrix.shape[0]
  # set the cost in the diagonal to zero
  sim_matrix -= np.eye(n_texts)
  while not (sim_matrix <= thr).all()
        and n_texts > k_min:
    # compute the cost to remove each
    # text as sum of the similarity
    # between that text and all others.
    cost = sim_matrix.sum(axis=0)

    # remove the text with the highest
    # cost
    i = np.argmax(cost)

    # set the cost of the texts to be
    # removed to zero
    sim_matrix[i, :] = 0
    sim_matrix[:, i] = 0
    n_texts -= 1

  # compute the final cost for all texts
  cost = sim_matrix.sum(axis=0)
  # all texts whose cost is zero will be
  # removed
  remove_indices = np.where(cost==0)[0]
  # return the filtered texts
  return
   [caption
    for i,caption in enumerate(captions)
              if i not in remove_indices]
```

Algorithm 1: Python-like pseudocode of near-duplicate text removal algorithm.

From a thorough analysis of the results exhibited in Table A5, we note that none of the caption selection strategies significantly impacted the model performance. All strategies performed similarly to CAPIVARA with no caption selection. Specifically, the threshold-based caption selection strategy performed slightly better than the others but still in pair with CAPIVARA. This result suggests that BLIP2 is effective in generating captions related to images and, because of this, the caption selection methods did not affect the final performance. Nevertheless, Figure A8 and the results in Table A6 reveal that BLIP2 produces slightly different texts. Therefore, generating multiple captions per image has a limited effect on text augmentation. Note that adding 10 captions slightly improved compared to adding just one caption per image. Therefore, it is necessary to explore methods for generating more diverse texts, for instance, testing different sampling methods and other image captioning models, because we only used BLIP2 with default parameters.

Table A5: Experimental results for caption selection strategies. In this table, "threshold-based near-duplication", "threshold-based", and "rank-based" refer to caption selection methods, whereas CAPIVARA does not consider any caption selection strategy. For each setting, we report the average and the standard deviation of mean recall.

	Flickr30k		MS COCO		PraCegoVer	
Method	txt2img	img2txt	txt2img	img2txt	txt2img	img2txt
OPENCLIP (Baseline)	76.23	87.93	52.62	66.55	65.36	69.43
OPENCLIP + Fine-tuning	78.42 ± 0.02	90.02 ± 0.05	54.77 ± 0.01	70.06 ± 0.01	63.79 ± 0.01	60.10 ± 0.00
Threshold-based near-duplication	79.59 ± 0.01	90.02 ± 0.02	56.37 ± 0.01	71.14 ± 0.01	66.72 ± 0.01	65.33 ± 0.01
Threshold-based	79.65 ± 0.03	89.72 ± 0.02	56.39 ± 0.02	71.11 ± 0.02	66.77 ± 0.01	65.47 ± 0.01
Rank-based	79.60 ± 0.01	89.13 ± 0.04	56.32 ± 0.01	70.64 ± 0.02	66.85 ± 0.00	65.96 ± 0.01
CAPIVARA	79.56 ± 0.01	89.95 ± 0.04	56.27 ± 0.01	71.24 ± 0.01	66.40 ± 0.01	64.75 ± 0.01

Table A6: Impact of multiple captions. This table presents the results of models trained with different numbers of synthetic captions translated into Portuguese. We report the average and the standard deviation of mean recall for each setting across Flickr30k, MS COCO, and PraCegoVer datasets.

	Flickr30k		MS COCO		PraCegoVer	
Method	txt2img	img2txt	txt2img	img2txt	txt2img	img2txt
OPENCLIP (Baseline)	76.23	87.93	52.62	66.55	65.36	**69.43**
OPENCLIP + Fine-tuning	78.42 ± 0.02	90.02 ± 0.05	54.77 ± 0.01	70.06 ± 0.01	63.79 ± 0.01	60.10 ± 0.00
CAPIVARA + 10 synth. captions	**79.56 ± 0.01**	**89.95 ± 0.04**	**56.27 ± 0.01**	**71.24 ± 0.01**	**66.40 ± 0.01**	64.75 ± 0.01
CAPIVARA + 5 synth. captions	79.17 ± 0.02	90.72 ± 0.02	55.62 ± 0.01	70.95 ± 0.00	65.18 ± 0.01	62.14 ± 0.01
CAPIVARA + 1 synth. caption	79.46 ± 0.01	90.02 ± 0.05	56.26 ± 0.01	71.27 ± 0.01	66.09 ± 0.01	63.95 ± 0.01

A.3.2 Impact of Increasing the Batch Size

Among the different hyperparameters used to train the model, batch size has significant potential to improve model results. As batch size increases, more examples are observed per training step, and more examples might be discriminated by contrastive learning. Therefore, to determine the optimal batch size to use in our method, we conducted experiments fixing the number of steps in 5863 and varying this value considering our GPU memory limitation. We experimented three different batch sizes: 1000, 2816, and 4300. Each setting was tested with traditional fine-tuning and with CAPIVARA, the results are presented in Table A7.

Overall, we do not observe a significant gain in increasing the batch size. Intriguingly, in the

Table A7: Comparison between different batch sizes in fine-tuning and CAPIVARA settings.

		Flickr30k		MS COCO		PraCegoVer	
Method	Batch size	txt2img	img2txt	txt2img	img2txt	txt2img	img2txt
OpenCLIP + Fine-tunning	1000	78.68 ± 0.02	90.02 ± 0.02	54.45 ± 0.01	69.06 ± 0.01	66.38 ± 0.01	66.49 ± 0.02
	2816	78.71 ± 0.02	89.85 ± 0.02	54.57 ± 0.00	69.17 ± 0.03	66.44 ± 0.01	66.57 ± 0.01
	4300	78.70 ± 0.01	89.86 ± 0.02	54.62 ± 0.04	69.22 ± 0.02	66.42 ± 0.05	66.76 ± 0.19
CAPIVARA + Opt. (5863 steps)	1000	79.71 ± 0.03	90.51 ± 0.05	55.36 ± 0.03	69.58 ± 0.03	67.00 ± 0.03	68.01 ± 0.01
	2816	79.81 ± 0.03	90.65 ± 0.02	55.56 ± 0.01	69.64 ± 0.04	67.07 ± 0.02	68.14 ± 0.01
	4300	79.87 ± 0.01	90.63 ± 0.04	55.63 ± 0.01	69.70 ± 0.04	67.08 ± 0.01	68.19 ± 0.01

context of CAPIVARA, the performance slightly improves across the datasets as we increase the batch size from 1000 to 2816. However, it declines when we use a batch size of 4300. For this reason, the CAPIVARA models were trained with an average batch size of 2816, while the optimized CAPIVARA models were trained with a batch size of 1000. This study shows that using smaller batches to train the optimized models does not result in significant loss. At the same time, it saves memory and training time.

A.4 Qualitative Analysis

We conducted experiments on Flickr30k for a qualitative analysis of the model's ability in cross-modal retrieval tasks, the outcomes are presented in Figures A6 and A7. Figure A6 shows the result of the image-to-text retrieval task, where the five texts in Portuguese more similar to a given image are retrieved by our model. For the first example, all the texts retrieved describe correctly the image content, which consists of a group of women running in a race. However, in the second example, none of the retrieved text matches the input image. It illustrates the limitations of our model.

Similarly, we analyze qualitatively our model in text-to-image retrieval. In Figure A7, we present four examples of texts and the top-5 images more similar to each of them. We can see that overall the model ranks the correct images on the top. Regarding the other images, although the scene representations match the texts, there is still a lack of details in the images that are not considered by the model, such as the number of people, objects, and colors. This can happen because there are no images that contain all elements from the text within the dataset, and it tries to retrieve the most similar images, or by model limitations. Thus, in the last example, we present an instance in which the model fails. Given the text "Woman and man walking across wooden rope bridge with a caution sign beside it.", the model does not rank the expected image among the top-5 most similar.

A.5 Synthetic Captions Generated by BLIP2

In the process of text augmentation, the BLIP2 model (Li et al., 2023) was used to generate new captions for the images. However, this model presents some issues regarding text generation. For example, it may generate text that does not match the image and repeat words. Several strategies have been used to mitigate these problems in our work. They are best described in Sec. 3. Figure A8 shows three images from CC3M along with their original caption and 10 captions generated with BLIP2.

The first image represents an example where the generated captions are good and diverse, as all captions correctly describe the image, there are no repeated words, and there is a high diversity of words used to describe the scene. The captions generally describe the image and add new elements to the description, although they still contain repetitive structures. In the second example, we present a scenario of good caption and low textual diversity. The captions describe the image, but there is a high level of repetition in the sentence structures. In the third example, we illustrate a case of badly generated captions and low textual diversity. In this example, the model not only shows a lot of word repetition, but also fails to represent the image, hallucinating.

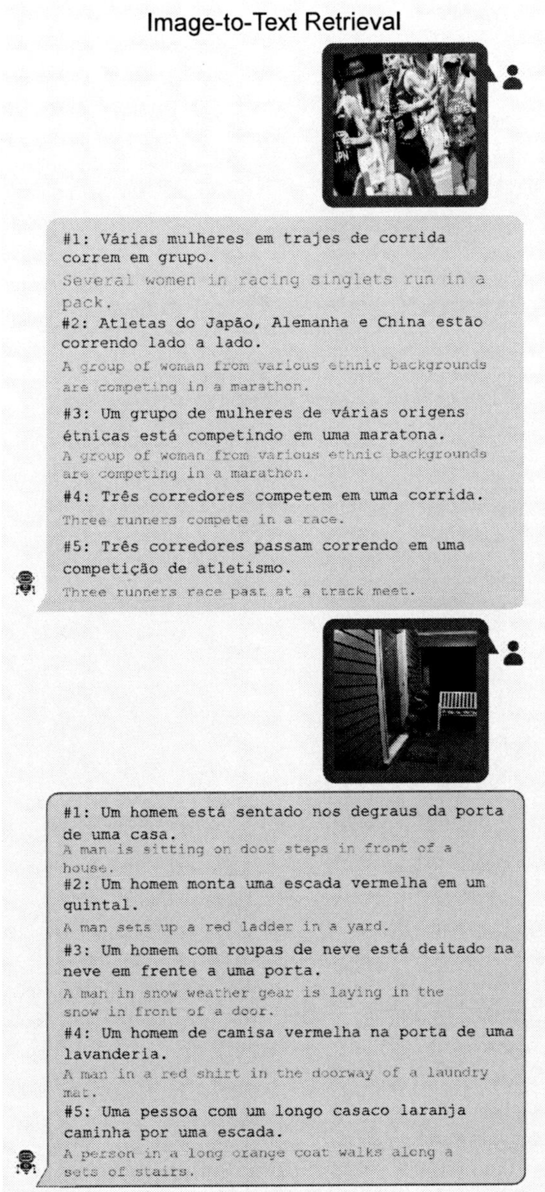

Figure A6: Examples of image-to-text retrieval using CAPIVARA + Opt.

Figure A7: Examples of text-to-image retrieval using CAPIVARA + Opt.

Good captions, high diversity

Original Caption:

a toting airship flying around the blue skies

Generated Captions:

the foreground features 's a large airship with an american flag painted on it - stock image
a photo of airship blimp flying in the sky with palm trees in the background - stock image
a picture of airship flying in the sky with palm trees in the background - stock image
this is a scene depicting airship blimp flying in the sky with palm trees in the background - stock image
an image of airship blimp flying in the sky with palm trees in the background - stock image
portrait of a airship flying in the sky with palm trees in the background - stock image
this image captures a moment of a blimp flying in the sky with palm trees in the background - stock image
a painting of airship with american flag flying in the sky - stock image
an art of airship flying in the sky with palm trees in the background - stock image
the picture shows the american flag blimp flying in the sky with palm trees in the background - stock image

---

Good captions, low diversity

Original Caption:

a teenager from the rural town of person , was shocked to find a koala behind the wheel.

Generated Captions:

the foreground features koalas sitting in the driver's seat of a vehicle
a photo of koala sitting on the steering wheel of a vehicle
a picture of a koala sitting on the steering wheel of a vehicle
this is a scene depicting of a koala sitting on the steering wheel of a vehicle
an image of koala sitting on the steering wheel of a vehicle
portrait of a a koala sitting on the steering wheel of a vehicle
this image captures a moment of a koala sitting in the driver's seat of a vehicle
a painting of of a koala sitting on the steering wheel of a vehicle
an art of koala sitting on the steering wheel of a vehicle
the picture shows a koala sitting in the driver's seat of a vehicle

---

Bad captions, low diversity

Original Caption:

waterfall on a small stream.

Generated Captions:

the foreground features a man holding a bird in his hand
a photo of of a man holding a bird in his hand
a picture of a man holding a bird in his hand
this is a scene depicting of a person holding a bird
an image of of a man holding a bird in his hand
portrait of a of a man holding a bird in the water
this image captures a moment of a man holding a bird in the water
a painting of a man holding a bird in the water
an art of of a man holding a bird in the water
the picture shows a man holding a bird in the water

Figure A8: Examples of images with synthetic captions generated by BLIP2.

A.6 Model Cards

This section was done using the Model Cards for Model Reporting (Mitchell et al., 2019) tool.

Model Details

- Developed by researchers from the Natural Language Processing Group of the Artificial Intelligence and Cognitive Architectures Hub – H.IAAC.
- CAPIVARA, 2023, v1.
- CAPIVARA is a cost-efficient framework designed to enhance the performance of multilingual CLIP models in low-resource languages.
- CAPIVARA augments text data using image captioning and machine translation to generate multiple synthetic captions in low-resource languages. The training pipeline is optimized with LiT, LoRA, and gradient checkpointing to alleviate the computational cost.
- More information can be found on CAPIVARA's official GitHub `https://github.com/hiaac-nlp/CAPIVARA`.
- For further information or questions, please contact Sandra Avila `avilas@unicamp.br`.

Intended Use

- Intended to be used for general tasks focused on finding a representation in a common space for texts and images. Examples of tasks are image-to-text and text-to-image retrieval and image classification.
- Particularly intended for scientific researchers.
- Not intended to be used with aspects, positions, and cultural values from an under-represented region (e.g., Brazilian memes) due to the lack of representativeness of the datasets used for training. It cannot be used with long texts (more than 77 tokens).

Factors

- Based on known problems with image and language models, potential relevant factors include groups for under-represented and minority people. In order to adapt the model to languages with low resources, texts were initially translated from English; thus, the model does not represent the cultural and geographical aspects of the countries that speak these target languages. The datasets used are made of texts collected from the Internet; therefore, the model may not perform as well for data collected from other sources and may carry biases from the original texts.

Metrics

- Evaluation metrics include Mean Recall, representing the average recall value across the recall@K instances, where K = 1, 5, 10, for cross-modal retrieval, which is the main task of CAPIVARA, and top-1 accuracy metrics for image classification task on ImageNet-1k. Moreover, the ELEVATER benchmark was used for the image classification task, and Appendix A.2 provides the specific metrics used (see Table A4).
- Each experiment was run three times, and the mean and standard deviation were reported for all experiments performed (see Section 4).

Quantitative Analyses

- Quantitative Analyses can be seen in Figure 1 and Section 4.

Evaluation Data

- Evaluation data include Flickr30k, MS COCO, and PraCegoVer datasets for cross-modal retrieval task, and all 20 datasets from ELEVATOR benchmark and ImageNet-1k for image classification task (see Table A3).
- These datasets were chosen because they are the most widely used datasets in the literature, except for PraCegoVer. PraCegoVer is a dataset with images and texts originally in Portuguese that was used precisely to evaluate linguistic and cultural aspects present in the Portuguese language. (NOTE: Data originally in English that has been translated into the target language will be made available with the model).
- See Section 3.2 for more details about data preprocessing.

Training Data

- Training data was CC3M dataset.
- This dataset was chosen because of the amount of example data provided and the better quality of the data. In addition, our limited computing infrastructure for training the model was considered.
- See Section 3.2 for more details about data preprocessing.
- It is possible that the model was trained with data where group distributions are not homogeneous and, therefore, encoded some type of bias.

Ethical Considerations

- CAPIVARA does not deliberately use sensitive data in training. However, since it uses data collected from the Internet consisting of images and annotations about the image's content, it is possible that data with political, religious, or cultural positioning have been used.
- CAPIVARA does not generate any type of data that could pose a risk to human life. However, our model can be adapted for other specific tasks, e.g., image or text generation, which could contribute to generating false information and harming people.
- The model's training data was translated via Google Translate from English into the target language. This can lead to linguistic biases and a lack of representativeness for the target groups.
- CAPIVARA adopts training time optimizers, resulting in a smaller carbon footprint than traditional fine-tuning. Therefore, it presents a better financial and environmental alternative to improve the performance of pre-trained models.

Caveats and Recommendations

- Further work is needed to assess the impact of adding more samples from the target language and how much this brings the performance of the target language closer to English, which currently has the best performances. See Section 5 for more future works.
- People and groups who do not have access to the Internet and, therefore, do not produce digital content were under-represented in the training set. However, CAPIVARA is intended to be applied to languages with low digital resources. CAPIVARA offers the technique to improve performance for low-resource languages, however there is still a gap in performance between English texts and texts in low-resource languages. Future studies are required to improve performance for different languages and include cultural and linguistic aspects of the target language in the model.
- An ideal evaluation dataset would additionally include annotations made in the target language, which also considers cultural and linguistic aspects and has a background of minority and under-represented groups.

- Current literature is constantly evaluating the ethical risks and impacts that vision and language models can have on society. Keeping up with this work is extremely important, as these studies can point to risks and negative impacts that have not yet been considered in this current version of Model Cards.
- Ideally, when using CAPIVARA as a base model for other applications, a study of the ethical impacts of the application should be carried out before it is implemented.
- It is highly recommended to read this Model Cards in conjunction with the article that introduces CAPIVARA, as the article contains detailed information on the entire life cycle of the proposed model.

Code-switching as a cross-lingual Training Signal: an Example with Unsupervised Bilingual Embedding

Félix Gaschi [2,3], **Ilias El Baamrani**[1], **Barbara Gendron**[1], **Parisa Rastin** [2], **Yannick Toussaint** [2]
[1]École des Mines de Nancy, [2]LORIA, [3] SAS Posos
{felix.gaschi,parisa.rastin,yannick.toussaint}@loria.fr

Abstract

Code-switching is the occurrence of words from different languages in the same utterance. This paper shows that code-switching is largely present in a popular dataset for training word embeddings, and demonstrates that it can be a useful training signal for unsupervised cross-lingual embeddings. `CoSwitchMap`, the proposed method for leveraging this signal, outperforms other unsupervised mapping-based methods for cross-lingual embeddings on two of the three tested language pairs and suggests that code-switching can be a useful training signal for multilingual representations.

1 Introduction

Code-switching occurs when words from multiple languages are used in a single sentence. Some examples of code-switching, randomly sampled from a Wikipedia dump, are shown in Figure 1. While code-switching can be expected in speech data, or in informal writing, this paper shows that it can be found in more formally written data like in Wikipedia, in an amount that is sufficient to use as a training signal for learning fair multilingual representations.

While artificially induced code-switching was already shown to help build cross-lingual embeddings (Xiao and Guo, 2014; Gouws and Søgaard, 2015), this paper investigates whether it is possible to leverage naturally-occurring code-switching for the same objective.

To demonstrate the usefulness of code-switching, this work builds cross-lingual word embeddings using code-switching as a training signal. But rather than the proposed method itself, we believe that the most important part of our contribution is to show that code-switching is present in sufficient amount in a typical monolingual pre-training dataset that it can be used as a cross-lingual training signal, with our proposed method or with another.

Exemple 1 : 1999年歐洲歌唱大賽(eurovision song contest 1999) 為歐洲歌唱大賽之第44屆比賽
Exemple 2 : as a result , " li " (禮) , meaning " ritual " or " etiquette , "governed the conduct of the nobles , whilst " xing " (刑) , the rules of punishment
Exemple 3 : 是一款由鬼游(ghost town games)公司, team 17 行的烹模游. 玩家通多人合作或多角控制, 控制多游角色挑各种房里的机

Figure 1: Examples of code-switching

The experiments in this paper focus on static word embeddings built with FastText (Bojanowski et al., 2016) rather than contextualized ones, obtained with deeper models such as BERT (Devlin et al., 2019). Static embeddings are preferred in this work for their simplicity and because there is already a whole line of work for creating cross-lingual static embeddings (Mikolov et al., 2013a; Conneau et al., 2017, inter alia), whereas pre-training contextualized embeddings require more resource and methods for improving their multilingual properties might not be consistently effective (Wu and Dredze, 2020).

There are several methods to obtain cross-lingual static embeddings. Mikolov et al. (2013a) introduce one of the pioneering methods for supervised alignment that consists of learning a mapping between the source and target language. Following the observation that word translations tend to have similar geometric properties, they leverage parallel data through a bilingual dictionary to learn a linear projection between the two languages. Even if such an approach proved efficient, it still has the drawback of being supervised. This has motivated the emergence of less supervised or even completely unsupervised alignment methods as developed in Conneau et al. (2017). Leveraging isomorphic properties between embedding spaces,

Proceedings of the The 3rd Workshop on Multi-lingual Representation Learning (MRL), pages 208–217
December 7, 2023 ©2023 Association for Computational Linguistics

they describe a method to deduce a bilingual dictionary that provides an accurate word alignment and matches supervised baselines. However, fully unsupervised approaches may not be stable enough as pointed out by Søgaard et al. (2018a). They claim that the reason why unsupervised alignment can sometimes lead to lower performances is that the original embedding spaces are not really isomorphic. In addition, they showed that retrieving identical words in order to form a seed dictionary brings a weak supervision signal which is enough to improve the robustness of the approach.

To evaluate the potential of code-switching as a cross-lingual signal, this work first provides quantitative insights about the presence of code-switching in Wikipedia, showing that it covers a large part of the most frequent words of the studied languages. Thus, this paper proposes `CoSwitchMap` (**Code-Switching**-based bilingual **Mapping**), which uses code-switching as a weak supervision signal to learn bilingual word embeddings for languages in different scripts. `CoSwitchMap` allows to overcome some known limitations of unsupervised mapping-based methods for learning multilingual word embeddings.

2 Related Works

In the following, code-switching will be referred to as the use of words from multiple languages in a single sentence or discourse. This is different from language contamination, which simply refers to the presence of whole sentences from other languages in a supposedly monolingual corpus. With code-switching, two words from different languages can share the same context, contrary to language contamination. According to Blevins and Zettlemoyer (2022), language contamination is almost surely found in large English corpora, and it might explain the cross-lingual transfer abilities of monolingual models. Indeed, even with less than 1% of contamination, supposedly monolingual models based on Transformers (Vaswani et al., 2017) such as BERT (Devlin et al., 2019) or RoBERTa (Liu et al., 2019) reach surprising performances on target languages which are positively correlated to the amount of contaminated data on POS tagging task.

Because token contamination does not combine different languages in the same context, only code-switching is studied in this work. Artificially adding some code-switching is a way to create cross-lingual embeddings. Several approaches were developed in that sense (Xiao and Guo, 2014; Gouws and Søgaard, 2015). They all have in common that some tokens are randomly replaced with their translation in monolingual training data, ensuring that translation pairs keep having the same embedding representation. According to Ruder (2017), pseudo-bilingual corpora and bilingual mapping methods are in fact equivalent because they boil down to optimizing the same objective.

On the other hand, code-switching can improve the pre-training of deep multilingual models. In order to improve the learning of contextual information mostly in mBERT, the multilingual version of BERT, Qin et al. (2020) developed a data augmentation approach by generating sentences with randomly chosen code-switched tokens. This method, used during the fine-tuning step, systematically improves the performances of baseline models on all five tasks and for each pair of languages. With the same goal of achieving language neutrality, Krishnan et al. (2021) also leverage multilingual code-switching within some model training. The main contribution of such methods is to be able to perform cross-lingual generalization with a reasonable amount of parallel data from different languages. The cross-lingual signal used for the cited methods is indeed smaller that the pre-training corpus of mBERT. A similar approach proposed by Yang et al. (2020) outperforms existing Transformer-based models with an enhanced version of the Masked Language Modeling (MLM) task performed during mBERT pre-training. By training on code-switched sentences, the model is expected to learn a cross-lingual embedding.

The previously mentioned methods focus either on multilingual models to improve their cross-lingual generalization or on alignment methods using artificially created code-switching. In this work, the aim is to leverage the code-switching naturally present in a corpus, in order to train alignment methods on static embeddings without any supervised cross-lingual signal. To the best of our knowledge, there isn't any existing method that relies on naturally occurring code-switching to produce multilingual static embeddings.

3 Method

Our goal is (1) to identify code-switching situations in monolingual corpora like Wikipedia, (2) to learn an orthogonal mapping between two monolingual embeddings by applying a modified skip-gram loss to pairs of code-switched words, and (3) to refine this orthogonal mapping with self-learning.

3.1 Identifying code-switching with different scripts

To identify code-switching situations we must find paragraphs that contain words coming from different languages. However, determining whether a word belongs to the vocabulary of one given language is not straightforward. Without resorting to additional resources like a dictionary, the vocabulary of one language can be obtained based on occurrences in a monolingual corpus. However, if this monolingual corpus potentially contains code-switching, the vocabulary we would obtain might not help identify code-switching situations as it might include words from other languages.

If two languages are written using different scripts, most code-switching situations can be extracted by identifying paragraphs where the two scripts occur, using regular expressions with relevant character ranges. This method has, by design, a high recall, as it should only miss some situations where the word from one language is transcribed into the script of the other, which can still be seen as code-switching, or rather script-switching, situations. However, it can lack precision in some cases, because the same script can be used in different languages. For example, when extracting pairs of code-switched words involving English in a Chinese corpus, we might also retrieve German-Chinese pairs.

In our experiments, this code-switching extraction method allows us to obtain pairs of code-switched words to use as a weak supervision signal for `CoSwitchMap`.

3.2 Code-switching pairs as a supervision signal

We refer to code-switching pairs as pairs of words from two different languages present in the same context. The goal is to leverage these pairs as a multilingual signal to learn a mapping matrix W that allows us to project the words of a source language (src) to the target language (tgt). It must be noted that multi-word expressions are not getting a particular treatment, like in most word embedding algorithms. Code-switching pairs are pairs of words from different scripts found in the same sliding window of context. A multi-word expression like "Eurovision Song Contest" (cf. Figure 1) is broken down and each word that composes it will appear individually in pairs with Chinese neighboring words.

Given two monolingual embeddings for source and target languages obtained with skip-gram (Mikolov et al., 2013b) or a variant like FastText (Bojanowski et al., 2016), we can retrieve two embedding matrices for each language: the central embedding of each word x_i, i.e. the embedding that is usually used in downstream application, and the context embedding $\tilde{x}_j$, used to embed context words in the skip-gram algorithm. The goal is to continue the training of skip-gram with code-switched words in order to learn a matrix W mapping the source embedding x_i^{src} to the target embedding x_j^{tgt}. During the training, the W matrix will be either applied to the context word or central word depending on the training pair. Thus, we freeze the embedding matrices and initialize W with the identity matrix before training it.

The original monolingual skip-gram loss from (Mikolov et al., 2013b) is the following :

$$L = -\frac{1}{|C|} \sum_{w_i \in C} \sum_{w_j \in \mathcal{N}(w_i)} \log P(w_j|w_i) \quad (1)$$

Where C is the corpus, w_i is a central word from the corpus, and w_j is a word found in $\mathcal{N}(w_i)$, the context window of the central word. $P(w_j|w_i)$ is computed with negative sampling as :

$$\begin{aligned} \log P(w_j|w_i) &= \log \sigma(\tilde{x}_j^\top x_i) \\ &+ \sum_{w_k \sim P_V}^{n} \log \sigma(-\tilde{x}_k^\top x_i) \end{aligned} \quad (2)$$

x_i is the embedding of w_i and $\tilde{x}_j$ is the context embedding of w_j. n negative examples of context words w_k are sampled randomly from a distribution P over the vocabulary V. Minimizing L in Equation 1 is maximizing the similarity of x_i with $\tilde{x}_j$ with respect to the similarity of x_i with any other randomly sampled word.

`CoSwitchMap` learns the mapping matrix W with a similar negative sampling loss, but replaces the source word embedding, either central or context, by their projection with W. The initial embedding obtained with skip-gram applied to monolingual corpora is frozen and the modified skip-gram loss is only computed for pairs of code-switched words. For a code-switching pair $(w_i^{\text{src}}, w_j^{\text{tgt}})$, where the central word w_i^{src} is in the source language script, and w_j^{tgt} is a context word in the target language script, The goal is to project w_i^{src} to the target language. The probability $P(w_j^{\text{tgt}}|w_i^{\text{src}})$ becomes:

$$\log P(w_j^{\text{tgt}}|w_i^{\text{src}}) = \log \sigma(\tilde{x}_j^{\text{tgt}\top} W x_i^{\text{src}}) + \sum_{w_k^{\text{tgt}} \sim \mathcal{U}_{V_{\text{tgt}}}}^{n} \log \sigma(-\tilde{x}_k^{\text{tgt}\top} W x_i^{\text{src}}) \quad (3)$$

For the reversed case, where a code-Switching pair $(w_i^{\text{tgt}}, w_j^{\text{src}})$ is given, the central word is in the target language, and the context word in the source language. The mapping matrix must then be applied to the context embedding:

$$\log P(w_j^{\text{src}}|w_i^{\text{tgt}}) = \log \sigma(\tilde{x}_j^{\text{src}\top} W^\top x_i^{\text{tgt}}) + \sum_{w_k^{\text{src}} \sim \mathcal{U}_{V_{\text{src}}}}^{n} \log \sigma(-\tilde{x}_k^{\text{src}\top} W^\top x_i^{\text{tgt}}) \quad (4)$$

By enforcing the orthogonality of W, applying it to the source context embedding is actually equivalent to applying its inverse to the source central embedding. Using an orthogonal matrix also allows to preserve the distance between words from the source language. Thus, during the training steps, we orthogonalize the mapping matrix W after each update of the loss of a training batch as it was done in Conneau et al. (2017):

$$W \leftarrow (1+\beta)W - \beta(WW^T)W \quad (5)$$

Where β is a hyper-parameter, fixed to 0.01 following (Conneau et al., 2017).

3.3 Self-learning

The method from the previous section learns a mapping between two languages which might need some refining as it is obtained from noisy data. Indeed, as mentioned in Section 3.1, the unsupervised extraction of code-switching pairs can produce some unwanted pairs between other languages using the same script. CoSwitchMap thus involves an additional refinement step using self-learning as in many other existing unsupervised mapping-based methods.

For the proposed method, the self-learning procedure of VecMap (Artetxe et al., 2018b) is used, allowing for a controlled comparison with different kinds of initialization. The principle of this self-learning loop is to improve the alignment by iteratively learning a new bilingual dictionary from the previously learned mapping, and then a new mapping from this bilingual dictionary, and so on. In VecMap, each new dictionary is obtained with a nearest-neighbor search, and each new mapping with Procrustes (Artetxe et al., 2018b).

The self-learning procedure needs a seed dictionary to start. CoSwitchMap uses the same nearest-neighbor search as in the further steps of VecMap to calculate a new bilingual dictionary from the W mapping learned with code-switched pairs. The obtained dictionary can then be used as the first dictionary of the self-learning procedure of VecMap.

4 Experimental details

Our experiments are performed in three pairs of languages (English-Arabic, English-Russian, and English-Chinese) and based on tokenized Wikipedia dumps. We use FastText (Bojanowski et al., 2016) monolingual embeddings[1] and keep only the 200,000 most frequent words.

4.1 Code-switched pairs extraction

CoSwitchMap considers a word to belong to a given language if all its characters are in the character range of the relevant script. Character ranges for each language can be found in Appendix A.

For each non-English language (Arabic, Russian, and Chinese), code-switched pairs of words involving the non-English language and English are extracted from the non-English corpus and the English one. The pairs retained are all pairs of words in the same context, such that one matches one script and the other matches the other script. Two words are considered to be in the same context if they are in the same window of width 5, to match the default window size of the monolingual embedding we use.

pair	number
en-ar	7,848,024
en-ru	50,182,802
en-zh	23,097,625

Table 1: Number of code-switching pairs extracted

The total number of pairs for each language pair is reported in Table 1.

4.2 Learning the W mapping

Word embedding and context embedding matrices are obtained from already pre-trained FastText

[1] https://fasttext.cc/docs/en/pretrained-vectors.html

monolingual embeddings. The embedding matrices are l2-normalized and frozen while only the mapping is trained.

In each epoch, each pair of words is passed twice, with the English word as the central word and with the non-English word as the central word. Five negative samples are drawn uniformly from the context word language vocabulary, although limited to the 200,000 most frequent words since we filtered our monolingual embeddings.

The mapping is trained for five epochs with SGD optimizer, learning rate 0.1, momentum 0.9, and a batch size of 1024 pairs (including negative samples). The orthogonalization step is applied after each batch with $\beta = 0.01$ (cf. Equation 5).

4.3 Inference of the first dictionary

From the embeddings, roughly aligned with W, we obtain a seed dictionary with a nearest-neighbor search. For each word in the English vocabulary, we retrieve its nearest neighbor in the non-English embedding. Following Artetxe et al. (2018b), we also retrieve the nearest neighbor in the English embedding for each word in the non-English one.

The retrieval criterion is the Cross-domain Similarity with Local Scaling (CSLS) (Joulin et al., 2018), a modified cosine similarity that mitigates the effects of hubs, which are words that are nearest neighbor of many others. This criterion has a hyper-parameter which is the number of neighbors to include in the computation to mitigate the cosine similarity. We use 10 following Artetxe et al. (2018b).

4.4 Self-learning

For the self-learning iteration, we use the VecMap algorithm (Artetxe et al., 2018b)[2]. We simply replace the initialization with ours. All parameters are left with default values.

4.5 Evaluation

Following previous work, the aligned embeddings obtained are evaluated with Bilingual Lexicon Induction (BLI). Given a bilingual dictionary containing pairs of English words with their translation in a given language, we evaluate the top-1 accuracy of a nearest-neighbor search to retrieve the translation of a given word. We use the same CSLS criterion as before and as in VecMap for the nearest-neighbor search.

The dictionaries used for evaluation are the evaluation dictionaries containing 1500 distinct words provided by Conneau et al. (2017)[3].

5 Results

Results show that (1) despite being infrequent, code-switching in a large unlabelled non-English corpus involves a large majority of the most frequent words of an English dictionary and that (2) `CoSwitchMap` provides a higher accuracy in bilingual lexicon induction that other unsupervised isometric mapping-based methods.

5.1 Amount of code-switching in text corpora

To evaluate the amount of code-switching in a corpus, we must rely on a dictionary or rather a list of words that are guaranteed to originate from a given language. Indeed if we rely only on different scripts, as in `CoSwitchMap`, we might have an issue with the precision of the code-switching retrieval as the same script can be used in different languages. Using a dictionary can lack a bit of recall, as a dictionary can hardly contain all the vocabulary used in English with all their inflections. But if the dictionary is comprehensive enough, it should provide a good lower bound of the number of code-switching situations.

We use the `3of6game` dictionary from the 6th version of the `12dicts`[4]. This dictionary contains 64,662 words. It was chosen because it is said to be oriented towards common words and was manually checked for errors, which should reduce the chance of the dictionary itself being polluted by code-switching. It is obtained from 6 advanced learners' ESL dictionaries, and contains American and British English, with inflections and neologisms.

We differentiate between token contamination and code-switching. Token contamination is simply the fact of finding an English token in a non-English corpus, but is not necessarily a code-switching situation, where the English word must be found in the same context as a non-English word (identified with its script). A code-switching situation is thus also a token contamination situation. But the reciprocal is not necessarily true.

Table 2 shows that code-switching is present in all the tested datasets. From around 500,000 situations in Arabic to more than 4 million in Russian.

[2] https://github.com/artetxem/vecmap

[3] https://github.com/facebookresearch/MUSE

[4] http://wordlist.aspell.net/12dicts-readme

lang	tokens	token contamination			code-switching		
		coverage (%)	count	count digits	coverage (%)	count	count digits
ar	229M	44.9	1,043,396	6,511,347	38.0	486,764	6,360,450
ru	685M	55.1	5,237,773	26,063,394	50.7	4,158,232	25,637,900
zh	319M	47.6	1,720,247	3,220,332	39.4	1,174,912	3,117,309

Table 2: Presence of words from an English dictionary in three non-English Wikipedia dumps. Contamination considers all words that were found in the corpus, and code-switching considers them only if they are in the vicinity of a word written in the non-English script. "coverage" is the proportion of the dictionary that was found and "count", the number of single occurrences. The occurrences of digit tokens are given for comparison.

ranks	ar	ru	zh
1-10	100.0	100.0	100.0
11-100	100.0	100.0	100.0
101-1,000	99.3	99.1	99.7
1,001-10,000	86.8	93.2	90.0
$\geq$10,001	30.9	45.8	32.1

Table 3: Proportion (in %) of English words in a dictionary covered by code-switching situations, split by buckets of frequency rank. e.g. line "1-10" indicates the proportion of the ten most frequent words in the dictionary that are covered by code-switching situations in each non-English language.

This is a small fraction of the hundreds of millions of tokens present in each corpus. But, to comprehend what the frequency of code-switching represents, Table 2 shows that code-switching is 3 to 15 times rarer than digits. This goes on to show that code-switching is not an exceptional occurrence in a monolingual corpus like Wikipedia.

While code-switching is relatively scarce, it however covers an important portion of the English vocabulary. Indeed, Table 2 shows that code-switching situations cover up to half of the English dictionary. A breakdown by frequency shows that the most frequent words are almost all involved in code-switching situations, as shown in Table 3.

Figure 2 compares the frequency of English words in the English corpus with their frequency in a non-English corpus. It shows that the frequency of a code-switched word rarely exceeds 10^{-4}, with frequent words in English being generally more frequently code-switched than infrequent ones. While code-switching occurs mainly for the most frequent words, Table 2 shows that it covers a high proportion of the 10,000 most frequent words, which is comparable with the number of words kept for learning alignment in several unsupervised alignment methods. VecMap, for example, learns its mapping on the 20,000 most frequent words of both languages involved. This advocates for learning an orthogonal mapping based on code-switching pairs, as proposed in `CoSwitchMap` rather than learning entirely new embeddings.

The results of this section suggest that code-switching, despite being infrequent, amounts to a non-negligible number of code-switched tokens in a large corpus that covers a large part of the most frequent words from the code-switched language, which might be sufficient to learn a mapping between the respective embeddings of two languages.

5.2 Results of `CoSwitchMap`

`CoSwitchMap` introduces a new way to learn a seed bilingual dictionary from code-switching. This seed dictionary can then be used as initialization for a self-learning loop. `CoSwitchMap` reuses the self-learning algorithm of VecMap. We thus compare the method to VecMap and other unsupervised mapping-based methods.

Wasserstein-Procrustes (**WP**) (Grave et al., 2018) is a method relying on optimal transport. The initial dictionary is provided through the convex relaxation of a graph-matching problem between the graphs, for each monolingual embedding, of similarities between each word. Self-learning is then performed. At each step, a new mapping is learned from a given dictionary with Procrustes as in most other methods. A new dictionary is obtained from a given mapping by solving an optimal transport problem using Wasserstein distance.

MUSE (Conneau et al., 2017) relies on adversarial learning. A linear mapping is trained to maximize the loss of a discriminator that is simultaneously trained to distinguish embeddings from both languages that are being aligned. The mapping is orthogonalized at each step using the same update as ours (cf. Equation 5). The obtained mapping is then refined with self-learning. Each new mapping is obtained with Procrustes. Each new dictionary is obtained through a nearest-neighbor search.

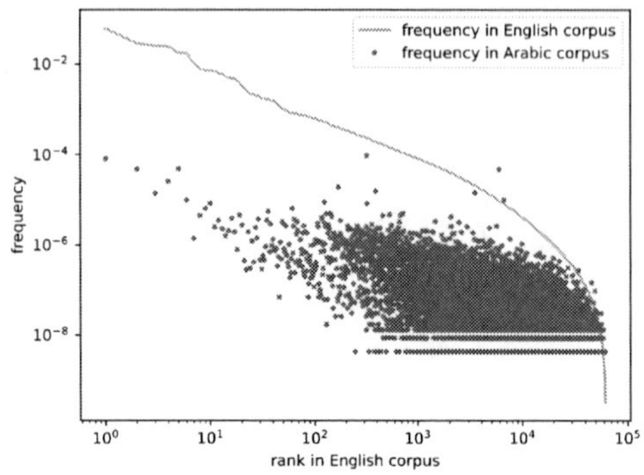

(a) Arabic

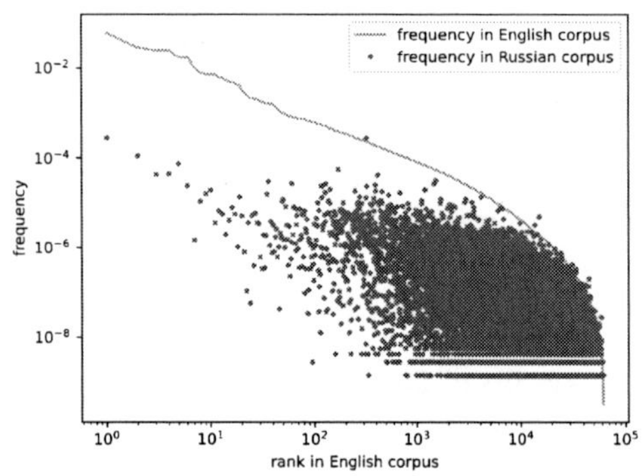

(b) Russian

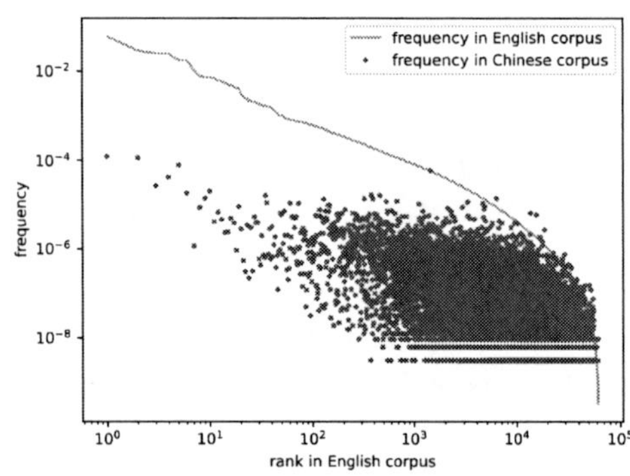

(c) Chinese

Figure 2: Frequency of words from an English dictionary in the English corpus (line) and non-English one (dots) according to the rank in frequency in the English corpus.

VecMap (Artetxe et al., 2018b) relies, like WP, on graph-matching for initialization: each word is represented by a vector containing the distance to all other words. After taking the square root of each embedding matrix, sorting the values in each vector, and normalizing them, a nearest-neighbor

method	en-ar	en-ru	en-zh
Methods with other self-learning procedures			
WP	$10.7_{\pm 9.9}$	$36.9_{\pm 1.4}$	$0.6_{\pm 0.8}$
MUSE	$30.9_{\pm 3.3}$	$41.7_{\pm 2.9}$	$0.0_{\pm 3.3}$
Different initializations for the same self-learning			
VecMap	$36.4_{\pm 1.8}$	**49.1**$_{\pm 0.4}$	$0.0_{\pm 0.0}$
w/ MUSE init.	$37.4_{\pm 2.6}$	$48.3_{\pm 0.4}$	$0.0_{\pm 0.1}$
w/ WP init.	$38.6_{\pm 0.7}$	$45.8_{\pm 2.8}$	$0.1_{\pm 0.0}$
w/ identical init.	$\underline{39.8}_{\pm 0.3}$	$\underline{48.9}_{\pm 0.2}$	$36.8_{\pm 0.8}$
CoSwitchMap (ours)	**39.9**$_{\pm 0.1}$	$\underline{49.0}_{\pm 0.3}$	**37.9**$_{\pm 0.9}$
supervised	*43.0*	*52.7*	*43.3*

Table 4: Comparison of `CoSwitchMap` with other unsupervised mapping-based methods. The score is the top-1 accuracy of a nearest-neighbor search with CSLS criterion for BLI. Results are averaged over 5 seeds and the standard deviation is provided (except for the deterministic supervised baseline). Bold indicates the best score for a given language pair and all scores that are within the standard deviation of the best one are underlined.

search provides the initial dictionary. Self-learning then consists of Procrustes for learning each new mapping and nearest-neighbor search for learning each new dictionary.

Søgaard et al. (2018b) showed that fully unsupervised mapping-based methods can fail in certain conditions, namely when languages are distant. They obtain better results using a seed dictionary built with identical words found in both vocabularies instead of one resulting from graph-matching algorithms or adversarial mapping that might rely too heavily on the need for isometry between embeddings. We use this initialization with VecMap self-learning to compare with ours and VecMap.

Table 4 shows how `CoSwitchMap` fares compared to the other aforementioned mapping-based methods in a Bilingual Lexicon Induction (BLI) task. For the three language pairs tested, fully unsupervised mapping-based methods (WP, MUSE, and VecMap) are outperformed or matched by `CoSwitchMap`. The gap is the most significant for the English-Chinese pair, where fully unsupervised methods largely fail, while initialization with identical words scores slightly behind `CoSwitchMap`. For the two other language pairs, the differences are less pronounced but `CoSwitchMap` is still among the best-performing ones.

In `CoSwitchMap` code-switching is used only for the initialization, the self-learning being the same as VecMap. Thus, Table 4 also compares different initializations with the same self-learning from VecMap. It must be noted that the initial-

method	results for different seeds				
WP	14.9	5.7	28.0	5.1	0.0
MUSE	34.1	33.9	26.5	32.4	27.3
Vecmap	37.8	37.4	35.9	33.2	37.9
id. init.	40.3	39.7	39.9	39.4	39.8
ours	40.1	39.8	39.7	39.5	40.1

Table 5: Breakdown of the BLI accuracy for each of the tested random seeds for the English-Arabic language pair. Each column represents a different random seed used for the algorithms.

ization methods of MUSE and WP provide better results when used with the VecMap self-learning method than with their original self-learning procedure. This validates the choice of the self-learning procedure for our method. But most importantly, it shows that the initialization provided by the code-switching training signal is significantly better than any other except the identical initialization for Arabic and Russian, and the original initialization for Russian. But `CoSwitchMap` always at least matches, if not outperforms, the best unsupervised baseline.

However, two things must be noted about the identical initialization. First, it might indirectly rely on code-switching, since the most frequently code-switched words will be present in the vocabulary of both languages[5]. Second, `CoSwitchMap` still outperforms this baseline for the English-Chinese pair, suggesting that explicitly relying on code-switching can sometimes provide more accurate alignment.

Table 4 also shows the results of a competitive supervised baseline, from the same framework as VecMap (Artetxe et al., 2018a) trained on a bilingual dictionary of 5,000 different words with their translations, distinct from those used for evaluation, but from the same origin (Conneau et al., 2017). Being unsupervised, `CoSwitchMap` is unsurprisingly outperformed by the supervised baseline, but falls short only by a few points, from 3.1 to 5.6. The supervised method has the unfair advantage of relying on a training bilingual dictionary, which is similar to the test dictionary used for evaluating BLI.

It is also worth noting that `CoSwitchMap`, along with all methods using VecMap self-learning, has results with a smaller standard deviation than the others. This suggests that there is a need for robust self-learning algorithms in unsupervised mapping-based methods. Table 5 shows the same algorithm can sometimes give different results according to the random seed used. WP and MUSE show more instability than methods with VecMap self-learning. However, it must be noted that the initialization might also play an important role in the stability of the results since VecMap provides slightly less stable results with its original initialization than with the two others (id. init. and ours).

6 Conclusion

In a corpus like Wikipedia, code-switching is an infrequent signal that nonetheless involves a large portion of the most frequent vocabulary. It can thus be harnessed to learn cross-lingual word representations. We proposed `CoSwitchMap` to extract code-switching situations in an unsupervised manner and to use them to build a seed dictionary for learning a bilingual word embedding.

The method is limited to pairs of languages written in different scripts. But it is often for those pairs of languages that existing unsupervised methods fail, due to the languages being too distant. Our analysis shows that code-switched words seem to never have a frequency above a certain threshold, which suggests that a frequency-based method for code-switching extraction could be devised to adapt our method to pairs of same-script languages.

`CoSwitchMap` outperforms other unsupervised mapping-based methods in Bilingual Lexicon Induction for languages of different scripts. It shows that, with the right initialization, unsupervised mapping-based methods can work with distant languages. But, most of all, it demonstrates that code-switching can be valuable cross-lingual training signal.

7 Limitations

The reader should note that `CoSwitchMap` is thought of as a way to demonstrate the utility of code-switching as a cross-lingual signal, rather than as a method with direct practical utility. Indeed, the method only works for different scripts. It requires one to know the character ranges of the script at hand, which can still be seen as a very weak level of supervision, and which has prevented us from testing the method on a larger set of languages.

[5]Only the most frequently code-switched words because vocabularies are usually truncated before alignment typically to 200,000 words

References

Mikel Artetxe, Gorka Labaka, and Eneko Agirre. 2018a. Generalizing and improving bilingual word embedding mappings with a multi-step framework of linear transformations. In *Proceedings of the Thirty-Second AAAI Conference on Artificial Intelligence*, pages 5012–5019.

Mikel Artetxe, Gorka Labaka, and Eneko Agirre. 2018b. A robust self-learning method for fully unsupervised cross-lingual mappings of word embeddings. In *Proceedings of the 56th Annual Meeting of the Association for Computational Linguistics (Volume 1: Long Papers)*, pages 789–798, Melbourne, Australia. Association for Computational Linguistics.

Terra Blevins and Luke Zettlemoyer. 2022. Language contamination helps explain the cross-lingual capabilities of english pretrained models.

Piotr Bojanowski, Edouard Grave, Armand Joulin, and Tomás Mikolov. 2016. Enriching word vectors with subword information. *CoRR*, abs/1607.04606.

Alexis Conneau, Guillaume Lample, Marc'Aurelio Ranzato, Ludovic Denoyer, and Hervé Jégou. 2017. Word translation without parallel data. *CoRR*, abs/1710.04087.

Jacob Devlin, Ming-Wei Chang, Kenton Lee, and Kristina Toutanova. 2019. BERT: Pre-training of deep bidirectional transformers for language understanding. In *Proceedings of the 2019 Conference of the North American Chapter of the Association for Computational Linguistics: Human Language Technologies, Volume 1 (Long and Short Papers)*, pages 4171–4186, Minneapolis, Minnesota. Association for Computational Linguistics.

Stephan Gouws and Anders Søgaard. 2015. Simple task-specific bilingual word embeddings. In *Proceedings of the 2015 Conference of the North American Chapter of the Association for Computational Linguistics: Human Language Technologies*, pages 1386–1390, Denver, Colorado. Association for Computational Linguistics.

Edouard Grave, Armand Joulin, and Quentin Berthet. 2018. Unsupervised alignment of embeddings with wasserstein procrustes. *arXiv preprint arXiv:1805.11222*.

Armand Joulin, Piotr Bojanowski, Tomas Mikolov, Hervé Jégou, and Edouard Grave. 2018. Loss in translation: Learning bilingual word mapping with a retrieval criterion. In *Proceedings of the 2018 Conference on Empirical Methods in Natural Language Processing*, pages 2979–2984, Brussels, Belgium. Association for Computational Linguistics.

Jitin Krishnan, Antonios Anastasopoulos, Hemant Purohit, and Huzefa Rangwala. 2021. Multilingual code-switching for zero-shot cross-lingual intent prediction and slot filling. *CoRR*, abs/2103.07792.

Yinhan Liu, Myle Ott, Naman Goyal, Jingfei Du, Mandar Joshi, Danqi Chen, Omer Levy, Mike Lewis, Luke Zettlemoyer, and Veselin Stoyanov. 2019. Roberta: A robustly optimized BERT pretraining approach. *CoRR*, abs/1907.11692.

Tomás Mikolov, Quoc V. Le, and Ilya Sutskever. 2013a. Exploiting similarities among languages for machine translation. *CoRR*, abs/1309.4168.

Tomas Mikolov, Ilya Sutskever, Kai Chen, Greg Corrado, and Jeffrey Dean. 2013b. Distributed representations of words and phrases and their compositionality. In *Proceedings of the 26th International Conference on Neural Information Processing Systems - Volume 2*, NIPS'13, page 3111–3119, Red Hook, NY, USA. Curran Associates Inc.

Libo Qin, Minheng Ni, Yue Zhang, and Wanxiang Che. 2020. Cosda-ml: Multi-lingual code-switching data augmentation for zero-shot cross-lingual NLP. *CoRR*, abs/2006.06402.

Sebastian Ruder. 2017. A survey of cross-lingual embedding models. *CoRR*, abs/1706.04902.

Anders Søgaard, Sebastian Ruder, and Ivan Vulic. 2018a. On the limitations of unsupervised bilingual dictionary induction. *CoRR*, abs/1805.03620.

Anders Søgaard, Sebastian Ruder, and Ivan Vulić. 2018b. On the limitations of unsupervised bilingual dictionary induction. In *Proceedings of the 56th Annual Meeting of the Association for Computational Linguistics (Volume 1: Long Papers)*, pages 778–788, Melbourne, Australia. Association for Computational Linguistics.

Ashish Vaswani, Noam Shazeer, Niki Parmar, Jakob Uszkoreit, Llion Jones, Aidan N. Gomez, Lukasz Kaiser, and Illia Polosukhin. 2017. Attention is all you need.

Shijie Wu and Mark Dredze. 2020. Do explicit alignments robustly improve multilingual encoders? In *Proceedings of the 2020 Conference on Empirical Methods in Natural Language Processing (EMNLP)*, pages 4471–4482, Online. Association for Computational Linguistics.

Min Xiao and Yuhong Guo. 2014. Distributed word representation learning for cross-lingual dependency parsing. In *Proceedings of the Eighteenth Conference on Computational Natural Language Learning*, pages 119–129, Ann Arbor, Michigan. Association for Computational Linguistics.

Jian Yang, Shuming Ma, Dongdong Zhang, Shuangzhi Wu, Zhoujun Li, and Ming Zhou. 2020. Alternating language modeling for cross-lingual pre-training. In *AAAI Conference on Artificial Intelligence*.

A Character ranges for each language

For each of the languages experimented, we use the following character ranges:

- English: [a–zA–Z]
- Arabic: [\u0621–\u064A]
- Russian: [\u0401\u0451\u0410–\u044f]
- Chinese: [\u4e00–\u9fff\u3400–\u4dbf \U00020000–\U0002a6df\U0002a700–\U0002ebef\U00030000–\U000323af\ufa0e \ufa0f\ufa11\ufa13\ufa14\ufa1f\ufa21\ufa23 \ufa24\ufa27\ufa28\ufa29\u3006\u3007][\ufe00–\ufe0f\U000e0100–\U000e01ef]?

The regular expressions in English, Arabic and Russian are simple ranges. For Chinese (Han script), a more complex regular expression is used as it must take into account variation selectors that can be added after an ideogram. The whole regular expression was obtained from https://ayaka.shn.hk/hanregex

Learning to translate by learning to communicate

C.M. Downey[α*] **Xuhui Zhou** [β*] **Leo Z. Liu**[γ] **Shane Steinert-Threlkeld**[α]
[α]Department of Linguistics, University of Washington
[β]Language Technologies Institute, Carnegie Mellon University
[γ]Department of Computer Science, The University of Texas at Austin
{cmdowney,shanest}@uw.edu
zliu@cs.utexas.edu, xuhuiz@cs.cmu.edu

Abstract

We formulate and test a technique to use Emergent Communication (EC) with a pre-trained multilingual model to improve on modern Unsupervised NMT systems, especially for low-resource languages. It has been argued that the current dominant paradigm in NLP of pre-training on text-only corpora will not yield robust natural language understanding systems, and the need for grounded, goal-oriented, and interactive language learning has been highlighted. In our approach, we embed a multilingual model (mBART, Liu et al., 2020) into an EC image-reference game, in which the model is incentivized to use multilingual generations to accomplish a vision-grounded task. The hypothesis is that this will align multiple languages to a shared task space. We present two variants of EC Fine-Tuning (Steinert-Threlkeld et al., 2022), one of which outperforms a backtranslation-only baseline in all four languages investigated, including the low-resource language Nepali.

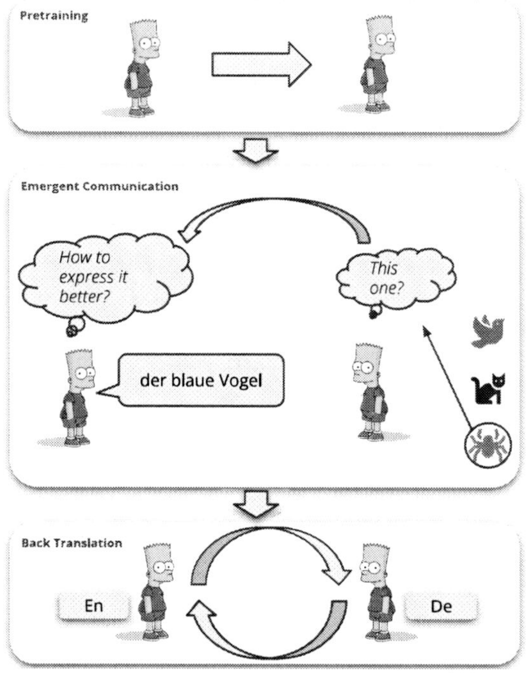

Figure 1: Illustration of our modeling process. For the *pre-training* stage, we use the off-the-shelf mBART (Lewis et al., 2020). We fine-tune the model for translation with Emergent Communication.

1 Introduction

While neural machine translation (NMT) systems are one of the great success stories of natural language processing (Sutskever et al., 2014; Bahdanau et al., 2015; Wu et al., 2016), typical methods rely on large quantities of *parallel text* (i.e. existing human translated texts) as gold data for supervised learning. These approaches are thus difficult to apply to low-resource languages, which lack large bodies of such data (Joshi et al., 2020). To extend this vital language technology to low-resource languages, many have focused on *Unsupervised NMT* (UNMT) — the task of building NMT systems without any parallel text (Artetxe et al., 2018; Lample et al., 2018a,c; Lample and Conneau, 2019; Conneau et al., 2020).

Typical approaches to UNMT rely on large pre-trained multilingual models (Lample and Conneau, 2019; Conneau et al., 2020; Liu et al., 2020; Song et al., 2019) and the method of *back-translation* (Sennrich et al., 2016b) to iteratively generate synthetic parallel text. These approaches, however, still rely on plain text information alone. For that reason, the resulting models are considered *ungrounded* (there is no link between the text and the external world). This may limit model abilities.

Despite NLP breakthroughs stemming from large-scale pre-training on raw text corpora with self-supervised learning (Howard and Ruder, 2018; Peters et al., 2018; Devlin et al., 2019; Liu et al., 2019; Conneau et al., 2020; Liu et al., 2020; Brown

*Equal contribution. We also include a detailed Author Contribution Statement at the end of the paper.

Proceedings of the The 3rd Workshop on Multi-lingual Representation Learning (MRL), pages 218–238
December 7, 2023

et al., 2020, i.a.), several recent results suggest limitations in model generalization (McCoy et al., 2019; Niven and Kao, 2019; Ettinger, 2020; Rogers et al., 2020, i.a.). More fundamentally, several have argued that pre-training on text alone will not deliver fully general and robust NLP systems.[1]

For example, using several detailed thought experiments, Bender and Koller (2020) argue that models trained on text alone will not, in principle, be able to recover either the conventional meaning of expressions or the communicative intent of an expression in context. Their arguments highlight the importance of the interaction between linguistic expressions and extra-linguistic communicative intents (e.g. acting in the world, executing programs).[2] Similarly, Bisk et al. (2020) articulate progressively broader *world scopes* in which language use is embedded, and argue that present pre-training methods work at a relatively limited scope. They too emphasize the importance of embodied interaction with the environment and with the social world for future NLP systems.[3]

In this paper, we propose to use methods from the field of *emergent communication* (EC) (Wagner et al., 2003; Skyrms, 2010; Lazaridou and Baroni, 2020) to improve UNMT systems. EC studies artificial agents communicating with each other to accomplish particular environmental goals. EC is a subfield of reinforcement learning, wherein language (i.e. the communcation protocol) is shaped by rewards determined by interacting with an external environment and with other agents. Typical work in this area starts from a *tabula rasa* and studies under what conditions —e.g. environments, tasks/goals, social settings—the resulting communication protocols among agents resembles human language, along axes like word length economy (Chaabouni et al., 2019a), word-order biases (Chaabouni et al., 2019b), and compositionality (Andreas, 2019; Chaabouni et al., 2020; Steinert-Threlkeld, 2020; Geffen Lan et al., 2020), among others (Mu and Goodman, 2021).

Our approach leverages the insight that people learn new languages by using them to do things (e.g. order food, buy train tickets); our machines should do the same. We improve upon a standard UNMT system by taking a large pre-trained multilingual model (mBART) and embedding it in an EC task, having it participate in goal-directed communication (in addition to back-translation). Communication should promote translation in the following way. Translation can be viewed as 'aligning' model representations for sentences in several languages. In the supervised case, parallel text instructs the model how to do this alignment. In the unsupervised case, through communication, each model aligns its language representations *with the same shared environment*, thereby promoting alignment between the languages themselves. This work is thus an instance of the wider framework of Emergent Communication Fine-tuning (EC-FT) (Steinert-Threlkeld et al., 2022).

In what remains, we describe our pipeline for EC fine-tuning (Section 2) and the experiments that we conduct to demonstrate its benefit for UNMT (Section 3), overview our experimental results, in which we show EC yields benefits for every language we study with particularly strong gains for the low-resource language Nepali (Section 4). We then study some manipulations on our training pipeline (Section 5) before discussing the implications of these experiments (Section 6), and situating them in the context of existing work (Section 7).

Our contributions are the following: (i) We demonstrate that EC-FT can be used to improve upon UNMT baselines. (ii) We give a proof-of-concept for the viability of using modern pre-trained language models in an EC scenario. (iii) We articulate a view for EC-FT as a generalized and parameterizable framework.

2 Methodology

As shown in Figure 1, the pipeline that we introduce here consists of three main phases: (1) Begin with a pre-trained multilingual model, which either already has an encoder and decoder, or from which this *seq2seq* stack can be initialized. (2) Conduct emergent-communication training using image and/or text embeddings (Figure 2). (3) Use iterative backtranslation (Sennrich et al., 2016a; Section 7) to tune the model for translation.[4]

[1] This is largely what (Linzen, 2020) calls the pre-training Agnostic Independently Distributed (PAID) evaluation paradigm. We discuss pre-training on multimodal (i.e. not text-only) data in § 7.

[2] See Merrill et al. (2021) for a formalization of argument in Bender and Koller (2020) about learning a programming language from form alone.

[3] As noted by Bender and Koller (2020), many of these arguments can be seen as detailed elaborations of the need for NLU systems to solve the *symbol grounding* problem (Harnad, 1990; Taddeo and Floridi, 2005).

[4] The code to run all experiments described here can be found at `https://github.com/CLMBRs/communication-translation`.

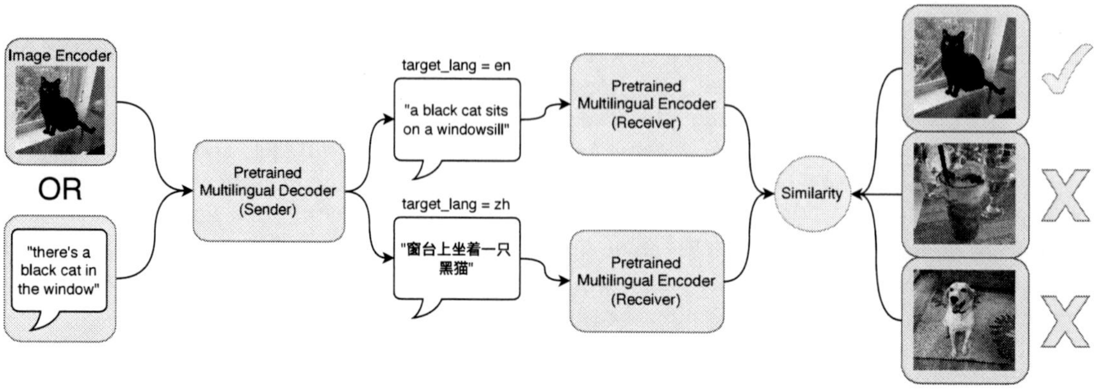

Figure 2: Emergent Communication Fine-Tuning: the task is a standard image reference game from the EC literature, but with the sender and receiver initialized from a pre-trained multilingual decoder and encoder. The communication language alternates between the two languages in the translation pair that is being fine-tuned.

For step (2), we test two versions of the EC fine-tuning task. In the first (I2I-EC), the EC step uses *only image embeddings*, and the model must select the original input image from among distractors, based on a text generation (akin to a caption). In the second (T2I-EC), the communication game involves gold captions, instead of only image features: based on a caption, the model must generate a translation of it, on the basis of which the original image must be selected from amongst distractors.

First, we introduce some notation. We use E_m and D_m for the multilingual encoder and decoder, respectively, which are parameterized by θ_E and θ_D. $\mathbf{x}_E \in \mathbb{R}^{N\times|V|}$ and $\mathbf{x}_D \in \mathbb{R}^{K\times|V|}$ are sequences of symbols of length N and K respectively. $E_m(\mathbf{x}_E;\theta_E) \in \mathbb{R}^{N\times d_m}$, where d_m is the model hidden dimension, is the encoder output. Similarly, the decoder output is $D_m(\mathbf{x}_D,\mathbf{e};\theta_D) \in \mathbb{R}^{K\times|V|}$, where $\mathbf{e} \in \mathbb{R}^{N\times d_m}$ is a set of vectors for cross-attention of the decoder.

This formulation of our pipeline leaves many concrete choices open. In the remainder of this section, we describe the specific implementation of this process used in our experiments.

2.1 Pipeline Components

Pre-trained Model We use mBART(-large) (Liu et al., 2020), which has demonstrated strong unsupervised translation performance in several languages. mBART employs *seq2seq* pre-training, encoding a "noised" input sequence and then reconstructing the original sequence with the decoder, over a collection of 25 languages. mBART's encoder-decoder architecture and corresponding seq2seq training make it a natural fit for our EC experiments, in which a multilingual decoder and encoder are used to send and receive natural language messages. We use $\theta_{E_{PT}}$ to denote the parameters of the pretrained encoder, and *mutatis mutandis* for the pretrained decoder.

Backtranslation Iterative backtranslation allows a model (usually pre-trained) to achieve some level of translation performance while only training on monolingual data (Section 7). Our baseline system is mBART fine-tuned with backtranslation only. In the EC-FT case, backtranslation is always performed last so that the model is tuned for translation immediately before it is evaluated.

Image-to-Image EC (I2I-EC) Our emergent communication framework consists of two main subtasks. First, an agent (the sender, a decoder) must take in an image encoding and produce a natural language description of it. The generation language may vary; there will be several in our experiments. Next, another agent (the receiver, an encoder) takes in the generated text and uses it to pick the described image from a set of distractors. In the EC literature, this is referred to as a standard image reference game (see Figure 2).[5]

Let $i \in \mathbb{R}^{d_i}$ be an image embedding (d_i is the dimension of these embeddings, which may come from a vision model). We also assume that we have

[5]The image reference game, as used in much of the EC literature, is very similar to? training an image caption module to produce discriminative captions via self-retrieval, as pursued in (Liu et al., 2018). They first train the text-to-image pipeline from gold captions, and then pursue training a caption generator via image selection both with and without supervision from gold captions. We thank an anonymous reviewer for calling our attention to this work.

a reshaper $R(i; \theta_R)$ which maps images to $\mathbb{R}^{d_m}$.

Because mBART is not natively multi-modal, some adaptations are made to allow it to generate a description of an image. In particular, the image embedding cannot simply be the first token to the sender since mBART reserves this for a special language identification token. Further, it is not obvious that a pre-trained transformer decoder's cross-attention can be "turned off" without effecting overall performance. For these reasons, we pass the image embedding into an "unroller" U (one auto-regressive transformer layer) to generate a sequence of embeddings $U(R(i); \theta_U) \in \mathbb{R}^{M \times d_m}$ where M is a hyperparameter. This sequence is then used as the keys and values in the sender's cross-attention.

We auto-regressively generate from the sender's distributions $S := D_m(\langle \text{LID}, T_{<K} \rangle, U(R(i))) \in \mathbb{R}^{K \times |V|}$, where LID is a language ID token and $T_{<K}$ is the prefix of text T generated at the previous time step. The sampling required for discrete generation is not differentiable, so we use the straight-through Gumbel-Softmax estimator (Jang et al., 2017; Maddison et al., 2017) with temperature $\tau = 1.0$. $T := \text{GS-ST}(S)$ is the sequence of one-hot vectors sampled in this way.

The receiver consumes this generated 'caption': $E_m(T) \in \mathbb{R}^{K \times d_m}$. To produce a single representation of the image, we use an 'aggregator' A which takes this sequence of representations and pools them into a single one $A(E_m(T); \theta_A) \in \mathbb{R}^{d_m}$.[6]

The score for each of the candidate images is the inverse of the mean squared error between the image and the receiver's final representation. The loss for the image selection task is then cross-entropy among the image candidates. This loss partially follows Lee et al. (2018), though they jointly train on supervised caption generation during EC.

Given the original image i, and a set $\{i_m\}_{m=1}^{M}$ of distractor images, let the image selection loss be

$$\ell_{\text{IS}}(i, \Theta) := - \log \text{softmax} \frac{1}{\|A(E_m(T)) - R(i)\|_2^2} \quad (1)$$

where $\Theta = \{\theta_D, \theta_E, \theta_R, \theta_A, \theta_U\}$ and the softmax is taken over the distractor images $\{R(i_m)\}$.

Finally, because EC can cause significant language drift (Lee et al., 2018, 2019; Lu et al., 2020; Lazaridou et al., 2020), we use KL regularization (Havrylov and Titov, 2017; Baziotis et al., 2020) to ensure that the sender's output distribution does not drift too far from the distribution of an auxiliary causal language model (CLM; this model is not trained as part of EC):[7]

$$\ell_{\text{KL}} := \frac{1}{K} \sum_k \text{KL}\left(S_k \,||\, D_{\text{CLM}}(\langle LID, T_{<k} \rangle)_k\right) \quad (2)$$

Combining equations (1) and (2) and averaging over iterations of the game, the final EC loss is

$$\mathcal{L}_{\text{EC}} := \mathbb{E}_i \left[\ell_{\text{IS}} + \lambda \ell_{\text{KL}}\right] \quad (3)$$

with λ a hyperparameter.

Text-to-Image EC (T2I-EC) The text-to-image EC task is identical to I2I-EC, except in what is presented to the sender via cross-attention. In T2I-EC, monolingual gold captions are used in the cross-attention for the emergent generation after being embedded by the encoder E_m.

In other words, given c_i as a caption for image i, T2I-EC still uses $\mathcal{L}_{\text{EC}}$ (equation (3)), but without the unroller for the sender. Now, we have $S = D_m(\langle \text{LID}, S_{<K} \rangle, E_m(c_i; \theta_E))$.

As in I2I-EC, the image descriptions are generated in *either* the caption language (here, English) or another translation target language. Importantly, the emergent generation need not be identical to the gold caption. This is desirable, since there may be several valid paraphrases of a given translation/caption. Similarly, we only require gold captions in one language, not every language; for this reason, there is no implicitly parallel text data and so the translation task can still be considered unsupervised.

The motivation for this version of EC comes from the observation that the encodings used in the sender's cross-attention should be fairly similar to those generated by the model's encoder, since the model is being fine-tuned to be an encoder-decoder translation model. Generating into varying target languages incentivizes the model to use the same encodings for generating different languages, rather than copying the input text to the output. In contrast, there is no guarantee that the image encodings used in I2I-EC are at all similar to those produced by the model's encoder.

[6]Pilot experiments suggested that a small aggregator worked better than simply using mean pooling.

[7]We finetune the original mBART decoder as a CLM for this purpose; see the end of Appendix A for details.

Initial Supervision Because multilingual EC is a complicated task with sparse training signal, we first ground the agents in their visual sub-tasks independently of the combined communication task. We train the sender to produce gold-standard captions in a high-resource language (English in our experiments) while simultaneously training the receiver to pick out the correct image based on the gold-standard caption. Critically, this stage only assumes that you have gold-standard captions in *one* language. The model is never trained on gold captions in non-English languages. This step is conducted independently, before EC.

2.2 Data

Training We use two main sources of training data: monolingual corpora for backtranslation, and pairings of images and captions in a single high-resource language. We train translation systems between English and four other languages: Chinese (zh), German (de), Nepali (ne), and Sinhala (si).

Backtranslation creates synthetic translation pairs by generating sentences in the second language given natural sentences in the first. Following experiments using mBART for unsupervised translation (Liu et al., 2020), we use small portions of the Common Crawl 25 dataset, which is the pre-training data for mBART. In this way, no novel data is introduced to establish our UNMT baseline.

For the EC stage, the data required differs between I2I-EC and T2I-EC. The former requires only image embeddings. The latter requires paired images and captions, since the true caption is used to prompt the sender's generation. As mentioned, we assume that captions are *only available for one language*. Since English is in every translation pair, we use English captions. Our image-caption pairs come from the MS-COCO dataset (Lin et al., 2014), and our image embeddings are extracted from ResNet 50 (He et al., 2016b) (these are also used during the supervised captioning stage).

Validation and Test Translation validation and test sets are the only parallel data used in our experiments. For Nepali and Sinhala, we use the standard splits of the FLoRes evaluation datasets (Guzmán et al., 2019). For Chinese and German, we use the `newstest2018` and `newsdev2019` splits of the WMT'19 release as validation data (Barrault et al., 2019). For test data in these two languages, we sample 4096 examples from News Commentary v14 subset of the same release.

3 Experiments

We evaluate a UNMT baseline and our two proposed EC-FT pipelines on translation performance for each language pair. Checkpoints are picked by highest mean BLEU on the validation set. We first describe these models and then our evaluation. More extensive details can be found in Appendix A.

Baseline For our UNMT baseline, we start with mBART-25 and perform iterative backtranslation for 8192 steps in each direction. mBART employs language control tokens at the beginning of sequences, but it is *not* pre-trained to decode one language from another (Liu et al., 2020), which is a key feature of (back-)translation. To overcome the model's tendency to copy the input sequence to the output, we establish language-controlled generation using language control tokens and language masks (Liu et al., 2020). Concretely, we obtain token counts from the mBART training data, and these are used to create a logit mask, only allowing the model to generate tokens which make up the top p percent of the probability mass of the data in the given language. For the first 2048 backtranslation steps, we use a masking threshold of $p = 0.9$. After that, we raise the threshold to $p = 0.99$.

(I2I/T2I)-EC In both of our EC-FT models, we keep the total number of backtranslation steps the same (8192), and add 2048 steps each of supervised caption training and EC-FT. The language of generation can also be controlled during EC, so we use language-control tokens and a logit mask to ensure the sender generates in the specified language. The language of the emergent generation is selected uniformly at random per example.

Evaluation For our final evaluation, we report both BLEU and COMET (Rei et al., 2020) scores in both translation directions for each language pair. COMET provides the output of a regression model trained to predict the human direct-assessment translation quality score of a translation pair. Based on normalized quality scores, a COMET score of 0 means the translation is predicted to be of average quality. Postive scores indicate above-average quality, and vice-versa. We use the `wmt22-comet-da` model.

4 Results

Table 1 shows the results from our main experiment. Firstly, our UNMT baseline based on iterative back-

Model	Language	BLEU				COMET		
		en→X	X→en	mean	Δ	en→X	X→en	mean
baseline (mBART + BT)	zh	18.45	11.36	14.90	-	0.03	0.15	0.09
	de	19.06	25.73	22.39	-	0.20	0.38	0.29
	ne	2.14	5.07	3.60	-	-0.24	-0.34	-0.29
	si	1.18	4.73	2.95	-	-0.18	-0.28	-0.23
I2I-EC	zh	18.72	11.88	15.30	+3%	0.04	0.17	0.10
	de	18.26	25.60	21.93	-2%	0.20	0.40	**0.30**
	ne	1.51	5.34	3.43	-5%	-0.24	-0.31	-0.28
	si	0.01	0.08	0.04	-99%	-1.31	-1.05	-1.28
T2I-EC	zh	19.25	11.91	**15.58**	+5%	0.06	0.18	**0.12**
	de	18.64	26.20	**22.42**	+0.1%	0.19	0.41	**0.30**
	ne	2.36	5.92	**4.14**	+15%	-0.20	-0.27	**-0.24**
	si	1.29	4.76	**3.02**	+2%	-0.18	-0.27	**-0.22**

Table 1: Results of our main experiment. Values reported here are the maximum across 3 random seeds per row; see Appendix C for full variation. T2I-EC shows consistent improvement for each language in terms of both mean BLEU and COMET. Δ shows percent improvement over the baseline.

translation (BT) shows a marked decrease in performance from the two higher-resource languages (Chinese and German) to the two lower-resource languages (Nepali and Sinhala). This is expected since BT-based UNMT often requires a strong initialization (Lample et al., 2018c) and multilingual models (like mBART) do not perform as well for lower-resource languages (Wu and Dredze, 2020).

Our model fine-tuned with both backtranslation and I2I-EC remains close to or exceeds the baseline for the two higher-resource languages and Nepali but achieves very poor performance on Sinhala. It appears that EC provides a worse initialization for backtranslation for this language.

In contrast, our "text-to-image" variant of EC-FT (T2I-EC) yields the best performing model in terms of mean BLEU for all four of our languages. In particular, we see significant gains for both lower-resource languages. Most striking is the Nepali-English pair, which sees a +15% BLEU improvement over the baseline. While there are improvements in both directions, the Nepali→English direction has the largest gain. By contrast, Sinhala shows improvements in both directions, with the larger improvement in the to-Sinhala direction (partially due to a stronger baseline). The improvements are smallest for German, which is both very high-resource and the most similar to English of our languages. The COMET scores were broadly correlated with BLEU scores in all of our settings.

These results show that EC-FT of a pre-trained multilingual model can provide real improvement over a backtranslation-only baseline, giving proof-of-concept of communication for fine-tuning.

5 Manipulations

To better understand which components of the pipeline affect the results in T2I-EC, we conducted several follow-up experiments. For each manipulation, we looked at one high-resource language (German) and one low-resource langauge (Sinhala). See Appendix B for full methodological details.

Image Encoder To test the effect of the image encoder, we replaced the ResNet image encoder with the best performing one from CLIP (Radford et al., 2021). This image encoder is based on the Vision Transformer (Dosovitskiy et al., 2021) architecture and trained jointly with a text encoder via a contrastive loss to pair image encodings with caption encodings.

Initial Backtranslation Because the EC component of training is the first time that language ID codes are being used to generate text from the decoder with input other than representations of the same language from the encoder, we experimented with splitting the backtranslation training into two parts. Instead of doing all 8192 steps after EC, we did 2048 steps after image supervision but before EC, and the final 6144 steps after EC.

Interleaved Training Inspired by Lowe et al. (2020), who showed that inter-leaving EC with a supervised learning objective can improve EC results, we ran a version of our training pipeline where we alternated between EC and BT four times. The total number of training steps remained the same (2048 and 8192, respectively), but this was now done in 4 equal-sized EC-to-BT pieces.

Results Table 2 shows the results of these ablations. Evaluation is in terms of BLEU on the test set, and the Δ column reports the percent difference from the best value for a language in Table 1. We find significant reduction in translation quality with the CLIP image encoder and inconsistent performance for both an initial BT phase and interleaved training, with performance dropping for German but slightly increasing for Sinhala when compared to T2I-EC (as seen in the Δ column).

Manipulation	Lang	en→X	X→en	mean	Δ
CLIP-img	de	18.52	25.93	22.23	-1%
CLIP-img	si	1.05	4.18	2.61	-14%
Init BT	de	18.20	25.39	21.80	-3%
Init BT	si	1.24	4.84	3.04	+0.6%
Interleave	de	18.29	25.69	21.99	-2%
Interleave	si	1.25	4.84	3.05	+1%

Table 2: Results from several training pipeline manipulations. BLEU scores reported; Δ is the percentage difference from the corresponding mean value in T2I-EC in Figure 1.

6 Discussion

We have demonstrated that (at least one variant of) EC fine-tuning provides improvement on unsupervised translation over a standard backtranslation baseline. The gains are especially pronounced for the low-resource language Nepali, which is ideal since under-resourced languages constitute the expected use case for unsupervised translation techniques. Furthermore, since the hyperparameters for the EC-FT portion of our pipeline were mostly determined empirically, our approach may be *under-optimized*, meaning future work may yield further improvement using the same technique.

I2I-EC However, it is also clear that our formulation and implementation of "standard" EC (I2I-EC) does not improve upon the baseline, and even degrades performance in many cases. Our interpretation of this behavior is linked to our motivation for formulating T2I-EC in the first place.

As mentioned in Section 2.1, the image representations used in the sender's cross-attention, in the image-to-image setup, are not guaranteed to be at all similar to the representations that the receiver learns to encode. Because we seek to fine-tune for a standard *seq2seq* task (translation), it is desirable that the sender (mBART decoder) be trained to use the same or similar representations to those produced by the receiver (mBART encoder). Thus, we hypothesize that the null and negative effects of I2I-EC may be due to this mismatch between the representations the sender is trained to use, and those that the receiver is trained to produce.

However, we do **not** believe we have shown that I2I-EC will not be useful under slightly different formulations. In particular, the image representations may be able to be constrained to be similar to those of the receiver, either during EC or during the initial supervision phase. This could be accomplished using an auxillary distance loss, or by normalizing the mean and variance of the representations in both places.

EC Fine-Tuning Lastly, we view EC fine-tuning as a broader framework in which we have tested two distinct formulations (Steinert-Threlkeld et al., 2022). We will assume that the invariant element of EC is a model's use of discrete, natural-language generations as input to a second model, which must use them to accomplish some task.

Given this definition, there are several choice points for applying EC-FT. The parameter we explicitly explore in our experiments is whether the input to the sender is *image-based* or *text-based*. In both of our formulations, the receiver is trained by a contrastive image-choice loss. Another parameter for future work concerns whether this loss applies to images or texts. The receiver could be trained to choose the correct sentence out of a set of distractors via the similarity of the sentence embeddings.

A third parameter is whether the receiver is trained by a *contrastive* loss or a *generative* one (i.e. exactly reproducing a target sequence, as in *seq2seq* training).[8] In fact, an EC parameterization with text input, text output, and generative loss has already been formulated elsewhere, though it is not referred to as such. Niu et al. (2019) design a formulation of backtranslation, in which the artificial intermediate text is generated with straight-through

[8]Known as "reference game" versus "reconstruction game" in the EC literature (Lazaridou and Baroni, 2020).

Gumbel Softmax, instead of generated separately first. Future work will explore using this method with pre-trained models, i.e. in an EC-FT context.

These and other parameter choices leave extensive room for exciting future work with EC-FT as a general framework, both for UNMT and beyond.

7 Related Work

UNMT Unsupervised NMT uses only monolingual texts in each language of interest. Lample et al. (2018c) describe three principles for successful UNMT systems: 1. *initialization*, the initial model must leverage aligned representations between languages; 2. *language modeling*, there should be a strong "data driven prior" over the text patterns of each language; and 3. *backtranslation* which turns the unsupervised problem into a noisily-supervised one, through the use of semi-synthetic translations.

Significant progress has been made in improving each of these aspects of UNMT. Pre-trained multilingual language models (Lample and Conneau, 2019; Conneau et al., 2020; Liu et al., 2020; Song et al., 2019) have vastly improved the tractability of principles 1 and 2, largely replacing initialization techniques using inferred bilingual dictionaries (e.g. Lample et al., 2018b).

For the third principle, *iterative backtranslation* is widely used (Sennrich et al., 2016a; He et al., 2016a; Lample et al., 2018a; Haddow et al., 2022). On this approach, synthetic data is generated "on the fly", during training. The model is updated before each new batch of synthetic text is generated, leading to simultaneous incremental improvement in generated data quality and model quality.

In this work, we adhere to all three principles, but add EC as a training signal. It has been noted that UNMT baselines still perform relatively poorly for low-resource languages (Guzmán et al., 2019). We improve upon low-resource UNMT pipelines by leveraging goal-directed, multimodal fine-tuning via emergent communication.

EC and NLP A few other papers combine EC and NMT specifically. Lee et al. (2018) use EC and image captioning to build UNMT models, showing that EC promotes better translation than the multimodal alignment technique of Nakayama and Nishida (2017). Our approach differs in several important respects: we initialize our EC environment with *pre-trained language models*; we use both EC and backtranslation; and we do not simultaneously train on the EC objective and image captioning objective. Moreover, because we use one multilingual model, our caption grounding only uses one language, instead of all languages. Our results show that EC promotes unsupervised translation in the context of advanced methods that combine pre-training with backtranslation.

Li et al. (2020b) use emergent communication as a pre-training step for NMT systems. They have agents play an EC game, and then use those parameters to initialize an NMT system. They find that (together with adapters and weight-distance regularization) EC pre-training improves in BLEU over a standard NMT baseline, with especially large gains coming in the few-shot setting. While this shows that EC can provide a good initialization for a recurrent NMT system, our present work shows that EC can provide a good fine-tuning signal for a pre-trained multilingual language model. We also note two differences with respect to both works: (i) they use recurrent networks, whereas we start from a pre-trained transformer, and (ii) they use separate models for each language, whereas we use one multilingual model.

Lee et al. (2019) cast translation as a communication game with a third pivot language as the latent space in order to study (i) language drift from a pre-trained supervised MT model and (ii) using visual grounding (via gold image captions) plus language modeling to counter such drift. This approach thus does use EC with a pre-trained model, but it is a small model trained on the target task (translation). Our approach encourages using EC in conjunction with large-scale pre-trained language models which are intended to be general-purpose.

Finally, Lazaridou et al. (2020) study various ways of combining EC with a standard vision-language task, namely image captioning. They identify several forms of language drift and explore ways of incorporating auxillary losses. This work heavily inspires our own, since many of their settings correspond to using a pre-trained image-caption system. Our focus, however, has been on using EC to fine-tune large-scale pre-trained models on a language-only task, which introduces its own challenges and has its own benefits.

Multimodal pre-training Recently, efforts in multimodal pre-training are surging, especially in vision-language (V-L) pre-training (Du et al., 2022). Most of the works create joint V-L representations through a fusion encoder (Li et al., 2020a, 2019; Tan and Bansal, 2019), where the fused representation is the joint representation of image and text, as learned by a single encoder. Other recent works such as CLIP (Radford et al., 2021) and ALIGN (Jia et al., 2021) attempt to use different encoders for images and text to make the framework more efficient. While V-L pre-training models image and text data jointly (Du et al., 2022; Wang et al., 2021), we start with an existing pre-trained language model and further train it through the communication process in an image referential game. Although we expect the alignment between image and text to arise through this process, we view the visual modality as an additional signal to ground the multilingual communication process.

We also note that most previous work on V-L pre-training is evaluated solely on vision or V-L tasks (Li et al., 2019; Radford et al., 2021; Jia et al., 2021). The advantage of this joint pre-training for language-only tasks remains unclear (Yun et al., 2021; Pezzelle et al., 2021). In this paper, we focus on a language-only task (UNMT) to evaluate whether visual grounding can improve such tasks.

Finally, we note that EC-FT is more general than typical approaches to multimodal pre-training. While the image-based task we employ here works by promoting multimodal alignment, the range of possible tasks that can be used in EC-FT is huge, from directing other agents (Mordatch and Abbeel, 2018) to controlling a robot (Das et al., 2019) to playing games and reasoning about social dilemmas (Jaques et al., 2019). This wide range of tasks can incorporate many dimensions of communication that should be beneficial for NLP systems—e.g. other agents with their own private goals, social context, embodied control—that are not easily captured by multimodal pre-training (Bender and Koller, 2020; Bisk et al., 2020). In terms of Bisk et al. (2020)'s *world scopes* mentioned in the introduction, multimodal pre-training corresponds to world scope 3 (perception); EC-FT has the ability to move us much closer towards the final scopes 4 (embodiment and action) and 5 (the social world).

Multimodal Fine-tuning A related body of work focuses on adapting pre-trained language-only models for use in multi-modal tasks. For example, Tsimpoukelli et al. (2021) show that using a frozen language model and adapting a visual encoder to produce embeddings aligned with the LM's can be useful for few-shot learning in multimodal tasks like visual question answering. Liang et al. (2022) make this approach more modular by additionally freezing the visual encoder and learning separate prompt vectors. In the EC-FT context, these works suffer some of the same limitations in world scope, but could provide very useful methods for the environment-to-sender adapter step discussed in Section 2.1.

8 Conclusion

We have shown that Emergent Communication can be used as a fine-tuning signal for a large pre-trained multilingual model; this grounding in a goal-oriented multimodal task yields improvements over an unsupervised NMT baseline in all four languages studied. There is likely room to further improve upon the specific EC variants we propose here, since we believe the EC process is under-optimized for hyperparameters. We have further noted that the framework we propose leaves extensive room for further experimentation, since there are many choice points of the general EC setup that we have not yet tested, and may be promising avenues for future improvement. The general EC-FT framework may also be applied to other tasks beyond UNMT in future work.

Author Contribution Statement

Following a practice in several other fields, we here list author contributions according to the Contributor Role Taxonomy (CRediT; Allen et al., 2019). **C.M. Downey:** Conceptualization, Methodology, Software, Validation, Investigation, Writing - original draft, Writing - review and editing, Visualization. **Xuhui Zhou:** Conceptualization, Methodology, Software, Validation, Investigation, Data curation, Writing - review and editing. **Zeyu Liu:** Conceptualization, Methodology, Software, Validation, Investigation, Data curation, Writing - review and editing. **Shane Steinert-Threkeld:** Conceptualization, Methodology, Resources, Writing - original draft, Writing - review and editing, Supervision, Project administration, Funding acquisition.

Limitations

One limitation of our work concerns analysis. Much remains to be learned about the mechanisms by which EC can help translation. By evaluating the model more comprehensively, we could gain insight into whether and how the grounding helps task performance. Based on such analysis, a better version of the pipeline could be developed.

We observed significant variability across random seeds in our EC training; methods for stabilizing this variability could ensure the reliability of EC as a fine-tuning process for models.

Finally, we investigated only four non-English languages, two 'high-resource' and two 'low-resource'. It would be valuable to explore a wider range of typologically diverse languages to validate that these methods apply across the board and, if not, to understand what language factors drive success.

Ethics Statement

This work on unsupervised translation should have a positive impact on many under-served language communities by extending the reach of a core language technology (translation) to languages which lack the extensive parallel data required for supervised translation systems.

That being said, there are ethical risks with the present approach. The pre-training of mBART depends on the CommonCrawl dataset, so there might be some offensive language and even identity leakage due to CommonCrawl's preprocessing pipeline. It is possible that the model will generate toxic and biased utterances in our experiments. We didn't evaluate the toxicity of our generation. Our intuition is that the caption grounding will bias the model towards descriptive captions and thus suppress the toxic generation.

Acknowledgments

We thank Emily M Bender, Emmanuel Chemla, Chris Potts, Tania Rojas-Esponda, and the anonymous reviewers of and audience at the ICLR 2022 Emergent Communication workshop for helpful discussion. This work was partially supported by funding from the University of Washington Royalty Research Fund (RRF), grant number A167354 "Learning to translate by learning to communicate".

References

Liz Allen, Alison O'Connell, and Veronique Kiermer. 2019. How can we ensure visibility and diversity in research contributions? How the Contributor Role Taxonomy (CRediT) is helping the shift from authorship to contributorship. *Learned Publishing*, 32(1):71–74.

Jacob Andreas. 2019. Measuring compositionality in representation learning. In *7th International Conference on Learning Representations, ICLR 2019, New Orleans, LA, USA, May 6-9, 2019*. OpenReview.net.

Mikel Artetxe, Gorka Labaka, Eneko Agirre, and Kyunghyun Cho. 2018. Unsupervised neural machine translation. In *International Conference of Learning Representations*. _eprint: 1710.11041.

Dzmitry Bahdanau, Kyunghyun Cho, and Yoshua Bengio. 2015. Neural Machine Translation by Jointly Learning to Align and Translate. In *International Conference of Learning Representations (ICLR)*, pages 1–15. _eprint: 1409.0473.

Loïc Barrault, Ondřej Bojar, Marta R. Costa-jussà, Christian Federmann, Mark Fishel, Yvette Graham, Barry Haddow, Matthias Huck, Philipp Koehn, Shervin Malmasi, Christof Monz, Mathias Müller, Santanu Pal, Matt Post, and Marcos Zampieri. 2019. Findings of the 2019 conference on machine translation (WMT19). In *Proceedings of the Fourth Conference on Machine Translation (Volume 2: Shared Task Papers, Day 1)*, pages 1–61, Florence, Italy. Association for Computational Linguistics.

Christos Baziotis, Barry Haddow, and Alexandra Birch. 2020. Language model prior for low-resource neural machine translation. In *Proceedings of the 2020 Conference on Empirical Methods in Natural Language Processing (EMNLP)*, pages 7622–7634, Online. Association for Computational Linguistics.

Emily M. Bender and Alexander Koller. 2020. Climbing towards NLU: On meaning, form, and understanding in the age of data. In *Proceedings of the 58th Annual Meeting of the Association for Computational Linguistics*, pages 5185–5198, Online. Association for Computational Linguistics.

Yonatan Bisk, Ari Holtzman, Jesse Thomason, Jacob Andreas, Yoshua Bengio, Joyce Chai, Mirella Lapata, Angeliki Lazaridou, Jonathan May, Aleksandr Nisnevich, Nicolas Pinto, and Joseph Turian. 2020. Experience grounds language. In *Proceedings of the 2020 Conference on Empirical Methods in Natural Language Processing (EMNLP)*, pages 8718–8735, Online. Association for Computational Linguistics.

Tom Brown, Benjamin Mann, Nick Ryder, Melanie Subbiah, Jared D Kaplan, Prafulla Dhariwal, Arvind Neelakantan, Pranav Shyam, Girish Sastry, Amanda Askell, Sandhini Agarwal, Ariel Herbert-Voss, Gretchen Krueger, Tom Henighan, Rewon Child, Aditya Ramesh, Daniel Ziegler, Jeffrey Wu, Clemens Winter, Chris Hesse, Mark Chen, Eric Sigler, Mateusz Litwin, Scott Gray, Benjamin Chess, Jack Clark, Christopher Berner, Sam McCandlish, Alec Radford, Ilya Sutskever, and Dario Amodei. 2020. Language Models Are Few-Shot Learners. In *Advances in Neural Information Processing Systems*, volume 33, pages 1877–1901. Curran Associates, Inc.

Rahma Chaabouni, Eugene Kharitonov, Diane Bouchacourt, Emmanuel Dupoux, and Marco Baroni. 2020. Compositionality and Generalization In Emergent

Languages. In *Proceedings of the 58th Annual Meeting of the Association for Computational Linguistics*, pages 4427–4442, Stroudsburg, PA, USA. Association for Computational Linguistics. _eprint: 2004.09124.

Rahma Chaabouni, Eugene Kharitonov, Emmanuel Dupoux, and Marco Baroni. 2019a. Anti-efficient encoding in emergent communication. In *Proceedings of the 33rd Conference on Neural Information Processing Systems (NeurIPS 2019)*. _eprint: 1905.12561v4.

Rahma Chaabouni, Eugene Kharitonov, Alessandro Lazaric, Emmanuel Dupoux, and Marco Baroni. 2019b. Word-order Biases in Deep-agent Emergent Communication. In *Proceedings of the 57th Annual Meeting of the Association for Computational Linguistics*, pages 5166–5175, Stroudsburg, PA, USA. Association for Computational Linguistics.

Alexis Conneau, Kartikay Khandelwal, Naman Goyal, Vishrav Chaudhary, Guillaume Wenzek, Francisco Guzmán, Edouard Grave, Myle Ott, Luke Zettlemoyer, and Veselin Stoyanov. 2020. Unsupervised cross-lingual representation learning at scale. In *Proceedings of the 58th Annual Meeting of the Association for Computational Linguistics*, pages 8440–8451, Online. Association for Computational Linguistics.

Abhishek Das, Théophile Gervet, Joshua Romoff, Dhruv Batra, Devi Parikh, Mike Rabbat, and Joelle Pineau. 2019. TarMAC: Targeted Multi-Agent Communication. In *Proceedings of the 36th International Conference on Machine Learning*, volume 97 of *Proceedings of Machine Learning Research*, pages 1538–1546. PMLR.

Jacob Devlin, Ming-Wei Chang, Kenton Lee, and Kristina Toutanova. 2019. BERT: Pre-training of deep bidirectional transformers for language understanding. In *Proceedings of the 2019 Conference of the North American Chapter of the Association for Computational Linguistics: Human Language Technologies, Volume 1 (Long and Short Papers)*, pages 4171–4186, Minneapolis, Minnesota. Association for Computational Linguistics.

Alexey Dosovitskiy, Lucas Beyer, Alexander Kolesnikov, Dirk Weissenborn, Xiaohua Zhai, Thomas Unterthiner, Mostafa Dehghani, Matthias Minderer, Georg Heigold, Sylvain Gelly, Jakob Uszkoreit, and Neil Houlsby. 2021. An image is worth 16x16 words: Transformers for image recognition at scale. In *International Conference of Learning Representations (ICLR)*.

Yifan Du, Zikang Liu, Junyi Li, and Wayne Xin Zhao. 2022. A survey of vision-language pre-trained models. *CoRR*, abs/2202.10936.

Allyson Ettinger. 2020. What BERT is not: Lessons from a new suite of psycholinguistic diagnostics for language models. *Transactions of the Association for Computational Linguistics*, 8:34–48.

Nur Geffen Lan, Emmanuel Chemla, and Shane Steinert-Threlkeld. 2020. On the Spontaneous Emergence of Discrete and Compositional Signals. In *Proceedings of the 58th Annual Meeting of the Association for Computational Linguistics*, pages 4794–4800, Stroudsburg, PA, USA. Association for Computational Linguistics.

Francisco Guzmán, Peng-Jen Chen, Myle Ott, Juan Pino, Guillaume Lample, Philipp Koehn, Vishrav Chaudhary, and Marc'Aurelio Ranzato. 2019. The FLORES evaluation datasets for low-resource machine translation: Nepali–English and Sinhala–English. In *Proceedings of the 2019 Conference on Empirical Methods in Natural Language Processing and the 9th International Joint Conference on Natural Language Processing (EMNLP-IJCNLP)*, pages 6098–6111, Hong Kong, China. Association for Computational Linguistics.

Barry Haddow, Rachel Bawden, Antonio Valerio Miceli Barone, Jindřich Helcl, and Alexandra Birch. 2022. Survey of Low-Resource Machine Translation. Technical Report arXiv:2109.00486, arXiv. ArXiv:2109.00486 [cs] type: article.

Stevan Harnad. 1990. The Symbol Grounding Problem. *Physica D: Nonlinear Phenomena*, 42(1):335–346.

Serhii Havrylov and Ivan Titov. 2017. Emergence of Language with Multi-agent Games: Learning to Communicate with Sequences of Symbols. In *Proceedings of the 31st Conference on Neural Information Processing Systems (NeurIPS 2017)*. _eprint: 1705.11192.

Di He, Yingce Xia, Tao Qin, Liwei Wang, Nenghai Yu, Tie-Yan Liu, and Wei-Ying Ma. 2016a. Dual learning for machine translation. In *Advances in Neural Information Processing Systems*, volume 29. Curran Associates, Inc.

Kaiming He, Xiangyu Zhang, Shaoqing Ren, and Jian Sun. 2016b. Deep Residual Learning for Image Recognition. In *2016 IEEE Conference on Computer Vision and Pattern Recognition (CVPR)*, pages 770–778.

Jeremy Howard and Sebastian Ruder. 2018. Universal language model fine-tuning for text classification. In *Proceedings of the 56th Annual Meeting of the Association for Computational Linguistics (Volume 1: Long Papers)*, pages 328–339, Melbourne, Australia. Association for Computational Linguistics.

Eric Jang, Shixiang Gu, and Ben Poole. 2017. Categorical Reparameterization with Gumbel-Softmax. In *Proceedings of the International Conference on Learning Representations*.

Natasha Jaques, Angeliki Lazaridou, Edward Hughes, Caglar Gulcehre, Pedro Ortega, Dj Strouse, Joel Z. Leibo, and Nando De Freitas. 2019. Social Influence as Intrinsic Motivation for Multi-Agent Deep Reinforcement Learning. In *Proceedings of the 36th*

International Conference on Machine Learning, volume 97 of *Proceedings of Machine Learning Research*, pages 3040–3049. PMLR.

Chao Jia, Yinfei Yang, Ye Xia, Yi-Ting Chen, Zarana Parekh, Hieu Pham, Quoc V. Le, Yun-Hsuan Sung, Zhen Li, and Tom Duerig. 2021. Scaling up visual and vision-language representation learning with noisy text supervision. In *Proceedings of the 38th International Conference on Machine Learning, ICML 2021, 18-24 July 2021, Virtual Event*, volume 139 of *Proceedings of Machine Learning Research*, pages 4904–4916. PMLR.

Pratik Joshi, Sebastin Santy, Amar Budhiraja, Kalika Bali, and Monojit Choudhury. 2020. The State and Fate of Linguistic Diversity and Inclusion in the NLP World. In *Proceedings of the 58th Annual Meeting of the Association for Computational Linguistics*, pages 6282–6293, Stroudsburg, PA, USA. Association for Computational Linguistics.

Guillaume Lample and Alexis Conneau. 2019. Cross-lingual Language Model Pretraining. In *33rd Conference on Neural Information Processing Systems (NeurIPS 2019)*. _eprint: 1901.07291.

Guillaume Lample, Alexis Conneau, Ludovic Denoyer, and Marc'Aurelio Ranzato. 2018a. Unsupervised machine translation using monolingual corpora only. In *International Conference of Learning Representations (ICLR)*.

Guillaume Lample, Alexis Conneau, Marc'Aurelio Ranzato, Ludovic Denoyer, and Hervé Jégou. 2018b. Word translation without parallel data. In *International Conference on Learning Representations*.

Guillaume Lample, Myle Ott, Alexis Conneau, Ludovic Denoyer, and Marc'Aurelio Ranzato. 2018c. Phrase-based & neural unsupervised machine translation. In *Proceedings of the 2018 Conference on Empirical Methods in Natural Language Processing*, pages 5039–5049, Brussels, Belgium. Association for Computational Linguistics.

Angeliki Lazaridou and Marco Baroni. 2020. Emergent Multi-Agent Communication in the Deep Learning Era. pages 1–24. _eprint: 2006.02419.

Angeliki Lazaridou, Anna Potapenko, and Olivier Tieleman. 2020. Multi-agent communication meets natural language: Synergies between functional and structural language learning. In *Proceedings of the 58th Annual Meeting of the Association for Computational Linguistics*, pages 7663–7674, Online. Association for Computational Linguistics.

Jason Lee, Kyunghyun Cho, and Douwe Kiela. 2019. Countering language drift via visual grounding. In *Proceedings of the 2019 Conference on Empirical Methods in Natural Language Processing and the 9th International Joint Conference on Natural Language Processing (EMNLP-IJCNLP)*, pages 4385–4395, Hong Kong, China. Association for Computational Linguistics.

Jason Lee, Kyunghyun Cho, Jason Weston, and Douwe Kiela. 2018. Emergent translation in multi-agent communication. *6th International Conference on Learning Representations, ICLR 2018 - Conference Track Proceedings*, pages 1–18. _eprint: 1710.06922.

Mike Lewis, Yinhan Liu, Naman Goyal, Marjan Ghazvininejad, Abdelrahman Mohamed, Omer Levy, Veselin Stoyanov, and Luke Zettlemoyer. 2020. BART: Denoising Sequence-to-Sequence Pre-training for Natural Language Generation, Translation, and Comprehension. In *Proceedings of the 58th Annual Meeting of the Association for Computational Linguistics*, pages 7871–7880, Stroudsburg, PA, USA. Association for Computational Linguistics. _eprint: 1910.13461.

Gen Li, Nan Duan, Yuejian Fang, Ming Gong, and Daxin Jiang. 2020a. Unicoder-vl: A universal encoder for vision and language by cross-modal pre-training. In *The Thirty-Fourth AAAI Conference on Artificial Intelligence, AAAI 2020, The Thirty-Second Innovative Applications of Artificial Intelligence Conference, IAAI 2020, The Tenth AAAI Symposium on Educational Advances in Artificial Intelligence, EAAI 2020, New York, NY, USA, February 7-12, 2020*, pages 11336–11344. AAAI Press.

Liunian Harold Li, Mark Yatskar, Da Yin, Cho-Jui Hsieh, and Kai-Wei Chang. 2019. Visualbert: A simple and performant baseline for vision and language. *CoRR*, abs/1908.03557.

Yaoyiran Li, Edoardo Maria Ponti, Ivan Vulić, and Anna Korhonen. 2020b. Emergent communication pretraining for few-shot machine translation. In *Proceedings of the 28th International Conference on Computational Linguistics*, pages 4716–4731, Barcelona, Spain (Online). International Committee on Computational Linguistics.

Sheng Liang, Mengjie Zhao, and Hinrich Schütze. 2022. Modular and Parameter-Efficient Multimodal Fusion with Prompting. *arXiv:2203.08055 [cs]*. ArXiv: 2203.08055.

Tsung-Yi Lin, Michael Maire, Serge J. Belongie, Lubomir D. Bourdev, Ross B. Girshick, James Hays, Pietro Perona, Deva Ramanan, Piotr Dollár, and C. Lawrence Zitnick. 2014. Microsoft COCO: Common Objects in Context. *CoRR*, abs/1405.0312. ArXiv: 1405.0312.

Tal Linzen. 2020. How can we accelerate progress towards human-like linguistic generalization? In *Proceedings of the 58th Annual Meeting of the Association for Computational Linguistics*, pages 5210–5217, Online. Association for Computational Linguistics.

Xihui Liu, Hongsheng Li, Jing Shao, Dapeng Chen, and Xiaogang Wang. 2018. Show, Tell and Discriminate: Image Captioning by Self-retrieval with Partially Labeled Data. In Vittorio Ferrari, Martial Hebert, Cristian Sminchisescu, and Yair Weiss, editors, *Computer*

Vision – ECCV 2018, volume 11219, pages 353–369. Springer International Publishing, Cham.

Yinhan Liu, Jiatao Gu, Naman Goyal, Xian Li, Sergey Edunov, Marjan Ghazvininejad, Mike Lewis, and Luke Zettlemoyer. 2020. Multilingual denoising pre-training for neural machine translation. *Transactions of the Association for Computational Linguistics*, 8:726–742.

Yinhan Liu, Myle Ott, Naman Goyal, Jingfei Du, Mandar Joshi, Danqi Chen, Omer Levy, Mike Lewis, Luke Zettlemoyer, and Veselin Stoyanov. 2019. RoBERTa: A Robustly Optimized BERT Pretraining Approach. *ArXiv*, abs/1907.11692.

Ryan Lowe, Abhinav Gupta, Jakob Foerster, Douwe Kiela, and Joelle Pineau. 2020. On the interaction between supervision and self-play in emergent communication. In *International Conference on Learning Representations*.

Yuchen Lu, Soumye Singhal, Florian Strub, Aaron Courville, and Olivier Pietquin. 2020. Countering Language Drift with Seeded Iterated Learning. In *Proceedings of the 37th International Conference on Machine Learning*, volume 119 of *Proceedings of Machine Learning Research*, pages 6437–6447. PMLR.

Chris J Maddison, Andriy Mnih, Yee Whye Teh, United Kingdom, and United Kingdom. 2017. The Concrete Distribution: A Continuous Relaxation of Discrete Random Variables. In *International Conference of Learning Representations (ICLR)*.

Tom McCoy, Ellie Pavlick, and Tal Linzen. 2019. Right for the wrong reasons: Diagnosing syntactic heuristics in natural language inference. In *Proceedings of the 57th Annual Meeting of the Association for Computational Linguistics*, pages 3428–3448, Florence, Italy. Association for Computational Linguistics.

William Merrill, Yoav Goldberg, Roy Schwartz, and Noah A. Smith. 2021. Provable Limitations of Acquiring Meaning from Ungrounded Form: What Will Future Language Models Understand? *Transactions of the Association for Computational Linguistics*, 9:1047–1060.

Igor Mordatch and P. Abbeel. 2018. Emergence of Grounded Compositional Language in Multi-Agent Populations. In *AAAI*.

Jesse Mu and Noah D. Goodman. 2021. Emergent Communication of Generalizations. In *Proceedings of Neural Information Processing Systems (NeurIPS)*.

James Mullenbach, Yada Pruksachatkun, Sean Adler, Jennifer Seale, Jordan Swartz, Greg McKelvey, Hui Dai, Yi Yang, and David Sontag. 2021. CLIP: A dataset for extracting action items for physicians from hospital discharge notes. In *Proceedings of the 59th Annual Meeting of the Association for Computational Linguistics and the 11th International Joint Conference on Natural Language Processing (Volume 1: Long Papers)*, pages 1365–1378, Online. Association for Computational Linguistics.

Hideki Nakayama and Noriki Nishida. 2017. Zero-resource machine translation by multimodal encoder–decoder network with multimedia pivot. *Machine Translation*, 31(1-2):49–64. Publisher: Springer Netherlands _eprint: 1611.04503.

Xing Niu, Weijia Xu, and Marine Carpuat. 2019. Bi-directional differentiable input reconstruction for low-resource neural machine translation. In *Proceedings of the 2019 Conference of the North American Chapter of the Association for Computational Linguistics: Human Language Technologies, Volume 1 (Long and Short Papers)*, pages 442–448, Minneapolis, Minnesota. Association for Computational Linguistics.

Timothy Niven and Hung-Yu Kao. 2019. Probing neural network comprehension of natural language arguments. In *Proceedings of the 57th Annual Meeting of the Association for Computational Linguistics*, pages 4658–4664, Florence, Italy. Association for Computational Linguistics.

Adam Paszke, Sam Gross, Francisco Massa, Adam Lerer, James Bradbury, Gregory Chanan, Trevor Killeen, Zeming Lin, Natalia Gimelshein, Luca Antiga, Alban Desmaison, Andreas Köpf, Edward Z. Yang, Zachary DeVito, Martin Raison, Alykhan Tejani, Sasank Chilamkurthy, Benoit Steiner, Lu Fang, Junjie Bai, and Soumith Chintala. 2019. Pytorch: An imperative style, high-performance deep learning library. In *Advances in Neural Information Processing Systems 32: Annual Conference on Neural Information Processing Systems 2019, NeurIPS 2019, December 8-14, 2019, Vancouver, BC, Canada*, pages 8024–8035.

Matthew E. Peters, Mark Neumann, Mohit Iyyer, Matt Gardner, Christopher Clark, Kenton Lee, and Luke Zettlemoyer. 2018. Deep contextualized word representations. In *Proceedings of the 2018 Conference of the North American Chapter of the Association for Computational Linguistics: Human Language Technologies, Volume 1 (Long Papers)*, pages 2227–2237, New Orleans, Louisiana. Association for Computational Linguistics.

Sandro Pezzelle, Ece Takmaz, and Raquel Fernández. 2021. Word Representation Learning in Multimodal Pre-Trained Transformers: An Intrinsic Evaluation. *Transactions of the Association for Computational Linguistics*, 9:1563–1579.

Alec Radford, Jong Wook Kim, Chris Hallacy, Aditya Ramesh, Gabriel Goh, Sandhini Agarwal, Girish Sastry, Amanda Askell, Pamela Mishkin, Jack Clark, Gretchen Krueger, and Ilya Sutskever. 2021. Learning Transferable Visual Models From Natural Language Supervision. In *Proceedings of the 38th International Conference on Machine Learning*, volume 139 of *Proceedings of Machine Learning Research*, pages 8748–8763. PMLR.

Ricardo Rei, Craig Stewart, Ana C Farinha, and Alon Lavie. 2020. COMET: A neural framework for MT evaluation. In *Proceedings of the 2020 Conference on Empirical Methods in Natural Language Processing (EMNLP)*, pages 2685–2702, Online. Association for Computational Linguistics.

Anna Rogers, Olga Kovaleva, and Anna Rumshisky. 2020. A primer in BERTology: What we know about how BERT works. *Transactions of the Association for Computational Linguistics*, 8:842–866.

Rico Sennrich, Barry Haddow, and Alexandra Birch. 2016a. Improving neural machine translation models with monolingual data. In *Proceedings of the 54th Annual Meeting of the Association for Computational Linguistics (Volume 1: Long Papers)*, pages 86–96, Berlin, Germany. Association for Computational Linguistics.

Rico Sennrich, Barry Haddow, and Alexandra Birch. 2016b. Neural machine translation of rare words with subword units. In *Proceedings of the 54th Annual Meeting of the Association for Computational Linguistics (Volume 1: Long Papers)*, pages 1715–1725, Berlin, Germany. Association for Computational Linguistics.

Brian Skyrms. 2010. *Signals: Evolution, Learning, and Information*. Oxford University Press.

Kaitao Song, Xu Tan, Tao Qin, Jianfeng Lu, and Tie-Yan Liu. 2019. MASS: Masked Sequence to Sequence Pre-training for Language Generation. In *Proceedings of the 36th International Conference on Machine Learning*, volume 97 of *Proceedings of Machine Learning Research*, pages 5926–5936. PMLR.

Shane Steinert-Threlkeld. 2020. Toward the Emergence of Nontrivial Compositionality. *Philosophy of Science*, 87(5):897–909. Publisher: The University of Chicago Press.

Shane Steinert-Threlkeld, Leo Z. Liu, Xuhui Zhou, and C.M. Downey. 2022. Emergent communication fine-tuning (EC-FT) for pretrained language models. In *Proceedings of the 5th Annual Workshop on Emergent Communication, ICLR*.

Ilya Sutskever, Oriol Vinyals, and Quoc V. Le. 2014. Sequence to Sequence Learning with Neural Networks. In *Advances in Neural Information Processing Systems 27 (NIPS 2014)*. _eprint: 1409.3215.

Mariarosaria Taddeo and Luciano Floridi. 2005. Solving the Symbol Grounding Problem: A Critical Review of Fifteen Years of Research. *Journal of Experimental & Theoretical Artificial Intelligence*, 17(4):419–445. Publisher: Taylor & Francis.

Hao Tan and Mohit Bansal. 2019. LXMERT: Learning cross-modality encoder representations from transformers. In *Proceedings of the 2019 Conference on Empirical Methods in Natural Language Processing and the 9th International Joint Conference on Natural Language Processing (EMNLP-IJCNLP)*, pages 5100–5111, Hong Kong, China. Association for Computational Linguistics.

Maria Tsimpoukelli, Jacob Menick, and Serkan Cabi. 2021. Multimodal Few-Shot Learning with Frozen Language Models. In *Neural Information Processing Systems*.

Kyle Wagner, James A. Reggia, Juan Uriagereka, and Gerald Wilkinson. 2003. Progress in the Simulation of Emergent Communication and Language. *Adapt. Behav.*, 11(1):37–69.

Jianfeng Wang, Xiaowei Hu, Zhe Gan, Zhengyuan Yang, Xiyang Dai, Zicheng Liu, Yumao Lu, and Lijuan Wang. 2021. UFO: A unified transformer for vision-language representation learning. *CoRR*, abs/2111.10023.

Thomas Wolf, Lysandre Debut, Victor Sanh, Julien Chaumond, Clement Delangue, Anthony Moi, Pierric Cistac, Tim Rault, Rémi Louf, Morgan Funtowicz, and Jamie Brew. 2019. Huggingface's transformers: State-of-the-art natural language processing. *CoRR*, abs/1910.03771.

Shijie Wu and Mark Dredze. 2020. Are all languages created equal in multilingual BERT? In *Proceedings of the 5th Workshop on Representation Learning for NLP*, pages 120–130, Online. Association for Computational Linguistics.

Yonghui Wu, Mike Schuster, Zhifeng Chen, Quoc V. Le, Mohammad Norouzi, Wolfgang Macherey, Maxim Krikun, Yuan Cao, Qin Gao, Klaus Macherey, Jeff Klingner, Apurva Shah, Melvin Johnson, Xiaobing Liu, \Lukasz Kaiser, Stephan Gouws, Yoshikiyo Kato, Taku Kudo, Hideto Kazawa, Keith Stevens, George Kurian, Nishant Patil, Wei Wang, Cliff Young, Jason Smith, Jason Riesa, Alex Rudnick, Oriol Vinyals, Greg Corrado, Macduff Hughes, and Jeffrey Dean. 2016. Google's Neural Machine Translation System: Bridging the Gap between Human and Machine Translation. _eprint: 1609.08144.

Tian Yun, Chen Sun, and Ellie Pavlick. 2021. Does vision-and-language pretraining improve lexical grounding? In *Findings of the Association for Computational Linguistics: EMNLP 2021*, pages 4357–4366, Punta Cana, Dominican Republic. Association for Computational Linguistics.

A Main Experiments Training Details

We here include more details about the training protocol for the results reported in Section 4. Our codebase is built upon the mBART code from `huggingface` (Wolf et al., 2019) and PyTorch (Paszke et al., 2019). We use one NVIDIA RTX 8000 GPU for each experiment. Backtranslation is the most expensive part of the entire training pipeline. It takes around 24-28 hours to finish, depending on the languages. The combined training time for caption grounding and emergent communication is within 1 hour.

Baseline As discussed in section 3, our UNMT baseline is established by starting with mBART and performing 8192 steps of iterative backtranslation for each translation pair. We use a batch size of 32 and a maximum generated sequence length of 64. See more hyperparameter choices in Table 3.

I2I-EC For our I2I-EC fine-tuned model, training consists of the following pipeline

1. 2048 steps of backtranslation
2. 2048 steps of supervised captioning training (English-only)
3. 2048 steps of EC fine-tuning
4. 6144 steps of backtranslation

Backtranslation uses the same exact hyperparameters as in the baseline, but with training split between the first 2048 and last 6144 steps (Table 3).

Supervised caption training is described in Section 2.1. We have 8 choices for the image selection task (7 distractors and 1 correct choice). As part of Sender agent, we use a one-layer autoregressive transformer to serialize (or, "unroll") a single ResNet image representation to a sequence of vectors to imitate the sequential data mBART observes during its pre-training. The unrolled sequence is used in the sender's cross-attention, and the sender is trained to generate the gold-standard caption.

Also during the supervised captioning stage, the receiver takes in the gold-standard caption, and a one-layer RNN is used to aggregate its final hidden states and choose the correct image. The image selection (cross-entropy) loss is scaled with λ, before being added to the caption-generation loss. Full hyperparameter choices are detailed in Table 4.

I2I-EC fine-tuning is also described in Section 2.1. Different from caption grounding, we have a total of 16 image choices instead of 8. The adapter unrolls the ResNet image representation to a length of 32. The emergent generation is language-constrained as described in Section 3 with a threshold. A repetition penalty is applied to the generations, and they are constrained to not repeat any 4-grams or longer. KL-regularization with a separate mBART instance fine-tuned on causal language modeling is applied with a λ parameter. Full hyperparameter choices are detailed in Table 5.

T2I-EC For our T2I-EC fine-tuned model, training is performed slightly differently for empirical reasons

1. 2048 steps of supervised captioning training (English-only)
2. 2048 steps of EC fine-tuning
3. 8192 steps of backtranslation

T2I-EC hyperparameters are very similar to I2I-EC. See full parameters in Tables 3, 4, and 5.

Auxiliary CLM To have a language model for use in KL regularization (see equation (2)), we fine-tuned just the mBART decoder on the same common crawl data used for its pretraining in all of the languages of interest. We trained for 100000 steps, batch size 32, sequence length 96, and learning rate of 6×10^{-6}. This model was then frozen during EC training and only used to compute the KL divergence which was used in updating the sender's parameters.

B Manipulations Training Details

All manipulations are performed on the main T2I-EC process. Interleaved training uses versions of the the learning rate schedules used for the main experiments shortened by a factor of 4.

C Full results

In Table 6, we include full results for our main experiment (summarized in Table 1). Although we found the EC process to help with machine translation, it also leads to instability in model training. We a systematic study of this variation to future work.

In Table 7 we show experiments with a more modern choice of image encoder — CLIP-Large (Mullenbach et al., 2021). We find that the CLIP-Large encoder under-performs ResNet.

The full results from our manipulation experiments (Section 5) are found in Table 8.

Name	Values
optimizer	`Adam(betas=(0.9, 0.999))` (default in PyTorch)
LR scheduler	`constant_w_warmup`
`grad_clip`	1.0
`batch_size`	32
`evaluate_bleu_every`	256
|validation_set|	4096
#beams	5
first `#vocab_constrained_steps`	2048
threshold (after `#vocab_constrained_steps`)	0.99
#warmup_steps	$\frac{1}{4}\cdot$ #steps

(a) Backtranslation shared parameters

(b) Baseline

Name	Values
Learning rate	2.0e-5
#steps	8192
first_threshold	0.90

(c) I2I-EC (Initial BT)

Name	Values
Learning rate	1.0e-5
#steps	2048
first_threshold	0.96

(d) I2I-EC (Secondary BT)

Name	Values
Learning rate	1.0e-5
#steps	6144

(e) T2I-EC

Name	Values
Learning rate	1.0e-5
#steps	8192
first_threshold	0.96

Table 3: Hyper-parameters for backtranslation.

Name	Values
optimizer	`Adam(betas=(0.9, 0.999))` (default in PyTorch)
#steps	2048
learning rate	4.0e-5
LR scheduler	`linear_w_warmup`
#warm-up steps	0
batch_size	16
#distractors	7
Reshaper (Sender & Receiver)	linear projection
Dropout (anywhere)	0.0
Image Unroll	one (auto-regressive) transformer layer
Image Unroll length	32
Receiver aggregation	RNN
Sender	no freezing
Receiver	no freezing
beam_width	1 (Greedy)
temperature	1.0
gumble_softmax sample	one-hot
`repetition_penalty`	1.0
`max_seq_length`	32

(a) Captioning shared parameters

(b) I2I-EC

Name	Values
Image selection loss λ	4.0
grad_clip	1.0

(c) T2I-EC

Name	Values
Image selection loss λ	8.0
grad_clip	0.5

Table 4: Hyper-parameters for caption grounding part of emergent communication.

Name	Values
optimizer	`Adam(betas=(0.9, 0.999))` (default in PyTorch)
#steps	2048
LR scheduler	`linear_w_warmup`
#warm-up steps	0
batch_size	12
#distractors	15
Reshaper (Sender & Receiver)	linear projection
Dropout (anywhere)	0.0
Image Unroll	one (auto-regressive) transformer layer
Image Unroll length	32
Receiver aggregation	RNN
Sender	no freezing
Receiver	no freezing
beam_width	1 (Greedy)
temperature	1.0
gumble_softmax sample	one-hot
`vocab_constraint_threshold`	0.99
`repetition_penalty`	1.0
`max_seq_length`	32

(a) Emergent communication shared parameters

(b) I2I-EC

Name	Values
Language modeling loss λ	0.125
Learning rate	6.0e-6
grad_clip	1.0

(c) T2I-EC. *: length of text string in place of series of "pseudo-images" from image unroller

Name	Values
Language modeling loss λ	0.0625
Learning rate	1.0e-6
grad_clip	0.5
`max_text_seq_length`*	128

Table 5: Hyper-parameters for emergent communication.

Model	Language	Seed	BLEU			COMET		
			en→X	X→en	mean	en→X	X→en	mean
baseline (mBART + BT)	zh	1	17.21	11.35	14.28	-0.04	0.14	0.05
		2	18.38	11.39	14.89	0.02	0.14	0.08
		3	18.45	11.36	14.90	0.03	0.15	0.09
	de	1	18.66	25.83	22.24	0.18	0.39	0.29
		2	19.06	25.73	22.39	0.20	0.38	0.29
		3	18.79	25.88	22.33	0.22	0.40	0.31
	ne	1	1.94	4.74	3.34	-0.19	-0.36	-0.27
		2	1.84	4.94	3.39	-0.20	-0.34	-0.27
		3	2.14	5.07	3.60	-0.24	-0.34	-0.29
	si	1	1.29	4.53	2.91	-0.29	-0.31	-0.30
		2	1.18	4.73	2.95	-0.18	-0.28	-0.23
		3	1.21	4.35	2.78	-0.20	-0.32	-0.26
I2I-EC	zh	1	17.31	10.96	14.13	-0.03	0.12	0.05
		2	17.03	11.24	14.14	0.00	0.15	0.07
		3	18.72	11.88	15.30	0.04	0.17	0.10
	de	1	18.22	25.41	21.81	0.18	0.39	0.29
		2	18.26	25.60	21.93	0.18	0.39	0.29
		3	18.06	25.28	21.67	0.20	0.40	0.30
	ne	1	1.24	5.13	3.19	-0.25	-0.31	-0.28
		2	1.22	5.30	3.26	-0.25	-0.36	-0.31
		3	1.51	5.34	3.43	-0.24	-0.33	-0.29
	si	1	0.01	0.08	0.04	-1.63	-1.05	-1.34
		2	0.00	0.02	0.01	-1.31	-1.28	-1.30
		3	0.01	0.05	0.03	-1.40	-1.15	-1.28
T2I-EC	zh	1	19.25	11.91	15.58	0.06	0.18	0.12
		2	0.09	0.11	0.10	-1.75	-1.60	-1.68
		3	18.60	12.27	15.43	0.05	0.18	0.11
	de	1	17.91	25.72	21.81	0.18	0.38	0.28
		2	18.64	26.20	22.42	0.19	0.41	0.30
		3	18.56	25.82	22.19	0.19	0.39	0.29
	ne	1	0.06	0.03	0.04	-1.27	-1.14	-1.20
		2	0.02	0.11	0.07	-1.33	-1.06	-1.20
		3	2.36	5.92	4.14	-0.20	-0.27	-0.24
	si	1	1.10	4.33	2.72	-0.25	-0.29	-0.27
		2	0.01	0.19	0.10	-1.42	-1.12	-1.27
		3	1.28	4.76	3.02	-0.18	-0.27	-0.22

Table 6: Full results of our main experiment with ResNet image representation.

Model	Language	Seed	BLEU			COMET		
			en→X	X→en	mean	en→X	X→en	mean
baseline (mBART + BT)	zh	1	17.21	11.35	14.28	-0.04	0.14	0.05
		2	18.38	11.39	14.89	0.02	0.14	0.08
		3	18.45	11.36	14.90	0.03	0.15	0.09
	de	1	18.66	25.83	22.24	0.18	0.39	0.29
		2	19.06	25.73	22.39	0.20	0.38	0.29
		3	18.79	25.88	22.33	0.22	0.40	0.31
	ne	1	1.94	4.74	3.34	-0.19	-0.36	-0.27
		2	1.84	4.94	3.39	-0.20	-0.34	-0.27
		3	2.14	5.07	3.60	-0.24	-0.34	-0.29
	si	1	1.29	4.53	2.91	-0.29	-0.31	-0.30
		2	1.18	4.73	2.95	-0.18	-0.28	-0.23
		3	1.21	4.35	2.78	-0.20	-0.32	-0.26
I2I-EC	zh	1	16.66	10.94	13.80	-0.07	0.13	0.03
		2	17.46	10.87	14.16	-0.01	0.13	0.06
		3	18.84	11.64	15.24	0.03	0.16	0.10
	de	1	18.64	26.17	22.40	0.22	0.40	0.31
		2	17.98	25.20	21.59	0.20	0.38	0.29
		3	18.09	25.35	21.72	0.20	0.40	0.30
	ne	1	1.02	4.68	2.85	-0.41	-0.38	-0.39
		2	1.87	5.19	3.53	-0.26	-0.33	-0.29
		3	1.79	5.29	3.54	-0.20	-0.34	-0.27
	si	1	0.30	1.64	0.97	-1.14	-0.59	-0.87
		2	0.16	0.55	0.36	-0.88	-0.88	-0.88
		3	0.76	4.88	2.82	-0.37	-0.29	-0.33
T2I-EC	zh	1	0.04	0.09	0.07	-1.69	-1.43	-1.56
		2	17.77	12.02	14.90	0.00	0.18	0.09
		3	17.24	11.23	14.24	-0.03	0.13	0.05
	de	1	10.45	14.14	12.29	-0.42	-0.30	-0.36
		2	18.52	25.93	22.23	0.20	0.40	0.30
		3	18.26	25.61	21.94	0.19	0.38	0.28
	ne	1	0.75	2.49	1.62	-0.85	-0.58	-0.71
		2	0.09	0.07	0.08	-1.37	-1.18	-1.28
		3	0.02	0.04	0.03	-1.35	-1.17	-1.26
	si	1	0.02	0.15	0.09	-2.00	-1.45	-1.72
		2	0.04	0.19	0.12	-2.02	-1.32	-1.67
		3	1.05	4.18	2.61	-0.33	-0.28	-0.30

Table 7: Full results of our main experiment with CLIP-Large image representation.

Manipulation	Language	Seed	BLEU			COMET		
			en→X	X→en	mean	en→X	X→en	mean
CLIP-img	de	1	10.45	14.14	12.29	-0.42	-0.30	-0.36
		2	18.52	25.93	22.23	0.20	0.40	0.30
		3	18.26	25.61	21.94	0.19	0.38	0.28
	si	1	0.02	0.15	0.09	-2.00	-1.45	-1.72
		2	0.04	0.19	0.12	-2.02	-1.32	-1.67
		3	1.05	4.18	2.61	-0.33	-0.28	-0.30
Init BT	de	1	18.49	25.87	22.18	0.19	0.40	0.30
		2	17.28	24.89	21.08	0.12	0.32	0.22
		3	18.20	25.39	21.80	0.22	0.40	0.31
	si	1	0.94	4.56	2.75	-0.43	-0.27	-0.35
		2	1.24	4.84	3.04	-0.28	-0.25	-0.27
		3	0.09	0.62	0.35	-1.24	-0.84	-1.04
Interleave	de	1	18.23	25.56	21.90	0.15	0.39	0.27
		2	18.29	25.69	21.99	0.18	0.38	0.28
		3	17.93	25.81	21.87	0.16	0.39	0.27
	si	1	0.01	0.02	0.02	-1.57	-1.34	-1.46
		2	1.25	4.84	3.05	-0.34	-0.25	-0.30
		3	1.04	4.37	2.70	-0.46	-0.28	-0.37

Table 8: Results from several T2I-EC training pipeline manipulations.

Contrastive Learning for Universal Zero-Shot NLI with Cross-Lingual Sentence Embeddings

Md. Kowsher[1], **Md. Shohanur Islam Sobuj**[2], **Nusrat Jahan Prottasha**[1], **Mohammad Shamsul Arefin**[3], **Yasuhiko Morimoto**[4]

[1]Stevens Institute of Technology, USA
[2]Hajee Mohammad Danesh Science and Technology University, Bangladesh
[3]Chittagong University of Engineering and Technology, Bangladesh
[4]Graduate School of Engineering, Hiroshima University, Japan
{ga.kowsher,shohanursobuj,jahannusratprotta}@gmail.com
sarefin@cuet.ac.bd   morimo@hiroshima-u.ac.jp

Abstract

Natural Language Inference (NLI) is a crucial task in natural language processing, involving the classification of sentence pairs into entailment, contradiction, or neutral categories. This paper introduces a novel approach to achieve universal zero-shot NLI by employing contrastive learning with cross-lingual sentence embeddings. We utilize a large-scale pretrained multilingual language model trained on NLI data from 15 diverse languages, enabling our approach to achieve zero-shot performance across other unseen languages during the training, including low-resource ones. Our method incorporates a Siamese network-based contrastive learning framework to establish semantic relationships among similar sentences in the 15 languages. By training the zero-shot NLI model using contrastive training on this multilingual data, it effectively captures meaningful semantic relationships. Leveraging the fine-tuned language model's zero-shot learning capabilities, our approach extends the zero-shot capability to additional languages within the multilingual model. Experimental results demonstrate the effectiveness of our approach in achieving universal zero-shot NLI across diverse languages, including those with limited resources. We showcase our method's ability to handle previously unseen low-resource language data within the multilingual model, highlighting its practical applicability and broad language coverage.

1 Introduction

Natural Language Processing (NLP) has seen significant advancements in recent years, primarily due to the development of powerful pre-trained languages models like BERT (Devlin et al., 2019a), RoBERTa (Liu et al.), and XLM-RoBERTa (Conneau et al., 2020a). These models have achieved state-of-the-art performance on a wide range of NLP tasks, including Natural Language Inference (NLI) (Bowman et al., 2015; Williams et al., 2018). However, most existing NLI models are limited to the languages they have been explicitly trained on, hindering their applicability across diverse languages and regions. Consequently, there is a growing interest in developing universal zero-shot NLI models capable of generalizing to multiple languages without explicit training data.

Cross-lingual representation learning has emerged as an effective approach to develop models that can understand and process different languages (Ruder et al., 2019). A prominent example is the XLM-RoBERTa model (Conneau et al., 2020a), which leverages a masked language modeling (MLM) objective to learn language-agnostic representations. Despite its effectiveness, XLM-RoBERTa can still benefit from further fine-tuning on specific tasks, such as NLI, to enhance its cross-lingual understanding.

In this paper, we present a novel approach to achieving universal zero-shot Natural Language Inference by leveraging contrastive learning with cross-lingual sentence embeddings depicted in the Figure 1. Our method addresses the challenge of zero-shot NLI, where a model trained on one set of languages can accurately classify sentence pairs in languages it has never seen before. This capability enables the extension of NLI to a vast number of languages without the need for extensive labeled data in each language.

To achieve universal zero-shot NLI, we leverage large-scale pre-trained multilingual language models. Specifically, we utilize an extensively trained multilingual language model, such as XLM-RoBERTa-large, which has been pre-trained on NLI data from 15 diverse languages. This pretraining ensures that the model captures meaningful semantic relationships across different languages.

Proceedings of the The 3rd Workshop on Multi-lingual Representation Learning (MRL), pages 239–252
December 7, 2023

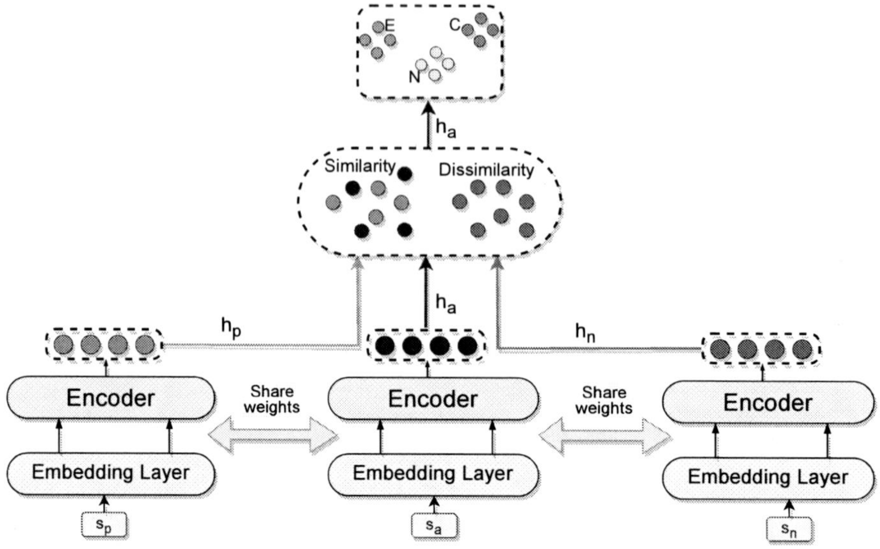

Figure 1: Overview of the proposed methodology for achieving universal zero-shot NLI. The approach incorporates contrastive learning with cross-lingual sentence embeddings, leveraging a large-scale pre-trained multilingual language model trained on NLI data from diverse languages. The Siamese network-based contrastive learning framework establishes semantic relationships among similar sentences, enabling the zero-shot NLI model to capture meaningful semantic representations. By extending the zero-shot capability to additional languages within the multilingual model, the approach achieves universal zero-shot NLI across a broad range of languages, including low-resource ones. In this framework, "a" serves as an anchor, "n" as negative, and "p" as positive in defining the relationships between three categories: entailment (E), neutral (N), or contradiction (C) (for more details, refer to Model Architecture in 5.1).

We exploit the power of contrastive learning by employing a Siamese network-based framework to establish semantic relationships among similar sentences in the 15 languages. Contrastive learning enables the model to learn robust representations that can effectively discriminate between entailment and contradiction.

By training the zero-shot NLI model using contrastive training on this multilingual dataset, we equip the model with the ability to generalize to unseen languages. The fine-tuned language model's zero-shot learning capabilities allow us to extend the zero-shot NLI capability to additional languages within the multilingual model. This approach significantly broadens the language coverage and practical applicability of the NLI model, especially for low-resource languages where labeled data is scarce.

2 Related Work

Text classification is a typical task of categorizing texts into groups, including sentiment analysis, question answering, etc. Due to the unstructured nature of the text, extracting useful information from texts can be very time-consuming and inefficient. With the rapidly development of deep learning, neural network methods such as RNN (Hochreiter and Schmidhuber, 1997; Chung et al., 2014) and CNN (Kim, 2014; Zhang et al., 2015) have been widely explored for efficiently encoding the text sequences. However, their capabilities are limited by computational bottlenecks and the problem of long-term dependencies. Recently, large-scale pre-trained language models (PLMs) based on transformers (Vaswani et al., 2017) has emerged as the art of text modeling. Some of these auto-regressive PLMs include GPT (Radford et al., 2018) and XLNet (Yang et al., 2019), auto-encoding PLMs such as BERT (Devlin et al., 2019b), RoBERTa (Liu et al.) and ALBERT (Lan et al., 2019). The stunning performance of PLMs mainly comes from the extensive knowledge in the large scale corpus used for pre-training.

Despite the optimality of the cross-entropy in supervised learning, a large number of studies have revealed the drawbacks of the cross-entropy loss, e.g., vulnerable to noisy labels (Zhang et al., 2018), poor margins (Elsayed et al., 2018) and weak adversarial robustness (Pang et al., 2019). Inspired by the InfoNCE loss (Oord et al., 2018), contrastive learning (Hadsell et al., 2006) has been widely used in unsupervised learning to learn good generic representations for downstream tasks. For example, (He et al., 2020) leverages a momentum encoder to maintain a look-up dictionary for encoding the input examples. (Chen et al., 2020) produces multiple views of the input example using data augmentations as the positive samples, and compare them to the negative samples in the datasets. (Gao et al., 2021) similarly dropouts each sentence twice to generate positive pairs. In the supervised scenario, (Khosla et al., 2020) clusters the training examples by their labels to maximize the similarity of representations of training examples within the same class while minimizing ones between different classes. (Gunel et al., 2021) extends supervised contrastive learning to the natural language domain with pre-trained language models. (Lopez-Martin et al., 2022) studies the network intrusion detection problem using well-designed supervised contrastive loss.

3 Background

3.1 NLI

Natural Language Inference (NLI) is a task in natural language processing (NLP) where the goal is to determine the relationship between two sentences. Given two input sentences s_1 and s_2, the task is to classify their relationship as one of three categories: entailment (E), neutral (N), or contradiction (C).

Formally, let S_1 and S_2 be sets of sentences in two different languages, and let $L = E, N, C$ be the set of possible relationship labels. Given a pair of sentences $(s_1, s_2) \in S_1 \times S_2$, the task is to predict the label $l \in L$ that represents the relationship between the two sentences, i.e., $l = NLI(s_1, s_2)$.

3.2 Siamese Networks

Siamese networks are neural network architectures specifically designed for comparing the similarity or dissimilarity between pairs of inputs (Chen and He, 2021). Given two input samples x_1 and x_2, a Siamese network learns a shared representation for both inputs and measures their similarity based on this shared representation.

Let f denote the shared subnetwork of the Siamese network. The shared subnetwork consists of multiple layers, such as convolutional or recurrent layers, followed by fully connected layers. It aims to extract relevant features from the input samples and map them into a common representation space.

The Siamese network takes two input samples, x_1 and x_2, and applies the shared subnetwork to each input to obtain the respective representations:

$$h_1 = f(x_1), \quad h_2 = f(x_2)$$

To measure the similarity between h_1 and h_2, a distance metric is commonly employed, such as Euclidean distance or cosine similarity. For example, cosine similarity can be calculated as:

$$\text{similarity} = \frac{h_1 \cdot h_2}{\|h_1\| \cdot \|h_2\|}$$

During training, Siamese networks utilize a contrastive loss function to encourage similar inputs to have close representations and dissimilar inputs to have distant representations. The contrastive loss penalizes large distances for similar pairs and small distances for dissimilar pairs.

Siamese networks have demonstrated effectiveness in various domains, enabling tasks such as similarity-based classification, retrieval, and clustering. The ability to learn meaningful representations for similarity estimation has made Siamese networks widely applicable in research and practical applications.

3.3 Contrastive learning

Let $\mathcal{D} = (x_i, y_i)_{i=1}^N$ be a dataset of N samples, where x_i is a sentence and y_i is a label. Let ϕ be an embedding function that maps a sentence x_i to a low-dimensional vector representation $\phi(x_i) \in \mathbb{R}^d$, where d is the dimensionality of the embedding space. The goal of contrastive learning is to learn an embedding function ϕ such that the similarity between the representation of a sentence x_i and its positive sample x_j is greater than that of its negative samples x_k.

Given a pair of sentences (x_i, x_j), the contrastive loss can be defined as follows:

$$L = -\log \frac{\exp\left(\frac{\text{sim}(x_i,x_j)}{\theta}\right)}{\exp\left(\frac{\text{sim}(x_i,x_k)}{\theta}\right)} + \sum_{k=1}^{N} [y_k = y_i] \exp\left(\frac{\text{sim}(x_i,x_k)}{\theta}\right) + \sum_{k=1}^{N} [y_k \neq y_i] \exp\left(\frac{\text{sim}(x_i,x_k)}{\theta}\right) \quad (1)$$

where $\text{sim}(x_i, x_j) = \frac{\phi(x_i)^\top \phi(x_j)}{\|\phi(x_i)\|\|\phi(x_k)\|}$ is the cosine similarity between the embeddings of the sentences x_i and x_j, θ is the temperature parameter that controls the sharpness of the probability distribution over the similarity scores, $[y_k = y_i]$ is the Iverson bracket that takes the value 1 if $y_k = y_i$ and 0 otherwise, and $[y_k \neq y_i]$ is the Iverson bracket that takes the value 1 if $y_k \neq y_i$ and 0 otherwise.

The contrastive loss encourages the model to learn to generate similar embeddings for sentences with the same meaning across different languages, as they will be positively paired during training. This can help enhance the model's cross-lingual understanding and zero-shot learning performance.

4 Problem Definition

Let $\mathcal{S}$ denote the set of all sample data, where each sample $s \in \mathcal{S}$ contains multilingual textual data $s^1, s^2, \ldots, s^z \in s$, which are semantically similar. Here, s_i^z represents the z-th language data for the i-th sample. Each textual data of a language consists of a premise and a hypothesis, separated by a special token, such as [SEP] $(s_{i,p}^z, s_{i,h}^z \in s_i^z)$.

The subscripts p and h refer to the hypothesis and premise, respectively.

Now, let $\mathcal{L} = \text{E}, \text{N}, \text{C}$ be the set of labels for natural language inference (NLI), representing entailment, neutral, and contradiction, respectively. Our objective is to address the task of NLI across multiple languages under the zero-shot learning setting.

Given an input sentence pair $(s_{i,p}^z, s_{i,h}^z)$, the task is to determine their semantic relationship by assigning an NLI label $l \in \mathcal{L}$. We assume limited or no training data is available for some languages, and our goal is to leverage a multilingual pre-trained language model to generalize to unseen languages.

To achieve this, we aim to learn a mapping function $\phi : \mathcal{S} \rightarrow \mathbb{R}^d$, where $\phi(s) \in \mathbb{R}^d$ represents the dense vector representation of a sentence s in an embedding space of dimensionality d. The embedding function ϕ is trained to generate similar embeddings for semantically equivalent sentences across different languages, while producing dissimilar embeddings for sentences with different meanings.

We formulate our NLI model as a multi-task learning problem by simultaneously optimizing two loss functions: the cross-entropy loss and the contrastive loss. The cross-entropy loss is employed to predict the NLI label l_i for a given sentence pair $s_i^z = (s_{i,p}^z, s_{i,h}^z)$. The contrastive loss ensures that cross-lingual sentence embeddings with similar semantics are close together in the embedding space, i.e., for two languages $\alpha, \beta \in z$, $sim(s^\alpha, s^\beta) = \frac{\mathbf{h}^\alpha \cdot \mathbf{h}^\beta}{|\mathbf{h}^\alpha||\mathbf{h}^\beta|} > \tau$, while dissimilar sentence embeddings are far apart, i.e., $sim(s^\alpha, s^\beta) = \frac{\mathbf{h}^\alpha \cdot \mathbf{h}^\beta}{|\mathbf{h}^\alpha||\mathbf{h}^\beta|} < \tau$. Here, τ represents the similarity threshold.

We optimize both loss functions using stochastic gradient descent with appropriate hyperparameters to train our model for universal zero-shot NLI across multiple languages.

5 Methodology

5.1 NLI Model Architecture

Let $s_a = s_i^1, s_i^2, \ldots, s_i^z \in \mathcal{S}$ denote the i-th sample, considered as the **anchor** batch, which contains z samples from z different languages that are semantically similar. Similarly, we need to find a **negative** batch s_n, denoted as $s_n = s_j^1, s_j^2, \ldots, s_j^z \in \mathcal{S}$, where $i \neq j$ and s_n is the farthest from s_a among all samples in $\mathcal{S}$. We employ a clustering approach (Yang et al., 2019) to obtain s_n. Initially, we cluster the set $\mathcal{S}$ into k clusters using sentence embedding techniques (Hochreiter and Schmidhuber, 1997). For any text in the α-th language in the i-th batch, denoted as $s_i^\alpha \in \mathcal{S}$, we determine its corresponding cluster membership, denoted as τ_i. Subsequently, we identify the cluster τ_j in s_n for the j-th batch that is the farthest from the current cluster τ_i, considering it as a non-semantic cluster. From this non-semantic cluster τ_j, we randomly select a sample as s_n. During the training phase, we opt for random selection instead of using a deterministic approach. Since we select the α-th language for clustering, we refer to it as the clustering priority language. If $C(\cdot)$ represents the trained cluster model, mathematically, we obtain the cluster number of s_a as follows:

$$e_a = T(s_a)$$
$$\tau_a = C(e_a)$$

Here, $T(\cdot)$ is the sentence embedding transformer, and τ_a is the cluster ID for s_a. Now, we need to find the most distant cluster τ_n by calculating the Euclidean distance between the centers of the two clusters, given by $||c_a - c_n||_2^2$, where $c_a \in \mathbb{R}^d$ is the center of cluster τ_a, and $c_n \in \mathbb{R}^d$ is the center of cluster τ_n.

Next, for every sample in the cluster, we map the farthest distance cluster as $D(\tau_a) = \tau_n$.

Finally, we obtain the most dissimilar batch s_n to s_a. To obtain the similar batch s_p (positive), we randomly shuffle s_a to introduce cross-lingual similarity.

The dense vector representation of the i-th batch is obtained by passing s_a through the model:

$$h_a = \phi(s_a),$$

where $h_a \in \mathbb{R}^{z \times d}$ represents the hidden state of the i-th batch, z is the number of samples (i.e., the total number of languages in $\mathcal{S}$), and d is the embedding space dimensionality.

Using a Siamese network, the hidden states of s_p and s_n are also obtained as follows:

$$h_p = \phi(s_p)$$
$$h_n = \phi(s_n)$$

To measure the similarity between sentences within the i-th batch, we define the similarity function $sim(s_{i,a}, s_{i,p})$, which computes the cosine similarity between their embeddings:

$$sim(s_{i,a}, s_{i,p}) = \frac{h_a \cdot h_p}{||h_a|| ||h_p||},$$

The contrastive loss function is used to learn similar embeddings for semantically equivalent sentences across different languages and dissimilar embeddings for semantically non-equivalent sentences across different languages. We combine both the similarity and dissimilarity losses into a single contrastive loss function using the triplet loss, given by:

$$\mathcal{L}c = \sum_{i=1}^{N} \left[|h_a - h_p|_2^2 - |h_a - h_n| \, 2^2 + \gamma \right]_+ \tag{2}$$

where γ is the temperature parameter that controls the smoothness of the similarity function.

The goal of the triplet loss is to encourage the feature vectors for the anchor and positive embeddings to be closer together in the embedding space than the anchor and negative embeddings. The function $[x]_+$ denotes the hinge loss, which penalizes the model if the distance between the anchor and positive embedding is greater than the distance between the anchor and negative embedding by more than a margin γ.

Here, similar embeddings correspond to semantically equivalent sentences across different languages, and dissimilar embeddings correspond to semantically non-equivalent sentences across different languages.

For the NLI task, the cross-entropy loss is used. Given a sentence pair $(s_p, s_h) \in \mathcal{S}$, the predicted NLI label p_i is obtained as:

$$p_i = G(h_a)$$

where $G(\cdot)$ is a classifier, and $p_i \in \mathbb{R}^{z \times m}$ represents the softmax scores, with $m = 3$ as the number of classes for the NLI labels $\mathcal{L} = \mathrm{E, N, C}$.

The cross-entropy loss function is defined as:

$$\mathcal{L}_{\mathrm{CE}} = -\sum_{i=1}^{z} \sum_{k=1}^{m} y_{i,k} \log(p_{i,k}),$$

where $y_{i,k}$ is the indicator function, defined as

$$y_{i,k} = \begin{cases} 1, & \text{if the NLI label of the ith batch is } k, \\ 0, & \text{otherwise.} \end{cases}$$

The overall loss function is a combination of the contrastive loss and the cross-entropy loss:

$$L = \mathcal{L}_{\mathrm{C}} + (1 - \lambda)\mathcal{L}_{\mathrm{CE}}$$

where λ is a hyperparameter controlling the trade-off between the two losses.

5.2 Training for Zero-Shot Classification

The pseudocode for training the NLI model is outlined in Algorithm 1. The algorithm takes as input an NLI multilingual dataset S, where $S = S^1, S^2, \ldots, S^z$. Each batch $s_1, s_2, \ldots, s_b$ is randomly sampled from S, and the target labels for each batch are denoted as $y_1, y_2, \ldots, y_b$. Additionally, the algorithm utilizes a trained cluster model $C(.)$, a pre-trained masked language model $F(.)$, and a classifier $G(.)$. The objective is to train a universal zero-shot LM model. The training process

Algorithm 1 Pseudocode for NLI Model Training

Require:
XNLI dataset $S = \{S^1, S^2, \ldots, S^z\}$
Batch $\{s_1, s_2, \ldots, s_b\} \in S$
Label for every batch $\{y_1, y_2, \ldots, y_b\} \in Y$
Trained cluster model $C(.)$
Pre-trained MLM $F(.)$
Classifier $G(.)$
Mapping maximum distance $D(.)$
Ensure: Trained universal zero-shot LM model
for each epoch **do**
  for each batch $(s_i, y_i) \in (S, Y)$ **do**
    $s_a, y_i \leftarrow$ Randomly Shuffle (s_i, y_i)
    $s_p \leftarrow$ Randomly Shuffle s_i
    $c \leftarrow D(C(s_i^z))$
    $s_n \leftarrow$ Randomly Shuffle s_c
    $h_a \leftarrow \phi(s_a)$
    $h_p \leftarrow \phi(s_p)$
    $h_n \leftarrow \phi(s_n)$
    $\hat{y}_i \leftarrow G(h_a)$
    $\mathcal{L}_{CE} \leftarrow L_{CE}(\hat{y}_i, y_i)$
    $\mathcal{L}_C \leftarrow L_C(h_a, h_p, h_n)$
    $\mathcal{L}_{total} \leftarrow \lambda\mathcal{L}_C + \leftarrow (1-\lambda)\mathcal{L}_{CE}$
  end for
  backpropagate and update model parameters using optimizer such as Adam
end for

consists of iterating over each epoch and each batch within an epoch. In each batch, the samples s_i and their corresponding labels y_i are randomly shuffled. Then, a positive batch s_p is created by randomly shuffling s_i. The clustering model is used to find the most distant cluster from the current cluster of s_i, denoted as s_c. A negative batch s_n is created by randomly shuffling the samples in s_c. The sentence embeddings h_a, h_p, and h_n are obtained by passing s_a, s_p, and s_n through the model function ϕ. The classifier $G(.)$ predicts the NLI label $\hat{y}i$ for s_a. The cross-entropy loss $\mathcal{L}CE$ is computed between $\hat{y}i$ and y_i. The contrastive loss $\mathcal{L}C$ is computed using h_a, h_p, and h_n. The total loss $\mathcal{L}_{total}$ is a combination of the contrastive loss and the cross-entropy loss, weighted by the hyperparameter λ. After computing the loss, the model parameters are updated using an optimizer such as Adam. This process is repeated for each batch in each epoch.

For the training, we use the XNLI dataset (Conneau et al., 2018), which is a multilingual extension of the MNLI dataset. XNLI consists of a few thousand examples from MNLI that have been translated into 15 different languages, including Arabic, Bulgarian, Chinese, English, French, German, Greek, Hindi, Russian, Spanish, Swahili, Thai, Turkish, Urdu, and Vietnamese. The dataset includes three labels: entailment, neutral, and contradiction.

In the hyperparameter configuration, we used a margin of 1.0 for the Triplet loss. The distance metric used was the Euclidean distance, with a 15 batch size. In addition, we used a 8 gradient accumulation step. We used the Adam optimizer during the training procedure, with a decay rate of 0.01. Starting at $2e-6$, the learning rate was linear scheduled.

5.3 Fine-Tuning for Zero-Shot Classification

The objective of fine-tuning the NLI model is to enable zero-shot classification, where the model trained on a particular language can work for other unseen languages with similar objectives. The fine-tuning process is similar to NLI training, with a few key differences. In this approach, we do not use a Siamese network architecture. Instead, there is only one forward representation denoted as h_a. Additionally, there is no contrastive learning involved.

The fine-tuning process begins by organizing the data in a specific way. We concatenate 60% of the data with its correct label, which is considered as an entailment (E) relationship. The remaining 40% of the data is concatenated with another incorrect label, which is considered as a contradiction (C) relationship. An example table illustrating the organization of the data is shown in Table 2.

To fine-tune the NLI model, we leveraged rich and resourceful language resources, including English (Maas et al., 2011), (Keung et al., 2020a), Arabic (ElSahar and El-Beltagy, 2015), France (Le et al., 2019), Russian (Fenogenova et al., 2022), Chines (Li et al., 2018). These resources provided diverse and extensive linguistic data for training and enhancing the model's performance. By incorporating data from multiple languages, we aimed to improve the model's generalization capabilities and enable it to handle various languages effectively (Experimental analysis is discussed in the Ablation study 6.4).

6 Experiments

We employed two multilingual language models (LM) for our zero-shot learning experiments using the XNLI datasets: XLM-RoBERTa (Conneau

Model / Dataset	XLM-RoBERTa		mDeBERTa-v3		mT5		mBERT		mDistilBERT		XLM-RoBERTa*		mDeBERTa-v3*	
	F1	Acc	F1	Acc	F1	Acc	F1	Acc	F1	Acc	F1	Acc	F1	Acc
DKHate	0.65	0.63	0.64	0.63	0.64	0.62	0.56	0.53	0.53	0.54	**0.69**	**0.67**	0.68	0.66
+ few-shot	0.68	0.66	0.67	0.66	0.67	0.67	0.60	0.58	0.55	0.54	**0.71**	**0.70**	**0.71**	0.69
MARC-ja	0.78	0.79	0.80	0.80	0.80	0.81	0.73	0.70	0.53	0.53	**0.81**	**0.82**	**0.81**	**0.82**
+ few-shot	0.84	0.85	0.85	0.86	**0.87**	**0.88**	0.77	0.75	0.55	0.54	0.86	0.87	**0.87**	**0.88**
Kor-3i4k	0.72	0.82	0.75	0.83	0.76	0.85	0.71	0.80	0.69	0.79	0.77	**0.87**	**0.78**	**0.87**
+ few-shot	0.75	0.86	0.77	0.87	0.78	0.88	0.73	0.82	0.72	0.81	**0.79**	0.88	**0.79**	**0.89**
Id-clickbait	0.73	0.71	0.71	0.69	0.75	0.73	0.66	0.65	0.62	0.61	**0.79**	**0.78**	0.77	0.75
+ few-shot	0.76	0.74	0.75	0.72	0.80	0.80	0.69	0.69	0.67	0.68	**0.83**	**0.83**	0.81	0.81
MCT4	0.77	0.78	0.75	0.75	0.76	0.76	0.70	0.68	0.68	0.67	**0.83**	**0.83**	0.80	0.80
+ few-shot	0.83	0.83	0.83	0.83	0.83	0.83	0.78	0.78	0.76	0.76	**0.87**	**0.87**	0.86	0.86
MCT7	0.74	0.75	0.75	0.75	0.76	0.76	0.72	0.71	0.68	0.67	**0.79**	0.78	**0.79**	**0.79**
+ few-shot	0.80	0.79	0.80	0.80	0.81	0.81	0.76	0.75	0.74	0.74	**0.83**	**0.83**	**0.83**	**0.83**
ToLD-br	0.58	0.59	0.59	0.59	0.60	0.60	0.55	0.55	0.52	0.53	**0.63**	**0.63**	**0.63**	**0.63**
+ few-shot	0.63	0.63	0.66	0.65	0.67	0.67	0.59	0.60	0.57	0.57	0.69	0.70	**0.70**	**0.71**

Table 1: Performance comparison of various multilingual models on unseen and low-resource NLI datasets in both zero-shot and few-shot settings in terms of accuracy, the higher the better. The models with an asterisk (*) denote our proposed universal zero-shot models. The **best results** are highlighted in **bold** and the second best results are highlighted with underline.

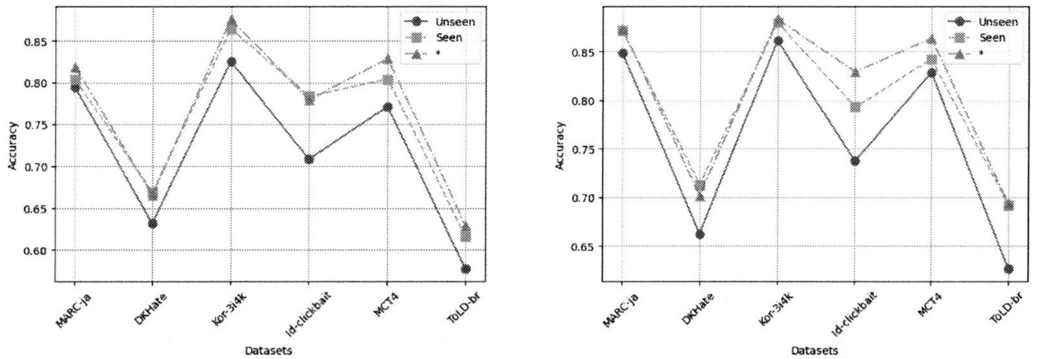

Figure 2: Accuracy comparison of various NLI models in both zero-shot (Left Figure) and few-shot (Right Figure) settings across different low-resource datasets. The performances of the unseen multilingual XLM-RoBERTa, seen XLM-RoBERTa, and our proposed XLM-RoBERTa* are depicted. In this context, seen alludes to the language data that has been employed in training the zero-shot model, while unseen pertains to data that hasn't been incorporated into the zero-shot training process.

Text	Label	Relationship
You are capable of achieving great things	This is an example of positive text	Entailment
You are capable of achieving great things	This is an example of negative text	Contradiction

Table 2: Illustration of text-label relationships for two example sentences, showcasing entailment and contradiction.

et al., 2020b) and mDeBERTa-v3 (He et al., 2023), as outlined in training sections 5.2 and 5.3. In our universal behavior experiments, both models were tested on languages not seen during the zero-shot training phase. Furthermore, we benchmarked our universal zero-shot models against several other prominent multilingual models—mT5 (Xue et al., 2021), mBERT (Devlin et al., 2019b), mDistill-BERT (Sanh et al., 2020), XLM-RoBERTa (Conneau et al., 2020b), and mDeBERTa-v3 (He et al., 2023) in a zero-shot setting to gauge their performance. Additionally, we've provided a detailed comparison between our universal zero-shot models and the trained baseline results in Appendix A.3.

6.1 Dataset

We used couple of low-resource datasets to conduct the experiment such as MARC-ja (Keung et al., 2020b), DKHate (Sigurbergsson and Derczynski, 2020), kor_3i4k (Cho et al., 2018), id_clickbait (William and Sari, 2020), BanglaMCT (Sobuj et al., 2021), ToLD-Br (Leite et al., 2020). The dataset description is described in the Appendix A.2.

6.2 Experimental Results

Based on the presented results in Table 1, our universal zero-shot models, XLM-RoBERTa* and mDeBERTa-v3*, consistently outperformed other multilingual models across various unseen and low-resource datasets. Specifically, in the zero-shot setting, our models achieved the highest accuracy on datasets such as DKHate, MARC-ja, Kor-3i4k, and Id-clickbait. The trend was further emphasized in the few-shot learning scenario, where our models maintained their lead. For instance, on the Id-clickbait dataset, XLM-RoBERTa* achieved an F1 score of 0.83 and an accuracy of 0.83, noticeably surpassing other models. While traditional multilingual models such as mT5 and mBERT demonstrated competitive performance in some scenarios, they did not consistently match the prowess of our proposed models. These results underscore the effectiveness of our approach in handling low-resource languages, emphasizing its potential for broader linguistic applications in the realm of Natural Language Inference.

In Figure 2, we observe a comparative analysis of model accuracy across various unseen and low-resource datasets. Notably, for the zero-shot setting, our proposed XLM-RoBERTa* consistently outperformed the unseen multilingual XLM-RoBERTa and closely matched or even exceeded the performance of the seen version on datasets such as MARC-ja, Kor-3i4k, and MCT4. This trend continues into the few-shot scenario, where our model's accuracy remains competitive, particularly outshining both unseen and seen mDeBERTa-v3 on datasets like Id-clickbait and MCT4. The parity, or in some instances superiority, of our universal zero-shot model compared to the seen model accentuates the potency of our approach, demonstrating its capability to generalize well even to languages it hasn't been explicitly trained on, a crucial trait for practical NLI tasks across diverse linguistic landscapes. More experiment has been described in the Appendix A.3

6.3 Ablation Study

6.4 Effect of Fine-Tuning on Cross-Lingual

After training a universal zero-shot NLI model, we conducted fine-tuning experiments on specific tasks to assess their impact on cross-lingual sentiment analysis. We utilized a multilingual sentiment analysis dataset (Tyqiangz, 2023) for our evaluation. Initially, we fine-tuned the model on sentiment prediction using datasets in English (En), German (De), Spanish (Es), and French (Fr). Subsequently, we evaluated the model's performance on sentiment analysis tasks in Japanese (Ja), Chinese (Zh), Arabic (Ar), Hindi (Hi), Indonesian (In), Italian (It), and Portuguese (Pt). The results presented in Table 3 demonstrate that fine-tuning for specific tasks in one language significantly enhances sentiment analysis performance across various languages, as measured by Accuracy, Precision, and F1-score metrics.

Method / Language	Before Fine-tuning			After Fine-tuning		
	Acc	Pre	F1	Acc	Pre	F1
English (En)	0.51	0.53	0.52	0.54	0.55	0.55
German (De)	0.52	0.54	0.53	0.55	0.57	0.56
Spanish (Es)	0.50	0.52	0.51	0.53	0.55	0.54
French (Fr)	0.53	0.55	0.54	0.56	0.58	0.57
Japanese (Ja)	0.51	0.53	0.52	0.54	0.56	0.55
Chinese (Zh)	0.50	0.52	0.51	0.53	0.55	0.54
Arabic (Ar)	0.50	0.52	0.51	0.53	0.55	0.54
Hindi (Hi)	0.52	0.54	0.53	0.54	0.57	0.56
Indonesian (In)	0.51	0.53	0.52	0.54	0.56	0.55
Italian (It)	0.53	0.55	0.54	0.55	0.58	0.57
Portuguese (Pt)	0.52	0.54	0.53	0.54	0.55	0.56

Table 3: Performance Metrics Before and After Fine-Tuning Across Multiple Languages

7 Conclusion

In conclusion, this work presents a novel approach to achieving universal zero-shot Natural Language Inference (NLI) across a wide range of languages, including low-resource ones. By leveraging contrastive learning with cross-lingual sentence embeddings and a large-scale pre-trained multilingual language model, we have demonstrated the effectiveness of our approach in capturing meaningful semantic relationships and achieving high-performance NLI classification.

Through the use of a Siamese network-based contrastive learning framework, our approach establishes semantic connections among similar sentences in 15 diverse languages. By training the zero-shot NLI model on this multilingual data, it acquires the ability to generalize to unseen languages, effectively extending the zero-shot capability to a broader range of languages within the multilingual model.

Our experimental findings across different languages and tasks showcase the generalizability and flexibility of our zero-shot approach. By fine-tuning the zero-shot models on a limited amount of task-specific labeled data, we are able to bridge the performance gap and achieve competitive results.

References

Samuel R Bowman, Gabor Angeli, Christopher Potts, and Christopher D Manning. 2015. A large annotated corpus for learning natural language inference. In *Proceedings of the 2015 Conference on Empirical Methods in Natural Language Processing*, pages 632–642.

Ting Chen, Simon Kornblith, Mohammad Norouzi, and Geoffrey Hinton. 2020. A simple framework for contrastive learning of visual representations. In *International conference on machine learning*, pages 1597–1607. PMLR.

Xinlei Chen and Kaiming He. 2021. Exploring simple siamese representation learning. In *Proceedings of the IEEE/CVF conference on computer vision and pattern recognition*, pages 15750–15758.

Won Ik Cho, Hyeon Seung Lee, Ji Won Yoon, Seok Min Kim, and Nam Soo Kim. 2018. Speech intention understanding in a head-final language: A disambiguation utilizing intonation-dependency. *arXiv preprint arXiv:1811.04231*.

Junyoung Chung, Çaglar Gülçehre, KyungHyun Cho, and Yoshua Bengio. 2014. Empirical evaluation of gated recurrent neural networks on sequence modeling. In *Advances in neural information processing systems*, pages 2253–2261.

Alexis Conneau, Kartikay Khandelwal, Naman Goyal, Vishrav Chaudhary, Guillaume Wenzek, Francisco Guzmán, Edouard Grave, Myle Ott, Luke Zettlemoyer, and Veselin Stoyanov. 2020a. Unsupervised cross-lingual representation learning at scale. In *Proceedings of the 58th Annual Meeting of the Association for Computational Linguistics*, pages 8440–8451.

Alexis Conneau, Kartikay Khandelwal, Naman Goyal, Vishrav Chaudhary, Guillaume Wenzek, Francisco Guzmán, Edouard Grave, Myle Ott, Luke Zettlemoyer, and Veselin Stoyanov. 2020b. Unsupervised cross-lingual representation learning at scale.

Alexis Conneau, Ruty Rinott, Guillaume Lample, Adina Williams, Samuel R Bowman, Holger Schwenk, and Veselin Stoyanov. 2018. Xnli: Evaluating cross-lingual sentence representations. In *Proceedings of the 2018 Conference on Empirical Methods in Natural Language Processing*, pages 2475–2485.

Jacob Devlin, Ming-Wei Chang, Kenton Lee, and Kristina Toutanova. 2019a. BERT: Pre-training of deep bidirectional transformers for language understanding. In *Proceedings of the 2019 Conference of the North American Chapter of the Association for Computational Linguistics: Human Language Technologies, Volume 1 (Long and Short Papers)*, pages 4171–4186, Minneapolis, Minnesota. Association for Computational Linguistics.

Jacob Devlin, Ming-Wei Chang, Kenton Lee, and Kristina Toutanova. 2019b. Bert: Pre-training of deep bidirectional transformers for language understanding.

Hady ElSahar and Samhaa R El-Beltagy. 2015. Building large arabic multi-domain resources for sentiment analysis. In *Computational Linguistics and Intelligent Text Processing: 16th International Conference, CICLing 2015, Cairo, Egypt, April 14-20, 2015, Proceedings, Part II 16*, pages 23–34. Springer.

Gamaleldin F Elsayed, Vaishaal Shankar, Ngai-Man Cheung, Nicolas Papernot, and Alexey Kurakin. 2018. Large margin deep networks for classification. In *Advances in Neural Information Processing Systems*, pages 9155–9166.

Muhammad N. Fakhruzzaman, Saidah Z. Jannah, Ratih A. Ningrum, and Indah Fahmiyah. 2021. Clickbait headline detection in indonesian news sites using multilingual bidirectional encoder representations from transformers (m-bert).

Alena Fenogenova, Maria Tikhonova, Vladislav Mikhailov, Tatiana Shavrina, Anton Emelyanov, Denis Shevelev, Alexandr Kukushkin, Valentin Malykh, and Ekaterina Artemova. 2022. Russian superglue 1.1: Revising the lessons not learned by russian nlp models. *arXiv preprint arXiv:2202.07791*.

Xiaohan Gao, Wei Chen, Jing Guo, and Junzhou Huang. 2021. Clr-bert: Contrastive learning for robust pretraining. In *Proceedings of the 2021 Conference on Empirical Methods in Natural Language Processing*, pages 275–287.

Beliz Gunel, Jingfei Du, Alexis Conneau, and Ves Stoyanov. 2021. Supervised contrastive learning for pretrained language model fine-tuning.

Raia Hadsell, Sumit Chopra, and Yann LeCun. 2006. Dimensionality reduction by learning an invariant mapping. *Computer vision and pattern recognition, 2006 IEEE computer society conference on*, 2:1735–1742.

Kaiming He, Haoqi Fan, Yuxin Wu, Saining Xie, and Ross Girshick. 2020. Momentum contrast for unsupervised visual representation learning. In *Proceedings of the IEEE/CVF Conference on Computer Vision and Pattern Recognition*, pages 9729–9738.

Pengcheng He, Jianfeng Gao, and Weizhu Chen. 2023. Debertav3: Improving deberta using electra-style pretraining with gradient-disentangled embedding sharing.

Sepp Hochreiter and Jürgen Schmidhuber. 1997. Long short-term memory. *Neural computation*, 9(8):1735–1780.

Phillip Keung, Yichao Lu, György Szarvas, and Noah A Smith. 2020a. The multilingual amazon reviews corpus. *arXiv preprint arXiv:2010.02573*.

Phillip Keung, Yichao Lu, György Szarvas, and Noah A. Smith. 2020b. The multilingual Amazon reviews corpus. In *Proceedings of the 2020 Conference on Empirical Methods in Natural Language Processing (EMNLP)*, pages 4563–4568, Online. Association for Computational Linguistics.

Prannay Khosla, Piotr Teterwak, Chen Wang, Aaron Sarna, Yonglong Tian, Phillip Isola, Aaron Maschinot, Ce Liu, and Dilip Krishnan. 2020. Supervised Contrastive Learning. In *Advances in Neural Information Processing Systems*, volume 33, pages 18661–18673. Curran Associates, Inc.

Yoon Kim. 2014. Convolutional neural networks for sentence classification. *arXiv preprint arXiv:1408.5882*.

Md Kowsher, Abdullah As Sami, Nusrat Jahan Prottasha, Mohammad Shamsul Arefin, Pranab Kumar Dhar, and Takeshi Koshiba. 2022. Bangla-bert: transformer-based efficient model for transfer learning and language understanding. *IEEE Access*, 10:91855–91870.

Kentaro Kurihara, Daisuke Kawahara, and Tomohide Shibata. 2022. JGLUE: Japanese general language understanding evaluation. In *Proceedings of the Thirteenth Language Resources and Evaluation Conference*, pages 2957–2966, Marseille, France. European Language Resources Association.

Zhenzhong Lan, Mingda Chen, Sebastian Goodman, Kevin Gimpel, Piyush Sharma, and Radu Soricut. 2019. ALBERT: A lite BERT for self-supervised learning of language representations. *CoRR*, abs/1909.11942.

Hang Le, Loïc Vial, Jibril Frej, Vincent Segonne, Maximin Coavoux, Benjamin Lecouteux, Alexandre Allauzen, Benoit Crabbé, Laurent Besacier, and Didier Schwab. 2019. Flaubert: Unsupervised language model pre-training for french. *arXiv preprint arXiv:1912.05372*.

João Augusto Leite, Diego Silva, Kalina Bontcheva, and Carolina Scarton. 2020. Toxic language detection in social media for Brazilian Portuguese: New dataset and multilingual analysis. In *Proceedings of the 1st Conference of the Asia-Pacific Chapter of the Association for Computational Linguistics and the 10th International Joint Conference on Natural Language Processing*, pages 914–924, Suzhou, China. Association for Computational Linguistics.

Yue Li, Xutao Wang, and Pengjian Xu. 2018. Chinese text classification model based on deep learning. *Future Internet*, 10(11):113.

Yinhan Liu, Myle Ott, Naman Goyal, Jingfei Du, Mandar Joshi, Danqi Chen, and Omer and Levy. Roberta: A robustly optimized bert pretraining approach.

Manuel Lopez-Martin, Antonio Sanchez-Esguevillas, Juan Ignacio Arribas, and Belen Carro. 2022. Supervised contrastive learning over prototype-label embeddings for network intrusion detection. *Information Fusion*, 79:200–228.

Andrew Maas, Raymond E Daly, Peter T Pham, Dan Huang, Andrew Y Ng, and Christopher Potts. 2011. Learning word vectors for sentiment analysis. In *Proceedings of the 49th annual meeting of the association for computational linguistics: Human language technologies*, pages 142–150.

Aaron van den Oord, Yazhe Li, and Oriol Vinyals. 2018. Representation learning with contrastive predictive coding. *arXiv preprint arXiv:1807.03748*.

Tianyu Pang, Chuanxiong Xu, Hongtao Du, Ningyu Zhang, and Jun Zhu. 2019. Improving adversarial robustness via promoting ensemble diversity. In *Proceedings of the IEEE/CVF Conference on Computer Vision and Pattern Recognition*, pages 6440–6449.

Adam Paszke, Sam Gross, Francisco Massa, Adam Lerer, James Bradbury, Gregory Chanan, Trevor Killeen, Zeming Lin, Natalia Gimelshein, Luca Antiga, Alban Desmaison, Andreas Köpf, Edward Yang, Zach DeVito, Martin Raison, Alykhan Tejani, Sasank Chilamkurthy, Benoit Steiner, Lu Fang, Junjie Bai, and Soumith Chintala. 2019. PyTorch: An Imperative Style, High-Performance Deep Learning Library. *Advances in Neural Information Processing Systems*, 32.

Alec Radford, Karthik Narasimhan, Tim Salimans, and Ilya Sutskever. 2018. Improving language understanding by generative pre-training. *URL:* `https://s3-us-west-2.amazonaws.com/openai-assets/researchcovers/languageunsupervised/language_understanding_paper.pdf`.

Sebastian Ruder, Ivan Vulic, and Anders Søgaard. 2019. A survey of cross-lingual word embedding models. *Journal of Artificial Intelligence Research*, 65:569–630.

Victor Sanh, Lysandre Debut, Julien Chaumond, and Thomas Wolf. 2020. Distilbert, a distilled version of bert: smaller, faster, cheaper and lighter.

Gudbjartur Ingi Sigurbergsson and Leon Derczynski. 2020. Offensive language and hate speech detection for Danish. In *Proceedings of the Twelfth Language Resources and Evaluation Conference*, pages 3498–3508, Marseille, France. European Language Resources Association.

Md. Shohanur Islam Sobuj, Md. Kowsher, and Md. Fahim Shahriar. 2021. Bangla multi class text dataset. `https://www.kaggle.com/datasets/shohanursobuj/banglamct`.

Tyqiangz. 2023. Multilingual sentiments dataset. `https://huggingface.co/datasets/tyqiangz/multilingual-sentiments`.

Ashish Vaswani, Noam Shazeer, Niki Parmar, Jakob Uszkoreit, Llion Jones, Aidan N Gomez, Łukasz Kaiser, and Illia Polosukhin. 2017. Attention is all you need. In *Advances in neural information processing systems*, pages 5998–6008.

Andika William and Yunita Sari. 2020. CLICK-ID: A novel dataset for Indonesian clickbait headlines. *Data in Brief*, 32:106231.

Adina Williams, Nikita Nangia, and Samuel Bowman. 2018. A broad-coverage challenge corpus for sentence understanding through inference. In *Proceedings of the 2018 Conference of the North American Chapter of the Association for Computational Linguistics: Human Language Technologies, Volume 1 (Long Papers)*, pages 1112–1122.

Thomas Wolf, Lysandre Debut, Victor Sanh, Julien Chaumond, Clement Delangue, Anthony Moi, Pierric Cistac, Tim Rault, Rémi Louf, Morgan Funtowicz, Joe Davison, Sam Shleifer, Patrick von Platen, Clara Ma, Yacine Jernite, Julien Plu, Canwen Xu, Teven Le Scao, Sylvain Gugger, Mariama Drame, Quentin Lhoest, and Alexander M. Rush. 2019. HuggingFace's Transformers: State-of-the-art Natural Language Processing.

Linting Xue, Noah Constant, Adam Roberts, Mihir Kale, Rami Al-Rfou, Aditya Siddhant, Aditya Barua, and Colin Raffel. 2021. mt5: A massively multilingual pre-trained text-to-text transformer.

Zhilin Yang, Zihang Dai, Yiming Yang, Jaime Carbonell, Ruslan Salakhutdinov, and Quoc V Le. 2019. Xlnet: Generalized autoregressive pretraining for language understanding. *arXiv preprint arXiv:1906.08237*.

Hongyi Zhang, Moustapha Cisse, and Yann N Dauphin. 2018. Generalized cross entropy loss for training deep neural networks with noisy labels. *arXiv preprint arXiv:1805.07836*.

Xiang Zhang, Junbo Zhao, and Yann LeCun. 2015. Character-level convolutional networks for text classification. In *Advances in neural information processing systems*, pages 649–657.

A Appendix

A.1 Hardware and Software

We perform our experiments on a double NVIDIA RTX3090 GPU with 24GB memory. We use PyTorch (Paszke et al., 2019) as the deep learning framework and Hugging Face's Transformers library (Wolf et al., 2019) to work with the XLM-RoBERTa-large model. We use the official evaluation scripts provided with the XNLI dataset to compute the evaluation metrics.

A.2 Dataset

The dataset provided in this paper is described in this section.

A.2.1 MARC-ja

The Multilingual Amazon Reviews Corpus (MARC), from which the Japanese dataset MARC-ja was built (Keung et al., 2020b), was used to create the JGLUE benchmark (Kurihara et al., 2022). This study focuses on text classification, and to that end, 4- and 5-star ratings were converted to the "positive" class, while 1- and 2-star ratings were assigned to the "negative" class. The dev and test set each contained 5,654 and 5,639 occurrences, compared to 187,528 instances in the training set. The extensive collection of product reviews provided by MARC-ja makes it possible to evaluate NLP models in-depth. The characteristics of the dataset and the accuracy metric used for evaluation help to provide a thorough examination of how well models perform on tasks involving Japanese text classification.

A.2.2 DKHate

The Danish hate speech dataset, used in this study, is a significant resource that consists of anonymized Twitter data that has been properly annotated for hate speech. The dataset offers a targeted and thorough collection for hate speech detection and was produced by Sigurbergsson and Derczynski for their article titled "Offensive Language and Hate Speech Detection for Danish" (Sigurbergsson and Derczynski, 2020). Each element in the collection contains a tweet and a label designating whether or not it is offensive ("OFF" or "NOT"). It has a training split of 2,960 tweets and a test split of 329 tweets.

A.2.3 Kor-3i4k

The Korean speaker intentions dataset 3i4K used in this study is an invaluable tool for this purpose (Cho et al., 2018). Along with manually crafted commands and inquiries, it includes commonly used Korean terms from the corpus of the Seoul National University Speech Language Processing Lab. It includes classifications for utterances that depend on intonation as well as fragments, statements, inquiries, and directives. This dataset offers essential information on precisely determining speaker intents given the importance of intonation in languages like Korean. With a training set of 55,134 examples and a test set of 6,121 examples, this domain can effectively train and evaluate models.

A.2.4 Id-clickbait

The CLICK-ID dataset used in this study is made up of a selection of headlines from Indonesian news sources (William and Sari, 2020). There are two primary components to it: Specifically, a subset of 15,000 annotated sample headlines that have been classified as clickbait or non-clickbait and 46,119 raw article data. Three annotators separately examined each headline during the annotation process, and the majority conclusion was taken as the actual truth. There are 6,290 clickbait headlines and 8,710 non-clickbait headlines in the annotated sample. We only trained and evaluated models on the annotated example for the classification task used in this study.

A.2.5 BanglaMCT

The BanglaMCT dataset, known as the Bangla Multi Class Text Dataset, is a comprehensive collection of Bengali news tags sourced from various newspapers (Sobuj et al., 2021) (Kowsher et al., 2022). It offers two versions, MCT4 and MCT7. MCT4 consists of four tags, while MCT7 includes seven tags. The dataset contains a total of 287,566 documents for MCT4 and 197,767 documents for MCT7. The dataset is split into a balanced 50/50 ratio for training and testing, making it suitable for text classification tasks in Bengali, particularly for news-related content across different categories.

A.2.6 ToLD-br

The ToLD-Br dataset is a valuable resource for investigating toxic tweets in Brazilian Portuguese (Leite et al., 2020). The dataset provides thorough coverage of LGBTQ+phobia, Xenophobia, Obscene, Insult, Misogyny, and Racism with contributions from 42 annotators chosen to reflect various populations. The binary version of the dataset was used in this study, to evaluate whether a tweet is toxic or not. There are 21,000 examples total in the dataset, with 16,800 examples in the training set, 2,100 examples in the validation set, and 2,100 examples in the test set. This large dataset helps the construction and testing of models for identifying toxicity in Brazilian Portuguese tweets.

A.3 Universal Zero-shot vs Trained model

In this section, we present the experimental results of our zero-shot and hence few-shot NLI model compared to previously established datasets and trained models. Typically, models that are specifically trained for a task perform better than zero-shot models. However, our models stood up well when compared to these trained models. We demonstrate the performance of our model across various languages and tasks. In our experimental setup, including the training, validation, and test phases, we closely followed the settings defined in the baseline papers.

Model	Accuracy	
	Dev	Test
Human	0.989	0.990
Tohoku BERT$_{BASE}$	0.958	0.957
Tohoku BERT$_{BASE}$ (char)	0.956	0.957
Tohoku BERT$_{LARGE}$	0.955	0.961
NICT BERT$_{BASE}$	0.958	0.96
Waseda RoBERTa$_{BASE}$	0.962	0.962
XLM-RoBERTa$_{BASE}$	0.961	0.962
XLM-RoBERTa$_{LARGE}$	0.964	0.965
XLM-RoBERTa*	0.820	0.819
+ few shot	0.896	0.873
mDeBERTa-v3*	0.829	0.820
+ few shot	0.882	0.878

Table 4: JGLUE performance on the DEV/TEST sets of the MARC-ja dataset. The $*$ represents our NLI model for zero-shot classification. The baseline performances are taken from (Kurihara et al., 2022)

Table 4 shows the performance of different models on the DEV and TEST sets of the MARC-ja dataset. The baseline models, such as Tohoku BERT$BASE$, Tohoku BERT$LARGE$, NICT BERT$BASE$, Waseda RoBERTa$BASE$, XLM-RoBERTa$BASE$, and XLM-RoBERTa$LARGE$, are explicitly trained models. Our zero-shot models, XLM-RoBERTa$LARGE$* and mDeBERTa-v3$base$*, initially exhibit lower accuracy but achieve notable improvement after few-shot training. This demonstrates the potential of our zero-shot approach combined with limited fine-tuning data to bridge the performance gap with explicitly trained models.

Table 5 presents the results from sub-task A in Danish. Existing models, such as Logistic Regression DA, Learned-BiLSTM (10 Epochs) DA, Fast-BiLSTM (100 Epochs) DA, and AUX-Fast-BiLSTM (50 Epochs) DA, are trained models. Our zero-shot models, XLM-RoBERTa$LARGE$* and mDeBERTa-v3$base$*, achieve competitive performance, and their accuracy further improves after few-shot training.

For the FCI module in the Korean language, Ta-

Model	Macro F1
Logistic Regression DA	0.699
Learned-BiLSTM (10 Epochs) DA	0.658
Fast-BiLSTM (100 Epochs) DA	0.630
AUX-Fast-BiLSTM (50 Epochs) DA	0.675
XLM-RoBERTa*	0.685
+ few shot	0.711
mDeBERTa-v3*	0.680
+ few shot	0.709

Table 5: Results from sub-task A in Danish. The baseline performances are taken from (Sigurbergsson and Derczynski, 2020)

Models	F1 score	accuracy
charCNN	0.7691	0.8706
charBiLSTM	0.7811	0.8807
charCNN + charBiLSTM	0.7700	0.8745
charBiLSTM-Att	0.7977	0.8869
charCNN + charBiLSTM-Att	0.7822	0.8746
XLM-RoBERTa*	0.7741	0.8760
+ few-shot	0.7913	0.8839
mDeBERTa-v3*	0.7817	0.8722
+ few-shot	0.7989	0.8901

Table 6: Model Performance for FCI module for the Korean Language. The baseline performances are taken from (Cho et al., 2018)

ble 6 displays the performance comparison of different models. Existing models, including charCNN, charBiLSTM, charCNN + charBiLSTM, and charBiLSTM-Att, are trained models. Our zero-shot models, XLM-RoBERTa$LARGE*$ and mDeBERTa-v3$base*$, exhibit comparable performance initially and achieve notable improvement after few-shot training.

In the context of clickbait headline detection in Indonesian news sites (Table 7), the average accuracy of established models like M-BERT, Bi-LSTM, CNN, and XGBoost is provided. Our zero-shot models, XLM-RoBERTa$LARGE*$ and mDeBERTa-v3$base*$, demonstrate competitive performance initially and show significant enhancement after few-shot training.

Table 8 presents the results of Bengali multi-class text classification. The models compared include biLSTM, CNN, CNN-biLSTM, DNN, Logistic Regression, and MNB. Our zero-shot models, XLM-RoBERTa$LARGE*$ and mDeBERTa-v3$base*$, initially show lower accuracy but achieve notable improvement after few-shot training.

Finally, Table 9 displays the model evaluation for toxic language detection in Brazilian

Model Name	Average Accuracy
M-BERT	0.9153
Bi-LSTM	0.8125
CNN	0.7958
XGBoost	0.8069
XLM-RoBERTa*	0.7794
+ few-shot	0.8294
mDeBERTa-v3*	0.7492
+ few-shot	0.8061

Table 7: Performance Comparison of Clickbait Headline Detection in Indonesian News Sites. The baseline performances are taken from (Fakhruzzaman et al., 2021)

Portuguese social media. Existing methods, such as BoW + AutoML, BR-BERT, M-BERT-BR, M-BERT(transfer), and M-BERT(zero-shot), are compared. Our zero-shot models, XLM-RoBERTa$LARGE*$ and mDeBERTa-v3$base*$, exhibit competitive performance initially and demonstrate improvement after few-shot training. Overall, our zero-shot NLI models demonstrate the ability to perform reasonably well without explicit training on the target language. Although their initial performance might be lower compared to explicitly trained models, few-shot training significantly

	Model	Accuracy	f1-score
MCT4	biLSTM	0.9652	0.9653
	CNN	0.9723	**0.9723**
	CNN-biLSTM	0.9673	0.9673
	DNN	0.9707	0.9708
	Logistic Regression	0.9586	0.9587
	MNB	0.9357	0.9359
	XLM-RoBERTa*	0.8316	0.8290
	+ few-shot	0.8713	0.8639
	mDeBERTa-v3*	0.8012	0.8007
	+ few-shot	0.8518	0.8600
MCT7	biLSTM	0.9236	0.9237
	CNN	0.9204	0.9204
	CNN-biLSTM	0.9115	0.9114
	DNN	0.9289	0.9290
	Logistic Regression	0.9156	0.9156
	MNB	0.8858	0.8859
	XLM-RoBERTa*	0.7418	0.7562
	+ few-shot	0.8234	0.8221
	mDeBERTa-v3*	0.7441	0.7612
	+ few-shot	0.8309	0.8237

Table 8: Bengali Multi-Class Text Classification Model Performance. The baseline performances are taken from (Sobuj et al., 2021)

Methods	Precision	Recall	F1-score
BoW + AutoML	0.74	0.74	0.74
BR-BERT	0.76	0.76	0.76
M-BERT-BR	0.75	0.75	0.75
M-BERT(transfer)	0.76	0.76	0.76
M-BERT(zero-shot)	0.61	0.58	0.56
XLM-RoBERTa*	0.64	0.63	0.62
+ few-shot	0.71	0.70	0.69
mDeBERTa-v3*	0.64	0.62	0.62
+ few-shot	0.72	0.71	0.70

Table 9: Model Evaluation for Toxic Language Detection in Brazilian Portuguese Social Media. The baseline performances are taken from (Leite et al., 2020)

UD-MULTIGENRE – a UD-Based Dataset Enriched with Instance-Level Genre Annotations

Vera Danilova and Sara Stymne
Department of Linguistics and Philology
Uppsala University, Sweden
first_name.last_name@lingfil.uu.se

Abstract

Prior research on the impact of genre on cross-lingual dependency parsing has suggested that genre is an important signal. However, these studies suffer from a scarcity of reliable data for multiple genres and languages. While Universal Dependencies (UD), the only available large-scale resource for cross-lingual dependency parsing, contains data from diverse genres, the documentation of genre labels is missing, and there are multiple inconsistencies. This makes studies of the impact of genres difficult to design. To address this, we present a new dataset, UD-MULTIGENRE, where 17 genres are defined and instance-level annotations of these are applied to a subset of UD data, covering 38 languages. It provides a rich ground for research related to text genre from a multilingual perspective. Utilizing this dataset, we can overcome the data shortage that hindered previous research and reproduce experiments from earlier studies with an improved setup. We revisit a previous study that used genre-based clusters and show that the clusters for most target genres provide a mix of genres. We compare training data selection based on clustering and gold genre labels and provide an analysis of the results. The dataset is publicly available.[1]

1 Introduction

In the context of cross-lingual transfer to low-resource target languages, a significant effort is put into identifying the most suitable source data for the transfer process. The source language, as a pivotal transfer factor, is subject to comprehensive research (e.g. Lin et al., 2019; Lauscher et al., 2020; Turc et al., 2021). Within cross-lingual dependency parsing, a direction of research explores the additional impact of the text genre dimension (Stymne, 2020; Müller-Eberstein et al., 2021a). These studies use data from Universal Dependencies (UD) (Nivre et al., 2020), which provides detailed cross-linguistically consistent morphosyntactic annotations for over 100 languages. Genre[2] information is represented by labels that are assigned at the treebank level. While UD has extensive guidelines for morphosyntactic annotations, Nivre et al. (2020) note that genre labels lack both exclusive boundaries and consistent criteria, and there is a lack of comprehensive descriptions of UD genres. This means that each contributor of a UD treebank may interpret the genre labels in a different way, leading to inconsistencies. Our investigation shows that it is indeed often the case that the actual texts included in a treebank do not match the assigned genre label(s). The inconsistencies in genre annotation in UD, limit the possibilities of exploring the effect of genre on parsing and other studies based on UD, and is a confounding factor in previous studies, such as Müller-Eberstein et al. (2021a).

We present UD-MULTIGENRE, a dataset of instance-level genre annotations for a highly multilingual subset of UD, based on a comprehensive manual analysis of documentation and metadata for individual UD treebanks. We analyze the existing UD genres, and propose modifications to achieve more coherent genres, resulting in a set of 17 target genres. We then go through a subset of UD treebanks and reorganize them into controlled single-genre subsets. The training and development part of the corpus covers all 17 genres and 38 languages from 63 UD treebanks. We also create a smaller test set covering 5 genres and 16 languages, based on 17 UD treebanks. In addition, we perform an experiment on genre-aware cross-lingual dependency parsing, where we revisit the most successful method in Müller-Eberstein et al. (2021a) and reanalyze it based on our gold genre

[1] https://github.com/UppsalaNLP/UD-MULTIGENRE

[2] We follow the terminology of UD, and use the term *genre* for the distinction between categories. We note though, that some of the categories used in UD are not strictly genres, such as *medical* (topic/theme) and *spoken* (medium).

Proceedings of the The 3rd Workshop on Multi-lingual Representation Learning (MRL), pages 253–267
December 7, 2023 ©2023 Association for Computational Linguistics

annotations.

Our work makes two contributions. First, it addresses the lack of morphosyntactically annotated multilingual multigenre datasets. Some of its potential applications include 1) exploring the impact of genre on cross-lingual transfer learning, 2) understanding the role of genre in the adaptation to languages with few or no resources, and 3) learning multilingual genre representations for genre prediction. Secondly, we build on Müller-Eberstein et al. (2021a) and investigate the performance of dependency parsing when sampling multilingual training instances by gold genre compared to clustering-based sampling.

2 Related Work

Besides UD, several cross-lingual datasets exist for multiple tasks, for instance, XGLUE (Liang et al., 2020) and XTREME (Hu et al., 2020), which, however, are not focused on genres, and typically mainly have a single genre per task. There are also many datasets available annotated for genre, including corpora of raw text collected from different genres for a single language, such as the BNC.[3] Multilingual genre corpora, also annotated for other aspects are less common; one example is MultiNERD, which covers 10 languages and 2 genres, annotated for NER (Tedeschi and Navigli, 2022).

Compared to other datasets, UD stands out as covering a high number of languages for a diverse set of genres, and annotation of morphosyntax. The UD treebanks are contributed by independent teams, who are expected to follow the UD guidelines, which, however, are missing for genres. There is a mix between single-genre treebanks, and multi-genre treebanks, containing a mix of different genres. Some treebanks contain additional sentence-level annotations. However, these are specific to each treebank and are not standardized. In addition, each treebank comes with some additional documentation, more or less detailed, and in some cases refers to papers that describe some aspect of the treebank. Previous work has explored the distribution and properties of genres in UD (Müller-Eberstein et al., 2021b), noticing the diverse and contradictory nature of UD genre labels. Besides the available single-genre treebanks in UD, they were able to identify readily available instance-level annotations from 6 treebanks with training data and 20 with test data only. They then explored methods to automatically classify genres in the remaining multi-genre treebanks.

There has also been work attempting to improve parsing by using genre information from UD. Stymne (2020) focused on two genres, spoken and Twitter, a sub-genre of social, showing that using in-genre data from other languages led to improvements compared to using only out-of-genre data from the same or related languages. Müller-Eberstein et al. (2021a) continue this line of research and present findings showing the significance of genre features in the training data. They propose a set of data-driven methods for collecting training data for a specific target genre, mainly based on clustering. They found that it was better to use genre-based clustering or bootstrapping, rather than to just match sentences using an LLM. Including all multi-genre treebanks containing a given target genre, led to worse results than even a random baseline, even though this gave the largest training data sets. One of their best methods is clustering based on Gaussian mixture models (GMMs), originally explored by Aharoni and Goldberg (2020) for monolingual domain clustering. The idea is to cluster each multi-genre treebank into the same number of clusters as their assigned genres, and then select the cluster that is closest to a target genre embedding, calculated based on 100 sentences from the target treebanks.

Another line of work has tried to improve UD parsing for a given language by combining all treebanks for the language. While not directly related to genre, it is one of the relevant aspects. Overall the findings are that concatenation of treebanks does not work well and that a more advanced method is needed to take advantage of the different treebanks, such as single-treebank fine-tuning (Che et al., 2017; Shi et al., 2017), treebank embeddings (Stymne et al., 2018), or adversarial networks (Sato et al., 2017).

3 UD-MULTIGENRE Dataset

The main purpose of this effort is to provide consistent and comprehensive instance-level genre annotation of UD treebanks covering many genres and multiple languages per genre. We achieve this by splitting existing UD treebanks into subsets with a single genre, which we reclassify by going through treebank documentation. The dataset enables new research as well as re-evaluation and a deeper un-

[3] https://www.english-corpora.org/bnc/

derstanding of prior research on genre-based data selection for cross-lingual dependency parsing. In addition, it is highly relevant for the research direction that investigates cross-lingual genre representation and classification (Petrenz, 2012).

Our dataset is based on treebanks from UD version 2.11 and focuses mainly on training and development sets. Additionally, for the experiments carried out in this paper, we collected a small test set including additional languages. Collecting test sets across all covered genres is left for future work.

3.1 General Overview

The main part of the dataset is made up of training and development data, collected from training and development sets of 25 single-genre and 38 multi-genre UD treebanks in 38 languages from 15 language families, as well as the English-Tweebank (Liu et al., 2018), which contains Twitter data in UD format.[4] Currently, the total size of the dataset (training and development) in tokens is 11096.9k, and in sentences - 657.4k. In addition, the test set currently includes data from 17 treebanks for five genres and 14 low-resource languages (119k tokens and 7.2k sentences).

In order to get a coherent and useful dataset, we decided on the following limitations, and excluded:

- data in ancient languages including data attributed, among others, to the *bible* and *poetry* genres. Genres in ancient languages are likely to have their distinctive properties and their annotation requires further analysis, which will be addressed in future research;
- data that requires paid subscription;
- subsets of training instances with less than 500 tokens per genre in a treebank;
- data corresponding to UD labels *grammar_examples* and *web*, which cannot be viewed as single genres.

3.2 Genres in UD

UD contains 18 treebank-level genre labels, see Müller-Eberstein et al. (2021b)) for an overview. As pointed out by Nivre et al. (2020) for UD v2.7, the distribution of the 18 genre labels is skewed towards a few genres. In UD v2.11, which we work on, *news* is the most frequent label included in 60% of all treebanks in training data. While it might seem to be the most consistent in terms of text sources, this is not always the case. We found it to be represented both by daily mainstream news and long reads from magazines and periodicals. *Nonfiction* is the second most frequent and diverse genre in UD that subsumes many subgenres including *academic*, *legal*, and others, as noted earlier in Müller-Eberstein et al. (2021b).

The descriptions in the underlying documentation often mismatch the assigned genre labels, even for single-genre treebanks. To provide some examples, the Dutch-Alpino treebank is labelled as *news*, however, its metadata description on GitHub lists several types of genre annotation patterns that cover both news and data from other sources, such as a QA project, the Dutch reference grammar, suites for grammar maintenance, periodicals and magazines. English-Atis and Turkish-Atis are labelled as *news* and *non-fiction*, however, they belong to the *spoken* genre in fact, since they include transcriptions of human speech interactions where people request flight information through automated inquiry systems. Tamil-MWTT is labeled as *news* and it comprises sentences primarily sourced from a grammar on Tamil. Development and test sets of the same treebank may have different genre distributions. We identified similar issues by analyzing the documentation and metadata in other treebanks including those that have multiple genre labels.

41% of UD treebanks contain only test sets and have no data for training. Only a small portion (35%) of treebanks that have training data are single-genre, and many of them are small. Single-genre treebanks cover 13 genre labels where 18% of labels belong to *bible*, *grammar_examples*, and *medical*. Moreover, some of the genres are not adequately represented in single-genre treebanks, which complicates the use of methodologies from prior research in Müller-Eberstein et al. (2021a,b). While *news* constitutes 32% of single-genre treebanks in training data, *nonfiction* is represented only by data in ancient languages (Latin-ITTB, Old East Slavic-Birchbark, Sanskrit-Vedic).

3.3 Genres in UD-MULTIGENRE

The 18 original treebank-level UD genre tags serve as an initial reference. Our label set uses 11 out of these tags, for which we provide new definitions. This led to reassigning some treebanks that do not fit the new definitions. In addition, we add 6 new tags, based on coherent subgenres, most of which are currently subsumed under *nonfiction*. Table 1

[4]Converted to avoid multiple roots following Stymne (2020).

genre	in UD	Criteria
academic	✓	scientific articles and reports from different fields (medicine, oil and gas, humanities, computer science), and popular science articles
blog	✓	texts proceeding from blogging platforms like WordPress
email	✓	email messages
fiction	✓	fiction novels, stories, fairy tales. Documentation and patterns tend to include author or story names
guide		Wikihow, travel guides, instructions
interviews		prepared interviews with celebrities, politicians and businessmen
learner_essays	✓	essays of language learners on different topics that tend to contain grammar errors
legal	✓	legal and administrative texts, including texts from governmental webs
news	✓	mainstream daily (online) news, Wikinews. We stick to short articles and exclude long-read newspaper articles since they often belong to popular science
nonfiction_prose		documentary prose, biographies, autobiographical narratives, memoirs, essays
parliament		transcriptions of parliamentary speeches and debates
QA		data from Question Answering competitions
reviews	✓	messages containing reviews and opinions
social	✓	informal social media posts and discussions (e.g., Twitter, Telegram, Reddit, forum messages and comments etc.)
spoken	✓	transcriptions of spontaneous spoken speech: monologues and conversations
textbook		educational literature, textbooks
wiki	✓	main Wikipedia articles. Wikihow, Wikinews, Wikitravel, and Wikianswers are not considered in this category

Table 1: Genre selection criteria

gives an overview of all our genres with definitions.

As stated earlier, we exclude both labels and data related to treebanks in ancient languages and the extremely diverse UD genres *web* and *grammar_examples*. *nonfiction* and "topical" labels (*medical*, *government*) are discarded as labels, but the underlying data is categorized based on the analysis of the documentation and metadata patterns. Within *nonfiction*, we find the following major types of data sources that correspond to a specific metadata pattern in each treebank: 1) academic reports and popular science articles, 2) guides (wikihow, Wiki travel) and instructions, 3) textbooks, 4) nonfictional prose that includes documentary prose, biographical narratives, and essays, 5) interviews. We group the sources in 1), 2) and 4) into the corresponding new metadata-based genres. The categorization is based on concepts shared by these sources that closely align with the idea of communicative purpose. Although communicative purpose is itself a complex and multilayer concept as discussed in Askehave and Swales (2001), it has often been considered a key characteristic feature for genre identification and categorization. Academic reports and popular science articles deliver scientific knowledge and are attributed to *academic*. Guides and instructions provide step-by-step guidance on how to perform a specific task or function and are assigned the *guide* label. Documentary prose, biographical narratives and essays are literary works based mainly on factual information[5] and are assigned the *nonfiction_prose* label. Textbooks and interviews are assigned the labels *textbook* and *interviews*, respectively.

The UD *medical* label is quite rare, and the underlying data is categorized as *academic*. It is mostly represented by Romanian-SiMoNERo where texts predominantly come from scientific books. Moreover, it includes European Medicines Agency reports where medicines are their properties are mainly discussed.

The UD *government* label contains texts from governmental websites or parliamentary debates. We categorize the data from governmental websites as *legal*, since it generally aims to provide legal and administrative guidance. Parliamentary debates are attributed to *parliament*. The UD label *spoken* also contains parliamentary debates, which we include in *parliament* since we limit the *spoken* genre to contain spontaneous speech, rather than speech that is planned or scripted.

Finally, we include *QA* as a new genre. This data originates mostly from Question Answering competitions and its purpose is roughly to provide clear answers to specific questions in various domains. In UD, *QA* is mostly included in *news* or *web*.

The final assignment of a subset of instances to a genre is based on the criteria for data sources listed

[5]encyclopedia Britannica: https://www.britannica.com/topic/nonfictional-prose

Genre	*L*	*T*	*S*
academic	13	960.0k	42.8k
blog	6	92.9k	5.4k
email	1	51.2k	4.3k
fiction	20	769.3k	57.9k
guide	2	48.5k	3.5k
interview	4	62.8k	3.7k
learner_essays	1	28.6k	952
legal	11	217.0k	9.6k
news	29	6534.0k	361.6k
nonfiction_prose	9	85.0k	5.8k
parliament	11	191.7k	8.5k
QA	4	154.2k	12.2k
reviews	5	475.8k	44.0k
social	11	455.0k	32.6k
spoken	12	410.6k	34.0k
textbook	1	9.1k	430
wiki	14	549.3k	29.8k
Total	155	11096.9k	657.4k

Table 2: Number of covered languages (L) and size of each genre in tokens (T) and sentences (S) in the training and development sets.

in Table 1. As a result, annotation patterns that cannot be associated with any of these criteria are not considered and the corresponding subsets of instances are not included in UD-MULTIGENRE.

3.4 Procedure

UD-MULTIGENRE contains subsets of treebanks with consistent genres. Each subset contains information about genre, source UD treebank, language, and language family, as well as all sentences matching the subset identifiers. These subsets may originate both from multi-genre and single-genre UD treebanks. Due to the diversity of descriptions in the repositories of different UD treebanks, proper assignment of annotated subsets of instances to the corresponding genres required significant manual effort and is done as follows. For a given UD treebank (multi-genre or single-genre) we use information from the UD github repository, as well as any documentation of source corpora and treebank-related papers, and available document- and/or sentence-leval metadata. To ensure higher confidence in the retrieved patterns, original data sources are identified and provided for less clear cases. We compare the original UD labels with the official description of sources in the corresponding GitHub repositories and reclassify (parts of) treebanks when necessary. We also identify metadata patterns for each of the genres in UD-MULTIGENRE, and attribute sentences matching this metadata to the corresponding genre.[6]

[6]A detailed description of metadata patterns is available in the UD-MULTIGENRE repository.

Treebanks are considered good candidates to be included in the dataset when their documentation provides references to text sources, bibliographies and metadata patterns of various granularity together with the lists of genres. The procedure is more complex when detailed genre descriptions can only be found in project papers and additional documents that are available on original corpora websites. For some treebanks, scarce information on metadata patterns and their correspondence to genres is available. In this case, we verify whether the number of patterns corresponds to the number of genres and examine each annotation pattern in detail. We specifically focus on sentence-level metadata patterns `sent_id`, `newdoc id`, `genre`. For sources like *wiki*, *blog*, *fiction* and others, they often contain the exact genre names or their parts. In the case of *fiction*, they tend to contain the names of authors or literary pieces. Aligning patterns with treebank genres becomes more challenging when annotations include genre names or other identifiers in the language of the treebank. For instance, the annotations of fiction in Estonian-EDT start with `sent_id = ilu` where ilu refers to *Ilukirjandus* (eng. "fiction"). In less clear cases, we determine the origin of the texts by tracing the sources they come from.

Table 2 summarizes the size of the resulting genres in tokens and sentences, as well as the number of languages available for each genre.

3.5 Limitations in Training and Development Data

Some of the UD treebanks included in our dataset either lack development data or do not have some of their genres available in the development data. In these cases, where possible, a 20% split of training data is left for development. At least 10k tokens are left for training since our experiments require this minimum. It was done for the following treebanks and their corresponding genres: Russian-Taiga (*reviews* and *QA*), Lithuanian-ALKSNIS (*academic*), Dutch-Alpino (*QA* and *news*), Indonesian-CSUI (*news*), Slovenian-SST (*spoken*), Slovak-SNK (*fiction*), Russian-Syntagrus (*news* and *nonfiction_prose*). Slovak-SNK treebank's genres in training and development do not match. The development set contains only Wikipedia data and, since its size is sufficient to share between training and development, we use 0.9 of it (10.8k instances) as training data. For

Italian-ParlaMint, which lacks development data and its training data size is lower than 10k, we add 4.8k test instances to the development set since it has a test set of over 9k tokens,

3.6 Test Data

The current test data is targeted at the experiment described in Section 4, and covers five genres. We plan to collect test sets across all genres and for more languages in future work. Test data is extracted from 17 UD treebanks including test-only treebanks that satisfy the requirement of our experimental setup: maximum genetic distance should be achieved between test and training data to minimize transfer from close languages. Hence, we select test sets of treebanks in languages that do not belong to the language families of the training set. In some cases, this was not possible, such as for *fiction*, where all the available test sets belong to the Uralic language family. Consequently, we exclude Uralic languages from the training set during the experiments. UD includes PUD corpora (*wiki* and *news*) that have only test sets available. We retrieve instances for these genres for our test data in Indonesian, Japanese, Chinese, and Thai, and split them into subsets for *news* and *wiki*.

4 Experiment

We present a pilot experiment, designed to shed some further light on genre-based data selection, explored in Müller-Eberstein et al. (2021a). We limit the experiments to five genres explored in their work: *news*, *wiki*, *spoken*, *social*, *fiction*, excluding *grammar_examples*, which is not in UD-MULTIGENRE. We analyze their GMM clustering strategy for data selection and compare it to using gold genre annotated data. In addition, we aim to control for dataset size as well as minimize the impact of related languages in the data selection.

4.1 Experiment Motivation

As we have pointed out, earlier research on genres in cross-lingual UD parsing is affected by the inconsistent genre annotations in UD. In this experiment, we validate whether by addressing the limitations of prior research and obtaining a cleaner genre signal, we can confirm the statement of the previous work. Specifically, we revisit the GMM clustering method of Müller-Eberstein et al. (2021a), taking advantage of the clean genre annotations in UD-MULTIGENRE, which allows us to explore the content of GMM clusters with respect to the gold genre. In addition, we modify the GMM strategy compared to Müller-Eberstein et al. (2021a) to avoid using the target data for mean genre embedding calculation, made possible by the fact that UD-MULTIGENRE provides target genre annotations for multiple languages that are necessary to calculate mean genre embeddings for genre representation. We also control for the size of the training data and exclude all languages that are closely related to the target language from the training data, in order to isolate the genre feature as far as possible.

Our main questions can be formulated as follows: 1) Does the GMM clustering approach, based on Müller-Eberstein et al. (2021a), extract genre-specific subsets? 2) Is selecting gold target genre instances better or worse than GMM clusters? 3) What is the mix of genres in GMM clusters, especially when GMM outperforms gold?

4.2 Training Data Selection

We compare the performance of a parser trained on two types of training sets for each genre. The first type uses gold multilingual training instances from UD-MULTIGENRE subsets. The second is based on instances selected from multigenre UD treebanks using GMM, inspired by Müller-Eberstein et al. (2021a), as well as sentences from single-genre treebanks. For GMM, we use multigenre UD treebanks, from which subsets are derived. It allows us to clearly see how gold instances are distributed within clusters.

We consider several enhancements to the workflow in Müller-Eberstein et al. (2021a). First, we avoid target-like data when calculating the mean genre embeddings to represent genres. The data come neither from the same treebank (training data) nor from the same language. It is based entirely on UD-MULTIGENRE subsets derived from single-genre UD treebanks with verified labels and single-subset treebanks in UD-MULTIGENRE. This allows us to exclude the bias towards topical and language features of target data. Secondly, we minimize the influence of genetically close languages by excluding the members of the target language family from the training data for each genre.

Gold: For the gold data, we collect all subsets from UD-MULTIGENRE that are labelled with the target genre. This includes both data that was originally from UD single-genre as well as multigenre treebanks.

GMM: For each genre, mean genre embeddings are calculated by mean pooling XLMRoberta-base embeddings of $n = 100$ instances that are randomly selected from all single-genre subsets. All subsets in UD-MULTIGENRE that originate from a multi-genre UD treebank that contains the target genre are then clustered. The number of clusters is set to the number of genres in each set. Next, we compute cluster centroids and measure the cosine distance from each cluster centroid to our mean genre embeddings. The closest cluster is selected, and all sentences in it are added to the GMM training data for that genre. In addition, we add data from all matching single-genre UD treebanks, controlled in UD-MULTIGENRE, since such data is readily available.

In order to balance the size of the training data for each target, we select the number of sentences in the smallest set of gold and GMM, and sample that amount of sentences from the larger set. This ensures that the two datasets for each genre have the same size. Table 8 (Appendix) shows the sizes of the training sets.

4.3 Training Setup

We use the MaChAmp v4.2 (van der Goot et al., 2021) for dependency parsing. An older version of the same framework was used in the previous work (Müller-Eberstein et al., 2021a). Instead of mBERT, as used there, XLMRoberta base is used as the base MLM. XLMRoberta was observed to be more suitable for multigenre data since it was trained not only on Wikipedia but on a large selection of multilingual CommonCrawl resources (Lepekhin and Sharoff, 2022) and it typically gives better results for cross-lingual parsing than mBERT (see e.g. de Lhoneux et al., 2022). The performance is assessed using labelled attachment scores (LAS). We use the test data described in Section 3.6, controlling for language family in the training sets. Therefore, we remove Uralic languages from the training data for *fiction* and *social* (Finnish-OOD). It allows us to add Uralic development sets from UD-MULTIGENRE to the evaluation (Estonian-EDT *fiction*, Finnish-TDT *fiction*, Estonian-EWT *social*).

4.4 Results and Discussion

Table 3 shows the proportion of genres in the GMM clusters. It is clear that all clusters contain a mix of genres, with *news* and *fiction* containing the largest part of matching genre data, and *spoken* very little from its own genre. Only for *news*, the majority of instances come from this genre (66.64%). This indicates that GMM clustering is not solely capturing genre, but also other aspects, as also noted by Aharoni and Goldberg (2020), who suggest that cluster assignments are sensible to the presence of topical terms. Note that when using GMM for training, we concatenate it with data from single-genre treebanks, which means that additional in-genre data is added for each target genre. The proportion of such data is 24% for *fiction*, and over 50% for all other genres, up to 88% for *spoken*

	news	wiki	fiction	spoken	social
news	***66.73***	*33.80*	26.77	20.52	*23.77*
wiki	1.86	**9.13**	1.89	0.75	0.90
fiction	8.42	23.12	***43.19***	*39.74*	10.29
spoken	0.47	0.02	2.63	**18.60**	0.75
social	3.30	15.99	12.07	3.41	**21.20**
academic	8.60	4.20	1.92	0.36	0.00
blog	0.86	2.53	0.45	1.56	1.77
email	0.00	0.00	0.00	0.00	4.55
guide	0.80	0.00	0.95	3.28	0.00
interview	0.62	1.27	2.68	3.83	0.00
legal	1.92	2.85	0.69	0.00	0.00
nf_prose	1.94	2.70	3.25	5.13	1.85
parliament	3.04	1.38	3.14	0.65	0.00
QA	1.34	2.79	0.00	0.06	15.88
reviews	0.07	0.21	0.19	1.69	19.04
textbook	0.03	0.00	0.16	0.42	0.00

Table 3: Distribution in percent of gold genres in GMM-based training data for each genre. The matching genre is marked in bold, and the largest genre in each cluster is marked in italics. *nf_prose* is short for *nonfiction_prose*

The results of zero-shot dependency parsing are shown in Table 4. The performance with data selected with the GMM-based approach is generally on par with data based on gold instances. The average score is slightly higher for GMM, whereas gold is better for 12 out of 21 targets. For *fiction*, gold is the best option in all cases, with an average improvement over GMM of 2 LAS points. For all other genres, however, there is a variation between target treebanks of which option performs the best. In two cases, both in spoken, the LAS scores are equal, but very low, showing that neither of the training sets are a good fit in that case.

To further investigate the impact of genres, we additionally performed cross-genre experiments, applying the GMM and gold models for each genre, to all target genres. The full results of this experiment are shown in Table 7 (Appendix). Here we did not fully control for language relatedness, and

		GMM	gold
fiction	Erzya_JR	17.33	**18.28**
	Estonian_EDT	72.35	**74.22**
	Finnish_TDT	74.45	**75.31**
	Komi-Zyrian_Lattice	14.56	**17.34**
	Moksha_JR	18.51	**19.80**
news	Chinese_PUD	**45.88**	45.61
	Japanese_PUD	**41.50**	40.71
	Tamil_TTB	46.61	**47.76**
	Thai_PUD	57.59	**58.30**
social	Estonian_EWT	59.71	**60.75**
	Finnish_OOD	66.78	**67.85**
	Irish_TwittIrish	**47.01**	45.62
spoken	Abaza_ATB	3.07	3.07
	Beja_NSC	0.82	0.82
	Cantonese_HK	**33.40**	32.32
	Chukchi_HSE	10.60	**10.92**
	Gheg_GPS	32.61	**33.78**
	Komi-Zyrian_IKDP	**21.96**	20.57
wiki	Albanian_TSA	**82.97**	79.83
	Indonesian_PUD	**73.54**	73.37
	Japanese_PUD	33.14	**31.65**
	Average	**40.8**	**40.7**

Table 4: Zero-shot dependency parsing results (LAS)

it is clear that the best results for both gold and GMM when the training data include the same language, as for Indonesian_PUD, when trained on *news* containing Indonesian_CSUI, or when trained on related languages, such as for Irish_Twittrish trained on *news*, containing Scottish Gaelic data. This shows the importance of controlling for languages. However, there are still cases when it is preferable to train on other genres than the target genre. This is the case for *spoken*, where training on *social* is the best option for Chukchi and Cantonese and training on *fiction* is best for Komi Zyrian. This to some extent matches the content of these treebanks, which include folk stories and fairy tales in Komi Zyrian and political discussions in Cantonese.

When GMM outperforms gold we mainly observe 2 scenarios. In the first case, GMM-based training data contains a significant portion of a non-target genre g, and, at the same time, the gold parser for g scores the highest across all parsers. In the second case, gold underperforms GMMs in all or most genres, which suggests that another genre beyond the five target genres of this experiment contributes to the performance. The latter is the case for Japanese *news* and Albanian *wiki*. Examples of the former are *spoken* Cantonese and Komi Zyrian, discussed above, where we note that the *spoken* GMM cluster contains a relatively high proportion of both *fiction* and *social*. For Cantonese-HK, the parser trained on gold *social* achieves the best score of 37.4 LAS. This test set includes sentences from a council meeting discussion and an interview. Social media discussions on political issues involving several participants are quite typical of the *social* genre. Hence, although this test set contains unprepared speech with many disfluencies, characteristic of the *spoken* genre, we assume that the input from *social* in the GMM-based training data (18.47%) contributes useful instances and increases the performance. For Indonesian *wiki*, the scores when training on *news* are high, and the GMM cluster contains a high proportion of it.

This experiment provides valuable knowledge on the influence of genre distribution on dependency parsing performance. Gold training data is more advantageous in *fiction*. GMMs work better for several treebanks in *social*, *spoken*, *news*, and *wiki*, where we assume a larger diversity in terms of topics and author styles. Therefore, input from other genres can be useful. Nevertheless, on the majority of test treebanks, GMM-based genre distributions do not improve performance. On the one hand, it may be explained by a higher genre consistency. On the other hand, genre distributions may not match the target due to the use of single-genre sets instead of the target test samples for mean genre embedding calculation as in the original paper (Müller-Eberstein et al., 2021a). As stated earlier, we attempt to isolate genre from topic and language features, which would be impossible if we calculated mean genre embeddings based on target test data. In summary, the results of our experiment indicate that the distribution of genre in the training data influences the results of zero-shot dependency parsing, and minimizing the differences between distributions in training and target sets can improve the results.

5 Conclusions

This paper presents UD-MULTIGENRE, a UD-based dataset with instance-level genre annotations for 17 genres in 38 languages. It provides fine-grained verified labels for 63 treebanks with training data and 17 test-only treebanks. It constitutes a robust basis for further exploration of text genre from a multilingual perspective.

A pilot experiment illustrates the application of UD-MULTIGENRE to genre-related research. We revisit previous work that builds on treebank-level UD labels to perform training data selection for zero-shot dependency parsing. Our dataset has facilitated in-depth analysis of training sets produced by a top-performing clustering approach. We show that GMM clusters are not limited to the target genre, but contain a mix of different genres. Instead, this approach can sometimes produce training data containing genre mixtures that are advantageous for certain test treebanks. However, gold training data from UD-MULTIGENRE produces better results on the majority of test treebanks.

6 Limitations

Genre data in UD-MULTIGENRE is grouped based on UD data sources and documentation. This information is more or less detailed, however, we cannot be completely confident about it. Also, it should not be the sole basis for defining terms. More comprehensive and UD-independent genre definitions can help to further reorganize and improve the dataset.

Furthermore, genre descriptions and instance-level patterns are not available for all UD treebanks. Therefore, UD-MULTIGENRE currently cannot provide full coverage of UD. The documentation and referenced project reports contain detailed descriptions of genres for a few treebanks, such as Pomak-PHILOTIS and Welsch-CCG, however, instance-level annotations cannot be associated with them and no source documents corresponding to the annotation patterns are available on the project websites. Also, UD-MULTIGENRE currently does not cover genres encountered in ancient texts, which is a limitation for the investigation of genre-aware dependency parsing of ancient languages. Finally, additional collaboration with contributors of less documented treebanks is needed to increase confidence in annotation patterns and further enhance the clarity of genres.

Acknowledgements

This work is supported by the Swedish strategic research programme eSSENCE. Computations were enabled by resources in project UPPMAX 2020/2-2 at the Uppsala Multidisciplinary Center for Advanced Computational Science. We want to thank all contributors to UD treebanks for their work; without your effort, this work would not have been possible.

References

Roee Aharoni and Yoav Goldberg. 2020. Unsupervised domain clusters in pretrained language models. In *Proceedings of the 58th Annual Meeting of the Association for Computational Linguistics*, pages 7747–7763, Online. Association for Computational Linguistics.

Inger Askehave and John M. Swales. 2001. Genre identification and communicative purpose: a problem and a possible solution. *Applied Linguistics*, 22(2):195–212.

Wanxiang Che, Jiang Guo, Yuxuan Wang, Bo Zheng, Huaipeng Zhao, Yang Liu, Dechuan Teng, and Ting Liu. 2017. The HIT-SCIR system for end-to-end parsing of Universal Dependencies. In *Proceedings of the CoNLL 2017 Shared Task: Multilingual Parsing from Raw Text to Universal Dependencies*, pages 52–62, Vancouver, Canada. Association for Computational Linguistics.

Miryam de Lhoneux, Sheng Zhang, and Anders Søgaard. 2022. Zero-shot dependency parsing with worst-case aware automated curriculum learning. In *Proceedings of the 60th Annual Meeting of the Association for Computational Linguistics (Volume 2: Short Papers)*, pages 578–587, Dublin, Ireland. Association for Computational Linguistics.

Junjie Hu, Sebastian Ruder, Aditya Siddhant, Graham Neubig, Orhan Firat, and Melvin Johnson. 2020. XTREME: A massively multilingual multi-task benchmark for evaluating cross-lingual generalisation. In *Proceedings of the 37th International Conference on Machine Learning*, volume 119 of *Proceedings of the 37th International Conference on Machine Learning*, pages 4411–4421. PMLR.

Anne Lauscher, Vinit Ravishankar, Ivan Vulić, and Goran Glavaš. 2020. From zero to hero: On the limitations of zero-shot language transfer with multilingual Transformers. In *Proceedings of the 2020 Conference on Empirical Methods in Natural Language Processing (EMNLP)*, pages 4483–4499, Online. Association for Computational Linguistics.

Mikhail Lepekhin and Serge Sharoff. 2022. Estimating confidence of predictions of individual classifiers and TheirEnsembles for the genre classification task. In *Proceedings of the Thirteenth Language Resources and Evaluation Conference*, pages 5974–5982, Marseille, France. European Language Resources Association.

Yaobo Liang, Nan Duan, Yeyun Gong, Ning Wu, Fenfei Guo, Weizhen Qi, Ming Gong, Linjun Shou, Daxin Jiang, Guihong Cao, Xiaodong Fan, Ruofei Zhang, Rahul Agrawal, Edward Cui, Sining Wei, Taroon Bharti, Ying Qiao, Jiun-Hung Chen, Winnie Wu, Shuguang Liu, Fan Yang, Daniel Campos, Rangan Majumder, and Ming Zhou. 2020. XGLUE: A new benchmark dataset for cross-lingual pre-training, understanding and generation. In *Proceedings of the*

2020 Conference on Empirical Methods in Natural Language Processing (EMNLP), pages 6008–6018, Online. Association for Computational Linguistics.

Yu-Hsiang Lin, Chian-Yu Chen, Jean Lee, Zirui Li, Yuyan Zhang, Mengzhou Xia, Shruti Rijhwani, Junxian He, Zhisong Zhang, Xuezhe Ma, Antonios Anastasopoulos, Patrick Littell, and Graham Neubig. 2019. Choosing transfer languages for cross-lingual learning. In *Proceedings of the 57th Annual Meeting of the Association for Computational Linguistics*, pages 3125–3135, Florence, Italy. Association for Computational Linguistics.

Yijia Liu, Yi Zhu, Wanxiang Che, Bing Qin, Nathan Schneider, and Noah A. Smith. 2018. Parsing tweets into Universal Dependencies. In *Proceedings of the 2018 Conference of the North American Chapter of the Association for Computational Linguistics: Human Language Technologies, Volume 1 (Long Papers)*, pages 965–975, New Orleans, Louisiana. Association for Computational Linguistics.

Max Müller-Eberstein, Rob van der Goot, and Barbara Plank. 2021a. Genre as weak supervision for cross-lingual dependency parsing. In *Proceedings of the 2021 Conference on Empirical Methods in Natural Language Processing*, pages 4786–4802, Online and Punta Cana, Dominican Republic. Association for Computational Linguistics.

Max Müller-Eberstein, Rob van der Goot, and Barbara Plank. 2021b. How universal is genre in Universal Dependencies? In *Proceedings of the 20th International Workshop on Treebanks and Linguistic Theories (TLT, SyntaxFest 2021)*, pages 69–85, Sofia, Bulgaria. Association for Computational Linguistics.

Joakim Nivre, Marie-Catherine de Marneffe, Filip Ginter, Jan Hajič, Christopher D. Manning, Sampo Pyysalo, Sebastian Schuster, Francis Tyers, and Daniel Zeman. 2020. Universal Dependencies v2: An evergrowing multilingual treebank collection. In *Proceedings of the Twelfth Language Resources and Evaluation Conference*, pages 4034–4043, Marseille, France. European Language Resources Association.

Philipp Petrenz. 2012. Cross-lingual genre classification. In *Proceedings of the Student Research Workshop at the 13th Conference of the European Chapter of the Association for Computational Linguistics*, pages 11–21, Avignon, France. Association for Computational Linguistics.

Motoki Sato, Hitoshi Manabe, Hiroshi Noji, and Yuji Matsumoto. 2017. Adversarial training for cross-domain Universal Dependency parsing. In *Proceedings of the CoNLL 2017 Shared Task: Multilingual Parsing from Raw Text to Universal Dependencies*, pages 71–79, Vancouver, Canada. Association for Computational Linguistics.

Tianze Shi, Felix G. Wu, Xilun Chen, and Yao Cheng. 2017. Combining global models for parsing Universal Dependencies. In *Proceedings of the CoNLL 2017 Shared Task: Multilingual Parsing from Raw Text to Universal Dependencies*, pages 31–39, Vancouver, Canada. Association for Computational Linguistics.

Sara Stymne. 2020. Cross-lingual domain adaptation for dependency parsing. In *Proceedings of the 19th International Workshop on Treebanks and Linguistic Theories*, pages 62–69, Düsseldorf, Germany. Association for Computational Linguistics.

Sara Stymne, Miryam de Lhoneux, Aaron Smith, and Joakim Nivre. 2018. Parser training with heterogeneous treebanks. In *Proceedings of the 56th Annual Meeting of the Association for Computational Linguistics (Volume 2: Short Papers)*, pages 619–625, Melbourne, Australia. Association for Computational Linguistics.

Simone Tedeschi and Roberto Navigli. 2022. MultiNERD: A multilingual, multi-genre and fine-grained dataset for named entity recognition (and disambiguation). In *Findings of the Association for Computational Linguistics: NAACL 2022*, pages 801–812, Seattle, United States. Association for Computational Linguistics.

Iulia Turc, Kenton Lee, Jacob Eisenstein, Ming-Wei Chang, and Kristina Toutanova. 2021. Revisiting the primacy of english in zero-shot cross-lingual transfer. *ArXiv*, abs/2106.16171.

Rob van der Goot, Ahmet Üstün, Alan Ramponi, Ibrahim Sharaf, and Barbara Plank. 2021. Massive choice, ample tasks (MaChAmp): A toolkit for multi-task learning in NLP. In *Proceedings of the 16th Conference of the European Chapter of the Association for Computational Linguistics: System Demonstrations*, pages 176–197, Online. Association for Computational Linguistics.

A Target data selection

Table 5 provides a detailed description of test sets including their size in tokens and the information on text sources. Also, for some treebanks, metadata patterns are used to extract data corresponding to target genres. The use of patterns is explained in the description column. PUD *news* test treebanks in Thai, Japanese, and Chinese represent translations of sentences randomly extracted from multiple daily news media in English: The Washington Post, The Independent, BBC and others. From PUD treebanks, *news* instances are selected using metadata where `sent_id` starting with `n` and `w` correspond to *news* and *wiki*, respectively.

B Genre in UD and UD-MULTIGENRE

Table 6 lists all UD treebanks included in UD-MULTIGENRE, and, for each of them, the official UD labels (treebank-level) and the ones that we assign to subsets of instances derived from these treebanks based on the performed analysis.

C Additional Results

Cross-genre evaluation results are shown in Table 7. As stated earlier, we control for language family distribution in the training data for each genre. Therefore, within a specific genre, we manage to avoid the influence of genetically close language. However, when we perform cross-genre evaluation, this influence takes place for some targets. Japonic, Dravidian, Caucasian, Chukotko-Kamchatkan, and IE.Albanian language families are not present in either of the training sets. Therefore, for the corresponding targets, we assume no transfer from genetically close languages across genres.

Instances from a Sino-Tibetan language (Chinese-GSD) are included only in the *wiki* training sets. Therefore, the higher scores of the *wiki* parsers on Chinese-PUD *news* and Cantonese-HK *spoken* are not taken into consideration.

Austronesian language family instances (Indonesian-CSUI) are included only in the *news* training data. Hence, the higher scores of the *news* parsers on Indonesian-PUD *wiki* are not considered.

A Celtic language, Scottish Gaelic, is present in *spoken*, *news*, and *fiction*. Therefore, the higher performance of parsers on the Irish-Twittirish test set in these genres can be due to the transfer of language features from a genetically close language.

Instances from Afroasiatic languages (Hebrew, Maltese) are part of *news*, *wiki*, and *fiction* training data. For the Beja test set, we exclude from consideration the scores of the corresponding genre-specific parsers.

Uralic languages are present in *news* and *wiki* training data. Hence, the scores of the corresponding parsers for Estonian, Finnish, Komi Zyrian, Erzya, and Moksha test sets are not taken into account.

The results where the transfer from genetically close languages takes place are marked in bold italics in Table 7.

D Additional Statistics

Table 8 shows, for each genre, the number of instances in the single-genre set (shared), in gold and GMM samples derived from the multigenre set together with the total number of instances in the balanced training data. To save computational resources, we reduce the size of the training data based on the multigenre set for news to the mean multigenre set size (38436 instances). We randomly select this number of instances from the corresponding gold and GMM training data.

Table 9 shows the distribution of language families in the clustering-based training data. Language families are the same in the gold data since it is based on the same multigenre sets. Table 10 displays the distribution of language families in the single-genre sets.

genre	treebank	language family	description	tokens
spoken	Abaza-ATB	Caucasian	spontaneous stories about the speakers' lives, village traditions, tales and legends (source: corpus website)	652
spoken	Beja-NSC	Afroasiatic	a collection of fairy tales and stories narrated by Beja speakers(source: corpus website)	856
spoken	Cantonese-HK	Sino-Tibetan	2 parts of this test set correspond to spontaneous spoken speech: send_id = 411 to 547, interview with unprepared dialogues, and send_id = 651 to 1004, meeting of the legislation council with unprepared dialogues	10231
spoken	Chukchi-HSE	Chukotko-Kamchatkan	anecdotes, songs, parables, autobiographical stories, fairy tales, everyday dialogues, retellings of silent movie fragments (source: corpus website)	5389
spoken	Gheg-GPS	IE.Albanian	narrations of Wallace Chafe's Pear Stories video (pearstories.org) by heritage speakers of Gheg Albanian. To extract the instances, metadata starting with `[sent_id = P]` is used (speakers from Prishtina), we exclude the instances of speakers from Switzerland since they contain a lot of code-switching (mostly Swiss-German).	2312
spoken	Komi Zyrian-IKDP	Uralic	Iźva dialect transcriptions of spoken Komi Zyrian (source: corpus website)	2304
wiki	Albanian-TSA	IE.Albanian	Wikipedia	922
wiki	Indonesian-PUD	Austronesian	Wikipedia	9823
wiki	Japanese-PUD	Japonic	Wikipedia	15124
news	Japanese-PUD	Japonic	traslated: Washington Post, BBC, etc.	13664
news	Tamil-TTB	Dravidian	daily news media (source: corpus website)	1772
news	Chinese-PUD	Sino-Tibetan	traslated: Washington Post, BBC, etc.	10531
news	Thai-PUD	Sino-Tibetan	traslated: Washington Post, BBC, etc.	10831
fiction	Erzya-JR	Uralic	texts from various authors of fiction who created original works in the Erzya language	10357
fiction	Komi Zyrian-Lattice	Uralic	all `sent_id` variants belong to *fiction* except for those that start with `kpv` (news) and `OKK` (grammar examples)	2662
fiction	Moksha-JR	Uralic	all instances belong to *fiction*, except for those `sent_id` starting with `MKS` (grammar examples)	1004
social	Irish-Twittirish	Celtic	Twitter data	15433
social	Finnish-OOD	Uralic	instances with `sent_id` starting with `thread` belong to forum discussions and `tweet` - to Twitter posts	5134

Table 5: Description of the test data grouped by genre. The selection of metadata patterns for the extraction of genre-specific subsets of instances is explained in the description column. IE stands for Indo-European language family

Treebank name	UD labels	UD-MULTIGENRE labels
Afrikaans-AfriBooms	legal, nonfiction	legal
Armenian-ArmTDP	blog, fiction, grammar-examples, legal, news, nonfiction	nonfiction_prose, blog, fiction, news, legal
Armenian-BSUT	blog, fiction, government, legal, news, nonfiction, web, wiki	nonfiction_prose, blog, fiction, news, legal, wiki
Belarusian-HSE	fiction, legal, news, nonfiction, poetry, social, wiki	social, news, nonfiction_prose, fiction, wiki
Bulgarian-BTB	fiction, legal, news	fiction, legal, academic, nonfiction_prose, news, interview
Catalan-AnCora	news	news
Chinese-GSD	wiki	wiki
Croatian-SET	news, web, wiki	news
Czech-CAC	legal, medical, news, nonfiction, reviews	legal, news, academic
Czech-FicTree	fiction	fiction
Czech-PDT	news, nonfiction, reviews	news, academic
Dutch-Alpino	news	news, QA
Dutch-LassySmall	wiki	wiki
English-Atis	news, nonfiction	spoken
English-EWT	blog, email, reviews, social, web	social, QA, reviews, blog, email
English-GUM	academic, blog, fiction, government, news, nonfiction, social, spoken, web, wiki	news, fiction, academic, nonfiction_prose, parliament, spoken, guide, interview, textbook
English-GUMReddit	blog, social	social
English-LinES	fiction, nonfiction, spoken	fiction, parliament
English-Tweebank		social
Erzya-JR	fiction	nonfiction_prose, fiction
Estonian-EDT	academic, fiction, news, nonfiction	news, academic, fiction
Estonian-EWT	blog, social, web	social
Finnish-TDT	blog, fiction, grammar-examples, legal, news, wiki	wiki, news, legal, blog, fiction, parliament
French-ParisStories	spoken	spoken
French-Rhapsodie	spoken	spoken
French-Sequoia	medical, news, nonfiction, wiki	wiki, academic, parliament, news
German-GSD	news, reviews, wiki	reviews
German-HDT	news, nonfiction, web	news
Greek-GDT	news, spoken, wiki	news, parliament
Hebrew-HTB	news	news
Hebrew-IAHLTwiki	wiki	wiki
Hindi English-HIENCS	social	social
Hindi-HDTB	news	news
Icelandic-Modern	news, nonfiction	parliament, news
Indonesian-CSUI	news, nonfiction	news
Italian-ISDT	legal, news, wiki	news, parliament, QA, wiki, legal
Italian-MarkIT	grammar-examples	learner_essays
Italian-ParlaMint	government, legal	parliament
Italian-PoSTWITA	social	social
Italian-TWITTIRO	social	social
Lithuanian-ALKSNIS	fiction, legal, news, nonfiction	academic, legal, news, fiction
Maltese-MUDT	fiction, legal, news, nonfiction, wiki	fiction, parliament
Naija-NSC	spoken	spoken
Norwegian-Nynorsk	blog, news, nonfiction	blog, parliament, legal, news
Norwegian-NynorskLIA	spoken	spoken
Polish-LFG	fiction, news, nonfiction, social, spoken	social, news, fiction, academic, spoken
Portuguese-PetroGold	academic	academic
Romanian-RRT	academic, fiction, legal, medical, news, nonfiction, wiki	legal, news, fiction, academic, wiki
Romanian-SiMoNERo	medical	academic
Russian-GSD	wiki	wiki
Russian-SynTagRus	fiction, news, nonfiction	news, fiction, academic, nonfiction_prose, interview, wiki
Russian-Taiga	blog, fiction, news, poetry, social, wiki	social, QA, reviews
Scottish Gaelic-ARCOSG	fiction, news, nonfiction, spoken	fiction, news, spoken, interview
Slovak-SNK	fiction, news, nonfiction	fiction, legal, nonfiction_uc, news, wiki
Slovenian-SSJ	fiction, news, nonfiction	wiki
Slovenian-SST	spoken	spoken
Swedish-LinES	fiction, nonfiction, spoken	fiction, parliament

Treebank name	UD labels	UD-MULTIGENRE labels
Turkish German-SAGT	spoken	spoken
Turkish-Atis	news, nonfiction	spoken
Turkish-BOUN	news, nonfiction	news, guide, nonfiction_prose
Turkish-Tourism	reviews	reviews
Uyghur-UDT	fiction	fiction
Western Armenian-ArmTDP	blog, fiction, news, nonfiction, reviews, social, spoken, web, wiki	nonfiction_prose, academic, news, fiction, blog, reviews, social, wiki, spoken

Table 6: Initial UD treebank-level genre labels compared to labels that correspond to each treebank in UD-MULTIGENRE

	fiction_GMM	fiction_gold	news_GMM	news_gold	social_GMM	social_gold	spoken_GMM	spoken_gold	wiki_GMM	wiki_gold
fiction_Erzya_JR	17.3	18.3	***16.3***	***15.3***	16.7	17.2	15.4	14.2	***16.2***	***15.5***
fiction_Estonian_EDT	72.3	74.2	***84.8***	***85.7***	70.1	71.3	71.7	70.9	***78.3***	***78.9***
fiction_Finnish_TDT	74.5	75.3	***86.4***	***82.8***	74.9	75.6	73.6	73.2	***85.9***	***87.0***
fiction_Komi-Zyrian_Lattice	14.6	17.3	***12.5***	***13.6***	16.0	13.6	14.6	10.9	***13.5***	***15.0***
fiction_Moksha_JR	18.5	19.8	***16.5***	***15.6***	16.0	18.8	15.1	13.5	***14.0***	***16.7***
news_Chinese_PUD	43.7	42.3	45.9	45.6	48.5	49.2	42.1	39.6	***64.4***	***64.7***
news_Japanese_PUD	27.0	26.3	41.5	40.7	36.1	35.6	20.0	18.7	32.0	29.8
news_Tamil_TTB	35.3	38.4	46.6	47.8	42.8	43.0	32.0	33.5	37.0	35.2
news_Thai_PUD	55.5	55.6	57.6	58.3	56.8	56.9	55.2	54.8	54.3	55.0
social_Estonian_EWT	58.5	61.0	***73.7***	***73.9***	59.7	60.7	59.3	59.2	***63.5***	***64.1***
social_Finnish_OOD	66.0	65.9	***76.3***	***74.2***	66.8	67.8	64.5	63.3	***76.1***	***76.3***
social_Irish_TwittIrish	***49.2***	***52.3***	***47.1***	***42.4***	47.0	45.6	***50.0***	***49.8***	45.0	41.8
spoken_Abaza_ATB	5.5	3.5	2.1	2.6	3.5	3.8	3.1	3.1	2.0	2.3
spoken_Beja_NSC	***5.1***	***7.9***	***3.2***	***2.0***	4.1	2.9	0.8	0.8	***1.8***	***2.2***
spoken_Cantonese_HK	32.6	33.8	32.6	35.1	36.5	37.4	33.4	32.3	***37.2***	***35.3***
spoken_Chukchi_HSE	16.2	14.5	11.9	12.2	17.8	16.1	10.6	10.9	13.1	14.4
spoken_Gheg_GPS	34.3	35.0	36.7	31.4	36.3	38.7	32.6	33.8	38.4	37.5
spoken_Komi-Zyrian_IKDP	24.1	25.7	***21.0***	***21.5***	23.7	23.0	22.0	20.6	***21.8***	***22.7***
wiki_Albanian_TSA	84.2	81.7	80.4	78.2	79.0	79.3	77.7	75.9	83.0	79.8
wiki_Indonesian_PUD	75.5	76.0	***82.5***	***82.4***	74.7	72.8	74.2	74.8	73.5	73.4
wiki_Japanese_PUD	27.1	25.4	39.1	39.8	37.1	35.1	19.3	19.2	33.1	31.7

Table 7: Complete results of zero-shot dependency parsing evaluation (LAS). In bold italics, we mark the results of cross-genre evaluation where the same and/or genetically close languages are present in the training data

	news	wiki	fiction	spoken	social
shared	190272	19552	11816	24156	14424
gold	131894	6548	29714	3062	14373
GMM	113643	22408	27222	4907	23311
Total balanced	228708*	26100	39038	27218	28797

Table 8: For each genre, the number of instances in shared (single-genre set), gold and GMM samples derived from the multigenre set, as well as the total number of instances in the balanced data (details on balancing are given in Section 4.2). *To save computational resources, the mean multigenre set size is used for *news* (38436 instances)

Language families	news	wiki	fiction	spoken	social
IE.Slavic	68.03	66.32	68.62	58.84	80.30
IE.Germanic	15.49	0.00	19.47	14.92	16.48
Uralic	7.80	9.45	0.00	0.00	0.00
IE.Romance	3.75	19.37	2.80	0.00	0.00
Altaic	1.88	0.00	0.00	0.00	0.00
IE.Armenian	1.34	4.86	3.94	14.56	3.22
IE.Greek	1.12	0.00	0.00	0.00	0.00
IE.Celtic	0.60	0.00	2.02	11.68	0.00
Afro-Asiatic	0.00	0.00	1.69	0.00	0.00
IE.Baltic	0.00	0.00	1.47	0.00	0.00

Table 9: Distribution of language families in clustering-based training data (from multigenre sets) for each genre (in percent)

Language families	news	wiki	fiction	spoken	social
IE.Germanic	80.43	29.61	0.00	31.82	22.62
IE.Indic	6.99	0.00	0.00	0.00	0.00
IE.Romance	6.90	0.00	0.00	11.09	63.29
Afro-Asiatic	2.75	21.98	0.00	0.00	0.00
IE.Slavic	2.65	27.97	85.99	6.88	0.00
Austronesian	0.28	0.00	0.00	0.00	0.00
Sino-Tibetan	0.00	20.44	0.00	0.00	0.00
Altaic	0.00	0.00	14.01	17.69	0.00
Creole	0.00	0.00	0.00	30.13	0.00
Code-switch	0.00	0.00	0.00	2.39	14.09

Table 10: Distribution of language families in single-genre sets for each genre (in percent)

Embedding Structure Matters: Comparing Methods to Adapt Multilingual Vocabularies to New Languages

C.M. Downey[α] **Terra Blevins**[β] **Nora Goldfine**[α] **Shane Steinert-Threlkeld**[α]

[α]Department of Linguistics, University of Washington

[β]Paul G. Allen School of Computer Science & Engineering, University of Washington

{cmdowney,shanest}@uw.edu

blvns@cs.washington.edu

ngoldfine@gmail.com

Abstract

Pre-trained multilingual language models underpin a large portion of modern NLP tools outside of English. A strong baseline for specializing these models for specific languages is Language-Adaptive Pre-Training (LAPT). However, retaining a large cross-lingual vocabulary and embedding matrix comes at considerable excess computational cost during adaptation. In this study, we propose several simple techniques to replace a cross-lingual vocabulary with a compact, language-specific one. Namely, we address strategies for re-initializing the token embedding matrix after vocabulary specialization. We then provide a systematic experimental comparison of our techniques, in addition to the recently-proposed FOCUS method. We demonstrate that: 1) Embedding-replacement techniques in the monolingual transfer literature are inadequate for adapting multilingual models. 2) Replacing cross-lingual vocabularies with smaller specialized ones provides an efficient method to improve performance in low-resource languages. 3) Simple embedding re-initialization techniques based on script-wise sub-distributions rival techniques such as FOCUS, which rely on similarity scores obtained from an auxiliary model.

1 Introduction

For languages other than English and a handful of other very high-resource languages, pre-trained multilingual language models form the backbone of most current NLP systems. These models address the relative data scarcity in most non-English languages by pooling text data across many languages to train a single model that (in theory) covers all training languages (Devlin, 2019; Conneau and Lample, 2019; Conneau et al., 2020; Liu et al., 2020; Scao et al., 2023, i.a.). These models often include language-agnostic tokenization and an increased vocabulary capacity over monolingual models (Conneau et al., 2020).

However, Wu and Dredze (2020) show that these massively multilingual models still underperform on lower-resource languages. Recent efforts to cover these languages instead pre-train models that are specialized to specific languages or language families (Ogueji et al., 2021; Ogunremi et al., 2023). These approaches nonetheless require training a new model from scratch and do not leverage transferable information in existing models.

Our study builds on a line of work which instead *adapts* a pre-trained cross-lingual model (such as XLM-R; Conneau et al., 2020) to a single language, or a smaller set of languages. Language-Adaptive Pre-Training (LAPT)—continuing the MLM or CLM pre-training task on only the target language(s)—is a simple and strong baseline in this regard (Chau et al., 2020).

However, LAPT with no change to the cross-lingual vocabulary comes with considerable excess computational cost: when adapting to a single language or small subset of languages, only a small fraction of the cross-lingual vocabulary is used. The excess vocabulary still contributes to the computational cost on both the forward and backward pass, and embedding/output matrices often constitute a large fraction of the total trainable model parameters (for XLM-R-base, 192M / 278M ≈ 69% of parameters). Additionally, the information-theoretic tokenization modules for cross-lingual models are usually under-optimized for any given language, and especially low-resource languages (Ács, 2019; Conneau and Lample, 2019, i.a.)

For this reason, we propose several simple techniques to replace the large cross-lingual vocabulary of a pre-trained model with a compact, language-specific one during model specialization. Training a new SentencePiece or BPE tokenizer poses no special difficulties. However, re-initializing the embedding matrix for a new vocabulary, which will almost certainly introduce many new tokens lacking pre-trained embeddings, poses significant

Proceedings of the The 3rd Workshop on Multi-lingual Representation Learning (MRL), pages 268–281
December 7, 2023 ©2023 Association for Computational Linguistics

challenges. We compare several methods for such embedding re-initialization.

After reviewing related literature in Section 2, we conduct a qualitative exploration of the pre-trained embedding space for a standard multilingual model: XLM-R (Section 3.1). This exploration informs our formalization of simple techniques to align new vocabulary embeddings with the pre-trained embedding distribution of our base model (Section 3.2). We then provide a systematic experimental comparison of the embedding re-initialization techniques we propose, plus the recently proposed FOCUS re-initialization method (Dobler and de Melo, 2023, Section 4). Our experiments cover a wide selection of low- and mid-resource target languages (i.e. those that have the most to gain from language specialization).[1]

The results of our experiments (Sections 5, 6) demonstrate the following: 1) Embedding-replacement techniques proposed in the monolingual model adaptation literature are inadequate for adapting multilingual models. 2) Replacing large cross-lingual vocabularies with smaller language-specific ones provides a computationally-efficient method to improve task performance in low-resource languages. 3) The simple re-initialization techniques we propose here, based on script-wise embedding sub-distributions, rival techniques such as FOCUS, which rely on model-driven semantic similarity.

2 Related Work

Pre-trained Model Adaptation Extensive work has proposed re-using and modifying pre-trained models for new settings in order to retain existing model knowledge and reduce pre-training costs. Gururangan et al. (2020) show that continued training on domain-specific data effectively adapts pre-trained models to new domains in both high- and low-resource settings. This approach is also used to adapt models to new languages (i.e. Language-Adaptive Pre-Training / LAPT; Chau et al., 2020).

Other approaches involve training new, language-specific adapter layers to augment a frozen monolingual (Artetxe et al., 2020) or multilingual encoder (Pfeiffer et al., 2020; Üstün et al., 2020; Faisal and Anastasopoulos, 2022). A comparison of these cross-lingual adaptation approaches (Ebrahimi and Kann, 2021) found that continued pre-training often outperforms more complex setups, even in low-resource settings. With this in mind, our experiments evaluate the success of models tuned for target languages with LAPT, starting from variable initializations depending on a choice of embedding adaptation technique.

Cross-lingual Vocabulary Adaptation A major limitation in adapting pre-trained models to new languages is the subword vocabulary, which often fails to cover an unseen script (Pfeiffer et al., 2021) or tokenizes target text inefficiently (Ács, 2019). Muller et al. (2021) demonstrate that script is an extremely important factor in predicting transfer success. Specifically, the pre-trained coverage of closely-related languages improves transfer, but only if the target language is written in the same script as its pre-trained relative.

One adaptation technique is to initialize new subword embeddings that cover the target language, e.g. by expanding the existing vocabulary with new tokens as necessary, then training the new (randomly initialized) embeddings (Chau et al., 2020; Wang et al., 2020). When transferring a monolingual model to a new language, Artetxe et al. (2020) and de Vries and Nissim (2021) instead completely re-initialize the embedding matrix, corresponding to a new subword vocabulary. These embeddings are then trained into alignment with the pre-trained, frozen transformer encoder. We show that this technique is not successful when adapting a multilingual model (Section 5).

Other work reuses information in pre-trained embeddings rather than initializing new ones at random. This may include scaling up smaller embedding spaces from models trained on the target language (de Vries and Nissim, 2021; Ostendorff and Rehm, 2023) or copying embeddings from the original vocabulary where there is exact vocabulary overlap (Pfeiffer et al., 2021). When transferring to a target language written in a poorly-covered script, Muller et al. (2021) show that transliterating the target to the script of a well-covered relative can lead to significant performance gains.

Finally, recent work has proposed more complex methods for mapping source embeddings onto semantically similar ones in the target space either through cross-lingually aligned static word embeddings (e.g. the WESCHEL method; Minixhofer et al., 2022) or with bilingual lexicons (Zeng et al., 2023). In concurrent work to ours, Dobler and de Melo (2023) extend WECHSEL with the FO-

[1]The software used to run all experiments may be found at https://github.com/cmdowney88/EmbeddingStructure

CUS method to specialize multilingual vocabularies to a single language. Ostendorff and Rehm (2023) use a cross-lingual progressive transfer learning approach to combine information from the source embeddings and a smaller target language model to initialize higher-dimension target embeddings. Unlike earlier initialization methods and our proposed setup, these methods all require additional information outside the source model and often require significant additional compute. We compare one method from this family (FOCUS) to our proposed heuristic-based initialization schemes.

3 Vocabulary Replacement & Embedding Re-initialization

Research transferring monolingual models from one language to another (e.g. Artetxe et al., 2020; de Vries and Nissim, 2021), has shown that random re-initialization of embeddings +LAPT is sufficient. However, our experiments show that this technique performs poorly when transferring from a multilingual model (Section 5). For this reason, we propose several simple techniques for initializing new embeddings based on a qualitative exploration of the embedding space for XLM-R (Section 3.1), and include the more complex FOCUS technique, developed concurrently with our work, for comparison (Dobler and de Melo, 2023).

3.1 XLM-R Embedding-Space Analysis

To better understand the task of initializing new embeddings for a multilingual model, we explore the token-embedding space of XLM-R through PCA projection. Our hypothesis is that multilingual models do not process all languages homogeneously. This seems to be demonstrated in Figures 1a and 1b, where word embeddings are colored by their respective Unicode script block. We see that the highest-resource scripts in XLM-R (Common, Latin, and Cyrillic) have relatively divergent distributions, while others cluster closer together. This heterogeneity may help explain the finding from Muller et al. (2021) that pre-trained models do not transfer well to even closely-related target languages if the target script does not match that of the pre-trained relative.

Secondly, each script can be further divided into two sub-distributions, roughly corresponding to a shift in the second principal component. Figure 1c shows that this division corresponds to whether a token is word-initial or word-medial. To preserve whitespace information, SentencePiece tokens include a leading underscore to indicate tokens that should be preceded by a space (word-initial tokens).[2] Although the model does not have access to the internal makeup of its tokens, we hypothesize that it learns to discern which tokens can begin a word and which cannot.

Thus when proposing methods to initialize new embeddings for XLM-R, we hypothesize that initializing according script- and position-wise sub-distributions will help to align new vocabulary items with the pre-trained embedding distribution.

3.2 Embedding Re-initialization Techniques

We now formalize simple techniques for embedding re-initialization based on our exploration of XLM-R's embedding space, as well as one recently proposed technique based on an auxiliary embedding model (FOCUS). Figure 2 provides PCA visualizations of the re-initialized embeddings from each technique on a subword vocabulary specialized for languages of the Uralic family (we experiment with these languages in Section 4). The visualization for these languages' respective scripts (Common, Latin, Cyrillic) in the base model can be found in Figure 1b for comparison.

Re-initialization by Identity REINIT-IDENT first identifies tokens in the new vocabulary that exactly match a token in the original vocabulary, then sets the new embeddings of shared tokens to be identical to those in the original embedding table (Figure 2a). This is a common approach to preserve information from the original model, even when the other embeddings are randomly re-initialized (e.g., Pfeiffer et al., 2021). When identity re-initialization is applied in conjunction with another technique (such as REINIT-SCRIPT), identity takes precedence.

Re-initialization by Script For REINIT-SCRIPT, all base XLM-R tokens are first categorized by Unicode block, as a stand-in for identifying the script/orthography. We then calculate the mean and standard deviation for each script in the original embedding space. Finally, new token embeddings for each script are distributed according to a Normal distribution with the corresponding mean and standard deviation (Figure 2b).

[2]E.g., "_the" and "the" are word-initial and word-medial tokens of the same character sequence.

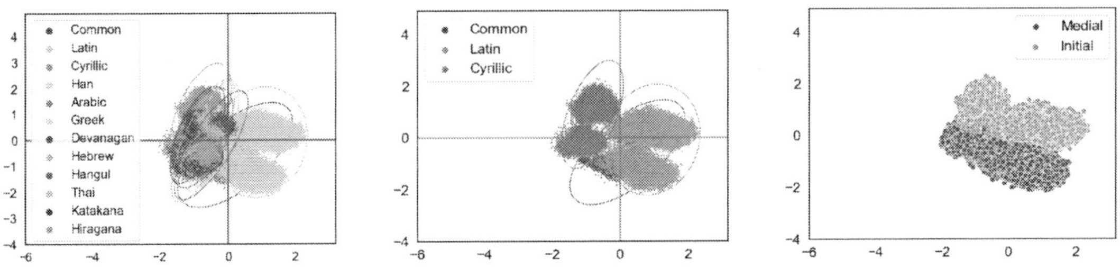

(a) (b) (c)

Figure 1: PCA visualizations of the embedding space for XLM-R. Subplots: (a) Distribution of embeddings for the 12 most common Unicode scripts. (b) Plot reduced to only Common, Latin, and Cyrillic scripts for simplicity. (c) Embeddings colored by whether the token begins a word (initial) or occurs in the middle of one (medial)

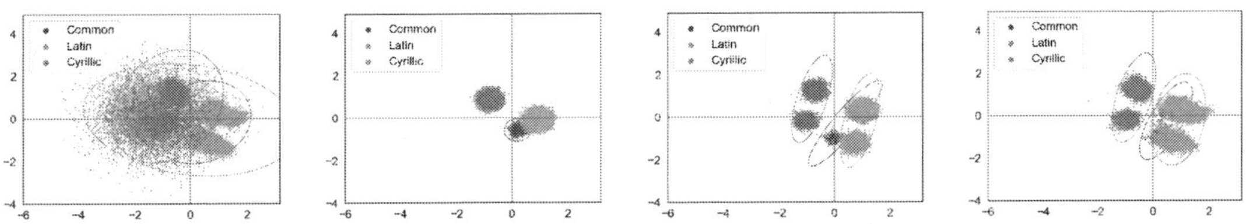

(a) IDENT (b) SCRIPT (c) SCRIPT+POSN (d) SCRIPT+POSN+IDENT

Figure 2: PCA visualizations embedding re-initialized using the heuristic techniques introduced in Section 3.2

Re-initialization by Position REINIT-POSN is based on the observation that within each script, embeddings seem to cluster according their word-initial vs. word-medial status (Figure 1c). Similarly to REINIT-SCRIPT, we identify the mean and standard deviation of embeddings that belong to each category. Because positional status seems to be a sub-cluster within script clusters, we only use REINIT-POSN in combination with REINIT-SCRIPT. The mean and standard deviation for each (script, position) combination is calculated and new embeddings are initialized accordingly (Figure 2c).

FOCUS Re-initialization In addition to the heuristic-based methods introduced above, we investigate a pre-existing method for embedding transfer, termed FOCUS (Dobler and de Melo, 2023). FOCUS works by extrapolating from the embedding space of an existing model, like our heuristic methods, but further introduces an auxiliary embedding model trained on the new language(s). This auxiliary model (based on FastText; Bojanowski et al., 2017) is used to obtain similarity measures between the new vocabulary items. Embeddings corresponding to overlapping tokens in the new vocabulary keep their values from the source model (REINIT-IDENT). Completely new tokens are initialized as a weighted combination of the overlapping items, with weights obtained according to similarity in the auxiliary model.

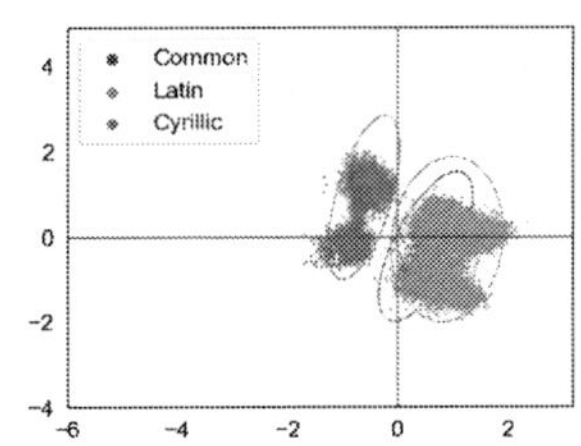

Figure 3: PCA: REINIT-FOCUS embeddings

Random Re-initialization Embeddings not initialized through the above methods are initialized according to a Standard Normal Distribution about the origin. This includes the non-overlapping tokens when REINIT-IDENT is applied on its own, and REINIT-RANDOM, where all embeddings are initialized this way.

Inspection of re-initialized embeddings Figures 2 and 3 show PCA visualizations for the re-initialization techniques described here. Figure 2a shows that while REINIT-IDENT captures some of the pre-trained embedding structure, a large number also remain randomly scattered throughout the space. REINIT-SCRIPT (2b) initializes all embeddings in a Normal distribution about the centroid for each script, but misses key embedding structure, such as the fact that each script has two position-wise sub-distributions. REINIT-SCRIPT+POSN (2c) takes these sub-distributions into account, forming six Normal clusters instead of three.[3] Finally, REINIT-SCRIPT+POSN+IDENT (2d) and FOCUS (3) give the closest emulation of the original XLM-R embedding structure (1b).

4 Experiments

In our experiments, we replace the large cross-lingual embedding matrix of XLM-R and re-initialize it for a new, language-specific vocabulary. We then conduct LAPT to specialize the model for the new language(s), and evaluate performance on downstream tasks. We consider both multilingual→monolingual and multilingual→multilingual transfer scenarios, the latter being transfer to a much smaller set of languages than the original cross-lingual training set. We compare our vocabulary-replacement techniques against the baseline performance of XLM-R off-the-shelf, as well as LAPT while retaining the original, full-sized vocabulary.

Another manipulation we consider is whether the transformer-specific parameters are frozen during LAPT. This follows from the literature on transferring monolingual models, which proposes freezing the encoder parameters and only training the new embedding matrix to mitigate catastrophic forgetting during transfer learning (Artetxe et al., 2020; de Vries and Nissim, 2021). In our tables, we denote LAPT with trainable transformer layers as LAPT-FULL, and training with the transformer frozen (but trainable embeddings) as LAPT-EMB.

Target Languages We select our target languages for a wide selection of language families, scripts, typological characteristics, and resource availability, while still having standard evaluation sets for comparison. Training data for all languages is obtained from OSCAR v.22.01 (Abadji et al., 2022). For our lowest-resource languages, supplemental data is obtained from monolingual splits of the OPUS translation corpus (Tiedemann and Nygaard, 2004) and the Johns Hopkins University Bible Corpus (McCarthy et al., 2020). More data curation details may be found in Appendix A.

Our multilingual→monolingual transfer languages can be found in Table 1. In these experiments, the replacement vocabulary and LAPT training are constrained to a single target language. In addition, we include two multilingual→multilingual experiments. In the first, we simply transfer to the set of languages used in our monolingual experiments. Most of these languages are unrelated and cover a variety of scripts and levels of resource-availability. In the second, we transfer to a set of languages belonging to a single language family — Uralic. These languages come from the same ancestor language, and share broad grammatical features, but also use both Cyrillic and Latin scripts. These differing settings are designed to demonstrate whether language relatedness has an effect on the success of multilingual vocabulary-replacement techniques.

Vocabulary Replacement / Re-initialization When replacing model vocabulary, we train new Sentencepiece models on a subset of the training data. For targets with less than 1GB of data, we use the entire dataset. For those with more, we use a random subset of about 250MB. For multilingual models, we sample 5 million lines according to the same distribution as the training data. All new Sentencepiece models have a total vocabulary size of 32,770 including special tokens. We then initialize the embedding matrix for each new vocabulary according to one or a combination of the techniques described in Section 3.[4]

Training All of our experiments use XLM-R as a starting point (base size; Conneau et al., 2020). We conduct LAPT for 100k training steps, with evaluation checkpoints every 1000 steps. For LAPT-FULL experiments, the transformer blocks are frozen for the first 10k steps, then unfrozen for the last 90k, so that the model does not overfit to initial (possibly poor) embedding initializations. For LAPT-EMB experiments, transformer blocks remain frozen throughout training. The checkpoint obtaining the best MLM loss on a development set is selected for task fine-tuning and evaluation.

For multilingual training, we sample languages according to a multinomial distribution parameterized by $\alpha = 0.2$, following Conneau and Lample (2019), Conneau et al. (2020), i.a. Languages are sampled sentence-wise rather than batch-wise.

Evaluation We evaluate model quality with POS-tagging and NER tasks. For each task and each language, the trained model is fine-tuned on task

[3]Figure 5b in the Appendix verifies that these clusters capture the initial vs. medial token distinction

[4]The auxiliary FastText model for FOCUS initialization is trained on the same set as the vocabulary

training data until evaluation set convergence or the maximum number of epochs is reached, across four random seeds. POS performance is evaluated on Universal Dependencies (UD) treebanks (de Marneffe et al., 2021), and NER is measured on the WikiAnn benchmark (Pan et al., 2017).

5 Results

The results for monolingual adaptation can be found in Tables 1-2 and general multilingual adaptation in Tables 3-4. Because the results for multilingual adaptation to the Uralic family mostly echo overall trends, we provide these results in Appendix C.[5] In order to adhere to our overall computational budget, we only conduct full-vocabulary LAPT experiments for three languages in the monolingual setting.[6]

We first note that across re-initialization methods, LAPT-FULL always outperforms LAPT-EMB. I.e. training with trainable transformer layers outperforms training with frozen ones, despite the risk of catastrophic forgetting with the former. This trend persists across monolingual and multilingual experiments. For example, REINIT-FOCUS+IDENT shows a 6.9 average POS accuracy drop between LAPT-FULL and LAPT-EMB (Table 1).

Second, although FOCUS is the best performing re-initialization method when averaged across languages, for individual languages, it does not perform significantly differently than script-based methods. For instance, Armenian and Telugu POS tagging with script-based initialization performs on-par with or better than FOCUS (Tables 1, 3).[7] In the case of the very low-resource language Erzya, script-based methods mostly outperform FOCUS.[8]

Third, for the languages with the largest amount of data in XLM-R (Estonian, Hebrew, and Russian), the off-the-shelf performance of XLM-R (top row) is slightly better than any re-initialization method. This is not unexpected, since we can expect the highest-resource languages in XLM-R to receive adequate vocabulary coverage, and their embeddings are likely the most robustly trained.

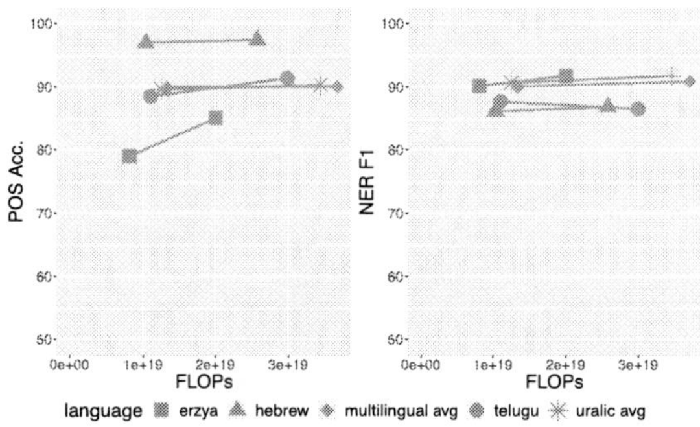

Figure 4: Evaluation scores plotted against total floating point operations of LAPT (computational cost). Left point represents cost of LAPT with reduced vocabulary, right point with full vocabulary

Finally, LAPT with the full, original XLM-R vocabulary, results in marginally better performance than other techniques. On one hand, this might be surprising given the inefficiency with which cross-lingual vocabularies often tokenize low-resource languages (Ács, 2019). On the other hand, these original pre-trained embeddings are also likely robustly aligned with the transformer encoder, which might contribute to slightly better performance.

Part of the motivation for this work, however, is to investigate *efficient* ways to specialize multilingual models. LAPT with the full XLM-R vocabulary is much more computationally costly than training new vocabulary. Figure 4 shows the trade-off between computation (in FLOPs) and performance gain in our experiments: the (often) small gains in performance we see from fine-tuning with the original vocabulary come at the cost of two to three times more FLOPs during adaptation.

Erzya POS performance provides one exception to the pattern of full-vocab LAPT providing only marginal benefits (85.1 accuracy with the full vocabulary vs. 79.0 with the reduced vocabulary). This seems surprising, given Erzya is not included in XLM-R's pre-training data, and intuitively should benefit the most from a specialized vocabulary. It could be that the reduced vocabulary size of 32k is sub-optimal for this particular target language, and/or that the new vocabulary does not overlap enough with the original (full-size) one to inherit useful Cyrillic-script embeddings. Investigating the dynamics of target vocabulary size dur-

[5]While training on related languages may be beneficial for low-resource Uralic languages like Erzya, family-based training vs. general multilingual training does not seem to alter the relative ranking of embedding initialization techniques, which is our primary research interest

[6]We select Erzya, Telugu, and Hebrew for these full-size experiments, spanning very-low, low, and medium resource-availability levels

[7]Overall performance/ranking of SCRIPT+POSN+IDENT vs. SCRIPT+IDENT remains uncertain. For LAPT-FULL averaged across languages, the former performs better in 2/3 POS settings, but only 1/3 NER settings

[8]However, script-based methods show significant variation on Erzya POS after multilingual training (Table 3)

LAPT	REINIT	Armenian	Basque	Erzya	Estonian	Hebrew	Russian	North Sami	Telugu	Avg
*	*	93.4 ± 2.2	95.1 ± 0.7	56.3 ± 5.3	95.6 ± 0.1	97.5 ± 0.1	98.6 ± 0.1	71.2 ± 1.8	83.8 ± 0.1	86.4
FULL	*	-	-	85.1 ± 1.8	-	97.5 ± 0.1	-	-	91.4 ± 4.3	-
FULL	FOCUS+IDENT	**92.3 ± 1.9**	**96.0 ± 0.6**	76.1 ± 2.0	**95.1 ± 0.3**	**97.2 ± 0.1**	**98.4 ± 0.1**	**92.1 ± 0.8**	**86.9 ± 3.5**	**91.7**
FULL	SCRIPT+POSN+IDENT	**93.1 ± 1.7**	93.8 ± 0.5	**79.0 ± 0.7**	94.0 ± 0.2	96.7 ± 0.1	98.2 ± 0.04	86.9 ± 0.7	**88.5 ± 3.2**	91.3
FULL	SCRIPT+IDENT	91.7 ± 1.9	93.6 ± 0.3	70.8 ± 12.8	94.0 ± 0.1	96.7 ± 0.1	98.1 ± 0.1	83.4 ± 1.3	**87.1 ± 3.4**	89.4
FULL	SCRIPT+POSN	90.9 ± 2.0	92.1 ± 0.7	74.6 ± 2.2	90.4 ± 0.6	95.4 ± 0.1	97.2 ± 0.02	78.7 ± 0.5	**87.5 ± 1.4**	88.3
FULL	SCRIPT	89.6 ± 1.5	90.9 ± 0.2	71.5 ± 2.1	89.4 ± 0.9	95.0 ± 0.05	96.9 ± 0.03	77.9 ± 0.2	84.0 ± 1.5	86.9
FULL	IDENT	81.6 ± 0.4	83.6 ± 0.6	59.1 ± 3.1	86.4 ± 0.4	91.1 ± 0.1	96.2 ± 0.04	70.7 ± 0.5	78.0 ± 2.5	80.9
FULL	RANDOM	67.4 ± 2.0	72.7 ± 0.6	53.3 ± 2.8	72.0 ± 0.1	81.0 ± 0.6	86.5 ± 0.6	64.7 ± 0.9	76.4 ± 1.0	72.4
EMB	FOCUS+IDENT	**92.3 ± 1.7**	**95.1 ± 0.6**	48.6 ± 0.1	**94.5 ± 0.05**	**96.9 ± 0.3**	**98.3 ± 0.04**	**73.6 ± 1.6**	**86.2 ± 3.8**	**84.8**
EMB	SCRIPT+POSN+IDENT	87.6 ± 1.3	88.2 ± 0.7	**55.6 ± 4.8**	89.6 ± 0.1	95.3 ± 0.1	97.1 ± 0.05	69.8 ± 1.4	81.8 ± 1.2	82.5
EMB	SCRIPT+IDENT	87.7 ± 1.8	87.9 ± 0.4	**53.8 ± 5.4**	89.2 ± 0.5	95.2 ± 0.1	97.0 ± 0.1	68.6 ± 1.8	82.0 ± 1.3	82.0
EMB	SCRIPT+POSN	56.5 ± 7.6	61.3 ± 12.0	48.7 ± 0.1	71.4 ± 1.4	82.5 ± 0.3	92.1 ± 0.4	59.8 ± 1.5	70.1 ± 7.4	69.4
EMB	SCRIPT	47.6 ± 6.4	59.6 ± 8.1	48.6 ± 0.1	65.7 ± 5.2	80.4 ± 2.2	89.7 ± 1.0	55.5 ± 5.0	73.4 ± 5.5	67.6
EMB	IDENT	80.3 ± 1.1	80.1 ± 0.6	47.9 ± 1.5	82.5 ± 1.8	88.7 ± 0.2	95.2 ± 0.4	60.6 ± 1.2	76.6 ± 1.4	75.9
EMB	RANDOM	47.6 ± 1.8	55.2 ± 2.8	46.3 ± 0.2	63.5 ± 1.8	67.6 ± 2.5	80.2 ± 0.6	44.7 ± 4.0	56.7 ± 6.7	59.2

Table 1: Monolingual Language-Adaptive Pre-Training (LAPT): POS tagging accuracy after fine-tuning. * indicates XLM-R off-the-shelf. Within each division, best result and results within 1 standard deviation are bolded; overall best result indicated with added underline. Best result determined by *mean - stdev*. LAPT with full XLM-R vocab only conducted for three languages due to prohibitive computational cost

LAPT	REINIT	Armenian	Basque	Erzya	Estonian	Hebrew	Russian	Telugu	Avg
*	*	94.1 ± 0.1	94.3 ± 0.1	89.5 ± 0.6	93.3 ± 0.2	85.9 ± 0.1	90.9 ± 0.2	85.4 ± 0.5	90.5
FULL	*	-	-	91.8 ± 0.5	-	86.9 ± 0.1	-	86.6 ± 1.9	-
FULL	FOCUS+IDENT	**95.1 ± 0.9**	**94.9 ± 0.4**	**89.9 ± 0.8**	**92.6 ± 0.2**	**86.2 ± 0.3**	**90.6 ± 0.1**	**87.7 ± 0.5**	**91.0**
FULL	SCRIPT+POSN+IDENT	93.9 ± 0.1	94.3 ± 0.2	**90.2 ± 0.7**	92.0 ± 0.3	83.2 ± 0.4	89.8 ± 0.2	83.5 ± 1.8	89.6
FULL	SCRIPT+IDENT	93.8 ± 0.3	94.3 ± 0.1	**89.8 ± 0.2**	89.3 ± 0.2	83.4 ± 0.3	89.4 ± 0.2	84.0 ± 0.5	89.5
FULL	SCRIPT+POSN	92.0 ± 0.6	92.1 ± 0.04	89.1 ± 0.5	88.3 ± 0.4	78.7 ± 0.1	86.5 ± 0.1	81.0 ± 0.9	86.8
FULL	SCRIPT	91.4 ± 0.4	91.1 ± 0.1	87.7 ± 0.5	87.5 ± 0.2	78.5 ± 0.2	85.7 ± 0.1	79.6 ± 1.1	85.9
FULL	IDENT	86.2 ± 0.4	90.7 ± 0.2	79.0 ± 0.6	89.3 ± 0.2	72.0 ± 0.4	86.7 ± 0.1	69.3 ± 0.4	81.9
FULL	RANDOM	74.1 ± 1.4	81.5 ± 0.3	72.6 ± 3.3	45.8 ± 27.2	54.4 ± 0.9	70.3 ± 0.7	47.2 ± 8.2	63.7
EMB	FOCUS+IDENT	**93.5 ± 0.5**	**94.2 ± 0.2**	81.7 ± 2.2	**92.0 ± 0.2**	**84.9 ± 0.1**	**90.3 ± 0.1**	**86.1 ± 0.3**	**89.0**
EMB	SCRIPT+POSN+IDENT	91.5 ± 0.2	92.3 ± 0.1	**87.2 ± 0.3**	89.8 ± 0.2	79.1 ± 0.2	88.9 ± 0.1	74.1 ± 1.2	86.1
EMB	SCRIPT+IDENT	90.9 ± 0.3	92.0 ± 0.3	86.1 ± 1.0	89.6 ± 0.3	78.7 ± 0.3	88.6 ± 0.1	79.1 ± 0.5	86.4
EMB	SCRIPT+POSN	86.5 ± 0.4	87.3 ± 0.3	84.1 ± 1.2	81.8 ± 0.8	71.0 ± 0.9	81.0 ± 0.2	64.3 ± 1.9	79.4
EMB	SCRIPT	83.9 ± 0.4	73.0 ± 0.8	84.0 ± 1.2	79.5 ± 0.9	67.8 ± 0.6	77.4 ± 0.2	56.8 ± 3.2	74.6
EMB	IDENT	80.9 ± 0.8	87.9 ± 0.4	61.8 ± 3.8	85.3 ± 0.3	64.8 ± 1.4	84.8 ± 0.4	54.9 ± 1.5	74.3
EMB	RANDOM	59.6 ± 2.5	0.0 ± 0.0	51.8 ± 2.7	0.0 ± 0.0	17.1 ± 17.2	47.5 ± 6.9	22.4 ± 5.5	28.3

Table 2: Monolingual LAPT: entity-wise NER F1 score after fine-tuning. A score of 0.0 results from the model learning to output only class O (not a named entity) which is the majority class. Sami does not have enough NER data for fine-tuning

ing vocabulary specialization would be a fruitful direction for future work.

6 Discussion

Embedding-only training is inadequate for multilingual model transfer Our experiments show that language transfer methods developed for monolingual models, which freeze the transformer blocks and re-train only the embedding matrix (Artetxe et al., 2020; de Vries and Nissim, 2021), yield poor results when transferring a multilingual model. This work in the monolingual literature not only keeps transformer layers frozen, but initializes new embeddings randomly. This setup (LAPT-EMB, REINIT-RANDOM) performs much worse than the off-the-shelf baseline in all of our experiments.

It is worth noting that Artetxe et al. (2020) do not necessarily suggest that freezing the main model is the *optimal* language transfer method. However, it does demonstrate that for monolingual→monolingual adaptation, embedding-only training is competitive with an off-the-shelf multilingual model. We see no such comparability in our experiments. We believe this is partly caused by the heterogeneity of the XLM-R embeddings, where different languages (or at least scripts) are encoded in different spaces. When new embeddings are randomly and homogeneously initialized, they fail to align with the pre-trained subspaces expected by the frozen transformer.

Vocab replacement efficiently specializes models We demonstrate that for languages inadequately covered by a pre-trained multilingual model, replacing and re-training the cross-lingual model vocabulary with a language-specific one is a computationally efficient way to create a compact model specialized for the target language(s). In our monolingual adaptation experiments, vocabulary replacement performs better than off-the-shelf XLM-R in 5/8 languages for POS tagging and 5/7 languages

LAPT	REINIT	Armenian	Basque	Erzya	Estonian	Hebrew	Russian	North Sami	Telugu	Avg
*	*	93.4 ± 2.2	95.1 ± 0.7	56.3 ± 5.3	95.6 ± 0.1	97.5 ± 0.1	98.6 ± 0.1	71.2 ± 1.8	83.8 ± 0.1	86.4
FULL	*	91.3 ± 0.1	95.9 ± 0.6	71.7 ± 5.3	95.5 ± 0.2	97.4 ± 0.2	98.6 ± 0.04	80.6 ± 1.4	89.7 ± 3.6	90.1
FULL	FOCUS+IDENT	91.0 ± 0.1	**95.8 ± 0.1**	**72.5 ± 1.3**	**95.5 ± 0.2**	**97.1 ± 0.1**	**98.4 ± 0.03**	**80.4 ± 1.2**	**89.4 ± 3.2**	**90.0**
FULL	SCRIPT+POSN+IDENT	**92.9 ± 2.1**	95.0 ± 0.6	**63.6 ± 9.8**	94.8 ± 0.3	97.0 ± 0.1	**98.4 ± 0.04**	**80.4 ± 1.1**	**89.6 ± 2.6**	89.0
FULL	SCRIPT+IDENT	**93.8 ± 1.8**	95.3 ± 0.03	**66.1 ± 10.2**	94.7 ± 0.2	**97.1 ± 0.1**	**98.4 ± 0.03**	**80.1 ± 1.2**	**91.7 ± 0.8**	89.7
FULL	SCRIPT+POSN	85.3 ± 3.5	87.9 ± 3.5	70.5 ± 1.5	89.0 ± 0.8	93.7 ± 0.6	97.2 ± 0.01	72.8 ± 2.1	81.6 ± 0.4	84.7
FULL	SCRIPT	83.3 ± 1.9	85.8 ± 2.7	66.6 ± 1.9	85.4 ± 1.7	90.5 ± 0.8	96.8 ± 0.03	68.6 ± 1.1	81.0 ± 0.3	82.2
FULL	IDENT	**93.2 ± 0.7**	93.0 ± 0.5	58.1 ± 0.9	93.6 ± 0.2	96.6 ± 0.1	98.3 ± 0.03	71.5 ± 1.2	89.0 ± 4.1	86.7
FULL	RANDOM	64.5 ± 2.9	67.4 ± 0.4	50.0 ± 4.6	71.9 ± 0.3	80.0 ± 0.8	84.6 ± 0.9	62.7 ± 0.5	75.0 ± 6.2	70.2
EMB	FOCUS+IDENT	**93.1 ± 2.2**	**95.2 ± 0.7**	**63.7 ± 2.0**	**94.7 ± 0.1**	**97.1 ± 0.04**	**98.5 ± 0.03**	71.2 ± 2.1	**87.5 ± 2.9**	**86.8**
EMB	SCRIPT+POSN+IDENT	**91.3 ± 1.6**	93.5 ± 0.6	57.2 ± 7.0	93.5 ± 0.1	96.7 ± 0.03	98.3 ± 0.1	**74.5 ± 1.1**	**85.6 ± 2.9**	85.6
EMB	SCRIPT+IDENT	**92.2 ± 2.0**	93.2 ± 0.7	58.5 ± 6.9	93.3 ± 0.1	96.9 ± 0.1	98.3 ± 0.02	**72.0 ± 3.0**	**86.5 ± 2.4**	85.5
EMB	SCRIPT+POSN	61.5 ± 1.9	76.0 ± 1.3	51.9 ± 3.1	75.7 ± 0.2	87.2 ± 1.2	95.3 ± 0.3	65.3 ± 0.2	77.3 ± 0.3	75.5
EMB	SCRIPT	44.7 ± 0.0	71.0 ± 1.0	48.5 ± 0.2	73.5 ± 2.2	83.6 ± 0.3	93.5 ± 0.5	63.8 ± 1.4	77.7 ± 0.5	73.1
EMB	IDENT	89.4 ± 0.8	90.5 ± 0.6	49.3 ± 4.6	91.8 ± 0.5	96.2 ± 0.1	98.1 ± 0.1	65.6 ± 1.1	84.0 ± 1.7	82.2
EMB	RANDOM	48.7 ± 2.4	61.2 ± 5.6	46.0 ± 0.3	66.3 ± 3.9	73.7 ± 3.4	85.1 ± 1.2	44.7 ± 4.6	67.5 ± 5.0	63.5

Table 3: Multilingual LAPT: POS tagging accuracy after fine-tuning

LAPT	REINIT	Armenian	Basque	Erzya	Estonian	Hebrew	Russian	Telugu	Avg
*	*	94.1 ± 0.1	94.3 ± 0.1	89.5 ± 0.6	93.3 ± 0.2	85.9 ± 0.1	90.9 ± 0.2	85.4 ± 0.5	90.5
FULL	*	94.0 ± 0.5	94.5 ± 0.2	90.5 ± 0.3	93.7 ± 0.2	86.2 ± 0.1	91.1 ± 0.2	85.9 ± 0.7	90.9
FULL	FOCUS+IDENT	**94.2 ± 0.3**	**94.0 ± 0.2**	**89.6 ± 1.0**	**92.0 ± 0.5**	**85.2 ± 0.1**	**90.0 ± 0.5**	**85.4 ± 0.4**	**90.1**
FULL	SCRIPT+POSN+IDENT	**94.1 ± 0.2**	**94.0 ± 0.1**	88.8 ± 0.9	**92.3 ± 0.1**	85.0 ± 0.2	**90.4 ± 0.1**	84.8 ± 0.4	89.9
FULL	SCRIPT+IDENT	**94.2 ± 0.2**	**94.1 ± 0.2**	**90.1 ± 0.6**	**92.4 ± 0.1**	84.9 ± 0.3	90.3 ± 0.1	84.5 ± 0.2	90.0
FULL	SCRIPT+POSN	91.2 ± 0.5	91.5 ± 0.1	88.9 ± 0.5	88.4 ± 0.4	77.3 ± 0.4	86.3 ± 0.1	76.2 ± 0.4	85.7
FULL	SCRIPT	90.9 ± 0.1	91.3 ± 0.3	86.4 ± 1.9	87.7 ± 0.2	75.8 ± 0.3	85.7 ± 0.1	75.1 ± 0.9	84.7
FULL	IDENT	93.2 ± 0.1	93.4 ± 0.2	80.9 ± 2.4	91.5 ± 0.4	83.5 ± 0.3	89.8 ± 0.1	83.2 ± 0.5	87.9
FULL	RANDOM	69.9 ± 4.4	80.9 ± 0.5	75.2 ± 1.5	70.5 ± 2.1	37.7 ± 21.8	68.6 ± 0.7	42.1 ± 1.6	63.6
EMB	FOCUS+IDENT	**93.9 ± 0.3**	**93.7 ± 0.2**	**89.7 ± 0.4**	**91.9 ± 0.4**	**84.8 ± 0.2**	**89.9 ± 0.3**	**85.2 ± 0.5**	**89.9**
EMB	SCRIPT+POSN+IDENT	**93.7 ± 0.2**	93.5 ± 0.1	87.2 ± 1.0	**91.9 ± 0.2**	84.0 ± 0.2	**89.9 ± 0.2**	84.0 ± 0.5	89.2
EMB	SCRIPT+IDENT	93.3 ± 0.5	93.4 ± 0.2	85.8 ± 1.4	**91.9 ± 0.3**	83.7 ± 0.2	**89.9 ± 0.1**	82.5 ± 1.3	88.7
EMB	SCRIPT+POSN	87.5 ± 0.3	88.8 ± 0.3	81.0 ± 3.1	84.8 ± 0.4	72.8 ± 0.1	82.7 ± 0.3	67.1 ± 1.3	80.7
EMB	SCRIPT	85.2 ± 0.3	81.3 ± 7.1	80.0 ± 1.1	84.3 ± 0.3	68.3 ± 0.9	80.6 ± 1.0	59.7 ± 3.5	77.1
EMB	IDENT	91.2 ± 0.3	92.3 ± 0.2	76.7 ± 1.3	90.8 ± 0.3	81.6 ± 0.2	89.3 ± 0.2	78.6 ± 1.8	85.8
EMB	RANDOM	62.8 ± 0.9	74.9 ± 1.6	66.1 ± 1.1	62.7 ± 1.9	23.9 ± 18.2	53.1 ± 4.7	37.7 ± 2.6	54.4

Table 4: Multilingual LAPT: entity-wise NER F1 score after fine-tuning

for NER. Only the high-resource languages of Estonian, Hebrew, and Russian seem to be adequately covered in XLM-R to outperform our specialization techniques. Language-Adaptive Pre-Training with the full (cross-lingual) XLM-R vocabulary often produces marginally better results overall, but at a much greater computational cost, and without making the model more compact in size. Further training and inference after LAPT will continue to suffer from the memory and compute wasted on unused vocabulary items, which constitute a large percentage of the total model parameters.

Script-distribution initialization rivals semantic similarity methods We introduced several methods for embedding re-initialization in Section 3, namely using the insight that token embeddings for XLM-R cluster by script and position within a word, then distributing new vocabulary items according to these pre-trained sub-distributions. We compare this to the FOCUS re-initialization method, which initializes new embeddings as a weighted combination of existing ones according to similarity scores from an auxiliary model.

Averaged across languages, FOCUS yields the best performance in downstream tasks by a slight margin. Within languages, it often overlaps significantly with the performance of our script-distribution methods. For very low-resource languages like Erzya, script-based methods even show a slight advantage. This seems to show that, at least in combination with LAPT, the majority of the benefit in re-initialization can be achieved by a method that takes the structure of the pre-trained embedding distribution into account, whether or not it uses advanced methods to precisely initialize the representations of new vocabulary items.

We do note that the advantage of FOCUS is more clear-cut when LAPT is conducted with transformer blocks frozen. This lends credence to the idea that FOCUS more precisely mimics the embedding distribution expected by the pre-trained transformer. However, the overall best results come when the transformer blocks are unfrozen/trainable.

Fully random initialization performs poorly Finally, our experiments demonstrate that fully random re-initialization of embeddings during vocabulary replacement leads to overall poor performance. Across LAPT-FULL experiments, random initialization performs an average of 19.4 points worse than the next-best re-initialization method, and 24.7 points worse than the off-the-shelf baseline. The poor performance of random initialization has been noted in other works such as Dobler and de Melo (2023), but we emphasize that even incredibly simple methods such as REINIT-IDENT and REINIT-SCRIPT work far better than the random baseline.

7 Conclusion

This work presents a systematic comparison of methods to specialize the subword vocabularies and embeddings of multilingual models for new languages. We propose simple methods for re-initializing embeddings, motivated by a qualitative exploration of the XLM-R embedding space. Our experiments show that (1) updating the encoder layers during LAPT is crucial for downstream performance, (2) vocabulary replacement provides a computationally-efficient method to improve task performance in low-resource languages, and (3) our re-initialization techniques employing script-wise sub-distributions perform on par with more involved similarity-based methods. We hope these findings can be built upon in future work on multilingual model specialization, with the goal of providing the best performance for under-resourced languages while also making language modeling more accessible through more manageable compute cost and model sizes.

Limitations

One limitation of our work is the relatively narrow set of evaluation tasks available for our languages of interest. The model-adaptation techniques we compare here are most applicable to low- and medium-resource languages that are not optimally covered by pre-existing multilingual models. For most of these languages, the only standard evaluation datasets that exist are for relatively low-level tasks like Part of Speech tagging and Named Entity Recognition. Evaluation of embedding-reinitialization techniques could be improved in future work if datasets for higher-level tasks like Natural Language Inference, question answering, and paraphrase detection were curated for these under-resourced languages.

We also make several simplifying choices to maintain a feasible scope for our work. First, we conduct model adaptation from only a single base model: XLM-R. A valuable addition in future work would be to determine whether the trends we observe here generalize to other model types (i.e. causal and seq2seq language models) and to larger model scales. Secondly, we consider only one size for newly-initialized target vocabularies (32k). Because effective per-language vocabulary allocation has been shown to be an important factor in multilingual modeling (Conneau et al., 2020, i.a.), investigating the dynamics of target vocabulary size during vocabulary re-initialization will be important for future work on this topic.

Acknowledgements

We thank Ibrahim Sharaf, Anita Silva, and Peter Zuckerman for early investigation of data availability for low-resource languages. We are also gracious to Emily P. Ahn, Gina-Anne Levow, Sara Ng, and our anonymous MRL reviewers for useful feedback and discussion.

References

Julien Abadji, Pedro Ortiz Suarez, Laurent Romary, and Benoît Sagot. 2022. Towards a cleaner document-oriented multilingual crawled corpus. In *Proceedings of the Thirteenth Language Resources and Evaluation Conference*, pages 4344–4355, Marseille, France. European Language Resources Association.

Judit Ács. 2019. Exploring BERT's vocabulary.

Mikel Artetxe, Sebastian Ruder, and Dani Yogatama. 2020. On the cross-lingual transferability of monolingual representations. In *Proceedings of the 58th Annual Meeting of the Association for Computational Linguistics*, pages 4623–4637, Online. Association for Computational Linguistics.

Mikko Aulamo, Sami Virpioja, and Jörg Tiedemann. 2020. OpusFilter: A configurable parallel corpus filtering toolbox. In *Proceedings of the 58th Annual Meeting of the Association for Computational Linguistics: System Demonstrations*, pages 150–156, Online. Association for Computational Linguistics.

Piotr Bojanowski, Edouard Grave, Armand Joulin, and Tomas Mikolov. 2017. Enriching word vectors with subword information. *Transactions of the Association for Computational Linguistics*, 5:135–146.

Ethan C. Chau, Lucy H. Lin, and Noah A. Smith. 2020. Parsing with multilingual BERT, a small corpus, and a small treebank. In *Findings of the Association for Computational Linguistics: EMNLP 2020*, pages 1324–1334, Online. Association for Computational Linguistics.

Alexis Conneau, Kartikay Khandelwal, Naman Goyal, Vishrav Chaudhary, Guillaume Wenzek, Francisco

Guzmán, Edouard Grave, Myle Ott, Luke Zettlemoyer, and Veselin Stoyanov. 2020. Unsupervised cross-lingual representation learning at scale. In *Proceedings of the 58th Annual Meeting of the Association for Computational Linguistics*, pages 8440–8451, Online. Association for Computational Linguistics.

Alexis Conneau and Guillaume Lample. 2019. Cross-lingual Language Model Pretraining. In *Advances in Neural Information Processing Systems*, volume 32, Vancouver, Canada. Curran Associates, Inc.

Marie-Catherine de Marneffe, Christopher D. Manning, Joakim Nivre, and Daniel Zeman. 2021. Universal Dependencies. *Computational Linguistics*, 47(2):255–308.

Wietse de Vries and Malvina Nissim. 2021. As good as new. how to successfully recycle English GPT-2 to make models for other languages. In *Findings of the Association for Computational Linguistics: ACL-IJCNLP 2021*, pages 836–846, Online. Association for Computational Linguistics.

Jacob Devlin. 2019. Multilingual BERT Readme. `https://github.com/google-research/bert/blob/master/multilingual.md`.

Konstantin Dobler and Gerard de Melo. 2023. Focus: Effective embedding initialization for specializing pretrained multilingual models on a single language. *arXiv preprint arXiv:2305.14481*.

Abteen Ebrahimi and Katharina Kann. 2021. How to adapt your pretrained multilingual model to 1600 languages. In *Proceedings of the 59th Annual Meeting of the Association for Computational Linguistics and the 11th International Joint Conference on Natural Language Processing (Volume 1: Long Papers)*, pages 4555–4567, Online. Association for Computational Linguistics.

Fahim Faisal and Antonios Anastasopoulos. 2022. Phylogeny-inspired adaptation of multilingual models to new languages. In *Proceedings of the 2nd Conference of the Asia-Pacific Chapter of the Association for Computational Linguistics and the 12th International Joint Conference on Natural Language Processing (Volume 1: Long Papers)*, pages 434–452, Online only. Association for Computational Linguistics.

Suchin Gururangan, Ana Marasović, Swabha Swayamdipta, Kyle Lo, Iz Beltagy, Doug Downey, and Noah A. Smith. 2020. Don't stop pretraining: Adapt language models to domains and tasks. In *Proceedings of the 58th Annual Meeting of the Association for Computational Linguistics*, pages 8342–8360, Online. Association for Computational Linguistics.

Diederik Kingma and Jimmy Ba. 2015. Adam: A Method for Stochastic Optimization. In *3rd International Conference on Learning Representations, ICLR 2015, Conference Track Proceedings*, San Diego, CA, USA.

Julia Kreutzer, Isaac Caswell, Lisa Wang, Ahsan Wahab, Daan van Esch, Nasanbayar Ulzii-Orshikh, Allahsera Tapo, Nishant Subramani, Artem Sokolov, Claytone Sikasote, Monang Setyawan, Supheakmungkol Sarin, Sokhar Samb, Benoît Sagot, Clara Rivera, Annette Rios, Isabel Papadimitriou, Salomey Osei, Pedro Ortiz Suarez, Iroro Orife, Kelechi Ogueji, Andre Niyongabo Rubungo, Toan Q. Nguyen, Mathias Müller, André Müller, Shamsuddeen Hassan Muhammad, Nanda Muhammad, Ayanda Mnyakeni, Jamshidbek Mirzakhalov, Tapiwanashe Matangira, Colin Leong, Nze Lawson, Sneha Kudugunta, Yacine Jernite, Mathias Jenny, Orhan Firat, Bonaventure F. P. Dossou, Sakhile Dlamini, Nisansa de Silva, Sakine Çabuk Ballı, Stella Biderman, Alessia Battisti, Ahmed Baruwa, Ankur Bapna, Pallavi Baljekar, Israel Abebe Azime, Ayodele Awokoya, Duygu Ataman, Orevaoghene Ahia, Oghenefego Ahia, Sweta Agrawal, and Mofetoluwa Adeyemi. 2022. Quality at a glance: An audit of web-crawled multilingual datasets. *Transactions of the Association for Computational Linguistics*, 10:50–72.

Yinhan Liu, Jiatao Gu, Naman Goyal, Xian Li, Sergey Edunov, Marjan Ghazvininejad, Mike Lewis, and Luke Zettlemoyer. 2020. Multilingual denoising pre-training for neural machine translation. *Transactions of the Association for Computational Linguistics*, 8:726–742.

Arya D. McCarthy, Rachel Wicks, Dylan Lewis, Aaron Mueller, Winston Wu, Oliver Adams, Garrett Nicolai, Matt Post, and David Yarowsky. 2020. The Johns Hopkins University Bible corpus: 1600+ tongues for typological exploration. In *Proceedings of the Twelfth Language Resources and Evaluation Conference*, pages 2884–2892, Marseille, France. European Language Resources Association.

Benjamin Minixhofer, Fabian Paischer, and Navid Rekabsaz. 2022. WECHSEL: Effective initialization of subword embeddings for cross-lingual transfer of monolingual language models. In *Proceedings of the 2022 Conference of the North American Chapter of the Association for Computational Linguistics: Human Language Technologies*, pages 3992–4006, Seattle, United States. Association for Computational Linguistics.

Benjamin Muller, Antonios Anastasopoulos, Benoît Sagot, and Djamé Seddah. 2021. When being unseen from mBERT is just the beginning: Handling new languages with multilingual language models. In *Proceedings of the 2021 Conference of the North American Chapter of the Association for Computational Linguistics: Human Language Technologies*, pages 448–462, Online. Association for Computational Linguistics.

Kelechi Ogueji, Yuxin Zhu, and Jimmy Lin. 2021. Small data? no problem! exploring the viability of pretrained multilingual language models for low-resourced languages. In *Proceedings of the 1st Workshop on Multilingual Representation Learning*, pages 116–126, Punta Cana, Dominican Republic. Association for Computational Linguistics.

Tolulope Ogunremi, Dan Jurafsky, and Christopher Manning. 2023. Mini but mighty: Efficient multilingual pretraining with linguistically-informed data selection. In *Findings of the Association for Computational Linguistics: EACL 2023*, pages 1251–1266, Dubrovnik, Croatia. Association for Computational Linguistics.

Malte Ostendorff and Georg Rehm. 2023. Efficient Language Model Training through Cross-Lingual and Progressive Transfer Learning. ArXiv:2301.09626 [cs].

Xiaoman Pan, Boliang Zhang, Jonathan May, Joel Nothman, Kevin Knight, and Heng Ji. 2017. Cross-lingual name tagging and linking for 282 languages. In *Proceedings of the 55th Annual Meeting of the Association for Computational Linguistics (Volume 1: Long Papers)*, pages 1946–1958, Vancouver, Canada. Association for Computational Linguistics.

Jonas Pfeiffer, Ivan Vulić, Iryna Gurevych, and Sebastian Ruder. 2020. MAD-X: An Adapter-Based Framework for Multi-Task Cross-Lingual Transfer. In *Proceedings of the 2020 Conference on Empirical Methods in Natural Language Processing (EMNLP)*, pages 7654–7673, Online. Association for Computational Linguistics.

Jonas Pfeiffer, Ivan Vulić, Iryna Gurevych, and Sebastian Ruder. 2021. UNKs everywhere: Adapting multilingual language models to new scripts. In *Proceedings of the 2021 Conference on Empirical Methods in Natural Language Processing*, pages 10186–10203, Online and Punta Cana, Dominican Republic. Association for Computational Linguistics.

Teven Le Scao, Angela Fan, Christopher Akiki, Ellie Pavlick, Suzana Ilić, Daniel Hesslow, Roman Castagné, Alexandra Sasha Luccioni, François Yvon, Matthias Gallé, Jonathan Tow, Alexander M. Rush, Stella Biderman, Albert Webson, Pawan Sasanka Ammanamanchi, Thomas Wang, and Inter Alia. 2023. Bloom: A 176b-parameter open-access multilingual language model.

Jörg Tiedemann and Lars Nygaard. 2004. The OPUS corpus - parallel and free: `http://logos.uio.no/opus`. In *Proceedings of the Fourth International Conference on Language Resources and Evaluation (LREC'04)*, Lisbon, Portugal. European Language Resources Association (ELRA).

Ahmet Üstün, Arianna Bisazza, Gosse Bouma, and Gertjan van Noord. 2020. UDapter: Language adaptation for truly Universal Dependency parsing. In *Proceedings of the 2020 Conference on Empirical Methods in Natural Language Processing (EMNLP)*, pages 2302–2315, Online. Association for Computational Linguistics.

Zihan Wang, Karthikeyan K, Stephen Mayhew, and Dan Roth. 2020. Extending multilingual BERT to low-resource languages. In *Findings of the Association for Computational Linguistics: EMNLP 2020*, pages 2649–2656, Online. Association for Computational Linguistics.

Shijie Wu and Mark Dredze. 2020. Are all languages created equal in multilingual BERT? In *Proceedings of the 5th Workshop on Representation Learning for NLP*, pages 120–130, Online. Association for Computational Linguistics.

Qingcheng Zeng, Lucas Garay, Peilin Zhou, Dading Chong, Yining Hua, Jiageng Wu, Yikang Pan, Han Zhou, Rob Voigt, and Jie Yang. 2023. GreenPLM: Cross-Lingual Transfer of Monolingual Pre-Trained Language Models at Almost No Cost. volume 6, pages 6290–6298. ISSN: 1045-0823.

A Data Details

General information about the language data used in this study can be found in Table 5. All training data used in our experiments is cleaned and deduplicated using the OpusFilter package (Aulamo et al., 2020). For the lowest-resource languages (Erzya and Sami) we additionally filter out lines that are identified as English with a probability of 90% or higher, since positive automatic language-identification for low-resource languages is likely not robust (Kreutzer et al., 2022). We additionally filter out lines composed of less than 2 tokens, lines with an average token length of greater than 16 characters, lines with tokens longer than 32 characters, and lines composed of fewer than 50% alphabetic characters.

For POS tagging evaluation, most languages have a standard train/dev/test split curated the original Universal Dependencies dataset (de Marneffe et al., 2021). Erzya, however, only has a standard train/test split. To form a dev split, we randomly sample 300 sentences from the train split. The WikiAnn dataset (Pan et al., 2017) does not ship with standard train/dev/test splits, so we create random 85/5/10% splits of each language for this purpose, with a minimum dev/test size of 256 and 512 sentences respectively.

B Training Details

The main details of our experimental process can be found in Section 4. Here we provide our choice of hyperparameters and other details relevant to reproducibility. The code used to run all experiments will be released in a later version of this

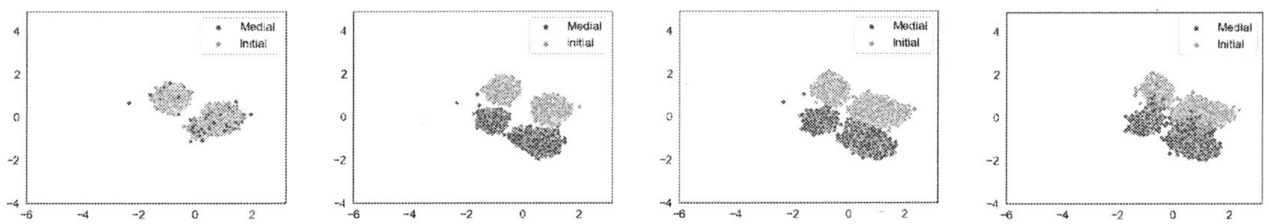

(a) SCRIPT (b) SCRIPT+POSN (c) SCRIPT+POSN+IDENT (d) FOCUS

Figure 5: PCA visualization of re-initialized embeddings with word-initial vs word-medial tokens highlighted. For REINIT-SCRIPT, position-wise clustering seen in the base XLM-R embeddings (Figure 1c) is not captured. REINIT-SCRIPT+POSN and REINIT-SCRIPT+POSN+IDENT show expected positional clustering. REINIT-FOCUS seems to allow slightly more positional overlap

Language	Code	Family	Script	XLM-R Data (GB)	LAPT Data (GB)
Armenian	hy	Indo-European	Armenian	5.5	1.2
Basque	eu	isolate	Latin	2.0	0.35
Erzya	myv	Uralic	Cyrillic	0	0.006
Estonian	et	Uralic	Latin	6.1	3.0
Finnish	fi	Uralic	Latin	54.3	9.1
Hebrew	he	Afro-Asiatic	Hebrew	31.6	7.7
Hungarian	hu	Uralic	Latin	58.4	13.0
Russian	ru	Indo-European	Cyrillic	278.0	10.0
Sami	sme	Uralic	Latin	0	0.004
Telugu	te	Dravidian	Telugu	4.7	0.9

Table 5: Training data breakdown by language. XLM-R data is the amount of data used in the pre-training of that model. LAPT data is the amount used for training in our current experiments, after cleaning/deduplicating.

paper. All models are trained and fine-tuned on Nvidia Quadro RTX 6000 GPUs using the Adam optimizer (Kingma and Ba, 2015).

Hyperparameters for Language-Adaptive Pre-Training (LAPT) can be found in Table 6. If NaN losses were encountered during training, `max_gradient_norm` was reduced to 0.5. For multilingual sampling during training, each language's training data is capped at approximately 2GB.

Hyperparameters for task fine-tuning on POS and NER are in Table 7. For NER, the reported evaluation metric is entity-wise F1, meaning tokens with label `O` are ignored. In order to prevent models from learning to output only the majority class `O` during training, the loss for the `O` tokens in each batch is down-weighted to have the same influence as the tokens that actually correspond to a named entity. We cap fine-tuning training data at 32,768 sequences.

C Uralic Results

The results for multilingual adaptation to the Uralic family can be found in Tables 8 and 9. These results mostly follow the trends discussed in Section 5 (LAPT-EMB consistently underperforms LAPT-FULL, off-the-shelf performance is best for high-resource languages, LAPT with full cross-lingual vocab performs marginally better than other methods). It should be noted that for both Erzya and Hungarian, the best POS accuracy is achieved with SCRIPT+POSN+IDENT initialization (better even than LAPT with the fully cross-lingual vocabulary). Results for the very low-resource language Erzya are generally higher than with multilingual training on unrelated languages, which could suggest a benefit to training with closely-related languages. This observation does not clearly hold for Sami (the other very low-resource language), however. Note that Russian is not a Uralic language — we include it for multilingual training in order to robustly train embeddings for the Cyrillic script, in which Erzya is written. Erzya is also spoken primarily within the Russian Federation, making loan-words likely.

Hyperparameter	Value
mlm_masking_prob	0.15
max_sequence_length	256
learning_rate	1e-5
lr_schedule	linear
batch_size	200
max_gradient_norm	1.0

Table 6: Hyperparameters for model training (LAPT)

Hyperparameter	Value
max_sequence_length	256
learning_rate	5e-6
lr_schedule	constant
max_epochs	64
eval_interval (epochs)	2
patience (epochs)	8 (POS) / 4 (NER)
batch_size	72
max_gradient_norm	1.0

Table 7: Hyperparameters for model task fine-tuning

LAPT	REINIT	Erzya	Estonian	Finnish	Hungarian	North Sami	Russian	Avg
*	*	56.3 ± 5.3	95.6 ± 0.1	97.5 ± 0.1	93.7 ± 1.5	71.2 ± 1.8	98.6 ± 0.1	85.9
FULL	*	72.5 ± 2.6	95.8 ± 0.1	97.7 ± 0.2	94.1 ± 1.9	82.9 ± 0.4	98.6 ± 0.04	90.3
FULL	FOCUS+IDENT	**73.8 ± 2.7**	**95.3 ± 0.2**	**97.2 ± 0.1**	92.5 ± 1.6	**80.1 ± 1.4**	**98.4 ± 0.04**	**89.6**
FULL	SCRIPT+POSN+IDENT	**73.0 ± 1.4**	94.7 ± 0.3	96.6 ± 0.1	**94.8 ± 0.7**	**78.0 ± 2.3**	**98.4 ± 0.01**	89.3
FULL	SCRIPT+IDENT	67.7 ± 11.0	94.3 ± 0.3	96.4 ± 0.1	**94.7 ± 0.7**	**78.8 ± 2.2**	**98.4 ± 0.03**	88.4
FULL	SCRIPT+POSN	71.2 ± 2.7	88.7 ± 0.4	90.6 ± 0.1	86.8 ± 0.4	72.9 ± 2.0	97.2 ± 0.02	84.7
FULL	SCRIPT	65.9 ± 4.6	85.6 ± 1.3	89.1 ± 0.3	85.2 ± 0.2	73.5 ± 1.6	96.9 ± 0.05	82.7
FULL	IDENT	59.8 ± 1.2	92.2 ± 0.03	95.2 ± 0.04	91.8 ± 2.8	68.9 ± 0.9	98.2 ± 0.03	84.3
FULL	RANDOM	53.7 ± 3.2	71.9 ± 0.6	73.1 ± 0.2	59.6 ± 1.6	63.9 ± 0.9	84.9 ± 1.9	67.8
EMB	FOCUS+IDENT	**66.3 ± 1.2**	**94.7 ± 0.1**	**96.8 ± 0.2**	**94.2 ± 0.8**	**73.3 ± 1.6**	**98.4 ± 0.05**	**87.3**
EMB	SCRIPT+POSN+IDENT	64.2 ± 2.8	93.0 ± 0.1	95.5 ± 0.03	**93.6 ± 0.8**	**72.7 ± 2.6**	98.3 ± 0.05	86.2
EMB	SCRIPT+IDENT	55.8 ± 4.1	92.8 ± 0.2	95.4 ± 0.04	92.3 ± 1.6	69.8 ± 1.6	98.3 ± 0.04	84.1
EMB	SCRIPT+POSN	54.5 ± 4.3	74.2 ± 0.8	79.5 ± 0.7	62.1 ± 2.6	65.2 ± 2.0	94.8 ± 0.4	71.7
EMB	SCRIPT	48.7 ± 0.04	56.9 ± 15.6	71.6 ± 3.2	54.3 ± 4.4	58.0 ± 1.7	91.4 ± 1.8	63.5
EMB	IDENT	49.2 ± 1.7	90.6 ± 0.4	94.4 ± 0.03	84.8 ± 2.9	64.7 ± 1.3	97.9 ± 0.1	80.3
EMB	RANDOM	48.6 ± 0.2	64.5 ± 4.1	66.4 ± 1.2	43.6 ± 0.1	45.8 ± 4.2	84.0 ± 1.4	58.8

Table 8: Uralic family multilingual LAPT: POS tagging accuracy after fine-tuning

LAPT	REINIT	Erzya	Estonian	Finnish	Hungarian	Russian	Avg
*	*	89.5 ± 0.6	93.3 ± 0.2	90.7 ± 0.1	<u>92.4 ± 0.1</u>	<u>90.9 ± 0.2</u>	91.4
FULL	*	<u>90.5 ± 0.5</u>	<u>93.8 ± 0.2</u>	<u>91.0 ± 0.2</u>	92.4 ± 0.3	91.0 ± 0.2	<u>91.8</u>
FULL	FOCUS+IDENT	**89.4 ± 1.7**	**92.5 ± 0.1**	**89.8 ± 0.2**	**91.2 ± 0.4**	**90.4 ± 0.1**	**90.7**
FULL	SCRIPT+POSN+IDENT	88.7 ± 0.5	92.2 ± 0.4	89.2 ± 0.2	90.9 ± 0.2	90.1 ± 0.1	90.2
FULL	SCRIPT+IDENT	**89.3 ± 0.4**	**92.7 ± 0.3**	89.2 ± 0.4	**91.3 ± 0.1**	90.0 ± 0.2	90.5
FULL	SCRIPT+POSN	**89.5 ± 1.0**	87.9 ± 0.2	84.2 ± 0.3	86.3 ± 0.3	86.2 ± 0.2	86.8
FULL	SCRIPT	**88.9 ± 0.8**	87.5 ± 0.3	83.3 ± 0.1	86.3 ± 0.2	85.5 ± 0.1	86.3
FULL	IDENT	81.1 ± 0.8	91.6 ± 0.1	88.2 ± 0.2	90.7 ± 0.3	89.6 ± 0.1	88.2
FULL	RANDOM	73.7 ± 2.7	53.1 ± 30.7	0.0 ± 0.0	32.9 ± 33.0	65.1 ± 2.2	45.0
EMB	FOCUS+IDENT	**88.6 ± 0.6**	**92.4 ± 0.3**	**89.6 ± 0.1**	**91.1 ± 0.1**	**90.0 ± 0.1**	**90.3**
EMB	SCRIPT+POSN+IDENT	86.6 ± 1.1	91.4 ± 0.2	88.8 ± 0.3	90.5 ± 0.2	89.9 ± 0.1	89.4
EMB	SCRIPT+IDENT	87.0 ± 1.3	91.8 ± 0.1	88.6 ± 0.3	**91.0 ± 0.2**	89.6 ± 0.2	89.6
EMB	SCRIPT+POSN	85.0 ± 1.2	84.2 ± 0.4	78.1 ± 0.3	81.9 ± 0.5	82.1 ± 0.2	82.3
EMB	SCRIPT	82.9 ± 2.6	82.4 ± 1.3	72.5 ± 1.3	80.7 ± 0.4	79.0 ± 0.2	79.5
EMB	IDENT	71.0 ± 4.4	90.1 ± 0.3	87.0 ± 0.4	89.9 ± 0.2	88.7 ± 0.1	85.3
EMB	RANDOM	64.9 ± 1.9	0.0 ± 0.0	13.6 ± 23.5	0.0 ± 0.0	54.4 ± 2.2	26.6

Table 9: Uralic family multilingual LAPT: entity-wise NER F1 score after fine-tuning. A score of 0.0 results from the model learning to output only class O (not a named entity) which is the majority class. Sami does not have enough NER data for fine-tuning

Multi-EuP: The Multilingual European Parliament Dataset for Analysis of Bias in Information Retrieval

Jinrui Yang* **Timothy Baldwin*†** **Trevor Cohn***
*School of Computing & Information Systems, The University of Melbourne
†Mohamed bin Zayed University of Artificial Intelligence, UAE
jinruiy@student.unimelb.edu.au {tbaldwin,trevor.cohn}@unimelb.edu.au

Abstract

We present Multi-EuP, a new multilingual benchmark dataset, comprising 22K multilingual documents collected from the European Parliament, spanning 24 languages. This dataset is designed to investigate fairness in a multilingual information retrieval (IR) context to analyze both language and demographic bias in a ranking context. It boasts an authentic multilingual corpus, featuring topics translated into all 24 languages, as well as cross-lingual relevance judgments. Furthermore, it offers rich demographic information associated with its documents, facilitating the study of demographic bias. We report the effectiveness of Multi-EuP for benchmarking both monolingual and multilingual IR. We also conduct a preliminary experiment on language bias caused by the choice of tokenization strategy.

1 Introduction

Information retrieval (IR) classically uses a retrieval model to query a document collection and return a ranked list of documents which are predicted to be (decreasingly) relevant to the query. Retrieval models have increasingly been based on supervised learning, involving the annotation of documents with relevance scores relative to a given query, and the training of models to predict the relative association between a query and document (Karpukhin et al., 2020; Khattab and Zaharia, 2020).

In parallel with these advances, the democratisation of the internet has led to a surge of individual contributors serving as information disseminators, hailing from various countries and regions, and posting in different languages. This has created possibilities for exploration of cross-lingual and multilingual text retrieval. Cross-lingual retrieval pertains to scenarios where queries are formulated in one language but documents are retrieved from another language. On the other hand, multilingual retrieval involves a query in one language but retrieval of documents across multiple languages simultaneously. An important consideration in any such work is both robustness and fairness across different combinations of languages – for instance, are results from one language consistently ranked higher than another for certain types of query.

While progress towards multilingual retrieval through the release of datasets such as Mr. TYDI (Zhang et al., 2021) and mMARCO (Bonifacio et al., 2021), both are limited in that they evaluate monolingual retrieval for a range of languages, rather than true multilingual retrieval, using multiple languages simultaneously. Additionally, mMARCO was created by machine translation of MS MARCO (Nguyen et al., 2016), introducing a confounding factor of translation errors.

We present a multilingual dataset based on the European Parliament debate archive with queries in 24 distinct languages, and relevance judgements also across all 24 languages. This ensures the "multilingual" nature of the dataset in terms of both query-to-document and document-to-query associations. We additionally augment each document with comprehensive metadata of the author, including gender, nationality, political affiliation, and age, for use in exploring fairness with respect to protected attributes.

Our work contributes to the field in three main ways: (1) we construct and release the Multi-EuP dataset, a resource for multilingual retrieval over 24 languages, effectively capturing the multilingual nature of both queries and documents; (2) we explore language bias within the realm of multilingual retrieval, revealing that multilingual IR using BM25 indeed exhibits notable language bias; and (3) we supplement the dataset with rich author metadata to enable research on fairness and demographic bias in IR.[1]

[1]The Multi-EuP dataset is available for download from `https://github.com/jrnlp/Multi-EuP`.

Proceedings of the The 3rd Workshop on Multi-lingual Representation Learning (MRL), pages 282–291
December 7, 2023 ©2023 Association for Computational Linguistics

2 Background and Related Work

The European Parliament (EP) serves as an important forum for political debates and decision-making at the European Union level. Members of the European Parliament (MEP) are elected in direct elections across the EU. The European Parliament debate is presided over by the President, who guides MEPs in discussing specific subjects.

EP debates have been the source of three key datasets. First, *Europarl-2005* was crafted by Koehn (2005) by collecting EP debates documents from 1996 to 2011, and extracting translations as a parallel corpus for statistical machine translation, enriched with attributes including *debate date, chapter id, MEP id, language, MEP name*, and *MEP party*.

Later, Rabinovich et al. (2017) built *Europarl-2017* upon *Europarl-2005*, by introducing additional demographic attributes: *MEP gender* and *MEP age*. These were sourced from sources such as Wikidata (Vrandečić and Krötzsch, 2014) and automatic annotation tools such as *Genderize*[2] and *AlchemyVision*.[3] However, *Europarl-2017* is limited to only two language pairs: English–German and English–French. *Europarl-2018* (Vanmassenhove and Hardmeier, 2018) expanded upon *Europarl-2017* to add twenty additional language pairs, based on the manual translations in the EP archives. These corpora have been used primarily for machine translation research.

Since 2020, the EU has publicly released raw debates in the form of transcribed source-language speeches with rich multilingual topic index data, along with the original video and audio recordings. This forms the basis of the Multi-EuP dataset, with additional attributes for each speaking MEP such as an image, birthplace, and nationality.

Zhang et al. (2021) introduced Mr. TYDI, an evaluation benchmark dataset for dense retrieval assessment over 11 languages. This dataset is constructed from TYDI (Clark et al., 2020), a question answering dataset. For each language, annotators assign relevance scores as judgments for questions, derived from Wikipedia articles. Notably, the questions for different languages are crafted independently, and relevance judgements are provided in-language only. Based on the dataset, the authors evaluate on monolingual retrieval tasks for non-English languages using BM25 and mDPR as zero-shot baselines. However, Mr. TYDI's scope is limited in that it is not truly multilingual, in that queries in a given language are only performed over documents in that language. This is part of the void our work aims to address.

MS MARCO (Nguyen et al., 2016) is a widely-used dataset, sourced from Bing's search query logs, but for English queries and documents only. To mitigate this, Bonifacio et al. (2021) introduced mMARCO, a multilingual variant of the MS MARCO passage ranking dataset, spanning 13 languages and created through machine translation, based on one open-source approach (Tiedemann and Thottingal, 2020) and one commercial system in the form of Google Translate.[4] Analysis of the authors' results reveals a positive correlation between translation quality and retrieval performance, with higher translation BLEU scores yielding improved retrieval MRR outcomes. However, similar to Mr. TYDI, mMARCO focuses on in-language retrieval only for multiple languages, rather than multilingual retrieval.

Throughout the past few decades, numerous datasets and tasks pertaining to multilingual retrieval have been developed for evaluation, through efforts such as CLEF, TREC, and FIRE, each contributing standardized document collections and evaluation procedures. These evaluation datasets facilitate genuine multilingual IR research such as Rahimi et al. (2015) and Lawrie et al. (2023). However, the scope of these datasets is generally limited to a small number of queries. For example, in the case of CLEF 2001-2003, each edition encompasses a mere few dozen queries. This limitation tends to confine research predominantly to evaluation and not offer a resource for training a multilingual ranking model. Our dataset is of a scale to accommodate both large-scale training and evaluation of multilingual retrieval methods.

Compared with the related work above, our work augments the multilingual mixture of queries and documents compared to Mr.TYDI, preserves the authenticity of multilingual contexts compared to mMARCO's translation-based approach, and surpasses the query count limitations of tasks like CLEF.

[2] https://genderize.io/

[3] https://www.ibm.com/smarterplanet/us/en/ibmwatson/developercloud/alchemy-vision.html

[4] https://cloud.google.com/translate

3 Multi-EuP

In our approach, we consider the debate topics to be the queries, and the text of each individual speech delivered by an MEP to be a document.

Topics The topics are officially annotated by the EU, and professionally translated into 24 different languages.[5] During preprocessing, we filter out procedural debate topics such as *agenda*, leaving 1.1K unique topics. They will serve as a valuable resource for assessing language bias in multilingual ranking methods, given that all the topics across different languages are semantically consistent.

Documents The 22K multilingual documents within the Multi-EuP dataset originate from MEP speeches during parliamentary debates. Each document annotated with additional metadata, including the date of the speech, the MEP ID, and a link to the video recording for potential multimodal research but not used here. Table 1 shows a detailed breakdown of the language distribution and descriptive statistics of the dataset. We include in our corpus documents only in the original language, as spoken by the MEP, but not their translations into other languages. Our only use of translations is the debate topics themselves.

Judgments To assess the relevance of documents to a given query, we use a binary relevance judgment, based on whether the speech was part of a debate on the given topic, resulting in one positive relevance judgment per document, meaning that the document collection is much less sparse than Mr. TYDI and MS MARCO, for example.

Languages Multi-EuP covers 24 EU languages from seven families (Germanic, Romance, Slavic, Uralic, Baltic, Semitic, Hellenic), each of which is the official language of one or more member states. Table 1 provides a breakdown of each language's EU usage, member state distribution, and population, using ISO-639 codes.

MEP Multi-EuP encompasses 705 members elected across the 27 member states of the EU. We constructed the MEP dictionary by collecting MEP attributes such as *name, photo, id in EU, nationality, place of birth, party affiliation,* and *spoken language*. We further annotated MEPs with gender and their birthdate, based on Wikipedia profiles and Rabinovich et al. (2017), and manually checked if difference existing. Figure 1 illustrates the gender and age distribution across MEPs, with male MEPs being more than twice as numerous as female MEPs, and the majority falling within the 40–70 age range. This corpus is rare, perhaps unique, due to its richly detailed speaker demographic information, which enables research on fairness and bias in information retrieval.

Data Split For data splitting, we select two sets with 100 language-specific and distinct topics for development and test set in 24 languages, and keep the remaining topics to the training set. This design choice was made to maintain an ample supply of topics and judgment samples essential for the training of deep learning models, and also facilitate subsequent cross-lingual comparative research.

Supported Task Similarly to Mr.TYDI (Zhang et al., 2021), Multi-EuP can be used for monolingual retrieval in English as well as non-English languages (eg. Swedish queries against Swedish documents). However, unlike Mr.TYDI, Multi-EuP encompasses multilingual documents and identical multilingual topics, ensuring that queries in different languages can be compared. Consequently, Multi-EuP can support diverse information retrieval experimental tasks. These including *one-vs-one* scenarios with single one language queries against single one language documents, in other words, monolingual or cross-lingual IR, *one-vs-many* scenarios with single-language queries against multilingual documents, i.e., multilingual IR, and *many-vs-many* scenarios involving multilingual queries against multilingual documents, i.e, mixed multilingual IR).

4 Experiments and Findings

We conduct preliminary experiments in both one-vs-one and one-vs-many settings, as described above.

Methods We base our experiments on BM25 with default settings ($k_1 = 0.9$ and $b = 0.4$), a popular traditional information retrieval baseline. Our implementation is based on Pyserini (Lin et al., 2021), which is built upon Lucene (Yang et al., 2017). Notably, the latest LUCENE 8.5.1 API offers language-specific tokenizers, [6] covering 19

[5] https://www.europarl.europa.eu/translation/en/translation-at-the-european-parliament/

[6] Provided by the Anaylzer package in LUCENE. https://lucene.apache.org/core/8_5_1/analyzers-common/index.html

Language	ISO code	Countries where official lang.	Native Usage	Total Usage	# Docs	Words per Doc
English	EN	United Kingdom, Ireland, Malta	13%	51%	7123	286/200
German	DE	Germany, Belgium, Luxembourg	16%	32%	3433	180/164
French	FR	France, Belgium, Luxembourg	12%	26%	2779	296/223
Italian	IT	Italy	13%	16%	1829	190/175
Spanish	ES	Spain	8%	15%	2371	232/198
Polish	PL	Poland	8%	9%	1841	155/148
Romanian	RO	Romania	5%	5%	794	186/172
Dutch	NL	Netherlands, Belgium	4%	5%	897	184/170
Greek	EL	Greece, Cyprus	3%	4%	707	209/205
Hungarian	HU	Hungary	3%	3%	614	126/128
Portuguese	PT	Portugal	2%	3%	1176	179/167
Czech	CS	Czech Republic	2%	3%	397	167/149
Swedish	SV	Sweden	2%	3%	531	175/165
Bulgarian	BG	Bulgaria	2%	2%	408	196/178
Danish	DA	Denmark	1%	1%	292	218/198
Finnish	FI	Finland	1%	1%	405	94/87
Slovak	SK	Slovakia	1%	1%	348	151/158
Lithuanian	LT	Lithuania	1%	1%	115	142/127
Croatian	HR	Croatia	<1%	<1%	524	183/164
Slovene	SL	Slovenia	<1%	<1%	270	201/163
Estonian	ET	Estonia	<1%	<1%	58	160/158
Latvian	LV	Latvia	<1%	<1%	89	111/123
Maltese	MT	Malta	<1%	<1%	178	117/115
Irish	GA	Ireland	<1%	<1%	33	198/172

Table 1: Multi-EuP statistics, broken down by language: ISO language code; EU member states using the language officially; proportion of the EU population speaking the language (Chalkidis et al., 2021); number of debate speech documents; and words per document (mean/median).

out of the 24 languages present in Multi-EuP. For the remaining languages — namely Polish (PL), Croatian (HR), Slovak (SK), Slovenian (SL), and Maltese (MT) — we use a whitespace tokenizer.

Evaluation Our primary evaluation metric is Mean Reciprocal Rank (MRR). For a single query, the reciprocal rank is $RR = \frac{1}{\text{rank}}$ where rank is the position of the highest-ranked relevant document. If no correct answer was returned, then the reciprocal rank is defined to be 0. For multiple queries Q, the MRR is the mean of the Q reciprocal ranks.

$$MRR = \frac{1}{Q}\sum_{i=1}^{Q}\frac{1}{\text{rank}_i}$$

MRR@k denotes MRR computed at a depth of k results. Note that the higher the number the better, and that a perfect retriever achieves an MRR of 1 (assuming every query has at least one relevant document). The choice of setting $k = 100$ aligns with prior endeavors over MS MARCO (Nguyen et al., 2016).

4.1 Monolingual IR (*one-vs-one*)

Experimental Setup We first present results over Multi-EuP in a monolingual setting across the 24 different languages. Specifically, we evaluate single-language queries against documents in the same language. In this configuration, we partitioned our original collection of 22K documents into 24 distinct language-specific sub-collections. Table 2 presents the results broken down across languages.

Results and Findings Table 2 presents the MRR@100 results for BM25 on Multi-EuP. There are two high-level findings:

First, Multi-EuP is a relatively easy benchmark for monolingual information retrieval, as the MRR@100 is always around 40 or greater (meaning that the first relevant document is in the top-

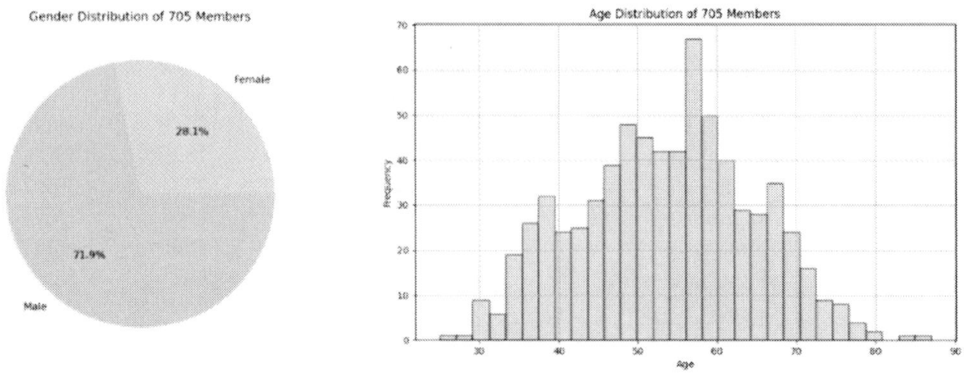

Figure 1: The gender and birth year distributions of the 705 MEPs in Multi-EuP dataset. The birth year corresponds to the current age calculation.

	GERMANIC					ROMANCE					SLAVIC			URALIC		
	EN	DA	DE	NL	SV	RO	ES	FR	IT	PT	PL	BG	CS	HU	FI	EL
One-vs-one (Queries and documents in the same language.)																
num_q	839	208	840	458	330	434	680	765	659	557	628	273	259	404	251	360
num_d	7123	268	3433	897	531	794	2371	2779	1829	1176	1841	408	397	614	405	707
num_r	7123	3433	3433	897	531	794	2371	2779	1829	1176	1841	408	397	614	405	707
MRR	**73.79**	**45.51**	**56.70**	**39.02**	**45.77**	**42.58**	**54.25**	**46.57**	**56.40**	**56.51**	**47.68**	**44.70**	**47.12**	**39.99**	**46.46**	**39.58**
One-vs-many (A fixed set of queries in the given language, with documents in all 24 languages.)																
num_q	100	100	100	100	100	100	100	100	100	100	100	100	100	100	100	100
num_d	22K	22K	22K	22K	22K	22K	22K	22K	22K	22K	22K	22K	22K	22K	22K	22K
num_r	2902	1997	1995	1992	1996	1996	1996	1924	1994	1997	1996	1996	1997	1996	1997	1996
MRR	**62.79**	**16.15**	**28.27**	**20.88**	**19.40**	**16.10**	**22.57**	**24.22**	**14.24**	**18.7**	**4.80**	**7.57**	**9.52**	**7.51**	**17.61**	**11.16**

Table 2: Details of Multi-EuP for the 16 most widely spoken EU official languages, in terms of the number of queries (q), documents (d) and relevance judgements (r). Results are for BM25 in one-vs-one and one-vs-many settings based on MRR@100 (%). See Table 3 in the Appendix for results across all languages. Note that as each document has a unique topic which in turn defines the relevance judgements, num_d= num_r in the one-vs-one setting.

3 results on average). Indeed, the average MRR across the 24 test languages is 49.61. While direct comparison is not possible, it is noteworthy that for Mr. TYDI, the average MRR is 32.1 across 11 languages. Part of this difference can be attributed to the fact that our relevance judgments are not as sparse as theirs.

Second, similar to Mr. TYDI, direct comparison of absolute scores between languages is not meaningful in a monolingual setting, as the document collection size differs.

4.2 Multilingual IR (*one-vs-many*)

Experimental Setup In contrast to Mr. TYDI (Zhang et al., 2021), Multi-EuP supports one-vs-many retrieval, and allows us to systematically explore the effect of querying the same document collection with the same set of topics in different languages. This is because we have translations of the topics in all languages, documents span multiple languages, and judgments are cross-lingual (e.g., English queries potentially yield relevant Polish documents). For this experiment, we use the default whitespace tokenizer in the Pyserini library.

Results and Findings Table 2 presents the MRR results for BM25 for multilingual information retrieval on 100 topics from the Multi-EuP test set. It's worth noting that these topics have translation-equivalent content in the different languages. Consequently, the one-vs-many approach allows us to analyze language bias. We made several key observations:

First, unsurprisingly, having more relevance judgments tends to improve ranking accuracy. Therefore, when comparing English topics with other languages, English exhibits notably better MRR performance.

Second, despite there being consistency in the topics, document collection, and relevance judgments, there is a significant disparity in MRR scores across languages, an effect we investigate further in the next section.

5 Language Bias Discussion

In light of our findings in a one-vs-many setting, we were keen to delve further into the underlying causes of the disparity between languages.

5.1 Bias Detection

Language bias is likely if the query language aligns better with one document language than another. As mentioned earlier, Pyserini supports different tokenizers, specifically language-specific tokenizers or simple whitespace tokenization. Therefore, in the one-vs-many setting, we analyze the composition of the top-100 rankings for the 100 topics. During indexing of the document collection, we used the simple whitespace tokenizer, given the multilingual nature of the collection. However, over the queries during retrieval, we employed two different tokenizers — a language-specific tokenizer, and the whitespace tokenizer.

We conducted a correlation analysis between the language of the topics and the language of the top 100 relevant documents. From Table 2, we can see that relevance judgments in our test cases are consistent across languages, ensuring uniformity in the correlation matrix within the test set. However, Figure 2 reveals that both approaches generate strong language bias. In both cases, the query language aligns better with documents in its own language than others. The right plot appears to show that languages from the same family has strong correlation (e.g., PL, CS) and (IT, ES) since they may have some shared vocabulary.

5.2 Collection Distribution Factors

Initially, we hypothesized that the disparity for each language may be a contributing factor to this bias. Figure 3 presents the regression line between the number of documents in a given language and MRR, which explains much of the variation across languages.

However, note the outlier above the regression line (Polish: PL), which has a substantial number of documents but surprisingly low MRR performance. We refer to this phenomenon as a "BM25 unfriendly" language. According to Wojtasik et al. (2023), the main reason for the low performance of Polish lies in its highly-inflected morphology, giving rise to a a multitude of word forms per lexeme, including inflections of proper names, and complex morphological structure. In such cases, lexical matching is less effective than in other morphologically-simpler languages. Furthermore, LUCENE 8.5.1 API does not have a language-specific tokenizer for Polish. Conversely, languages below the regression line can be termed "BM25 friendly" languages, as they require fewer documents to achieve higher MRR in retrieval.

5.3 Language Tokenizer Factors

Secondly, we speculated that the choice of language-specific Analyzer in LUCENE might be a contributing factor, as it influences word tokenization, token filter, synonym expansion and other processing. [7] To investigate this, we conducted a controlled experiment in the one-vs-many setting. When indexing the collection, given the multilingual nature of the collection, we employed whitespace as the tokenizer. However, over the queries, we experimented with either a language-specific tokenizer or whitespace tokenizer. We then compared the linear regression of MRR against the number of documents in Figure 3. On the right side of the plot, we can see a strong correlation when using whitespace tokenization for both the collection and the queries, reducing language bias.

Furthermore, when transitioning from language-specific tokenizers to whitespace tokenizers, the overall MRR across all languages declined modestly, from 15.02 to 14.18. That is, the original performance level was largely preserved, but language bias was diminished in using simple whitespace tokenization.

6 Conclusion

In this paper, we introduce Multi-EuP, a novel dataset for multilingual information retrieval across

[7] https://lucene.apache.org/core/8_0_0/core/org/apache/lucene/analysis/package-summary.html#package.description

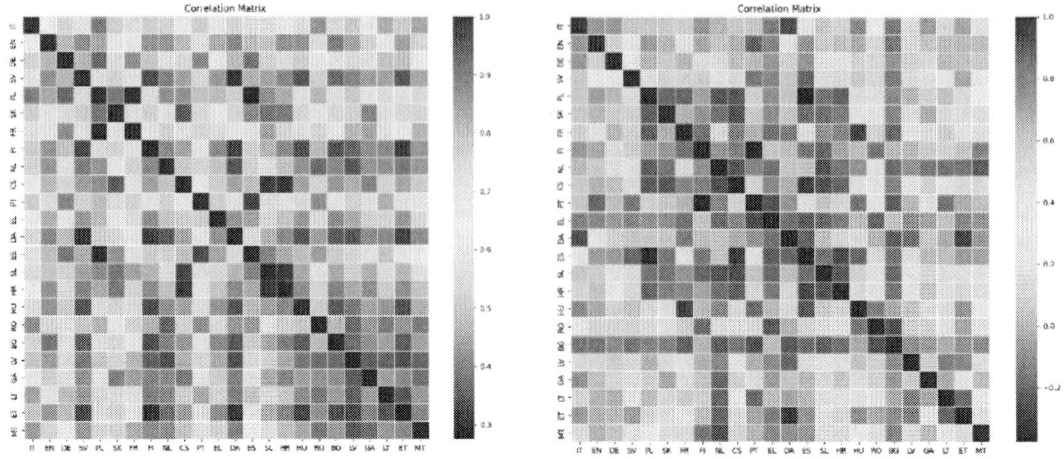

Figure 2: Language correlation matrix between topics and the ranking output top 100 relevant documents in a one-vs-many setting. The row is the topic languages, the columns is the document languages. The left matrix displays results using a language-specific tokenizer, while the right matrix represents the experiment with a simple whitespace tokenizer. Both of them show strong language bias between the language of the topic and the retrieved documents.

24 languages, collected from European Parliament debates. The demographic information provided by the Multi-EuP dataset serves a dual purpose: not only does it contribute to multilingual retrieval tasks, but it also holds significant potential for advancing research in the realm of fairness and bias. This dataset can play a pivotal role in investigating issues of equitable representations and mitigation of biases within document ranking settings.

Multi-EuP facilitates diverse information retrieval (IR) scenarios, encompassing one-vs-one, one-vs-many, and many-vs-many settings. We demonstrated the utility of Multi-EuP as a benchmark for evaluating both monolingual and multilingual IR. Our study reveals the presence of language bias in multilingual IR when employing BM25. We further validate the effectiveness of mitigating this bias through the strategic implementation of whitespace as a language tokenizer.

We propose to conduct future work in three main areas. First, we intend to expand our investigation of language bias to encompass a broader range of ranking methods, including neural methods such as mDPR (Zhang et al., 2021), mColBERT (Lawrie et al., 2023) and PLAID-X(Santhanam et al., 2022). Second, we will expand the dataset by developing an automated API to retrieve data published by the European Parliament (EP), thereby ensuring real-time synchronization of our dataset. Lastly, our current experiments have explored language bias only, but we plan to further investigate gender bias, age bias, and nationality bias.

Limitations

The limitations of the Multi-EuP dataset are notable but navigable. Primarily, the temporal coverage of the dataset is confined to the past three years. This temporal constraint arises due to the fact that, preceding 2020, documents released by the EU were predominantly available in mono-lingual versions only. However, a potential remedy lies in the amalgamation of the Europarl (Koehn, 2005) collection, enabling a more comprehensive and holistic Multi-EuP dataset.

Furthermore, it is worth noting the domain skew of the dataset, in that Multi-EuP inevitably centers on political matters. While this presents challenges, particularly in terms of the intricate nuances of political language, it inherently serves as an excellent foundational stepping stone for delving into the intricacies of multilingual retrieval. We believe, however, that this dataset can serve as a launching pad for broader explorations encompassing cross-domain and open-domain transfer learning scenarios, thus contributing to the broader landscape of language understanding and retrieval.

Ethics Statement

The dataset contains publicly-available EP data that does not include personal or sensitive information,

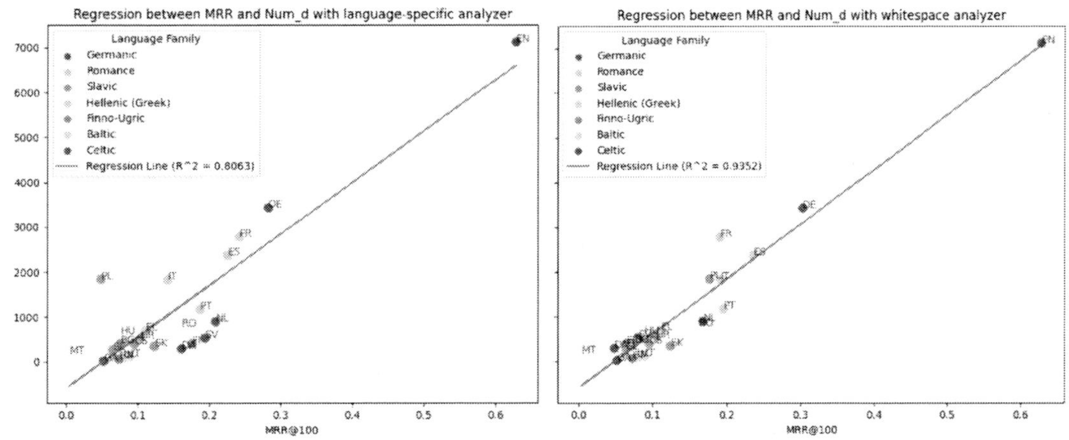

Figure 3: Linear regression between MRR@100 and the number of documents per language. The left plot is based on collection indexing with a whitespace tokenizer but a language-specific tokenizer over the queries. The right plot uses a whitespace tokenizer for both indexing the collection and the queries. The higher R^2 for the right plot suggests that using a whitespace tokenizer for both the collection and queries reduces language bias in multilingual IR.

with the exception of information relating to public officeholders, e.g., the names of the active members of the European Parliament, European Council, or other official administration bodies. The collected data is licensed under the Creative Commons Attribution 4.0 International licence. [8]

Acknowledgements

This research was funded by Melbourne Research Scholarship and undertaken using the LIEF HPC-GPGPU Facility hosted at the University of Melbourne. This facility was established with the assistance of LIEF Grant LE170100200. We would like to thank George Buchanan for providing valuable feedback.

References

Luiz Henrique Bonifacio, Israel Campiotti, Roberto de Alencar Lotufo, and Rodrigo Frassetto Nogueira. 2021. mMARCO: A multilingual version of MS MARCO passage ranking dataset. *CoRR*, abs/2108.13897.

Ilias Chalkidis, Manos Fergadiotis, and Ion Androutsopoulos. 2021. MultiEURLEX - a multi-lingual and multi-label legal document classification dataset for zero-shot cross-lingual transfer. In *Proceedings of the 2021 Conference on Empirical Methods in Natural Language Processing*, pages 6974–6996, Online and Punta Cana, Dominican Republic. Association for Computational Linguistics.

[8] `https://eur-lex.europa.eu/content/legal-notice/legal-notice.html`

Jonathan H. Clark, Eunsol Choi, Michael Collins, Dan Garrette, Tom Kwiatkowski, Vitaly Nikolaev, and Jennimaria Palomaki. 2020. TyDi QA: A benchmark for information-seeking question answering in typologically diverse languages. *Transactions of the Association for Computational Linguistics*, 8:454–470.

Vladimir Karpukhin, Barlas Oguz, Sewon Min, Patrick Lewis, Ledell Wu, Sergey Edunov, Danqi Chen, and Wen-tau Yih. 2020. Dense passage retrieval for open-domain question answering. In *Proceedings of the 2020 Conference on Empirical Methods in Natural Language Processing (EMNLP)*, pages 6769–6781, Online. Association for Computational Linguistics.

Omar Khattab and Matei Zaharia. 2020. Colbert: Efficient and effective passage search via contextualized late interaction over BERT. *CoRR*, abs/2004.12832.

Philipp Koehn. 2005. Europarl: A parallel corpus for statistical machine translation. In *Proceedings of Machine Translation Summit X: Papers*, pages 79–86, Phuket, Thailand.

Dawn Lawrie, Eugene Yang, Douglas W. Oard, and James Mayfield. 2023. Neural approaches to multilingual information retrieval. arXiv cs.IR 2209.01335.

Jimmy Lin, Xueguang Ma, Sheng-Chieh Lin, Jheng-Hong Yang, Ronak Pradeep, and Rodrigo Nogueira. 2021. Pyserini: A Python toolkit for reproducible information retrieval research with sparse and dense representations. `https://github.com/castorini/pyserini`.

Tri Nguyen, Mir Rosenberg, Xia Song, Jianfeng Gao, Saurabh Tiwary, Rangan Majumder, and Li Deng. 2016. MS MARCO: A human generated machine reading comprehension dataset. *CoRR*, abs/1611.09268.

Ella Rabinovich, Raj Nath Patel, Shachar Mirkin, Lucia Specia, and Shuly Wintner. 2017. Personalized machine translation: Preserving original author traits. In *Proceedings of the 15th Conference of the European Chapter of the Association for Computational Linguistics: Volume 1, Long Papers*, pages 1074–1084, Valencia, Spain. Association for Computational Linguistics.

Razieh Rahimi, Azadeh Shakery, and Irwin King. 2015. Multilingual information retrieval in the language modeling framework. *Information Retrieval Journal*, 18:246–281.

Keshav Santhanam, Omar Khattab, Christopher Potts, and Matei Zaharia. 2022. PLAID: An efficient engine for late interaction retrieval. In *Proceedings of the 31st ACM International Conference on Information & Knowledge Management*, CIKM '22, page 1747–1756, New York, NY, USA. Association for Computing Machinery.

Jörg Tiedemann and Santhosh Thottingal. 2020. OPUS-MT – building open translation services for the world. In *Proceedings of the 22nd Annual Conference of the European Association for Machine Translation*, pages 479–480, Lisboa, Portugal. European Association for Machine Translation.

Eva Vanmassenhove and Christian Hardmeier. 2018. Europarl datasets with demographic speaker information. In *Proceedings of the 21st Annual Conference of the European Association for Machine Translation*, page 391, Alicante, Spain.

Denny Vrandečić and Markus Krötzsch. 2014. Wikidata: A free collaborative knowledge base. *Communications of the ACM*, 57:78–85.

Konrad Wojtasik, Vadim Shishkin, Kacper Wołowiec, Arkadiusz Janz, and Maciej Piasecki. 2023. BEIR-PL: Zero shot information retrieval benchmark for the Polish language. arXiv cs.IR 2305.19840.

Peilin Yang, Hui Fang, and Jimmy Lin. 2017. Anserini: Enabling the use of lucene for information retrieval research. In *Proceedings of the 40th International ACM SIGIR Conference on Research and Development in Information Retrieval*, pages 1253–1256.

Xinyu Zhang, Xueguang Ma, Peng Shi, and Jimmy Lin. 2021. Mr. TyDi: A multi-lingual benchmark for dense retrieval. arXiv cs.CL 2108.08787.

A Appendix

	GERMANIC						ROMANCE					SLAVIC						URALIC			BALTIC		HELLENTICH	CELTC
	EN	DA	DE	NL	SV	MT	RO	ES	FR	IT	PT	PL	BG	CS	SK	SL	HR	HU	FI	ET	LV	LT	EL	GA
One-vs-one (Queries in one language against documents in the same language, test on the whole set.)																								
num_q	839	208	840	458	330	138	434	680	765	659	557	628	273	259	236	205	311	404	251	52	75	99	360	14
num_d	7123	292	3433	897	531	178	794	2371	2779	1829	1176	1841	408	397	348	270	524	614	405	58	89	115	707	16
num_r	7123	292	3433	897	531	178	794	2371	2779	1829	1176	1841	408	397	348	270	524	614	405	58	89	115	707	16
MRR	**73.79**	**45.51**	**56.70**	**39.02**	**45.77**	**65.17**	**42.58**	**54.25**	**56.51**	**47.68**	**56.40**	**47.12**	**44.70**	**47.12**	**44.51**	**45.47**	**39.83**	**39.99**	**46.46**	**41.59**	**58.04**	**50.03**	**39.58**	**72.22**
One-vs-many (Queries in one language against documents in many languages, test on semantically consistent topics.)																								
num_q	100	100	100	100	100	100	100	100	100	100	100	100	100	100	100	100	100	100	100	100	100	100	100	100
num_d	22K	22K	22K	22K	22K	22K	22K	22K	22K	22K	22K	22K	22K	22K	22K	22K	22K	22K	22K	22K	22K	22K	22K	22K
num_r	2902	1997	1996	1996	1996	1996	1996	1924	1996	1997	1996	1996	1996	1997	1996	1996	1923	1996	1997	1909	1996	1997	1996	1992
MRR	**62.79**	**16.15**	**28.27**	**20.88**	**19.40**	**0.40**	**16.10**	**22.57**	**24.22**	**14.24**	**18.70**	**4.80**	**7.57**	**9.52**	**12.35**	**6.46**	**10.41**	**7.51**	**17.61**	**7.31**	**7.95**	**8.94**	**11.16**	**5.21**

Table 3: Details of Multi-EuP for the all 24 spoken EU official languages, in terms of the number of queries (q), documents (d) and relevance judgements (r). Results are for BM25 in one-vs-one and one-vs-many settings based on MRR@100 (%). Note that as each document has a unique topic which in turn defines the relevance judgements, num_d= num_r in the one-vs-one setting.

Generating Continuations in Multilingual Idiomatic Contexts

Rhitabrat Pokharel and **Ameeta Agrawal**
PortNLP Lab, Department of Computer Science, Portland State University
{pokharel,ameeta}@pdx.edu

Abstract

The ability to process idiomatic or literal multiword expressions is a crucial aspect of understanding and generating any language. The task of generating contextually relevant continuations for narratives containing idiomatic (or literal) expressions can allow us to test the ability of generative language models (LMs) in understanding nuanced language containing non-compositional figurative text. We conduct a series of experiments using datasets in two distinct languages (English and Portuguese) under three different training settings (zero-shot, few-shot, and fine-tuned). Our results suggest that the models are only slightly better at generating continuations for literal contexts than idiomatic contexts, with exceedingly small margins. Furthermore, the models studied in this work perform equally well across both languages, indicating the robustness of generative models in performing this task.

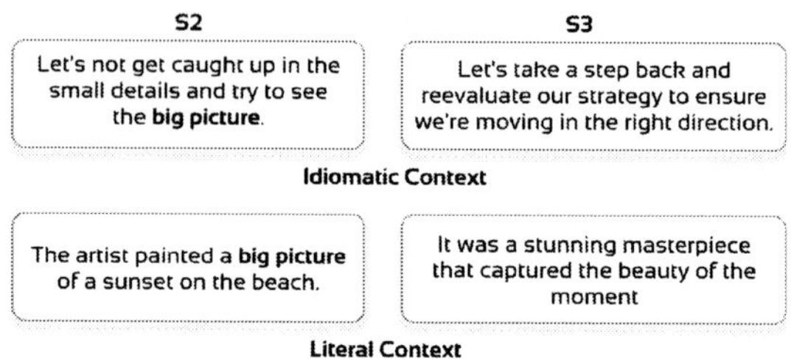

Figure 1: An example where a sentence (S2) contains the same multiword expression used in two contexts – idiomatic and literal. The task is to generate a coherent follow-up continuation (S3).

1 Introduction

Idiomatic expressions are a common feature of all human languages and are often used to convey emotions, cultural references, and implied meanings. These are phrases or expressions that have a figurative meaning that is different from the literal meaning of the words that make it up. In particular, it is the notion of non-compositionality that makes an idiomatic phrase often challenging as it requires understanding the phrase's meaning as a whole. As such, the ability to understand and generate idiomatic expressions is an important task for natural language processing systems, as it allows them to better understand and generate human languages. This is particularly important for applications such as machine translation, language generation, and dialogue systems, where idiomatic expressions are often used to convey meaning. As an example, consider Figure 1 where the multiword expression "big picture" can convey vastly different meanings depending on the context (idiomatic vs. literal) in which it is being used.

In the field of idiomaticity, prior works have focused on detecting idioms (Tayyar Madabushi et al., 2021; Tan and Jiang, 2021; Tedeschi et al., 2022; Tedeschi and Navigli, 2022), paraphrasing idiomatic sentences to literal paraphrases (Zhou et al., 2022), cloze task such as fill-in-the-blank language comprehension (Zheng et al., 2019), classifying idiomatic and literal expressions (Peng et al., 2015), translating idiomatic language (Tang, 2022), and generating continuations for idiomatic contexts (Chakrabarty et al., 2022).

The question remains whether generative language models (LMs), typically trained on extensive text corpora of human language, perform differently or similarly under contexts containing literal and idiomatic expressions, particularly in multilingual settings. We explore this by generating text continuations within contexts featuring multiword expressions in both idiomatic and literal forms. Our investigation considers two distinct languages – English and Portuguese. Both languages use Latin script and subject-verb-object sentence structure. However, notable differences exist between these two languages. English is classified as a language with the highest resource level ('5'), whereas Portuguese is categorized as '4' according

Proceedings of the The 3rd Workshop on Multi-lingual Representation Learning (MRL), pages 292–301
December 7, 2023 ©2023 Association for Computational Linguistics

Paper	Task	Languages
Tayyar Madabushi et al. (2021)	Idiomaticity detection	en, pt
Tedeschi et al. (2022)	Idiomaticity detection	en, de, it, es
Tedeschi and Navigli (2022)	Idiomaticity detection	en, pt, gl
Tan and Jiang (2021)	Idioms interpretation	en
Chakrabarty et al. (2022)	Idioms interpretation	en
Moussallem et al. (2018)	Idiom translation, idiom linking	en, de, it, pt, ru
Fadaee et al. (2018)	Idiom translation	en, de
Tang (2022)	Idiom translation	cz, en
Korkontzelos et al. (2013)	Semantic similarity	en, fr, de, it
Peng et al. (2015)	Idiomatic and literal expression classification	en
Zheng et al. (2019)	Cloze test	cz
Chakrabarty et al. (2021)	Idiomatic continuation generation	en
Dashtipour et al. (2022)	Sentiment analysis of idiomatic sentences	fa
Zhou et al. (2022)	Paraphrasing idioms	en

Table 1: A survey of works that have focused on idioms in different languages.

to the linguistic diversity taxonomy (Joshi et al., 2020), which could potentially impact how well the models process texts in these languages. Moreover, the distinct traditions and historical influences of Portuguese-speaking and English-speaking cultures lead to differences in social norms and idiomatic expressions.

Using existing datasets of sentence sequences where multiword expressions are used in both literal and idiomatic senses, we empirically evaluate several language models under various settings including zero-shot, few-shot, and fully supervised, by generating logical continuations of narratives. Our findings suggest that while the models show a slight preference for the literal and compositional use of multiword expressions, resulting in more coherent continuations in literal contexts compared to idiomatic ones, this trend is only consistently observed in approximately half of the cases (with the performance being comparable in the other half). Moreover, the difference is extremely minor, typically not exceeding 0.02 metric points. In terms of multilingual models, our study indicates that all models perform comparably well in both languages, which is an encouraging outcome. Interestingly, the best results are obtained under the zero-shot setting (rather than few-shot setting) using the GPT-3 `davinci` model for both English and Portuguese, suggesting that for creative text generation tasks like continuation generation, zero-shot settings are not only effective but also efficient in terms of cost.

The main contributions of this research include:

- Investigating the ability of generative language models to generate coherent subsequent sentences for idiomatic as well as literal contexts;
- Studying and evaluating four generative models under three training settings (zero-shot, few-shot, and fully supervised) in two distinct languages (English and Portuguese).

2 Related Work

Prior research focusing on idioms can be broadly categorized into two areas: *classification* and *generative*. Although our work relates to the latter, i.e., generating continuations in multilingual idiomatic contexts, we provide an overview of the background and current developments within both fields of research, and a brief summary in Table 1. In this context, the terms "idiomatic" and "figurative" are used interchangeably as they both denote language that conveys a meaning that is distinct from its literal or compositional interpretation.

2.1 Idioms-related Classification Tasks

Tayyar Madabushi et al. (2021) studied several transformer-based models such as BERT, XLNet, and XLM-RoBERTa for detection of idiomatic expressions in a sentence as a binary classification task, and additionally, proposed a similarity metric to assess the similarity between idiomatic and

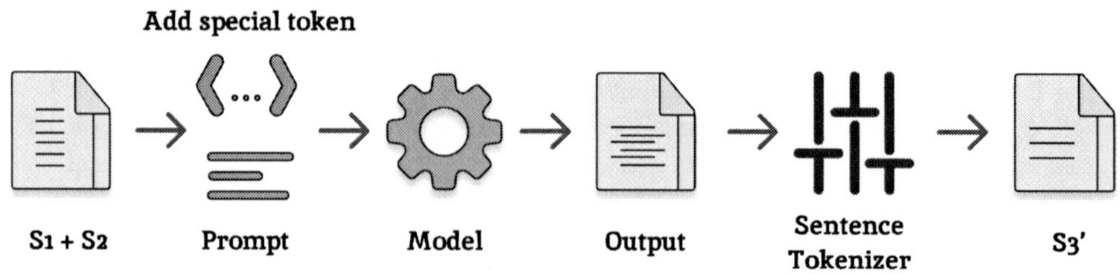

Figure 2: Overview of the modeling process.

non-idiomatic expressions. Tedeschi et al. (2022) utilized a BERT-based architecture for idiomatic expression detection, while Tedeschi and Navigli (2022) measured the similarity between a potentially idiomatic expression and its context to detect idiomatic usage.

In addition to idiom detection, the classification method has also been applied to the comprehension of idioms, encompassing a variety of subjects. One of them is the classification of different sentiments conveyed through idiomatic expressions (Dashtipour et al., 2022). Jhamtani et al. (2021) investigated whether dialogue models are able to handle figurative language usage and concluded that they do not perform well in this area. Tan and Jiang (2021) evaluated the ability of BERT to understand idioms by selecting the correct paraphrase from a set of options. Liu et al. (2022) examined models by having them choose the correct metaphorical phrase between two opposite metaphorical phrases, concluding that language models do not make use of context when dealing with metaphorical phrases. In addition, one of the tasks conducted by Chakrabarty et al. (2022) involved the selection of a plausible continuation from two candidate options.

2.2 Idioms-related Generative Tasks

In contrast to classification tasks, there has been limited exploration of generative tasks related to idiomatic expressions. Zhou et al. (2022) used the paraphrasing task to study the ability of models to understand idioms by replacing idiomatic expressions with literal paraphrases. They employed BART model and several metrics to compare the generated text with the reference text. Chakrabarty et al. (2022) explored the task of generating a coherent next sentence for English idiomatic contexts.

While similar in spirit, there are some notable differences between our work and prior work. Chakrabarty et al. (2022) exclusively focused on idiomatic usages, whereas our study takes a more comprehensive approach by encompassing and comparing the performance of generative models across *both* idiomatic and literal language expressions, which is a novel analysis in this area. It offers a deeper understanding of how these models interpret idiomatic context. Specifically, it sheds light on whether these models consistently interpret idiomatic phrases in the same manner (either literally or idiomatically), or if their interpretation varies depending on the surrounding context. Moreover, whereas their work was conducted only in English, our investigation extends its reach to two languages: English (EN) and Portuguese (PT).

3 Method

3.1 Problem Description

Given a text sequence of two consecutive sentences $S1$ and $S2$, such that $S2$ contains a multiword expression used either in a literal sense or an idiomatic sense, the goal is to generate the next sentence $S3'$ that reasonably and logically continues the narrative and is relevant within the context formed by $S1$ and $S2$. To evaluate the quality of the generated continuation $S3'$, we can either compare $S3'$ to the reference text $S3$ or assess it within the context formed by $S1$ and $S2$.

3.2 Models

Figure 2 presents an overview of the modeling process. Generative language models are used to generate text by learning patterns and structures from large collections of data, allowing them to generate new, coherent sentences based on the learned patterns. To generate the $S3'$ sentences, we use three generative language models: GPT-2[1] (117M), OPT[2] (125M), GPT-3[3] (ada and `davinci` models),

[1]`https://huggingface.co/gpt2`
[2]`https://huggingface.co/facebook/opt-125m`
[3]`https://openai.com`

under three training settings:
(a) *Zero-shot*: using the models without any further training,
(b) *Few-shot*: fine-tuning the models using a few examples each from idiomatic and literal contexts (full details in Table 2), and
(c) *Fully supervised*: fine-tuning the models using the entire training dataset.

To fine-tune the models (GPT-2 and OPT), we first tokenized the input sentences using the GPT2Tokenizer[4]. We then appended the special token $< |endoftext| >$ at the end of each sample to ensure that the models could correctly recognize the end of the input text. After the output text was generated, we tokenized it using the NLTK tokenizer (Bird, 2006) and extracted only the first sentence of the generated output as $S3'$ in cases where the models generate more than one sentence.

For GPT-3 models, we only use few-shot and zero-shot settings with the default settings. As input, we provide the context using $S1$ and $S2$, followed by the prompt:

"`\n\nQuestion: Generate a logical next sentence.\nAnswer:`"

appended to the end of each context. The generated text was cleaned by removing any HTML tags or trailing white spaces.

3.3 Implementation Details

We experimented with three temperature settings (0.6, 0.8, and 1.0) which control the diversity or randomness of the generated output, with temperature = 1 generating the most diverse and creative text, and temperature = 0 generating the least diverse text. The GPT-2 and OPT models were trained for 20 epochs, while the GPT-3 models were trained for 4 epochs. We set the learning rate to $2e^{-5}$ and use AdamW optimizer to train the models. The maximum sequence length was set to 400 and the batch size to 16. We used HuggingFace's utility function `generate`[5] by turning on sampling. When sampling is turned on, the model generates text by randomly selecting the next word based on its predicted probabilities. This allows for more diverse and creative outputs, as compared to deterministic approaches like greedy decoding. Since the model does not know when to stop the text generation, we set the generated text's minimum length to 20 and maximum length to 100.

	Train			Test
	ZS	FS	Full	
EN	-	87	3412	364
PT	-	53	1217	238

Table 2: Dataset statistics. The test dataset for a language was the same under all the settings (zero-shot (ZS), few-shot (FS), and fully supervised (Full)).

4 Evaluation

4.1 Datasets

We use an exiting dataset called Multilingual Idiomaticity Detection and Sentence Embedding dataset[6] (Tayyar Madabushi et al., 2021). Specifically, we use the English and Portuguese subsets of the data which were collected by a team of 12 judges from naturally occurring sources. The dataset contains sequences of three consecutive sentences with the middle sentence $S2$ containing multiword expressions in either idiomatic or literal sense. Note that this dataset describes these multiword expressions as *potentially idiomatic expressions* (PIE), which means $S2$ contains PIEs, which may or may not necessarily be idioms. However, this is the only available dataset that is closest to the task at hand and includes data from two languages. Table 2 presents the dataset's statistics, and some sample instances are shown in Table 3. In the test data[7], the number of idiomatic and non-idiomatic instances was balanced using random undersampling.

4.2 Metrics

We conduct automatic and human evaluations of the generated continuations. For automatic evaluation, we use the following three metrics which compare the generated sentence $S3'$ with a reference sentence $S3$ that is already available in the dataset.

- **ROUGE-L** (Lin, 2004), typically used to compare machine-generated text with human ref-

[4] `https://huggingface.co/docs/transformers/v4.25.1/en/model_doc/gpt2#transformers.GPT2Tokenizer`

[5] `https://huggingface.co/docs/transformers/v4.25.1/en/main_classes/text_generation#transformers.GenerationMixin.generate`

[6] `https://github.com/H-TayyarMadabushi/SemEval_2022_Task2-idiomaticity`

[7] We consider the development set from the original dataset as the test data in our experiments as we did not have access to the ground truth labels for the test set.

MWE	$S1$	$S2$	$S3$	Label	Lang.
night owl	I explain that a cicada is a locust, while circadian refers to patterns of sleep and wakefulness in relationship to light and darkness.	He has always been a night owl and I have always been an early morning person.	If the day comes that I am not up by 5, I am probably seriously ill. Or — as I recently read in someone's obituary — "not able to do lunch."	*I*	EN
night owl	However, you need the internet for the remote access features (no monthly fees for remote viewing).	The Night Owl system is a good option for small retail or service businesses.	Reolink Eight Channel PoE Video Surveillance System	*L*	EN
coração partido	Fiz isso, inclusive, na exibição do último episódio da série, quando era editor da Rolling Stone. [*I did this during the airing of the last episode of the series, while I was editor of Rolling Stone.*]	Li o resumão (era contra até então), fiz um textão completamente desacreditado pelo que virou a minha profissão e de coração partido pelo episódio mequetrefe. [*I read the summary (I was against it until then) and wrote a longish response completely disillusioned with what my profession had become and heartbroken by the mediocre episode.*]	O final era estranhamente confuso, talvez condizente com o que vinha acontecendo na série. [*The finale was oddly confusing, though perhaps in line with what had been happening in the series.*]	*I*	PT
coração partido	Isso ocorre pois os altos índices de estresse provoca aumento da frequência cardíaca, pressão arterial mais alta, coloca mais pressão no coração e prejudica o sistema imunológico. [*This occurs because the high stress levels bring about elevated heart rate and higher blood pressure, increase the load on the heart and damage the immune system.*]	Se você sofre de Síndrome do Coração Partido, parte do seu órgão aumentará temporariamente e não conseguirá bombear sangue tão bem quanto antes. [*If you suffer from Broken Heart Syndrome, part of your heart will temporarily become enlarged and be unable to pump blood as well as it could before.*]	Enquanto isso, o restante do coração continuará trabalhando normalmente ou será exigido um esforço dobrado. [*Meanwhile, the rest of the heart will continue to work normally, or it will require extra effort.*]	*L*	PT

Table 3: A few samples from the English and Portuguese training sets. In this table, we include the translations of Portuguese samples only for the sake of enhanced interpretation but these are not part of the dataset. Labels *I* and *L* indicate the presence of a multiword expression in $S2$ used in an idiomatic or literal sense, respectively.

erence text, measures the longest common subsequence between the two texts.

- **METEOR** (Banerjee and Lavie, 2005) is another widely used evaluation metric that aims to measure the degree of lexical and phrasal overlap between a machine-generated text and one or more reference texts.

- **BERTScore** (Zhang et al., 2019) is a semantic similarity metric that uses cosine similarity between the sentence embeddings to compare the meaning of two sentences. The embedding model we used was `microsoft/deberta-xlarge-mnli` (He et al., 2021).

While the automatic evaluation measuring the similarity between $S3'$ and an existing $S3$ serves as a quick and cost-effective method of evaluation, it may not comprehensively capture the nuances of natural language, particularly when several valid outputs are possible. Therefore, we complement our evaluation by obtaining human assessment of the outputs where $S3'$ is evaluated within the contexts formed by $S1$ and $S2$.

5 Results and Discussion

The results of our experiments are evaluated automatically, through human assessment, and qualitatively, as discussed next.

Lang.		Model	ROUGE-L		METEOR		BERTScore	
			I	L	I	L	I	L
EN	ZS	GPT2	**0.10**	0.09	**0.11**	0.10	0.55	0.55
		OPT	0.10	0.10	0.11	**0.12**	0.55	0.55
		GPT3 ada	0.11	**0.12**	0.11	**0.13**	0.55	0.55
		GPT3 davinci	0.12	**0.13***	0.12	**0.14***	0.59	**0.60***
	FS	GPT2	0.10	0.10	0.10	**0.11**	0.53	**0.54**
		OPT	0.09	**0.10**	0.11	0.11	0.55	**0.56**
		GPT3 ada	0.10	0.10	0.13	0.13	0.52	**0.53**
		GPT3 davinci	0.10	**0.11**	**0.14**	0.13	0.54	**0.55**
	Full	GPT2	0.10	0.10	0.13	0.13	0.53	0.53
		OPT	0.10	**0.11**	0.12	0.12	0.55	0.55
PT	ZS	GPT2	0.07	0.07	0.08	0.08	0.50	**0.52**
		OPT	0.10	**0.11**	0.12	0.12*	0.56	**0.57**
		GPT3 ada	0.06	0.06	0.07	0.07	0.51	**0.52**
		GPT3 davinci	**0.12***	0.11	**0.11**	0.10	0.60	**0.61***
	FS	GPT2	0.08	0.08	0.09	0.09	0.52	0.52
		OPT	0.10	**0.11**	0.11	0.11	0.58	0.58
		GPT3 ada	0.09	**0.10**	0.08	0.08	0.56	**0.58**
		GPT3 davinci	0.11	**0.12**	0.10	0.10	0.58	0.58
	Full	GPT2	0.09	**0.10**	0.11	0.11	0.54	**0.55**
		OPT	0.10	**0.11**	0.11	0.11	0.57	**0.59**

Table 4: Performance of the models for different metrics with temperature set to 1.0. I = Idiomatic, L = Literal, ZS = Zero Shot, FS = Few Shot, Full = Fully finetuned. The higher score between idiomatic and literal comparison is shown in **bold**, for each metric the best result for each training setting is underlined, and for each metric the best overall result for each dataset is shown with an *asterisk (where multiple best overall results exist, the one in the more cost-effective setting is shown). The differences between idiomatic and literal scores are found to be *not* statistically significant, with p-values > 0.4 using t-test.

5.1 Automatic Evaluation

Table 4 presents the main results of our experiments, from which we make some observations to answer the following questions.

Are literal contexts easier for language models than idiomatic contexts? Overall, in both the language datasets and all three metrics, the literal continuations obtain slightly higher scores than idiomatic continuations. However, in looking closely, we observe that the lexical continuations are better than idiomatic continuations in only about half the scenarios or less (11/20, 4/20, and 12/20 for ROUGE-L, METEOR, and BERTScore, respectively). When we consider the absolute difference in performance, it is interesting to note that the lexical continuations are superior to idiomatic continuations only by a very small margin (maximum difference of 0.01, 0.02, and 0.02 points for ROUGE-L, METEOR, and BERTScore, respectively). The results of statistical significance testing (t-test) yield p-values > 0.4, indicating that the disparities between idiomatic and literal results lack statistical significance. Taken together, these results lead us to conclude that the generative language models process these distinct contexts somewhat similarly, and that idiomatic contexts are not necessarily more challenging than literal contexts in this task.

We analyze the lengths of the different context sentences (Figure 3). It is observed that the lengths of $S1$, $S2$, and $S3$ are comparable between the idiomatic and literal contexts. Moreover, in both contexts, $S3'$ generated under the zero-shot setting is similar in length as the original $S3$, while $S3'$ under the few-shot setting is slightly longer. Furthermore, consistent results are obtained under all three temperature settings studied (Figure 4).

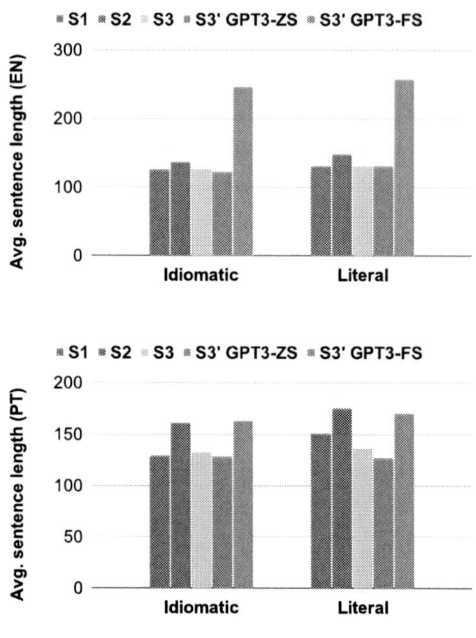

Figure 3: The graph comparing the average lengths of the sentences (numbers of words) for English (top) and Portuguese (bottom).

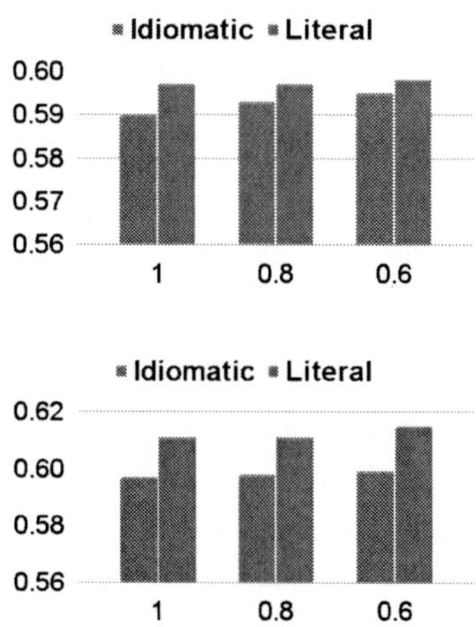

Figure 4: The results (BERTScore) of GPT-3 `davinci` under zero-shot for different temperature settings for English (top) and Portuguese (bottom).

How do language models compare between English and Portuguese? In terms of comparing the performance of all LMs between the two different languages, it appears that the results are comparable, which is encouraging given that English is considered the highest resource language (level '5') whereas Portuguese is '4', a high resource level, in the taxonomy of linguistic diversity (Joshi et al., 2020). For all the metrics, performance on English dataset is superior to that of Portuguese dataset by a maximum of 0.05 metric points, and in cases where Portuguese set performs better than English set, it is with at most about 0.04 points, suggesting that the performance across both languages remains largely similar.

	METEOR		**BERTScore**	
	I	**L**	**I**	**L**
Only $S2$ is used				
EN	0.10	**0.11**	0.58	**0.59**
PT	**0.09**	0.08	0.59	**0.61**
$S1$ and $S2$ are used				
EN	0.12	**0.14**	0.59	**0.60**
PT	0.10	0.10	0.59	**0.61**

Table 5: Performance of GPT-3 `davinci` model under zero-shot setting when only $S2$ is used (without $S1$). 'I' denotes idiomatic contexts where 'L' denotes literal contexts. As comparison, we also add the corresponding results here, borrowing from Table 4.

How do the models perform across different training settings? In line with general expectations, the newer and larger model (GPT-3 `davinci`) generally outperforms the older and smaller models (GPT-2, OPT, GPT-3 `ada`), even with no training (zero-shot) or little training (few-shot), although the difference remains small. In comparing the freely available models such as GPT-2 and OPT, a few interesting results emerge: (i) OPT generally outperforms GPT-2 across all settings, but more clearly in Portuguese, (ii) these models benefit from some training especially in the case of Portuguese, and (iii) for English, zero-shot setting yields better results than few-shot setting, but for Portuguese, few-shot setting yields better results than zero-shot setting.

How is the performance under limited context? As further analysis, we modify our experimental set up to use only $S2$ as the input context (instead of both $S1$ and $S2$). The results in Table 5 show that, as expected, the results are generally lower when only $S2$ is provided. However, this gap is noticeably larger in English than in Portuguese, suggesting that additional contexts are more useful in English than in Portuguese.

5.2 Human Evaluation

For conducting the human evaluation of the generated outputs, two annotators were invited to estimate the relevance and grammatical accuracy of

S1	S2	S3	S3'	Label
He believes Mueller's report on Russian interference in the 2016 election is devastating, but too complicated for mass consumption.	Attorney General William P. Barr spins up a dust storm of inaccuracies while Mueller "chose to submit his unreadable — and unread — report and then go away without a sound," Comey writes.	He could have found a way to speak to the American people in their language.	Mueller's report favours the idea that US intelligence agencies were not effectively informed of the backdrop of Russian activity before the election, and Syria is details which could support or prove the theory's inches.	*I*
Plant-based food has become a part of the mainstream culinary world.	It's exciting to be leading this conversation at Flower Child.	We work hard to maintain consistency and quality throughout the seasons.	We believe that everyone, regardless of their diet preference or lifestyle, should have options for amazing plant-based food that not only tastes great but is also good for you."~~#~~POSITION: We are currently looking for an experienced dynamic Vice President of Engineering to join our team.https	*L*

Table 6: Qualitative analysis of output generated ($S3'$) by GPT-3 `davinci` under zero-shot setting.

the third sentence ($S3'$) in the context of first ($S1$) and second ($S2$) sentences across 25 randomly selected English samples (12 idiomatic and 13 literal samples) generated from GPT-3 `davinci` model.

The annotators were assigned two tasks.

Task 1 involved rating the relevance of $S3'$ on a scale of 0 to 2, with 0 indicating no relevance, 1 representing neutrality, and 2 signifying relevance. The annotators reached an agreement on 15 samples, which accounts for approximately 60% of the total. For these 15 samples, both annotators assigned the same relevance scale. Within this subset, 9 samples (about 60%) were idiomatic, indicating a consistent interpretation across both idiomatic as well as literal contexts by both annotators. Additionally, within this subset, the majority of samples labeled as relevant were idiomatic (7 out of 8). This observation suggests that the model's generated idiomatic continuations were generally preferred.

Overall, considering all the 50 annotations (25 each per annotator), the annotators marked a total of 26 samples (52%) as relevant (16 idiomatic and 10 literal), 21 (42%) as neutral (5 idiomatic and 16 literal), and 3 (0.06%) as not relevant at all (3 idiomatic). These findings indicate that GPT-3 performed well in generating relevant continuations across both the contexts, but particularly so for idiomatic cases.

Task 2 involved identifying any grammatical errors in the generated outputs. These errors primarily included instances where $S3'$ failed to form complete sentences or had some punctuation issues. Other errors included missing spaces after sentence endings, unexpected numbers or symbols inserted into the text, random dates appearing, sentences with unclear or nonsensical content, or unexpected underlined sections. 45 out of 50 annotations were flagged as having some kind of abovementioned grammatical errors to some degree and the errors were distributed almost equally between the idiomatic and literal samples. In addition to highlighting the importance of human assessment in natural language generation tasks such as this one, these results suggest that natural language generation continues to present a challenge for these models.

5.3 Qualitative Analysis

The evaluation of generative tasks, such as narrative continuation, often benefits from qualitative investigation. In this regard, Table 6 presents a selection of texts generated by the GPT-3 `davinci` model. It demonstrates that $S3'$ is a logical sentence when considered within its context. However, one can observe certain grammatical errors in the generated text, which contribute to the inconsistency in the results obtained from automated metrics.

6 Conclusion

In this work, we investigate the ability of generative language models to generate reasonable continuations under idiomatic and literal contexts. The results suggest that literal continuations seem less challenging for the models than idiomatic continuations, but only slightly so. In particular, the human annotators found the continuations in idiomatic contexts to be fairly relevant. These observations were consistent across English and Portuguese datasets. The GPT-3 `davinci` model consistently outperformed all other models, and, interestingly, its performance under a zero-shot setting was better than under a few-shot setting.

We have multiple directions for future work that we intend to explore. For example, in this work, we experimented with only a handful of prompts. There are several ways in any language to write the same prompt. As such, the generated text might depend on how the prompt is designed, which eventually affects the meaning of the generated text (Lu et al., 2021). In terms of models, especially in the case of GPT-3 models, we were somewhat limited to the number of versions that we could experiment with due to limited computational resources and accessing it as a paid service. Recent versions of the ChatGPT model as well as more open source models could also be studied. Additionally, given the non-deterministic nature of text generations, multiple $S3'$ continuations could be generated and studied. Although this paper focused primarily on higher-resource languages within the same language family, we plan to extend the inquiry to include lower-resource languages from different language families.

Ethics Consideration

The use of idiomatic expressions in natural language can potentially alter the intended meaning of a message. If a language model is unable to accurately interpret these idiomatic expressions, it can easily lead to a misinterpretation of the message and negatively impact the overall effectiveness of the model. Language models have also been shown to contain gender biases (Lucy and Bamman, 2021). As we used existing datasets from credible sources (SemEval 2022, Task 2) in our experiments, we did not verify every instance manually but considering that the data originated from 'naturally occurring sentences', it is possible that the data may contain unintended biases or offensive content.

Limitations

We explored only a handful of prompts in this work. There are several ways in any language to write the same prompt. As such, the generated text might depend on how the prompt is designed eventually affecting the meaning of the generated text (Lu et al., 2021). Another limitation of our work is that human assessment was only conducted on English samples. In terms of models, especially in the case of GPT-3 models, we were limited to the number of variants we could experiment with due to limited computational resources and accessing it as a paid service.

Acknowledgments

We would like to thank the anonymous reviewers and the PortNLP research group for their insightful feedback. This research was supported by the National Science Foundation under Grant No. CRII:RI-2246174.

References

Satanjeev Banerjee and Alon Lavie. 2005. Meteor: An automatic metric for mt evaluation with improved correlation with human judgments. In *Proceedings of the acl workshop on intrinsic and extrinsic evaluation measures for machine translation and/or summarization*, pages 65–72.

Steven Bird. 2006. Nltk: the natural language toolkit. In *Proceedings of the COLING/ACL 2006 Interactive Presentation Sessions*, pages 69–72.

Tuhin Chakrabarty, Yejin Choi, and Vered Shwartz. 2022. It's not rocket science: Interpreting figurative language in narratives. *Transactions of the Association for Computational Linguistics*, 10:589–606.

Tuhin Chakrabarty, Debanjan Ghosh, Adam Poliak, and Smaranda Muresan. 2021. Figurative language in recognizing textual entailment. In *Findings of the Association for Computational Linguistics: ACL-IJCNLP 2021*, pages 3354–3361, Online. Association for Computational Linguistics.

Kia Dashtipour, Mandar Gogate, Alexander Gelbukh, and Amir Hussain. 2022. Extending persian sentiment lexicon with idiomatic expressions for sentiment analysis. *Social Network Analysis and Mining*, 12(1):1–13.

Marzieh Fadaee, Arianna Bisazza, and Christof Monz. 2018. Examining the tip of the iceberg: A data set for idiom translation. *arXiv preprint arXiv:1802.04681*.

Pengcheng He, Xiaodong Liu, Jianfeng Gao, and Weizhu Chen. 2021. Deberta: Decoding-enhanced bert with disentangled attention. In *International Conference on Learning Representations*.

Harsh Jhamtani, Varun Gangal, Eduard Hovy, and Taylor Berg-Kirkpatrick. 2021. Investigating robustness of dialog models to popular figurative language constructs. *arXiv preprint arXiv:2110.00687*.

Pratik Joshi, Sebastin Santy, Amar Budhiraja, Kalika Bali, and Monojit Choudhury. 2020. The state and fate of linguistic diversity and inclusion in the NLP world. In *Proceedings of the 58th Annual Meeting of the Association for Computational Linguistics*, pages 6282–6293, Online. Association for Computational Linguistics.

Ioannis Korkontzelos, Torsten Zesch, Fabio Massimo Zanzotto, and Chris Biemann. 2013. Semeval-2013 task 5: Evaluating phrasal semantics. In *Second Joint Conference on Lexical and Computational Semantics (* SEM), Volume 2: Proceedings of the Seventh International Workshop on Semantic Evaluation (SemEval 2013)*, pages 39–47.

Chin-Yew Lin. 2004. Rouge: A package for automatic evaluation of summaries. In *Text summarization branches out*, pages 74–81.

Emmy Liu, Chen Cui, Kenneth Zheng, and Graham Neubig. 2022. Testing the ability of language models to interpret figurative language. *arXiv preprint arXiv:2204.12632*.

Yao Lu, Max Bartolo, Alastair Moore, Sebastian Riedel, and Pontus Stenetorp. 2021. Fantastically ordered prompts and where to find them: Overcoming few-shot prompt order sensitivity. *arXiv preprint arXiv:2104.08786*.

Li Lucy and David Bamman. 2021. Gender and representation bias in gpt-3 generated stories. In *Proceedings of the Third Workshop on Narrative Understanding*, pages 48–55.

Diego Moussallem, Mohamed Ahmed Sherif, Diego Esteves, Marcos Zampieri, and Axel-Cyrille Ngonga Ngomo. 2018. Lidioms: A multilingual linked idioms data set. *arXiv preprint arXiv:1802.08148*.

Jing Peng, Anna Feldman, and Hamza Jazmati. 2015. Classifying idiomatic and literal expressions using vector space representations. In *Proceedings of the International Conference Recent Advances in Natural Language Processing*, pages 507–511.

Minghuan Tan and Jing Jiang. 2021. Does bert understand idioms? a probing-based empirical study of bert encodings of idioms. In *Proceedings of the International Conference on Recent Advances in Natural Language Processing (RANLP 2021)*, pages 1397–1407.

Kenan Tang. 2022. Petci: A parallel english translation dataset of chinese idioms. *arXiv preprint arXiv:2202.09509*.

Harish Tayyar Madabushi, Edward Gow-Smith, Carolina Scarton, and Aline Villavicencio. 2021. AStitchInLanguageModels: Dataset and methods for the exploration of idiomaticity in pre-trained language models. In *Findings of the Association for Computational Linguistics: EMNLP 2021*, pages 3464–3477, Punta Cana, Dominican Republic. Association for Computational Linguistics.

Simone Tedeschi, Federico Martelli, and Roberto Navigli. 2022. Id10m: Idiom identification in 10 languages. In *Findings of the Association for Computational Linguistics: NAACL 2022*, pages 2715–2726.

Simone Tedeschi and Roberto Navigli. 2022. Ner4id at semeval-2022 task 2: Named entity recognition for idiomaticity detection. In *Proceedings of the 16th International Workshop on Semantic Evaluation (SemEval-2022). Association for Computational Linguistics*.

Tianyi Zhang, Varsha Kishore, Felix Wu, Kilian Q Weinberger, and Yoav Artzi. 2019. Bertscore: Evaluating text generation with bert. *arXiv preprint arXiv:1904.09675*.

Chujie Zheng, Minlie Huang, and Aixin Sun. 2019. Chid: A large-scale chinese idiom dataset for cloze test. *arXiv preprint arXiv:1906.01265*.

Jianing Zhou, Ziheng Zeng, Hongyu Gong, and Suma Bhat. 2022. Idiomatic expression paraphrasing without strong supervision. In *Proceedings of the AAAI Conference on Artificial Intelligence*, volume 36, pages 11774–11782.

CUNI Submission to MRL 2023 Shared Task on Multi-lingual Multi-task Information Retrieval

Jindřich Helcl* and **Jindřich Libovický***
Charles University, Faculty of Mathematics and Physics
Institute of Formal and Applied Linguistics
V Holešovičkách 747/2, 180 00 Prague, Czech Republic
{helcl,libovicky}@ufal.mff.cuni.cz

Abstract

We present the Charles University system for the MRL 2023 Shared Task on Multi-lingual Multi-task Information Retrieval. The goal of the shared task was to develop systems for named entity recognition and question answering in several under-represented languages. Our solutions to both subtasks rely on the translate-test approach. We first translate the unlabeled examples into English using a multilingual machine translation model. Then, we run inference on the translated data using a strong task-specific model. Finally, we project the labeled data back into the original language. To keep the inferred tags on the correct positions in the original language, we propose a method based on scoring the candidate positions using a label-sensitive translation model. In both settings, we experiment with finetuning the classification models on the translated data. However, due to a domain mismatch between the development data and the shared task validation and test sets, the finetuned models could not outperform our baselines.

1 Introduction

Pre-trained language models reach state-of-the-art results in most current natural language processing (NLP) tasks. Whereas in high-resource languages such as English, we observe in-context learning capabilities and emergent abilities (Wei et al., 2022), in less-resourced languages, the results are more modest (Lai et al., 2023a), mostly due to the lack of necessary data needed to train really large models. Moreover, there is usually not enough task-specific data available in these languages. This leads to attempts to reuse the (high-resource) language model capabilities in other (low-resource) languages.

Most of the proposed methods are either based on transfer learning (Lauscher et al., 2020; Yu and Joty, 2021; Zheng et al., 2021; Schmidt et al., 2022) or machine translation (MT), both during training and at test time (e.g. mentioned as a baseline by Conneau et al., 2020, 2018).

The MRL 2023 Shared Task on Multi-lingual Multi-task Information Retrieval aims to explore these methods further, applied to many low-resource languages. The participants were tasked to build models for two subtasks: named entity recognition (NER) and question answering (QA).

The shared task setup is inspired by the XTREME-UP dataset (Ruder et al., 2023), which focuses on the most needed tasks for under-resourced languages: gathering data in a digital form (speech recognition, optical character recognition, transliteration) and making information in these languages accessible (NER, QA, retrieval for QA). This dataset contains a relatively small amount of data for multiple tasks on low-resource languages, featuring 88 languages in total, including QA datasets for 4 languages and NER datasets for 20 languages.

The shared task evaluation campaign focused on Igbo, Indonesian (QA only), Alsatian,[1] Turkish, Uzbek (QA only), and Yoruba. Out of these languages, only Indonesian is among the XTREME-UP QA datasets, and only Igbo and Yoruba have available NER task data in the benchmark. Upon releasing the validation data close to the end of the campaign, Azerbaijani was added as a surprise language for evaluation (with no data for QA or NER in XTREME-UP).

This setting left the participants with a choice to either collect external training data for languages not present in the benchmark (which was implicitly discouraged by the inclusion of the surprise language) or to develop language-agnostic systems.

Even though a lot of research effort is invested in developing systems that are inherently multilingual, typically based on pre-trained massively multilingual models (Artetxe and Schwenk, 2019; Lauscher et al., 2020; Pfeiffer et al., 2020; Xue

* The author order was determined by a coin toss.

[1] Mistakenly labeled as Swiss German on the task website.

Proceedings of the The 3rd Workshop on Multi-lingual Representation Learning (MRL), pages 302–309
December 7, 2023 ©2023 Association for Computational Linguistics

et al., 2021, inter alia), our submission is based on the translate-test approach that was recently shown to perform better than the community previously thought (Artetxe et al., 2023). We rely on the translation quality of a multi-lingual machine translation (MT) system, combined with the strong performance of pre-trained LLMs in English. The main ideas that are common to our approaches to both subtasks are described in Section 2. The particularities of our models which are specific to the NER and QA subtasks, are presented in Sections 3 and 4, respectively, including our results on those tasks.

Overall, we find that the translate-test approach can be useful in a multilingual setting. Our results do not outperform supervised, language-specific models, but are considerably better than zero-shot approaches.

To maximize reproducibility, we built our systems using an automated end-to-end development pipeline implemented in Snakemake (Köster and Rahmann, 2012); we release the code online.[2]

2 Main Ideas

In both tasks, we employ the translate-test approach, which can be summarized in the following three steps: First, we translate unlabeled examples from the task language into English using a multilingual MT model. Second, we use a pre-trained LLM to perform the task which assigns the labels to the example. Third, we use a label-aware translation model to project the inferred labels back to the target language.

Translation into English. In the first step, we translate the unlabeled data into English. In both subtasks, we use the NLLB-3.3B[3] multilingual MT model (Costa-jussà et al., 2022). We discuss the task-specific data processing details further in Sections 3 and 4.

Task-specific models. In each subtask, we apply a RoBERTa-large model, which has been finetuned on the task (Liu et al., 2019). This predicts labels for the English data. For NER, these are BIO-encoded labels, marking the span and type of each named entity in the example. Specifically, the output is a sequence of labels of the same length as the input sentence. For QA, the labels mark a span in the context representing the answer. This is encoded using two numbers, which denote character offsets in the detokenized version of the context paragraph.

Translation into the target language. The translate-test approach is less challenging when the labels are language-independent, which is also the case of both subtasks. However, span labeling tasks (such as NER and QA) require careful handling of the projection of the spans, i.e., we need to find the corresponding spans in the original language.

Our systems adopt the label projection method for cross-lingual transfer, originally meant for the translate-train approach (Chen et al., 2023). The authors of the paper finetune the NLLB model[4] to translate texts containing inserted tags so that the tags generated in the translation mark equivalent parts of the source sentence. In contrast to the original use-case of generating the whole target sentence with tags, we already know the target sentence in the shared task scenario. Therefore, we are only interested in the placement of the tags.

To find the best possible placement of the tags, we propose to use the aforementioned finetuned model as a scorer. We place the tags at all possible positions (subject to minimum/maximum span length constraints) and select the highest-scoring candidate. We then either reconstruct the label sequence (in the case of NER) or extract the appropriate passage from the context (for QA).

3 Named Entity Recognition

The goal of the NER subtask was to classify words and phrases into one of four categories: person (PER), organization (ORG), location (LOC), and date (DAT). Since most state-of-the-art NER classifiers (including the one we used) use a richer set of labels, we apply rule-based mapping to reduce the label set to the four categories: geopolitical entities (GPE) and facilities (FAC) are replaced with LOC, time with DAT.

The XTREME-UP benchmark contains two NER datasets, MasakhaNER (Adelani et al., 2021) and MasakhaNER 2 (Adelani et al., 2022), both using texts from local news stories and covering 10 and 20 African languages respectively.

The scheme of the translate-test pipeline for this task is shown in Figure 1.

[2] https://github.com/ufal/mrl2023-multilingual-ir-shared-task

[3] https://huggingface.co/facebook/nllb-200-3.3B-easyproject

[4] https://huggingface.co/ychenNLP/nllb-200-3.3B-easyproject

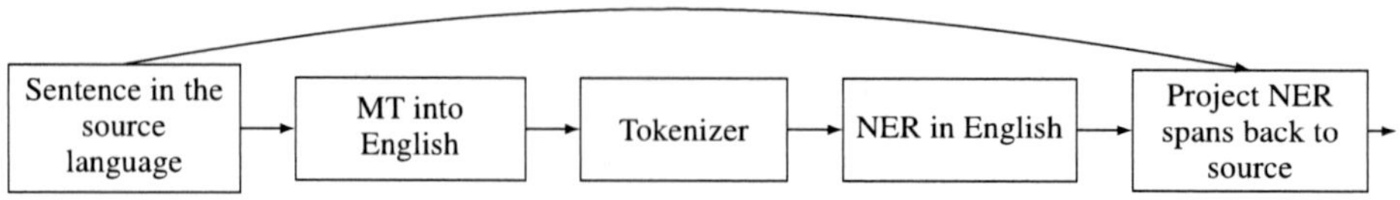

Figure 1: A scheme of the NER translate-test pipeline.

English NER models. For experiments with English NER, we use the tNER toolkit (Ushio and Camacho-Collados, 2021), which provides several models for this task. We selected two RoBERTa-based models for experiments, finetuned either on Ontonotes5 (Hovy et al., 2006) or on the CoNLL2003 (Tjong Kim Sang and De Meulder, 2003) dataset. We found that using the model built with Ontonotes5[5] leads to better results than the one finetuned on the CoNLL data.[6] Ontonotes5 contains news stories, television and radio transcripts, and web pages. The CoNLL 2003 data is international news from 1996–1997. This means there is a domain mismatch between the most available named entity recognizers and the MasakhaNER datasets.

Finetuning. To overcome the domain mismatch, we finetuned the tNER models using the MasakhaNER data. We translated the MasakhaNER training data into English and performed the span projection the same way as at inference time. The finetuning step serves not only as domain adaptation to news stories from the non-English speaking world but also as an adaptation to texts which have been automatically translated from low-resource languages.

Results. Table 1 presents the results on the MasakhaNER 1 dataset. Our translate-test approach significantly outperforms zero-shot transfer from English using the XLM-R (Conneau et al., 2020) and XLM-V (Liang et al., 2023) models; however, there is still a large performance gap between the translate-test approach and supervised in-language training.

The MasakhaNER 2 results are shown in Table 2. Similarly to MasakhaNER 1, our results are strictly worse than supervised training. The second line of the table shows the results of a model trained on MasakhaNER 1 but tested on MasakhaNER 2, which contains ten more languages than the first dataset. The results on these additional languages (shown in boxes) mark zero-shot transfer between African languages. Our translate-test approach via English is better than zero-shot using African languages for 5 of the 10 languages.

When compared to related work, our results (average score 61.3%) without finetuning outperform transfer from English using mDeBERTav3 (He et al., 2023) (average score 55.5%). However, they are worse when compared to the translate-train results reported by Chen et al. (2023) (average score 63.4%) that used additional parallel data with projected labels for training.

On both MasakhaNER benchmarks, the Ontonotes5 model is slightly better than CoNLL 2003. Finetuning (which involves training data of the respective datasets) leads to consistent improvements. On MasakhaNER 2, the finetuned model outperforms Chen et al. (2023); however, the training data setups are not easily comparable.

The results on the shared task validation data are in Table 3. Because of the domain mismatch (the shared task validation data are not local news but rather Wikipedia articles), the original Ontonotes5 model performs better. Based on this observation, we decided to use the pipeline using the original Ontonotes5 model *without* finetuning. We omit Yoruba from calculating the average score because most entities are left without annotation in the data.

4 Question Answering

The goal of this task is to find an answer to a given question within a given context. In the generative version of this task, the answer may not be taken from the context directly. Figure 2 shows the question-answering processing pipeline we use in our experiments.

Data Preprocessing. The XTREME-UP datasets for QA consist of three fields: The question, the context, and the answer. Since the context might be several sentences long, we apply sentence splitting using `wtpsplit` (Minixhofer et al., 2023). Since the toolkit does not support Alsatian or Swahili,

[5] `https://huggingface.co/tner/roberta-large-ontonotes5`

[6] `https://huggingface.co/tner/roberta-large-conll2003`

	amh	hau	ibo	kin	lug	luo	pcm	swa	wol	yor	AVG
Best baseline (supervised)	78.0	91.5	87.7	77.8	84.7	75.3	90.0	89.5	86.3	83.7	84.4
XLM-R (zero-shot)	25.1	43.5	11.6	9.4	9.5	8.4	36.8	48.9	5.3	10.0	20.9
XLM-V (zero-shot)	20.6	35.9	45.9	25.0	48.7	10.4	38.2	44.0	16.7	35.8	32.1
Spacy	59.2	58.3	57.7	48.5	52.6	45.8	9.0	60.0	48.1	47.2	48.6
tNER: ConLL2003	57.3	66.7	72.8	57.0	69.4	49.7	65.8	69.4	53.7	59.3	62.1
tNER: Ontonotes5	60.8	62.8	73.3	60.2	69.9	52.5	74.2	70.1	51.4	57.5	63.3
+ finetuning	61.8	70.0	76.4	65.4	70.2	57.5	77.9	74.5	58.2	59.6	67.2

Table 1: F1 scores on the MasakhaNER 1 dataset.

	bam	bbj	ewe	fon	hau	ibo	kin	lug	mos	nya
Best supervised in paper	82.2	75.2	90.3	82.7	87.4	89.6	87.5	89.6	76.4	92.4
Trained on MasakhaNER 1	50.9	49.8	76.2	57.1	88.7	90.1	87.6	90.0	75.0	80.4
Spacy	38.1	16.8	57.0	39.9	48.1	52.0	55.3	65.7	31.5	53.0
tNER: ConLL2003	49.0	21.9	67.5	51.7	66.3	64.9	60.6	74.8	42.5	66.0
tNER: Ontonotes5	46.8	20.5	67.3	48.8	63.6	63.6	64.6	75.2	39.8	69.0
+ finetuning	**60.9**	25.9	73.7	53.0	67.0	75.3	65.7	75.2	44.7	72.1
	pcm	sna	swa	tsn	twi	wol	xho	yor	zul	AVG
Best supervised in paper	90.1	96.2	92.7	89.4	81.8	86.8	89.9	89.3	90.6	87.1
Trained on MasakhaNER 1	90.2	42.5	93.1	79.4	57.3	87.0	47.4	89.7	64.3	74.0
Spacy	52.5	60.6	67.4	63.4	53.7	46.5	47.7	42.3	56.2	49.9
tNER: ConLL2003	67.7	69.7	70.8	74.8	67.6	61.9	67.0	52.9	66.0	61.2
tNER: Ontonotes5	72.8	72.4	72.7	73.1	62.0	57.7	67.9	55.6	70.3	61.3
+ finetuning	79.2	**81.7**	75.1	76.2	**68.4**	65.6	**75.8**	60.5	**70.4**	66.7

Table 2: F1 scores on the MasakhaNER 2 dataset. The numbers in boxes denote zero-shot transfer between African languages (i.e., languages that are in MasakhaNER 2 but not in MasakhaNER 1). Bold numbers are results where our approach is better than the zero-shot transfer between African languages.

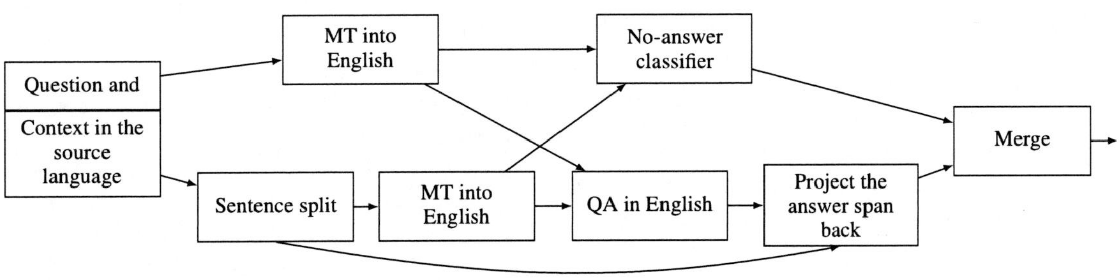

Figure 2: A scheme of the QA translate-test pipeline.

	als	aze	tur	yor	AVG
CoNLL 2003	38.4	54.6	48.0	4.4	47.0
Ontonotes5	40.3	62.8	54.7	3.1	52.4
+ finetuned	40.9	62.3	51.3	5.9	51.7

Table 3: Results on the shared task validation data. The average does not include Yoruba.

we use the English variant instead. After sentence splitting, we translate everything into English using the NLLB model. Since NLLB does not support Alsatian, we set the source language to German.

Answering Questions. For the extractive question answering task, we use a RoBERTa-based model[7] finetuned for question answering to mark the answer spans in the English context. Once the spans are found, we insert tags into the English sentence. To find the right spans in the original language, we use the tag-preserving NLLB model as a scorer and select the highest-scoring span according to the model.

No Answer Classification. Since there are examples with no answer in XTREME-UP, we train a classifier to detect such cases. We again use the QA-tuned RoBERTa, which we finetune on 3 epochs of the translated XTREME-UP data. We set the learning rate to 10^{-5}, weight decay to 0.01, and keep the default values of the rest of the hyper-parameters. The classifier achieves 93% accuracy on the development set. However, because the shared task validation set contains only a very small amount of examples with no answer, we decided not to use this classifier in our submissions.

In-domain Finetuning. We also implemented in-domain finetuning of the QA RoBERTa model on the XTREME-UP dataset translated into English. Because the answers are represented as spans within the context, we use the same technique to project the spans onto the English translation of the context as we use in span projecting to the original language. Performing grid search and measuring model performance on the development set, we found a learning rate of 5×10^{-6}, gradient norm of 1, warmup ratio of 0.5, and weight decay of 0.1 are the most suitable hyper-parameters.

Using Generative Models. We noticed that the shared task validation data did not actually contain examples of extractive question answering. Instead, the answers were likely written by a human annotator. Therefore, we decided also to submit a contrastive experiment using a generative model, namely Llama 2 (Touvron et al., 2023).[8] For the generation, we use the prompt `"Context: {context} Question: {question} Short answer:"`. We apply rule-based post-processing to remove potential continuations generated after the answer. Details can be found in the corresponding `Snakefile` in the code repository.

Results. Table 4 shows the results of the shared task validation set. Since there is a considerable domain mismatch between the XTREME-UP dataset and the shared task validation and test sets, we see that the in-domain finetuning does not improve the performance – we, therefore, use the baseline systems as our primary submission. Using the generative model, however, achieves a substantial improvement. Because the task was originally aimed at extractive QA, we decided to submit the generative model as a contrastive experiment.

5 Conclusions and Discussion

The research community long overlooked the translate-test approach until recently, when Artetxe et al. (2023) showed that it might outperform both translate-train and cross-lingual transfer with sufficiently strong machine translation systems.

With the increasing number of attempts to use large generative language models in cross-lingual setups, we speculate that the translate-test approach will become an important baseline that might not be easy to cross. Methods that work well with multilingual encoders enforce alignment of the intermediate representation (Wu and Dredze, 2020; Hämmerl et al., 2022; Pfeiffer et al., 2022, inter alia). However, in generative setups, this would lead to undesirable language mixing (Li and Murray, 2023). Generative models are also known not to be consistent across languages (Lai et al., 2023b; Wang et al., 2023). Translate-test does not suffer from either of these disadvantages.

We successfully tested the translate-test method in the shared task setup involving span-labeling tasks. We translated the input into English, performed the task using state-of-the-art English models, and projected the results back to the original language. The main technical challenge is that after labeling the spans in English, we need to find

[7]`https://huggingface.co/deepset/roberta-large-squad2`

[8]`https://huggingface.co/meta-llama/Llama-2-13b-chat-hf`

	als	aze	ind	tur	uzn	yor	AVG
Roberta-large	8.34	17.87	30.36	14.84	23.13	18.56	18.85
Finetuned	7.88	15.83	30.94	12.64	18.60	19.65	17.59
Llama 2	17.43	31.96	34.61	24.51	30.81	19.80	26.52

Table 4: Question answering results on the shared task validation data (chrF).

the corresponding span in the original text. For that purpose, we used an MT model specifically finetuned to preserve tags encoded as brackets. Furthermore, we finetuned the task-specific models on XTREME-UP data automatically translated into English.

Although the shared task claimed to be based on the XTREME-UP benchmark, the actual shared task data have many different characteristics. Instead of local news outlets, the NER data used Wikipedia text, often on generic topics rather than local ones. The QA validation and test data were abstractive, not extractive. Because of that, our finetuned models performed worse than the original ones. Also, generative QA using LlaMA 2 outperformed our original extractive system.

The final results show that building a translate-test pipeline is a viable approach to both cross-lingual NER and QA.

Limitations

Both validation and test datasets from the shared task are considerably small, especially for QA, where they contain only around 100 examples per language. This might lead to an unreliable comparison between the submitted systems.

The paper does not contain experimental results that would sufficiently back stronger claims about translate-test approaches. We made decisions that appeared to lead to a good performance in the context of the shared task. However, the paper misses ablations that would reliably show that the span projection method is the best. More importantly, this paper does not compare our results with a strong system based on cross-lingual transfer.

None of the system authors speak the languages in the shared task, and neither is particularly familiar with the culture of the respective language communities. The authors did not check the system outputs for harmful or otherwise inappropriate content.

Acknowledgments

The work was supported by the Charles University project PRIMUS/23/SCI/023. The work described herein has been using services provided by the LINDAT/CLARIAH-CZ Research Infrastructure (https://lindat.cz), supported by the Ministry of Education, Youth and Sports of the Czech Republic (Project No. LM2023062).

References

David Adelani, Graham Neubig, Sebastian Ruder, Shruti Rijhwani, Michael Beukman, Chester Palen-Michel, Constantine Lignos, Jesujoba Alabi, Shamsuddeen Muhammad, Peter Nabende, Cheikh M. Bamba Dione, Andiswa Bukula, Rooweither Mabuya, Bonaventure F. P. Dossou, Blessing Sibanda, Happy Buzaaba, Jonathan Mukiibi, Godson Kalipe, Derguene Mbaye, Amelia Taylor, Fatoumata Kabore, Chris Chinenye Emezue, Anuoluwapo Aremu, Perez Ogayo, Catherine Gitau, Edwin Munkoh-Buabeng, Victoire Memdjokam Koagne, Allahsera Auguste Tapo, Tebogo Macucwa, Vukosi Marivate, Mboning Tchiaze Elvis, Tajuddeen Gwadabe, Tosin Adewumi, Orevaoghene Ahia, Joyce Nakatumba-Nabende, Neo Lerato Mokono, Ignatius Ezeani, Chiamaka Chukwuneke, Mofetoluwa Oluwaseun Adeyemi, Gilles Quentin Hacheme, Idris Abdulmumin, Odunayo Ogundepo, Oreen Yousuf, Tatiana Moteu, and Dietrich Klakow. 2022. MasakhaNER 2.0: Africa-centric transfer learning for named entity recognition. In *Proceedings of the 2022 Conference on Empirical Methods in Natural Language Processing*, pages 4488–4508, Abu Dhabi, United Arab Emirates. Association for Computational Linguistics.

David Ifeoluwa Adelani, Jade Abbott, Graham Neubig, Daniel D'souza, Julia Kreutzer, Constantine Lignos, Chester Palen-Michel, Happy Buzaaba, Shruti Rijhwani, Sebastian Ruder, Stephen Mayhew, Israel Abebe Azime, Shamsuddeen H. Muhammad, Chris Chinenye Emezue, Joyce Nakatumba-Nabende, Perez Ogayo, Aremu Anuoluwapo, Catherine Gitau, Derguene Mbaye, Jesujoba Alabi, Seid Muhie Yimam, Tajuddeen Rabiu Gwadabe, Ignatius Ezeani, Rubungo Andre Niyongabo, Jonathan Mukiibi, Verrah Otiende, Iroro Orife, Davis David, Samba Ngom, Tosin Adewumi, Paul Rayson, Mofetoluwa Adeyemi, Gerald Muriuki, Emmanuel Anebi, Chiamaka Chukwuneke, Nkiruka Odu, Eric Peter Wairagala, Samuel

Oyerinde, Clemencia Siro, Tobius Saul Bateesa, Temilola Oloyede, Yvonne Wambui, Victor Akinode, Deborah Nabagereka, Maurice Katusiime, Ayodele Awokoya, Mouhamadane MBOUP, Dibora Gebreyohannes, Henok Tilaye, Kelechi Nwaike, Degaga Wolde, Abdoulaye Faye, Blessing Sibanda, Orevaoghene Ahia, Bonaventure F. P. Dossou, Kelechi Ogueji, Thierno Ibrahima DIOP, Abdoulaye Diallo, Adewale Akinfaderin, Tendai Marengereke, and Salomey Osei. 2021. MasakhaNER: Named entity recognition for African languages. *Transactions of the Association for Computational Linguistics*, 9:1116–1131.

Mikel Artetxe, Vedanuj Goswami, Shruti Bhosale, Angela Fan, and Luke Zettlemoyer. 2023. Revisiting machine translation for cross-lingual classification. *arXiv preprint arXiv:2305.14240*.

Mikel Artetxe and Holger Schwenk. 2019. Massively multilingual sentence embeddings for zero-shot cross-lingual transfer and beyond. *Transactions of the Association for Computational Linguistics*, 7:597–610.

Yang Chen, Chao Jiang, Alan Ritter, and Wei Xu. 2023. Frustratingly easy label projection for cross-lingual transfer. In *Findings of the Association for Computational Linguistics: ACL 2023*, pages 5775–5796, Toronto, Canada. Association for Computational Linguistics.

Alexis Conneau, Kartikay Khandelwal, Naman Goyal, Vishrav Chaudhary, Guillaume Wenzek, Francisco Guzmán, Edouard Grave, Myle Ott, Luke Zettlemoyer, and Veselin Stoyanov. 2020. Unsupervised cross-lingual representation learning at scale. In *Proceedings of the 58th Annual Meeting of the Association for Computational Linguistics*, pages 8440–8451, Online. Association for Computational Linguistics.

Alexis Conneau, Ruty Rinott, Guillaume Lample, Adina Williams, Samuel Bowman, Holger Schwenk, and Veselin Stoyanov. 2018. XNLI: Evaluating cross-lingual sentence representations. In *Proceedings of the 2018 Conference on Empirical Methods in Natural Language Processing*, pages 2475–2485, Brussels, Belgium. Association for Computational Linguistics.

Marta R Costa-jussà, James Cross, Onur Çelebi, Maha Elbayad, Kenneth Heafield, Kevin Heffernan, Elahe Kalbassi, Janice Lam, Daniel Licht, Jean Maillard, et al. 2022. No language left behind: Scaling human-centered machine translation. *arXiv preprint arXiv:2207.04672*.

Katharina Hämmerl, Jindřich Libovický, and Alexander Fraser. 2022. Combining static and contextualised multilingual embeddings. In *Findings of the Association for Computational Linguistics: ACL 2022*, pages 2316–2329, Dublin, Ireland. Association for Computational Linguistics.

Pengcheng He, Jianfeng Gao, and Weizhu Chen. 2023. Debertav3: Improving deberta using electra-style pre-training with gradient-disentangled embedding sharing. In *The Eleventh International Conference on Learning Representations, ICLR 2023, Kigali, Rwanda, May 1-5, 2023*. OpenReview.net.

Eduard Hovy, Mitchell Marcus, Martha Palmer, Lance Ramshaw, and Ralph Weischedel. 2006. OntoNotes: The 90% solution. In *Proceedings of the Human Language Technology Conference of the NAACL, Companion Volume: Short Papers*, pages 57–60, New York City, USA. Association for Computational Linguistics.

Johannes Köster and Sven Rahmann. 2012. Snakemake—a scalable bioinformatics workflow engine. *Bioinformatics*, 28(19):2520–2522.

Viet Dac Lai, Nghia Trung Ngo, Amir Pouran Ben Veyseh, Hieu Man, Franck Dernoncourt, Trung Bui, and Thien Huu Nguyen. 2023a. Chatgpt beyond english: Towards a comprehensive evaluation of large language models in multilingual learning. *arXiv preprint arXiv:2304.05613*.

Viet Dac Lai, Nghia Trung Ngo, Amir Pouran Ben Veyseh, Hieu Man, Franck Dernoncourt, Trung Bui, and Thien Huu Nguyen. 2023b. Chatgpt beyond english: Towards a comprehensive evaluation of large language models in multilingual learning. *CoRR*, abs/2304.05613.

Anne Lauscher, Vinit Ravishankar, Ivan Vulić, and Goran Glavaš. 2020. From zero to hero: On the limitations of zero-shot language transfer with multilingual Transformers. In *Proceedings of the 2020 Conference on Empirical Methods in Natural Language Processing (EMNLP)*, pages 4483–4499, Online. Association for Computational Linguistics.

Tianjian Li and Kenton Murray. 2023. Why does zero-shot cross-lingual generation fail? an explanation and a solution. In *Findings of the Association for Computational Linguistics: ACL 2023*, pages 12461–12476, Toronto, Canada. Association for Computational Linguistics.

Davis Liang, Hila Gonen, Yuning Mao, Rui Hou, Naman Goyal, Marjan Ghazvininejad, Luke Zettlemoyer, and Madian Khabsa. 2023. XLM-V: overcoming the vocabulary bottleneck in multilingual masked language models. *CoRR*, abs/2301.10472.

Yinhan Liu, Myle Ott, Naman Goyal, Jingfei Du, Mandar Joshi, Danqi Chen, Omer Levy, Mike Lewis, Luke Zettlemoyer, and Veselin Stoyanov. 2019. Roberta: A robustly optimized bert pretraining approach. *arXiv preprint arXiv:1907.11692*.

Benjamin Minixhofer, Jonas Pfeiffer, and Ivan Vulić. 2023. Where's the point? self-supervised multilingual punctuation-agnostic sentence segmentation. In *Proceedings of the 61st Annual Meeting of the Association for Computational Linguistics (Volume 1:*

Long Papers), pages 7215–7235, Toronto, Canada. Association for Computational Linguistics.

Jonas Pfeiffer, Naman Goyal, Xi Lin, Xian Li, James Cross, Sebastian Riedel, and Mikel Artetxe. 2022. Lifting the curse of multilinguality by pre-training modular transformers. In *Proceedings of the 2022 Conference of the North American Chapter of the Association for Computational Linguistics: Human Language Technologies*, pages 3479–3495, Seattle, United States. Association for Computational Linguistics.

Jonas Pfeiffer, Ivan Vulić, Iryna Gurevych, and Sebastian Ruder. 2020. MAD-X: An Adapter-Based Framework for Multi-Task Cross-Lingual Transfer. In *Proceedings of the 2020 Conference on Empirical Methods in Natural Language Processing (EMNLP)*, pages 7654–7673, Online. Association for Computational Linguistics.

Sebastian Ruder, Jonathan H Clark, Alexander Gutkin, Mihir Kale, Min Ma, Massimo Nicosia, Shruti Rijhwani, Parker Riley, Jean-Michel A Sarr, Xinyi Wang, et al. 2023. Xtreme-up: A user-centric scarce-data benchmark for under-represented languages. *arXiv preprint arXiv:2305.11938*.

Fabian David Schmidt, Ivan Vulić, and Goran Glavaš. 2022. Don't stop fine-tuning: On training regimes for few-shot cross-lingual transfer with multilingual language models. In *Proceedings of the 2022 Conference on Empirical Methods in Natural Language Processing*, pages 10725–10742, Abu Dhabi, United Arab Emirates. Association for Computational Linguistics.

Erik F. Tjong Kim Sang and Fien De Meulder. 2003. Introduction to the CoNLL-2003 shared task: Language-independent named entity recognition. In *Proceedings of the Seventh Conference on Natural Language Learning at HLT-NAACL 2003*, pages 142–147.

Hugo Touvron, Louis Martin, Kevin Stone, Peter Albert, Amjad Almahairi, Yasmine Babaei, Nikolay Bashlykov, Soumya Batra, Prajjwal Bhargava, Shruti Bhosale, Dan Bikel, Lukas Blecher, Cristian Canton Ferrer, Moya Chen, Guillem Cucurull, David Esiobu, Jude Fernandes, Jeremy Fu, Wenyin Fu, Brian Fuller, Cynthia Gao, Vedanuj Goswami, Naman Goyal, Anthony Hartshorn, Saghar Hosseini, Rui Hou, Hakan Inan, Marcin Kardas, Viktor Kerkez, Madian Khabsa, Isabel Kloumann, Artem Korenev, Punit Singh Koura, Marie-Anne Lachaux, Thibaut Lavril, Jenya Lee, Diana Liskovich, Yinghai Lu, Yuning Mao, Xavier Martinet, Todor Mihaylov, Pushkar Mishra, Igor Molybog, Yixin Nie, Andrew Poulton, Jeremy Reizenstein, Rashi Rungta, Kalyan Saladi, Alan Schelten, Ruan Silva, Eric Michael Smith, Ranjan Subramanian, Xiaoqing Ellen Tan, Binh Tang, Ross Taylor, Adina Williams, Jian Xiang Kuan, Puxin Xu, Zheng Yan, Iliyan Zarov, Yuchen Zhang, Angela Fan, Melanie Kambadur, Sharan Narang, Aurelien Rodriguez, Robert Stojnic, Sergey Edunov, and Thomas Scialom. 2023. Llama 2: Open foundation and fine-tuned chat models.

Asahi Ushio and Jose Camacho-Collados. 2021. T-NER: An all-round python library for transformer-based named entity recognition. In *Proceedings of the 16th Conference of the European Chapter of the Association for Computational Linguistics: System Demonstrations*, pages 53–62, Online. Association for Computational Linguistics.

Bin Wang, Zhengyuan Liu, Xin Huang, Fangkai Jiao, Yang Ding, Ai Ti Aw, and Nancy F. Chen. 2023. Seaeval for multilingual foundation models: From cross-lingual alignment to cultural reasoning. *CoRR*, abs/2309.04766.

Jason Wei, Yi Tay, Rishi Bommasani, Colin Raffel, Barret Zoph, Sebastian Borgeaud, Dani Yogatama, Maarten Bosma, Denny Zhou, Donald Metzler, Ed H. Chi, Tatsunori Hashimoto, Oriol Vinyals, Percy Liang, Jeff Dean, and William Fedus. 2022. Emergent abilities of large language models. *Transactions on Machine Learning Research*. Survey Certification.

Shijie Wu and Mark Dredze. 2020. Do explicit alignments robustly improve multilingual encoders? In *Proceedings of the 2020 Conference on Empirical Methods in Natural Language Processing (EMNLP)*, pages 4471–4482, Online. Association for Computational Linguistics.

Linting Xue, Noah Constant, Adam Roberts, Mihir Kale, Rami Al-Rfou, Aditya Siddhant, Aditya Barua, and Colin Raffel. 2021. mT5: A massively multilingual pre-trained text-to-text transformer. In *Proceedings of the 2021 Conference of the North American Chapter of the Association for Computational Linguistics: Human Language Technologies*, pages 483–498, Online. Association for Computational Linguistics.

Tao Yu and Shafiq Joty. 2021. Effective fine-tuning methods for cross-lingual adaptation. In *Proceedings of the 2021 Conference on Empirical Methods in Natural Language Processing*, pages 8492–8501, Online and Punta Cana, Dominican Republic. Association for Computational Linguistics.

Bo Zheng, Li Dong, Shaohan Huang, Wenhui Wang, Zewen Chi, Saksham Singhal, Wanxiang Che, Ting Liu, Xia Song, and Furu Wei. 2021. Consistency regularization for cross-lingual fine-tuning. In *Proceedings of the 59th Annual Meeting of the Association for Computational Linguistics and the 11th International Joint Conference on Natural Language Processing (Volume 1: Long Papers)*, pages 3403–3417, Online. Association for Computational Linguistics.

Findings of the 1st Shared Task on Multi-lingual Multi-task Information Retrieval at MRL 2023

Francesco Tinner
University of Amsterdam
14497425@uva.nl

David Ifeoluwa Adelani
University College London
d.adelani@ucl.ac.uk

Chris Emezue
TU Munich
chris.emezue@gmail.com

Mammad Hajili
Microsoft
mammadhajili@microsoft.com

Omer Goldman
Bar-Ilan University
omer.goldman@gmail.com

Muhammad Farid Adilazuarda
Institut Teknologi Bandung
faridlazuarda@gmail.com

Muhammad Dehan Al Kautsar
Institut Teknologi Bandung
faridlazuarda@gmail.com

Aziza Mirsaidova
Northwestern University
azizakhon@u.northwestern.edu

Müge Kural
Koç University
mugekural@ku.edu.tr

Dylan Massey
University of Zurich
dylan.massey@uzh.ch

Chiamaka Chukwuneke
Lancaster University, UK
chukwunekechiamaka3@gmail.com

Chinedu Mbonu
Nnamdi Azikiwe University
ce.mbonu@unizik.edu.ng

Damilola Oluwaseun Oloyede
Federal University of Agriculture, Abeokuta
oloyededo.19@student.funaab.edu.ng

Kayode Olaleye
University of Pretoria
kayode.olaleye@up.ac.za

Jonathan Atala
Anglia Ruskin University
Olaatala7@gmail.com

Benjamin A. Ajibade
University of Alabama
baajibade@crimson.ua.edu

Saksham Bassi
New York University
sakshambassi@nyu.edu

Rahul Aralikatte
MILA
rahul.aralikatte@mila.quebec

Najoung Kim
Boston University
najoung@bu.edu

Duygu Ataman
New York University
ataman@nyu.edu

Abstract

Large language models (LLMs) excel in language understanding and generation, especially in English which has ample public benchmarks for various natural language processing (NLP) tasks. Nevertheless, their reliability across different languages and domains remains uncertain. Our new shared task introduces a novel benchmark to assess the ability of multilingual LLMs to comprehend and produce language under sparse settings, particularly in scenarios with under-resourced languages, with an emphasis on the ability to capture logical, factual, or causal relationships within lengthy text contexts. The shared task consists of two subtasks crucial to information retrieval: Named Entity Recognition (NER) and Reading Comprehension (RC), in 7 data-scarce languages: Azerbaijani, Igbo, Indonesian, Swiss German, Turkish, Uzbek and Yorùbá, which previously lacked annotated resources in information retrieval tasks. Our evaluation of leading LLMs reveals that, despite their competitive performance, they still have notable weaknesses such as producing output in the non-target language or providing counterfactual information that cannot be inferred from the context. As more advanced models emerge, the benchmark will remain essential for supporting fairness and applicability in information retrieval systems.

Proceedings of the The 3rd Workshop on Multi-lingual Representation Learning (MRL), pages 310–323
December 7, 2023 ©2023 Association for Computational Linguistics

1 Introduction

Access to information on diverse subjects, recent events, or historical occurrences is of paramount significance in bolstering educational, media, and economic applications. Recent advancements in organizing online knowledge facilitated by Large Language Models (LLMs) have fundamentally reshaped the way we approach information retrieval. Extensive analysis of models have shown promising capabilities in competitive natural language processing (NLP) tasks, such as question answering (Mao et al., 2023), machine translation (Garcia and Firat, 2022; Hendy et al., 2023), and different types of reasoning (Zhou et al., 2021; Wei et al., 2022; Liu et al., 2023).

LLMs, or foundation models, are typically trained on extensive multilingual data sets, thereby enhancing their accessibility across a spectrum of languages (Floridi and Chiriatti, 2020; Touvron et al., 2023a; Muennighoff et al., 2022; Anil et al., 2023). However, this performance is limited in low-resources languages which lack representation in the public space (Yong et al., 2023). Recently, initiatives for creating standardized benchmarks for evaluating natural language processing (NLP) systems in a more linguistically inclusive setting had been proposed by corpora like XTREME (Hu et al., 2020) and XTREME-UP (Ruder et al., 2023). Although these data sets bring together large multilingual corpora they lack in generative human prepared data related to information access.

By organizing the 1st Shared Task on Multilingual Multi-task Information Retrieval (MMIR), we aim to provide a common means where multilingual LLMs can be evaluated in terms of their applicability and fairness in providing access to users speaking languages from different regions across the world. As the evaluation resource we use Wikipedia which we find representative of the inclusion of languages online. We pick 7 languages with varying degrees of resources and linguistic typology from 4 different language families: Azerbaijani, Turkish and Uzbek (Turkic), Igbo and Yoruba, (Niger-Congo), Indonesian (Austronesian), and Swiss German (Germanic), and produce annotations in two tasks crucial for IR: named entity recognition (NER) and reading comprehension (RC). We present our data curation and annotation process as well as the findings of the evaluation in the resulting benchmark including prominent LLMs trained on multi-lingual multi-task settings: MT-0 (Muennighoff et al., 2022) and GPT-4 (OpenAI, 2023a), in addition to the system submissions. We also release this benchmark on CodaBench (Xu et al., 2022), where we provide a possibility to obtain the test sets and evaluate future submissions[1] until MRL 2024 .

2 Task Description

With the advancement of language models accessing and processing vast amounts of information in different formats and languages, it has become of great importance to be able to assess their capabilities to access and provide the right information useful to different audiences. In this shared task, we provide a multi-task evaluation format that assesses information retrieval capabilities of language models in terms of two subtasks: named entity recognition (NER) and Reading Comprehension (RC).

2.1 Named Entity Recognition (NER)

NER is a classification task that identifies phrases in a text that refer to entities or predefined categories (such as dates, person, organization and location names) and it is an important capability for information access systems that perform entity lookups for knowledge verification, spell-checking or localization applications. The XTREME-UP dataset (Ruder et al., 2023) contains processed data from MasakhaNER (Adelani et al., 2021b)) and MasakhaNER 2.0 (Adelani et al., 2022) in the following languages: Amharic, Ghomálá, Bambara, Ewe, Hausa, Igbo, (Lu)Ganda, (Dho)Luo, Mossi (Mooré), Nyanja (Chichewa), Nigerian Pidgin, Kinyarwanda, Shona, Swahili, Tswana (Setswana), Twi, Wolof, Xhosa, Yorùbá and Zulu.

The objective of the system is to tag the named entities in a given text, either as a person (PER), organization (ORG), or location (LOC).

2.2 Reading Comprehension (RC)

RC is an important capability that enables responding to natural language questions with answers found in text. Here we focus on the information-seeking scenario where questions can be asked without knowing the answer. It is the system's task to locate a suitable answer passage (if any). Examples can be found in Table 2.

[1]https://www.codabench.org/competitions/1672/?secret_key=c68a56e8-542b-4c85-b4f5-7ce6b65643c7

Narendrabhai Damodardas Modi ni Mínśítà àgbà India kẹrìnlá àti mínísítà àgbà tí India lọ́wọ́ lọ́wọ́ lati ọdun 2014. O jẹ oloselu kan lati Bharatiya Janata Party, agbari-iṣẹ oluyọọda ara ilu Hindu kan. Oun ni Prime Minister akọkọ ni ita ti Ile-igbimọjọ ti Orilẹ-ede India lati ṣẹgun awọn ofin itẹlera meji pẹlu opoju to kun ati ekeji lati pari diẹ sii ju ọdun marun ni ọfiisi lẹhin Atal Bihari Vajpayee.

Table 1: Example of named entities in Yorùbá language. PER, LOC, and ORG are in colours red, green, and blue respectively. We make use of Label Studio for annotation (Tkachenko et al., 2020-2022).

The information-seeking question-answer pairs tend to exhibit less lexical and morphosyntactic overlap between the question and answer since they are written separately, which is a more suitable setting to evaluate typologically-diverse languages. Here, the system is given a question, title, and a passage and must provide the answer — if any — or otherwise return that the question has "no answer" in the passage. The XTREME-UP benchmark currently contains data only in Indonesian, Bengali, Swahili and Telugu (Ruder et al., 2023). The competing systems will therefore be required to infer information from different language annotations.

3 Languages

Table 3 provides an overview of the variety in our data set in terms of language families.

3.1 Azerbaijani (AZ)

Azerbaijani is a member of the Turkic language family, and spoken largely in Azerbaijan and Iran. Azerbaijani shares a high degree of linguistic characteristics with other Turkic languages, especially languages in the Western Oghuz subgroup such as Turkish, Gagauz and Turkmen. Azerbaijani has an agglutinative morphology, the language also uses a Subject-Object-Verb (SOV) word order, and does not have a gender in grammar. Azerbaijanis in Azerbaijan are using Latin script since its readoption in 1991. Arabic script is also used by Iranian Azerbaijanis. The data preparation for this study is done using text in Latin script.

3.2 Igbo (IG)

Igbo belongs to the Benue Congo group of the NigerCongo language family and is spoken by over 27 million people (Eberhard et al., 2021). It is native to the southeastern Nigeria, but also spoken in some parts of Equatorial Guinea and Cameroon. There are several Igbo dialects but the most used one is the central Igbo that was standardized in 1962 (Ohiri-Aniche, 2007). The standard Igbo consists 28 consonants and 8 vowels. There are two tones: high and low. High tone is marked with an acute accent, e.g., á, while low tone is marked with a grave accent, e.g, à. These are not normally represented in the orthography. Igbo along with other African languages have been include in several benchmarks by Masakhane such as MasakhaNER (Adelani et al., 2021b, 2022), AfriQA (Ogundepo et al., 2023), MasakhaPOS (Dione et al., 2023), AfriSenti (Muhammad et al., 2023) and so on.

3.3 Indonesian (ID)

Indonesian is a member of the Austronesian language family and official language in Indonesia. The language itself is well-standarized in terms of orthography and grammar through the country, however, it has high variety on usages, especially for registers and styles influenced by the cultural influences which creates dialect variances (Aji et al., 2022). In the colloquial setting, the language usage is more challenging due to new creative abbreviations and jargons created by the speakers, which is only popular for a particular generation. The research progress on Indonesian has been tremendously improved due to the recent advancement on benchmarks (IndoNLU (Wilie et al., 2020), IndoNLG (Cahyawijaya et al., 2021), NusaCrowd (Cahyawijaya et al., 2023a), IndoLEM (Koto et al., 2020)) and datasets (NusaX (Winata et al., 2023), NusaWrites (Cahyawijaya et al., 2023b)).

3.4 Swiss German (ALS)

Swiss German is a member of the Germanic language family and the subgroup of Alemannic dialects. In contrast to Standard German, Swiss German provides a unique challenge for multilingual NLP methods, as it is a non-standardized dialect continuum with a great variety in terms of lexicon, phonetics, morphology and syntax. Especially challenging is that there exists no official orthography, and therefore each dialect variant and also each person tends to write words differently following their own interpretation of the phonetic spelling. As it is not one of Switzerland's official languages, it is mainly used in the spoken form and in informal contexts. Formal writing is done in Standard German.

Context	Question	Answer
Zaqatala" qəzeti redaksiyası 1923-cü ilin mart ayından fəaliyyətə başlamışdır. İlk əvvəllər "Zaqatala kəndlisi" adlanan qəzet sonralar "Kolxozun səsi", "Bolşevik kolxozu uğrunda", "Qırmızı bayraq" və s. başlıqlarla fəaliyyət göstərmişdir. 1991-ci ilin oktyabr ayından isə "Zaqatala" adı ilə fəaliyyətini davam etdirir. Hal-hazırda "Zaqatala" qəzeti redaksiyasında 5 nəfər çalışır.	İndi qəzetdə neçə nəfər çalışır?	İndi "Zaqatala" qəzetində 5 nəfər işləyir.
Noch de jüngere Version isch de Eurytos vom Herakles töödt woore. Us Raach nämmli, well de em sini Töchter Iole nöd hett wöle gee, hett er d Stadt Oichalia eroberet, de Eurytos und all sini Söö töödt und d Iole graubt.	Was isch de Grund gsi für di tötig vom Eurytos?	Will de Eurytos am Herakles nöd sis Töchterli - d Iole - het welle geh.
Jembatan Siak atau Jembatan Tengku Agung Sultanah Latifah adalah jembatan sepanjang 1.196 m yang terletak di kota Siak Sri Indrapura. Jembatan ini membentang di atas Sungai Siak dan diresmikan pada tanggal 11 Agustus 2007. Pembangunan jembatan ini dimulai sejak 27 Desember 2002 dan nama jembatan ini diambil dari nama gelar Tengku Syarifah Mariam binti Fadyl, permaisuri dari Sultan Syarif Kasim II, sultan terakhir di Kerajaan Siak.	Berapa panjang jembatan siak?	Jembatan siak membentang sepanjang 1.196 m yang terletak di kota siak sri indrapura
Bugünkü arokarya ağacının akrabası olan bulunmuş fosiller 50 milyon yaşındadır. Dolayısıyla dünyanın en eski ağaç familyalarından birinin üyesidir.	Arokarya ağacının dünyanın en eski ağaç familyasına ait olduğu neden düşünülmektedir?	Bulunan akraba fosillerinin 50 milyon yaşında olması sebebiyle Arokarya ağacının dünyanın eski ağaç familyasına ait olduğu düşünülmektedir.
A bi Aisha Adamu Augie ni Zaria, Ipinle Kaduna, Nigeria, Augie-Kuta jẹ ọmọbinrin oloogbe Senator Adamu Baba Augie (oloselu / olugbohunsafefe), ati Onidajọ Amina Augie (JSC). Augie-Kuta bere si ni nifẹ si fọtoyiya nigbati baba rẹ fun u ni kamẹra ni ọdọ.	Ki ni ibaṣepọ to wa laarin Aisha Adamu Augie ati Senator Adamu Baba Augie?	Aisha Adamu jẹ ọmọ fun Senator Adamu Baba Augie
A bi Aisha Adamu Augie ni Zaria, Ipinle Kaduna, Nigeria, Augie-Kuta jẹ ọmọbinrin oloogbe Senator Adamu Baba Augie (oloselu / olugbohunsafefe), ati Onidajọ Amina Augie (JSC). Augie-Kuta bere si ni nifẹ si fọtoyiya nigbati baba rẹ fun u ni kamẹra ni ọdọ.	Ki ni ibaṣepọ to wa laarin Aisha Adamu Augie ati Senator Adamu Baba Augie?	Aisha Adamu jẹ ọmọ fun Senator Adamu Baba Augie

Table 2: Examples from the RC validation data in different languages.

Language	Family
Azerbaijani	Turkic
Igbo	Niger-Congo
Indonesian	Austronesian
Swiss German	Indo-European
Turkish	Turkic
Uzbek	Turkic
Yorùbá	Niger-Congo

Table 3: List of languages and language families.

Consequently, very few textual resources are available. Most notably, Hollenstein and Aepli compiled a text corpus for PoS tagging using the following sources: Alemannic Wikipedia, the Swatch Group's annual report, novels of Viktor Schobinger, newspaper articles and blog posts (Hollenstein and Aepli, 2014). Further resources are available in the format of speech corpora, such as the SDS-200 corpus (Plüss et al., 2022), Swiss Parliaments Corpus (Plüss et al., 2020), SwissDial corpus (Dogan-Schönberger et al., 2021), Radio Rottu Oberwallis corpus (Garner et al., 2014), ArchiMob corpus (Samardžić et al., 2016), SST4SG-350 (Plüss et al., 2023). Some of these also provide Swiss German transcriptions.

3.5 Turkish (TR)

As the highest-resourced language from the Turkic language family, Turkish is distinguished with its agglutinative morphology and employs an Subject-Object-Verb (SOV) word order. While lacking grammatical gender, it also features a rich case system. Verbs are inflected to indicate tense, mood, and person, while personal pronouns are used for person reference. The language incorporates vowel harmony and sound rules, with a significant number of palatalized consonants. Turkish has no definite or indefinite articles, relying on context for specificity. Additionally, it has phonemic vowel length, which affects word meaning. These properties collectively make Turkish a unique and complex language, distinct from many Indo-European languages, however its adoption of the Latin script allows meaningful comparison to representatives from the Indo-European family.

Corpus studies in Turkish include plenty monolingual (Aksan et al., 2012) and parallel resources (Tyers and Alperen, 2010; Cettolo et al., 2012; Ataman, 2018). Previous efforts also allowed the development of different tree banks, such as for Universal Dependencies (Sulubacak et al., 2016; Sulubacak and Eryiğit, 2018), semantic parsing (Şahin and Adalı, 2018) and a WordNET (Ehsani et al., 2018). Turkish is now part of many public multilingual benchmarks including the mc4 corpus (Raffel et al., 2019), and it is recognized in different multilingual NLP benchmarks to create human-annotated resources, such as for machine translation (Cettolo et al., 2013; Bojar et al., 2017) and morphological analysis (Pimentel et al., 2021). There are also annotated resources for Turkish which were created through automatic annotation using label transfer from other languages or translating existing resources, in tasks including natural language inference (Conneau et al., 2018), NER (Sahin et al., 2017), and summarization (Scialom et al., 2020).

3.6 Uzbek (UZ)

The Uzbek language is spoken by over 44 million speakers globally, securing its position as the second most spoken language in the Turkic Languages group, following Turkish. It accommodates both Cyrillic and Latin scripts in its writing systems. Agglutination is a significant characteristic of Uzbek, where suffixes are appended to morphemes. It shares a high degree of agglutination with the Azeri language among Turkic languages.

Uzbek is enriched with a diversity of dialects influenced by East-Iranian (Tajik) and Turkish languages. However, the presence of multiple dialects across various regions in Uzbekistan, each with unique orthographic rules, make it challenging to standardize grammatical conventions across the language. Additionally, the Uzbek lexicon has been heavily influenced by the Russian language, resulting in a blend and substitution of words. This linguistic amalgamation poses substantial challenges in the realm of computational linguistics due to its complexity and variability.

There are few notable resources available in Uzbek. Such as (Gribanova, 2012-2020), who developed a dataset on morphological word formation involving copular and non-copular verbs including some regional and other dialectal variation of Uzbek. Further, (Gribanova, 2018-2020) compiled a dataset including native Uzbek speakers' assessment about sentences involving verb-stranding and argument ellipsis. Other resources include, Uzbek WordNET (Agostini et al., 2021), a collection of similar word pairs, (Salaev et al., 2022) and rule based Uzbek POS tagger (Sharipov et al., 2023).

3.7 Yorùbá (YO)

Yorùbá belongs to the Volta-Niger subgroup of the Niger-Congo language, native to the South-Western part of Nigeria, Benin and Togo. It is spoken by over 45 million speakers according to Ethnologue, making it one of the top-5 most spoken African language after Nigerian-Pidgin, Swahili, Hausa, and Amharic (Eberhard et al., 2021). Yorùbá makes use of the Latin script with modified alphabet: it omits the letters "c,q,v,x,z" and adds "ẹ, gb, ọ, ṣ". The language is tonal, the tones includes high, low, and neutral. The high (as in à) and low (as in á) tones are indicated when writing texts in the language. The tones are important for the correct understanding and pronunciation of the words in Yorùbá. Despite the importance of the tones, many texts written online do not support the writing of the tonal marks, and this may pose a challenge on some downstream NLP applications e.g. machine translation (Adelani et al., 2021a) and text-to-speech (Ogunremi et al., 2023).

4 Data Preparation

We obtain the textual data for the generative task from the XML dumps provided on Wikimedia downloads[2] and sample 200 articles, which are split paragraph-wise for annotation. For the NE annotation, we ensure we sample only biographical articles and also only include articles available in all six languages.

We use Label Studio for RC and NER annotation (Tkachenko et al., 2020-2022) with the tag set (Person (PER), Organization (ORG), Location (LOC)) and ensure an annotation overlap of 2% for NER. The question-answer pairs were always produced from two separate annotators. We recruited two annotators per language, for IG and TR respectively four annotators contributed, and five persons annotated YO. The resulting data statistics for the validation and test splits can be found in Table 4. The scripts used to obtain the data, as well as pre- and post-processing methods required to create and export Label Studio annotation projects is included in this GitHub repository [3].

[2]https://dumps.wikimedia.org/

[3]https://github.com/Fenerator/wikiDataProcessingForQAandNER

5 Experimental Methodology

5.1 Baseline Systems

MT0 is the open-source multi-lingual multi-task model developed by Big Science (Muennighoff et al., 2022). We use the mT0-large version of the model with 24 Transformer layers, which is based on the mT5 model that supports 101 languages. The model is finetuned on 46 additional languages with English and translated prompts.

GPT-4 OpenAI (2023b) is a Transformer-style large language model pre-trained to predict the next token similar to GPT-3 (Brown et al., 2020) followed by additional training to follow an instruction in a prompt and provide a response. The instruction training is based on Reinforcement Learning from Human Feedback (RLHF), similar to InstructGPT (Ouyang et al., 2022).

5.2 Evaluation

We evaluate and report results in the generative task using ROGUE-L (Lin and Hovy, 2003), chrF (Popović, 2015), chrF+, chrF++ (Popović, 2017), and BERTScore (Zhang et al., 2019) F1 computed with RoBERTaBase (Liu et al., 2019a) [4] embeddings. Implementation is based on HuggingFace's evaluate library[5]. Overall performance in the NER task is computed in terms of precision, recall and F-1 scores using the CoNLL Evaluation Scripts[6], implemented in accordance with (Tjong Kim Sang and Buchholz, 2000).

We obtain a final score per task and system by weighting the performance per language inversely by the total number of tokens in the test sets per language. We also perform human evaluation of the RC outputs (context-question-answer pairs) of all baselines, and the best performing submission. Two annotators judge whether the generated answer is correct, in a binary sense, and optionally add observations on the characteristics of the generated grammar, adequacy between the answer and the context, as well as any typical behavior from models related to strengths, fall backs and stylistic properties.

5.3 Submissions

The shared task received a valid submission from Charles University (CUNI) which was also the win-

[4]https://huggingface.co/roberta-base

[5]https://github.com/huggingface/evaluate

[6]https://github.com/sighsmile/conlleval

Lang	Task	# Paragraphs Val	# Paragraphs Test	# Sentences Val	# Sentences Test	# Tokens Val	# Tokens Test
AZ	NER	-	-	126	124	7,774	8,200
IG	NER	-	-	711	143	54,526	11,668
ID	NER	-	-	0	0	0	0
ALS	NER	-	-	130	166	8,761	11,610
TR	NER	-	-	113	151	7,375	11,736
YO	NER	-	-	100	303	4,166	11,490
AZ	RC	38	64	116	220	2,138	3,618
IG	RC	100	175	240	469	6,263	12,175
ID	RC	100	175	230	488	4,789	10,293
ALS	RC	100	175	434	728	7,516	13,430
TR	RC	100	175	551	697	8,876	12,707
YO	RC	100	175	370	680	8,258	15,259

Table 4: Dataset statistics for the validation and test splits.

	Prompt Template
mT0	<CONTEXT> <QUESTION>
GPT-4	I will provide you with a passage and a question, please provide a precise answer Passage: <CONTEXT> Question: <QUESTION>

Table 5: Zero-shot prompt template used to obtain answers from the systems.

ning system. In this section we describe notable details from the system developed by CUNI which aims to perform multi-lingual multi-task information retrieval by providing a pivoting approach where any input is translated into English to perform the end task, and translated back to the original language for final comparison.

CUNI Question Answering (CQA) system uses the RoBERTa model (Liu et al., 2019b) fine-tuned on the question answering task using XTREME-UP (Ruder et al., 2023) and span matching based on the label projection approach by Chen et al. (2023).

CUNI Contrastive (CCo) In order to generate more naturalistic language and overcome issues related to domain mismatch, CUNI provided also contrastive generations (*i.e.*) in the RC task where they compared their output quality on the validation sets with the LLAMA-2 (Touvron et al., 2023b) model and make an additional experimental submission, which we also include in our evaluation.

CUNI NER also deploys multi-lingual fine-tuning including the MasakhaNER (Adelani et al., 2021b) data in order to increase robustness of the model to domain mismatch.

w. score	CQA	CCo	mT0	GPT-4
ChrF	0.23	0.27	0.26	0.45
ChrF+	0.22	0.25	0.24	0.44
ChrF++	0.21	0.23	0.23	0.42
RougeL	0.25	0.20	0.28	0.36
BERT F1	0.83	0.84	0.82	0.87

Table 6: RC system evaluation. Results indicate weighted average of the metrics over 6 languages. Results are weighted by the number of paragraphs in the testset.

6 Results

6.1 Automatic Evaluation

We evaluate the overall system performance on the generative task using automatic metrics weighted by the number of articles in the test set containing individual context used for answering the RC questions Table 6. Detailed results per system and language are presented in Table 7. We also present NER results for the CUNI system submission in Table 8.

6.2 Human Evaluation

Table 11 provides an overview of the relative amount of times the system generated an answer judged as correct by the human annotators.

Pearson correlation coefficients between the automatic metrics and the human annotations can be

system	language	ChrF aut.	ChrF r	ChrF+ aut.	ChrF+ r	ChrF++ aut.	ChrF++ r	RougeL aut.	RougeL r	BERTScore F1 aut.	BERTScore F1 r
CQA	AZ	0.42	-	0.40	-	0.39	-	0.44	-	0.90	-
CQA	ID	0.37	-	0.34	-	0.32	-	0.39	-	0.84	-
CQA	IG	0.14	-	0.14	-	0.13	-	0.19	-	0.79	-
CQA	TR	0.15	-	0.15	-	0.14	-	0.19	-	0.82	-
CQA	UZ	0.44	-	0.43	-	0.42	-	0.47	-	0.89	-
CQA	YO	0.23	-	0.22	-	0.21	-	0.24	-	0.82	-
CQA	ALS	0.12	-	0.11	-	0.11	-	0.09	-	0.79	-
CCo	AZ	0.34	0.36	0.33	0.37	0.31	0.35	0.28	0.34	0.87	0.25
CCo	ID	0.39	-0.04	0.36	-0.02	0.33	-0.02	0.30	0.07	0.86	0.01
CCo	IG	0.24	0.38	0.24	0.39	0.22	0.37	0.24	0.30	0.85	0.23
CCo	TR	0.24	0.04	0.24	0.05	0.22	0.06	0.21	0.07	0.85	0.08
CCo	UZ	0.36	0.44	0.34	0.42	0.31	0.43	0.22	0.38	0.85	0.32
CCo	YO	0.19	0.39	0.18	0.41	0.17	0.41	0.17	0.28	0.81	-0.04
CCo	ALS	0.19	0.27	0.19	0.28	0.17	0.27	0.07	0.33	0.82	0.39
mT0 (1B)	AZ	0.33	0.67	0.32	0.67	0.31	0.68	0.37	0.59	0.86	0.35
mT0 (1B)	ID	0.48	0.38	0.44	0.37	0.42	0.36	0.48	0.16	0.88	0.25
mT0 (1B)	IG	0.14	0.34	0.14	0.37	0.14	0.38	0.20	0.51	0.79	0.22
mT0 (1B)	TR	0.12	0.09	0.12	0.10	0.11	0.12	0.15	0.26	0.80	0.02
mT0 (1B)	UZ	0.49	0.47	0.47	0.47	0.46	0.47	0.55	0.52	0.90	0.31
mT0 (1B)	YO	0.28	0.47	0.27	0.47	0.26	0.47	0.30	0.47	0.82	0.21
mT0 (1B)	ALS	0.12	0.46	0.11	0.47	0.11	0.46	0.09	0.47	0.78	0.39
GPT-4	AZ	0.41	0.42	0.41	0.44	0.39	0.44	0.31	0.32	0.86	0.27
GPT-4	ID	0.51	0.08	0.49	0.09	0.47	0.10	0.47	0.11	0.88	0.08
GPT-4	IG	0.52	0.28	0.52	0.28	0.49	0.28	0.45	0.21	0.89	0.17
GPT-4	TR	0.57	0.02	0.57	0.03	0.53	0.03	0.49	0.05	0.92	0.11
GPT-4	UZ	0.53	0.02	0.52	0.02	0.51	0.02	0.43	0.01	0.87	0.09
GPT-4	YO	0.28	0.52	0.27	0.52	0.26	0.53	0.21	0.59	0.82	0.48
GPT-4	ALS	0.34	0.26	0.34	0.27	0.30	0.26	0.19	0.26	0.85	0.30

Table 7: Detailed RC results per system and language. "aut." denotes automatic evaluation results on the entire test set, r denotes the Pearson correlation coefficient between the respective metric and the binary human judgement on the annotated subset of the test data.

Lang.	All Tags acc	All Tags pre	All Tags rec	All Tags F1	LOC pre	LOC rec	LOC F1	ORG pre	ORG rec	ORG F1	PER pre	PER rec	PER F1
ALS	0.87	0.37	0.41	0.39	0.50	0.41	0.45	0.30	0.27	0.28	0.57	0.43	0.49
AZ	0.87	0.49	0.47	0.48	0.68	0.40	0.50	0.49	0.40	0.44	0.72	0.55	0.62
IG	0.89	0.46	0.58	0.51	0.67	0.51	0.58	0.33	0.34	0.33	0.78	0.68	0.72
TR	0.89	0.52	0.48	0.50	0.66	0.43	0.52	0.53	0.31	0.39	0.80	0.53	0.64
YO	0.84	0.52	0.63	0.57	0.73	0.44	0.55	0.49	0.51	0.50	0.85	0.81	0.83
w. average	0.87	0.47	0.52	0.49	0.64	0.44	0.52	0.42	0.36	0.39	0.75	0.60	0.66

Table 8: Test results for CUNI NER submission. Averages are weighted by number of tokens per language.

	$r(ChrF, h)$	$r(ChrF+, h)$	$r(ChrF++, h)$	$r(RougeL, h)$	$r(BERTF1, h)$
CCo	0.26	0.27	0.27	0.25	0.18
mT0 (1B)	0.41	0.42	0.42	0.43	0.25
GPT-4	0.23	0.23	0.24	0.22	0.21

Table 9: Pearson correlation r between metrics and human binary annotation (h) averaged over languages.

	$r(ChrF, h)$	$r(ChrF+, h)$	$r(ChrF++, h)$	$r(RougeL, h)$	$r(BERTF1, h)$
AZ	0.48	0.49	0.49	0.42	0.29
ID	0.14	0.15	0.15	0.11	0.11
IG	0.33	0.35	0.34	0.34	0.20
TR	0.05	0.06	0.07	0.13	0.07
UZ	0.31	0.30	0.31	0.30	0.24
YO	0.46	0.47	0.47	0.45	0.22
ALS	0.33	0.34	0.33	0.35	0.36

Table 10: Pearson correlation r between metrics and human binary annotation (h) averaged over systems.

Lang.	**mT0 (1B)**	**GPT-4**	**CCo**
AZ	0.42	0.78	0.68
ID	0.85	0.98	0.54
IG	0.44	0.92	0.42
TR	0.44	0.90	0.60
UZ	0.80	0.92	0.78
YO	0.52	0.64	0.36
ALS	0.48	0.92	0.48

Table 11: Relative amount of answers that were judged as correct by human annotators.

found in detail in Table 8. Table 10 provides an overview of the correlations by language, and Table 9 condenses the correlations per system.

According to our analysis, we find the GPT-4 as a strong baseline in the RC task and it has competitive rephrasing and reasoning capabilities. We notice when GPT-4 generates an answer it often rephrases the question into a statement which might cause some grammatical errors if the case do not directly translate and may need additional inflectional changes. In general, we find although grammatical errors exist, they do not always lead to complete semantic loss in the sentence and might allow check the information.

An important remark is the factuality of the GPT-4 answers which we also approach skeptically. We find a small percentage of the time GPT-4 generates information that do not exist in the provided context.

Especially in dialects and low-resourced languages, we observe incorrect language in the output. The majority of these incorrect outputs are in Swiss German (ALS) and Azerbaijani (AZ). We also find this problem reciprocates in understanding the prompt, whereas observing in Swiss German similar words such as "zwei" (translation: two) and "zwor" (translation: hence) are misinterpreted. The ability to understand and generate output in the desired language might be limited by data availability and current observations state it is not trivial for GPT-4 to directly allow usage in low-resourced languages.

The second baseline, MT-0, was found to be relatively different in the style and characteristics of the language generated. Most answers were precise and rather short although, in light of our human evaluation results, majorly correct in some languages like Indonesian (ID) and Uzbek (UZ). We find MT-0 to be more prone to spelling errors which might lead to more semantic losses. For Igbo (IG), Turkish (TR) and Swiss German (ALS) we find the majority of answers are incorrect. We also observe multiple typographical errors, such as the way to write metrics (e.g., “k" instead of “km") in ID, although the values are correct.

The answers provided by CUNI were generally fluent and presented plausible language. The system tended more frequently to make up non-factual information or information that cannot be inferred from the given context. We also observed incorrect language in the output, which was at a significant level in Swiss German (ALS) and Uzbek (UZ).

7 Conclusion and Future Work

We presented a new multi-lingual multi-task benchmark on information retrieval from Wikipedia in seven languages from typologically-diverse and low-resourced language families. We organized a shared task to call for system development on this challenging benchmark where we conducted a detailed analysis on how state-of-the-art LLMs perform in language understanding and generation under low-resourced settings. In addition to finding strong evidence on fall backs in both understanding and generation capabilities of LLMs in low-resourced languages, we also find it crucial to invest in better automatic evaluation metrics for generation in different languages. While we do not find this task to be solved, we plan to keep the competition open and promote more investment into the progress of information retrieval for languages with non-prominent and low-resourced characteristics. Our leaderboard that will continue to promote open access evaluation of new submissions of specialized systems will be available until MRL 2024 on the competition website.

Limitations

We have presented a multilingual evaluation benchmark for information retrieval which was created relying on Wikipedia articles in different languages. Using Wikipedia has inherent limitations such as limitations in variety of content and styles across languages making it challenging to ensure a uniform difficulty level for comprehension questions. Additionally, relying solely on Wikipedia may introduce biases, as certain languages might have more comprehensive or detailed articles than others. Moreover, evaluating language models on Wikipedia-centric benchmarks may not fully reflect their generalization abilities, as the models might excel at leveraging the more structured and well-formulated information found on Wikipedia but may struggle more with more diverse and unstructured text from other sources. These limitations underscore the need for diverse and contextually rich benchmarks to provide a comprehensive assessment of LLMs across multiple languages.

Ethics Statement

This research involved using human annotators to prepare data sets. All annotators were provided with clear instructions and guidelines to ensure the responsible and unbiased annotation of the data. We ensured ethical practices by providing clear guidelines and obtaining informed consent. We appreciate their contributions, and ethical treatment remains a key focus in our research.

Acknowledgements

We thank our sponsors Google Deepmind and Bloomberg to make this shared task possible. We also thank HumanSignal for providing us access to Label Studio's Enterprise version which allowed us execute the large-scale collaboration to perform human annotations in multiple tasks.

References

David Adelani, Graham Neubig, Sebastian Ruder, Shruti Rijhwani, Michael Beukman, Chester Palen-Michel, Constantine Lignos, Jesujoba Alabi, Shamsuddeen Muhammad, Peter Nabende, et al. 2022. Masakhaner 2.0: Africa-centric transfer learning for named entity recognition. In *Proceedings of the 2022 Conference on Empirical Methods in Natural Language Processing*, pages 4488–4508.

David Adelani, Dana Ruiter, Jesujoba Alabi, Damilola Adebonojo, Adesina Ayeni, Mofe Adeyemi, Ayodele Esther Awokoya, and Cristina España-Bonet. 2021a. The effect of domain and diacritics in Yoruba–English neural machine translation. In *Proceedings of Machine Translation Summit XVIII: Research Track*, pages 61–75, Virtual. Association for Machine Translation in the Americas.

David Ifeoluwa Adelani, Jade Abbott, Graham Neubig, Daniel D'souza, Julia Kreutzer, Constantine Lignos, Chester Palen-Michel, Happy Buzaaba, Shruti Rijhwani, Sebastian Ruder, et al. 2021b. Masakhaner: Named entity recognition for african languages. *Transactions of the Association for Computational Linguistics*, 9:1116–1131.

Alessandro Agostini, Timur Usmanov, Ulugbek Khamdamov, Nilufar Abdurakhmonova, and Mukhammadsaid Mamasaidov. 2021. UZWORDNET: A lexical-semantic database for the Uzbek language. In *Proceedings of the 11th Global Wordnet Conference*, pages 8–19, University of South Africa (UNISA). Global Wordnet Association.

Alham Fikri Aji, Genta Indra Winata, Fajri Koto, Samuel Cahyawijaya, Ade Romadhony, Rahmad Mahendra, Kemal Kurniawan, David Moeljadi, Radityo Eko Prasojo, Timothy Baldwin, et al. 2022. One country, 700+ languages: Nlp challenges for underrepresented languages and dialects in indonesia. In *Proceedings of the 60th Annual Meeting of the Association for Computational Linguistics (Volume 1: Long Papers)*, pages 7226–7249.

Yesim Aksan, Mustafa Aksan, Ahmet Koltuksuz, Taner Sezer, Ümit Mersinli, Umut Ufuk Demirhan, Hakan Yilmazer, Gülsüm Atasoy, Seda Öz, Ipek Yildiz, et al. 2012. Construction of the turkish national corpus (tnc). In *LREC*, pages 3223–3227.

Rohan Anil, Andrew M Dai, Orhan Firat, Melvin Johnson, Dmitry Lepikhin, Alexandre Passos, Siamak Shakeri, Emanuel Taropa, Paige Bailey, Zhifeng Chen, et al. 2023. Palm 2 technical report. *arXiv preprint arXiv:2305.10403*.

Duygu Ataman. 2018. Bianet: A parallel news corpus in turkish, kurdish and english. In *LREC 2018 Workshop*, page 14.

Ondřej Bojar, Rajen Chatterjee, Christian Federmann, Yvette Graham, Barry Haddow, Shujian Huang, Matthias Huck, Philipp Koehn, Qun Liu, Varvara Logacheva, Christof Monz, Matteo Negri, Matt Post, Raphael Rubino, Lucia Specia, and Marco Turchi. 2017. Findings of the 2017 conference on machine translation (WMT17). In *Proceedings of the Second Conference on Machine Translation*, pages 169–214.

Tom Brown, Benjamin Mann, Nick Ryder, Melanie Subbiah, Jared D Kaplan, Prafulla Dhariwal, Arvind Neelakantan, Pranav Shyam, Girish Sastry, Amanda Askell, Sandhini Agarwal, Ariel Herbert-Voss, Gretchen Krueger, Tom Henighan, Rewon Child, Aditya Ramesh, Daniel Ziegler, Jeffrey Wu, Clemens Winter, Chris Hesse, Mark Chen, Eric Sigler, Mateusz Litwin, Scott Gray, Benjamin Chess, Jack Clark, Christopher Berner, Sam McCandlish, Alec Radford, Ilya Sutskever, and Dario Amodei. 2020. Language models are few-shot learners. In *Advances in Neural Information Processing Systems*, volume 33, pages 1877–1901. Curran Associates, Inc.

Samuel Cahyawijaya, Holy Lovenia, Alham Fikri Aji, Genta Winata, Bryan Wilie, Fajri Koto, Rahmad Mahendra, Christian Wibisono, Ade Romadhony, Karissa Vincentio, et al. 2023a. Nusacrowd: Open source initiative for indonesian nlp resources. In *Findings of the Association for Computational Linguistics: ACL 2023*, pages 13745–13818.

Samuel Cahyawijaya, Holy Lovenia, Fajri Koto, Dea Adhista, Emmanuel Dave, Sarah Oktavianti, Salsabil Maulana Akbar, Jhonson Lee, Nuur Shadieq, Tjeng Wawan Cenggoro, et al. 2023b. Nusawrites: Constructing high-quality corpora for underrepresented and extremely low-resource languages. *arXiv preprint arXiv:2309.10661*.

Samuel Cahyawijaya, Genta Indra Winata, Bryan Wilie, Karissa Vincentio, Xiaohong Li, Adhiguna Kuncoro, Sebastian Ruder, Zhi Yuan Lim, Syafri Bahar, Masayu Khodra, et al. 2021. Indonlg: Benchmark and resources for evaluating indonesian natural language generation. In *Proceedings of the 2021 Conference on Empirical Methods in Natural Language Processing*, pages 8875–8898.

Mauro Cettolo, Christian Girardi, and Marcello Federico. 2012. Wit3: Web inventory of transcribed and translated talks. In *Proceedings of the Conference of European Association for Machine Translation (EAMT)*, pages 261–268.

Mauro Cettolo, Jan Niehues, Sebastian Stüker, Luisa Bentivogli, and Marcello Federico. 2013. Report on the 10th iwslt evaluation campaign. In *Proceedings of the 10th International Workshop on Spoken Language Translation: Evaluation Campaign*.

Yang Chen, Chao Jiang, Alan Ritter, and Wei Xu. 2023. Frustratingly easy label projection for cross-lingual transfer. In *Findings of the Association for Computational Linguistics: ACL 2023*, pages 5775–5796, Toronto, Canada. Association for Computational Linguistics.

Alexis Conneau, Ruty Rinott, Guillaume Lample, Adina Williams, Samuel Bowman, Holger Schwenk, and Veselin Stoyanov. 2018. Xnli: Evaluating cross-lingual sentence representations. In *Proceedings of the 2018 Conference on Empirical Methods in Natural Language Processing*, pages 2475–2485.

Cheikh M. Bamba Dione, David Ifeoluwa Adelani, Peter Nabende, Jesujoba Alabi, Thapelo Sindane, Happy Buzaaba, Shamsuddeen Hassan Muhammad, Chris Chinenye Emezue, Perez Ogayo, Anuoluwapo Aremu, Catherine Gitau, Derguene Mbaye, Jonathan Mukiibi, Blessing Sibanda, Bonaventure F. P. Dossou, Andiswa Bukula, Rooweither Mabuya, Allahsera Auguste Tapo, Edwin Munkoh-Buabeng, Victoire Memdjokam Koagne, Fatoumata Ouoba Kabore, Amelia Taylor, Godson Kalipe, Tebogo Macucwa, Vukosi Marivate, Tajuddeen Gwadabe, Mboning Tchiaze Elvis, Ikechukwu Onyenwe, Gratien Atindogbe, Tolulope Adelani, Idris Akinade, Olanrewaju Samuel, Marien Nahimana, Théogène Musabeyezu, Emile Niyomutabazi, Ester Chimhenga, Kudzai Gotosa, Patrick Mizha, Apelete Agbolo, Seydou Traore, Chinedu Uchechukwu, Aliyu Yusuf, Muhammad Abdullahi, and Dietrich Klakow. 2023. MasakhaPOS: Part-of-speech tagging for typologically diverse African languages. In *Proceedings of the 61st Annual Meeting of the Association for Computational Linguistics (Volume 1: Long Papers)*, pages 10883–10900, Toronto, Canada. Association for Computational Linguistics.

Pelin Dogan-Schönberger, Julian Mäder, and Thomas Hofmann. 2021. Swissdial: Parallel multidialectal corpus of spoken swiss german.

David M. Eberhard, Gary F. Simons, and Charles D. Fennig. 2021. Ethnologue: Languages of the world. twenty-third edition.

Razieh Ehsani, Ercan Solak, and Olcay Taner Yildiz. 2018. Constructing a wordnet for turkish using manual and automatic annotation. *ACM Transactions on Asian and Low-Resource Language Information Processing (TALLIP)*, 17(3):1–15.

Luciano Floridi and Massimo Chiriatti. 2020. Gpt-3: Its nature, scope, limits, and consequences. *Minds and Machines*, 30:681–694.

Xavier Garcia and Orhan Firat. 2022. Using natural language prompts for machine translation. *arXiv preprint arXiv:2202.11822*.

Philip N. Garner, David Imseng, and Thomas Meyer. 2014. Automatic speech recognition and translation of a swiss german dialect: Walliserdeutsch. In *Interspeech*.

Vera Gribanova. 2012-2020. The combinatorics of the Uzbek verbal complex in polar questions: Stanford digital repository.

Vera Gribanova. 2018-2020. Argument ellipsis and verb-stranding ellipsis in Uzbek: Stanford digital repository.

Amr Hendy, Mohamed Abdelrehim, Amr Sharaf, Vikas Raunak, Mohamed Gabr, Hitokazu Matsushita, Young Jin Kim, Mohamed Afify, and Hany Hassan Awadalla. 2023. How good are gpt models at machine translation? a comprehensive evaluation. *arXiv e-prints*, pages arXiv–2302.

Nora Hollenstein and Noëmi Aepli. 2014. Compilation of a Swiss German dialect corpus and its application to PoS tagging. In *Proceedings of the First Workshop on Applying NLP Tools to Similar Languages, Varieties and Dialects*, pages 85–94, Dublin, Ireland. Association for Computational Linguistics and Dublin City University.

Junjie Hu, Sebastian Ruder, Aditya Siddhant, Graham Neubig, Orhan Firat, and Melvin Johnson. 2020. Xtreme: A massively multilingual multi-task benchmark for evaluating cross-lingual generalisation. In *International Conference on Machine Learning*, pages 4411–4421. PMLR.

Fajri Koto, Afshin Rahimi, Jey Han Lau, and Timothy Baldwin. 2020. Indolem and indobert: A benchmark dataset and pre-trained language model for indonesian nlp. In *Proceedings of the 28th International Conference on Computational Linguistics*, pages 757–770.

Chin-Yew Lin and Eduard Hovy. 2003. Automatic evaluation of summaries using n-gram co-occurrence statistics. In *Proceedings of the 2003 human language technology conference of the North American chapter of the association for computational linguistics*, pages 150–157.

Hanmeng Liu, Ruoxi Ning, Zhiyang Teng, Jian Liu, Qiji Zhou, and Yue Zhang. 2023. Evaluating the logical reasoning ability of chatgpt and gpt-4. *arXiv preprint arXiv:2304.03439*.

Yinhan Liu, Myle Ott, Naman Goyal, Jingfei Du, Mandar Joshi, Danqi Chen, Omer Levy, Mike Lewis, Luke Zettlemoyer, and Veselin Stoyanov. 2019a. Roberta: A robustly optimized BERT pretraining approach. *CoRR*, abs/1907.11692.

Yinhan Liu, Myle Ott, Naman Goyal, Jingfei Du, Mandar Joshi, Danqi Chen, Omer Levy, Mike Lewis, Luke Zettlemoyer, and Veselin Stoyanov. 2019b. Roberta: A robustly optimized bert pretraining approach. *arXiv preprint arXiv:1907.11692*.

Rui Mao, Guanyi Chen, Xulang Zhang, Frank Guerin, and Erik Cambria. 2023. Gpteval: A survey on assessments of chatgpt and gpt-4. *arXiv preprint arXiv:2308.12488*.

Niklas Muennighoff, Thomas Wang, Lintang Sutawika, Adam Roberts, Stella Biderman, Teven Le Scao, M Saiful Bari, Sheng Shen, Zheng-Xin Yong, Hailey Schoelkopf, et al. 2022. Crosslingual generalization through multitask finetuning. *arXiv e-prints*, pages arXiv–2211.

Shamsuddeen Hassan Muhammad, Idris Abdulmumin, Abinew Ali Ayele, Nedjma Djouhra Ousidhoum, David Ifeoluwa Adelani, Seid Muhie Yimam, Ibrahim Said Ahmad, Meriem Beloucif, Saif M. Mohammad, Sebastian Ruder, Oumaima Hourrane, Pavel Brazdil, Felermino D'ario M'ario Ant'onio Ali, Davis C. Davis, Salomey Osei, Bello Shehu Bello, Falalu Ibrahim, Tajuddeen Rabiu Gwadabe, Samuel Rutunda, Tadesse Destaw Belay, Wendimu Baye Messelle, Hailu Beshada Balcha, Sisay Adugna Chala, Hagos Tesfahun Gebremichael, Bernard Opoku, and Steven Arthur. 2023. Afrisenti: A twitter sentiment analysis benchmark for african languages. *ArXiv*, abs/2302.08956.

Odunayo Ogundepo, Tajuddeen R. Gwadabe, Clara E. Rivera, Jonathan H. Clark, Sebastian Ruder, David Ifeoluwa Adelani, Bonaventure F. P. Dossou, Abdou Aziz DIOP, Claytone Sikasote, Gilles Hacheme, Happy Buzaaba, Ignatius Ezeani, Rooweither Mabuya, Salomey Osei, Chris Emezue, Albert Njoroge Kahira, Shamsuddeen H. Muhammad, Akintunde Oladipo, Abraham Toluwase Owodunni, Atnafu Lambebo Tonja, Iyanuoluwa Shode, Akari Asai, Tunde Oluwaseyi Ajayi, Clemencia Siro, Steven Arthur, Mofetoluwa Adeyemi, Orevaoghene Ahia, Aremu Anuoluwapo, Oyinkansola Awosan, Chiamaka Chukwuneke, Bernard Opoku, Awokoya Ayodele, Verrah Otiende, Christine Mwase, Boyd Sinkala, Andre Niyongabo Rubungo, Daniel A. Ajisafe, Emeka Felix Onwuegbuzia, Habib Mbow, Emile Niyomutabazi, Eunice Mukonde, Falalu Ibrahim Lawan, Ibrahim Said Ahmad, Jesujoba O. Alabi, Martin Namukombo, Mbonu Chinedu, Mofya Phiri, Neo Putini, Ndumiso Mngoma, Priscilla A. Amuok, Ruqayya Nasir Iro, and Sonia Adhiambo. 2023. Afriqa: Cross-lingual open-retrieval question answering for african languages.

Tolulope Ogunremi, Kola Tubosun, Anuoluwapo Aremu, Iroro Orife, and David Ifeoluwa Adelani. 2023. Ìròyìnspeech: A multi-purpose yorùbá speech corpus.

Chinyere Ohiri-Aniche. 2007. Stemming the tide of centrifugal forces in Igbo orthography. *Dialectical Anthropology*, 31(4):423–436.

OpenAI. 2023a. Gpt-4 technical report.

OpenAI. 2023b. Gpt-4 technical report. *ArXiv*, abs/2303.08774.

Long Ouyang, Jeff Wu, Xu Jiang, Diogo Almeida, Carroll L. Wainwright, Pamela Mishkin, Chong Zhang, Sandhini Agarwal, Katarina Slama, Alex Ray, John Schulman, Jacob Hilton, Fraser Kelton, Luke E. Miller, Maddie Simens, Amanda Askell, Peter Welinder, Paul Francis Christiano, Jan Leike, and Ryan J. Lowe. 2022. Training language models to follow instructions with human feedback. *ArXiv*, abs/2203.02155.

Tiago Pimentel, Maria Ryskina, Sabrina J Mielke, Shijie Wu, Eleanor Chodroff, Brian Leonard, Garrett Nicolai, Yustinus Ghanggo Ate, Salam Khalifa, Nizar Habash, et al. 2021. Sigmorphon 2021 shared task on morphological reinflection: Generalization across languages. In *Proceedings of the 18th SIGMORPHON Workshop on Computational Research in Phonetics, Phonology, and Morphology*, pages 229–259.

Michel Plüss, Jan Deriu, Yanick Schraner, Claudio Paonessa, Julia Hartmann, Larissa Schmidt, Christian Scheller, Manuela Hürlimann, Tanja Samardžić, Manfred Vogel, and Mark Cieliebak. 2023. STT4SG-350: A speech corpus for all Swiss German dialect regions. In *Proceedings of the 61st Annual Meeting of the Association for Computational Linguistics (Volume 2: Short Papers)*, pages 1763–1772, Toronto, Canada. Association for Computational Linguistics.

Michel Plüss, Manuela Hürlimann, Marc Cuny, Alla Stöckli, Nikolaos Kapotis, Julia Hartmann, Malgorzata Anna Ulasik, Christian Scheller, Yanick Schraner, Amit Jain, Jan Deriu, Mark Cieliebak, and Manfred Vogel. 2022. SDS-200: A Swiss German speech to Standard German text corpus. In *Proceedings of the Thirteenth Language Resources and Evaluation Conference*, pages 3250–3256, Marseille, France. European Language Resources Association.

Michel Plüss, Lukas Neukom, and Manfred Vogel. 2020. Swiss parliaments corpus, an automatically aligned swiss german speech to standard german text corpus. *ArXiv*, abs/2010.02810.

Maja Popović. 2015. chrf: character n-gram f-score for automatic mt evaluation. In *Proceedings of the tenth workshop on statistical machine translation*, pages 392–395.

Maja Popović. 2017. chrf++: words helping character n-grams. In *Proceedings of the second conference on machine translation*, pages 612–618.

Colin Raffel, Noam Shazeer, Adam Roberts, Katherine Lee, Sharan Narang, Michael Matena, Yanqi Zhou, Wei Li, and Peter J. Liu. 2019. Exploring the limits of transfer learning with a unified text-to-text transformer. *arXiv e-prints*.

Sebastian Ruder, Jonathan H Clark, Alexander Gutkin, Mihir Kale, Min Ma, Massimo Nicosia, Shruti Rijhwani, Parker Riley, Jean-Michel A Sarr, Xinyi Wang, et al. 2023. Xtreme-up: A user-centric scarce-data benchmark for under-represented languages. *arXiv preprint arXiv:2305.11938*.

Bahadir Sahin, Mustafa Tolga Eren, Caglar Tirkaz, Ozan Sonmez, and Eray Yildiz. 2017. English/turkish wikipedia named-entity recognition and text categorization dataset. *Mendeley Data, V1*.

Gözde Gül Şahin and Eşref Adalı. 2018. Annotation of semantic roles for the turkish proposition bank. *Language Resources and Evaluation*, 52:673–706.

Ulugbek Salaev, Elmurod Kuriyozov, and Carlos Gómez-Rodríguez. 2022. Simreluz: Similarity and relatedness scores as a semantic evaluation dataset for uzbek language.

Tanja Samardžić, Yves Scherrer, and Elvira Glaser. 2016. ArchiMob - a corpus of spoken Swiss German. In *Proceedings of the Tenth International Conference on Language Resources and Evaluation (LREC'16)*, pages 4061–4066, Portorož, Slovenia. European Language Resources Association (ELRA).

Thomas Scialom, Paul-Alexis Dray, Sylvain Lamprier, Benjamin Piwowarski, and Jacopo Staiano. 2020. Mlsum: The multilingual summarization corpus. In *2020 Conference on Empirical Methods in Natural Language Processing (EMNLP)*, pages 8051–8067. Association for Computational Linguistics.

Maksud Sharipov, Elmurod Kuriyozov, Ollabergan Yuldashev, and Ogabek Sobirov. 2023. Uzbektagger: The rule-based pos tagger for uzbek language.

Umut Sulubacak and Gülşen Eryiğit. 2018. Implementing universal dependency, morphology, and multiword expression annotation standards for turkish language processing. *Turkish Journal of Electrical Engineering and Computer Sciences*, 26(3):1662–1672.

Umut Sulubacak, Memduh Gökırmak, Francis Tyers, Çağrı Çöltekin, Joakim Nivre, and Gülşen Eryiğit. 2016. Universal dependencies for turkish. In *Proceedings of COLING 2016, the 26th international conference on computational linguistics: Technical papers*, pages 3444–3454.

Erik F. Tjong Kim Sang and Sabine Buchholz. 2000. Introduction to the CoNLL-2000 shared task chunking. In *Fourth Conference on Computational Natural Language Learning and the Second Learning Language in Logic Workshop*.

Maxim Tkachenko, Mikhail Malyuk, Andrey Holmanyuk, and Nikolai Liubimov. 2020-2022. Label Studio: Data labeling software. Open source software available from https://github.com/heartexlabs/label-studio.

Hugo Touvron, Thibaut Lavril, Gautier Izacard, Xavier Martinet, Marie-Anne Lachaux, Timothée Lacroix, Baptiste Rozière, Naman Goyal, Eric Hambro, Faisal Azhar, et al. 2023a. Llama: Open and efficient foundation language models. *arXiv preprint arXiv:2302.13971*.

Hugo Touvron, Louis Martin, Kevin Stone, Peter Albert, Amjad Almahairi, Yasmine Babaei, Nikolay Bashlykov, Soumya Batra, Prajjwal Bhargava, Shruti Bhosale, et al. 2023b. Llama 2: Open foundation and fine-tuned chat models. *arXiv preprint arXiv:2307.09288*.

Francis M Tyers and Murat Serdar Alperen. 2010. South-east european times: A parallel corpus of balkan languages. In *Proceedings of the LREC workshop on exploitation of multilingual resources and tools for Central and (South-) Eastern European Languages*, pages 49–53.

Jason Wei, Xuezhi Wang, Dale Schuurmans, Maarten Bosma, Fei Xia, Ed Chi, Quoc V Le, Denny Zhou, et al. 2022. Chain-of-thought prompting elicits reasoning in large language models. *Advances in Neural Information Processing Systems*, 35:24824–24837.

Bryan Wilie, Karissa Vincentio, Genta Indra Winata, Samuel Cahyawijaya, Xiaohong Li, Zhi Yuan Lim, Sidik Soleman, Rahmad Mahendra, Pascale Fung, Syafri Bahar, et al. 2020. Indonlu: Benchmark and resources for evaluating indonesian natural language understanding. In *Proceedings of the 1st Conference of the Asia-Pacific Chapter of the Association for Computational Linguistics and the 10th International Joint Conference on Natural Language Processing*, pages 843–857.

Genta Winata, Alham Fikri Aji, Samuel Cahyawijaya, Rahmad Mahendra, Fajri Koto, Ade Romadhony, Kemal Kurniawan, David Moeljadi, Radityo Eko Prasojo, and Pascale Fung. 2023. Nusax: Multilingual parallel sentiment dataset for 10 indonesian local languages. In *Proceedings of the 17th Conference of the European Chapter of the Association for Computational Linguistics*, pages 815–834.

Zhen Xu, Sergio Escalera, Adrien Pavão, Magali Richard, Wei-Wei Tu, Quanming Yao, Huan Zhao, and Isabelle Guyon. 2022. Codabench: Flexible, easy-to-use, and reproducible meta-benchmark platform. *Patterns*, 3(7):100543.

Zheng-Xin Yong, Cristina Menghini, and Stephen H Bach. 2023. Low-resource languages jailbreak gpt-4. *arXiv preprint arXiv:2310.02446*.

Tianyi Zhang, Varsha Kishore, Felix Wu, Kilian Q Weinberger, and Yoav Artzi. 2019. Bertscore: Evaluating text generation with bert. *arXiv preprint arXiv:1904.09675*.

Xuhui Zhou, Yue Zhang, Leyang Cui, and Dandan Huang. 2021. Evaluating commonsense in pretrained language models.

Author Index

Association for Computational Linguistics
209 N. Eighth Street
Stroudsburg, Pennsylvania 18360

ISBN 978-1-7138-8602-0

CURRAN ASSOCIATES INC.
proceedings.com